SAMS

Teach Yourself

the C#
Language

in 21 Days

Brad ley L. Jones

SAMS

800 East 96th St., Indianapolis, Indiana, 46240 USA

Sams Teach Yourself the C# Language in 21 Days

Copyright © 2004 by Bradley L. Jones

International Standard Book Number: 0-672-32546-2

Library of Congress Catalog Card Number: 2003092624

Printed in the United States of America

First Printing: July 2003

06	05	04	03		4	3	2

Trademarks

All terms mentioned in this book that are known to be trademarks or service marks have been appropriately capitalized. Sams Publishing cannot attest to the accuracy of this information. Use of a term in this book should not be regarded as affecting the validity of any trademark or service mark.

Warning and Disclaimer

Every effort has been made to make this book as complete and as accurate as possible, but no warranty or fitness is implied. The information provided is on an "as is" basis. The author and the publisher shall have neither liability nor responsibility to any person or entity with respect to any loss or damages arising from the information contained in this book.

Bulk Sales

Sams Publishing offers excellent discounts on this book when ordered in quantity for bulk purchases or special sales. For more information, please contact:

U.S. Corporate and Government Sales
1-800-382-3419
corpsales@pearsontechgroup.com

For sales outside of the U.S., please contact:

International Sales
+1-317-428-3341
international@pearsontechgroup.com

ASSOCIATE PUBLISHER
Michael Stephens

EXECUTIVE EDITOR
Candace Hall

DEVELOPMENT EDITOR
Mark Renfrow

MANAGING EDITOR
Charlotte Clapp

PROJECT EDITOR
Matthew Purcell

COPY EDITOR
Krista Hansing

INDEXER
Mandie Frank

PROOFREADER
Paula Lowell

TECHNICAL EDITOR
Anand Narayanaswamy

TEAM COORDINATOR
Cindy Teeters

INTERIOR DESIGNER
Gary Adair

COVER DESIGNER
Alan Clements

PAGE LAYOUT
Michelle Mitchell

Contents at a Glance

Table of Contents

On CD-ROM

Answers

About the Author

BRADLEY L. JONES (Brad@TeachYourselfCSharp.com) is the site manager for a number of high-profile developer sites—including CodeGuru.com, Developer.com, and VBForums.com—and is an executive editor of Jupitermedia's EarthWeb channel, which is a part of Internet.com. Bradley has been working with C# longer than most developers because he was invited to Microsoft before the official beta release. Bradley's background includes experience developing in C, C++, PowerBuilder, SQL Server, and numerous other tools and technologies. Additionally, he is an internationally best-selling author who wrote the original 21 Days book: *Sams Teach Yourself C in 21 Days*. On Developer.com and CodeGuru.com, you find a number of articles from Bradley on topics ranging from .NET to mobile development to general developer topics.

Dedication

This book is dedicated to my wife, Melissa.

Acknowledgments

As I stated earlier, although I create the structure and write the words, I don't create a book like this on my own. Many people's contributions helped to make this a much better book.

First, however, let me thank my wife and family for being patient and understanding while I set the normal flow of life aside in order to focus on writing this book.

I'd also like to give my personal thanks to Mattias Sjögren and Anand Narayanaswamy. Mattias proved to be one of the best technical editors that I have had review one of my books. His suggestions and corrections to the first edition of this book truly brought it to a higher level of quality. Anand, a Microsoft MVP, stepped in to review the second edition. Although his suggestions caused more work for me, I believe the end result is an even better book for you, the reader.

In addition to the offical technical editor, this book has been read by thousands of others. I want to thank the readers who took the time to suggest changes, improvements, or clarifications. I take this feedback seriously and work a lot of it into reprints and errata.

I'd also like to thank the editors at Sams Publishing for their effort in building this book. This includes Candy Hall, Mark Renfrow, Krista Hansing, Matt Purcell, Brad Shannon, Nancy Albright, and others also spent large amounts of time focused on making this the best book possible. They deserve to be acknowledged as well.

On a different note, this book would have been impossible to do without the support of a number of people at Microsoft. Over the last several years, I have gained help from too many people to list all of them. A number of people on the C# team—such as Nick Hodapp, Tony Goodhew, and Eric Gunnerson—helped provide information on C# in addition to answering many of my questions.

Because this book provides the chance to publicly acknowledge people, I'd also like to thank a number of other people at Microsoft for their help over the last several years—either on this book or on many other projects. This includes Eric Ewing, Stacey Giard, Brad Goldberg, Tony Goodhew, Rob Howard, Jeff Ressler, Scott Guthrie, Connie Sullivan, Dee Dee Walsh, Dennis Bye, Bob Gaines, Robert Green, David Lazar, Greg Leake, Lizzie Parker, Charles Sterling, Susan Warren, and lots of others.

I'd like to thank you, the reader. There are a number of books on C# that you could have bought or could use. I appreciate your giving me the chance to teach you C#.

Finally, thanks goes to Bob, who still seems to always be blue.

Tell Us What You Think!

As the reader of this book, *you* are our most important critic and commentator. We value your opinion and want to know what we're doing right, what we could do better, what areas you'd like to see us publish in, and any other words of wisdom you're willing to pass our way.

As an Executive Editor for Sams, I welcome your comments. You can e-mail or write me directly to let me know what you did or didn't like about this book—as well as what we can do to make our books stronger.

Please note that I cannot help you with technical problems related to the topic of this book, and that due to the high volume of mail I receive, I might not be able to reply to every message.

When you write, please be sure to include this book's title and author as well as your name and phone or fax number. I will carefully review your comments and share them with the author and editors who worked on the book.

E-mail: feedback@samspublishing.com

Mail: Candace Hall, Executive Editor
           Sams Publishing
           800 East 96th Street
           Indianapolis, IN 46240 USA

Introduction

Welcome to *Sams Teach Yourself the C# Language in 21 Days*. As you can guess from the title of this book, I have written this book with the expectation that you will spend 21 days learning the C# programming language. The book is divided into 21 lessons that can each be accomplished in a couple of hours or a single evening. If you dedicate 2 to 3 hours for 21 days, you should easily be able to work through this book. This doesn't have to be consecutive evenings, nor does it even have to be evenings.

Each lesson can be read in an hour or two. Some will take longer to read; some will take less time. If you expect to learn C# by just reading, you will be greatly disappointed. Instead, you should expect to spend half your time reading and the other half entering the code from the daily lesson, doing the quizzes, and trying out the exercises. That might sound like a lot, but you can do each lesson in an evening, if you try.

The quizzes and exercises are part of the 21-day series, designed to help you confirm your understanding of that day's material. After reading a day's lesson, you should be able to answer all the questions in the quiz. If you can't, you may need to review parts of that lesson.

The exercises present you with a chance to apply what you've learned. The exercises generally focus on understanding code, identifying common code problems, and writing code based on the day's lesson.

Answers to the quizzes and most of the exercises are provided on the CD-ROM, "Answers", which can be found on the CD-ROM included with the book. Try to come up with the answers on your own before jumping to the CD-ROM.

You will notice several other features when reading this book. You'll find tips, notes, and caution boxes throughout the book. Tips provide useful suggestions. Notes provide additional information that you might find interesting. Cautions alert you to a common problem or issue that you might encounter. A special element of this series of books is the Q&A section at the end of each day. The Q&A section provides questions—along with the answers—you might have while reading that day's lesson. These questions might involve peripheral topics to the lesson.

A second special element is provided simply for fun. Throughout this book, you will find Type & Runs (T&Rs), which provide listings that you can enter, compile, and run. More important, you can make changes with the code in these listings; you an experiment and play. In most cases, you should find the T&Rs a bit more functional and fun than the more standard listings used to teach specific topics.

Assumptions I've Made

I've made a few assumptions about you. I've assumed that you have a C# compiler and a .NET runtime environment. Although you can read this book without them, you will have a harder time fully understanding what is being presented. To help ensure this assumption, this book comes with a CD-ROM that includes a C# editor and a C# runtime.

I've assumed that you are a beginning-level programmer. If you are not, you will still gain a lot from this book; however, you might find that in some areas you will progress slower than you'd like.

This book does not assume that you are using Microsoft Visual C# .NET or the Microsoft Visual Studio .NET development environment. You can use Microsoft's tools or a number of other tools. You'll learn more about this within the book. I don't even assume that you are using Microsoft Windows. After all, there are now C# compilers for other platforms such as Linux and FreeBSD.

Web Site Support

No one is perfect—especially me. Combine this with a programming language that is relatively new and that faces future changes. You can expect problems to crop up.

This book has been based on a previous edition, which has been read by thousands. Editorial, technical, and development reviews of the book have been done. Even with all the reviews, errors still happen. In case a problem did sneak through, errata for this book can be found on a number of Web sites. The publisher's Web site is located at `www.samspublishing.com/`.

Additionally, I have created a site specifically for the support of this book: `www.TeachYourselfCSharp.com`. I will post errata at this location.

Source Code

I believe that the best way to learn a programming language is to type the code and see it run. I believe that the best way to learn a programming language is to type in the programs. I also understand, however, that my beliefs are not the same as everyone else's. For that reason, the source code for this book is provided on the included CD.

This book is for learning. You can use the source code contained within it. You can adapt it. You can extend it. You can give it to your mom. Learn from it. Use it. By purchasing this book, you gain the right to use this code any way you see fit, with one exception: You can't repurpose this code for a C# tutorial.

CD-ROM

As already stated, this book includes a CD-ROM that contains the source code for this book, as well as a number of tools and utilities. When you run the CD-ROM, you will get information on its contents.

Getting Started

I applaud your efforts in reading this introduction; however, you're most likely more interested in learning about C#. "Week 1 at a Glance" gives you an overview of what you can expect in your first week of learning the C# programming language. What better time to get started than now?

Week 1

At a Glance

Welcome to *Sams Teach Yourself the C# Language in 21 Days, Second Edition*. If you are unsure what you need to know to get the most out of this book, you should review the Introduction. The Introduction also explains the elements used within this book.

You are getting ready to start the first of three weeks of lessons. These first lessons will help you gain a solid foundation for writing C# programs. Regardless of what C# compiler you are using, as long as it follows the C# standards, you should be able to learn and apply all of the information learned in this first week.

Starting with Day 1, "Getting Started with C#," you will be entering C# programs. In addition to learning about C# and some of the editors and tools available, you will learn how a C# program is created and run.

On Day 2, "Understanding C# Programs," you will learn how C# fits into the Microsoft .NET Framework. You will also be taught about the fundamental principles of an object-oriented language, and you will learn how basic information is held within a C# program.

Day 3, "Manipulating Values in Your Programs" and Day 4, "Controlling Your Program's Flow," teach you the core programming concepts required for C# programming. This includes manipulating data and controlling your program flow.

Days 5, "The Core of C# Programming: Classes," and 6, "Packaging Functionality: Class Methods and Member Functions," cover classes and class methods. Classes are a

1

2

3

4

5

6

7

core concept to object-oriented programming and, therefore, a core concept to C# programming.

The first week ends with coverage of a number of more complex ways for holding information in a program on Day 7, "Storing More Complex Stuff: Structures, Enumerators, and Arrays." On this day, you will learn how to organize your program's data in a number of ways.

By the end of the first week, you will have learned many of the foundational concepts for C# programming. You'll find that by the time you review this first week, you will have the tools and knowledge to build basic C# programs on your own.

DAY 1

Getting Started with C#

Welcome to *Sams Teach Yourself C# in 21 Days*! In today's lesson, you begin the process of becoming a proficient C# programmer. Today you…

- Learn why C# is a great programming language to use.
- Discover the steps in the program-development cycle.
- Understand how to write, compile, and run your first C# program.
- Explore error messages generated by the compiler and linker.
- Review the types of solutions that can be created with C#.
- Create your first console and Windows forms program.
- Learn about object-oriented concepts.

What Is C#?

It would be unusual if you bought this book without knowing what C# is. However, it would not be unusual if you didn't know a lot about the language. Released to the public as a beta in June 2000 and officially released in the spring of 2002, C#—pronounced "see sharp"—has not been around for very long.

C# is a language that was created by Microsoft and submitted to ECMA for standardization. Its creators were a team of people at Microsoft that included the guidance of Anders Hejlsberg. Interestingly, Hejlsberg is a Microsoft Distinguished Engineer who has created other products and languages, including Borland Turbo C++ and Borland Delphi. With C#, he and the team at Microsoft focused on using what was right about existing languages and adding improvements to make something better.

Although C# was created by Microsoft, it is not limited to just Microsoft platforms. C# compilers exist for FreeBSD, Linux, the Macintosh, and several of the Microsoft platforms.

C# is a powerful and flexible programming language. Like all programming languages, it can be used to create a variety of applications. The C# language does not place constraints on what you can do; therefore, your potential with it is limited only by your imagination. C# has already been used for projects as diverse as dynamic Web sites, development tools, and even compilers.

In the following section, you learn a process for creating and running a C# program. This is followed by some additional background information on the C# language.

Preparing to Program

You should take certain steps when solving a problem. First, you must define the problem. If you don't know what the problem is, you will never find the solution. After you know what the problem is, you can devise a plan to fix it. When you have a plan, you can usually implement it. After the plan is implemented, you must test the results to see whether the problem actually has been solved. This same logic can be applied to many other areas, including programming.

When creating a program in C# (or in any language), you should follow a similar sequence of steps:

1. Determine the objective(s) of the program.
2. Determine the methods you want to use in writing the program.
3. Create the program to solve the problem.
4. Run the program to see the results.

An example of an objective (see Step 1) is to write a word processor or database program. A much simpler objective is to display your name on the screen. If you don't have an objective, you won't be able to write an effective program.

The second step is to determine the method you want to use to write the program. Do you need a computer program to solve the problem? What information must be tracked? What formulas will be used? During this step, you should try to determine what you need and in what order the solution should be implemented.

As an example, assume that someone asks you to write a program to determine the area inside a circle. Step 1 is complete because you know your objective: Determine the area inside a circle. Step 2 is to determine what you need to know to calculate the area. In this example, assume that the user of the program will provide the radius of the circle. Knowing this, you can apply the formula πr^2 to obtain the answer. Now you have the pieces you need, so you can continue to Steps 3 and 4, which are called the program-development cycle.

The Program-Development Cycle

The program-development cycle has its own steps. In the first step, you use an editor to create a file that contains your source code. In the second step, you compile the source code to create an intermediate file called either an executable file or a library file. The third step is to run the program to see whether it works as originally planned.

Creating the Source Code

New Term *Source code* is a series of statements or commands used to instruct the computer to perform your desired tasks. These statements and commands are a set of keywords that have special meaning along with other text. As a whole, this text is readable and understandable.

As mentioned, the first step in the program-development cycle is to enter source code into an editor. For example, here is a snippet of C# source code:

```
System.Console.WriteLine("Hello, Mom!");
```

This single line of source code instructs the computer to display the message Hello, Mom! on the screen. Even without knowing how to program, you could speculate that this line of source code writes a line (WriteLine) to the system's console window (System.Console). It is also easy to understand that the line written will be Hello Mom!.

Using an Editor

New Term An *editor* is a program that can be used to enter and save source code. A number of editors can be used with C#. Some are made specifically for C#, and others are not.

Microsoft has added C# capabilities to Microsoft Visual Studio .NET, which now includes Microsoft Visual C# .NET. This is the most prominent editor available for C# programming; however, you don't need Visual Studio .NET or Visual C# .NET to create C# programs.

Other editors also are available for C#. Like Visual Studio .NET, many of these enable you to do all the steps of the development cycle without leaving the editor. Most of these editors also provide features such as color-coding the text that you enter. This makes it much easier to find possible mistakes. Many editors even give you information on what you need to enter and by providing a robust help system.

If you don't have a C# editor, don't fret. Most computer systems include a program that can be used as an editor. If you're using Microsoft Windows, you can use either Notepad or WordPad as your editor. If you're using a Linux or UNIX system, you can use such editors as ed, ex, edit, emacs, or vi.

 The editor SharpDevelop is included on the CD with this book. For more on this editor, see Appendix D, "Using SharpDevelop."

Word processors can also be used to enter C# source code. Most word processors use special codes to format their documents. Other programs can't read these codes correctly. Many word processors—such as WordPerfect, Microsoft Word, and WordPad—are capable of saving source files in a text-based form. When you want to save a word processor file as a text file, select the Text option when saving.

 Note

To find alternative editors, check computer stores or computer mail-order catalogs. Another place to look is in the ads in computer-programming magazines. The following are a few editors that were available at the time this book was written:

- **SharpDevelop, by Mike Krüger**—SharpDevelop is a free editor for C# and VB .NET projects on Microsoft's .NET platform. It is an open-source editor (GPL), so you can download both source code and executables from www.icsharpcode.net. This editor includes a forms designer, code completion, and more. A copy of this editor is included on the CD with this book.

- **CodeWright**—CodeWright is an editor that provides special support for ASP, XML, HTML, C#, Perl, Python, and more. A 30-day trial version of this editor is available at www.premia.com. CodeWright is now associated with Borland.

- **Poorman IDE**—Poorman provides a syntax-highlighted editor for both C# and Visual Basic .NET. It also enables you to run the compiler and capture the console output so that you don't need to leave the Poorman IDE. Poorman is located at `www.geocities.com/duncanchen/poormanide.htm`.

- **EditPlus**—EditPlus is an Internet-ready text editor, HTML editor, and programmer's editor for Windows. Although it can serve as a good replacement for Notepad, it also offers many powerful features for Web page authors and programmers, including the color-coding of code. It is located at `www.editplus.com`.

- **JEdit**—JEdit is an open-source editor for Java; however, it can be used for C#. It includes the capability of color-coding the code. It is located at `http://jedit.sourceforge.net`.

- **Antechinus C#**—This editor supports the C# programming language, provides color-coded syntax, and allows you to compile and run applications from the integrated environment. Other features include easy project generation, integration with .NET tools, unlimited undo/redo capability, bookmarks and brace matching, and Intellisense. It is located at `www.c-point.com`.

Naming Your Source Files

When you save a source file, you must give it a name. The name should describe what the program does. Although you could give your source file any extension, .cs is recognized as the appropriate extension to use for a C# program source file.

Tip

The name should describe what the program does. Some people suggest that the name of your source file should be the same as the name of your C# class.

Understanding the Execution of a C# Program

It is important to understand a little bit about how a C# program executes. C# programs are different from programs that you can create with many other programming languages.

C# programs are created to run on the .NET Common Language Runtime (CLR). This means that if you create a C# executable program and try to run it on a machine that doesn't have the CLR or a compatible runtime, the program won't execute.

The benefit of creating programs for a runtime environment is portability. If you wanted to create a program that could run on different platforms or operating systems with an older language such as C or C++, you had to compile a different executable program for each. For example, if you wrote a C application and you wanted to run it on a Linux machine and a Windows machine, you would have to create two executable programs—one on a Linux machine and one on a Windows machine. With C#, you create only one executable program, and it runs on either machine.

NEW TERM If you want your program to execute as fast as possible, you want to create a true executable. To become a true executable, a program must be translated from source code to machine language (digital, or *binary*, instructions). A program called a *compiler* performs this translation. The compiler takes your source code file as input and produces a disk file containing the machine-language instructions that correspond to your source-code statements. With programs such as C and C++, the compiler creates a file that can be executed with no further effort.

With C#, you use a compiler that does not produce machine language. Instead, it produces an Intermediate Language (IL) file. This IL file can be copied to any machine with a .NET CLR. Because this IL file isn't directly executable by the computer, you need something more to happen to translate or further compile the program for the computer. The CLR or a compatible C# runtime does this final compile just as it is needed.

Compiling the program is one of the first things the CLR does with an IL file. In this process, the CLR converts the code from the portable, IL code to a language (machine language) that the computer can understand and run. The CLR actually compiles only the parts of the program that are being used. This saves time. This final compile of a C# program is called Just In Time (JIT) compiling, or *jitting*.

Because the runtime needs to compile the IL file, it takes a little more time to initially run portions of a program than it does to run a fully compiled language such as C++. After the first time a portion of the program is executed, the time difference disappears because the fully compiled version is used from that point. In most cases, this initial time delay is minor. You can also choose to JIT a C# program when you install it to a specific platform.

Note

At the time this book was written, the .NET CLR and a command-line C# compiler were available for free from Microsoft as a part of the .NET Framework. Check the Microsoft Web site (www.microsoft.com) for the latest version of the .NET Framework.

> Additionally, limited versions of C# and the .NET Framework are available for other platforms. This includes the mono version of .NET. The mono project (www.go-mono.com) includes a compiler and a runtime that works for .NET. Currently, the mono project targets Windows, Linux, and the Macintosh.

Compiling C# Source Code to Intermediate Language

To create the IL file, you use the C# compiler. If you are using the Microsoft .NET Framework SDK, you can apply the csc command, followed by the name of the source file, to run the compiler. For example, to compile a source file called Radius.cs, you type the following at the command line:

```
csc Radius.cs
```

If you are not using Microsoft's .NET Framework, a different command may be necessary. For example, the mono compiler is mcs. To compile for mono, you use the following:

```
mcs Radius.cs
```

If you're using a graphical development environment such as Microsoft Visual C# .NET, compiling is even simpler. In most graphical environments, you can compile a program by selecting the Compile icon or selecting the appropriate option from the menu. After the code is compiled, selecting the Run icon or the appropriate option from the menus executes the program.

Note

> You should check your compiler's manuals for specifics on compiling and running a program.

New Term After you compile, you have an IL file. If you look at a list of the files in the directory or folder in which you compiled, you should find a new file that has the same name as your source file, but with an .exe (rather than a .cs) extension. The file with the .exe extension is your compiled program (called an *assembly*). This program is ready to run on the CLR. The assembly file contains all the information that the CLR needs to know to execute the program. According to .NET terminology, the code inside the assembly file is called *managed code*.

> **Note**   Managed code refers to the code that can be executed under only the .NET
> environment.

Figure 1.1 shows the progression from source code to executable.

FIGURE 1.1

*The C# source code
that you write is con-
verted to Intermediate
Language (IL) code by
the compiler.*

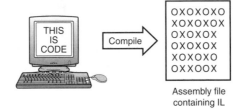

Assembly file
containing IL

> **Note**   In general, two primary types of deliverables are created as C# programs—
> executables and libraries. You can also use C# for other types of program-
> ming, including scripting on ASP.NET pages. Although you will primarily
> focus on executables in this book, you will also learn more about libraries
> and ASP.NET pages.

Completing the Development Cycle

After your program becomes a compiled IL file, you can run it by entering its name at
the command-line prompt or just as you would run any other program. However, the program requires that you have the .NET CLR. If you don't have the CLR installed, you
will get an error when you run the program. Installing the Microsoft .NET Framework
allows you to run your programs like all other programs. If you use other frameworks,
you might have to do something different. For example, when you compile a program
using the mono compiler (mcs), you can then run the program by entering it after mono.
For example, to run the radius program mentioned earlier, you would type the following
at the command line:

```
mono Radius.exe
```

1

If you run the program and receive different results than you thought you would, you need to go back to the first step of the development process. You must identify what caused the problem and correct it in the source code. When you make a change to the source code, you need to recompile the program to create a corrected version of the executable file. You keep following this cycle until you get the program to execute exactly as you intended.

The C# Development Cycle

Use an editor to write your source code. C# source-code files are usually given the .cs extension (for example, a_program.cs, database.cs, and so on).

Compile the program using a C# compiler. If the compiler doesn't find any errors in the program, it produces an assembly file with the extension .exe or .dll. For example, Myprog.cs compiles to Myprog.exe by default. If the compiler finds errors, it reports them. You must return to Step 1 to make corrections in your source code.

Execute the program on a machine with a C# runtime, such as the CLR. You should test to determine whether your program functions properly. If not, start again with Step 1, and make modifications and additions to your source code.

Figure 1.2 shows the program-development steps. For all but the simplest programs, you might go through this sequence many times before finishing your program. Even the most experienced programmers can't sit down and write a complete, error-free program in just one step. Because you'll be running through the edit-compile-test cycle many times, it's important to become familiar with your tools: the editor, compiler, and runtime environment.

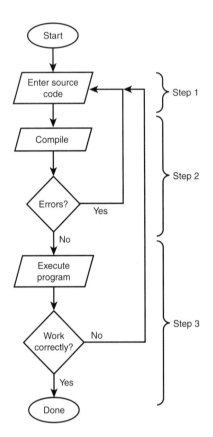

Creating Your First C# Program

You're probably eager to create your first program in C#. To help you become familiar with your compiler, Listing 1.1 contains a quick program for you to work through. You might not understand everything at this point, but you should still try to get a feel for the process of writing, compiling, and running a real C# program.

This demonstration uses a program named Hello.cs, which does nothing more than display the words Hello, World! on the screen. This program is the traditional one used to introduce people to programming. The source code for Hello.cs is in Listing 1.1. When you type this listing, don't include the line numbers on the left or the colons.

LISTING **1.1**   Hello.cs

```
1:  class Hello
2:  {
3:     public static void Main()
4:     {
5:         System.Console.WriteLine("Hello, World!");
6:     }
7:  }
```

Be sure that you have installed your compiler as specified in the installation instructions provided with the software. If you have installed the .NET Framework SDK, then you already have a C# compiler installed. It comes with a C# compiler.

When your compiler and editor are ready, follow the steps in the next section to enter, compile, and execute Hello.cs.

Entering and Compiling Hello.cs

To enter and compile the Hello.cs program, follow these steps:

1. Start your editor.
2. Enter the Hello.cs source code shown in Listing 1.1. Don't enter the line numbers or colons; these are provided only for reference within this book. Press Enter at the end of each line. Make sure that you enter the code using the same case. C# is case sensitive, so if you change the capitalization, you will get errors.

Caution

> In C and C++, main() is lowercase. In C#, Main() has a capital M. In C#, if you type a lowercase m, you will get an error.

3. Save the source code. You should name the file Hello.cs.
4. Verify that Hello.cs has been saved by listing the files in the directory or folder.
5. Compile Hello.cs. If you are using the Microsoft C# command-line compiler, enter the following:

   csc Hello.cs

   If you are using a mono command-line compiler, enter the following:

   mcs Hello.cs

   If you are using an Integrated Development Environment (IDE), select the appropriate icon, hot key, or menu option. You should get a message stating that there were no errors or warnings.

Tip

> If you are using Microsoft Visual Studio .NET, you can launch the command prompt from Start, Program Files, Microsoft Visual Studio .NET, Visual Studio .NET Tools, Visual Studio .NET Command Prompt. If you choose to use the command line, I recommend that you use this prompt for compiling and executing your C# programs because it has the correct path settings for the C# compiler.

6. Check the compiler messages. If you receive no errors or warnings, everything should be okay.

   If you made an error typing the program, the compiler will catch it and display an error message. For example, if you misspelled the word `Console` as `Consol`, you would see a message similar to the following:

   ```
   Hello.cs(5,7): error CS0234: The type or namespace name 'Consol' does not
   exist in the class or namespace 'System' (are you missing an assembly
   reference?)
   ```

7. Go back to Step 2 if this or any other error message is displayed. Open the Hello.cs file in your editor. Compare your file's contents carefully with Listing 1.1, make any necessary corrections, and continue with Step 3.

8. Your first C# program should now be compiled and ready to run. If you display a directory listing of all files named hello (with any extension), you should see the following:

   Hello.cs, the source code file you created with your editor
   Hello.exe, the executable program created when you compiled hello.cs

9. To *execute*, or run, Hello.exe, enter **Hello** at the command line. The message `Hello, World!` is displayed onscreen.

Note

> If you are using Windows and you run the hello program by double-clicking in Microsoft's Windows Explorer, you might not see the results. This program runs in a command prompt window. When you double-click in Windows Explorer, the program opens a command prompt window, runs the program, and—because the program is done—closes the window. This can happen so fast that it doesn't seem like anything happens. It is better to open a command prompt window, change to the directory containing the program, and then run the program from the command line.

> **Note**
>
> If you are not using the Microsoft .NET compiler and runtime, you might have to run the program differently. For example, to run the program using the mono runtime, you will need to enter the following on a command line:
>
> `mono Hello.exe`
>
> If you are using a different runtime, you will want to check its documentation for specific instructions for running a .NET program.

Congratulations! You have just entered, compiled, and run your first C# program. Admittedly, Hello.cs is a simple program that doesn't do anything overly useful, but it's a start. In fact, most of today's expert programmers started learning in this same way— by compiling a "hello world" program.

Understanding Compilation Errors

A compilation error occurs when the compiler finds something in the source code that it can't compile. A misspelling, a typographical error, or any of a dozen other things can cause the compiler to choke. Fortunately, modern compilers don't just choke; they tell you what they're choking on and where the problem is. This makes it easier to find and correct errors in your source code.

This point can be illustrated by introducing a deliberate error into the Hello.cs program that you entered earlier. If you worked through that example (and you should have), you now have a copy of hello.cs on your disk. Using your editor, move the cursor to the end of Line 5 and erase the terminating semicolon. Hello.cs should now look like Listing 1.2.

LISTING 1.2   Helloerr.cs—Hello.cs with an Error

```
1:  class Hello
2:  {
3:     public static void Main()
4:     {
5:         System.Console.WriteLine("Hello, World!")
6:     }
7:  }
```

Next, save the file. You're now ready to compile it. Do so by entering the command for your compiler. Remember, the command-line command is this:

`csc Helloerr.cs`

Because of the error you introduced, the compilation is not completed. Instead, the compiler displays a message similar to the following:

```
Helloerr.cs(5,48): error CS1002: ; expected
```

Looking at this line, you can see that it has three parts:

`Helloerr.cs`	The name of the file where the error was found
`(5,48):`	The line number and position where the error was noticed: Line 5, position 48
`error CS1002: ; expected`	A description of the error

This message is quite informative, telling you that when the compiler made it to the 48th character of Line 5 of Helloerr.cs, the compiler expected to find a semicolon but didn't.

Although the compiler is very clever about detecting and localizing errors, it's no Einstein. Using your knowledge of the C# language, you must interpret the compiler's messages and determine the actual location of any errors that are reported. They are often found on the line reported by the compiler, but if not, they are almost always on the preceding line. You might have a bit of trouble finding errors at first, but you should soon get better at it.

Before leaving this topic, take a look at another example of a compilation error. Load Helloerr.cs into your editor again, and make the following changes:

1. Replace the semicolon at the end of Line 5.
2. Delete the double quotation mark just before the word `Hello`.

Save the file to disk, and compile the program again. This time, the compiler should display an error message similar to the following:

```
Helloerr.cs(5,46): error CS1010: Newline in constant
```

The error message finds the correct line for the error, locating it in Line 5. The error messages found the error at location 46 on Line 5. This error message missed the point that a quotation mark was missing from the code. In this case, the compiler took its best guess at the problem. Although it was close to the area of the problem, it was not perfect.

Tip

> If the compiler reports multiple errors and you can find only one, fix that error and recompile. You might find that your single correction is all that's needed, and the program will compile without errors.

Understanding Logic Errors

You might get one other type of error: logic errors. Logic errors are not errors that you can blame on the code or the compiler; they are errors that can be blamed only on you. It is possible to create a program with perfect C# code that still contains an error. For example, suppose that you want to calculate the area of a circle by multiplying 2 multiplied by the value of pi, multiplied by the radius:

Area = $2\pi r$

You can enter this formula into your program, compile, and execute. You will get an answer. The C# program could be written syntactically correct; however, every time you run this program, you will get a wrong answer. The logic is wrong. This formula will never give you the area of a circle; it gives you its circumference. You should have used the formula πr^2.

No matter how good a compiler is, it will never be able to find logic errors. You have to find these on your own by reviewing your code and by running your programs.

Types of C# Programs

Before continuing with another program, it is worth reviewing the types of applications you can create with C#. You can build a number of types:

- **Console applications**—Console applications run from the command line. Throughout this book, you will create console applications, which are primarily character- or text-based and, therefore, remain relatively simple to understand.
- **Window forms applications**—You can also create Windows applications that take advantage of the graphical user interface (GUI) provided by Microsoft Windows.
- **Web Services**—Web Services are routines that can be called across the Web.
- **Web form/ASP.NET applications**—ASP.NET applications are executed on a Web server and generate dynamic Web pages.

In addition to these types of applications, C# can be used to do a lot of other things, including create libraries, create controls, and more. As you progress through this book, you will learn to create applications based on these four main types of applications.

Creating Your First Window Application

One of the most common types of application you will most likely create with C# is a Windows form application. You might also see these applications referred to as WinForm applications. These applications use the graphical-style windows like those that you see in Microsoft Windows. Because a standardized library (from the .NET Framework) is used, you can actually expect the Windows application to match your operating system's look and feel. In Listing 1.3, an extremely simple windows form is created. You'll notice that this application takes a little more code than the previous console application that was created. However, you will also notice that the application's output is much nicer.

If you are using the Microsoft .NET runtime, you will be able to do forms-based (Windows) applications. If you are using a different runtime, you will need to check its documentation to determine whether Window forms is currently supported. At the time this book was written, the support for Window forms applications were fully available only within the Microsoft Framework. The go-mono project was working to build the routines for doing forms-based (Windows) applications. Other versions of the .NET Framework are expected to support Windows forms as well as the other .NET Framework routines. This means that if your framework doesn't support these routines today, it will most likely support them in the future. More important, the routines follow Microsoft's structure, to make them portable.

Note

The routines for doing forms are a part of the .NET Framework rather than a part of the C# language. However, the C# language can tap into these routines.

LISTING 1.3   MyForm.cs: Hello Windows World!

```
 1:  using System;
 2:  using System.Windows.Forms;
 3:
 4:  namespace HelloWin
 5:  {
 6:    public class MyForm : Form
 7:    {
 8:      private TextBox txtEnter;
 9:      private Label   lblDisplay;
10:      private Button  btnOk;
11:
12:      public MyForm()
13:      {
14:        this.txtEnter   = new TextBox();
15:        this.lblDisplay = new Label();
16:        this.btnOk      = new Button();
17:        this.Text = "My HelloWin App!";
18:
```

LISTING 1.3   continued

```
19:        // txtEnter
20:        this.txtEnter.Location = new System.Drawing.Point(16, 32);
21:        this.txtEnter.Size = new System.Drawing.Size(264, 20);
22:
23:        // lblDisplay
24:        this.lblDisplay.Location = new System.Drawing.Point(16, 72);
25:        this.lblDisplay.Size = new System.Drawing.Size(264, 128);
26:
27:        // btnOk
28:        this.btnOk.Location = new System.Drawing.Point(88, 224);
29:        this.btnOk.Text = "OK";
30:        this.btnOk.Click +=
31:                new System.EventHandler(this.btnOK_Click);
32:        // MyForm
33:        this.Controls.AddRange(new Control[] {
34:                this.txtEnter, this.lblDisplay, this.btnOk});
35:    }
36:
37:    static void Main ()
38:    {
39:      Application.Run(new MyForm());
40:    }
41:
42:    private void btnOK_Click(object sender, System.EventArgs e)
43:    {
44:      lblDisplay.Text = txtEnter.Text + "\n" + lblDisplay.Text;
45:    }
46:  }
47: }
```

Just as you did with the previous program, enter the code from Listing 1.3 into your editor. Remember that the line numbers and colons are for reference in the book; you do not enter them when entering the listing. After you've entered the listing, you will compile it as shown earlier. If you are compiling at the command line, you enter this:

```
csc /t:winexe MyForm.cs
```

Note

> You can actually leave out the /t:winexe, and this program will still compile and run. By including /t:winexe on the command line, you tell the C# compiler to target this application as a Windows executable. Non-Microsoft compilers use a similar command.

If you are using an IDE you can select its button or menu option for compiling. If after you compile you receive an error, compare what you entered to the listing in the book to make sure you didn't type something wrong. As discussed earlier, the error messages should help you to identify where the problem is.

When you compile this listing without errors, you can run it in the same manner that you run any other program. Even though this is a Windows application, you can run it from the command line. You do this by simply entering the name of the program, MyForm. Regardless of where you run this program from, the result is a Windows form displayed, as shown in Figure 1.3.

OUTPUT

FIGURE 1.3

MyForm output.

ANALYSIS Enter text into the window dialog box and click the OK button. You can continue to enter text and click the OK button; the text is displayed on the form. As you enter additional text and click the OK button, you'll see the previously entered text scroll. Figure 1.4 shows the form after a few lines of text have been entered.

FIGURE 1.4

MyForm application after entering several lines of text.

As you can see, much more code is needed to display a form than is needed to display a simple message in a console window. Look through the code in Listing 1.3; however, don't expect to understand all of it right now. You'll see there is code for creating a text box (txtEnter), a button (btnOK), and a label control (lblDisplay). You'll learn more about this code when you learn about Windows forms.

Why C#?

Now that you've created your first applications in C#, it is time to step back and answer a simple question: Why C#? Many people believed that there was no need for a new programming language. Java, C++, Perl, Microsoft Visual Basic, and other existing languages were believed to offer all the functionality needed.

C# was created as an object-oriented programming (OOP) language. Other programming languages include object-oriented features, but very few are fully object-oriented. As you go through this book, you will learn all the details of what makes up an object-oriented language.

C# is a language derived from C and C++, but it was created from the ground up. Microsoft started with what worked in C and C++, and included new features that would make these languages easier to use. Many of these features are very similar to what is found in Java. Ultimately, Microsoft had a number of objectives when building the language. These objectives included the creation of a simple, yet modern language that was fully object-oriented.

Caution The following contains a lot of technical terms. Don't worry about understanding these; most of them don't matter to C# programmers. The ones that do matter are explained later in this book.

Other reasons exist for using C#, beyond Microsoft's reasons. C# removes some of the complexities and pitfalls of languages such as Java and C++, including macros, multiple inheritance, and virtual base classes. These are all areas that cause either confusion or potential problems for C++ developers. If you are learning C# as your first language, rest assured—these are topics that you won't have to spend time learning. Statements, expressions, operators, and other functions are taken directly from C and C++, but improvements make the language simpler. Some of the improvements include eliminating redundancies. Other areas of improvement include additional syntax changes. For example, C++ uses a number of different operators when working with members of a structure: ::, ., and ->. Knowing when to use each of these three operators can be very confusing. In C#, these all have been replaced with a single symbol—the "dot" operator. For newer programmers, changes like these make learning C# easier. You'll learn more about all of these features throughout this book.

C# is also a modern language. Features such as exception handling, garbage collection, extensible data types, and code security are expected in a modern language; C# contains all of these. If you are a new programmer, you might be asking what all these complicated-sounding features are. Again, you don't need to understand these now. By the end of your 21 days, you will understand how all of them apply to your C# programming.

C# Is Object-Oriented

NEW TERM   As mentioned earlier, C# is an object-oriented language. The keys to an object-oriented language are encapsulation, inheritance, and polymorphism. C# supports all of these. *Encapsulation* is the placing of functionality into a single package. *Inheritance* is a structured way of extending existing code and functionality into new programs and packages. *Polymorphism* is the capability of adapting to what needs to be done. Detailed explanations of each of these terms and a more detailed description of object orientation are provided in Day 5's lesson, "The Core of C# Programming: Classes." Additionally, because OOP is central to C#, these topics are covered in greater detail throughout this book.

C# Is Modular

NEW TERM   C# code can (and should) be written in chunks called *classes,* which contain routines called *member methods*. These classes and methods can be reused in other applications or programs. By passing pieces of information to the classes and methods, you can create useful, reusable code.

NEW TERM   Another term that is often associated with C# is *component*. C# can also be used to create components. Components are programs that can be incorporated into other programs. These may or may not include the C# code. Once created, a component can be used as a building block for other more complex programs.

C# Will Be Popular

C# is a newer programming language, but its popularity is already growing. One of the key reasons for this growth is Microsoft and the promises of .NET.

Microsoft wants C# to be popular. Although a company cannot make a product popular, it can help. Not long ago, Microsoft suffered the abysmal failure of the Microsoft Bob operating system. Although Microsoft wanted Bob to be popular, it failed.

C# stands a better chance of success than Microsoft Bob. I don't know whether people at Microsoft actually used Bob in their daily jobs. C#, however, *is* being used by Microsoft. Many of its products have already had portions rewritten in C#. By using it, Microsoft helps validate the capabilities of C# to meet the needs of programmers.

Microsoft .NET is another reason why C# stands a chance to succeed. .NET is a change in the way the creation and implementation of applications is done. Although virtually any programming language can be used with .NET, C# is proving to be the language of choice.

Starting with Microsoft Windows Server 2003, the .NET Framework will be included with Microsoft's operating systems. This means that there will be no need to install the runtime on future versions of Windows. This will give Windows developers the capability to use all of the functionality built into the .NET Framework, without needing to distribute it with their applications. This can result in smaller applications.

C# will also be popular for all the features mentioned earlier: simplicity, object-orientation, modularity, flexibility, and conciseness.

A High-Level View of .NET

C# is a language that was created to work with the .NET Framework. The .NET Framework consists of a number of pieces, including a runtime, a set of predefined routines, and a defined set of ways to store the information. C# programs take advantage of these features of the platform.

You have already learned about the runtime: the Common Language Runtime (CLR). The CLR offers a buffer between your compiled C# program and the specific operating system you are using to run your C# program.

The standard way of storing information is accomplished through the Common Type System (CTS). This is a set of storage types that a number of different programs can use. More specifically, all of the programming languages used with the .NET platform use these common types. By using a common system to define ways of storing information, it is possible for different programming languages to share this information. You'll learn more about the CTS and the common types in Day 2's lesson, "Understanding C# Programs."

The other key piece to the .NET platform is the set of defined routines that you can use. These routines are a part of the .NET Base Class library (BCL). Thousands of routines have been created that you can use from your C# programs. These include routines such as printing information to a console window, as you did in the "Hello World" application, or more complex routines for creating forms and controls. Routines also exist for doing file handling, working with XML, doing multitasking, and much more. You'll see lots of these routines used throughout this book.

 Note

Note that these routines are fully available in the Microsoft .NET Framework. In .NET Frameworks for other platforms, the routines were not completed at the time this book was written. For example, the go-mono project was still in the process of creating many of these routines. Projects such as go-mono are working to convert the routines so that they will work identically to the routines in Microsoft's .NET Framework.

The routines in the BCL, the CTS, and many other features of the .NET platform apply to other .NET languages in the same way they apply to C#. For example, the routines in the BCL are the same routines that are used by languages such as Microsoft Visual Basic .NET, Microsoft J# .NET, and JScript .NET.

Because of the shared features from the .NET Framework, you will find that after you learn C#, it is very simple to learn to use other .NET programming languages. In fact, you can create routines in C# that can be used by other .NET languages as well.

C# and Object-Oriented Programming (OOP)

You've covered a lot of material already today; however, one more foundational topic needs to be covered before jumping deep into the C# programming language. This is object-oriented programming (OOP).

As mentioned earlier, C# is considered an object-oriented language. To take full advantage of C#, you should understand the concepts of object-oriented languages. The following sections present an overview of objects and what makes a language object-oriented. You will learn how these concepts are applied to C# as you work through the rest of this book.

Object-Oriented Concepts

What makes a language object-oriented? The most obvious answer is that the language uses objects. However, this doesn't tell you much. As stated earlier, three concepts generally are associated with object-oriented languages:

- Encapsulation
- Polymorphism
- Inheritance

A fourth concept is expected as a result of using an object-oriented language: reuse.

Encapsulation

Encapsulation is the concept of making "packages" that contain everything you need. With object-oriented programming, this means that you can create an object (or package) such as a circle that does everything that you would want to do with a circle. This includes keeping track of everything about the circle, such as the radius and the center point. It also means knowing how to handle the functionality of a circle, such as calculating its radius and possibly knowing how to draw it.

By encapsulating a circle, you allow the user to be oblivious to how the circle works; the user needs to know only how to interact with the circle. This provides a shield to the inner workings of the circle. Why should users care how information about a circle is stored internally? As long as they can get the circle to do what they want, they shouldn't.

Polymorphism

Polymorphism is the capability of assuming many forms. This can be applied to two areas of object-oriented programming (if not more). First, it means that you can call an object or a routine in many different ways and still get the same result. Using a circle as an example, you might want to call a circle object to get its area. You can do this by using three points or by using a single point and the radius. Either way, you would expect to get the same results. In a procedure language such as C, you need two routines with two different names to address these two methods of getting the area. In C#, you still have two routines; however, you can give them the same name. Any programs that you or others write will simply call the circle routine and pass your information. The circle program automatically determines which of the two routines to use. Based on the information passed, the correct routine is used. Users calling the routine don't need to worry about which routine to use; they just call the routine.

A more important use of polymorphism is the capability to work with something even though you might not know exactly what it is. Your program can adapt. For example, you could have a number of different shapes, such as triangles, squares, and circles. You could write a program that used polymorphism that could work with shapes. Because triangles, squares, and circles are all shapes, your program could adapt to working with all three of these. Although this type of programming is more complex than basic programming, the power that it provides you is worth the complexity. You'll learn to program polymorphism in this manner on Day 12, "Tapping into OOP: Interfaces."

Inheritance

Inheritance is the most complicated of the object-oriented concepts. Having a circle is nice, but what if a sphere would be nicer? A sphere is just a special kind of circle: It has all the characteristics of a circle, with a third dimension added. You could say that a sphere is a special kind of circle that takes on all the properties of a circle and then adds a little more. By using the circle to create your sphere, your sphere can inherit all the properties of the circle. The capability of inheriting these properties is a characteristic of inheritance.

Reuse

One of the key reasons an object-oriented language is used is the concept of reuse. When you create a class, you can reuse it to create lots of objects. By using inheritance and some of the features described previously, you can create routines that can be used again in a number of programs and in a number of ways. By encapsulating functionality, you can create routines that have been tested and proven to work. This means that you won't have to test the details of how the functionality works—only that you are using it correctly. This makes reusing these routines quick and easy.

Objects and Classes

NEW TERM Now that you understand the concepts of an object-oriented language, it is important to understand the difference between a class and an object. A *class* is a definition for an item that will be created. The actual item that will be created is an *object*. Simply put, classes are definitions used to create objects.

An analogy often used to describe classes is a cookie cutter. A cookie cutter defines a cookie shape. It isn't a cookie, and it isn't edible. It is simply a construct that can be used to create shaped cookies repeatedly. When you use the cookie cutter to create cookies, you know that each cookie will look the same. You also know that you can use the cookie cutter to create lots of cookies.

As with a cookie cutter, a class can be used to create lots of objects. For example, you can have a circle class that can be used to create a number of circles. If you create a drawing program to draw circles, you could have one circle class and lots of circle objects. You could make each circle in the snowman an object; however, you would need only one class to define all of them.

You also can have a number of other classes, including a name class, a card class, an application class, a point class, a circle class, an address class, a snowman class (that can use the circle class), and more.

Note

Classes and objects are covered again in more detail throughout this book. Today's information gives you an overview of the object-oriented concepts and introduces you to some of the terminology. If you don't fully understand the terminology at this time, don't worry; you'll understand these concepts by the end of your 21 days.

Summary

At the beginning of today's lesson, you learned what C# has to offer, including its power, its flexibility, and its object orientation. You also learned that C# is considered simple and modern.

Today you explored the various steps involved in writing a C# program—the process known as program development. You should have a clear grasp of the edit-compile-test cycle before continuing.

Errors are an unavoidable part of program development. Your C# compiler detects errors in your source code and displays an error message, giving both the nature and the location of the error. Using this information, you can edit your source code to correct the error. Remember, however, that the compiler can't always accurately report the nature and location of an error. Sometimes you need to use your knowledge of C# to track down exactly what is causing a given error message.

You ended today's lesson with an overview of several object-oriented concepts. You were introduced to a number of technical concepts, including polymorphism, inheritance, encapsulation, and reuse. You also learned the conceptual difference between a class and an object. Because OOP is central to C#, you'll learn more about these concepts throughout this book.

A lot was covered in your first day of C#. Many of the concepts and technical terms will be covered again as you progress through this book. Before moving on to Day 2, you should make sure that you are comfortable with the steps of entering, compiling, and running a C# program, as shown earlier. Don't worry about understanding the actual C# code at this time. That is the focus of the rest of this book!

Q&A

Q **Will a C# program run on any machine?**

A No. A C# program will run only on machines that have the Common Language Runtime (CLR) installed. If you copy the executable program to a machine that does not contain the CLR, you get an error. On versions of Microsoft Windows without the CLR, you usually are told that a DLL file is missing.

Q **If I want to give people a program that I wrote, which files do I need to give them?**

A One of the nice things about C# is that it is a compiled language. This means that after the source code is compiled, you have an executable program. If you want to give the hello program to all your friends with computers, you can. You give them the executable program, Hello.exe. They don't need the source file, hello.cs, and they don't need to own a C# compiler. They do need to use a computer system that has a .NET runtime, such as the Common Language Runtime (CLR) from Microsoft.

Q **After I create an executable file, do I need to keep the source file (.cs)?**

A If you get rid of the source file, you have no easy way to make changes to the program in the future, so you should keep this file.

Most Integrated Development Environments create files in addition to the source file (.cs) and the executable file. As long as you keep the source file (.cs), you can almost always re-create the other files. If your program uses external resources, such as images and forms, you also need to keep those files in case you need to make changes and re-create the executable.

Q **If my compiler came with an editor, do I have to use it?**

A Definitely not. You can use any editor, as long as it saves the source code in text format. If the compiler came with an editor, you should try to use it. If you like a different editor better, use it. I use an editor that I purchased separately, even though all my compilers have their own editors. The editors that come with compilers are getting better. Some of them automatically format your C# code. Others color-code different parts of your source file, to make it easier to find errors.

Q **Do I need a copy of Microsoft Visual Studio .NET or Microsoft Visual C# .NET to do C# programming?**

A No. However, you do need a C# compiler and a copy of a .NET runtime. The Microsoft .NET Framework—which was free to download at the time this book was written—contains a C# compiler as well as the runtime that you need to execute your programs. You can also use different C# compilers and runtimes. For example, you can download a C# compiler and runtime from www.go-mono.com. The mono products will work with platforms such as Windows, Linux, and more.

One caution is that some of the available compilers and runtime might not fully support all of the functionality of the Microsoft platform. If a C# compiler has been released, it should fully support the C# language. The C# language is covered in the first 14 days of this book. During the last week, a number of the .NET Framework classes are covered. Compilers and runtimes that are not complete might not fully support everything in the last week. The Microsoft .NET Framework supports everything presented in this book.

Q Can I ignore warning messages?

A Some warning messages don't affect how the program runs, and some do. If the compiler gives you a warning message, it's a signal that something isn't right. Most compilers let you set the warning level. By setting the warning level, you can get only the most serious warnings, or you can get all the warnings, including the most minute. Some compilers even offer various levels between. In your programs, you should look at each warning and make a determination. It's always best to try to write all your programs with absolutely no warnings or errors. (With an error, your compiler won't create the executable file.)

Workshop

The Workshop provides quiz questions to help you solidify your understanding of the material covered and exercises to provide you with experience in using what you've learned. Try to understand the quiz and exercise answers before continuing to the day's lesson. Answers are provided on the CD.

Quiz

1. Give three reasons why C# is a great choice of programming language.
2. What do IL and CLR stand for?
3. What are the steps in the program-development cycle?
4. What command do you need to enter to compile a program called My_prog.cs with your compiler?
5. What extension should you use for your C# source files?
6. Is Filename.txt a valid name for a C# source file?

7. If you execute a program that you have compiled and it doesn't work as you expected, what should you do?

8. What is machine language?

9. On what line did the following error most likely occur?

   ```
   My_prog.cs(35,6): error CS1010: Newline in constant
   ```

10. Near what column did the following error most likely occur?

    ```
    My_prog.cs(35,6): error CS1010: Newline in constant
    ```

11. What are the key OOP concepts?

Exercises

1. Use your text editor to look at the EXE file created by Listing 1.1. Does the EXE file look like the source file? (Don't save this file when you exit the editor.)

2. Enter the following program and compile it. (Don't include the line numbers or colons.) What does this program do?

```
 1:  // Variables.cs - Using variables and literals
 2:  // This program calculates some circle stuff.
 3:  //---------------------------------------------
 4:
 5:  using System;
 6:
 7:  class Variables
 8:  {
 9:      public static void Main()
10:      {
11:          //Declare variables
12:
13:          int radius = 4;
14:          const double PI = 3.14159;
15:          double circum, area;
16:
17:          //Do calculations
18:
19:          area = PI * radius * radius;
20:          circum = 2 * PI * radius;
21:
22:          //Print the results
23:
24:          Console.WriteLine("Radius = {0}, PI = {1}", radius, PI );
25:          Console.WriteLine("The area is {0}", area);
26:          Console.WriteLine("The circumference is {0}", circum);
27:      }
28:  }
```

3. Enter and compile the following program. What does this program do?

```
1:  class AClass
2:  {
3:     public static void Main()
4:     {
5:        int x,y;
6:        for ( x = 0; x < 10; x++, System.Console.Write( "\n" ) )
7:           for ( y = 0; y < 10; y++ )
8:              System.Console.Write( "X" );
9:     }
10: }
```

4. **Bug Buster:** The following program has a problem. Enter it in your editor and compile it. Which lines generate error messages?

```
1:  class Hello
2:  {
3:     public static void Main()
4:     {
5:        System.Console.WriteLine(Keep Looking!);
6:        System.Console.WriteLine(You'll find it!);
7:     }
8:  }
```

5. Make the following change to the program in Exercise 3. Recompile and rerun this program. What does the program do now?

```
8:              System.Console.Write( "{0}",  (char) 1 );
```

Type & Run 1

Numbering Your Listings

Throughout this book, you will find a number of Type & Run sections. These sections present a listing that is a little longer than the listings within the daily lessons. The purpose of these listings is to give you a program to type in and run. The listings might contain elements not yet explained in the book.

These programs generally do something either fun or practical. For instance, the program included here, named NumberIT, adds line numbers similar to those included on the listings in this book. You can use this program to number your listings as you work through the rest of this book.

I suggest that after you type in and run these programs, you take the time to experiment with the code. Make changes, recompile, and then rerun the programs. See what happens. There won't be explanations on how the code works—only on what it does. Don't fret, though. By the time you complete this book, you should understand everything within these earlier listings. In the meantime, you will have had the chance to enter and run some listings that are a little more fun or practical.

The First Type & Run

Enter and compile the following program. If you get any errors, make sure you entered the program correctly.

The usage for this program is NumberIT *filename.ext*, where *filename.ext* is the source filename along with the extension. Note that this program adds line numbers to the listing. (Don't let this program's length worry you; you're not expected to understand it yet. It's included here to help you compare printouts of your programs with the ones given in the book.)

LISTING T&R 1.1   NumberIT.cs

```
 1: using System;
 2: using System.IO;
 3:
 4: /// <summary>
 5: /// Class to number a listing. Assumes fewer than 1000 lines.
 6: /// </summary>
 7:
 8: class NumberIT
 9: {
10:
11:    /// <summary>
12:    /// The main entry point for the application.
13:    /// </summary>
14:
15:    public static void Main( string[] args)
16:    {
17:
18:       // check to see if a file name was included on the
19:       // command line.
20:
21:       if ( args.Length <= 0 )
22:       {
23:          Console.WriteLine("\nYou need to include a filename.");
24:       }
25:       else
26:       {
27:          // declare objects for connecting to files...
28:          StreamReader InFile  = null;
29:          StreamWriter OutFile = null;
30:
31:          try
32:          {
33:             // Open file name included on command line...
34:             InFile  = File.OpenText(args[0]);
35:             // Create the output file...
```

LISTING T&R1.1   continued

```
36:              OutFile = File.CreateText("outfile.txt");
37:
38:              Console.Write("\nNumbering...");
39:
40:              // Read first line of the file...
41:              string line = InFile.ReadLine();
42:              int ctr = 1;
43:
44:              // loop through the file as long as not at the end...
45:              while ( line != null)
46:              {
47:                OutFile.WriteLine("{0}: {1}",
48:                        ctr.ToString().PadLeft(3,'0'), line);
49:                Console.Write("..{0}..", ctr.ToString());
50:                ctr++;
51:                line = InFile.ReadLine();
52:              }
53:            }
54:          catch (System.IO.FileNotFoundException)
55:            {
56:              Console.WriteLine ("Could not find the file {0}", args[0]);
57:            }
58:          catch (Exception e)
59:            {
60:              Console.WriteLine("Error: {0}", e.Message);
61:            }
62:          finally
63:            {
64:              if(InFile != null)
65:              {
66:                // Close the files
67:                InFile.Close();
68:                OutFile.Close();
69:                Console.WriteLine("...Done.");
70:              }
71:            }
72:        }
73:      }
74: }
```

You will also find that the Type & Runs don't contain line-by-line analysis like many of the listings within the books. Instead, a few key concepts are highlighted.

Enter the previous listing and compile it. If you need to, refer to Day 1, "Getting Started with C#," for the steps to enter, compile, and run a listing. When you run this listing on the command line as follows:

```
NumberIT
```

you will get this message:

 `You need to include a filename.`

This listing takes a command-line parameter that is the name of the file that you want numbered. For example, to number the NumberIT.cs listing, you would enter this:

```
NumberIT NumberIT.cs
```

When this program executes, it displays the following to the screen:

```
Numbering.....1....2....3....4....5....6....7....8....9....10....11....1
2....13....14....15....16....17....18....19....20....21....22....23....2
4....25....26....27....28....29....30....31....32....33....34....35....3
6....37....38....39....40....41....42....43....44....45....46....47....4
8....49....50....51....52....53....54....55....56.....Done.
```

In addition to displaying this output, the listing creates an additional file named outfile.txt. This file contains the numbered version of the listing that you passed as a command-line parameter. If you want the output to be a different name, you can change the name in Line 36.

 Note

The source code for this listing is available on the included CD. Any updates to the code will be available at www.TeachYourselfCSharp.com.

DAY **2**

Understanding C# Programs

In addition to understanding the basic composition of a program, you need to understand the structure of creating a C# program. Today you...

- Learn about the parts of a C# application.
- Understand C# statements and expressions.
- Explore the basic storage types for C# programs.
- Learn what a variable is.
- Discover how to create variable names in C#.
- Use different types of numeric variables.
- Evaluate the differences and similarities between character and numeric values.
- See how to declare and initialize variables.

Dissecting a C# Application

The first part of today's lesson focuses on a simple C# application. Using Listing 2.1, you will gain an understanding of some of the key parts of a C# application.

LISTING 2.1   App.cs—Example C# Application

```
 1:  // App.cs - A sample C# application
 2:  // Don't worry about understanding everything in
 3:  // this listing. You'll learn all about it later!
 4:  //----------------------------------------------
 5:
 6:  using System;
 7:
 8:  class App
 9:  {
10:      public static void Main()
11:      {
12:          //Declare variables
13:
14:          int radius = 4;
15:          const double PI = 3.14159;
16:          double area;
17:
18:          //Do calculation
19:
20:          area = PI * radius * radius;
21:
22:          //Print the results
23:
24:          Console.WriteLine("Radius = {0}, PI = {1}", radius, PI );
25:          Console.WriteLine("The area is {0}", area);
26:      }
27: }
```

You should enter this listing into your editor and then use your compiler to create the program. You can save the program as App.cs. When compiling the program, you enter the following at the command prompt:

`csc App.cs`

Alternatively, if you are using a visual editor, you should be able to select a compiler from the menu options.

Caution Remember, you don't enter the line numbers or the colons when you are entering the listing. The line numbers help in discussing the listing in the lessons.

When you run the program, you get the following output:

OUTPUT
```
Radius = 4, PI = 3.14159
The area is 50.26544
```

As you can see, the output from this listing is pretty straightforward. The value of a radius and the value of PI are displayed. The area of a circle based on these two values is then displayed.

In the following sections, you learn about some of the different parts of this program. Don't worry about understanding everything. In the lessons presented on later days, you will be revisiting this information in much greater detail. The purpose of the following sections is to give you a first look.

Starting with Comments

The first four lines of Listing 2.1 are comments. Comments are used to enter information in your program that can be ignored by the compiler. Why would you want to enter information that the compiler will ignore? There are a number of reasons.

Comments are often used to provide descriptive information about your listing—for example, identification information. Additionally, by entering comments, you can document what a listing is expected to do. Even though you might be the only one who uses a listing, it is still a good idea to put in information about what the program does and how it does it. Although you know what the listing does now—because you just wrote it— you might not be able to remember later what you were thinking. If you give your listing to others, the comments will help them understand what the code was intended to do. Comments can also be used to provide revision history of a listing.

The main thing to understand about comments is that they are for programmers using the listing. The compiler actually ignores them. In C#, you can use three types of comments:

- One-line comments
- Multiline comments
- Documentation comments

> **Tip**   The compiler removes comments, so there is no penalty for having them in your program listings. If in doubt, you should include a comment.

One-Line Comments

Listing 2.1 uses one-line—also called single-line—comments in Lines 1–4 and Lines 12, 18, and 22. One-line comments have the following format:

```
// comment text
```

The two slashes indicate that a comment is beginning. From that point to the end of the current line, everything is treated as a comment.

A one-line comment does not have to start at the beginning of the line. You can actually have C# code on the line before the comments; however, after the two forward slashes, the rest of the line is a comment.

Multiline Comments

Listing 2.1 does not contain any multiline comments, but sometimes you want a comment to go across multiple lines. In this case, you can either start each line with the double forward slash (as in Lines 1–4 of the listing), or you can use multiline comments.

Multiline comments are created with a starting and ending token. To start a multiline comment, you enter a forward slash followed by an asterisk:

```
/*
```

Everything after that token is a comment until you enter the ending token. The ending token is an asterisk followed by a forward slash:

```
*/
```

The following is a comment:

```
/* this is a comment */
```

The following is also a comment:

```
/* this is
a comment that
is on
a number of
lines */
```

You can also enter this comment as the following:

```
// this is
// a comment that
// is on
// a number of
// lines
```

The advantage of using multiline comments is that you can "comment out" a section of a code listing by simply adding `/*` and `*/`. The compiler ignores anything that appears between the `/*` and the `*/` as a comment.

> **Caution**
>
> You cannot nest multiline comments. This means that you cannot place one multiline comment inside of another. For example, the following is an error:
>
> ```
> /* Beginning of a comment...
>     /* with another comment nested */
> */
> ```

Documentation Comments

C# has a special type of comment that enables you to create external documentation automatically.

These comments are identified with three slashes instead of the two used for single-line comments. These comments also use Extensible Markup Language (XML)–style tags. XML is a standard used to mark up data. Although any valid XML tag can be used, common tags used for C# include `<c>`, `<code>`, `<example>`, `<exception>`, `<list>`, `<para>`, `<param>`, `<paramref>`, `<permission>`, `<remarks>`, `<returns>`, `<see>`, `<seealso>`, `<summary>`, and `<value>`.

These comments are placed in your code listings. Listing 2.2 shows an example of these comments being used. You can compile this listing as you have earlier listings. See Day 1, "Getting Started with C#," if you need a refresher.

LISTING 2.2   Xmlapp.cs—Using XML Comments

```
 1:  // Xmlapp.cs - A sample C# application using XML
 2:  //                documentation
 3:  //--------------------------------------------
 4:
 5:  /// <summary>
 6:  /// This is a summary describing the class.</summary>
 7:  /// <remarks>
 8:  /// This is a longer comment that can be used to describe
```

LISTING 2.2   continued

```
 9:  /// the class. </remarks>
10:  class Xmlapp
11:  {
12:      /// <summary>
13:      /// The entry point for the application.
14:      /// </summary>
15:      /// <param name="args"> A list of command line arguments</param>
16:      public static void Main(string[] args)
17:      {
18:          System.Console.WriteLine("An XML Documented Program");
19:      }
20:  }
```

When you compile and execute this listing, you get the following output:

 An XML Documented Program

To get the XML documentation, you must compile this listing differently from what you have seen before. To get the XML documentation, add the /doc parameter when you compile at the command line. If you are compiling at the command line, you enter this:

```
csc /doc:xmlfile Xmlapp.cs
```

When you compile, you get the same output as before when you run the program. The difference is that you also get a file called xmlfile that contains documentation in XML. You can replace xmlfile with any name that you want to give your XML file. For Listing 2.2, the XML file is this:

```
<?xml version="1.0"?>
<doc>
    <assembly>
        <name>Xmlapp</name>
    </assembly>
    <members>
        <member name="T:Xmlapp">
            <summary>
            This is a summary describing the class.</summary>
            <remarks>
            This is a longer comment that can be used to describe
            the class. </remarks>
        </member>
        <member name="M:Xmlapp.Main(System.String[])">
            <summary>
            The entry point for the application.
            </summary>
```

```
        <param name="args"> A list of command line arguments</param>
      </member>
    </members>
  </doc>
```

Note

XML and XML files are beyond the scope of this book.

Note

If you are compiling from within an Integrated Development Environment, you need to check the documentation or help system to learn how to generate the XML documentation. Even if you are using such a tool, you can compile your programs from the command line, if you want. If you are using Microsoft Visual Studio .NET, you can set the project to generate the XML documentation by doing the following:

1. Go to the Solution Explorer. See the documentation if you are unsure of what the Solution Explorer is.

2. Right-click the project name and select the Properties page.

3. Click the Configuration Properties folder to select it.

4. Click the Build option to select it.

5. In the dialog box (shown in Figure 2.1), enter a filename for the XML Documentation File property. In the dialog box in Figure 2.1, the name MyXMLDocs was entered.

FIGURE 2.1

Setting the documentation comments switch in Visual Studio .NET.

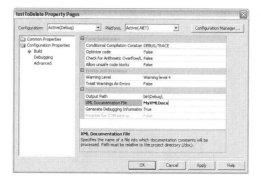

Basic Parts of a C# Application

A programming language is composed of a bunch of keywords that have special meanings. A computer program is the formatting and use of these words in an organized manner, along with a few additional words and symbols. The key parts of a C# language include the following:

- Whitespace
- C# keywords
- Literals
- Identifiers

Formatting with Whitespace

NEW TERM Listing 2.1 has been formatted so that the code lines up and is relatively easy to read. The blank spaces put into a listing are called *whitespace*. The basis of this term is that, on white paper, you can't see the spaces. Whitespace can consist of spaces, tabs, linefeeds, and carriage returns.

The compiler almost always ignores whitespace. Because of this, you can add as many spaces, tabs, and linefeeds as you want. For example, consider Line 14 from Listing 2.1:

```
int radius = 4;
```

This is a well-formatted line with a single space between items. This line could have had additional spaces:

```
int         radius        =        4         ;
```

This line with extra spaces executes the same way as the original. In fact, when the program is run through the C# compiler, the extra whitespace is removed. You could also format this code across multiple lines:

```
int
radius
=
4
;
```

Although this is not very readable, it still works.

The exception to the compiler ignoring whitespace has to do with the use of text within quotation marks. When you use text within double quotes, whitespace is important because the text is to be used exactly as presented. Text has been used within quotation marks with the listings you have seen so far. In Listing 2.1, Lines 24–25 contain text within double quotes. This text is written exactly as it is presented between the quotation marks.

Tip

Because the compiler ignores whitespace, you should make liberal use of it to help format your code and make it readable.

2

The Heart of C#: Keywords

Keywords are the specific terms that have special meaning and, therefore, make up a language. The C# language has a number of keywords, listed in Table 2.1.

TABLE 2.1   The C# Keywords

abstract	as	base	bool	break
byte	case	catch	char	checked
class	const	continue	decimal	default
delegate	do	double	else	enum
event	explicit	extern	false	finally
fixed	float	for	foreach	goto
if	implicit	in	int	interface
internal	is	lock	long	namespace
new	null	object	operator	out
override	params	private	protected	public
readonly	ref	return	sbyte	sealed
short	sizeof	stackalloc	static	string
struct	switch	this	throw	true
try	typeof	uint	ulong	unchecked
unsafe	ushort	using	virtual	void
while				

Note

A few other words are used in C# programs: get, set, and value. Although these reserved words are not keywords, they should be treated as though they are.

In future versions of C#, partial, yield, and where might also become keywords.

These keywords have a specific meaning when you program in C#. You will learn the meaning of these as you work through this book. Because all these words have a special meaning, they are reserved; you should not use them for your own use. If you compare the words in Table 2.1 to Listing 2.1 or any of the other listings in this book, you will see that much of the listing is composed of keywords.

 Note   Appendix A, "C# Keywords," contains short definitions for each of the C# keywords.

Literals

 Literals are straightforward hard-coded values. They are literally what they are! For example, the numbers 4 and 3.14159 are both literals. Additionally, the text within double quotes is literal text. Later today, you will learn more details on literals and their use.

Identifiers

 In addition to C# keywords and literals, other words are used within C# programs. These words are considered *identifiers*. Listing 2.1 contains a number of identifiers, including System in Line 6; sample in Line 8; radius in Line 14; PI in line 15; area in Line 16; and PI, radius, and area in Line 22.

Exploring the Structure of a C# Application

Words and phrases are used to make sentences, and sentences are used to make paragraphs. In the same way, whitespace, keywords, literals, and identifiers are combined to make expressions and statements. These, in turn, are combined to make a program.

Understanding C# Expressions and Statements

 Expressions are like phrases: They are snippets of code made up of keywords. For example, the following are simple expressions:

```
PI = 3.14159

PI * radius * radius
```

Statements are like sentences; they complete a single thought. A statement generally ends with a punctuation character—a semicolon (;). In Listing 2.1, Lines 14–16 are examples of statements.

The Empty Statement

One general statement deserves special mention: the empty statement. As you learned previously, statements generally end with a semicolon. You can actually put a semicolon on a line by itself. This is a statement that does nothing. Because there are no expressions to execute, the statement is considered an empty statement. You'll learn on Day 4, "Controlling Your Program's Flow," when you need to use an empty statement.

Analyzing Listing 2.1

ANALYSIS It is worth taking a closer look at Listing 2.1 now that you've learned of some of the many concepts. The following sections review each line of Listing 2.1.

Lines 1–4: Comments

As you already learned, Lines 1–4 contain comments that the compiler ignores. These are for you and anyone who reviews the source code.

Lines 5, 7, 13, 17, 21, and 23: Whitespace

Line 5 is blank. You learned that a blank line is simply whitespace that the compiler ignores. This line is included to make the listing easier to read. Lines 7, 13, 17, 21, and 23 are also blank. You can remove these lines from your source file, and there will be no difference in how your program runs.

Line 6—The using Statement

Line 6 is a statement that contains the keyword using and a literal System. As with most statements, this ends with a semicolon. The using keyword is used to condense the amount of typing you need to do in your listing. Generally, the using keyword is used with namespaces. Namespaces and details on the using keyword are covered in some detail on Day 5, "The Core of C# Programming: Classes."

Line 8—Class Declaration

C# is an object-oriented programming (OOP) language. Object-oriented languages use classes to declare objects. This program defines a class called App. Although classes are used throughout this entire book, the coding details concerning classes start on Day 5.

Lines 9, 11, 26, and 27: Punctuation Characters

Line 9 contains an opening bracket that is paired with a closing bracket in Line 27. Line 11 has an opening bracket that is paired with the closing one in Line 26. These sets of brackets contain and organize blocks of code. As you learn about different commands over the next four days, you will see how these brackets are used.

Line 10: `Main()`

NEW TERM
The computer needs to know where to start executing a program. C# programs start executing with the `Main()` function, as in Line 10. A *function* is a grouping of code that can be executed by calling the function's name. You'll learn the details about functions on Day 6, "Packaging Functionality: Class Methods and Member Functions." The `Main()` function is special because it is used as a starting point.

Lines 14–16: Declarations

Lines 14–16 contain statements used to create identifiers that will store information. These identifiers are used later to do calculations. Line 14 declares an identifier to store the value of a radius. The literal 4 is assigned to this identifier. Line 15 creates an identifier to store the value of PI. This identifier, PI, is filled with the literal value of 3.14159. Line 16 declares an identifier that is not given any value. You'll learn more about creating and using these identifiers, called variables, later today.

Line 20: The Assignment Statement

Line 20 contains a simple statement that multiplies the identifier PI by the radius twice. The result of this expression is then assigned to the identifier area. You'll learn more about creating expressions and doing operations in tomorrow's lesson.

Lines 24–25: Calling Functions

Lines 24–25 are the most complex expressions in this listing. These two lines call a predefined routine that prints information to the console (screen). You learned about these routines yesterday, and you'll see them used throughout this entire book.

Storing Information with Variables

When you start writing programs, you will quickly find that you need to keep track of different types of information. This might be tracking your clients' names, the amounts of money in your bank accounts, or the ages of your favorite movie stars. To keep track of this information, your computer programs need a way to store the values.

Storing Information in Variables

A *variable* is a named data storage location in your computer's memory. By using a variable's name in your program, you are, in effect, referring to the information stored there.

For example, you could create a variable called my_variable that holds a number. You would be able to store different numbers in the my_variable variable.

You could also create variables to store information other than a simple number. You could create a variable called BankAccount to store a bank account number, a variable called email to store an email address, or a variable called address to store a person's mailing address. Regardless of what type of information will be stored, a variable is used to obtain its value.

Naming Your Variables

To use variables in your C# programs, you must know how to create variable names. In C#, variable names must adhere to the following rules:

- The name can contain letters, digits, and the underscore character (_).
- The first character of the name must be a letter. The underscore is also a legal first character, but its use is not recommended at the beginning of a name. An underscore is often used with special commands. Additionally, it is sometimes hard to read.
- Case matters (that is, upper- and lowercase letters). C# is case sensitive; thus, the names count and Count refer to two different variables.
- C# keywords can't be used as variable names. Recall that a keyword is a word that is part of the C# language. (A complete list of the C# keywords can be found in Appendix A.)

The following list contains some examples of valid and invalid C# variable names:

Variable Name	Legality
Percent	Legal
y2x5__w7h3	Legal
yearly_cost	Legal
_2010_tax	Legal, but not advised
checking#account	Illegal; contains the illegal character #
double	Illegal; is a C keyword
9byte	Illegal; first character is a digit

Because C# is case-sensitive, the names percent, PERCENT, and Percent are considered three different variables. C# programmers commonly use only lowercase letters in variable names, although this isn't required; often programmers use mixed case as well. Using all-uppercase letters is usually reserved for the names of constants (which are covered later today).

Variables can have any name that fits the rules listed previously. For example, a program that calculates the area of a circle could store the value of the radius in a variable named radius. The variable name helps make its usage clear. You could also have created a variable named x or even billy_gates; it doesn't matter. Such a variable name, however, wouldn't be nearly as clear to someone else looking at the source code. Although it might take a little more time to type descriptive variable names, the improvements in program clarity make it worthwhile.

Many naming conventions are used for variable names created from multiple words. Consider the variable name circle_radius. Using an underscore to separate words in a variable name makes it easy to interpret. Another style is called *Pascal notation*. Instead of using spaces, the first letter of each word is capitalized. Instead of circle_radius, the variable would be named CircleRadius. Yet another notation that is growing in popularity is *camel notation*. Camel notation is like Pascal notation, except that the first letter of the variable name is also lowercase. A special form of camel notation is called Hungarian notation. With Hungarian notation, you also include information in the name of the variable—such as whether it is numeric, has a decimal value, or is text—that helps to identify the type of information being stored. The underscore is used in this book because it's easier for most people to read. You should decide which style you want to adopt.

Do	Don't
Do use variable names that are descriptive.	Don't name your variables with all capital letters unnecessarily.
Do adopt and stick with a style for naming your variables.	

Note

C# supports a Unicode character set, which means that letters from any language can be stored and used. You can also use any Unicode character to name your variables.

Using Your Variables

Before you can use a variable in a C# program, you must declare it. A variable declaration tells the compiler the name of the variable and the type of information that the variable will be used to store. If your program attempts to use a variable that hasn't been declared, the compiler generates an error message.

Declaring a variable also enables the computer to set aside memory for the variable. By identifying the specific type of information that will be stored in a variable, you can gain the best performance and avoid wasting memory.

Declaring a Variable

A variable declaration has the following form:

```
typename varname;
```

typename specifies the variable type. In the following sections, you will learn about the types of variables that are available in C#. *varname* is the name of the variable. To declare a variable that can hold a standard numeric integer, you use the following line of code:

```
int my_number;
```

The name of the variable declared is `my_number`. The data type of the variable is `int`. As you will learn in the following section, the type `int` is used to declare integer variables, which is perfect for this example.

You can also declare multiple variables of the same type on one line by separating the variable names with commas. This enables you to be more concise in your listings. Consider the following line:

```
int count, number, start;
```

This line declares three variables: `count`, `number`, and `start`. Each of these variables is type `int`, which is for integers.

Note   Although declaring multiple variables on the same line can be more concise, I don't recommend that you always do this. Sometimes it is easier to read and follow your code by using multiple declarations. There will be no noticeable performance loss by doing separate declarations.

Assigning Values to Your Variables

Now that you know how to declare a variable, it is important to learn how to store values. After all, the purpose of a variable is to store information.

The format for storing information in a variable is as follows:

varname = *value*;

You have already seen that *varname* is the name of the variable. *value* is the value that will be stored in the variable. For example, to store the number 5 in the variable, my_variable, you enter the following:

my_variable = 5;

You can assign a value to a variable any time after it has been declared. You can even do this at the same time you declare a variable:

int my_variable = 5;

A variable's value can also be changed. To change the value, you simply reassign a new value:

my_variable = 1010;

Listing 2.3 illustrates assigning values to a couple of variables. It also shows that you can overwrite a value.

LISTING 2.3   var_values.cs—Assigning Values to a Variable

```
01: // var_values.cs - A listing to assign and print the value
02: //                 of variables
03: //--------------------------------------------------------
04:
05: using System;
06:
07: class var_values
08: {
09:     public static void Main()
10:     {
11:         // declare first_var
12:         int first_var;
13:
14:         // declare and assign a value to second_var
15:         int second_var = 200;
16:
17:         // assign an initial value to first_var...
18:         first_var = 5;
19:
```

LISTING 2.3   continued

```
20:        // print values of variables...
21:        Console.WriteLine("\nfirst_var contains the value {0}", first_var);
22:        Console.WriteLine("second_var contains the value {0}", second_var);
23:
24:        // assign a new value to the variables...
25:        first_var = 1010;
26:        second_var = 2020;
27:
28:        // print new values...
29:        Console.WriteLine("\nfirst_var contains the value {0}", first_var);
30:        Console.WriteLine("second_var contains the value {0}", second_var);
31:    }
32: }
```

OUTPUT
```
first_var contains the value 5
second_var contains the value 200

first_var contains the value 1010
second_var contains the value 2020
```

ANALYSIS Enter this listing into your editor, compile it, and execute it. If you need a refresher on how to do this, refer to Day 1. The first three lines of this listing are comments. Lines 11, 14, 17, 20, 24, and 28 also contain comments. Remember that comments provide information; the compiler ignores them. Line 5 includes the System namespace that you need to do things such as write information. Line 7 declares the class that will be your program (var_values). Line 9 declares the entry point for your program, the Main() function. Remember, Main() must be capitalized or you'll get an error.

Line 12 declares the variable first_var of type integer (int). After this line has executed, the computer knows that a variable called first_var exists and enables you to use it. Note, however, that this variable does not yet contain a value. In Line 15, a second variable called second_var is declared and also assigned the value of 200. In Line 18, the value of 5 is assigned to first_var. Because first_var was declared earlier, you don't need to include the int keyword again.

Lines 21–22 print the values of first_var and second_var. In Lines 25–26, new values are assigned to the two variables. Lines 29–30 then reprint the values stored in the variables. You can see when the new values print that the old values of 5 and 200 are gone.

Caution
You must declare a variable before you can use it.

Issues with Uninitialized Variables

You will get an error if you don't assign a value to a variable before it is used. You can see this by modifying Listing 2.3. Add the following line of code after Line 12:

```
Console.WriteLine("\nfirst_var contains the value {0}", first_var);
```

You can see that in Line 12, first_var is declared; however, it is not assigned any value. What value would you expect first_var to have when the preceding line tries to print it to the console? Because first_var hasn't been assigned a value, you have no way of knowing what the value will be. In fact, when you try to recompile the listing, you get an error:

```
var_values2.cs(13,63): error CS0165: Use of unassigned local variable
       'first_var'
```

It is best to always assign a value to a variable when you declare it. You should do this even if the value is temporary.

Note

> In other languages, such as C and C++, this listing would compile. The value printed for the uninitialized first_var in these other languages would be garbage. C# prevents this type of error from occurring.

Understanding Your Computer's Memory

Variables are stored in your computer's memory. If you already know how a computer's memory operates, you can skip this section. If you're not sure, read on. This information is helpful to understanding how programs store information.

What is your computer's memory (RAM) used for? It has several uses, but only data storage need concern you as a programmer. Data is the information with which your C# program works. Whether your program is maintaining a contact list, monitoring the stock market, keeping a budget, or tracking the price of snickerdoodles, the information (names, stock prices, expense amounts, or prices) is kept within variables in your computer's memory when it is being used by your running program.

A computer uses random access memory (RAM) to store information while it is operating. RAM is located in integrated circuits, or chips, inside your computer. RAM is volatile, which means that it is erased and replaced with new information as often as needed. Being volatile also means that RAM "remembers" only while the computer is turned on and loses its information when you turn the computer off.

A *byte* is the fundamental unit of computer data storage. Each computer has a certain amount of RAM installed. The amount of RAM in a system is usually specified in megabytes (MB), such as 64MB, 128MB, 256MB, or more. 1MB of memory is 1,024 kilobytes (KB). 1KB of memory consists of 1,024 bytes. Thus, a system with 8MB of memory actually has 8 × 1,024KB, or 8,192KB of RAM. This is 8,192KB × 1,024 bytes, for a total of 8,388,608 bytes of RAM. Table 2.2 provides you with an idea of how many bytes it takes to store certain kinds of data.

TABLE 2.2 Minimum Memory Space Generally Required to Store Data

Data	Bytes Required
The letter x	2
The number 500	2
The number 241.105	4
The phrase "Teach Yourself C#"	34
One typewritten page	Approximately 4,000

The RAM in your computer is organized sequentially, with one byte following another. Each byte of memory has a unique address by which it is identified—an address that also distinguishes it from all other bytes in memory. Addresses are assigned to memory locations in order, starting at 0 and increasing to the system limit. For now, you don't need to worry about addresses; it's all handled automatically.

Now that you understand a little about the nuts and bolts of memory storage, you can get back to C# programming and how C# uses memory to store information efficiently.

Introducing the C# Data Types

You know how to declare, initialize, and change the values of variables; it is important that you know the data types that you can use. You learned earlier that you have to declare the data type when you declare a variable. You've seen that the `int` keyword declares variables that can hold integers. An integer is simply a whole number that doesn't contain a fractional or decimal portion. The variables that you've declared to this point hold only integers. What if you want to store other types of data, such as decimals or characters?

Numeric Variable Types

C# provides several different types of numeric variables. You need different types of variables because different numeric values have varying memory storage requirements and differ in the ease with which certain mathematical operations can be performed on them. Small integers (for example, 1, 199, and -8) require less memory to store, and your computer can perform mathematical operations (addition, multiplication, and so on) with such numbers very quickly. In contrast, large integers and values with decimal points require more storage space and more time for mathematical operations. By using the appropriate variable types, you ensure that your program runs as efficiently as possible.

The following sections break the different numeric data types into four categories:

- Integral
- Floating point
- Decimal
- Boolean

The amount of memory used to store a variable is based on its data type. Listing 2.4 is a program that contains code beyond what you know right now; however, it provides you with the amount of information needed to store some of the different C# data types.

You must include extra information for the compiler when you compile this listing. This extra information is referred to as a "flag" to the compiler and can be included on the command line. Specifically, you need to add the /unsafe flag, as shown:

```
csc /unsafe sizes.cs
```

If you are using an Integrated Development Environment, you need to set the unsafe option as instructed by its documentation.

 Note

If you are using Microsoft Visual Studio .NET, you can set the unsafe flag in the same dialog box where you set the XML documentation filename.

LISTING 2.4   Sizes.cs—Memory Requirements for Data Types

```
1:  // Sizes.cs--Program to tell the size of the C# variable types
2:  //-------------------------------------------------------------
3:
4:  using System;
5:
6:  class Sizes
```

LISTING 2.4   continued

```
 7: {
 8:     unsafe public static void Main()
 9:     {
10:         Console.WriteLine( "\nA byte    is {0} byte(s)", sizeof( byte ));
11:         Console.WriteLine( "A sbyte    is {0} byte(s)", sizeof( sbyte ));
12:         Console.WriteLine( "A char     is {0} byte(s)", sizeof( char ));
13:         Console.WriteLine( "\nA short   is {0} byte(s)", sizeof( short ));
14:         Console.WriteLine( "An ushort  is {0} byte(s)", sizeof( ushort ));
15:         Console.WriteLine( "\nAn int    is {0} byte(s)", sizeof( int ));
16:         Console.WriteLine( "An uint    is {0} byte(s)", sizeof( uint ));
17:         Console.WriteLine( "\nA long    is {0} byte(s)", sizeof( long ));
18:         Console.WriteLine( "An ulong   is {0} byte(s)", sizeof( ulong ));
19:         Console.WriteLine( "\nA float   is {0} byte(s)", sizeof( float ));
20:         Console.WriteLine( "A double   is {0} byte(s)", sizeof( double ));
21:         Console.WriteLine( "\nA decimal is {0} byte(s)", sizeof( decimal
            ➥));
22:         Console.WriteLine( "\nA boolean is {0} byte(s)", sizeof( bool ));
23:     }
24: }
```

Caution

The C# keyword `sizeof` can be used, but you should generally avoid it. The `sizeof` keyword sometimes accesses memory directly to find out the size. Accessing memory directly should be avoided in pure C# programs.

You might get an error when compiling this program, saying that unsafe code can appear only if you compile with /unsafe. If you get this error, you need to add the /unsafe flag to the command-line compile:

```
csc /unsafe sizes.cs
```

If you are using an IDE, you need to set the /unsafe flag in the IDE settings.

OUTPUT

```
A byte     is 1 byte(s)
A sbyte    is 1 byte(s)
A char     is 2 byte(s)

A short    is 2 byte(s)
An ushort  is 2 byte(s)

An int     is 4 byte(s)
An uint    is 4 byte(s)

A long     is 8 byte(s)
An ulong   is 8 byte(s)

A float    is 4 byte(s)
A double   is 8 byte(s)
```

```
A decimal  is 16 byte(s)

A boolean  is 1 byte (s)
```

ANALYSIS Although you haven't learned all the data types yet, it is valuable to present this listing here. As you go through the following sections, refer to this listing and its output.

This listing uses a C# keyword called `sizeof`. The `sizeof` keyword tells you the size of a variable. In this listing, `sizeof` is used to show the size of the different data types. For example, to determine the size of an `int`, you can use this:

```
sizeof(int)
```

If you had declared a variable called x, you could determine its size—which would actually be the size of its data type—by using the following code:

```
sizeof(x)
```

Looking at the output of Listing 2.4, you see that you have been given the number of bytes that are required to store each of the C# data types. For an `int`, you need 4 bytes of storage. For a `short`, you need 2. The amount of memory used determines how big or small a number that is stored can be. You'll learn more about this in the following sections.

The `sizeof` keyword is not one that you will use very often; however, it is useful for illustrating the points in today's lesson. The `sizeof` keyword taps into memory to determine the size of the variable or data type. With C#, you avoid tapping directly into memory. In Line 8, the extra keyword `unsafe` is added. If you don't include the `unsafe` keyword, you get an error when you compile this program. For now, understand that `unsafe` is added because the `sizeof` keyword has the potential to work directly with memory.

The Integral Data Types

Until this point, you have been using one of the integral data types, `int`. Integral data types store integers. Recall that an integer is basically any numeric value that does not include a decimal or a fractional value. The numbers `1`, `1,000`, `56,000,000,000,000`, and `-534` are integral values.

C# provides nine integral data types, including the following:

- Integers (`int` and `uint`)
- Shorts (`short` and `ushort`)
- Longs (`long` and `ulong`)

- Bytes (`byte` and `sbyte`)
- Characters (`char`)

Integers

As you saw in Listing 2.4, an integer is stored in 4 bytes of memory. This includes both the `int` and `uint` data types. This data type cannot store just any number; it can store any signed whole number that can be represented in 4 bytes or 32 bits—any number between -2,147,483,648 and 2,147,483,647.

A variable of type `int` is signed, which means that it can be positive or negative. Technically, 4 bytes can hold a number as big as 4,294,967,295; however, when you take away one of the 32 bits to keep track of positive or negative, you can go only to 2,147,483,647. You can, however, also go to -2,147,483,648.

Note

> As you learned earlier, information is stored in units called bytes. A byte is actually composed of 8 bits. A *bit* is the most basic unit of storage in a computer. A bit can have one of two values—0 or 1. Using bits and the binary math system, you can store numbers in multiple bits. In Appendix C, "Understanding Number Systems," you can learn the details of binary math.

If you want to use a type `int` to go higher, you can make it unsigned. An unsigned number can be only positive. The benefit should be obvious. The `uint` data type declares an unsigned integer. The result is that a `uint` can store a value from 0 to 4,294,967,295.

What happens if you try to store a number that is too big? What about storing a number with a decimal point into an `int` or a `uint`? What happens if you try to store a negative number into a `uint`? Listing 2.5 answers all three questions.

LISTING 2.5   int_conv.cs—Doing Bad Things

```
 1:  // int_conv.cs
 2:  // storing bad values. Program generates errors and won't compile.
 3:  //-----------------------------------------------------------
 4:
 5:  using System;
 6:
 7:  class int_conv
 8:  {
 9:      public static void Main()
10:      {
11:          int val1, val2;    // declare two integers
```

LISTING 2.5   continued

```
12:          uint pos_val;        // declare an unsigned int
13:
14:          val1 = 1.5;
15:          val2 = 9876543210;
16:          pos_val = -123;
17:
18:          Console.WriteLine( "val1 is {0}", val1);
19:          Console.WriteLine( "val2 is {0}", val2);
20:          Console.WriteLine( "pos_val is {0}", pos_val);
21:      }
22:  }
```

OUTPUT

```
int_conv.cs(14,15): error CS0029: Cannot implicitly convert type
➥'double' to 'int'
int_conv.cs(15,15): error CS0029: Cannot implicitly convert type
➥'long' to 'int'
int_conv.cs(16,18): error CS0031: Constant value '-123' cannot be
➥converted to a 'uint'
```

Caution   This program gives compiler errors.

ANALYSIS   This program will not compile. As you can see, the compiler catches all three problems that were questioned. Line 14 tries to put a number with a decimal point into an integer. Line 15 tries to put a number that is too big into an integer. Remember, the highest number that can go into an int is 2,147,483,647. Finally, Line 16 tries to put a negative number into an unsigned integer (uint). As the output shows, the compiler catches each of these errors and prevents the program from being created.

Shorts

The int and uint data types used 4 bytes of memory for each variable declared. Sometimes you don't need to store numbers that are that big. For example, you don't need big numbers to keep track of the day of the week (numbers 1–7), to store a person's age, or to track the temperature to bake a cake.

When you want to store a whole number and you want to save some memory, you can use short and ushort. A short, like an int, stores a whole number. Unlike an int, it is only 2 bytes instead of 4. In the output from Listing 2.4, you see that sizeof returned 2 bytes for both short and ushort. If you are storing both positive and negative numbers, you'll want to use short. If you are storing only positive numbers and you want to use the extra room, you'll want to use ushort. The values that can be stored in a short are from -32,768 to 32,767. If you use a ushort, you can store whole numbers from 0 to 65,535.

Longs

If int and uint are not big enough for what you want to store, you can use the long data type. As with short and int, there is also an unsigned version of the long data type called ulong. In the output from Listing 2.4, you can see that long and ulong each use 8 bytes of memory. This gives them the capability of storing very large numbers. A long can store numbers from -9,223,372,036,854,775,808 to 9,223,372,036,854,775,807. A ulong can store a number from 0 to 18,446,744,073,709,551,615.

Bytes

As you have seen, you can store whole numbers in data types that take 2, 4, or 8 bytes of memory. When your needs are very small, you can also store a whole number in a single byte. To keep things simple, the data type that uses a single byte of memory for storage is called a byte. As with the previous integers, there is both a signed version, sbyte, and an unsigned version, byte. An sbyte can store a number from -128 to 127. An unsigned byte can store a number from 0 to 255.

 Caution   Unlike the other data types, it is byte and sbyte instead of byte and ubyte; there is no such thing as a ubyte.

Characters

In addition to numbers, you will often want to store characters. Characters are letters, such as A, B, or C, or even extended characters such as the smiley face. Additional characters that you might want to store are $, %, or *. You might even want to store foreign characters.

A computer does not recognize characters; it can recognize only numbers. To get around this, all characters are stored as numbers. To make sure that everyone uses the same values, a standard was created called Unicode. Within Unicode, each character and symbol is represented by a single whole number. This is why the character data type is considered an integral type.

To know that numbers should be used as characters, you use the data type char. A char is a number stored in 2 bytes of memory that is interpreted as a character. Listing 2.6 presents a program that uses char values.

LISTING 2.6   Chars.cs—Working with Characters

```
 1:  // Chars.cs

 2:  // A listing to print out a number of characters and their numbers
 3:  //------------------------------------------------------------
 4:
 5:  using System;
 6:
 7:  class Chars
 8:  {
 9:     public static void Main()
10:     {
11:         int ctr;
12:         char ch;
13:
14:         Console.WriteLine("\nNumber   Value\n");
15:
16:         for( ctr = 63; ctr <= 94; ctr = ctr + 1)
17:         {
18:             ch = (char) ctr;
19:             Console.WriteLine( "{0} is {1}", ctr, ch);
20:         }
21:     }
22:  }
```

OUTPUT

```
Number   Value

63 is ?
64 is @
65 is A
66 is B
67 is C
68 is D
69 is E
70 is F
71 is G
72 is H
73 is I
74 is J
75 is K
76 is L
77 is M
78 is N
79 is O
80 is P
81 is Q
82 is R
83 is S
84 is T
```

```
85 is U
86 is V
87 is W
88 is X
89 is Y
90 is Z
91 is [
92 is \
93 is ]
94 is ^
```

ANALYSIS This listing displays a range of numeric values and their character equivalents. Line 11 declares an integer called ctr. This variable is used to cycle through a number of integers. Line 12 declares a character variable called ch. Line 14 prints headings for the information that will be displayed.

Line 16 contains something new. For now, don't worry about fully understanding this line of code. On Day 4, you will learn all the glorious details. For now, know that this line sets the value of ctr to 63. It then runs Lines 18–19 before adding 1 to the value of ctr. It keeps doing this until ctr is no longer less than or equal to 94. The end result is that Lines 18–19 are run using the ctr with the value of 63, then 64, then 65, and on and on until ctr is 94.

Line 18 sets the value of ctr (first 63) and places it into the character variable ch. Because ctr is an integer, you have to tell the computer to convert the integer to a character, which the (char) statement does. You'll learn more about this later.

Line 19 prints the values stored in ctr and ch. As you can see, the integer ctr prints as a number. The value of ch, however, does not print as a number; it prints as a character. As you can see from the output of this listing, the character A is represented by the value 65. The value of 66 is the same as the character B.

Character Literals

How can you assign a character to a char variable? You place the character between single quotes. For example, to assign the letter a to the variable my_char, you use the following:

```
my_char = 'a';
```

In addition to assigning regular characters, you will most likely want to use several extended characters. You have actually been using one extended character in a number of your listings. The \n that you've been using in your listings is an extended character that prints a newline character. Table 2.3 contains some of the most common characters you might want to use. Listing 2.7 shows some of these special characters in action.

TABLE 2.3   Extended Characters

Characters	Meaning
\b	Backspace
\n	Newline
\t	Horizontal tab
\\	Backslash
\'	Single quote
\"	Double quote

Note   The extended characters in Table 2.3 are often called *escape characters* because the slash "escapes" from the regular text and indicates that the following character is special (or extended).

LISTING 2.7   chars_table.cs—The Special Characters

```
 1: // chars_table.cs
 2: //------------------------------------------------------------
 3:
 4: using System;
 5:
 6: class chars_table
 7: {
 8:    public static void Main()
 9:    {
10:       char ch1 = 'Z';
11:       char ch2 = 'x';
12:
13:       Console.WriteLine("This is the first line of text");
14:       Console.WriteLine("\n\n\nSkipped three lines");
15:       Console.WriteLine("one\ttwo\tthree <-tabbed");
16:       Console.WriteLine(" A quote: \' \ndouble quote: \"");
17:       Console.WriteLine("\n ch1 = {0}   ch2 = {1}", ch1, ch2);
18:    }
19: }
```

OUTPUT

```
This is the first line of text



Skipped three lines
one     two      three <-tabbed
 A quote: '
```

```
double quote: "

ch1 = Z    ch2 = x
```

ANALYSIS This listing illustrates two concepts. First, in Lines 10–11, you see how a character can be assigned to a variable of type char. It is as simple as including the character in single quotes. In Lines 13–17, you see how to use the extended characters. There is nothing special about Line 13. Line 14 prints three newlines followed by some text. Line 15 prints one, two, and three, separated by tabs. Line 16 displays a single quote and a double quote. Notice that there are two double quotes in a row at the end of this line. Finally, line 17 prints the values of ch1 and ch2.

Working with Floating-Point Values

Not all numbers are whole numbers. When you need to use numbers that have decimals, you must use different data types. As with storing whole numbers, you can use different data types, depending on the size of the numbers you are using and the amount of memory you want to use. The two primary types are float and double.

float

A float is a data type for storing numbers with decimal places. For example, in calculating the circumference or area of a circle, you often end up with a result that is not a whole number. Any time you need to store a number such as 1.23 or 3.1459, you need a nonintegral data type.

The float data type stores numbers in 4 bytes of memory. As such, it can store a number from approximately 1.5×10^{-45} to 3.4×10^{38}.

Note

10^{38} is equivalent to 10×10, 37 times. The result is 1 followed by 38 zeros, or 100,000,000,000,000,000,000,000,000,000,000,000,000. 10^{-45} is $10 \div 10$, 44 times. The result is 44 zeros between a decimal point and a 1, or .00000000000000000000000000000000000000000000001.

Caution

A float can retain only about seven digits of precision, which means that it is not uncommon for a float to be off by a fraction. For example, subtracting 9.90 from 10.00 might result in a number different from .10; it might result in a number closer to .099999999. Generally, such rounding errors are not noticeable.

double

Variables of type `double` are stored in 8 bytes of memory. This means that they can be much bigger than a `float`. A `double` can generally be from 5.0×10^{-324} to 1.7×10^{308}. The precision of a `double` is generally from 15 to 16 digits.

Note

> C# supports the 4-byte precision (32 bits) and 8-byte precision (64 bits) of the IEEE 754 format, so certain mathematical functions return specific values. If you divide a number by 0, the result is infinity (either positive or negative). If you divide 0 by 0, you get a *Not-a-Number* value. Finally, 0 can be both positive and negative. For more on this, check your C# documentation.

Gaining Precision with Decimal

C# provides another data type that can be used to store special decimal numbers: the `decimal` data type. This data type was created for storing numbers with greater precision. When you store numbers in a `float` or a `double`, you can get rounding errors. For example, storing the result of subtracting 9.90 from 10.00 in a `double` could result in the string `0.099999999999999645` instead of `.10`. If this math is done with `decimal` values, the `.10` is stored.

Tip

> If you are calculating monetary values or doing financial calculations in which precision is important, you should use a `decimal` instead of a `float` or a `double`.

A `decimal` number uses 16 bytes to store numbers. Unlike the other data types, there is no unsigned version of `decimal`. A `decimal` variable can store a number from 1.0×10^{-28} to approximately 7.9×10^{28}. It can do this while maintaining precision to 28 places.

Storing Boolean Values

The last of the simple data types is the Boolean. Sometimes you need to know whether something is on or off, true or false, or yes or no. Boolean numbers are generally set to one of two values: 0 or 1.

C# has a Boolean data type called a `bool`. As you can see in Listing 2.4, a `bool` is stored in 1 byte of memory. The value of a `bool` is either `true` or `false`, which are C# keywords. This means that you can actually store `true` and `false` in a data type of `bool`.

Caution Yes, no, on, and off are not keywords in C#. This means that you cannot set a Boolean variable to these values. Instead, you must use `true` or `false`.

Working Checked Versus Unchecked Code

Earlier in today's lesson, you learned that if you put a number that is too big into a variable, an error is produced. Sometimes you do not want an error produced. In those cases, you can have the compiler avoid checking the code. This is done with the `unchecked` keyword, as illustrated in Listing 2.8.

LISTING 2.8   Unchecked.cs—Marking Code as Unchecked

```
 1:  // Unchecked.cs
 2:  //---------------------------------------------------------------
 3:
 4:  using System;
 5:
 6:  class Unchecked
 7:  {
 8:     public static void Main()
 9:     {
10:        int val1 = 2147483647;
11:        int val2;
12:
13:        unchecked
14.        {
15:           val2 = val1 + 1;
16:        }
17:
18:        Console.WriteLine( "val1 is {0}", val1);
19:        Console.WriteLine( "val2 is {0}", val2);
20:     }
21:  }
```

OUTPUT
```
val1 is 2147483647
val2 is -2147483648
```

ANALYSIS This listing uses `unchecked` in Line 13. The brackets in Line 14 and 16 enclose the area to be unchecked. When you compile this listing, you do not get any errors. When you run the listing, you get what might seem like a weird result. The number 2,147,483,647 is the largest number that a signed `int` variable can hold. As you see in Line 10, this maximum value has been assigned to `var1`. In Line 15, the unchecked line, 1 is added to what is already the largest value `var1` can hold. Because this line is unchecked, the program continues to operate. The result is that the value stored in var1 rolls to the most negative number.

This operation is similar to the way an odometer works in a car. When the mileage gets to the maximum, such as 999,999, adding 1 more mile (or kilometer) sets the odometer to 000,000. It isn't a new car with no miles; it is simply a car that no longer has a valid value on its odometer. Rather than rolling to 0, a variable rolls to the lowest value it can store. In this listing, that value is -2,147,483,648.

Change Line 13 to the following, and recompile and run the listing:

```
13:        checked
```

The program compiled, but will it run? Executing the program causes an error. If you are asked to run your debugger, you'll want to say no. The error that you get will be similar to the following:

```
Exception occurred: System.OverflowException: An exception of type
  System.OverflowException was thrown.
    at Unchecked.Main()
```

On later days, you'll see how to deal with this error in your program. For now, you should keep in mind that if you believe there is a chance of putting an invalid value into a variable, you should force checking to occur. You should not use the unchecked keyword as a means of simply avoiding an error.

Data Types Simpler Than .NET

The C# data types covered so far are considered simple data types. The simple data types are sbyte, byte, short, ushort, int, uint, long, ulong, char, float, double, bool, and decimal. In yesterday's lesson, you learned that C# programs execute on the Common Language Runtime (CLR). Each of these data types corresponds directly to a data type that the CLR uses. Each of these types is considered simple because there is a direct relationship with the types available in the CLR and, thus, in the .NET Framework. Table 2.4 presents the .NET equivalent of the C# data types.

TABLE 2.4 C# and .NET Data Types

C# Data Type	.NET Data Type
sbyte	System.SByte
byte	System.Byte
short	System.Int16
ushort	System.UInt16
int	System.Int32

TABLE 2.4   continued

C# Data Type	.NET Data Type
uint	System.UInt32
long	System.Int64
ulong	System.UInt64
char	System.Char
float	System.Single
double	System.Double
bool	System.Boolean
decimal	System.Decimal

If you want to declare an integer using the .NET equivalent declaration—even though there is no good reason to do so—you use the following:

```
System.Int32 my_variable = 5;
```

As you can see, System.Int32 is much more complicated than simply using int. Listing 2.9 shows the use of the .NET data types.

LISTING 2.9   net_vars.cs—Using the .NET Data Types

```
 1:  // net_vars
 2:  // Using a .NET data declaration
 3:  //        . . . . . . . . . . . . . . . . . . . . . . . . . . . . . . .
 4:
 5:  using System;
 6:
 7:  class net_vars
 8:  {
 9:      public static void Main()
10:      {
11:          System.Int32 my_variable = 4;
12:          System.Double PI = 3.1459;
13:
14:          Console.WriteLine("\nmy_variable is {0}", my_variable );
15:          Console.WriteLine("\nPI is {0}", PI );
16:      }
17:  }
```

OUTPUT

```
my_variable is 4

PI is 3. 1459
```

Lines 11–12 declare an `int` and a `double`. Lines 14–15 print these values. This listing operates like those you've seen earlier, except that it uses the .NET data types.

In your C# programs, you should use the simple data types rather than the .NET types. All the functionality of the .NET types is available to you in the simpler commands that C# provides. However, you should understand that the simple C# data types translate to .NET equivalents. You'll find that all other programming languages that work with the Microsoft .NET types also have data types that translate to these .NET types.

> **Note**
>
> The *Common Type System* (CTS) is a set of rules that data types within the CLR must adhere to. The simple data types within C# adhere to these rules, as do the .NET data types. If a language follows the CTS in creating its data types, the data created and stored should be compatible with other programming languages that also follow the CTS.

Literals Versus Variables

Often you will want to type a number or value into your source code. A *literal value* stands on its own within the source code. For example, in the following lines of code, the number `10` and the value `"Bob is a fish"` are literal values.

```
int x = 10;
myStringValue = "Bob is a fish";
```

Working with Numeric Literals

In many of the examples, you have used numeric literals. By default, a numeric literal is either an integer or a `double`. It is an `int` if it is a whole number, and it is a `double` if it is a floating-point number. For example, consider the following:

```
nbr = 100;
```

By default, the numeric literal `100` is considered to be of type `int`, regardless of what data type the `nbr` variable is. Now consider the following:

```
nbr = 99.9;
```

In this example, `99.9` is also a numeric literal; however, it is of type `double` by default. Again, this is regardless of the data type that `nbr` is. This is true even though `99.9` could be stored in a type `float`. In the following line of code, is `100.` an `int` or a `double`?

```
x = 100.;
```

This is a tough one. If you guessed `int`, you are wrong. Because there is a decimal included with the `100`, it is a `double`.

Understanding the Integer Literal Defaults

When you use an integer value, it is actually put into an `int`, `uint`, `long`, or `ulong`, depending on its size. If it will fit in an `int` or a `uint`, it will be. If not, it will be put into a `long` or a `ulong`. If you want to specify the data type of the literal, you can use a suffix on the literal. For example, to use the number `10` as a literal `long` value (signed or unsigned), you write it like the following:

```
10L;
```

You can make an unsigned value by using a `u` or a `U`. If you want an unsigned literal `long` value, you can combine the two suffixes: `ul`.

Note

> The Microsoft C# compiler gives you a warning if you use a lowercase *l* to declare a `long` value literal. The compiler provides this warning to make you aware that it is easy to mistake a lowercase *l* with the number 1.

Understanding Floating-Point Literal Defaults

As stated earlier, by default, a decimal value literal is a `double`. To declare a literal that is of type `float`, you include `f` or `F` after the number. For example, to assign the number `4.4` to a `float` variable, `my_float`, you use the following:

```
my_float = 4.4f;
```

To declare a literal of type decimal, you use a suffix of `m` or `M`. For example, the following line declares `my_decimal` to be equal to the decimal number `1.32`.

```
my_decimal = 1.32m;
```

Working with Boolean Literals (`true` and `false`)

We have already covered Boolean literals. The values `true` and `false` are literal. They also happen to be keywords.

Understanding String Literals

When you put characters together, they make words, phrases, and sentences. In programming parlance, a group of characters is called a *string*. A string can be identified because it is contained within a set of double quotes. For example, the `Console.WriteLine` routine uses a string. A string literal is any set of characters between double quotes. The following are examples of strings:

`"Hello, World!"`

`"1234567890"`

Because the numbers are between quotation marks, the last example is treated as a string literal rather than as a numeric literal.

 Note   You can use any of the special characters from Table 2.3 inside a string.

Creating Constants

In addition to using literals, sometimes you want to put a value in a variable and freeze it. For example, if you declare a variable called PI and you set it to 3.14159, you want it to stay 3.14159. There is no reason to ever change it. Additionally, you want to prevent people from changing it.

To declare a variable to hold a constant value, you use the `const` keyword. For example, to declare PI as stated, you use the following:

`const float PI = 3.1459;`

You can use PI in a program; however, you will never be able to change its value. The `const` keyword freezes its contents. You can use the `const` keyword on any variable of any data type.

 Tip   To help make it easy to identify constants, you can enter their names in all capital letters.

A Peek at Reference Types

To this point, you have seen a number of different data types. C# offers two primary ways of storing information: by value (`byval`) and by reference (`byref`). The basic data types that you have learned about store information by value.

When a variable stores information by value, the variable contains the actual information. For example, when you store 123 in an integer variable called x, the value of x is 123. The variable x actually contains the value 123.

Storing information by reference is a little more complicated. If a variable stores by reference rather than storing the information in itself, it stores the location of the information. In other words, it stores a reference to the information. For example, if x is a "by reference" variable, it contains information on where the value 123 is located; it does not store the value 123. Figure 2.2 illustrates the difference.

FIGURE 2.2

By reference versus by value.

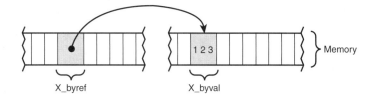

The data types used by C# that store by reference are listed here:

- Classes
- Strings
- Interfaces
- Arrays
- Delegates

Each of these data types is covered in detail throughout the rest of this book.

Summary

Today's lesson was the longest in the book. It builds some of the foundation that will be used to teach you C#. Today you started by learning about some of the basic parts of a C# application. You learned that comments help make your programs easier to understand.

In addition, you learned about the basic parts of a C# application, including whitespace, C# keywords, literals, and identifiers. Looking at an application, you saw how these parts are combined to create a complete listing. This included seeing a special identifier used as a starting point in an application: Main().

After you examined a listing, you dug into storing basic information in a C# application using variables. You learned how the computer stores information. You focused on the data types that store data by value, including int, uint, long, ulong, bool, char, short, ushort, float, double, decimal, byte, and ubyte. In addition to learning about the data types, you learned how to name and create variables. You also learned the basics of setting values in these variables, including the use of literals. Table 2.5 lists the data types and information about them.

TABLE 2.5   C# Data Types

C# Data Type	NET Data Type	Size in Bytes	Low Value	High Value
sbyte	System.Sbyte	1	-128	127
byte	System.Byte	1	0	255
short	System.Int16	2	-32,768	32,767
ushort	System.UInt16	2	0	65,535
int	System.Int32	4	-2,147,483,648	2,147,483,647
uint	System.UInt32	4	0	4,294,967,295
long	System.Int64	8	-9,223,372,036, 854,775,808	9,223,372,036,854,775,807
ulong	System.UInt64	8	0	18,446,744,073,709,551,615
char	System.Char	2	0	65,535
float	System.Single	4	1.5×10^{-45}	3.4×10^{38}
double	System.Double	8	5.0×10^{-324}	1.7×1010^{308}
bool	System.Boolean	1	false (0)	true (1)
decimal	System.Decimal	16	1.0×10^{-28}	approx. 7.9×10^{28}

Q&A

Q Why shouldn't all numbers be declared as the larger data types instead of the smaller data types?

A Although it might seem logical to use the larger data types, this would not be efficient. You should not use any more system resources (memory) than you need.

Q What happens if you assign a negative number to an unsigned variable?

A The compiler returns an error saying that you can't assign a negative number to an unsigned variable if you do this with a literal. If you do a calculation that causes an unsigned variable to go below 0, you get erroneous data. On later days, you will learn how to check for these erroneous values.

Q A `decimal` value is more precise than a `float` or a `double` value. What happens with rounding when you convert from these different data types?

A When converting from a `float`, `double`, or `decimal` to one of the whole-number variable types, the value is rounded. If a number is too big to fit into the variable, an error occurs.

When a `double` is converted to a `float` that is too big or too small, the value is represented as infinity or `0`, respectively.

When a value is converted from a `float` or a `double` to a `decimal`, the value is rounded. This rounding occurs after 28 decimal places and occurs only if necessary. If the value being converted is too small to be represented as a `decimal`, the new value is set to `0`. If the value is too large to store in the `decimal`, an error occurs.

For conversions from `decimal` to `float` or `double`, the value is rounded to the nearest value that the `float` or `double` can hold. Remember, a `decimal` has better precision than a `float` or a `double`. This precision is lost in the conversion.

Q What other languages adhere to the Common Type System (CTS) in the Common Language Runtime (CLR)?

A Microsoft Visual Basic .NET (Version 7) and Microsoft Visual C++ .NET (Version 7) both support the CTS. Additionally, versions of a number of other languages are ported to the CTS. These include Python, COBOL, Perl, Java, and more. Check out the Microsoft Web site for additional languages.

Workshop

The Workshop provides quiz questions to help you solidify your understanding of the material covered and exercises to provide you with experience in using what you've learned. Try to understand the quiz and exercise answers before continuing to the next day's lesson. Answers are provided on the CD.

Quiz

1. What three types of comments can you use in a C# program and how is each of the three types of comments entered into a C# program?

2. What impact does whitespace have on a C# program?

3. Which of the following are C# keywords?

   `field, cast, as, object, throw, baseball, catch, football, fumble, basketball`

4. What is a literal?

5. What by value data types are available in C#?

6. What is the difference between a signed variable and an unsigned variable?

7. What is the smallest data type that you can use to store the number 55?

8. What is the biggest number that a type short variable can hold?

9. What numeric value is the character B?

10. Name three of the reference data types.

11. Which floating-point data type has the best precision?

12. What .NET data type is equivalent to the C# int data type?

Exercises

1. Enter, compile, and run the following program. What does it do?

```
1:  // Ex0201.cs - Exercise 1 for Day 2
2:  //----------------------------------------------
3:
4:  class Ex0201
5:  {
6:      public static void Main()
7:      {
8:          int ctr;
9:
10:         for( ctr = 1; ctr <= 10; ctr++ )
11:         {
12:             System.Console.Write("{0:D3} ", ctr);
13:         }
14:     }
15: }
```

2. **Bug Buster:** The following program has a problem. Enter it in your editor and compile it. Which lines generate error messages?

```
1:  // Bugbust.cs
2:  //----------------------------------------------
3:
4:  class Bugbust
5:  {
6:      public static void Main()
7:      {
8:          System.Console.WriteLine("\nA fun number is {1}", 123 );
9:      }
10: }
```

3. Change the range of values in Listing 2.6 to print the lowercase letters.

4. Write the line of code that declares a variable named xyz of type float, and assign the value of 123.456 to it.

5. Which of the following variable names are valid?

   a. X

   b. PI

   c. 12months

   d. sizeof

   e. nine

6. **Bug Buster:** The following program has a problem. Enter it in your editor and compile it. Which lines generate error messages?

```
 1:  //BugBuster
 2:  //----------------------------------------------------------
 3:  using System;
 4:
 5:  class BugBuster
 6:  {
 7:      public static void Main()
 8:      {
 9:          double my_double;
10:          decimal my_decimal;
11:
12:          my_double = 3.14;
13:          my_decimal = 3.14;
14:
15:          Console.WriteLine("\nMy Double:  {0}", my_double);
16:          Console.WriteLine("\nMy Decimal: {0}", my_decimal);
17:
18:      }
19:  }
```

7. **On Your Own:** Write a program that declares two variables of each data type and assigns the values 10 and 1.879 to each variable.

DAY 3

Manipulating Values in Your Programs

Now that you know how to store information in variables, you'll want to do something with that information. Most likely, you'll want to manipulate it by making changes to it. For example, you might want to use the radius of a circle to find the area of the circle. Today you...

- Learn two ways of displaying basic information.
- Discover the types and categories of operators available in C#.
- Manipulate information using the different operators.
- Change program flow using the `if` command.
- Understand which operators have precedence over others.
- Investigate variable and value conversions.
- Explore bitwise operations—if you're brave enough.

Displaying Basic Information

Before you learn how to manipulate values stored in variables, it is worth taking a few minutes to learn how to display basic information. You can use two routines to display information. When you understand these routines, you will be able to display basic information to the console.

The two routines that you will use throughout this book to display basic information are as follows:

- `System.Console.WriteLine()`
- `System.Console.Write()`

Both print information to the screen in the same manner, with only one small difference. The `WriteLine()` routine writes information and then goes to a new line. The `Write()`routine does not go to a new line when information is written.

The information that you will display on the screen is written between the parentheses. If you are printing text, you include the text between the parentheses and within double quotes. For example, the following prints the text `Hello World`:

```
System.Console.WriteLine("Hello World");
```

This prints `Hello World` on the screen. The following examples illustrate other text being printed:

```
System.Console.WriteLine("This is a line of text");
System.Console.WriteLine("This is a second line of text");
```

If you execute these consecutively, you see the following displayed:

```
This is a line of text
This is a second line of text
```

Now consider the following two lines. If these execute consecutively, what do you see printed?

```
System.Console.WriteLine("Hello ");
System.Console.WriteLine("World!");
```

If you guessed that these would print

```
Hello World!
```

you are not correct! Instead, the following is printed:

```
Hello
World!
```

Notice that each word is on a separate line. If you execute the two lines using the `Write()` routine instead, you get the results you want:

```
Hello World!
```

As you can see, the difference between the two routines is that `WriteLine()` automatically goes to a new line after the text is displayed, whereas `Write()` does not.

Displaying Additional Information

In addition to printing text between quotation marks, you can pass values to be printed within the text. Consider the following example:

```
int nbr = 456;
System.Console.WriteLine("The following is a number: {0}", nbr);
```

This prints the following line:

```
The following is a number: 456
```

As you can see, the `{0}` gets replaced with the value that follows the quoted text. In this case, the value is that of a variable, `nbr`, which equals `456`. The format is as shown here:

```
System.Console.WriteLine("Text", value);
```

`Text` is almost any text that you want to display. The `{0}` is a placeholder for a value. The brackets indicate that this is a placeholder. The `0` is an indicator for using the first item following the quotation marks. A comma separates the text from the value to be placed in the placeholder.

You can have more than one placeholder in a printout. Each placeholder is given the next sequential number:

```
System.Console.Write("Value 1 is {0} and value 2 is {1}", 123, "Brad");
```

This prints the following line:

```
Value 1 is 123 and value 2 is Brad
```

Listing 3.1 presents `System.Console.Write` and `System.Console.WriteLine` in action.

LISTING 3.1   Display.cs—Using `WriteLine()` and `Write()`

```
1: // Display.cs - printing with WriteLine and Write
2: //-----------------------------------------------
3:
4: class Display
5: {
6:     public static void Main()
```

LISTING **3.1**   continued

```
 7:   {
 8:
 9:       int iNbr = 321;
10:       double dNbr = 123.45;
11:
12:       System.Console.WriteLine("First WriteLine Line");
13:       System.Console.WriteLine("Second WriteLine Line");
14:
15:       System.Console.Write("First Write Line");
16:       System.Console.Write("Second Write Line");
17:
18:       // Passing literal parameters
19:       System.Console.WriteLine("\nWriteLine: Parameter = {0}", 123 );
20:       System.Console.Write("Write: Parameter = {0}", 456);
21:
22:       // Passing variables
23:       System.Console.WriteLine("\nWriteLine: val1 = {0} val2 = {1}",
24:                                   iNbr, dNbr );
25:       System.Console.Write("Write: val1 = {0} val2 = {1}", iNbr, dNbr);
26:   }
27: }
```

Remember that to compile this listing from the command line, you enter the following:

`csc Display.cs`

If you are using an integrated development tool, you can select the Compile option.

OUTPUT
```
First WriteLine Line
Second WriteLine Line
First Write LineSecond Write Line
WriteLine: Parameter = 123
Write: Parameter = 456
WriteLine: val1 = 321 val2 = 123.45
Write: val1 = 321 val2 = 123.45
```

ANALYSIS This listing defines two variables that will be printed later in the listing. Line 9 declares an integer and assigns the value 321 to it. Line 10 defines a double and assigns the value 123.45.

Lines 12–13 print two pieces of text using System.Console.WriteLine(). You can see from the output that each of these prints on a separate line. Lines 15–16 show the System.Console.Write() routine. These two lines print on the same line. There is no return linefeed after printing. Lines 19–20 show each of these routines with the use of a parameter. Lines 23 and 25 also show these routines printing multiple values from variables.

You will learn more about using these routines throughout this book.

| Caution | The first placeholder is numbered 0, not 1. |

Manipulating Variable Values with Operators

Now that you understand how to display the values of variables, it is time to focus on manipulating the values in the variables. Operators are used to manipulate information. You have used a number of operators in the programming examples up to this point. Operators are used for addition, multiplication, comparison, and more.

Operators can be broken into a number of categories:

- The basic assignment operator
- Mathematical/arithmetic operators
- Relational operators
- The conditional operator
- Other operators (type, size)

Each of these categories and the operators within them are covered in detail in the following sections. In addition to these categories, it is important to understand the structure of operator statements. Three types of operator structures exist:

- Unary
- Binary
- Ternary

Unary Operator Types

Unary operators are operators that impact a single variable. For example, to have a negative 1, you type this:

```
-1
```

If you have a variable called x, you change the value to a negative by using this line:

```
-x
```

The negative requires only one variable, so it is unary. The format of a unary variable is one of the following, depending on the specific operator:

```
[operator][variable]
```

or

```
[variable][operator]
```

Binary Operator Types

Whereas unary operator types use only one variable, binary operator types work with two variables. For example, the addition operator is used to add two values. The format of the binary operator types is as follows:

```
[variable1][operator][variable2]
```

Examples of binary operations in action are shown here:

```
5 + 4

3 - 2

100.4 - 92348.67
```

You will find that most of the operators fall into the binary operator type.

Ternary Operator Types

Ternary operators are the most complex operator type to work with. As the name implies, this type of operator works on three variables. C# has only one true ternary operator, the conditional operator. You will learn about it later today. For now, know that ternary operators work with three variables.

Understanding Punctuators

Before jumping into the different categories and specific operators within C#, it is important to understand about punctuators. Punctuators are a special form of operator that helps you format your code, do multiple operations at once, and simply signal information to the compiler. The punctuators that you need to know about are listed here:

- **Semicolon**—The primary use of the semicolon is to end each C# statement. A semicolon is also used with a couple of the C# statements that control program flow. You will learn about the use of the semicolon with the control statements on Day 4, "Controlling Your Program's Flow."

- **Comma**—The comma is used to stack multiple commands on the same line. You saw the comma in use on Day 2, "Understanding C# Programs," in a number of the examples. The most common time to use the comma is when declaring multiple variables of the same type:

  ```
  int var1, var2, var3;
  ```

- **Parentheses,** ()—Parentheses are used in multiple places. You will see later in today's lesson that you can use parentheses to force the order in which your code will execute. Additionally, parentheses are used with functions.
- **Braces,** {}—Braces are used to group pieces of code. You have seen braces used to encompass classes in many of the examples. You also should have noticed that braces are always used in pairs.

Punctuators work the same way punctuation within a sentence works. For example, you end a sentence with a period or another form of punctuation. In C#, you end a "line" of code with a semicolon or other punctuator. The word *line* is in quotation marks because a line of code might actually take up multiple lines in a source listing. As you learned on Day 2, whitespace and new lines are ignored.

 Note

> You can also use braces within the routines that you create to block off code. The code put between two braces, along with the braces, is called a *block*.

Moving Values with the Assignment Operator

It is now time to learn about the specific operators available in C#. The first operator that you need to know about is the basic assignment operator, which is an equals sign (=). You've seen this operator already in a number of the examples in earlier lessons.

The basic assignment operator is used to assign values. For example, to assign the value 142 to the variable x, you type this:

```
x = 142;
```

This compiler places the value that is on the right side of the assignment operator in the variable on the left side. Consider the following:

```
x = y = 123;
```

This might look a little weird; however, it is legal C# code. The value on the right of the equals sign is evaluated. In this case, the far right is 123, which is placed in the variable y. Then the value of y is placed in the variable x. The end result is that both x and y equal 123.

Caution   You cannot do operations on the left side of an assignment operator. For example, you can't do this:

1 + x = y;

Nor can you put literals or constants on the left side of an assignment operator.

Working with Mathematical/Arithmetic Operators

Among the most commonly used operators are the mathematical operators. All the basic math functions are available within C#, including addition, subtraction, multiplication, division, and modulus (remaindering). Additionally, compound operators make doing some of these operations more concise.

Adding and Subtracting

For addition and subtraction, you use the additive operators. As you should expect, for addition, the plus operator (+) is used. For subtraction, the minus (-) operator is used. The general format of using these variables is as follows:

```
NewVal = Value1 + Value2;

NewVal2 = Value1 - Value2;
```

In the first statement, `Value2` is being added to `Value1` and the result is placed in `NewVal`. When this command is done, `Value1` and `Value2` remain unchanged. Any pre-existing values in `NewVal` are overwritten with the result.

For the subtraction statement, `Value2` is subtracted from `Value1` and the result is placed in `NewVal2`. Again, `Value1` and `Value2` remain unchanged, and the value in `NewVal2` is overwritten with the result.

`Value1` and `Value2` can be any of the value data types, constants, or literals. You should note that `NewVal` must be a variable; however, it can be the same variable as `Value1` or `Value2`. For example, the following is legal as long as `Variable1` is a variable:

```
Variable1 = Variable1 - Variable2;
```

In this example, the value in `Variable2` is subtracted from the value in `Variable1`. The result is placed into `Variable1`, thus overwriting the previous value that `Variable1` held. The following example is also valid:

```
Variable1 = Variable1 - Variable1;
```

In this example, the value of `Variable1` is subtracted from the value of `Variable1`. Because these values are the same, the result is `0`. This `0` value is then placed into `Variable1`, overwriting any previous value.

If you want to double a value, you enter the following:

```
Variable1 = Variable1 + Variable1;
```

`Variable1` is added to itself, and the result is placed back into `Variable1`. The end result is that you double the value in `Variable1`.

Doing Multiplicative Operations

An easier way to double the value of a variable is to multiply it by two. Three multiplicative operators commonly are used in C#:

- For multiplication, the multiplier (or times) operator, which is an asterisk (`*`)
- For division, the divisor operator, which is a forward slash (`/`)
- For obtaining remainders, the remaindering (also called modulus) operator, which is the percentage sign (`%`)

Multiplication and division are done in the same manner as addition and subtraction. To multiply two values, you use the following format:

```
NewVal = Value1 * Value2;
```

For example, to double the value in `Val1` and place it back into itself (as seen with the last addition example), you can enter the following:

```
Val1 = Val1 * 2;
```

This is the same as this line:

```
Val1 = 2 * Val1;
```

Again, division is done the same way:

```
NewVal = Value1 / Value2;
```

This example divides `Value1` by `Value2` and places the result in `NewVal`. To divide 2 by 3, you write the following:

```
answer = 2 / 3;
```

Sometimes when doing division, you want only the remainder. For example, I know that 3 will go into 4 one time; however, I also would like to know that I have 1 remaining.

You can get this remainder using the remaindering (also called modulus) operator, which is the percentage sign (%). For example, to get the remainder of 4 divided by 3, you enter this:

```
Val = 4 % 3;
```

The result is that `Val` is `1`.

Consider another example that is near and dear to my heart. You have three pies that can be cut into six pieces. If 13 people each want a piece of pie, how many pieces of pie are left over for you?

To solve this, take a look at Listing 3.2.

LISTING 3.2   Pie.cs—Number of Pieces of Pie for Me

```
 1:  // Pie.cs - Using the modulus operators
 2:  //-----------------------------------------------
 3:  class Pie
 4:  {
 5:      public static void Main()
 6:      {
 7:          int PiecesForMe = 0;
 8:          int PiecesOfPie = 0;
 9:
10:          PiecesOfPie = 3 * 6;
11:
12:          PiecesForMe =  PiecesOfPie % 13;
13:
14:          System.Console.WriteLine("Pieces Of Pie = {0}", PiecesOfPie);
15:          System.Console.WriteLine("Pieces For Me = {0}", PiecesForMe);
16:      }
17:  }
```

OUTPUT
```
Pieces Of Pie = 18
Pieces For Me = 5
```

ANALYSIS Listing 3.2 presents the use of the multiplication and modulus operators. Line 10 illustrates the multiplication operator, which is used to determine how many pieces of pie there are. In this case, there are six pieces in three pies (so, 6 × 3). Line 12 then uses the modulus operator to determine how many pieces are left for you. As you can see from the information printed in Lines 14–15, there are 18 pieces of pie, and 5 will be left for you.

Working with the Compound Arithmetic Assignment Operators

You've learned about the basic assignment operator; however, there are also other assignment operators—the compound assignment operators (see Table 3.1).

TABLE 3.1 Compound Arithmetic Assignment Operators

Operator	Description	Noncompound Equivalent
+=	x += 4	x = x + 4
-=	x -= 4	x = x - 4
*=	x *= 4	x = x * 4
/=	x /= 4	x = x / 4
%=	x %= 4	x = x % 4

The compound operators provide a concise method for performing a math operation and assigning it to a value. For example, if you want to increase a value by 5, you use the following:

```
x = x + 5;
```

Or, you can use the compound operator:

```
x += 5;
```

As you can see, the compound operator is much more concise.

Tip

> Although the compound operators are more concise, they are not always the easiest to understand in code. If you use the compound operators, make sure that what you are doing is clear, or remember to comment your code.

Doing Unary Math

All the arithmetic operators that you have seen so far have been binary. Each has required two values to operate. A number of unary operators also work with just one value or variable. The unary arithmetic operators include the increment operator (++) and the decrement operator (--).

These operators add 1 to the value or subtract 1 from the value of a variable. The following example adds 1 to x:

```
++x;
```

It is the same as saying this:

```
x = x + 1;
```

Additionally, the following subtracts 1 from x:

```
--x;
```

It is the same as saying this:

```
x = x - 1;
```

Tip   The increment and decrement operators are handy when you need to step through a lot of values one by one.

The increment and decrement operators have a unique feature that causes problems for a lot of newer programmers. Assume that the value of myNbr is 10. Look at the following line of code:

```
NewNbr = ++myNbr;
```

After this statement executes, what will the values of myNbr and newNbr be? You should be able to guess that the value of myNbr will be 11 after it executes. The value of newNbr will also be 11. Now consider the following line of code; again consider the value of myNbr to start at 10.

```
newNbr = myNbr++;
```

After this statement executes, what will the values of myNbr and newNbr be? If you said that they would both be 11 again, you are wrong! After this line of code executes, myNbr will be 11; however, newNbr will be 10. Confused?

It is simple: The increment operator can operate as a *pre*-increment operator or a *post*-increment operator. If it operates as a pre-increment operator, the value is incremented before everything else. If it operates as a post-increment operator, it happens after everything else. How do you know whether it is pre- or post-? Easy. If it is before the variable, ++myNbr, it is *pre*-. If it is after the variable, myNbr++, it is *post*-. The same is true of the decrement operator. Listing 3.3 illustrates the pre- and post- operations of the increment and decrement operators.

LISTING 3.3   Prepost.cs—Using the Increment and Decrement Unary Operators

```
 1:   // Prepost.cs - Using pre- versus post-increment operators
 2:   //------------------------------------------------
 3:
 4:   class Prepost
 5:   {
 6:       public static void Main()
 7:       {
 8:          int Val1 = 0;
 9:          int Val2 = 0;
10:
11:          System.Console.WriteLine("Val1 = {0}   Val2 = {1}", Val1, Val2);
12:
13:          System.Console.WriteLine("Val1 (Pre) = {0}   Val2 = (Post) {1}",
14:               ++Val1, Val2++);
15:
16:          System.Console.WriteLine("Val1 (Pre) = {0}   Val2 = (Post) {1}",
17:               ++Val1, Val2++);
18:
19:          System.Console.WriteLine("Val1 (Pre) = {0}   Val2 = (Post) {1}",
20:               ++Val1, Val2++);
21:       }
22:   }
```

OUTPUT
```
Val1 = 0   Val2 = 0
Val1 (Pre) = 1   Val2 = (Post) 0
Val1 (Pre) = 2   Val2 = (Post) 1
Val1 (Pre) = 3   Val2 = (Post) 2
```

ANALYSIS It is important to understand what is happening in Listing 3.3. In Lines 8–9, two variables are again being initialized to 0. These values are printed in Line 11. As you can see from the output, the result is that Val1 and Val2 equal 0. Line 13, which continues to Line 14, prints the values of these two variables again. The values printed, though, are ++Val1 and Val2++. As you can see, the pre-increment operator is being used on Val1, and the post-increment operator is being used on Val2. The results can be seen in the output. Val1 is incremented by 1 and then printed. Val2 is printed and then incremented by 1. Lines 16 and 19 repeat these same operations two more times.

Do	Don't
Do use the compound operators to make your math routines concise.	Don't confuse the post-increment and pre-increment operators. Remember that the pre-increment adds before the variable, and the post-increment adds after it.

Making Comparisons with Relational Operators

Questions are a part of life. In addition to asking questions, it is often important to compare things. In programming, you compare values and then execute code based on the answer. The relational operators are used to compare two values. The relational operators are listed in Table 3.2.

TABLE 3.2   Relational Operators

Operator	Description
>	Greater than
<	Less than
==	Equal to
!=	Not equal to
>=	Greater than or equal to
<=	Less than or equal to

When making comparisons with relational operators, you get one of two results: `true` or `false`. Consider the following comparisons made with the relational operators:

`5 < 10`	5 is less than 10, so this is true.
`5 > 10`	5 is not greater than 10, so this is false.
`5 == 10`	5 does not equal 10, so this is false.
`5 != 10`	5 does not equal 10, so this is true.

As you can see, each of these results is either true or false. Knowing that you can check the relationship of values should be great for programming. The question is, how do you use these relations?

Using the `if` Statement

The value of relational operators is that they can be used to make decisions to change the flow of the execution of your program. The `if` keyword can be used with the relational operators to change the program flow.

The `if` keyword is used to compare two values. The standard format of the `if` command is as follows:

```
if( val1 [operator] val2)
    statement(s);
```

operator is one of the relational operators; `val1` and `val2` are variables, constants, or literals; and `statement(s)` is a single statement or a block containing multiple statements. Remember that a block is one or more statements between brackets.

If the comparison of `val1` to `val2` is true, the statements are executed. If the comparison of `val1` to `val2` is false, the statements are skipped. Figure 3.1 illustrates how the `if` command works.

FIGURE 3.1

The `if` command.

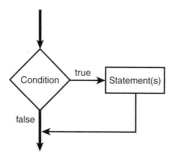

Applying this to an example helps make this clear. Listing 3.4 presents simple usage of the `if` command.

LISTING 3.4   iftest.cs—Using the `if` Command

```
 1:  // iftest.cs- The if statement
 2:  //.......    ...................................
 3:
 4:  class iftest
 5:  {
 6:     public static void Main()
 7:     {
 8:        int Val1 = 1;
 9:        int Val2 = 0;
10:
11:        System.Console.WriteLine("Getting ready to do the if...");
12:
13:        if (Val1 == Val2)
14:        {
15:            System.Console.WriteLine("If condition was true");
16:        }
17:        System.Console.WriteLine("Done with the if statement");
18:     }
19:  }
```

OUTPUT   Getting ready to do the if...
Done with the if statement

This listing uses the `if` statement in Line 13 to compare two values to see whether they are equal. If they are, it prints Line 15. If not, it skips Line 15. Because the values assigned to `Val1` and `Val2` in Lines 8–9 are not equal, the `if` condition fails and Line 15 is not printed.

Change Line 13 to this:

```
if (Val1 != Val2)
```

Rerun the listing. This time, because `Val1` does not equal `Val2`, the `if` condition evaluates to `true`. The following is the output:

```
Getting ready to do the if...
If condition was true
Done with the if statement
```

> **Caution**
>
> There is no semicolon at the end of the first line of the `if` command. For example, the following is incorrect:
>
> ```
> if( val != val );
> {
>     // Statements to do when the if evaluates to true (which will
>     // never happen)
> }
> ```
>
> `val` should always equal `val`, so `val != val` will be false and the line `// Statements to do when the if evaluates to true...` should never execute. Because there is a semicolon at the end of the first line, the `if` statement is ended. This means that the next statement *after* the `if` statement is executed—the line `//Statements to do when the if evaluates to true....` This line always executes, regardless of whether the `if` evaluates to `true` or, as in this case, to `false`. Don't make the mistake of including a semicolon at the end of the first line of an `if` statement.

Conditional Logical Operators

The world is rarely a simple place. In many cases, you will want to do more than one comparison to determine whether a block of code should be executed. For example, you might want to execute some code if a person is a female and at least 21 years old. To do this, you execute an `if` statement within another `if` statement. The following pseudocode illustrates this:

```
if( sex == female )
{
    if( age >= 21 )
    {
```

```
        // The person is a female that is 21 years old or older.
    }
}
```

There is an easier way to accomplish this—by using a conditional logical operator.

The conditional logical operators enable you to do multiple comparisons with relational operators. The two conditional logical operators that you will use are the AND operator (&&) and the OR operator (||).

The Conditional AND Operator

Sometimes you want to verify that a number of conditions are all met. The previous example was one such case. The logical AND operator (&&) enables you to verify that all conditions are met. You can rewrite the previous example as follows:

```
If( sex == female && age >= 21 )
{
    // This person is a female that is 21 years old or older.
}
```

3

You can actually place more than two relationships within a single if statement. Regardless of the number of comparisons, the comparisons on each side of the AND (&&) must be true. For example:

```
if( x < 5 && y < 10 && z > 10)
{
    // statements
}
```

The statements line is reached only if all three conditions are met. If any of the three conditions in the if statements is false, the statements are skipped.

The Conditional OR Operator

Also sometimes, you do not want all the conditions to be true: Instead, you need only one of a number of conditions to be true. For example, you want might want to execute some code if the day of week is Saturday or Sunday. In these cases, you use the logical OR operator (||). The following illustrates this with pseudocode:

```
if( day equals sunday OR day equals saturday )
{
    // do statements
}
```

In this example, the statements are executed if the day equals either *sunday* or *saturday*. Only one of these conditions needs to be true for the statements to be executed. Listing 3.5 presents both the logical AND and OR in action.

LISTING 3.5   and.cs—Using the Logical AND and OR

```
 1:  // and.cs- Using the conditional AND and OR
 2:  //-------------------------------------------------
 3:
 4:  class andclass
 5:  {
 6:      public static void Main()
 7:      {
 8:          int  day = 1;
 9:          char sex = 'f';
10:
11:          System.Console.WriteLine("Starting tests... (day:{0}, sex:{1})",
12:                                    day, sex );
13:
14:          if ( day >= 1 && day <=7 )       //day from 1 to 7?
15:          {
16:              System.Console.WriteLine("Day is from 1 to 7");
17:          }
18:          if (sex == 'm' || sex == 'f' )  // Male or female?
19:          {
20:              System.Console.WriteLine("Sex is male or female.");
21:          }
22:
23:          System.Console.WriteLine("Done with the checks.");
24:      }
25:  }
```

OUTPUT
```
Starting tests... (day:1, sex:f)
Day is from 1 to 7
Sex is male or female.
Done with the checks.
```

ANALYSIS This listing illustrates both the && and || operators. In Line 14, you can see the AND operator (&&) in action. For this if statement to evaluate to true, the day must be greater than or equal to 1 as well as less than or equal to 7. If the day is 1, 2, 3, 4, 5, 6, or 7, the if condition evaluates to true and Line 16 prints. Any other number results in the if statement evaluating to false, and thus Line 16 will be skipped.

Line 18 shows the OR (||) operator in action. Here, if the value in sex is equal to the character 'm' or the character 'f', line 20 is printed; otherwise, Line 20 is skipped.

Caution   Be careful with the if condition in Line 18. This checks for the characters 'm' and 'f'. Notice these are lowercase values, which are not the same as the uppercase values. If you set sex equal to 'F' or 'M' in Line 9, the if statement in line 18 would still fail.

Change the values in Lines 8–9, and rerun the listing. You'll see that you get different output results based on the values you select. For example, change Lines 8–9 to the following:

```
8:          int  day = 9;
9:          char sex = 'x';
```

Here are the results of rerunning the program:

```
Starting tests... (day:9, sex:x)
Done with the checks.
```

Other times you will want to use the AND (&&) and OR (||) commands together. For example, you might want to execute code if a person is 21 and is either a male or a female. This can be accomplished by using the AND and OR statements together. You must be careful when doing this, though. An AND operator expects the values on both sides of it to be true. An OR statement expects one of the values to be true. For the previous example, you might be tempted to enter the following (note that this is pseudocode):

```
if( age >= 21 AND gender == male OR gender == FEMALE)
    // statement
```

This will not accomplish what you want. If the person is 21 or older and is a female, the statement will not execute. The AND portion will result in being false. To overcome this problem, you can force how the statements are evaluated using the parenthesis punctuator. To accomplish the desired results, you would change the previous example to this:

```
if( age >= 21 AND (gender == male OR gender == female))
    // statement
```

The execution always starts with the innermost parenthesis. In this case, the statement (gender == male OR gender == female) is evaluated first. Because this uses OR, this portion of the statement will evaluate to true if either side is true. If this is true, the AND will compare the age value to see whether the age is greater than or equal to 21. If this proves to be true as well, the statement will execute.

Tip

Use parentheses to make sure that you get code to execute in the order you want.

Do	Don't
Do use parentheses to make complex math and relational operations easier to understand.	**Don't** confuse the assignment operator (=) with the relational equals operator (==).

Understanding Logical Bitwise Operators

You might want to use three other logical operators: the logical bitwise operators. Although the use of bitwise operations is beyond the scope of this book, I've included a section near the end of today's lesson called "For Those Brave Enough." This section explains bitwise operations, the three logical bitwise operators, and the bitwise shift operators.

The bitwise operators obtain their name from the fact that they operate on bits. A bit is a single storage location that stores either an on or an off value (equated to 0 or 1). In the section at the end of today's lesson, you will learn how the bitwise operators can be used to manipulate these bits.

Understanding the Type Operators

As you begin working with classes and interfaces later in this book, you will need the type operators. Without understanding interfaces and classes, it is hard to fully understand these operators. For now, be aware that you will need a number of operators later:

- `typeof`
- `is`
- `as`

Using the `sizeof` Operator

You saw the `sizeof` operator in action on Day 2. This operator is used to determine the size of a value in memory.

 Caution | Because the `sizeof` operator manipulates memory directly, avoid its use, if possible.

Shortcutting with the Conditional Operator

C# has one ternary operator: the conditional operator. The conditional operator has the following format:

```
Condition ? if_true_statement : if_false_statement;
```

As you can see, there are three parts to this operation, with two symbols used to separate them. The first part of the command is a condition. This is just like the conditions that you created earlier for the `if` statement. This can be any condition that results in either `true` or `false`.

After the condition is a question mark, which separates the condition from the first of two statements. The first of the two statements executes if the condition is true. The second statement is separated from the first with a colon and is executed if the condition is false. Listing 3.6 presents the conditional operator in action.

The conditional operator is used to create concise code. If you have a simple `if` statement that evaluates to doing a simple `true` and simple `false` statement, then the conditional operator can be used. In my opinion, you should avoid the use of the conditional operator. Because it is just a shortcut version of an `if` statement, just stick with using the `if` statement. Most people reviewing your code will find the `if` statement easier to read and understand.

LISTING 3.6   cond.cs—The Conditional Operator in Action

```
 1:  // cond.cs - The conditional operator
 2:  //----------------------------------------------
 3:
 4:  class cond
 5:  {
 6:     public static void Main()
 7:     {
 8:        int Val1 = 1;
 9:        int Val2 = 0;
10:        int result;
11:
12:        result = (Val1 == Val2) ? 1 : 0;
13:
14:        System.Console.WriteLine("The result is {0}", result);
15:     }
16:  }
```

OUTPUT   The result is 0

ANALYSIS   This listing is very simple. In Line 12, the conditional operator is executed and the result is placed in the variable `result`. Line 14 then prints this value. In this case, the conditional operator checks to see whether the value in `Val1` is equal to the value in `Val2`. Because 1 is not equal to 0, the false result of the conditional is set. Modify Line 8 so that `Val2` is set equal to 1, and then rerun this listing. You will see that because 1 is equal to 1, the result will be 1 instead of 0.

Caution The conditional operator provides a shortcut for implementing an if state-ment. Although it is more concise, it is not always the easiest to understand. When using the conditional operator, you should verify that you are not making your code harder to understand.

Understanding Operator Precedence

Rarely are these operators used one at a time. Often multiple operators are used in a single statement. When this happens, a lot of issues seem to arise. Consider the following:

```
Answer = 4 * 5 + 6 / 2 - 1;
```

What is the value of Answer? If you said 12, you are wrong. If you said 44, you are also wrong. The answer is 22.

NEW TERM Different types of operators are executed in a set order, called *operator precedence*. The word *precedence* is used because some operators have a higher level of precedence than others. In the example, multiplication and division have a higher level of precedence than addition and subtraction. This means that 4 is multiplied by 5, and 6 is divided by 2 *before* any addition occurs.

Table 3.3 lists all the operators. The operators at each level of the table are at the same level of precedence. In almost all cases, there is no impact on the results. For example, 5 × 4 / 10 is the same whether 5 is multiplied by 4 first or 4 is divided by 10.

TABLE 3.3   Operator Precedence

Level	Operator Types	Operators
1	Primary operators	() . [] x++ x-- new typeof sizeof checked unchecked
2	Unary	+ - ! ~ ++x --x
3	Multiplicative	* / %
4	Additive	+ -
5	Shift	<< >>
6	Relational	< > <= >= is
7	Equality	== !=
8	Logical AND	&
9	Logical XOR	^
10	Logical OR	|

TABLE 3.3   continued

Level	Operator Types	Operators
11	Conditional AND	&&
12	Conditional OR	||
13	Conditional	?:
14	Assignment	= *= /= %= += -= <<= >>= &= ^= |=

Changing Precedence Order

You learned how to change the order of precedence by using parentheses punctuators earlier in today's lessons. Because parentheses have a higher level of precedence than the operators, what is enclosed in them is evaluated before operators outside of them. Using the earlier example, you can force the addition and subtraction to occur first by using parentheses:

```
Answer = 4 * ( 5 + 6 ) / ( 2 - 1 );
```

Now what will Answer be? Because the parentheses are evaluated first, the compiler first resolves the code to this:

```
Answer = 4 * 11 / 1;
```

The final result is 44. You can also have parentheses within parentheses. For example, the code could be written as follows:

```
Answer = 4 * ( ( 5 + 6 ) / ( 2 - 1 ) );
```

The compiler would resolve this as follows:

```
Answer = 4 * ( 11 / 1 );
```

Then it would resolve it as this:

```
Answer = 4 * 11;
```

Finally, it would resolve it as the Answer of 44. In this case, the parentheses didn't cause a difference in the final answer; however, sometimes they do.

Converting Data Types

When you move a value from one variable type to another, a conversion must occur. Additionally, if you want to perform an operation on two different data types, a conversion might also need to occur. Two types of conversions can occur: implicit and explicit.

NEW TERM   *Implicit* conversions happen automatically without error. You've read about many of these within today's lesson. What happens when an implicit conversion is not available? For example, what if you want to put the value stored in a variable of type long into a variable of type int?

NEW TERM   *Explicit* conversions are conversions of data that are forced. For the value data types that you learned about today, the easiest way to do an explicit conversion is with a cast. A *cast* is the forcing of a data value to another data type. The format of a cast is shown here:

```
ToVariable = (datatype) FromVariable;
```

datatype is the data type that you want the FromVariable converted to. Using the example of converting a long variable to an int, you enter the following statement:

```
int IntVariable = 0;
long LongVariable = 1234;
IntVariable = (int) LongVariable;
```

In doing casts, you take responsibility for making sure that the variable can hold the value being converted. If the receiving variable cannot store the received value, truncation or other changes can occur. A number of times, you will need to do explicit conversions. Table 3.4 contains a list of those times.

 Note   Explicit conversions as a group also encompass all the implicit conversions. It is possible to use a cast even if an implicit conversion is available.

TABLE 3.4   Required Explicit Conversions

From Type	To Type(s)
sbyte	byte, ushort, uint, ulong, or char
byte	sbyte or char
short	sbyte, byte, ushort, uint, ulong, or char
ushort	sbyte, byte, short, or char
int	sbyte, byte, short, ushort, uint, ulong, or char
uint	sbyte, byte, short, ushort, int, or char
long	sbyte, byte, short, ushort, int, uint, ulong, or char
ulong	sbyte, byte, short, ushort, int, uint, long, or char
char	sbyte, byte, or short
float	sbyte, byte, short, ushort, int, uint, long, ulong, char, or decimal

TABLE 3.4   continued

From Type	To Type(s)
double	sbyte, byte, short, ushort, int, uint, long, ulong, char, float, or decimal
decimal	sbyte, byte, short, ushort, int, uint, long, ulong, char, float, or double

Understanding Operator Promotion

NEW TERM   Implicit conversions are also associated with *operator promotion,* which is the
automatic conversion of an operator from one type to another. When you do
basic arithmetic operations on two variables, they are converted to the same type before
doing the math. For example, if you add a byte variable to an int variable, the byte variable is promoted to an integer before it is added.

A numeric variable smaller than an int is promoted to an int. The order of promotion
after an int is as follows:

```
int

uint

long

ulong

float

double

decimal
```

Note   The following section contains advanced material that is not critical to know
at this time. You can cover this material now, or you can to skip to the end
of today's lesson and come back to this material later.

Bonus Material: For Those Brave Enough

For those brave enough, the following sections explain using the bitwise operators. This
includes using the shift operators and the logical bitwise operators. Bitwise operators are
a more advanced topic, so most beginning-level books skip over them. One reason they
are advanced is that before understanding how these operators work, you need to understand how variables are truly stored.

Tip

It is valuable to understand the bitwise operators and how memory works; however, it is not critical to your understanding C#. If you feel brave, continue forward. If not, feel free to jump to the Summary and Workshop at the end of today's lessons. You can always come back and read this later.

Storing Variables in Memory

To understand the bitwise operators, you must first understand bits. In yesterday's lesson on data types, you learned that the different data types take different numbers of bits to store. For example, a char data type takes 2 bytes. An integer takes 4 bytes. You also learned that maximum and minimum values can be stored in these different data types.

Recall that a byte is 8 bits of memory; 2 bytes is 16 bits of memory—2×8. Therefore, 4 bytes is 32 bits of memory. The key to all of this is to understand what a bit is.

A bit is simply a single storage unit of memory that can be either turned on or turned off just like a light bulb. If you are storing information on a magnetic medium, a bit can be stored as either a positive charge or a negative charge. If you are working with something such as a CD-ROM, the bit can be stored as a bump or as an indent. In all these cases, one value is equated to 0 and the other is equated to 1.

If a bit can store only a 0 or a 1, you are obviously very limited in what can be stored. To be able to store larger values, you use bits in groups. For example, if you use 2 bits, you can actually store four numbers, 00, 01, 10, and 11. If you use 3 bits, you can store eight numbers, 000, 001, 010, 011, 100, 101, 110, and 111. If you use 4 bits, you can store 16 numbers. In fact x bits can store 2^x numbers, so a byte (8 bits), can store 2^8, or 256 numbers. Two bytes can store 2^{16}, or 65536 values.

Translating from these 1s and 0s is simply a matter of using the binary number system. Appendix C, "Understanding Number Systems," explains how you can work with the binary number system in detail. For now, understand that the binary system is simply a number system.

You use the decimal number system to count. Whereas the decimal system uses 10 numbers (0 to 9), the binary system uses 2 numbers. When counting in the decimal system, you use 1s, 10s, 100s, 1,000s, and so forth. For example, the number 13 is one 10 and three 1s. The number 25 is two 10s and five 1s.

The binary system works the same way, except that there are only two numbers, 0 and 1. Instead of 10s and 100s, you have 1s, 2s, 4s, 8s, and so on. In fact, each group is based on taking 2 to the power of a number. The first group is 2 to the power of 0, the second is 2 to the power of 1, the third is 2 to the power of 3, and so on. Figure 3.2 illustrates this.

FIGURE 3.2

Binary versus decimal.

Presenting numbers in the binary system works the same way it does in the decimal system. The first position on the right is 1s, the second position from the right is 2s, the third is 4s, and so on. Consider the following number:

1101

To convert this binary number to decimal, you can multiply each value in the number times by positional value. For example, the value in the right column (1s) is 1. The 2s column contains a 0, the 4s column contains a 1, and the 8s column contains a 1. The result is this:

$$1 + (0 \times 2) + (1 \times 4) + (1 \times 8)$$

The final decimal result is this:

$$1 + 0 + 4 + 8$$

This is 13. So, 1101 in binary is equivalent to 13 in decimal. This same process can be applied to convert any binary number to decimal. As numbers get larger, you need more bit positions. To keep things simpler, memory is actually separated into 8-bit units—bytes.

Understanding the Shift Operators

C# has two shift operators that can be used to manipulate bits. These operators do exactly what their names imply—they shift the bits. The shift operators can shift the bits to the right using the >> operator or to the left using the << operator. These operators shift the bits within a variable by a specified number of positions. The format is as follows:

New_value = Value [shift-operator] number-of-positions;

Value is a literal or a variable, *shift-operator* is either the right (>>) or the left (<<) shift operator, and *number-of-positions* is how many positions you want to shift the bits. For example, if you have the number 13 stored in a byte, you know that its binary representation is as follows:

00001101

If you use the shift operator on this, you change the value. Consider the following:

```
00001101 >> 2
```

This shifts the bits in this number to the right two positions. The result is this:

00000011

This binary value is equivalent to the value of 3. In summary, 13 >> 2 equals 3. Consider another example:

```
00001101 << 8
```

This example shifts the bit values to the left eight positions. Because this is a single-byte value, the resulting number is 0.

Manipulating Bits with Logical Operators

In addition to being able to shift bits, you can combine the bits of two numbers. Three bitwise logical operators can be used, as shown in Table 3.5.

TABLE 3.5 Logical Bitwise Operators

Operator	Description
|	Logical OR bitwise operator
&	Logical AND bitwise operator
^	Logical XOR bitwise operator

Each of these operators is used to combine the bits of two binary values. Each has a different result.

The Logical OR Bitwise Operator

When combining two values with the logical OR bitwise operator (|), you get the following results:

- If both bits are 0, the result is 0.
- If either or both bits are 1, the result is 1.

Combining 2 byte values results in the following:

Value 1: 00001111

Value 2: 11001100

Result: 11001111

The Logical AND Bitwise Operator

When combining two values with the logical AND bitwise operator (&), you get the following result:

- If both bits are 1, the result is 1.
- If either bit is 0, the result is 0.

Combining 2 byte values results in the following:

Value 1: 00001111

Value 2: 11001100

Result: 00001100

The Logical XOR Operator

When combining two values with the logical XOR bitwise operator (^), you get the following result:

- If both bits are the same, the result is 0.
- If 1 bit is 0 and the other is 1, the result is 1.

Combining 2 byte values results in the following:

Value 1: 00001111

Value 2: 11001100

Result: 11000011

Listing 3.7 illustrates some of the bitwise operators.

LISTING 3.7 bitwise.cs—The Bitwise Operators

```
 1:  // bitwise.cs - Using the bitwise operators
 2:  //--------------------------------------------------
 3:
 4:  class bitwise
 5:  {
 6:      public static void Main()
 7:      {
 8:          int ValOne = 1;
 9:          int ValZero = 0;
10:          int NewVal;
11:
12:          // Bitwise XOR Operator
13:
14:          NewVal = ValZero ^ ValZero;
15:          System.Console.WriteLine("\nThe XOR Operator: \n  0 ^ 0 = {0}",
16:                                          NewVal);
17:          NewVal = ValZero ^ ValOne;
18:          System.Console.WriteLine("  0 ^ 1 = {0}", NewVal);
19:
20:          NewVal = ValOne ^ ValZero;
21:          System.Console.WriteLine("  1 ^ 0 = {0}", NewVal);
22:
23:          NewVal = ValOne ^ ValOne;
24:          System.Console.WriteLine("  1 ^ 1 = {0}", NewVal);
25:
26:          // Bitwise AND Operator
27:
28:          NewVal = ValZero & ValZero;
29:          System.Console.WriteLine("\nThe AND Operator: \n  0 & 0 = {0}",
             ➥NewVal);
30:
31:          NewVal = ValZero & ValOne;
32:          System.Console.WriteLine("  0 & 1 = {0}", NewVal);
33:
34:          NewVal = ValOne & ValZero;
35:          System.Console.WriteLine("  1 & 0 = {0}", NewVal);
36:
37:          NewVal = ValOne & ValOne;
38:          System.Console.WriteLine("  1 & 1 = {0}", NewVal);
39:
40:          // Bitwise OR Operator
41:
42:          NewVal = ValZero | ValZero;
43:          System.Console.WriteLine("\nThe OR Operator: \n  0 | 0 = {0}",
44:                                          NewVal);
45:          NewVal = ValZero | ValOne;
46:          System.Console.WriteLine("  0 | 1 = {0}", NewVal);
47:
```

LISTING 3.7   continued

```
48:          NewVal = ValOne | ValZero;
49:          System.Console.WriteLine("  1 | 0 = {0}", NewVal);
50:
51:          NewVal = ValOne | ValOne;
52:          System.Console.WriteLine("  1 | 1 = {0}", NewVal);
53:    }
54:  }
```

OUTPUT

```
The XOR Operator:
  0 ^ 0 = 0
  0 ^ 1 = 1
  1 ^ 0 = 1
  1 ^ 1 = 0

The AND Operator:
  0 & 0 = 0
  0 & 1 = 0
  1 & 0 = 0
  1 & 1 = 1

The OR Operator:
  0 | 0 = 0
  0 | 1 = 1
  1 | 0 = 1
  1 | 1 = 1
```

ANALYSIS   Listing 3.7 summarizes the logical bitwise operators. Lines 8–9 define two variables and assign the values 1 and 0 to them. These two variables are then used repeatedly with the bitwise operators. A bitwise operation is done, and the result is written to the console. You should review the output and see that the results are exactly as described in the earlier sections.

Flipping Bits with the Logical NOT Operator

One other bitwise operator is often used. The logical NOT operator (~) is used to flip the bits of a value. Unlike the logical bitwise operator mentioned in the previous sections, the NOT operator is unary—it works with only one value. The results are as follows:

- If the bit's value is 1, the result is 0.
- If the bit's value is 0, the result is 1.

Using this on an unsigned byte that contains the value of 1 (00000001) would result in the number 254 (11111110).

Summary

Today's lesson presents a lot of information regarding operators and their use. You learned about the types of operators, including arithmetic, multiplicative, relational, logical, and conditional. You also learned the order in which operators are evaluated (operator precedence). When working with values, you learned that there are both implicit and explicit conversions. Explicit conversions are ones that you make happen. Implicit conversions occur automatically. Finally, today's lesson ended with a section on bitwise operations and the bitwise operators, for those who were brave enough.

Q&A

Q How important is it to understand operators and operator precedence?

A You will use the operators in almost every application you create. Operator precedence is critical to understand. As you saw in today's lesson, if you don't understand operator precedence, you might end up with results that are different from what you expect.

Q Today's lesson covered the binary number system briefly. Is it important to understand this number system? Also, what other number systems are important?

A Although it is not critical to understand binary, it *is* important. With computers today, information is stored in a binary format. Whether it is a positive versus negative charge, a bump versus an impression, or some other representation, all data is ultimately stored in binary. Knowing how the binary system works will make it easier for you to understand these actual storage values.

In addition to binary, many computer programmers work with octal and hexadecimal. Octal is a base-8 number system, and hexadecimal is a base-16 number system. Appendix C, "Understanding Number Systems," covers these systems in more detail.

Workshop

The Workshop provides quiz questions to help you solidify your understanding of the material covered and exercises to provide you with experience in using what you've learned. Try to understand the quiz and exercise answers before continuing to the next day's lesson. Answers are provided on the CD.

Quiz

The following quiz questions will help verify your understanding of today's lessons.

1. What character is used for multiplication?
2. What is the result of 10 % 3?
3. What is the result of 10 + 3 * 2?
4. What are the conditional operators?
5. What C# keyword can be used to change the flow of a program?
6. What is the difference between a unary operator and a binary operator?
7. What is the difference between an explicit data type conversion and an implicit conversion?
8. Is it possible to convert from a long to an integer?
9. What are the possible results of a conditional operation?
10. What do the shift operators do?

Exercises

Please note that answers will not be provided for all exercises. The exercises will help you apply what you have learned in today's lessons.

1. What is the result of the following operation?

   ```
   2 + 6 * 3 + 5 - 2 * 4
   ```

2. What is the result of the following operation?

   ```
   4 * (8 - 3 * 2) * (0 + 1) / 2
   ```

3. Write a program that checks to see whether a variable is greater than 65. If the value is greater than 65, print the statement "The value is greater than 65!".

4. Write a program that checks to see whether a character contains the value of t or T.

5. Write the line of code to convert a long called MyLong to a short called MyShort.

6. **Bug Buster:** The following program has a problem. Enter it in your editor and compile it. Which lines generate error messages? What is the error?

   ```
   1:  class exercise
   2:  {
   3:      public static void Main()
   4:      {
   5:          int  value = 1;
   6:
   7:          if ( value > 100 );
   8:          {
   ```

```
 9:              System.Console.WriteLine("Number is greater than 100");
10:         }
11:     }
12:  }
```

7. Write the line of code to convert an integer, IntVal, to a short, ShortVal.

8. Write the line of code to convert a decimal, DecVal, to a long, LongVal.

9. Write the line of code to convert an integer, ch, to a character, charVal.

DAY 4

Controlling Your Program's Flow

You've learned a lot in the previous three days. This includes knowing how to store information, knowing how to do operations, and even knowing how to avoid executing certain commands by using the `if` statement. You have even learned a little about controlling the flow of a program using the `if` statement; however, often you need to be able to control the flow of a program even more. Today you...

- See the other commands to use for program flow control.
- Explore how to do even more with the `if` command.
- Learn to switch among multiple options.
- Investigate how to repeat a block of statements multiple times.
- Discover how to abruptly stop the repeating of code.

Controlling Program Flow

By controlling the flow of a program, you can create functionality that results in something useful. As you continue to program, you will want to change the flow of your programs in a number of additional ways. You will want to repeat a piece of code, skip a piece of code altogether, or switch among different pieces of code. Regardless of how you want to change the flow of a program, C# has an option for doing it. Most of the changes of flow can be categorized into two types:

- Selection statements
- Iterative statements

Using Selection Statements

Selection statements enable you to execute specific blocks of code based on the results of a condition. The `if` statement that you learned about previously is a selection statement, as is the `switch` statement.

Revisiting `if`

You've learned about the `if` statement; however, it is worth revisiting. Consider the following example:

```
if( gender == 'm' || gender == 'f' )
{
    System.Console.WriteLine("The gender is valid");
}
if( gender != 'm' && gender != 'f' )
{
    System.Console.WriteLine("The gender value, {0} is not valid", gender);
}
```

This example uses a character variable called `gender`. The first `if` statement checks to see whether `gender` is equal to an `'m'` or an `'f'`. This uses the OR operator (`||`) that you learned about in yesterday's lesson. A second `if` statement prints an error message when the gender is not equal to `'m'` or `'f'`. This second `if` statement is an example of making sure that the variable has a valid value. If there is a value other than `'m'` and `'f'`, an error message is displayed.

If you are looking at these two statements and think that something is just not quite optimal, you are correct. Like many other languages, C# offers another keyword that can be used with the `if` statement: the `else` statement. The `else` statement is used specifically with the `if` statement. The format of the `if...else` statement is shown here:

```
if ( condition )
{
   // If condition is true, do these lines
}
else
{
   // If condition is false, do these lines
}
// code after if... statement
```

The `else` statement gives you the capability to have code that executes when the `if` statement's `condition` fails. You should also note that either the block of code after the `if` or the block of code after the `else` executes—but not both. After either of these blocks of code is done executing, the program jumps to the first line after the `if...else condition`.

Listing 4.1 presents the gender code from earlier. This time, the code has been modified to use the `if...else` command. As you can see in the listing, this version is much more efficient and easier to follow than the one presented earlier.

LISTING 4.1   ifelse.cs—Using the `if...else` Command

```
 1:  //  ifelse.cs - Using the if...else statement
 2:  //------------------------------------------------------------
 3:
 4:  class ifelse
 5:  {
 6:      public static void Main()
 7:      {
 8:          char gender = 'x';
 9:
10:          if( gender == 'm' || gender == 'f' )
11:          {
12:              System.Console.WriteLine("The gender is valid");
13:          }
14:          else
15:          {
16:              System.Console.WriteLine("The gender value, {0}, is not valid",
17:                  gender);
18:          }
19:          System.Console.WriteLine("The if statement is now over!");
20:      }
21:  }
```

OUTPUT
```
The gender value, x, is not valid
The if statement is now over!
```

This listing declares a simple variable called `gender` of type `char` in Line 8. This variable is set to a value of `'x'` when it is declared. The `if` statement starts in Line 10, which checks to see whether `gender` is either `'m'` or `'f'`. If it is, a message is printed in Line 12 saying that `gender` is valid. If `gender` is not `'m'` or `'f'`, the `if` condition fails and control is passed to the `else` statement in Line 14. In this case, `gender` is equal to `'x'`, so the `else` command is executed. A message is printed stating that the `gender` value is invalid. Control is then passed to the first line after the `if...else` statement— Line 19.

Modify Line 8 to set the value of `gender` to either `'m'` or `'f'`. Recompile and rerun the program. This time the output will be as follows:

OUTPUT
```
The gender is valid
The if statement is now over!
```

> **Caution**
>
> What would you expect to happen if you set the value of gender to a capital M or F? Remember, C# is case sensitive.

Nesting and Stacking `if` Statements

NEW TERM *Nesting* is simply the inclusion of one statement within another. Almost all C# flow commands can be nested within each other.

To nest an `if` statement, you place a second `if` statement within the first. You can nest within the `if` section or the `else` section. Using the `gender` example, you could do the following to make the statement a little more effective (the nested statement appears in bold):

```
if( gender == 'm' )
{
   // it is a male
}
else
{
   if ( gender == 'f' )
   {
      // it is a female
   }
   else
   {
      //neither a male or a female
   }
}
```

A complete if...else statement is nested within the else section of the original if statement. This code operates just as you expect. If gender is not equal to 'm', the flow goes to the first else statement. Within this else statement is another if statement that starts from its beginning. This second if statement checks to see whether the gender is equal to 'f'. If not, the flow goes to the else statement of the nested if . At that point, you know that gender is neither 'm' nor 'f', and you can add appropriate coding logic.

Although nesting makes some functionality easier, you can also stack if statements. In the example of checking gender, stacking is actually a much better solution.

Stacking if Statements

Stacking if statements combines the else with another if. The easiest way to understand stacking is to see the gender example one more time, stacked (see Listing 4.2).

LISTING 4.2   Stacked.cs—Stacking an if Statement

```
 1:  //  Stacked.cs - Using the if...else statement
 2:  //-------------------------------------------------------------------
 3:
 4:  class Stacked
 5:  {
 6:      static void Main()
 7:      {
 8:          char gender = 'x';
 9:
10:          if( gender == 'm' )
11:          {
12:              System.Console.WriteLine("The gender is male");
13:          }
14:          else if ( gender == 'f' )
15:          {
16:              System.Console.WriteLine("The gender is female");
17:          }
18:          else
19:          {
20:              System.Console.WriteLine("The gender value, {0}, is not valid",
21:                                       gender);
22:          }
23:          System.Console.WriteLine("The if statement is now over!");
24:      }
25:  }
```

OUTPUT
```
The gender value, x, is not valid
The if statement is now over!
```

ANALYSIS The code presented in this example is very close to the code presented in the previous example. The primary difference is in Line 14. The `else` statement is
immediately followed by an `if`. There are no braces or a block. The format for stacking
is as follows:

```
if ( condition 1 )
{
   // do something about condition 1
}
else if ( condition 2 )
{
   // do something about condition 2
}
else if ( condition 3 )
{
   // do something about condition 3
}
else if ( condition x )
{
    // do something about condition x
else
{
   // All previous conditions failed
}
```

This is relatively easy to follow. With the `gender` example, you had only two conditions.
There are times when you might have more than two. For example, you could create a
computer program that checks the roll of a die. You could then do something different
depending on what the roll is. Each stacked condition could check for a different number
(from 1 to 6), with the final `else` statement presenting an error because there can be only
six numbers. The code for this would be as follows:

```
if ( roll == 1 )
   // roll is 1
else if (roll == 2)
        // roll is 2
else if (roll == 3)
        // roll is 3
else if (roll == 4)
        // roll is 4
else if (roll == 5)
        // roll is 5
else if (roll == 6)
        // roll is 6
else
   // it isn't a number from 1 to 6
```

This code is relatively easy to follow because it's easy to see that each of the six possible numbers is checked against the roll. If the roll is not one of the six, the final `else` statement can take care of any error logic or reset logic.

Note

> As you can see in the die code, no braces are used around the `if` statements. If you are using only a single statement within the `if` or the `else`, you don't need the braces. You include them only when you have more than one statement.

Discovering the `switch` Statement

C# provides a much easier way to modify program flow based on multiple values stored in a variable: the `switch` statement. The format of the `switch` statement is as follows:

```
switch ( value )
{
    case result_1 :
            // do stuff for result_1
            break;
    case result_2 :
            // do stuff for result_2
            break;
    ...
    case result_n :
            // do stuff for result_x
            break;
    default:
            // do stuff for default case
            break;
}
```

You can see by the format of the `switch` statement that there is no `condition`. Instead, a `value` is used. This value can be the result of an expression, or it can be a variable. This value is then compared to each of the values in each of the `case` statements until a match is found. If a match is not found, the flow goes to the `default` case. If there is not a `default` case, flow goes to the first statement following the `switch` statement.

When a match is found, the code within the matching `case` statement is executed. When the flow reaches another `case` statement, the `switch` statement ends. Only one `case` statement is executed at most. Flow then continues, with the first command following the `switch` statement. Listing 4.3 shows the `switch` statement in action, using the earlier example of a roll of a six-sided die.

4

LISTING 4.3   roll.cs—Using the switch Statement with the Roll of a Die

```
 1:  //  roll.cs- Using the switch statement.
 2:  //--------------------------------------------------------------
 3:
 4:  class roll
 5:  {
 6:     public static void Main()
 7:     {
 8:        int roll = 0;
 9:
10:        // The next two lines set the roll to a random number from 1 to 6
11:        System.Random rnd = new System.Random();
12:        roll = (int) rnd.Next(1,7);
13:
14:        System.Console.WriteLine("Starting the switch... ");
15:
16:        switch (roll)
17:        {
18:           case 1:
19:                   System.Console.WriteLine("Roll is 1");
20:                   break;
21:           case 2:
22:                   System.Console.WriteLine("Roll is 2");
23:                   break;
24:           case 3:
25:                   System.Console.WriteLine("Roll is 3");
26:                   break;
27:           case 4:
28:                   System.Console.WriteLine("Roll is 4");
29:                   break;
30:           case 5:
31:                   System.Console.WriteLine("Roll is 5");
32:                   break;
33:           case 6:
34:                   System.Console.WriteLine("Roll is 6");
35:                   break;
36:           default:
37:                   System.Console.WriteLine("Roll is not 1 through 6");
38:                   break;
39:        }
40:        System.Console.WriteLine("The switch statement is now over!");
41:     }
42:  }
```

OUTPUT

```
Starting the switch...
Roll is 1
The switch statement is now over!
```

Note
> Your answer for the roll in the output might be a number other than 1.

ANALYSIS This listing is a little longer than a lot of the previous listings; however, it is also more functional. The first thing to focus on is Lines 16–39. These lines contain the `switch` statement that is the center of this discussion. The `switch` statement uses the value stored in the roll. Depending on the value, one of the cases is selected. If the number is something other than 1–6, the `default` statement starting in Line 39 is executed. If any of the numbers is rolled (1–6), the appropriate `case` statement is executed.

You should note that at the end of each section of code for each `case` statement, there is a `break` command, which is required at the end of each set of code. This signals the end of the statements within a `case`. If you don't include the `break` command, you get a compiler error.

To make this listing more interesting, Lines 11–12 were added. Line 11 might look unfamiliar; it creates a variable called `rnd`, which is an object that holds a random number. In tomorrow's lesson, you revisit this line of code and learn the details of what it is doing. For now, simply know that it is setting up a variable for a random number.

Line 12 is also a line that will become more familiar over the next few days. The command `(int) rnd.Next(1,7)` provides a random number from 1 to 6.

Tip
> You can use Lines 11–12 to generate random numbers for any range by simply changing the values from 1 and 7 to the range you want numbers between. The first number is the lowest number that will be returned. The second number is one higher than the highest number that will be returned. For example, if you wanted a random number from 90 to 100, you could change Line 12 to this:
>
> ```
> Roll = (int) rnd.Next(90, 101);
> ```

Executing a Single Solution for Multiple Cases

Sometimes you want to execute the same piece of code for multiple values. For example, if you want to switch based on the roll of a six-sided die, but you want to do something based only on odd or even numbers, you could group multiple `case` statements. The `switch` statement is this:

```
switch (roll)
{
     case 1:
     case 3:
     case 5:
               System.Console.WriteLine("Roll is odd");
               break;
     case 2:
     case 4:
     case 6:
               System.Console.WriteLine("Roll is even");
               break;
     default:
               System.Console.WriteLine("Roll is not 1 through 6");
               break;
}
```

The same code is executed if the roll is 1, 3, or 5. Additionally, the same code is executed if the roll is 2, 4, or 6.

 Caution

> In other languages, such as C++, you can have code execute from multiple case statements by leaving out the break command. This causes the code to drop through to the next case statement. In C#, this is not valid. Code cannot drop through from one case to another. This means that if you are going to group case statements, you cannot place any code between them. You can place one only after the last case statement in each group.

Executing More Than One case Statement

You might want to execute more than one case statement within a switch statement. To do this in C#, you can use the goto command. The goto command can be used within the switch statement to go to either a case statement or the default command. The following code snippet shows the switch statement from the previous section executed with goto statements instead of simply dropping through:

```
switch (roll)
{
     case 1:
               goto case 5;
               break;
     case 2:
               goto case 6;
               break;
     case 3:
               goto case 5;
               break;
```

```
    case 4:
            goto case 6;
            break;
    case 5:
            System.Console.WriteLine("Roll is odd");
            break;
    case 6:
            System.Console.WriteLine("Roll is even");
            break;
    default:
            System.Console.WriteLine("Roll is not 1 through 6");
            break;
}
```

Although this example illustrates using the goto, it is much easier to use the previous
example of grouping multiple case statements. You will find times, however, when the
goto provides the solution you need.

Understanding the Governing Types for switch Statements

A switch statement has only certain types that can be used. The data type—or the "governing type" for a switch statement—is the type that the switch statement's expression
resolves to. If this governing type is sbyte, byte, short, ushort, int, uint, long, ulong, char,
or a text string, this type is the governing type. Another type, called an enum, is also valid
as a governing type. You will learn about enum types on Day 7, "Storing More Complex
Stuff: Structures, Enumerators, and Arrays."

If the data type of the expression is something other than these types, the type must have
a single implicit conversion that converts it to a type of sbyte, byte, short, ushort, int,
uint, long, ulong, or a string. If no conversion is available, or if there is more than one,
you get an error when you compile your program.

4

Note	If you don't remember what implicit conversions are, review Day 3, "Manipulating Values in Your Programs."

Do	**Don't**
Do use a switch statement when you are checking for multiple different values in the same variable.	**Don't** accidentally put a semicolon after the condition of a switch or if statement: if (condition);

Using Iteration Statements

In addition to changing the flow through selection statements, you might want to repeat a piece of code multiple times. When you want to repeat code, C# provides a number of iteration statements. Iteration statements can execute a block of code zero or more times. Each execution of the code is a single iteration.

The iteration statements in C# are listed here:

- while
- do
- for
- foreach

Executing Code with the `while` Statement

The `while` command is used to repeat a block of code as long as a condition is true. The format of the `while` statement is as follows

```
while ( condition )
{
    Statement(s)
}
```

This format is also presented in Figure 4.1.

FIGURE 4.1

The `while` command.

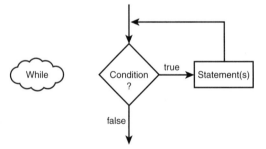

As you can see from the figure, a `while` statement uses a conditional statement. If this conditional statement evaluates to `true`, the statement(s) are executed. If the condition evaluates to `false`, the statements are not executed and program flow goes to the next command following the `while` statement. Listing 4.4 presents a `while` statement that enables you to print the average of 10 random numbers from 1 to 10.

LISTING 4.4   average.cs—Using the while Command

```
 1:  //  average.cs Using the while statement.
 2:  //  print the average of 10 random numbers that are from 1 to 10.
 3:  //-------------------------------------------------------------
 4:
 5:  class average
 6:  {
 7:     public static void Main()
 8:     {
 9:        int ttl = 0;  // variable to store the running total
10:        int nbr = 0;  // variable for individual numbers
11:        int ctr = 0;  // counter
12:
13:        System.Random rnd = new System.Random();  // random number
14:
15:        while ( ctr < 10 )
16:        {
17:           //Get random number
18:           nbr = (int) rnd.Next(1,11);
19:
20:           System.Console.WriteLine("Number {0} is {1}", (ctr + 1), nbr);
21:
22:           ttl += nbr;        //add nbr to total
23:           ctr++;             //increment counter
24:        }
25:
26:        System.Console.WriteLine("\nThe total of the {0} numbers is {1}",
27:                                 ctr, ttl);
28:        System.Console.WriteLine("\nThe average of the numbers is {0}",
29:                                 ttl/ctr );
30:     }
31:  }
```

4

Note

The numbers in your output will differ from those shown here. Because random numbers are assigned, each time you run the program, the numbers will be different.

OUTPUT

```
Number 1 is 2
Number 2 is 5
Number 3 is 4
Number 4 is 1
Number 5 is 1
Number 6 is 5
Number 7 is 2
Number 8 is 5
```

```
Number 9 is 10
Number 10 is 2

The total of the 10 numbers is 37

The average of the numbers is 3
```

 This listing uses the code for random numbers that you saw earlier in today's lesson. Instead of a random number from 1 to 6, this code picks numbers from 1 to 10. You see this in Line 18, where the value of 10 is multiplied against the next random number. Line 13 initialized the random variable before it was used in this manner.

The while statement starts in Line 15. The condition for this while statement is a simple check to see whether a counter is less than 10. Because the counter was initialized to 0 in Line 11, this condition evaluates to true, so the statements within the while are executed. This while statement simply gets a random number from 1 to 10 in Line 18 and adds it to the total counter, ttl in Line 22. Line 23 then increments the counter variable, ctr. After this increment, the end of the while is reached in Line 24. The flow of the program is automatically put back to the while condition in Line 15. This condition is re-evaluated to see whether it is still true. If it is true, the statements are executed again. This continues to happen until the while condition fails. For this program, the failure occurs when ctr becomes 10. At that point, the flow goes to Line 25, which immediately follows the while statement.

The code after the while statement prints the total and the average of the 10 random numbers that were found. The program then ends.

Caution

For a while statement to eventually end, you must make sure that you change something in the statement(s) that will impact the condition. If your condition can never be false, your while statement could end up in an infinite loop. There is one alternative to creating a false condition: the break statement. This is covered in the next section.

Breaking Out of or Continuing a while Statement

It is possible to end a while statement before the condition is set to false. It is also possible to end an iteration of a while statement before getting to the end of the statements.

To break out of a while and thus end it early, you use the break command. A break immediately takes control of the first command after the while.

You can also cause a while statement to jump immediately to the next iteration. This is done by using the continue statement. The continue statement causes the program's flow to go to the condition statement of the while. Listing 4.5 illustrates both the continue and the break statements within a while.

LISTING 4.5   even.cs—Using break and continue

```
 1:  //  even.cs- Using the while with the break and continue commands.
 2:  //------------------------------------------------------------
 3:
 4:  class even
 5:  {
 6:     public static void Main()
 7:     {
 8:        int ctr = 0;
 9:
10:        while (true)
11:        {
12:           ctr++;
13:
14:           if (ctr > 10 )
15:           {
16:              break;
17:           }
18:           else if ( (ctr % 2) == 1 )
19:           {
20:              continue;
21:           }
22:           else
23:           {
24:              System.Console.WriteLine("...{0}...", ctr);
25:           }
26:        }
27:        System.Console.WriteLine("Done!");
28:     }
29:  }
```

OUTPUT

```
...2...
...4...
...6...
...8...
...10...
Done!
```

ANALYSIS   This listing prints even numbers and skips odd numbers. When the value of the counter is greater than 10, the while statement ends with a break statement.

This listing declares and sets a counter variable, ctr, to 0 in Line 8. A while statement is then started in Line 10. Because a break is used to end the loop, the condition in Line 10 is simply set to true. This, in effect, creates an infinite loop. Because this is an infinite loop, a break statement is needed to end the while statement's iterations. The first thing done in the while statement is that ctr is incremented in Line 12. Line 14 then checks to see whether ctr is greater than 10. If ctr is greater than 10, Line 16 executes a break statement, which ends the while and sends the program flow to Line 27.

If ctr is less than 10, the else statement in Line 18 is executed. This else statement is stacked with an if statement that checks to see whether the current number is odd. This is done using the modulus operator. If the counter is even, by using the modulus operator with 2, you get a result of 0. If it is odd, you get a result of 1. When an odd number is found, the continue statement is called in Line 20. This sends control back to the top of the while statement, where the condition is checked again. Because the condition is always true (literally), the while statement's statements are executed again. This starts with the increment of the counter in Line 12 again, followed by the checks.

If the number is not odd, the else statement in Line 22 will execute. This final else statement contains a single call to WriteLine, which prints the counter's value.

Working with the do Statement

If a while statement's condition is false on the initial check, the while statement will never execute. Sometimes, however, you want statements to execute at least once. For these times, the do statement might be a better solution.

The format of the do statement is shown here:

```
Do
{
    Statement(s)
} while ( condition );
```

This format is also presented in Figure 4.2.

As you can see from the figure, a do statement first executes its statements. Then a while statement is presented with a condition. This while statement and condition operate the same as the while that you explored earlier in Listing 4.4. If the condition evaluates to true, program flow returns to the statements. If the condition evaluates to false, the flow goes to the next line after the do...while. Listing 4.6 presents a do command in action.

Note

Because of the use of the while with the do statement, a do statement is often referred to as a do...while statement.

FIGURE 4.2

The do *command.*

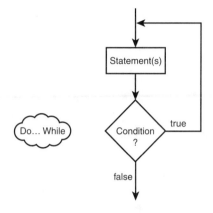

LISTING 4.6   do_it.cs—The do Command in Action

```
 1:  //  do_it.cs Using the do statement.
 2:  //  Get random numbers (from 1 to 10) until a 5 is reached.
 3:  //------------------------------------------------------------
 4:
 5:  class do_it
 6:  {
 7:     public static void Main()
 8:     {
 9:        int ttl = 0;  // variable to store the running total
10:        int nbr = 0;  // variable for individual numbers
11:        int ctr = 0;  // counter
12.
13:        System.Random rnd = new System.Random();  // random number
14:
15:        do
16:        {
17:           //Get random number
18:           nbr = (int) rnd.Next(1, 11);
19:
20:           ctr++;                //number of numbers counted
21:           ttl += nbr;           //add nbr to total of numbers
22:
23:           System.Console.WriteLine("Number {0} is {1}", ctr, nbr);
24:
25:        } while ( nbr != 5 );
26:
27:        System.Console.WriteLine("\n{0} numbers were read", ctr);
28:        System.Console.WriteLine("The total of the numbers is {0}", ttl);
29:        System.Console.WriteLine("The average of the numbers is {0}",
30:                                 ttl/ctr );
31:     }
32:  }
```

```
Number 1 is 1
Number 2 is 6
Number 3 is 5

3 numbers were read
The total of the numbers is 12
The average of the numbers is 4
```

ANALYSIS As with the previous listings that used random numbers, your output will most likely be different from what is displayed. You will have a list of numbers, ending with 5.

For this program, you want to do something at least once—get a random number. You want to then keep doing this until you have a condition met—you get a 5. This is a great scenario for the do statement. This listing is very similar to an earlier listing. In Lines 9–11, you set up a number of variables to keep track of totals and counts. In Line 13, you again set up a variable to get random numbers.

Line 15 is the start of your do statement. The body of the do (Lines 16–24) is executed. First, the next random number is obtained. Again, this is a number from 1 to 10 that is assigned to the variable nbr. Line 20 keeps track of how many numbers have been obtained by adding 1 to ctr each time a number is read. Line 21 then adds the value of the number read to the total. Remember, the code

```
ttl += nbr
```

is the same as this code:

```
ttl = ttl + nbr
```

Line 23 prints the obtained number to the screen with the count of which number it is.

Line 25 is the conditional portion of the do statement. In this case, the condition is that nbr is not equal to 5. As long as the number obtained, nbr, is not equal to 5, the body of the do statement continues to execute. When a 5 is received, the loop ends. In the output of your program, you will find that there is always only one 5, and it is always the last number.

Lines 27–29 print statistical information regarding the numbers you found.

Counting and More with the `for` Statement

Although the do...while and while statements give you all the functionality you really need to control iterations of code, they are not the only commands available. Before looking at the for statement, check out the code in the following snippet:

```
ctr = 1;
while ( ctr < 10 )
{
   //do some stuff
   ctr++;
}
```

In this snippet of code, you can see that a counter is used to loop through a `while` statement. The flow of this code is this:

1. Set a counter to the value of `1`.

   Check to see whether the counter is less than `10`.

   If the counter is not less than `10` (the condition fails), go to the end.

3. Do some stuff.

4. Add `1` to the counter.

5. Go to Step 2.

These steps are a very common use of iteration. Because this is a common use, you are provided with the `for` statement, which consolidates the steps into a much simpler format:

```
for ( initializer; condition; incrementor )
{
   Statement(s);
}
```

You should review the format presented here for the `for` statement, which contains three parts within parentheses: the `initializer`, the `condition`, and the `incrementor`. Each of these three parts is separated by a semicolon. If one of these expressions is to be left out, you still need to include the semicolon separators.

The `initializer` is executed when the `for` statement begins. It is executed only once at the beginning and then never again.

After executing the `initializer`, the `condition` statement is evaluated. Just like the condition in the `while` statement, this must evaluate to either `true` or `false`. If this evaluates to `true`, the statement(s) is executed.

After the statement or statement block executes, program flow is returned to the `for` statement where the `incrementor` is evaluated. This `incrementor` can actually be any valid C# expression; however, it is generally used to increment a counter.

After the `incrementor` is executed, the `condition` is again evaluated. As long as the `condition` remains true, the statements will be executed, followed by the `incrementor`. This continues until the `condition` evaluates to `false`. Figure 4.3 illustrates the flow of the `for` statement.

FIGURE 4.3

The for *statement.*

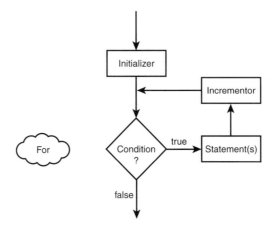

Before jumping into a listing, consider the while statement that was presented at the beginning of this section:

```
for ( ctr = 1; ctr < 10; ctr++ )
{
    //do some stuff
}
```

This for statement is much simpler than the code used earlier with the while statement. The steps that this for statement executes are as follows:

1. Set a counter to the value of 1.

2. Check to see whether the counter is less than 10.

    If the counter is not less than 10 (condition fails), go to the end of the for statement.

3. Do some stuff.

4. Add 1 to the counter.

5. Go to Step 2.

These are the same steps that were followed with the while statement snippet earlier. The difference is that the for statement is much more concise and easier to follow. Listing 4.7 presents a more robust use of the for statement. In fact, this is the same program that you saw in sample code earlier, only now it is much more concise.

LISTING 4.7   foravg.cs—Using the `for` Statement

```
 1: //  foravg.cs Using the for statement.
 2: //  print the average of 10 random numbers that are from 1 to 10.
 3: //-----------------------------------------------------------
 4:
 5: class average
 6: {
 7:    public static void Main()
 8:    {
 9:       int ttl = 0;  // variable to store the running total
10:       int nbr = 0;  // variable for individual numbers
11:       int ctr = 0;  // counter
12:
13:       System.Random rnd = new System.Random();  // random number
14:
15:       for ( ctr = 1; ctr <= 10; ctr++ )
16:       {
17:          //Get random number
18:          nbr = (int) rnd.Next(1, 11);
19:
20:          System.Console.WriteLine("Number {0} is {1}", (ctr), nbr);
21:
22:          ttl += nbr;         //add nbr to total
23:       }
24:
25:       System.Console.WriteLine("\nThe total of the 10 numbers is {0}",
26:                                ttl);
27:       System.Console.WriteLine("\nThe average of the numbers is {0}",
28:                                ttl/10 );
29:    }
30: }
```

OUTPUT

```
Number 1 is 10
Number 2 is 3
Number 3 is 6
Number 4 is 5
Number 5 is 7
Number 6 is 8
Number 7 is 7
Number 8 is 1
Number 9 is 4
Number 10 is 3

The total of the 10 numbers is 54

The average of the numbers is 5
```

ANALYSIS Much of this listing is identical to what you saw earlier in today's lessons. You should note the difference, however. In Line 15, you see the use of the `for` statement. The counter is initialized to 1, which makes it easier to display the value in the `WriteLine` routine in Line 20. The condition statement in the `for` statement is adjusted appropriately as well.

What happens when the program flow reaches the `for` statement? Simply put, the counter is set to 1. It is then verified against the condition. In this case, the counter is less than or equal to 10, so the body of the `for` statement is executed. When the body in Lines 16–23 is done executing, control goes back to the incrementor of the `for` statement in Line 15. In this `for` statement's incrementor, the counter is incremented by 1. The condition is then checked again and, if true, the body of the `for` statement executes again. This continues until the condition fails. For this program, this happens when the counter is set to 11.

Understanding the `for` Statement Expressions

You can do a lot with the initializer, condition, and incrementor. You can actually put any expressions within these areas. You can even put in more than one expression.

If you use more than one expression within one of the segments of the `for` statement, you need to separate them. The separator control is used to do this. The separator control is the comma. As an example, the following `for` statement initializes two variables and increments both:

```
for ( x = 1, y = 1; x + y < 100; x++, y++ )
   // Do something...
```

In addition to being able to do multiple expressions, you also are not restricted to using each of the parts of a `for` statement as described. The following example actually does all of the work in the `for` statement's control structure. The body of the `for` statement is an empty statement—a semicolon:

```
for ( x = 0; ++x <= 10; System.Console.WriteLine("{0}", x) )
   ;
```

This simple line of code actually does quite a lot. If you enter this into a program, it prints the numbers 1 to 10. You're asked to turn this into a complete listing in one of today's exercises at the end of the lesson.

Caution You should be careful about how much you do within the `for` statement's control structures. You want to make sure that you don't make your code too complicated to follow.

The `foreach` Statement

The `foreach` statement iterates in a way similar to the `for` statement. However, the `foreach` statement has a special purpose: It can loop through collections such as arrays. The `foreach` statement, collections, and arrays are covered on Day 7.

Revisiting `break` and `continue`

The `break` and `continue` commands were presented earlier with the `while` statement. Additionally, you saw the use of the `break` command with the `switch` statement. These two commands can also be used with the other program-flow statements.

In the `do...while` statement, `break` and `continue` operate exactly like the `while` statement. The `continue` command loops to the conditional statement. The `break` command sends the program flow to the statement following the `do...while`.

With the `for` statement, the `continue` statement sends control to the `incrementor` statement. The condition is then checked and, if true, the `for` statement continues to loop. The `break` statement sends the program flow to the statement following the `for` statement.

The `break` command exits the current routine. The `continue` command starts the next iteration.

Reviewing `goto`

The `goto` statement is fraught with controversy, regardless of the programming language you use. Because the `goto` statement can unconditionally change program flow, it is very powerful. With power comes responsibility. Many developers avoid the `goto` statement because it is easy to create code that is hard to follow.

The `goto` statement can be used in three ways. As you saw earlier, the `switch` statement is home to two of the uses of `goto`: `goto case` and `goto default`. You saw these in action earlier in the discussion on the `switch` statement.

The third `goto` statement takes the following format:

```
goto label;
```

With this form of the `goto` statement, you are sending the control of the program to a label statement.

Exploring Labeled Statements

A label statement is simply a command that marks a location. The format of a label is as follows:

label_name:

Notice that this is followed by a colon, not a semicolon. Listing 4.8 presents the goto statement being used with labels.

LISTING 4.8   score.cs—Using the goto Statement with a Label

```
 1:  //   score.cs    Using the goto and label statements.
 2:  //  Disclaimer: This program shows the use of goto and label
 3:  //              This is not a good use; however, it illustrates
 4:  //              the functionality of these keywords.
 5:  //-------------------------------------------------------------
 6:
 7:  class score
 8:  {
 9:     public static void Main()
10:     {
11:        int score = 0;
12:        int ctr = 0;
13:
14:        System.Random rnd = new System.Random();
15:
16:        Start:
17:
18:        ctr++;
19:
20:        if (ctr > 10)
21:           goto EndThis;
22:        else
23:           score = (int) rnd.Next(60, 101);
24:
25:        System.Console.WriteLine("{0} - You received a score of {1}",
26:                    ctr, score);
27:
28:        goto Start;
29:
30:     EndThis:
31:
32:        System.Console.WriteLine("Done with scores!");
33:     }
34:  }
```

OUTPUT
```
1 - You received a score of 83
2 - You received a score of 99
3 - You received a score of 72
4 - You received a score of 67
5 - You received a score of 80
6 - You received a score of 98
7 - You received a score of 64
8 - You received a score of 91
9 - You received a score of 79
10 - You received a score of 76
Done with scores!
```

ANALYSIS   The purpose of this listing is relatively simple; it prints 10 scores that are obtained by getting 10 random numbers from 60 to 100. This use of random numbers is similar to what you've seen before, except for one small change. In Line 23, instead of starting at 1 for the number to be obtained, you start at 60. Additionally, because the numbers that you want are from 60 to 100, the upper limit is set to 101. By using 101 as the second number, you get a number less than 101.

The focus of this listing is Lines 16, 21, 28, and 30. In Line 16, you see a label called Start. Because this is a label, the program flow skips past this line and goes to Line 18, where a counter is incremented. In Line 20, the condition within an if statement is checked. If the counter is greater than 10, a goto statement in Line 21 is executed, which sends program flow to the EndThis label in Line 30. Because the counter is not greater than 10, program flow goes to the else statement in Line 22. The else statement gets the random score in Line 23 that was already covered. Line 25 prints the score obtained. Program flow then hits Line 28, which sends the flow unconditionally to the Start label. Because the Start label is in Line 16, program flow goes back to Line 16.

This listing does a similar iteration to what can be done with the while, do, or for statements. In many cases, you will find that there are programming alternatives to using goto. If there is a different option, use it first.

Tip   Avoid using goto whenever possible. It can lead to what is referred to as *spaghetti code,* which is code that winds all over the place and is, therefore, hard to follow from one end to the next.

Nesting Flow

All of the program-flow commands from today can be nested. When nesting program-flow commands, make sure that the commands are ended appropriately. You can create a logic error and sometimes a syntax error if you don't nest properly.

Do	Don't
Do comment your code to make clearer what the program and program flow are doing.	Don't use a goto statement unless it is absolutely necessary.

Summary

You learned a lot in today's lesson, and you'll use this knowledge in virtually every C# application you create.

In today's lesson, you once again covered some of the constructs that are part of the basic C# language. You first expanded on your knowledge of the if statement by learning about the else statement. You then learned about another selection statement, the switch statement. Selection statements were followed by a discussion of iterative program flow-control statements. This included use of the while, do, and for statements. You learned that there is another command, foreach, that you will learn about on Day 7. In addition to learning how to use these commands, you discovered that they can be nested within each other. Finally, you learned about the goto statement and how it can be used with case, default, or labels.

Q&A

Q Are there other types of control statements?

A Yes—throw, try, catch, and finally. You will learn about these in future lessons.

Q Can you use a text string with a switch statement?

A Yes. A string is a "governing type" for switch statements. This means that you can use a variable that holds a string in the switch and then use string values in the case statements. Remember, a string is simply text in quotation marks. In one of the exercises, you create a switch statement that works with strings.

Q Why is goto considered so bad?

A The goto statement has gotten a bad rap. If used cautiously and in a structured, organized manner, the goto statement can help solve a number of programming problems. goto case and goto default are prime examples of good uses of goto. goto has a bad rap because the goto statement is often not used cleanly; programmers use it to get from one piece of code to another quickly and in an unstructured manner. In an object-oriented programming language, the more structure you can keep in your programs, the better—and more maintainable—they will be.

Workshop

The Workshop provides quiz questions to help you solidify your understanding of the material covered and exercises to provide you with experience in using what you've learned. Try to understand the quiz and exercise answers before continuing to the next day's lesson. Answers are provided on the CD.

Quiz

1. What commands are provided by C# for repeating lines of code multiple times?

2. What is the fewest number of times that the statements in a `while` will execute?

3. What is the fewest number of times that the statements in a `do` will execute?

4. Consider the following `for` statement:

   ```
   for ( x = 1; x == 1; x++ )
   ```

   What is the conditional statement?

5. In the `for` statement in Question 4, what is the incrementor statement?

6. What statement is used to end a `case` expression in a `select` statement?

7. What punctuation character is used with a label?

8. What punctuation is used to separate multiple expressions in a `for` statement?

9. What is nesting?

10. What command is used to jump to the next iteration of a loop?

Exercises

1. Write an `if` statement that checks to see whether a variable called `file-type` is `s`, `m`, or `j`. Print the following message based on the `file-type`:

   ```
   s    The filer is single

   m    The filer is married filing at the single rate

   j    The filer is married filing at the joint rate
   ```

2. Is the following `if` statement valid? If so, what is the value of `x` after this code executes?

   ```
   int x = 2;
   int y = 3;
   if (x==2) if (y>3) x=5; else x=9;
   ```

3. Write a `while` loop that counts from `99` to `1`.

4. Rewrite the `while` loop in Exercise 3 as a `for` loop.

5. **Bug Buster:** Is the following listing correct? If so, what does it do? If not, what is wrong with the listing (Ex04-05.cs)?

```
//  Ex0405.cs. Exercise 5 for Day 4
//-----------------------------------------------------------------

class score
{
    public static void Main()
    {
        int score = 99;

        if ( score == 100 );
        {
            System.Console.WriteLine("You got a perfect score!");
        }
        else
            System.Console.WriteLine("Bummer, you were not perfect!");
    }
}
```

6. Create a `for` loop that prints the numbers 1 to 10 all within the initializer, condition, and incrementor sections of the `for`. The body of the `for` should be an empty statement.

7. Write the code for a `switch` statement that switches on the variable `name`. If the name is `Robert`, print a message that says `Hi Bob`. If the name is `Richard`, print a message that says `Hi Rich`. If the name is `Barbara`, print a message that says `Hi Barb`. If the name is `Kalee`, print a message that says `You Go Girl!`. On any other name, print a message that says `Hi x`, where *x* is the person's name.

8. Write a program to roll a six-sided die 100 times. Print the number of times each of the sides of the die was rolled.

TYPE & RUN 2

Guess the Number!

This is the second Type & Run. Remember, you'll find a number of Type & Run sections throughout this book. These sections present a listing that is a little longer than the listings within the daily lessons. The purpose of these listings is to give you a program to type in and run. The listings might contain elements not yet explained in the book.

Two listings are provided in this Type & Run. The first does something a little more fun and a little less practical. The second does the same thing; however, it is done within a windows form.

Today's program is a number-guessing game. It enables you to enter a number from 0 to 10,000. You then are told whether the number is higher or lower. You should try to guess the number in as few tries as possible.

I suggest that you type in and run these programs. You can also copy them from the book's CD or download them. Regardless of how you start, take the time to experiment and play with the code. Make changes, recompile, and then rerun the programs. See what happens.

As with all of the Type & Runs, there isn't an explanation on how the code works. Don't fret, though. By the time you complete this book, you should understand everything within these listings. In the meantime, you will have had the chance to enter and run some listings that are a little more fun or practical.

The Guess Type & Run

Enter and compile the following program. If you get any errors, make sure you entered the program correctly.

LISTING T&R 2.1 Guess.cs

```
 1: // Guess.cs - Pick a Number
 2: //---------------------------------------------------------
 3:
 4: using System;
 5: using System.Drawing;
 6: using System.Text;
 7:
 8: public class Guess
 9: {
10:
11:
12:    private static int getRandomNumber( int nbr )
13:    {
14:      if ( nbr > 0 )
15:      {
16:         Random Rnd = new Random();
17:         return (Rnd.Next(0, nbr));
18:      }
19:      else
20:      {
21:         return 0;
22:      }
23:    }
24:
25:    private static void WriteStats(string Guess, int nbr, string err )
26:    {
27:      Console.WriteLine("\n===============================");
28:      Console.WriteLine("Current Guess: {0}", Guess);
29:      Console.WriteLine("Number of Guesses: {0}", nbr);
30:      if (err != "")
31:          Console.WriteLine( err );
32:      Console.WriteLine("Enter a number from 1 to 10000");
33:      Console.WriteLine("===============================");
34:
35:      return;
```

```
36:    }
37:
38:
39:    public static void Main( string[] args )
40:    {
41:      int    WinningNumber = Guess.getRandomNumber( 10000 );
42:      int    Guesses = 0;
43:      string Curr = "";
44:      int    val = 0;
45:      string errMsg;
46:
47:      bool cont = true;
48:
49:      WriteStats(Curr, Guesses, (string) "");
50:
51:
52:      while( cont == true)
53:      {
54:
55:        Console.Write("\nEnter Guess: ");
56:        Curr = Console.ReadLine();
57:
58:        try  // try, catch, and finally are covered on Day 9
59:        {
60:          val = Convert.ToInt32(Curr);
61:
62:          // If a number was not entered, an exception will be
63:          // throw. Program flow will go to catch statement below
64:
65:          Guesses += 1;      // Add one to Guesses
66:
67:          if( val < 0 || val > 10000 )
68:          {
69:            // bad value entered
70:            errMsg = "Number is out of range...Try again.";
71:            WriteStats(Curr, Guesses, errMsg);
72:          }
73:          else
74:          {
75:            if ( val < WinningNumber )
76:            {
77:              errMsg = "You guessed low...  Try again.";
78:              WriteStats(Curr, Guesses, errMsg);
79:            }
80:            else
81:            if ( val > WinningNumber )
82:            {
83:              errMsg = "You guessed high... Try again.";
84:              WriteStats(Curr, Guesses, errMsg);
85:            }
```

LISTING T&R 2.1   continued

```
 86:            else
 87:            {
 88:                Console.WriteLine("\n\nCurrent Guess: {0}\n", val);
 89:                Console.WriteLine("Number of Guesses: {0}\n", Guesses);
 90:                Console.WriteLine("You guessed correctly!!");
 91:                cont = false;
 92:            }
 93:          }
 94:        }
 95:        // Catch format errors....
 96:        catch( FormatException )
 97:        {
 98:          errMsg = "Please enter a valid number...";
 99:          WriteStats(Curr, Guesses, errMsg);
100:        }
101:      }
102:    }
103: }
```

Enter the previous listing and compile it. If you need to, refer to Day 1, "Getting Started with C#," for the steps to enter, compile, and run a listing. When this program executes, it displays the following to the screen:

```
===============================
Current Guess:
Number of Guesses: 0
Enter a number from 1 to 10000
===============================

Enter Guess:
```

You can enter a number between 0 and 10,000. You'll then be told that the number is either too high or too low. When you guess the number correctly, you're told so.

The WinGuess Type & Run

You may have been surprised to realize that you already have seen nearly everything presented in the Guess.cs listing. This Type & Run includes a second listing that contains a number of things that you have not seen. This is a program similar to the previous Guess program; the big difference is that this new listing uses a windows form.

You should note that support for windows forms comes from the .NET Framework classes rather than from the C# language. If you are using Microsoft's .NET Framework and compiler, this listing will be fully supported. If you are using a different compiler and .NET runtime, classes in this listing may not be supported. For example, at the time this book was written, the go-mono project had not completed development of the .NET forms classes. This means that if you are using the mono compiler and runtime, you may not be able to compile and run this listing—yet.

LISTING T&R 2.2   WinGuess.cs

```
 1: // WinGuess.cs - Pick a Number
 2: //--------------------------------------------------------
 3:
 4: using System;
 5: using System.Windows.Forms;
 6: using System.Drawing;
 7: using System.Text;
 8:
 9: public class WinGuess : Form
10: {
11:    private Label    lblTag1;
12:    private Button   btnGuess;
13:    private Label    lblInfo;
14:    private TextBox  txtEntry;
15:    private int      WinningNumber = 0;
16:    private int      Guesses = 0;
17:
18:    public WinGuess()
19:    {
20:        InitializeComponent();
21:    }
22:
23:    private void InitializeComponent()
24:    {
25:        // Get a random number from zero to 10000...
26:        WinningNumber = getRandomNumber( 10000 );
27:
28:        // Put title into window title bar
29:        this.Text = "WinGuess";
30:
31:        // Center form on screen
32:        this.StartPosition = FormStartPosition.CenterScreen;
33:
34:        // Set form style
35:        this.FormBorderStyle = FormBorderStyle.Fixed3D;
36:
37:        lblTag1 = new Label();        // Create label
38:        lblTag1.Text = "Enter A Number:";
39:        lblTag1.Location = new Point( 50, 20);
40:        this.Controls.Add(lblTag1);   // Add label to form
```

```
41:
42:        lblInfo = new Label();          // Create label
43:        lblInfo.Text = "Enter a number between 0 and 10000.";
44:        lblInfo.Location = new Point( 50, 80);
45:        lblInfo.Width = 200;
46:        lblInfo.Height = 40;
47:        this.Controls.Add(lblInfo);   // Add label to form
48:
49:        txtEntry = new TextBox();       // Create text  box
50:        txtEntry.Location = new Point( 150, 18 );
51:        this.Controls.Add(txtEntry);  // Add to form
52:
53:
54:        btnGuess = new Button();        // Create a button
55:        btnGuess.Text       = "Try Number";
56:        btnGuess.BackColor = Color.LightGray;
57:        // following centers button and puts it near bottom
58:        btnGuess.Location  = new Point( ((this.Width/2) -
59:                                        (btnGuess.Width / 2)),
60:                                        (this.Height - 75));
61:        this.Controls.Add(btnGuess); // Add button to form
62:
63:        // Add a click event handler using the default event handler
64:        btnGuess.Click += new System.EventHandler(this.btnGuess_Click);
65:    }
66:
67:    private int getRandomNumber( int nbr )
68:    {
69:        if ( nbr > 0 )
70:        {
71:            Random Rnd = new Random();
72:            return (Rnd.Next(0, nbr));
73:        }
74:        else
75:        {
76:            return 0;
77:        }
78:    }
79:
80:    protected void btnGuess_Click( object sender, System.EventArgs e)
81:    {
82:        int val = 0;
83:        StringBuilder tmpString = new StringBuilder();
84:        tmpString.Append("Current Guess: ");
85:        tmpString.Append(txtEntry.Text);
86:        tmpString.Append("\n");
87:
88:        try  // try, catch, and finally are covered on Day 9
89:        {
```

LISTING T&R 2.2 continued

```
 90:            val = int.Parse(txtEntry.Text);
 91:
 92:            // If a number was not entered, an exception will be
 93:            // throw. Program flow will go to catch statement below
 94:
 95:            tmpString.Append("Guesses: ");
 96:
 97:            Guesses += 1;        // Add one to Guesses
 98:
 99:            tmpString.Append(Guesses.ToString());
100:            tmpString.Append("\n");
101:
102:            if( val < 0 || val > 10000 )
103:            {
104:              // bad value entered
105:              tmpString.Append("Number is out of range...Try again.\n");
106:              tmpString.Append("Enter a number from 0 to 10000");
107:            }
108: else
109:            {
110:                if ( val < WinningNumber )
111:                {
112:                  tmpString.Append("You guessed low...  Try again.\n");
113:                  tmpString.Append("Enter a number from 0 to 10000");
114:                }
115:                else
116:                if ( val > WinningNumber )
117:                {
118:                  tmpString.Append("You guessed high... Try again.\n");
119:                  tmpString.Append("Enter a number from 0 to 10000");
120:                }
121:                else
122:                {
123:                    tmpString.Append("You guessed correctly!!");
124:                }
125:            }
126:        }
127:        // Catch format errors....
128:        catch( FormatException )
129:        {
130:            tmpString.Append("Please enter a valid number...\n");
131:            tmpString.Append("Enter a number from 0 to 10000");
132:        }
133:        finally
134:        {
135:            this.lblInfo.Text = tmpString.ToString();
136:            this.txtEntry.Text = "";
137:
```

LISTING T&R 2.2   continued

```
138:          // Next line will put winning number in window title
139:          // this.Text = WinningNumber.ToString();
140:      }
141:   }
142:
143:   public static void Main( string[] args )
144:   {
145:     Application.Run( new WinGuess() );
146:   }
147: }
```

OUTPUT

FIGURE TR2.1

T&R output.

As you can see in Figure TR2.1, this new listing has the same functionality as the previous listing. The difference is that this listing creates a windows form.

Note

The source code for this listing is available on the included CD. Any updates to the code will be available at www.TeachYourselfCSharp.com.

DAY 5

The Core of C#
Programming: Classes

As you learned on Day 1, "Getting Started with C#," classes are critical to an object-oriented language, including C#. Whether you've realized it or not, you have seen classes used in every example included in the book so far. Because classes are central to C#, today's lesson and tomorrow's are among the two most important in this book. Today you…

- Revisit the concepts involved in object-oriented programming.
- Learn how to declare a class.
- Learn how to define a class.
- Discover class members.
- Create your own data members.
- Implement properties in your classes.
- Take your first serious look at namespaces.

Digging into Object-Oriented Programming

On Day 1, you learned that C# is considered an object-oriented language. You also learned that to take full advantage of C#, you should understand the concepts of object-oriented languages. In the next few sections, you briefly revisit the concepts you learned about in Day 1. You will then begin to see how these concepts are applied to actual C# programs.

Recall from Day 1 the key characteristics that make up an object-oriented language:

- Encapsulation
- Polymorphism
- Inheritance
- Reuse

Encapsulation

Encapsulation is the concept of making classes (or "packages") that contain everything you need. In object-oriented programming, this means that you can create a class that stores all the variables that you need and all the routines to commonly manipulate this data. You can create a `Circle` class that stores information on a circle. This could include storing the location of the circle's center and its radius, plus storing routines commonly used with a circle. These routines could include getting the circle's area, getting its circumference, changing its center point, changing its radius, and much more.

By encapsulating a circle, you allow the user to be oblivious to how the circle works. You need to know only how to interact with the circle. This provides a shield to the inner workings of the circle, which means that the variables within the class could be changed and it would be invisible to the user. For example, instead of storing the radius of the circle, you could store the diameter. If you have encapsulated the functionality and the data, making this change impacts only your class. Any programs that use your class should not need to change. In today's and tomorrow's lessons, you see programs that work directly with a `Circle` class.

Note

Encapsulation is often referred to as "black boxing," which refers to hiding the functionality or the inner workings of a process. For a circle, if you send in the radius, you can get the area. You don't care how it happens, as long as you know that you are getting back the correct answer.

Inheritance

In many object-oriented programming books, an animal analogy is used to illustrate inheritance. The analogy starts with the concept of an animal as a living being.

Now consider reptiles, which are everything that an animal is; plus, they are cold-blooded. A reptile contains all of the features of an animal, but it also adds its own unique features. Now consider a snake. A snake is a reptile that is long and skinny and that has no legs. It has all the characteristics of a reptile, but it also has its own unique characteristics. A snake can be said to inherit the characteristics of a reptile. A reptile can be said to inherit the characteristics of an animal.

A second example of inheritance can be shown with a circle. A class can be created called shape. All shapes have a number of sides and an area. A circle can be created by inheriting from shape. It would still have the number of sides and the area that a shape provides. Additionally, it could have a center point. A triangle could also be created by inheriting from shape. The triangle would add its own unique characteristics to those that it gets from shape.

On Day 10, "Reusing Existing Code with Inheritance," you will see how this same concept is applied to classes and programming.

Polymorphism

Polymorphism is having the capability to assume many forms, which means that the programs can work with what you send them. For example, you could have a routine that gives the area of a shape. Because the area of a triangle is calculated differently than that of other shapes, the routine to calculate the area would need to adapt based on what is sent. Regardless of whether a triangle, a circle, or another shape is sent, the routine would be capable of treating them all as shapes and, thus, calculating the area. You will learn how to program polymorphism on Day 10.

Overloading is another concept that is often related to polymorphism. For example, you have used the WriteLine() routine in several of the previous days. You have seen that you can create a parameter field using {0}. What values does this field print? As you have seen, it can print a variable regardless of its type, or it can print another string. The WriteLine() routine takes care of how it gets printed. The routine is polymorphic, in that it adapts to most of the types that you can send it.

Using a circle as an example, you might want to call a circle object to get its area. You can do this by using three points or by using a single point and the radius. Either way,

5

you expect to get the same results. This polymorphic feature is done by using overloading. You'll learn more about overloading in tomorrow's lesson, "Packaging Functionality: Class Methods and Member Functions."

Reuse

When you create a class, you can reuse it to create lots of objects. By using inheritance and some of the features described previously, you can create routines that can be used repeatedly in many programs and in many ways. By encapsulating functionality, you can create routines that have been tested and are proven to work. You won't have to test the details of how the functionality works—only that you are using it correctly. This makes reusing these routines quick and easy.

Objects and Classes

On Day 1, an example of a cookie cutter and cookies illustrated classes and objects. Now you are done with cookies and snakes—it is time to jump into some code.

 Note You will learn about classes by starting with extremely simple examples and then building on them over the next several days.

Defining a Class

To keep things simple, a keyword called `class` is used to define classes. The basic structure of a class follows this format:

```
class identifier
{
    class-body ;
}
```

`identifier` is the name given to the class, and `class-body` is the code that makes up the class.

The name of a class is like any other variable name that can be declared. You want to give a class a meaningful name, something that describes what the class does.

The .NET Framework has a large number of built-in classes. You have actually been using one since the beginning of this book: the `Console` class. The `Console` class contains several data members and routines. You've already used many of these routines, including `Write` and `WriteLine`. The class name—the *identifier*—of this class is `Console`. The body of the `Console` class contains the code for the `Write` and `WriteLine` routines. By the end of tomorrow's lesson, you will be able to create and name your own classes that have their own routines.

Declaring Classes

After a class is defined, you use it to create objects. A class is just a definition used to create objects. A class by itself does not have the capability to hold information or actually perform routines. Instead, a class is used to declare objects. The object can then be used to hold the data and perform the routines as defined by the class.

> **Note**
>
> The declaration of an object is commonly referred to as *instantiation*. Said differently, an object is an instance of a class.

The format of declaring an object from a class is as follows:

```
class_name object_identifier = new class_name();
```

`class_name` is the name of the class, and `object_identifier` is the name of the object being declared. For example, if you have a class called `Point`, you can create an object called `startingPoint` with the following line of code:

```
point startingPoint = new Point();
```

The name of the class is `Point`, and the name of the object declared is `startingPoint`. Because `startingPoint` is an object, it can contain data and routines if they were defined within the `Point` class.

In looking at this declarative line of code, you might wonder what the other items are. Most important, a keyword is being used that you have not yet seen: `new`.

As its name implies, the `new` keyword is used to create new items. In this case, it creates a new point. Because `Point` is a class, an object is created. The `new` keyword indicates that a new instance is to be created. In this case, the new instance is a `Point` object.

When declaring an object with a class, you also have to provide parentheses to the class name on the right of the assignment. This enables the class to be constructed into a new object.

> **Caution**
>
> If you don't add the construction code `new class_name`, you will have declared a class, but the compiler won't have constructed its internal structure. You need to make sure that you assign the `new class_name` code to the declared object name to make sure everything is constructed. You will learn more about this initial construction in tomorrow's lesson.

5

Look at the statement again:

```
point startingPoint = new Point();
```

The following breaks down what is happening:

```
point startingPoint
```

The `Point` class is used to declare an object called `startingPoint`. This piece of the statement is like what you have seen with other data types, such as integers and decimals.

```
startingPoint =
```

As with variables, you assign the result of the right side of the assignment operator (the equals sign) to the variable on the left. In this case, the variable happens to be an object—which you now know is an object of type `Point` called `startingPoint`.

```
new Point()
```

This part of the statement does the actual construction of the `Point` object. The name of the class with parentheses is a signal to construct—create—an object of the class type—in this case, `Point`. The `new` keyword says to reserve some room in memory for this new object. Remember, a class is only a definition: It doesn't store anything. The object needs to store information, so it needs memory reserved. The `new` keyword reserves the memory.

Like all statements, this declaration is ended with a semicolon, which signals that the statement is done.

The Members of a Class

Now that you know the overall structure for creating an object with a class, it is time to look at what can be held in a class. Two primary types of items can be contained within the body of a class: data members and function members.

Data members include variables and constants. These include variables of any of the types that you learned about on Day 2, "Understanding C# Programs," and any of the more advanced types that you will learn about later. These data members can even be other classes.

The other type of element that is part of a class's body is function members. Function members are routines that perform an action. These actions can be as simple as setting a value to something more complex, such as writing a line of text using a variable number of values—as you have seen with `Write` and `WriteLine`. `Write` and `WriteLine` are member functions of the `Console` class. In tomorrow's lesson, you will learn how to create and use member functions of your own. For now, it is time to visit data members.

Working with Data Members, a.k.a. Fields

NEW TERM   Another name for a variable is a *field*. As stated previously, data members within a class are variables that are members of a class. In the Point class referenced earlier, you expect a data member to store the x and y coordinates of the point. These coordinates could be any of a number of data types; however, if these were integers, you would define the Point class as such:

```
class Point
{
   int x;
   int y;
}
```

That's it. This is effectively the code for a very simple Point class. You should include one other item for now: an access modifier called public. A variable is accessible only within the block where you declare it, unless you indicate otherwise. In this case, the block is the definition of the Point class. Without adding the word public, you cannot access x or y outside the Point class.

> **Note**
>
> Remember, a block is a section of code between two braces ({}). The body of a class is a block of code.

The change made to the Point class is relatively simple. With the public accessor added, the class becomes this:

```
class Point
{
   public int x;
   public int y;
}
```

Although the Point class contains two integers, you can actually use any data type within this class. For example, you can create a FullName class that contains three strings that store the first, middle, and last names. You can create an Address class that contains a name class and additional strings to hold the different address pieces. You can create a customer class that contains a long value for a customer number, an address class, a decimal account balance, a Boolean value for active or inactive, and more.

Accessing Data Members

When you have data members declared, you want to get to their values. As you learned, the public accessor enables you to get to the data members from outside the class.

You cannot simply access data members from outside the class by their name. For example, if you have a program that declares a startingPoint from the Point class, it would seem as if you should be able to get the point by using x and y—the names that are in the Point class. What happens if you declare both a startingPoint and an endingPoint in the same program? If you use x, which point is being accessed?

To access a data member, you use both the name of the object and the data member. The member operator, which is a period, separates these. To access the startingPoint's coordinates, you therefore use this

startingPoint.x

and this:

startingPoint.y

For the ending point, you use this

endingPoint.x

and this:

endingPoint.y

At this time, you have the foundation to try out a program. Listing 5.1 presents the Point class. This class is used to declare two objects, starting and ending.

LISTING 5.1   PointApp.cs—Declaring a Class with Data Members

```
 1:  //  PointApp.cs- A class with two data members
 2:  //-----------------------------------------------------------------
 3:
 4:  class Point
 5:  {
 6:      public int x;
 7:      public int y;
 8:  }
 9:
10:  class pointApp
11:  {
12:      public static void Main()
13:      {
14:          Point starting = new Point();
15:          Point ending   = new Point();
16:
17:          starting.x = 1;
18:          starting.y = 4;
19:          ending.x = 10;
20:          ending.y = 11;
```

LISTING 5.1   continued

```
21:
22:          System.Console.WriteLine("Point 1: ({0},{1})",
23:                                 starting.x, starting.y);
24:          System.Console.WriteLine("Point 2: ({0},{1})",
25:                                 ending.x, ending.y);
26:      }
27: }
```

OUTPUT
Point 1: (1,4)
Point 2: (10,11)

ANALYSIS A simple class called Point is declared in Lines 4–8. This class follows the structure that was presented earlier. In Line 4, the class keyword is being used, followed by the name of the class, Point. Lines 5–8 contain the braces that enclose the body
of the class. Within the body of this class, two integers are declared, x and y. These are
each declared as public so that you can use them outside of the class.

Line 10 contains the start of the main portion of your application. It is interesting to note
that the main portion of your application is also a class. In this case, the class containing
your application is called pointApp. You will learn more about this later.

Line 12 contains the main routine that you should now be very familiar with. In
Lines 14–15, two objects are created using the Point class, following the same format
that was described earlier. In Lines 17–20, values are set for each of the data members of
the Point objects. In Line 17, the value 1 is assigned to the x data member of the starting
class. The member operator, the period, separates the member name from the object
name. Lines 18–20 follow the same format.

Line 22 contains a WriteLine routine, which you have also seen before. This one is
unique because you print the values stored within the starting point object. The values
are stored in starting.x and starting.y, not just x and y. Line 24 prints the values for the
ending point.

Using Data Members

Listing 5.1 showed you how to assign a value to a data member, as well as how to get its
value. What if you want to do something more complex than a simple assignment or a
simple display?

The data members of a class are like any other variable type. You can use them in operations, control statements, or anywhere that a regular variable can be accessed. Listing 5.2
expands on the use of the point class. In this example, the calculation is performed to
determine the length of a line between two points. If you've forgotten your basic alge-
braic equation for this, Figure 5.1 illustrates the calculation to be performed.

5

Figure 5.1

*Calculating line length
from two points.*

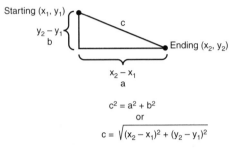

$$c^2 = a^2 + b^2$$
$$\text{or}$$
$$c = \sqrt{(x_2 - x_1)^2 + (y_2 - y_1)^2}$$

Listing 5.2   LineApp.cs—Working with Data Members

```
 1:  //  LineApp.cs- Calculate the length of a line.
 2:  //-------------------------------------------------------------
 3:
 4:  class Point
 5:  {
 6:      public int x;
 7:      public int y;
 8:  }
 9:
10:  class lineApp
11:  {
12:      public static void Main()
13:      {
14:          Point starting = new Point();
15:          Point ending   = new Point();
16:          double Line;
17:
18:          starting.x = 1;
19:          starting.y = 4;
20:          ending.x = 10;
21:          ending.y = 11;
22:
23:          Line = System.Math.Sqrt( (ending.x - starting.x)*
             ➥ (ending.x - starting.x) +
24:                                   (ending.y - starting.y)*
             ➥(ending.y - starting.y) );
25:
26:          System.Console.WriteLine("Point 1: ({0},{1})",
27:                                    starting.x, starting.y);
28:          System.Console.WriteLine("Point 2: ({0},{1})",
29:                                    ending.x, ending.y);
30:          System.Console.WriteLine(
31:                      "Length of line from Point 1 to Point 2: {0}",
32:                      Line);
33:      }
34:  }
```

```
Point 1: (1,4)
Point 2: (10,11)
Length of line from Point 1 to Point 2: 11.4017542509914
```

This listing is very similar to Listing 5.1. The biggest difference is the addition of a data member and some calculations that determine the length of a line. In Line 16, you see that the new data member is declared of type double and is called line. This variable will be used to hold the result of the length of the line between the two declared points.

Lines 23–24 are actually a single statement that looks more complex than it is. Other than the System.Math.Sqrt part, you should be able to follow what the line is doing. Sqrt is a routine within the System.Math object that calculates the square root of a value. If you compare this formula to the information presented in Figure 5.1, you will see that it is a match. The end result is the length of the line. The important thing to note is that the data members are being used within this calculation in the same manner that any other variable would be used. The only difference is the naming scheme.

Using Classes as Data Members

It was stated earlier that you can nest one class within another. A class is another type of data. As such, an object declared with a class type—which is just an advanced variable type—can be used in the same places as any other variable. Listing 5.3 presents an example of a line class. This class is composed of two points, starting and ending.

LISTING 5.3   line2.cs—Nested Classes

5

```
 1:  //  line2.cs- A class with two data members
 2:  //---------------------------------------------------------------
 3:
 4:  class Point
 5:  {
 6:      public int x;
 7:      public int y;
 8:  }
 9:
10:  class Line
11:  {
12:      public Point starting = new Point();
13:      public Point ending = new Point();
14:      public double len;
15:  }
16:
17:  class lineApp
18:  {
19:      public static void Main()
```

LISTING 5.3   continued

```
20:     {
21:         Line myLine = new Line();
22:
23:         myLine.starting.x = 1;
24:         myLine.starting.y = 4;
25:         myLine.ending.x = 10;
26:         myLine.ending.y = 11;
27:         myLine.len = System.Math.Sqrt(
28:             (myLine.ending.x - myLine.starting.x) *
29:             (myLine.ending.x - myLine.starting.x)  +
30:             (myLine.ending.y - myLine.starting.y)*
31:             (myLine.ending.y - myLine.starting.y) );
32:
33:         System.Console.WriteLine("Point 1: ({0},{1})",
34:                         myLine.starting.x, myLine.starting.y);
35:         System.Console.WriteLine("Point 2: ({0},{1})",
36:                         myLine.ending.x, myLine.ending.y);
37:         System.Console.WriteLine("Line Length: {0}",
38:                         myLine.len);
39:     }
40: }
```

OUTPUT
```
Point 1: (1,4)
Point 2: (10,11)
Line Length: 11.4017542509914
```

ANALYSIS Listing 5.3 is very similar to the previous listings. The Point class that you are coming to know and love is defined in Lines 4–8. There is nothing different about this from what you have seen before. In Lines 10–15, however, you see a second class being defined. This class, called line, is composed of three variables. The first two in Lines 12–13 are of type point, which is a class. These two variables are called starting and ending. When an object is declared using the Line class, the Line class, in turn, creates two Point objects. The third data member declared in Line 14 is a double that will be used to store the length of the line.

Continuing with the listing, you see in Line 21 that a new object is created using the Line class. This new Line object is given the name myLine. Line 21 follows the same format that you saw earlier for creating an object from a class.

Lines 23–31 access the data members of the Line class and assign them values. It is beginning to look a little more complex; however, looks can be deceiving. If you break this down, you will see that it is relatively straightforward. In Line 23, you assign the constant value 1 to the variable myLine.starting.x. In other words, you are assigning the value 1 to the x member of the starting member of myLine. Going from the other direction, you can say that you are assigning the value 1 to the myLine line object's start-ing member's x member. It is like a tree. Figure 5.2 illustrates the Line class's members.

The rest of this listing follows the same structure. Lines 27–31 might look complicated; however, this is the same formula that was used earlier to calculate the length of a line. The result, however, is placed into the len data member of the myLine object.

FIGURE 5.2

The myLine object's data members.

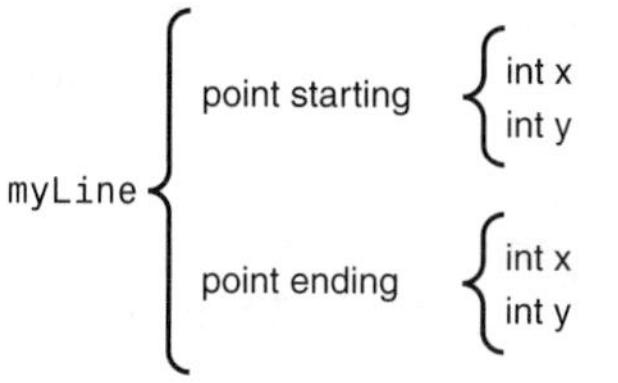

Working with Nested Types

On Day 2, you learned about the different standard data types that can be used. As you saw in Listing 5.3, an object created with a class can be used in the same places as any other variable created with a data type.

When used by themselves, classes really do nothing—they are only a description. For example, in Listing 5.3, the Point class in Lines 4–8 is only a description; nothing is declared and no memory is used. This description defines a type. In this case, the type is the class, or, specifically, a Point.

It is possible to nest a type within another class. If Point will be used only within the context of a line, it can be defined within the Line class. This enables Point objects to be used in the Line class.

The code for the nested Point type is as follows:

```
class Line
{
    public class Point
    {
        public int x;
        public int y;
    }

    public Point starting = new Point();
    public Point ending = new Point();
}
```

One additional change was made. The Point class had to be declared as public as well. If you don't declare the type as public, you get an error. The reason for the error should make sense if you think about it. How can the parts of a `Point` object be `public` if the point itself isn't `public`?

Using Static Variables

Sometimes you want a bunch of objects declared with the same class to share a value. For example, you might want to declare a number of line objects that all share the same originating point. If one `Line` object changes the originating point, you want all lines to change it.

To share a single data value across all the objects declared by a single class, you add the `static` modifier. Listing 5.4 revisits the `Line` class. This time, the same starting point is used for all objects declared with the `Line` class.

LISTING 5.4   StatLine.cs—Using the `static` Modifier with Data Members

```
 1:  //  StatLine.cs- A class with two data members
 2:  //-----------------------------------------------------------------
 3:
 4:  class Point
 5:  {
 6:      public int x;
 7:      public int y;
 8:  }
 9:
10:  class Line
11:  {
12:      static public Point origin= new Point();
13:      public Point ending = new Point();
14:  }
15:
16:  class lineApp
17:  {
18:      public static void Main()
19:      {
20:         Line line1 = new Line();
21:         Line line2 = new Line();
22:
23:         // set line origin
24:         Line.origin.x = 1;
25:         Line.origin.y = 2;
26:
27:
28:         // set line1's ending values
29:         line1.ending.x = 3;
30:         line1.ending.y = 4;
31:
```

LISTING 5.4   continued

```
32:            // set line2's ending values
33:            line2.ending.x = 7;
34:            line2.ending.y = 8;
35:
36:            // print the values...
37:            System.Console.WriteLine("Line 1 start: ({0},{1})",
38:                                      Line.origin.x, Line.origin.y);
39:            System.Console.WriteLine("line 1 end:   ({0},{1})",
40:                                      line1.ending.x, line1.ending.y);
41:            System.Console.WriteLine("Line 2 start: ({0},{1})",
42:                                      line.origin.x, line.origin.y);
43:            System.Console.WriteLine("line 2 end:   ({0},{1})\n",
44:                                      line2.ending.x, line2.ending.y);
45:
46:            // change value of line2's starting point
47:            Line.origin.x = 939;
48:            Line.origin.y = 747;
49:
50:            // and the values again...
51:
52:            System.Console.WriteLine("Line 1 start: ({0},{1})",
53:                                      Line.origin.x, Line.origin.y);
54:            System.Console.WriteLine("line 1 end:   ({0},{1})",
55:                                      line1.ending.x, line1.ending.y);
56:            System.Console.WriteLine("Line 2 start: ({0},{1})",
57:                                      line.origin.x, line.origin.y);
58:            System.Console.WriteLine("line 2 end:   ({0},{1})",
59:                                      line2.ending.x, line2.ending.y);
60:        }
61: }
```

OUTPUT
```
Line 1 start: (1,2)
line 1 end:   (3,4)
Line 2 start: (1,2)
line 2 end:   (7,8)

Line 1 start: (939,747)
line 1 end:   (3,4)
Line 2 start: (939,747)
line 2 end:   (7,8)
```

Caution   If you try to access a static data member with an object name, such as line1, you will get an error. You must use the class name to access a static data member.

ANALYSIS Listing 5.4 is not much different from what you have seen already. The biggest difference is in Line 12, where the origin point is declared as static in addition to being public. The static keyword makes a big difference in this Line class. Instead of each object that is created from the Line class containing an origin point, only one origin point is shared by all instances of Line.

Line 18 is the beginning of the Main routine. Lines 20–21 declare two Line objects, called line1 and line2. Lines 28–29 set the ending point of line1, and Lines 33–34 set the ending point of line2. Going back to Lines 24–25, you see something different from what you have seen before. Instead of setting the origin point of line1 or line2, these lines set the point for the class name, Line. This is important. If you try to set the origin on line1 or line2, you will get a compiler error. In other words, the following line of code is an error:

```
line1.origin.x = 1;
```

Because the origin object is declared static, it is shared across all objects of type Line. Because neither line1 nor line2 owns this value, these cannot be used directly to set the value. You must use the class name instead. Remember, a variable declared static in a class is owned by the class, not the individual objects that are instantiated.

Lines 37–44 print the origin point and the ending point for line1 and line2. Again, notice that the class name is used to print the origin values, not the object name. Lines 47–48 change the origin, and the final part of the program prints the values again.

> **Note** A common use of a static data member is as a counter. Each time an object does something, it can increment the counter for all the objects.

Inspecting the Application Class

If you haven't already noticed, a class being used in all your applications has not been fully discussed. In Line 16 of Listing 5.4, you see the following code:

```
class lineApp
```

You will notice a similar class line in every application that you have entered in this book. C# is an object-oriented language. This means that everything is an object—even your application. To create an object, you need a class to define it. Listing 5.4's application is lineApp. When you execute the program, the lineApp class is instantiated and creates a lineApp object, which just happens to be your program.

Like what you have learned already, your application class declares data members. In Listing 5.4, the lineApp class's data members are two classes: line1 and line2. There is additional functionality in this class as well. In tomorrow's lesson, you will learn that this additional functionality can be included in your classes as well.

Creating Properties

Earlier, it was stated that one of the benefits of an object-oriented program is the capability to control the internal representation and access to data. In the examples used so far in today's lesson, everything has been public, so access has been freely given to any code that wants to access the data members.

In an object-oriented program, you want to have more control over who can and can't get to data. In general, you won't want code to access data members directly. If you allow code to directly access these data members, you might lock yourself into being unable to change the data types of the values.

C# provides a concept called *properties* to enable you to create object-oriented fields within your classes. Properties use the reserved words get and set to get the values from your variables and set the values in your variables. Listing 5.5 illustrates the use of get and set with the Point class that you used earlier.

LISTING 5.5   prop.cs—Using Properties

```
 1:  //  PropApp.cs- Using Properties
 2:  //-------------------------------------------------------------
 3:
 4:  class Point
 5:  {
 6:      int my_X;   // my_X is private
 7:      int my_Y;   // my_Y is private
 8:
 9:      public int x
10:      {
11:        get
12:        {
13:           return my_X;
14:        }
15:        set
16:        {
17:            my_X = value;
18:        }
19:      }
20:      public int y
21:      {
```

5

LISTING 5.5   continued

```
22:            get
23:            {
24:                return my_Y;
25:            }
26:            set
27:            {
28:                my_Y = value;
29:            }
30:        }
31:    }
32:
33:    class PropApp
34:    {
35:        public static void Main()
36:        {
37:            Point starting = new Point();
38:            Point ending   = new Point();
39:
40:            starting.x = 1;
41:            starting.y = 4;
42:            ending.x = 10;
43:            ending.y = 11;
44:
45:            System.Console.WriteLine("Point 1: ({0},{1})",
46:                                    starting.x, starting.y);
47:            System.Console.WriteLine("Point 2: ({0},{1})",
48:                                    ending.x, ending.y);
49:        }
50:    }
```

OUTPUT   Point 1: (1,4)
Point 2: (10,11)

ANALYSIS   Listing 5.5 creates properties for both the x and y coordinates of the Point class. The Point class is defined in Lines 4–31. Everything on these lines is a part of the Point class's definition. In Lines 6–7, you see that two data members are created, my_x and my_Y. Because these are not declared as public, they cannot be accessed outside the class; they are considered private variables. You will learn more about keeping things private on Day 7, "Storing More Complex Stuff: Structures, Enumerators, and Arrays."

Lines 9–19 and Lines 20–30 operate exactly the same, except that the first set of lines uses the my_x variable and the second set uses the my_Y variable. These sets of lines create the property capabilities for the my_x and my_Y variables.

Line 9 looks like just another declaration of a data member. In fact, it is. In this line, you declare a public integer variable called x. Note that there is no semicolon at the end of this line; therefore, the declaration of the member variable is not complete. Instead, it also includes what is in the following code block in Lines 10–19. Within this block of code you have two commands. Line 11 begins a get statement, which is called whenever a program tries to get the value of the data member being declared—in this case, x. For example, if you assign the value of x to a different variable, you *get* the value of x and set it into the new variable. In this case, getting the value of x is the code that occurs in the block (Lines 12–14) following the get statement. When getting the value of x, you are actually getting the value of my_x, as you can see in Line 13.

The set statement in Line 15 is called whenever you are setting a value in the x variable. For example, setting x equal to 10 places the value of 10 in x.

When a program gets the value of x, the get property in Line 11 is called. This executes the code within the get, which is Line 13. Line 13 returns the value of my_x, which is the private variable in the Point class.

When a program places a value in x, the set property in Line 15 is called. This executes the code within the set, which is Line 17. Line 17 sets something called value into the private variable, my_x, in the Point class. value is the value being placed in x. (It is great when a name actually describes the contents.) For example, value is 10 in the following statement:

```
x = 10;
```

This statement places the value of 10 in x. The set property within x places this value in my_X.

Looking at the main application in Lines 33–50, you should see that x is used as it was before. There is absolutely no difference in how you use the Point class. The difference is that the Point class can be changed to store my_x and my_y differently, without impacting the program.

Although the code in Lines 9–30 is relatively simple, it doesn't have to be. You can do any coding and any manipulation that you want within the get and set. You don't even have to write to another data member.

5

Do	Don't
Do make sure that you understand data members and the class information presented in today's lesson before going to Day 6, "Packaging Functionality: Class Methods and Member Functions."	**Don't** forget to mark data members as `public` if you want to access them from outside your class.
Do use property accessors to access your class's data members in programs that you create.	

A First Look at Namespaces

As you begin to learn about classes, it is important to know that a large number of classes are available that do a wide variety of functions. The .NET Framework provides a substantial number of base classes that you can use. You can also obtain third-party classes that you can use.

 Note   Day 15, "Using Existing Routines from the .NET Base Classes," focuses specifically on using a number of key .NET base classes.

As you continue through this book, you will be exposed to a number of key classes. You've actually used a couple of base classes already. As mentioned earlier, `Console` is a base class. You also learned that `Console` has member routines, `Write` and `WriteLine`. For example, the following writes my name to the console:

```
System.Console.WriteLine("Bradley L. Jones");
```

You now know that `"Bradley L. Jones"` is a literal. You know that `WriteLine` is a routine that is a part of the `Console` class. You even know that `Console` is an object declared from a class. This leaves `System`.

Because of the number of classes, it is important that they be organized. Classes can be grouped into namespaces. A namespace is a named grouping of classes. The `Console` class is a part of the `System` namespace.

`System.Console.WriteLine` is a fully qualified name. With a fully qualified name, you point directly to where the code is located. C# provides a shortcut method for using classes and methods that doesn't require you to always include the full namespace name. This is accomplished with the `using` keyword.

The using keyword enables you to include a namespace in your program. When the namespace is included, the program knows to search the namespace for routines and classes that might be used. The format for including a namespace is as follows:

using *namespace_name*

namespace_name is the name of the namespace or the name of a nested namespace. For example, to include the System namespace, you include the following line of code near the top of your listing:

using System;

If you include this line of code, you do not need to include the System section when calling classes or routines within the namespace. Listing 5.6 calls the using statement to include the System namespace.

LISTING 5.6   NameApp.cs—Using using and Namespaces

```
 1:  //  NameApp.cs- Namespaces and the using keyword
 2:  //-------------------------------------------------------------
 3:
 4:  using System;
 5:
 6:  class name
 7:  {
 8:      public string first;
 9:      public string last;
10:  }
11:
12:  class NameApp
13:  {
14:      public static void Main()
15:      {
16:          // Create a name object
17:          name you = new name();
18:
19:          Console.Write("Enter your first name and press enter: ");
20:          you.first = Console.ReadLine();
21:          System.Console.Write("\n{0}, enter your last name and press enter: ",
22:                          you.first);
23:          you.last = System.Console.ReadLine();
24:
25:          Console.WriteLine("\nData has been entered.....");
26:          System.Console.WriteLine("You claim to be {0} {1}",
27:                          you.first, you.last);
28:      }
29:  }
```

5

OUTPUT

Enter your first name and press enter: **Bradley**

Bradley, enter your last name and press enter: **Jones**

Data has been entered.....
You claim to be Bradley Jones

Note

> The bold text in the output is text that I entered. You can enter any text in
> its place. I suggest using your own name rather than mine!

ANALYSIS   Line 4 of Listing 5.6 is the focal point of this program. The using keyword
includes the System namespace; when you use functions from the Console class,
you don't have to fully qualify their names. You see this in Lines 19, 20, and 25. By
including the using keyword, you are not precluded from continuing to use fully qualified names, as Lines 21, 23, and 26 show. However, there is no need to fully qualify
names because the namespace was included.

This program uses a second routine from the Console class, called ReadLine. As you can
see by running this program, the ReadLine routine reads what is entered by users up to
the time they press Enter. This routine returns what the user enters. In this case, the text
entered by the user is assigned with the assignment operator to one of the data members
in the name class.

Nested Namespaces

Multiple namespaces can be stored together and also are stored in a namespace. If a
namespace contains other namespaces, you can add them to the qualified name, or you
can include the subnamespace qualified in a using statement. For example, the System
namespace contains several other namespaces, including ones called Drawing, Data, and
Windows.Forms. When using classes from these namespaces, you can either qualify these
names or include them with using statements. To include a using statement for the Data
namespace within the System namespace, you enter the following:

using System.Data;

Note

> A namespace can also be used to allow the same class name to be used in
> multiple places. For example, I could create a class called person. You could
> also create a class called person. To keep these two classes from clashing,
> they could be placed into different namespaces. You'll learn how to do this
> on Day 8, "Advanced Method Access."

Summary

Today's and tomorrow's lessons are among two of the most important lessons in this book. Classes are the heart of object-oriented programming languages and, therefore, are the heart of C#. In today's lesson, you revisited the concepts of encapsulation, polymorphism, inheritance, and reuse. You then learned how to define the basic structure of a class and how to create data members within your class. You learned one of the first ways to encapsulate your program when you learned how to create properties using the set and get accessors. The last part of today's lesson introduced you to namespaces and the using statement. Tomorrow you will build on this by learning how to add more functionality to your classes.

Q&A

Q Would you ever use a class with just data members?

A Generally, you would not use a class with just data members. The value of a class and of object-oriented programming is the capability to encapsulate both functionality and data into a single package. You learned about only data today. In tomorrow's lesson, you learn how to add the functionality.

Q Should all data members always be declared public so people can get to them?

A Absolutely not! Although many of the data members were declared as public in today's lesson, sometimes you don't want people to get to your data. One reason is to allow the capability to change the way the data is stored.

Q It was mentioned that there are a bunch of existing classes. How can I find out about these?

A Microsoft has provided a bunch of classes called the .NET base classes, and also has provided documentation on what each of these classes can do. The classes are organized by namespace. At the time this book was written, the only way to get any information on them was through online help. Microsoft included a complete references section for the base classes. You will learn more about the base classes on Day 19, "Creating Remote Procedures (Web Services)."

5

Workshop

The Workshop provides quiz questions to help you solidify your understanding of the material covered and exercises to provide you with experience in using what you've learned. Try to understand the quiz and exercise answers before continuing to the next day's lesson. Answers are provided on the CD.

Quiz

1. What are the four characteristics of an object-oriented program?

2. What two key things can be stored in a class?

3. What is the difference between a data member declared as public and one that hasn't been declared as public?

4. What does adding the keyword `static` do to a data member?

5. What is the name of the application class in Listing 5.2?

6. What commands are used to implement properties?

7. When is `value` used?

8. Is `Console` a class, a data member, a namespace, a routine, or a type?

9. Is `System` a class, a data member, a namespace, a routine, or a type?

10. What keyword is used to include a namespace in a listing?

Exercises

1. Create a class to hold the center of a circle and its radius.

2. Add properties to the `Circle` class created in Exercise 1.

3. Create a class that stores an integer called `MyNumber`. Create properties for this number. When the number is stored, multiply it by `100`. Whenever it is retrieved, divide it by `100`.

4. **Bug Buster:** The following program has a problem. Enter it in your editor and compile it. Which lines generate error messages?

```
1:// A bug buster program
2:// Is something wrong? Or not?
3://-------------------------------------------
4:  using System;
5:  using System.Console;
6:
7:  class name
8:  {
9:      public string first;
10:  }
11:
12:  class NameApp
13:  {
14:      public static void Main()
15:      {
16:          // Create a name object
17:          name you = new name();
18:
19:          Write("Enter your first name and press enter: ");
```

```
20:        you.first = ReadLine();
21:        Write("\nHello {0}!", you.first);
22:    }
23: }
```

5. Write a class called die that will hold the number of sides of a die, sides, and the current value of a roll, value.

Use the class in Exercise 5 in a program that declares two dice objects. Set values into the side data members. Set random values into the stored roll values. (See Listing 5.3 for help with this program.)

5

DAY 6

Packaging Functionality: Class Methods and Member Functions

Yesterday you learned that a class has several parts. The most important thing you learned, though, is that a class has the capability of defining objects used for storing data and routines. Also, in yesterday's lesson you learned how data is stored. Today you learn about creating, storing, and using routines within your classes. These routines give your objects the power to do what you want. Although storing data can be important, manipulation of the information brings life to your programs. Today you...

- Build methods of your own.
- Pass information to your routines with parameters.
- Re-evaluate the concepts of "by value" and "by reference."
- Understand the concepts of calling methods.

- Discover the truth about constructors.

- Learn to finalize or destruct your classes.

Getting Started with Methods

On previous days, you learned how to store data and how to manipulate this data. You also learned how to manipulate your program's flow. Now you will learn to package this functionality into routines that you can reuse. Additionally, you will learn to associate these routines with the data members of a class.

Routines in C# are called functions or methods. There is no real distinction between these two terms, so you can use them interchangeably.

> **Note**
>
> Most Java, C++ and C# developers refer to routines as methods. Some programmers refer to them as functions. Regardless of what you call them, they all refer to the same thing.

 A *method* is a named piece of independent code that is placed in a reusable format. A method can operate without interference from other parts of an application. If created correctly, it should perform a specific task that is indicated by its name.

As you will learn in today's lesson, methods can return a value. Additionally, methods can have information passed to them.

Using Methods

You have already used a number of methods in this book. Write, WriteLine, and ReadLine are all methods that you've used that are associated with a Console object. Additionally, you have used the Main method in every program you have created. Listing 6.1 presents the Circle class that you have seen before. This time, the routines for calculating the area and circumference have been added to the class as methods.

LISTING 6.1   CircleApp.cs—A Class with Member Methods

```
 1: // CircleApp.cs - A simple circle class with methods
 2: //-----------------------------------------------------
 3:
 4: class Circle
 5: {
 6:     public int x;
 7:     public int y;
```

LISTING **6.1**   continued

```
 8:     public double radius;
 9:
10:     public double getArea()
11:     {
12:         double theArea;
13:         theArea = 3.14159 * radius * radius;
14:         return theArea;
15:     }
16:
17:     public double circumference()
18:     {
19:         double theCirc;
20:         theCirc = 2 * 3.14159 * radius;
21:         return theCirc;
22:     }
23: }
24:
25: class CircleApp
26: {
27:     public static void Main()
28:     {
29:         Circle first  = new Circle();
30:         Circle second = new Circle();
31:
32:         double area;
33:         double circ;
34:         first.x = 10;
35:         first.y = 14;
36:         first.radius = 3;
37:
38:         second.x = 10;
39:         second.y = 11;
40:         second.radius = 4;
41:
42:         System.Console.WriteLine("Circle 1: Center = ({0},{1})",
43:                                  first.x, first.y);
44:         System.Console.WriteLine("          Radius = {0}", first.radius);
45:         System.Console.WriteLine("          Area   = {0}", first.getArea());
46:         System.Console.WriteLine("          Circum = {0}",
47:                                  first.circumference());
48:         area = second.getArea();
49:         circ = second.circumference();
50:
51:         System.Console.WriteLine("\nCircle 2: Center = ({0},{1})",
52:                                  second.x, second.y);
53:         System.Console.WriteLine("          Radius = {0}", second.radius);
54:         System.Console.WriteLine("          Area   = {0}", area);
55:         System.Console.WriteLine("          Circum = {0}", circ);
56:     }
57: }
```

6

OUTPUT

```
Circle 1: Center = (10,14)
          Radius = 3
          Area   = 28.27431
          Circum = 18.84954

Circle 2: Center = (10,11)
          Radius = 4
          Area   = 50.26544
          Circum = 25.13272
```

ANALYSIS   Most of the code in Listing 6.1 should look familiar. The parts that might not seem familiar will be by the end of today's lesson.

Jumping into the listing, you see that Line 4 starts the class definition for the circle. In Lines 6–8, the same three data members that were declared in previous examples are declared. This includes an x and a y value to store the center point of the circle, and the variable radius to store the radius. The class continues after the declaration of the data members.

In Lines 10–15, you see the first definition of a member method. The details of how this method works are covered in the following sections. For now, you can see that the name of this method is getArea. Lines 12–14 are the code within this method; this code calculates the area and returns it to the calling program. Lines 12–13 should look familiar. You'll learn more about Line 14 later today. Lines 17–22 are a second method called circumference, which calculates the value of the circumference and returns it to the calling program.

Line 25 is the beginning of the application class for this listing. Line 27 contains the Main method that is the starting point of the application. This routine creates two circle objects (Lines 29–30) and then assigns values to the data members (Lines 34–40). In Lines 42–43, the data members are printed for the first circle. In Lines 45–46, you see the Console.WriteLine method that you've seen before; the difference is the value that you pass to be printed. In Line 45, you pass first.area(). This is a call to the first class's getArea member method, which was defined in Lines 10–15. The result of calling this method is then printed as the parameter in the WriteLine call.

Line 48 is a little more straightforward. It calls getArea for the second class and assigns the result to the area variable. Line 49 calls the circumference method and assigns its value to circ. These two variables are then printed in Lines 51–55 along with the other members of the second class.

Tip

> You know that getArea in the listing is a member method rather than a data member because the name is followed by parentheses when it is called. You'll learn more about this later.

If you haven't already, you should execute this listing and see what happens. The next few sections detail how to define your own methods and explain the way a method works. Additionally, you will learn how to send and receive values from a method.

Understanding Program Flow with Methods

As you were told earlier, a method is an independent piece of code that is packaged and named so that you can call it from your programs. When a method is called, program flow goes to the method, executes its code, and then returns to the calling routine. Figure 6.1 presents the order of flow for Listing 6.1. You can also see that a method can call another method with the same flow expectations.

FIGURE **6.1**

The program flow of the circle application in Listing 6.1.

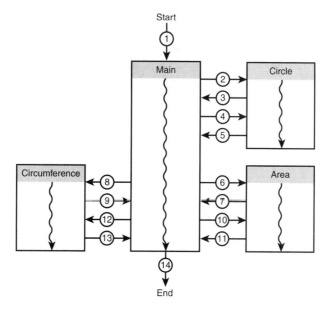

Exploring the Format of a Method

It is important to understand the format of a method. Listing 6.1 has hinted at the format and the procedure for calling a method. The basic format of a method is as follows:

```
Method_header
{
    Method_body
}
```

The Method Header

The method header is the entry point to a method that defines several things about the method:

- The access that programs have to the method
- The return data type of the method
- Any values that are being sent to the method
- The name of the method

In Line 10 of Listing 6.1, you see the header for the `getArea` method:

```
public double getArea()
```

This method is declared as `public`, which means that it can be accessed by programs outside this class. Additionally, you see that the method has a return type of `double`. The method can return one `double` value to the calling program. The method's name is `getArea`. Finally, because the parentheses are empty, no values are sent to this `getArea` method. Instead, it uses values that are data members within the same class. In a few moments, you will send information to the method.

 Caution | The method header does not end with a semicolon. If you place a semicolon at the end of the method header, you get an error.

Returning Data from a Method

A method has the capability to be declared using a return data type. This data type is indicated in the method's header. You can use any valid data type as the return data type for a method.

From within a method's body, a value of this data type must be returned to the program that called the method. To return a value from a method, you use the `return` keyword. The `return` keyword is followed by a value or variable of the same type specified in the header. For example, the `area` method in Listing 6.1 was declared with a return type of `double`. In Line 14 of the listing, the `return` keyword is used to return a variable of type `double`. The value of the `double` is returned to the calling program

What if a method does not need to return a value? What data type is used then? If a method does not return a value, you use the `void` keyword with the method. `void` indicates that no value is to be returned.

Naming Methods

It is important to name your methods appropriately. Several theories exist on naming methods; you need to decide what is best for you or your organization. One general rule is consistent: Always give your methods a meaningful name. If your method calculates and returns the area, the name getArea makes sense, as would names such as CalculateArea and CalcArea. Names such as routine1 or myRoutine make less sense.

One popular guideline for naming methods is to always use a verb/noun combination. Because a method performs some action, you can always use this type of combination. Using this guideline, a name such as area is considered a less useful name; however, the names CalculateArea or CalcArea are excellent choices.

Building the Method Body

The method body contains the code that will be executed when the method is called. This code starts with an opening brace and ends with a closing brace. The code in between can be any of the programming you've already seen. In general, however, the code modifies only the data members of the class that it is a part of or data that has been passed into the method.

If the method header indicates that the method has a return type, the method needs to return a value of that type. As stated earlier, you return a value by using the return keyword. The return keyword is followed by the value to be returned. Reviewing the getArea() method in Listing 6.1, you see that the method body is in Lines 11–15. The area of the circle is calculated and placed into a double field called theArea. In Line 14, this value is returned from the method using the return statement.

 Caution | The data type of the variable returned from a method must match the data type within the header of the method.

6

Using Methods

To use a method, you *call* it. A method is called the same way a data member is called: You enter the object name followed by a period and then the method name. The difference between calling a method and calling data members is that you must also include parentheses and any parameters that are needed. In Listing 6.1, the theArea method is called for the first object with the following code:

```
first.area()
```

As with a variable, if the method has a return type, it is returned to the spot where the method is called. For example, the getArea method returns the area of a circle as a double value. In Line 45 of Listing 6.1, this value is returned as the parameter to another method, Console.WriteLine. In Line 48, the return value from the second object's area method is assigned to another variable called area.

Using Data Members from a Method

The getArea method in Listing 6.1 uses the radius data member without identifying the class or object name. The code for the method is as follows:

```
public double getArea()
{
    double theArea;
    theArea = 3.14159 * radius * radius;
    return theArea;
}
```

Previously, you had to include the name of the object when you used a data member. No object name is included on this use of radius. How can the routine get away with omitting the object name? The answer is simple if you think it through.

When the getArea method is called, it is called using a specific object. If you call getArea with the circle1 object, you are calling the copy of the method within the circle1 object:

```
circle1.getArea()
```

The routine knows that you called with circle1, so all the regular data members and other methods within circle1 are available. You don't need to use the object name because you are within the member method for that specific object.

You also see that additional variables can be declared within a class's member method. These variables are valid only for the time the method is operating. These variables are said to be local to the method. In the case of the getArea method, a double variable called theArea is created and used. When the method exits, the value stored in theArea—as well as theArea—goes away.

Listing 6.2 illustrates the use of a local variable and the program flow.

LISTING 6.2   LocalsApp.cs—Using Local Versus Class Variables

```
1:  //  localsApp.cs - Local variables
2:  //----------------------------------------------------
3:
4:  using System;
5:
6:  class loco
```

LISTING 6.2   continued

```
 7:  {
 8:      public int x;
 9:
10:      public void count_x()
11:      {
12:         int x;
13:
14:         Console.WriteLine("In count_x method. Printing X values...");
15:         for ( x = 0; x <= 10; x++)
16:         {
17:             Console.Write("{0} - ", x);
18:         }
19:         Console.WriteLine("\nAt the end of count_x method. x = {0}", x);
20:      }
21:  }
22:
23:  class LocalsApp
24:  {
25:      public static void Main()
26:      {
27:         loco Locals = new loco();
28:
29:         int x = 999;
30:         Locals.x = 555;
31:
32:         Console.WriteLine("\nIn Main(), x = {0}", x);
33:         Console.WriteLine("Locals.x = {0}", Locals.x);
34:         Console.WriteLine("Calling Method");
35:         Locals.count_x();
36:         Console.WriteLine("\nBack From Method");
37:         Console.WriteLine("Locals.x = {0}", Locals.x);
38:         Console.WriteLine("In Main(), x = {0}", x);
39:  }
40:  }
```

OUTPUT
```
In Main(), x = 999
Locals.x = 555
Calling Method
In count_x method. Printing X values...
0 - 1 - 2 - 3 - 4 - 5 - 6 - 7 - 8 - 9 - 10 -
At the end of count_x method. x = 11

Back From Method
Locals.x = 555
In Main(), x = 999
```

6

ANALYSIS   Listing 6.2 does not contain good names for its variables; however, this listing illustrates a couple of key points that you should understand.

Several variables called x are declared in this listing. This includes a public int x declared in Line 8 as a part of the loco class. A local integer variable x also is declared in Line 12 as part of the count_x method. Finally, a third integer variable called x is declared in Line 29 as part of the Main method. Although all three of these variables have the same name, they are three totally different variables.

The first of these variables, the one in the loco class, is easiest to recognize. It is part of a class. As you've seen already, to use this variable outside the class, you use an object name. This is done in Line 30 of the listing, where an object declared with the name Locals is used to set a value its x data member to 555. The Main routine's x value was set to the value of 999 in Line 29. You can see in Lines 32–33 that these two variables contain their own values and are easy to differentiate from each other.

In Line 35, the Main method calls the count_x method of the Locals object. You can see the count_x method in the loco class. First, in Lines 10–21, a variable called x is declared (Line 12). This value overshadows any previous declarations of x, including the declaration of x in the class. In the rest of the method, this local variable x is used to loop and print numbers. When the loop is done, the value of x is printed one last time before the method ends.

With the end of the method, control is returned to the Main method, where the x variables are printed again. You can see from the output that the Locals data member x was not touched. Additionally, the x variable that was a local within Main retained its value of 999. Each of the variables operated independently.

What happens if you want to work with the class data member x in the count_x method? You learned earlier that within a class's method, you can call a data member without using the object name. In fact, you can't use the object name because it can vary. How, then, can you use the data member x within a method if there is a local variable with the same name—in this case, called x? Listing 6.3 is the previous locals listing, with a slight change.

LISTING 6.3   LocalsApp2.cs—Calling a Data Member Within a Method

```
1:  // LocalsApp2.cs - Local variables
2:  //-------------------------------------------------------
3:
4:  using System;
5:
6:  class loco
7:  {
8:      public int x;
9:
```

LISTING 6.3   continued

```
10:      public void count_x()
11:      {
12:         int x;
13:
14:         Console.WriteLine("In count x method. Printing X values...");
15:         for ( x = 0; x <= 10; x++)
16:         {
17:            Console.Write("{0} - ", x);
18:         }
19:
20:         Console.WriteLine("\nDone looping.  x = {0}", x);
21:         Console.WriteLine("The data member x's value: {0}", this.x);
22:         Console.WriteLine("At the end of count_x method.");
23:      }
24: }
25:
26: class LocalsApp
27: {
28:      public static void Main()
29:      {
30:         loco Locals = new loco();
31:
32:         int x = 999;
33:         Locals.x = 555;
34:
35:         Console.WriteLine("\nIn Main(), x = {0}", x);
36:         Console.WriteLine("Locals.x = {0}", Locals.x);
37:         Console.WriteLine("Calling Method");
38:         Locals.count_x();
39:         Console.WriteLine("\nBack From Method");
40:         Console.WriteLine("Locals.x = {0}", Locals.x);
41:         Console.WriteLine("In Main(), x = {0}", x);
42:      }
43: }
```

OUTPUT
```
In Main(), x = 999
Locals.x = 555
Calling Method
In count_x method. Printing X values...
0 - 1 - 2 - 3 - 4 - 5 - 6 - 7 - 8 - 9 - 10 -
Done looping.  x = 11
The data member x's value: 555
At the end of count_x method.

Back From Method
Locals.x = 555
In Main(), x = 999
```

6

ANALYSIS Line 21 is the unique part of this listing—a value called `this.x` is printed. The
keyword `this` always refers to the current object being used. In this case, `this`
refers to the `Locals` object on which the method was called. Because it refers to the current object, `this.x` refers to the object's x data member—not the local data member. So,
to access a data member from a method within the same class, you use the keyword `this`.

How can the class method access the value of x in the calling program—the local x variable declared in `Main` on Line 32 of Listing 6.3? It can't unless it is passed in as a parameter.

Passing Values to Methods

You now know how to access a method. You also know how to declare local variables
within the method and how to use data members within the same class. What if you want
to use a value, or multiple values, from another class or another method? For example,
suppose that you want a method that multiplies two numbers and returns the result. You
know how to return a single result, but how can you get the two numbers into the
method?

To receive values, the header must have been defined with parameters. The format of a
method header with parameters is as follows:

```
Modifiers ReturnType Name ( Parameters )
```

The parameters are passed within the parentheses of the method. Parameters are optional,
so if no parameters are sent, the parentheses are empty—just as you've seen in the previous examples.

The basic format for each parameter that is used is as follows:

```
[Attribute] Type Name
```

`Type` is the data type of the value being passed, and `Name` is the name of the variable being
passed. Optionally, you can have an attribute, which is covered later in today's lessons.
First, Listing 6.4 presents a simple program that multiplies two numbers and returns the
result.

LISTING 6.4   Mult.cs—Passing Values

```
1: //  MultiApp.cs · Passing values
2: //-------------------------------------------------
3:
4: using System;
5:
```

LISTING 6.4 continued

```
 6: class Multiply
 7: {
 8:     static public long multi( long nbr1, long nbr2 )
 9:     {
10:             return (nbr1 * nbr2);
11:     }
12: }
13: public class MultiApp
14: {
15:     public static void Main()
16:     {
17:         long x = 1234;
18:         long y = 5678;
19:         long a = 6789;
20:         long b = 9876;
21:
22:         long result;
23:
24:         result = Multiply.multi( x, y);
25:         Console.WriteLine("x * y : {0} * {1} = {2}", x, y, result);
26:
27:         result = Multiply.multi(a, b);
28:         Console.WriteLine("a * b : {0} * {1} = {2}", a, b, result);
29:
30:         result = Multiply.multi( 555L, 1000L );
31:         Console.WriteLine("With Long values passed, result is {0}", result);
32:     }
33: }
```

OUTPUT

```
x * y : 1234 * 5678 = 7006652
a * b : 6789 * 9876 = 67048164
With Long values passed, the result was 555000
```

ANALYSIS Listing 6.4 illustrates the point of passing two values; it also illustrates a couple of other items. First, take a look at the method definition in Lines 8–11. This method, called multi, has two parameters. These are each long data types and have been given the names nbr1 and nbr2. These two names are local variables that can be used in this method. In Line 10, the two variables are multiplied, and the resulting value is returned to the caller. In the method header in Line 8, the multi method is declared as a long, so it can return a single long value.

In Lines 24, 27, and 30, you see the multi method called three different times, each with different values. You can pass data variables, as in Lines 24 or 27. You can also pass literal values, as in Line 28. When the multi method is called, the values passed are sent to the method and are referenced with the variable names in the method header. So, for

6

Line 24, x and y are passed to nbr1 and nbr2. In Line 27, a and b are passed to nbr1 and nbr2. In Line 30, the values 555 and 1000 are passed to nbr1 and nbr2. These values are then used by the method.

It is important to note that the number of values sent to the method must match the number of parameters that were defined. In the case of the multi method, you must pass two values. If you don't, you get an error.

Note   There are no default parameters in C#, unlike in some other programming languages.

Working with Static Methods

You learned earlier that the static modifier caused a data member to be associated with a class instead of a specific object of a class. In Listing 6.4, a static method was used. Just as with data members, methods can be associated with the class by using the static modifier. The Multiply class in Listing 6.4 has a static method called multi. Just like with static data members, this method can be called using the class name instead of an object name.

In general, you will not declare your methods as static. If the multi method had not been static, you would have needed to declare a Multiply object to use it. Again, this is just like working with data members.

Access Attributes for Parameters

In the previous example, you passed the values to the method. The method had copies of what was originally passed. These copies were used and then thrown out when the method finished. This passing of values is known as passing by value. Passing by value to a method is only one means of interacting with the method and its parameters. There are three types of access attributes for parameters:

- Value
- Reference
- Out

Note   A method is defined with *parameters*. When you call a method, the values that you pass to the method are called *arguments*. The attributes listed previously are defined with the parameters of a method. As you will see, they impact how the arguments are treated.

Using Value Access on Parameters

As already stated, value access on a parameter refers to when a copy is made of the data being sent to the method. The method then uses a copy of the data being sent. The original values sent to the method are not impacted.

Using Reference Access on Parameters

Sometimes you will want to modify the data stored in the original variable being sent to a method. In this case, you can pass a reference to the variable instead of the variable's value. A reference is a variable that has access to the original variable. If you change the reference, you change the original variable's value as well.

In more technical terms, a reference variable points to a location in memory where the data is stored. Consider Figure 6.2. The variable number is stored in memory. A reference can be created that points to where number is stored. When the reference is changed, it changes the value in the memory, thus also changing the value of the number.

FIGURE 6.2

Reference variables versus value variables.

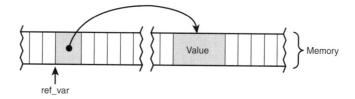

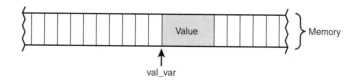

Because a reference variable can point to different places, it is not tied to a specific location in memory like a regular variable is. The reference points to the original variable's location. Any changes to the parameter variable's value also cause a change in the original variable. Each time a method that has a by reference parameter is called, the parameter points to the new variable that is being sent to the routine.

When declaring a parameter, its attribute defaults to the attribute type of the data type. For the basic data types, this is by value. To cause a basic data type, such as an integer, to be passed by reference, you add the ref keyword to the method header before the data type. Listing 6.5 illustrates using the ref keyword and shows the difference between using reference and value parameters. Listing 6.5 calls the method squareByVal and

6

passes a `double`. This `double` is being passed by value. It is followed by calling a method called `squareByRef`, in which a `double` is passed by reference. The difference between these two methods can be seen in the output that results.

Note

> As you learned in Day 2, "Understanding C# Programs," the basic data types are attributed as value types by default. This means that when you create a variable, it is given a specific location in memory where it can store its value. Data types such as classes are reference types by default. This means that the class name contains the address where the data within the class will be located rather than the data itself.

LISTING 6.5   RefVars.cs—Calling a Method by Value Versus by Reference

```
 1: //  RefVars.cs - reference vs by value variables.
 2: //-----------------------------------------------------
 3:
 4: using System;
 5:
 6: class nbr
 7: {
 8:     public double squareByVal( double x )
 9:     {
10:        x = x * x;
11:        return x;
12:     }
13:
14:     public double squareByRef( ref double x )
15:     {
16:        x = x * x;
17:        return x;
18:     }
19: }
20:
21: class RefVars
22: {
23:     public static void Main()
24:     {
25:        nbr doit = new nbr();
26:
27:        double nbr1 = 3;
28:        double retVal = 0;
29:
30:        // Calling method with a by value parameter:
31:        Console.WriteLine("Before square -> nbr1 = {0}, retVal = {1}",
32:                          nbr1, retVal);
33:
```

LISTING 6.5   continued

```
34:         retVal = doit.squareByVal( nbr1 );
35:
36:         Console.WriteLine("After square -> nbr1 = {0}, retVal = {1}",
37:                     nbr1, retVal);
38:
39:         Console.WriteLine("\n---------\n");
40:
41:         // Calling method with a by reference parameter:
42:         retVal = 0;    // reset return value to zero
43:
44:         Console.WriteLine("Before square -> nbr1 = {0}, retVal = {1}",
45:                     nbr1, retVal);
46:
47:         retVal = doit.squareByRef( ref nbr1 );
48:
49:         Console.WriteLine("After square -> nbr1 = {0}, retVal = {1}",
50:                     nbr1, retVal) ;
51:     }
52: }
```

OUTPUT

```
Before square -> nbr1 = 3, retVal = 0
After square -> nbr1 = 3, retVal = 9

---------

Before square -> nbr1 = 3, retVal = 0
After square -> nbr1 = 9, retVal = 9
```

ANALYSIS The output from these two listings tells the story of what is going on. In the squareByVal method (Lines 8–12), references are not used. As a result, the variable that is passed into the square method, var1, is not changed. It remains as the value of 3 both before and after the method is called. In the squareByRef method (Lines 14–18), a reference is passed. As you can see from the output of this listing, the variable passed to the square method is modified.

In the method header for the squareByRef method, the parameter is declared with the ref keyword added (see Line 14). A double is normally a value data type, so to pass it to the method as a reference, you need to add the ref keyword before the variable being passed in. You see this in Line 47.

Caution If you try to call the squareByRef method without passing a reference variable—or using the ref keyword with a value data type—you will get an error when you compile. In the case of the squareByRef method, you get an error saying that a double cannot be converted to a ref double.

6

Using out Access to Parameters

The return type enables you to send back a single variable from a method; however, sometimes you will want more than one value to be returned. Although reference variables could be used to do this, C# has also added a special attribute type specifically for returning data from a method.

You can add parameters to your method header specifically for returning values by adding the out keyword. This keyword signifies that a value is being returned out of the method but is not coming in. When you call a method that has an out parameter, you must be sure to include a variable to hold the value being returned. Listing 6.6 illustrates the use of the out attribute.

LISTING 6.6   Outter.cs—Using the out Attribute

```
 1:  // Outter.cs - Using output variables
 2:  //----------------------------------------------------
 3:
 4:  using System;
 5:
 6:  class nbr
 7:  {
 8:      public void math_routines( double x,
 9:                                 out double half,
10:                                 out double squared,
11:                                 out double cubed )
12:      {
13:          half = x / 2;
14:          squared = x * x;
15:          cubed = x * x * x;
16:      }
17:  }
18:
19:  class Outter
20:  {
21:      public static void Main()
22:      {
23:          nbr doit = new nbr();
24:
25:          double nbr = 600;
26:          double Half_nbr, Squared_nbr Cubed_nbr;
27:
28:          doit.math_routines( nbr, out Half_nbr,
29:                          out Squared_nbr, out Cubed_nbr );
30:          Console.WriteLine("After method -> nbr = {0}", nbr);
31:          Console.WriteLine("            Half_nbr = {0}", Half_nbr);
32:          Console.WriteLine("         Squared_nbr = {0}", Squared_nbr);
33:          Console.WriteLine("           Cubed_nbr = {0}", Cubed_nbr);
34:      }
35:  }
```

OUTPUT

```
After method -> nbr = 600
           Half_nbr = 300
        Squared_nbr = 360000
          Cubed_nbr = 216000000
```

ANALYSIS Two key pieces of code are in Listing 6.6. First is the method header in Lines 8–11. Remember, you can use whitespace to make your code easier to read. This method header has been formatted so that each argument is on a different line. Notice that the first argument, x, is a regular double variable. The remaining three arguments have been declared with the out attribute. This means that no value is being passed into the method. Rather, these three arguments are containers for values to be passed out of the method.

> **Note**
>
> If one of the variables passed to the method already contains a value, it is overwritten.

The second line of code to review is Line 28, the call to the math_routines method. The variables being passed must also be attributed with the out keyword when calling the method. If you leave off the out keyword when calling the method, you get an error.

Overall, the code in this listing is relatively straightforward. The math_routines method within the nbr class does three math calculations on a number. In Lines 30–33, the values are reprinted after having been filled within the math_routines method.

If you don't place a value in an output parameter, you get an error. It's important to know that you must assign a value to all output parameters within a method. For example, comment out Line 14 in Listing 6.6:

```
14:        // squared = x * x;
```

This removes the assignment to the square output variable. When you recompile this listing, you get the following error:

```
outter2.cs(8,17): error CS0177: The out parameter 'squared' must be assigned to
        before control leaves the current method
```

As you can see, if an output parameter is defined, it must be filled.

> **Note**
>
> A variable that is being used as an out variable does not have to be initialized before the method is called.

6

Do	Don't
Do use class and method names that are clear and descriptive.	**Don't** confuse by value variables with reference variables. Remember, passing a variable by value creates a copy. Passing by reference enables you to manipulate the original variable's value.

Types of Class Methods

You have learned the basics of using methods, but you should be aware of a few special types of methods as well:

- Property accessor methods
- Constructors
- Destructors/finalizers

Property Accessor Methods

You've already worked with property accessor methods—set and get. These methods enable you to keep data members private.

Constructors

When an object is first created, often you will want some setup to occur. A special type of method is used specifically for this initial setup—or construction—of objects. This method is called a constructor. Two types of constructors exist: instance constructors, used when each instance or object is created, and static constructors, called before any objects are created for a class.

Instance Constructors

An instance constructor is a method that is automatically called whenever an object is instantiated. This constructor can contain any type of code that a normal method can contain. A constructor is generally used to do initial setup for an object and can include functionality, such as initializing variables.

The format of a constructor is as follows:

```
modifiers classname()
{
    // Constructor body
}
```

This is a method that is defined using the class name that is to contain the constructor. Modifiers are the same modifiers that you can add to other methods. Generally, you use only public. You don't include any return data type.

It is important to note that every class has a default constructor that is called, even if you don't create one. By creating a constructor, you gain the capability to control some of the setup.

The constructor class is automatically called whenever you create an object. Listing 6.7 illustrates using a constructor.

LISTING 6.7   Constr.cs—Using a Constructor

```
 1:  // Constr.cs - constructors
 2:  //-------------------------------------------------------------
 3:
 4:  using System;
 5:
 6:  public class myClass
 7:  {
 8:      static public int sctr = 0;
 9:      public int ctr = 0;
10:
11:      public void routine()
12:      {
13:          Console.WriteLine("In the routine - ctr = {0} / sctr = {1}\n",
14:                            ctr, sctr );
15:      }
16:
17:      public myClass()
18:      {
19:          ctr++;
20:          sctr++;
21:          Console.WriteLine("In Constructor- ctr = {0} / sctr = {1}\n",
22:                            ctr, sctr );
23:      }
24:  }
25:
26:  class TestApp
27:  {
28:      public static void Main()
29:      {
30:          Console.WriteLine("Start of Main method...");
31:
32:          Console.WriteLine("Creating first object...");
33:          myClass first = new myClass();
34:          Console.WriteLine("Creating second object...");
35:          myClass second = new myClass();
```

6

LISTING 6.7   continued

```
36:
37:        Console.WriteLine("Calling first routine...");
38:        first.routine();
39:
40:        Console.WriteLine("Creating third object...");
41:        myClass third = new myClass();
42:        Console.WriteLine("Calling third routine...");
43:        third.routine();
44:
45:        Console.WriteLine("Calling second routine...");
46:        second.routine();
47:
48:        Console.WriteLine("End of Main method");
49:    }
50: }
```

OUTPUT

```
Start of Main method...
Creating first object...
In Constructor- ctr = 1 / sctr = 1

Creating second object...
In Constructor- ctr = 1 / sctr = 2

Calling first routine...
In the routine - ctr = 1 / sctr = 2

Creating third object...
In Constructor- ctr = 1 / sctr = 3

Calling third routine...
In the routine - ctr = 1 / sctr = 3

Calling second routine...
In the routine - ctr = 1 / sctr = 3

End of Main method
```

ANALYSIS   Listing 6.7 illustrates the use of a very simple constructor in Lines 17–23. This listing also helps to again illustrate the use of a static class data member versus a regular data member. In Lines 6–24, a class is defined called myClass. This class contains two data members that can be used as counters. The first data member is declared as static and is given the name sctr. The second data member is not static, so its name is ctr (without the s) .

Note   Remember, a class creates one copy of a static data member that is shared across all objects. For regular data members, each class has its own copy.

The test class contains two routines. The first is a method called routine, which prints a line of text with the current value of the two counters. The second routine has the same name as the class, myClass. Because of this, you automatically know that it is a constructor. This method is called each time an object is created. In this constructor, a couple of things are going on. First, each of the two counters is incremented by 1. For the ctr variable, this is the first time it is incremented because it is a new copy of the variable for this specific object. For sctr, the number might be something else. Because the sctr data member is static, it retains its value across all objects for the given class. The result is that for each copy of the class, sctr is incremented by 1. Finally, in Line 21, the constructor prints a message that displays the value stored in ctr and the value stored in sctr.

The application class for this program starts in Line 26. This class prints messages and instantiates test objects—nothing more. If you follow the messages that are printed in the output, you will see that they match the listing. The one interesting thing to note is that when you call the routine method for the second object in Line 46, the sctr is 3, not 2. Because sctr is shared across all objects, by the time you print this message, you have called the constructor three times.

You should note one final item about the constructor within your listing. Look at Line 33:

```
33:        myClass first = new myClass();
```

This is the line that creates your object. Although the constructor is called automatically, notice the myClass call in this line.

Note   Tomorrow you will learn how to pass parameters to a constructor.

6

Static Constructors

As with data members and methods, you can also create static constructors. A constructor declared with the static modifier is called before the first object is created. It is called only once and then is never used again. Listing 6.8 is a modified version of Listing 6.7. In this listing, a static constructor has been added to the test class.

Notice that this constructor has the same name as the other constructor. Because the static constructor includes the name static, the compiler can differentiate it from the regular constructor.

LISTING 6.8   StatCon.cs—Using a static Constructor

```
 1:  // StatCon.cs - static constructors
 2:  //-----------------------------------------------------------------
 3:
 4:  using System;
 5:
 6:  public class test
 7:  {
 8:      static public int sctr;
 9:      public int ctr;
10:
11:      public void routine()
12:      {
13:          Console.WriteLine("In the routine - ctr = {0} / sctr = {1}\n",
14:                            ctr, sctr );
15:      }
16:
17:      static test()
18:      {
19:          sctr = 100;
20:          Console.WriteLine("In Static Constructor - sctr = {0}\n", sctr );
21:      }
22:
23:      public test()
24:      {
25:          ctr++;
26:          sctr++;
27:          Console.WriteLine("In Constructor- ctr = {0} / sctr = {1}\n",
28:                            ctr, sctr );
29:      }
30:  }
31:
32:  class StatCon
33:  {
34:     public static void Main()
35:     {
36:         Console.WriteLine("Start of Main method...");
37:
38:         Console.WriteLine("Creating first object...");
39:         test first = new test();
40:         Console.WriteLine("Creating second object...");
41:         test second = new test();
42:
43:         Console.WriteLine("Calling first routine...");
```

LISTING 6.8   continued

```
44:            first.routine();
45:
46:            Console.WriteLine("Creating third object...");
47:            test third = new test();
48:            Console.WriteLine("Calling third routine...");
49:            third.routine();
50:
51:            Console.WriteLine("Calling second routine...");
52:            second.routine();
53:
54:            Console.WriteLine("End of Main method");
55:       }
56:   }
```

OUTPUT

```
Start of Main method...
Creating first object...
In Static Constructor - sctr = 100

In Constructor- ctr = 1 / sctr = 101

Creating second object...
In Constructor- ctr = 1 / sctr = 102

Calling first routine...
In the routine - ctr = 1 / sctr = 102

Creating third object...
In Constructor- ctr = 1 / sctr = 103

Calling third routine...
In the routine - ctr = 1 / sctr = 103

Calling second routine...
In the routine - ctr = 1 / sctr = 103

End of Main method
```

ANALYSIS   There is one key difference in the output of this listing from that of Listing 6.7. The third line printed in the output came from the static constructor. This printed the simple line In Static Constructor.... This constructor (in Lines 17–21) initializes the static data member, sctr, to 100 and then prints its message. The rest of the program operates exactly as it did for Listing 7.8. The output differs a little because the sctr variable now starts at 100 rather than at 0.

6

Destructors/Finalizers

You can perform some operations when an object is destroyed. These are accomplished in the destructor.

A destructor is automatically executed at some point after the program is finished using an object. Does "at some point after" sound vague? This is intentional. This destruction can happen from the point at which the object of a class is no longer used up to the point just before the program ends. In fact, it is possible that the program can end without calling the destructor, which means that it would never be called. You don't have any real control over when the destructor will execute; therefore, the value of a destructor is limited.

Caution In languages such as C++, a destructor can be called and the programmer can control when it will perform. This is not the case in C#.

Note From the technical side of things, a destructor is generally called by the C# runtime after an object of a class is no longer in use. The C# runtime normally calls destructors just before checking to see whether any available memory can be freed or released (a concept called garbage collection). If the C# runtime does not do any of this memory checking between the time the object is no longer used and the time the program ends, the destructor will never happen. It is possible to force garbage collection to happen; however, it makes more sense to just limit your use of destructors.

Using a Destructor

A C# destructor is defined by using a tilde (~) followed by the class name and empty parentheses. For example, the destructor for an xyz class is as follows

```
~xyz()
{
    // Destructor body
}
```

There are no modifiers or other keywords to be added to a destructor. Listing 6.9 presents a simpler version of Listing 6.7 with a destructor added.

LISTING 6.9   DestrApp.cs—Using a Destructor

```
 1:  //  DestrApp.cs - constructors
 2:  //-------------------------------------------------------------
 3:
 4:  using System;
 5:
 6:  public class test
 7:  {
 8:      static public int sctr = 0;
 9:      public int ctr = 0;
10:
11:      public void routine()
12:      {
13:         Console.WriteLine("In the routine - ctr = {0} / sctr = {1}",
14:                          ctr, sctr);
15:      }
16:
17:      public test()
18:      {
19:         ctr++;
20:         sctr++;
21:         Console.WriteLine("In Constructor");
22:      }
23:
24:      ~test()
25:      {
26:         Console.WriteLine("In Destructor");
27:      }
28:  }
29:
30:  class DestrApp
31:  {
32:     public static void Main()
33:     {
34:        Console.WriteLine("Start of Main method");
35:
36:        test first = new test();
37:        test second = new test();
38:
39:        first.routine();
40:
41:        test third = new test();
42:        third.routine();
43:
44:        second.routine();          // calling second routine last
45:
46:        Console.WriteLine("End of Main method");
47:     }
48:  }
```

6

```
Start of Main method
In Constructor
In Constructor
In the routine - ctr = 1 / sctr = 2
In Constructor
In the routine - ctr = 1 / sctr = 3
In the routine - ctr = 1 / sctr = 3
End of Main method
In Destructor
In Destructor
In Destructor
```

ANALYSIS The destructor in Lines 24 to 27 is called in the output after the final destruction of each of the objects. In this case, it happened after the Main() method ended; however, there is a chance that this destruction could have never happened.

Note It is worth repeating: Destructors are not guaranteed to happen. You might find that they don't execute when you run Listing 6.9.

Destructors and Finalization

Destructors are often called finalizers because of something that happens internally. A destructor is related to a method called Finalize. The compiler converts your constructor into the correct code for this finalization.

Summary

Today's lessons covered only a few topics; however, these topics are critical to your capability to program in C# and to program an object-oriented language. Yesterday you learned to add data members to your own classes. Today you learned how to add functionality in the form of methods to your classes. You learned that *methods*, *functions*, and *routines* are different terms that ultimately refer to the same thing.

After learning the basics of methods, you reviewed the difference between by value and by reference. You learned how to pass information as arguments to the parameters specified in a method's header. You learned that, by using keywords, such as ref and out, you can change the way the method treats the data passed.

Finally, you learned about a few special types of methods, including constructors and destructors.

In Day 7, "Storing More Complex Stuff: Structures, Enumerators, and Arrays," you expand on what you've learned about methods today. You will explore overloading, delegates, and a number of other more advanced features of methods.

Q&A

Q What is the difference between a parameter and an argument?

A A parameter is a definition of what will be sent to a method. A parameter occurs with the definition of a method in the method head. An argument is a value that is passed to a method. You pass arguments to a method. The method matches the arguments to the parameters that were set in the method definition.

Q Can you create a method outside a class?

A Although in other languages you can create methods that are outside a class, in C# you cannot. C# is object-oriented, so all code must be within the framework of a class.

Q Do methods and classes in C# operate the same way that they do for other languages, such as C++ and Java?

A For the most part, methods and classes operate similarly. However, differences exist between each language. It is beyond the scope of today's lesson to detail this here. As an example of a difference, C# does not allow defaulted parameters within a method. In languages such as C++, you can have a variable within a method default to a specified value if the calling method doesn't supply it. This is not the case with C#. Other differences exist as well.

Q If I'm not supposed to count on destructors, how can I do cleanup code?

A It is recommended that you create your own methods to do cleanup code and that you explicitly call these when you know that you are done with an object. For example, if you have a class that creates a file object, you will want to close the file when you are done with it. Because a destructor might not be called, or might not get called for a very long time, you should create your own closing method. You really don't want to leave the file sitting open longer than you need to.

6

Workshop

The Workshop provides quiz questions to help you solidify your understanding of the material covered and exercises to provide you with experience in using what you've learned. Try to understand the quiz and exercise answers before continuing to the next day's lesson. Answers are provided on the CD.

Quiz

1. What are the two key parts of a method?

2. What is the difference between a function and a method?

3. How many values can be returned from a method?

4. What keyword returns a value from a method?

5. What data types can be returned from a method?

6. What is the format of accessing a member method of a class? For example, if an object called `myObject` is instantiated from a class called `myClass`, which contains a method called `myMethod`, which of the following are correct for accessing the method?

    a. `myClass.myMethod`

    b. `myObject.myMethod`

    c. `myMethod`

    d. `myClass.myObject.myMethod`

7. What is the difference between passing a variable by reference and passing a variable by value?

8. When is a constructor called?

9. What is the syntax for a destructor that has no parameters?

10. When is a destructor called?

Exercises

1. Write the method header for a public method called `xyz`. This method will take no arguments and return no values.

2. Write the method header for a method called `myMethod`. This method will take three arguments as its parameters. The first will be a `double` passed by value, called `myVal`. The second will be an output variable called `myOutput`, and the third will be an integer passed by reference called `myReference`. The method will be publicly accessible and will return a byte value.

3. Using the `circle` class that you saw in Listing 6.1, add a constructor that defaults the center point to (5, 5) and the radius to 1. Use this class in a program that prints with both the defaulted values and prints after you have set values. Instead of printing the circle information from the `Main()` method, create a method to print the circle information.

4. **Bug Buster:** The following code snippet has a problem. Which lines generate error messages?

```
public void myMethod()
{
    System.Console.WriteLine("I'm a little teapot short and stout");
    System.Console.WriteLine("Down came the rain and washed the spider
    ↪out");

    return 0;
}
```

5. Using the dice class that you saw on previous days, create a new program. In this program, create a dice class that has three data members. These should be the number of sides of the dice, the value of the dice, and a static data member that contains the random number class (defined as rnd in previous examples). Declare a member method for this class called roll() that returns the next random value of the die.

6

DAY 7

Storing More Complex Stuff: Structures, Enumerators, and Arrays

You've learned about the basic data types and about classes. C# offers several other ways of storing information in your programs. In today's lesson, you learn about several of these alternative storage methods, including structures, enumerators, and arrays. More specifically, today you...

- Learn how to store values in structures.
- Discover how structures are similar to and different from classes.
- Understand what an enumerator is and how it can be used to make your programs easier to understand.
- See how to declare and use arrays to hold lots of values of the same data type.
- Work with the `foreach` keyword to manipulate arrays.

Working with Structures

Structures are a data type provided by C#. Like classes, structures can contain both data and method definitions. Also like a class, a structure can contain constructors, constants, fields, methods, properties, indexers, operators, and nested types.

Understanding the Difference Between Structures and Classes

Although a lot of similarities exist between classes and structures, there is one primary difference and a few minor differences. The primary difference between a structure and a class is centered on how a structure is stored and accessed. A structure is a value data type, and a class is a reference data type.

Although the difference between value and reference data types was covered before, it is worth covering several more times to ensure that you fully understand the difference. A value data type stores the actual values at the location identified by the data type's name. A reference data type actually stores a location that points to where the information is stored. Figure 7.1 is a repeat of the figure you saw on Day 6, "Packaging Functionality: Class Methods and Member Functions." This figure illustrates the difference between value and reference data type storage.

FIGURE 7.1

Storage by reference versus by value.

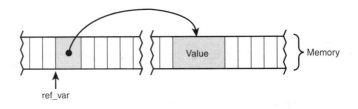

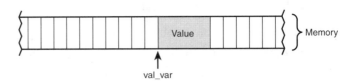

As you can see from Figure 7.1, a reference variable is actually more complicated to store than a value variable. However, the compiler takes care of this complexity for you. Although there are benefits to storing information by reference, this results in extra overhead in memory. If you are storing small amounts of information, the extra overhead can actually outweigh the amount of information being stored.

A structure is stored by value. The overhead of reference is not included, so it is preferred when dealing with small amounts of data or small data values.

When dealing with large amounts of data, a reference type such as a class is a better storage method. This is especially true when passing the data to a method. A reference variable passes only the reference, not the entire data value. A value variable such as a structure is copied and passed to the method. Such copying can cause fat, slower programs if the structures are large.

 Tip   If you need to decide between a class and a structure, and if the total size of the data members being stored is 16 bytes or less, use a structure. If it is greater than 16 bytes, consider how you will use the data.

Structure Members

Declaring members in a structure is identical to declaring data members in a class. The following is a structure for storing a point:

```
struct Point
{
    public int x;
    public int y;
}
```

This is similar to the class you saw on previous days. The only real difference is that the struct keyword is used instead of the class keyword. You can also use this in a listing as you would use a class. Listing 7.1 uses this Point structure.

LISTING 7.1   PointApp.cs—Using a Point Structure

```
 1: // PointApp.cs- A structure with two data members
 2: //-------------------------------------------------------------
 3:
 4: struct Point
 5: {
 6:     public int x;
 7:     public int y;
 8: }
 9:
10: class PointApp
11: {
12:     public static void Main()
13:     {
14:         Point starting = new Point();
```

7

LISTING 7.1   continued

```
15:         Point ending = new Point();
16:
17:         starting.x = 1;
18:         starting.y = 4;
19:         ending.x = 10;
20:         ending.y = 11;
21:
22:         System.Console.WriteLine("Point 1: ({0},{1})",
23:                                 starting.x, starting.y);
24:         System.Console.WriteLine("Point 2: ({0},{1})",
25:                                 ending.x, ending.y);
26:     }
27: }
```

OUTPUT
```
Point 1: (1,4)
Point 2: (10,11)
```

ANALYSIS   The primary difference between using the Point structure and using a class is the struct keyword when defining the class (Line 4). In fact, you could replace the struct keyword with the class keyword, and the listing would still work. As stated earlier, the biggest difference between using a structure and using a class is how they are stored in memory. Figure 7.2 illustrates how a starting Point object from a class could be placed in memory, versus how an instance of the starting Point structure could be stored.

FIGURE 7.2

Storing a starting
Point *structure and a*
class in memory.

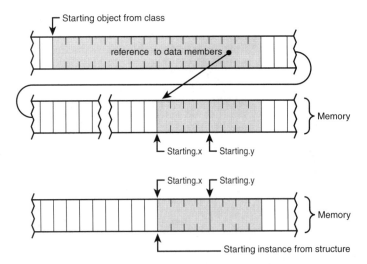

You can also see that members of a structure are accessed in the same manner in which members of a class are accessed. This is by using the name of the structure instance, followed by the member operator (a period), followed by the name of the data member. For example, Line 17 accesses the x data member of the starting instance of the Point structure.

Declaring an instance from a structure can be simpler. Declaring instances from structures does not require you to use the new keyword, which means that Lines 14–15 could be replaced with the following:

```
14:          Point starting;
15:          Point ending;
```

Make this change and recompile Listing 8.1. You will see that the listing still compiles and works. If you replace the struct keyword with the class keyword in this modified version of the listing, the result is an error when you compile:

```
PointApp.cs(17,7): error CS0165: Use of unassigned local variable 'starting'
PointApp.cs(19,7): error CS0165: Use of unassigned local variable 'ending'
```

Nesting Structures

Like classes, structures can contain any other data type, which includes other structures. Listing 7.2 illustrates a Line structure that contains two Point structures.

LISTING 7.2   LineApp.cs—A Line Structure

```
 1:  // line.cs- A line structure which contains point structures.
 2:  //-------------------------------------------------------------
 3:
 4:  struct Point
 5:  {
 6:      public int x;
 7:      public int y;
 8:  }
 9:
10:  struct Line
11:  {
12:      public Point starting;
13:      public Point ending;
14:  }
15:
16:  class LineApp
17:  {
18:      public static void Main()
19:      {
20:          Line myLine;
21:
```

7

LISTING 7.2   continued

```
22:          myLine.starting.x = 1;
23:          myLine.starting.y = 4;
24:          myLine.ending.x = 10;
25:          myLine.ending.y = 11;
26:
27:          System.Console.WriteLine("Point 1: ({0},{1})",
28:                                myLine.starting.x, myLine.starting.y);
29:          System.Console.WriteLine("Point 2: ({0},{1})",
30:                                myLine.ending.x, myLine.ending.y);
31:     }
32:  }
```

OUTPUT
```
Point 1: (1,4)
Point 2: (10,11)
```

ANALYSIS The Line structure is set up similarly to the way the Line class was set up on a previous day. The big difference is that when a line is instantiated, memory is allocated and directly stored.

In this listing, the Point structure is declared in Lines 4–8. In Lines 10–14, a Line structure is declared. Lines 12–13 contain Point structures that are publicly accessible. Each of these has its own x and y point values.

Lines 22–25 set the individual values in the Line structure. To access a value within a nested structure, you follow through the structure hierarchy. Member operators (periods) separate each step in the structure's hierarchy. In the case of Line 22, you are accessing the x data member of the starting point structure in the myLine line structure. Figure 7.3 illustrates the line hierarchy.

FIGURE 7.3

The hierarchy of the line structure.

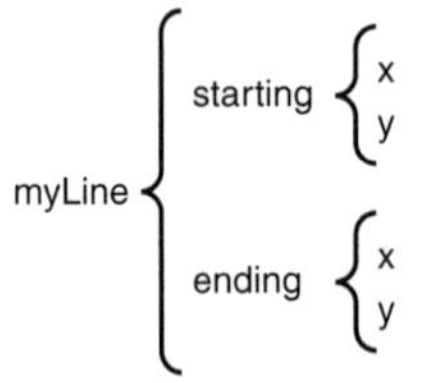

Structure Methods

Like classes, structures can also contain methods and properties. Methods and properties are declared exactly the same as classes. This includes using the modifiers and attributes used with classes. You can overload these methods, pass values, and return values. Listing 7.3 presents the Line class with a length method.

LISTING 7.3   LineApp2.cs—Adding Methods to Structures

```
 1:  //  LineApp2.cs- Adding methods to a structure.
 2:  //--------------------------------------------------------------
 3:
 4:  struct Point
 5:  {
 6:      public int x;
 7:      public int y;
 8:  }
 9:
10:  struct Line
11:  {
12:      public Point starting;
13:      public Point ending;
14:
15:      public double length()
16:      {
17:          double len = 0;
18:          len = System.Math.Sqrt( (ending.x - starting.x)*
             ➡(ending.x - starting.x) +
19:                                  (ending.y - starting.y)*
             ➡(ending.y - starting.y));
20:          return len;
21:      }
22:  }
23:
24:  class LineApp
25:  {
26:      public static void Main()
27:      {
28:          Line myLine;
29:
30:          myLine.starting.x = 1;
31:          myLine.starting.y = 4;
32:          myLine.ending.x = 10;
33:          myLine.ending.y = 11;
34:
35:          System.Console.WriteLine("Point 1: ({0},{1})",
36:                                  myLine.starting.x, myLine.starting.y);
37:          System.Console.WriteLine("Point 2: ({0},{1})",
38:                                  myLine.ending.x, myLine.ending.y);
39:          System.Console.WriteLine("Length of line Point 1 to Point 2: {0}",
40:                                  myLine.length());
41:      }
42:  }
```

7

OUTPUT
```
Point 1: (1,4)
Point 2: (10,11)
Length of from Point 1 to Point 2: 11.4017542509914
```

ANALYSIS Listing 7.3 adds the same `length` method you have seen in listings on previous days. This method is declared in Lines 15–21 within the `Line` structure. As was done previously, this structure uses the data members of the `Line` class to calculate the length of the line. This value is placed in the `len` variable and returned from the method in Line 20 as a `double` value.

The `length` method is used in the `lineApp` class. Its value is output using the `Console.WriteLine` method in Lines 39–40.

Although the `Line` class has only a single method, you could have created a number of methods and properties for the `Line` structure. You could also have overloaded these methods.

Structure Constructors

In addition to having regular methods, structures can have constructors. Unlike classes, if you decide to declare a constructor, you must include declarations with parameters. You cannot declare a constructor for a structure that has no parameters. Listing 7.4 includes the `Point` structure with a constructor added.

LISTING 7.4   PointApp2.cs—A `Point` Class with a Constructor

```
 1:  //  point2.cs- A structure with two data members
 2:  //----------------------------------------------------------------
 3:
 4:  struct Point
 5:  {
 6:      public int x;
 7:      public int y;
 8:
 9:      public Point(int x, int y)
10:      {
11:         this.x = x;
12:         this.y = y;
13:      }
14:  //    public Point() // parameterless constructors not allowed!
15:  //    {
16:  //       this.x = 0;
17:  //       this.y = 0;
18:  //    }
19:  }
20:
21:  class PointApp
22:  {
23:     public static void Main()
24:     {
25:         Point point1 = new Point();
```

LISTING 7.4   continued

```
26:          Point point2 = new Point(8, 8);
27:
28:          point1.x = 1;
29:          point1.y = 4;
30:
31:          System.Console.WriteLine("Point 1: ({0},{1})",
32:                              point1.x, point1.y);
33:          System.Console.WriteLine("Point 2: ({0},{1})",
34:                              point2.x, point2.y);
35:     }
36:  }
```

OUTPUT
```
Point 1: (1,4)
Point 2: (8,8)
```

ANALYSIS   A difference between structures and classes is that a structure cannot declare a constructor with no parameters. In Listing 7.4, you can see that such a constructor has been included in Lines 14–18; however, it has been excluded with comments. If you remove the single-line comments on these lines and compile, you get the following error:

```
PointApp2.cs(14,12): error CS0568: Structs cannot contain explicit parameterless
     constructors
```

Constructors with parameters can be declared. Lines 9–13 declare a constructor that can initialize the point values. The x and y values of the class are set with the x and y values passed into the constructor. To differ the passed-in x and y values from the structure instance x and y variables, the `this` keyword is used in Lines 11–12.

Line 25 illustrates a normal instantiation using the `Point` structure. You could also have instantiated `point1` by just entering this without the `new` operator and empty constructor call:

```
Point point1;
```

Line 26 illustrates using the constructor that you created with parameters.

A constructor in a structure has an obligation: It must initialize all the data members of the structure. When the default (parameterless) constructor of a structure is called, it automatically initializes each data member with its default value. Generally, the data members are initialized to 0s. If your constructor is called instead of this default constructor, you take on the obligation of initializing all the data members.

7

Caution Although you can avoid the new operator when using the default constructor, you cannot avoid it when instantiating an instance of a structure with parameters. Replacing Line 26 of Listing 7.4 with the following line gives you an error:

```
Point point2(8,8);
```

Structure Destructors

Whereas classes can have destructors, structures cannot. Recall that destructors are not to be relied upon in classes even though they are available for you to use. With structures, you cannot declare a destructor—if you try to add one, the compiler gives you an error.

Clarifying with Enumerators

Another type that can be used in C# is enumerators. Enumerators enable you to create variables that contain a limited number of values. For example, there are only seven days in a week. Instead of referring to the days of a week as 1, 2, 3, and so on, it would be much clearer to refer to them as Day.Monday, Day.Tuesday, Day.Wednesday, and so on. You could also have a toggle that could be either on or off. Instead of using values such as 0 and 1, you could use values such as Toggle.On and Toggle.Off.

An enumerator enables you to create these values. Enumerators are declared with the enum keyword. The format of creating an enumerator is as follows:

```
modifiers enum enumName
{
    enumMember1,
    enumMember2,
    ...
    enumMemberN
}
```

modifiers is either the new keyword or the access modifiers (public and private, which you are familiar with, or protected and internal, which you will learn about on later days). enumName is a name for the enumerator that is any valid identifier name. enumMember1, enumMember2 to enumMemberN are the members of the enumeration that contain the descriptive values.

The following declares a toggle enumerator with public access:

```
public enum toggle
{
    On,
```

```
        Off
}
```

The `enum` keyword is used, followed by the name of the enumerator, `toggle`. This enumeration has two values, `On` and `Off`, which are separated by a comma. To use the toggle `enum`, you declare a variable of type `toggle`. For example, the following declares a `myToggle` variable:

```
toggle myToggle;
```

This variable, `myToggle`, can contain two valid values—`On` or `Off`. To use these values, you use the name of the `enum` and the name of the value, separated by the member operator (a period). For example, `myToggle` can be set to `toggle.On` or `toggle.Off`. Using a `switch` statement, you can check for these different values. Listing 7.5 illustrates the creation of an enumerator to store a number of color values.

 Note By default, when an enumerator variable is initially declared, it is set to the value of 0.

LISTING 7.5 Colors.cs—Using an Enumeration

```
 1:  //  Color.cs- Using an enumeration
 2:  //           Note: Entering a nonnumeric number when running this
 3:  //                 program will cause an exception to be thrown.
 4:  //..............................                 ..............
 5:
 6:  using System;
 7:
 8:  class Colors
 9:  {
10:      enum Color
11:      {
12:          red,
13:          white,
14:          blue
15:      }
16:
17:      public static void Main()
18:      {
19:          string buffer;
20:          Color myColor;
21:
22:          Console.Write(
              ➥"Enter a value for a color: 0 = Red, 1 = White, 2 = Blue): ");
23:          buffer = Console.ReadLine();
```

7

LISTING 7.5   continued

```
24:
25:        myColor = (Color) Convert.ToInt32(buffer);
26:
27:        switch( myColor )
28:        {
29:           case Color.red:
30:               System.Console.WriteLine("\nSwitched to Red...");
31:               break;
32:           case Color.white:
33:               System.Console.WriteLine("\nSwitched to White...");
34:               break;
35:           case Color.blue:
36:               System.Console.WriteLine("\nSwitched to Blue...");
37:               break;
38:           default:
39:               System.Console.WriteLine("\nSwitched to default...");
40:               break;
41:        }
42:
43:        System.Console.WriteLine("\nColor is {0} ({1})",
44:                                 myColor, (int) myColor);
44:    }
45: }
```

OUTPUT

Enter a value for a color: 0 = Red, 1 = White, 2 = Blue): **1**

Switched to White...

Color is white (1)

OUTPUT

Enter a value for a color: 0 = Red, 1 = White, 2 = Blue): **5**

Switched to default...

Color is 5 (5)

ANALYSIS   This listing was executed twice for this output. The first time, the value of 1 was entered and recognized as being equivalent to white. In the second execution, the value of 5 was entered, which does not equate to any colors.

Looking closer at the listing, you can see that the Color enumerator was declared in Lines 10–15. This enumerator contains three members: red, white, and blue. When this enumerator is created, the value of 0 is automatically assigned to the first member (red), 1 is assigned to the second (white), and 2 is assigned to the third (blue). By default, all enumerators start with 0 as the first member and are then incremented by one for each additional member.

In Line 20, the enumerator is used to create a variable called `myColor` that can store a value from the `Color` enumerator. This variable is assigned a value in Line 25. The value that is assigned is worthy of some clarification. In Line 22, a prompt is displayed to the screen. In Line 23, the `ReadLine` method of the `Console` class is used to get a value entered by the user. Because the user can enter any value, the program is open to errors. Line 25 assumes that the value entered by the user can be converted to a standard integer. A method called `ToInt32` in the `Convert` class is used to convert the buffer that contains the value entered by the user. This is cast to a `Color` type and placed in the `myColor` variable. If a value other than a number is entered, you get an exception error from the runtime, and the program ends. On Day 9, "Handling Problems in Your Programs: Exceptions and Errors," you will learn one way to handle this type of error gracefully so that a runtime error isn't displayed and your program can continue to operate.

Line 27 contains a `switch` statement that switches based on the value in `myColor`. In Lines 29–35, the `case` statements in the `switch` don't contain literal numbers; they contain the values of the enumerators. The value in the `myColor` enumerator will actually match against the enumerator word values. This `switch` really serves no purpose other than to show you how to switch based on different values of an enumerator.

Line 43 is worth looking at closely. Two values are printed in this line. The first is the value of `myColor`. You might have expected the numeric value that was assigned to the variable to be printed; however, it isn't. Instead, the actual enumerator member name is printed. For the value of `1` in `myColor`, the value `white` is printed—not `1`. If you want the numeric value, you must explicitly force the number to print. This is done in Line 43 using a cast.

Changing the Default Value of Enumerators

The default value set to an enumerator variable is `0`. Even though this is the default value assigned to an enumerator variable, an enumerator does not have to have a member that is equal to `0`. Earlier, you learned that the values of the members in an enumerator definition start at `0` and are incremented by one. You can actually change these default values. For example, you will often want to start with the value of `1` rather than `0`.

You have two options for creating an enumerator with values that start at `1`. First, you can put a filler value in the first position of the enumerator. This is an easy option if you want the values to start at `1`; however, if you want the values of the enumerator to be larger numbers, this can be a bad option.

The second option is to explicitly set the value of your enumerator members. You can set these with literal values, the value of other enumerator members, or calculated values.

7

Listing 7.6 doesn't do anything complex for setting the values of an enumerator. Instead, it starts the first value at 1 rather than 0.

LISTING 7.6   Bday.cs—Setting the Numeric Value of Enumerator Members

```
 1:  //  Bday.cs- Using an enumeration, setting default values
 2:  //-------------------------------------------------------------------
 3:
 4:  using System;
 5:
 6:  public class Bday
 7:  {
 8:     enum Month
 9:     {
10:        January = 1,
11:        February = 2,
12:        March = 3,
13:        April = 4,
14:        May = 5,
15:        June = 6,
16:        July = 7,
17:        August = 8,
18:        September = 9,
19:        October = 10,
20:        November = 11,
21:        December = 12
22:     }
23:
24:     struct birthday
25:     {
26:        public Month bmonth;
27:        public int   bday;
28:        public int   byear;
29:      }
30:
31:     public static void Main()
32:     {
33:        birthday MyBirthday;
34:
35:        MyBirthday.bmonth = Month.August;
36:        MyBirthday.bday = 11;
37:        MyBirthday.byear = 1981;   // This is a lie...
38:
39:        System.Console.WriteLine("My birthday is {0} {1}, {2}",
40:            MyBirthday.bmonth, MyBirthday.bday, MyBirthday.byear);
41:     }
42:  }
```

OUTPUT

My birthday is August 11, 1981

ANALYSIS

This listing creates an enumerator type called Month. This enumerator type contains the 12 months of the year. Rather than using the default values, which would be from 0 to 11, this definition forces the values to be the more expected numbers of 1 to 12. Because the values would be incremented based on the previous value, it is not necessary to explicitly set February to 2 or any of the additional values; it is done here for clarity. You could just as easily have set these values to other numbers. You could even have set them to formulas. For example, June could have been set to this:

```
May + 1
```

Because May is considered equal to 5, this would set June to 6.

The Month enumerator type is used in Line 35 to declare a public data member within a structure. This data member, called bmonth, is declared as a public Month type. In Line 33, the structure, called birthday, is used to declare a variable called MyBirthday. The data members of this structure instance are then assigned values in Lines 26–28. The bmonth variable is assigned the value of Month.August. You could also have done the following to cast August to the MyBirthday.bmonth variable; however, the program would not have been as clear:

```
MyBirthday.bmonth = (Month) 8;
```

In Line 39, you again see that the value stored in MyBirthday.bmonth is August rather than a number.

Changing the Underlying Type of an Enumerator

In the examples so far, the underlying data type of the enumerators has been of type int. Enumerators can actually contain values of type byte, sbyte, int, uint, short, ushort, long, and ulong. If you don't specify the type, the default is type int. If you know that you need to have larger or smaller values stored in an enum, you can change the default underlying type to something else.

To change the default type, you use the following format:

```
modifiers enum enumName : typeName { member(s) }
```

This is the same definition as before, with the addition of a colon and the *typeName*, which is any of the types mentioned previously. If you change the type, you must make sure that any assigned values are of that type.

Listing 7.7 illustrates a new listing using the color enumerator shown earlier. This time, because the values are small, the enumerator is set to use bytes, to save a little memory.

7

LISTING 7.7   Colors2—Displaying Random Byte Numbers

```
 1:  // Colors2.cs- Using enumerations
 2:  //-----------------------------------------------------------------
 3:
 4:  using System;
 5:
 6:  class Colors2
 7:  {
 8:     enum Color : byte
 9:     {
10:         red,
11:         white,
12:         blue
13:     }
14:
15:     public static void Main()
16:     {
17:        Color myColor;
18:        byte   roll;
19:
20:        System.Random rnd = new System.Random();
21:
22:        for ( int ctr = 0; ctr < 10; ctr++ )
23:        {
24:           roll = (byte) (rnd.Next(0,3)); // random nbr from 0 to 2
25:           myColor = (Color) roll;
26:
27:           System.Console.WriteLine("Color is {0} ({1} of type {2})",
28:                   myColor, (byte) myColor, myColor.GetTypeCode());
29:        }
30:     }
31: }
```

OUTPUT

```
Color is white (1 of type Byte)
Color is white (1 of type Byte)
Color is red (0 of type Byte)
Color is white (1 of type Byte)
Color is blue (2 of type Byte)
Color is red (0 of type Byte)
Color is red (0 of type Byte)
Color is red (0 of type Byte)
Color is blue (2 of type Byte)
Color is red (0 of type Byte)
```

Note   Your output will vary from this because of the random generator.

ANALYSIS This listing does more than just declare an enumerator using a byte; you'll see this in a minute. First, look at Line 8. You can see that, this time, the Color enumerator type is created using bytes instead of type int values. You know this because of the inclusion of the colon and the byte keyword. This means that Color.red will be a byte value of 0, Color.white will be a byte value of 1, and Color.blue will be a byte value of 2.

In the Main method, this listing's functionality is different from the earlier listing. This listing uses the random logic that you have seen already. In Line 24, you can see that a random number from 0 to 2 is created and explicitly cast as a byte value into the roll variable. The roll variable was declared as a byte in Line 18. This roll variable is then explicitly cast to a Color type in Line 25 and is stored in the myColor variable.

Note

The Rnd.Next method returns a value that is equal to or greater than the first parameter, and less than the second parameter. In this example, it returns a value that is 0 or larger, yet less than 3.

Line 27 starts out similarly to what you have seen already. The WriteLine method is used to print the value of the myColor variable (which results in either red, white, or blue). This is followed by printing the numeric value using the explicit cast to byte. The third value being printed, however, is something new.

Enumerators are objects. Because of this, some built-in methods can be used on enumerators. The one that you will find most useful is the GetTypeCode method, which returns the type of the variable stored. For myColor, the return type is Byte, which is displayed in the output. If you add this parameter to one of the previous two listings, you will find that it prints Int32. Because the type is being determined at runtime, you get a .NET Framework data type instead of the C# data type.

Tip

To determine other methods of enumerators, check out the .NET Framework documentation. Look up the Enum class.

Do	Don't
Do use commas—not semicolons—to separate enumerator members.	**Don't** place filler values as enumerator members.

7

Using Arrays to Store Data

You've learned that you can store different types of related information together in classes and structure. Sometimes you will want to store a bunch of information that is the same data type. For example, a bank might keep track of monthly balances, or a teacher might want to keep track of the scores from a number of tests.

If you need to keep track of a number of items that are of the same data type, the best solution is to use an array. If you want to keep track of balances for each of the 12 months, without arrays you could create 12 variables to track these numbers:

```
decimal Jan_balance;
decimal Feb_balance;
decimal Mar_balance;
decimal Apr_balance;
decimal May_balance;
decimal Jun_balance;
decimal Jul_balance;
decimal Aug_balance;
decimal Sep_balance;
decimal Oct_balance;
decimal Nov_balance;
decimal Dec_balance;
```

To use these variables, you must determine which month it is and then switch among the correct variables. This requires several lines of code and could include a large switch statement, such as the following:

```
...
switch (month)
{
   case 1:  // do January stuff
            Jan_balance += new_amount;
            break;
   case 2:  // do February stuff
            Feb_balance += new_amount;
            break;
...
```

This is obviously not the complete switch statement; however, it is enough to see that a lot of code needs to be written to determine and switch among the 12 monthly balances.

> **Note**
>
> Although you could use an enumerator to make the switch statement more readable, this would still result in a lot of code to track and use the individual values.

Using an array, you can create much more efficient code. In this example, you could create an array of decimals to keep track of the monthly balances.

Creating Arrays

An array is a single data variable that can store multiple pieces of data that are each of the same data type. Each of these elements is stored sequentially in the computer's memory, thus making it easy to manipulate them and navigate among them.

Note

Because you declare one piece of data—or variable—after the other in a code listing does not mean that they will be stored together in memory. In fact, variables can be stored in totally different parts of memory, even though they are declared together. An array is a single variable with multiple elements. Because of this, an array stores its values one after the other in memory.

To declare an array, you use the square brackets after the data type when you declare the variable. The basic format of an array declaration is as shown here:

```
datatype[] name;
```

datatype is the type for the information you will store. The square brackets indicate that you are declaring an array, and the *name* is the name of the array variable. The following definition sets up an array variable called `balances` that can hold decimal values:

```
decimal[] balances;
```

This declaration creates the variable and prepares it to be capable of holding decimal values; however, it doesn't actually set aside the area to hold the variables. To do that, you need to do the same thing you do to create other objects, which is to initialize the variable using the `new` keyword. When you instantiate the array, you must indicate how many values will be stored. One way to indicate this number is to include the number of elements in square brackets when you do the initialization:

```
balances = new decimal[12];
```

You also can do this initialization at the same time that you define the variable:

```
decimal[] balances = new decimal[12];
```

As you can see, the format for initializing is as follows:

```
new datatype[nbr_of_elements]
```

7

datatype is the same data type of the array, and *nbr_of_elements* is a numeric value that indicates the number of items to be stored in the array. In the case of the `balances` variable, you can see that 12 decimal values can be stored.

New Term After you've declared and initialized an array, you can begin to use it. Each item in an array is called an *element*. Each element within the array can be accessed by using an index. An *index* is a number that identifies the offset—and, thus, the element—within the array.

The first element of an array is identified with an index of `0` because the first element is at the beginning of the array, and, therefore, there is no offset. The second element is indexed as `1` because it is offset by one element. The final index is at an offset that is one less than the size of the array. For example, the `balances` array declares 12 elements. The last element of the array will have an index of `11`.

To access a specific element within an array, you use the array name followed by the appropriate index within square brackets. To assign the value of `1297.50` to the first element of the `balances` array, you do the following (note that the `m` after the number indicates that it is a decimal):

```
balances[0] = 1297.50m;
```

To assign a decimal value to the third element of the `balances` array, you do the following:

```
balances[2] = 1000m;
```

The index of `2` is used to get to the third element. Listing 7.8 illustrates using the balances array; Figure 7.4 illustrates the concept of elements and indexes. This figure uses a simpler array of three characters, which are declared as follows:

```
char[] initials = new char[3];
```

FIGURE 7.4

An array in memory and its indexes.

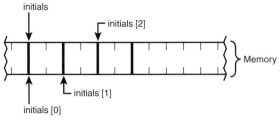

Caution   It is a very common mistake to forget that array indexes start at 0, not 1. In some languages, such as Visual Basic, you can start with an index of 1; however, most languages, including C#, start with an index of 0.

LISTING 7.8   Balances.cs—Using Arrays

```
 1: //  Balances.cs - Using a basic array
 2: //-----------------------------------------------------------------
 3:
 4: using System;
 5:
 6: public class Balances
 7: {
 8:    public static void Main()
 9:    {
10:       decimal[] balances = new decimal[12];
11:
12:       decimal ttl = 0m;
13:       System.Random rnd = new System.Random();
14:
15:       // Put random values from 0 to 100000 into balances array
16:
17:       for (int indx = 0; indx < 12; indx++ )
18:       {
19:          balances[indx] = (decimal) (rnd.NextDouble() * 10000);
20:       }
21:
22:       //values are initialized in balances
23:
24:       for( int indx = 0; indx < 12; indx++ )
25:       {
26:          Console.WriteLine("Balance {0}: {1}", indx, balances[indx]);
27:          ttl += balances[indx];
28:       }
29:
30:       Console.WriteLine("=================================");
31:       Console.WriteLine("Total of Balances = {0}", ttl);
32:       Console.WriteLine("Average Balance = {0}", (ttl/12));
33:    }
34: }
```

OUTPUT
```
Balance 0: 2276.50146106095
Balance 1: 4055.29556984794
Balance 2: 6192.0053633824
Balance 3: 2651.45477496621
Balance 4: 5885.39904257534
```

7

```
Balance 5: 2200.59107160223
Balance 6: 664.596651058922
Balance 7: 1079.63573237864
Balance 8: 2359.02580076783
Balance 9: 9690.85962031542
Balance 10: 934.673115114995
Balance 11: 7248.27192595614
==================================
Total of Balances = 45238.310129027017
Average Balance = 3771.54250645135085
```

ANALYSIS   Listing 7.8 illustrates the use of a basic array called `balances`. In Line 10, `balances` is declared as an array of decimal values. It is instantiated as a decimal array containing 12 elements. This listing creates a `Random` object called `rnd` (Line 13), which—as you've already seen—is used to create random numbers to store in the array. This assignment of random numbers occurs in Lines 17–20. Using an index counter, `indx`, this `for` loop goes from 0 to 11. This counter is then used as the index of the array in Line 19. The `NextDouble` method of the `Random` class returns a number between 0 and 1. To get a number between 0 and 10,000, the returned number is simply multiplied by 10,000.

After the values have been assigned, Lines 24–28 loop through the array a second time. Technically, this loop is redundant; however, you generally wouldn't get your values elsewhere than assigning random numbers. In this second `for` loop, each of the `balance` items is written to the console (Line 26). In Line 27, each `balance` array elements is added to a total called `ttl`. Lines 31–32 provide some summary information regarding the random balances. Line 31 prints the total of the balances. Line 32 prints the average of each.

The `balances` array is much simpler than the code would have been if you had had to use 12 different variables. When you use the indexes with the array name, such as `balance[2]`, it is like using a regular variable of the same data type.

Initializing Array Elements

You can initialize the values of the individual array elements at the same time that you declare and initialize the array. You can do this by declaring the values after the array declaration. The values are enclosed in a block and are separated by a comma. To initialize the values of the `balances` array, you do the following

```
decimal[] balances = new decimal[12] {1000.00m, 2000.00m, 3000.00m, 4000.00m,
                              5000m, 6000m, 0m, 0m, 9m, 0m, 0m, 12000m};
```

This declaration creates the `balances` array and preassigns values into it. The first value of 1000.00 is placed into the first element, `balances[0]`. The second value, 2000.00, is placed into the second element, `balances[1]`. The rest of the values are placed in the same manner.

It is interesting to note that if you initialize the values in this manner, you do not have to include the array size in the brackets. The following statement is equivalent to the previous statement:

```
decimal[] balances = new decimal[] {1000.00m, 2000.00m, 3000.00m, 4000.00m,
                                    5000m, 6000m, 0m, 0m, 9m, 0m, 0m, 12000m};
```

The compiler automatically defines this array as 12 elements because that is the number of items being initialized. Listing 7.9 creates and initializes a character array.

> **Note**
>
> You are not required to initialize all the values if you include the number of elements in your declaration. The following line of code is valid; the resulting array will have 12 elements, with the first 2 elements being initialized to 111:
>
> ```
> decimal[] balances = new decimal[12] {111m, 111m};
> ```
>
> However, if you don't include the number of elements, you can't add more later. In the following declaration, the `balances` array can hold only two elements; it cannot hold more than two.
>
> ```
> decimal[] balances = new decimal[] {111m, 111m};
> ```

LISTING 7.9   Fname.cs—Using Arrays

```
 1:  // Fname.cs - Initializing an array
 2:  //-------------------------------------------------------------------
 3:
 4:  using System;
 5:
 6:  public class Fname
 7:  {
 8:     public static void Main()
 9:     {
10:        char[] name = new char[] {'B','r','a','d','l','e','y', (char) 0 };
11:
12:        Console.WriteLine("Display content of name array...");
13:
14:        int ctr = 0;
15:        while (name[ctr] != 0)
16:        {
17:           Console.Write("{0}", name[ctr]);
18:           ctr++;
19:        }
```

7

LISTING 7.9   continued

```
20:          Console.WriteLine("\n...Done.");
21:     }
22: }
```

OUTPUT
```
Display content of name array...
Bradley
...Done.
```

ANALYSIS Listing 7.9 creates, initializes, and instantiates an array of characters called `name` in Line 10. The `name` array is instantiated to hold eight elements. You know it can hold eight elements, even though this is not specifically stated, because eight items were placed into the array when it was declared.

This listing does something that you have not seen in previous listings. It puts a weird value (a character value of 0) in the last element of the array. This weird value is used to signal the end of the array. In Lines 14–19, a counter called `ctr` is created for use as an index. The `ctr` is used to loop through the elements of the array until a character value of 0 is found. Then the `while` statement evaluates to `false` and the loop ends. This prevents you from going past the end of the array, which would result in an error.

Working with Multidimensional Arrays

A multidimensional array is an array of arrays. You can even have an array of arrays of arrays. The number of levels can quickly add up. This starts getting complicated, so I recommend that you don't store more than three levels (or three dimensions) of arrays.

An array of arrays is often referred to as a two-dimensional array because it can be represented in two dimensions. To declare a two-dimensional array, you expand on what you do with a regular (or one-dimensional) array:

```
byte[,] scores = new byte[15,30];
```

A comma is added to the first part of the declaration, and two numbers separated by a command are used in the second part. This declaration creates a two-dimensional array that has 15 elements, each containing an array of 30 elements. In total, the `scores` array holds 450 values of the data type `byte`.

To declare a simple multidimensional array that stores a few characters, you enter the following:

```
char[,] letters = new char[2,3];  // without initializing values
```

This declaration creates a two-dimensional array called `letters`, which contains two elements that are each arrays that have three character elements. You can initialize the elements within the `letters` array at declaration time:

```
char[,] letters = new char[,] { {'a','b','c'},
                                {'X','Y','Z'} };
```

Or, you can initialize each element individually. To access the elements of a multi-dimensional array, you again use the indexes. The first element of the `letters` array is `letters[0,0]`. Remember, the indexes start at offset 0, not 1. `letters[0,1]` is the second element, which contains the letter `'b'`. The letter `'X'` is `letter[1,0]` because it is in the second array (offset 1) and is the first element (offset 0). To initialize the letters array outside the declaration, you could do the following:

```
letters[0,0] = 'a';
letters[0,1] = 'b';
letters[0,2] = 'c';
letters[1,0] = 'X';
letters[1,1] = 'Y';
letters[1,2] = 'Z';
```

Creating an Array Containing Different-Size Arrays

In the previous section, an assumption was made that in a two-dimensional array, all the subarrays are the same size. This would make the arrays rectangular. What happens if you want to store arrays that are not the same size? Consider the following:

```
char[][] myname = new char[3][];
        myname[0] = new char[] { 'B', 'r', 'a', 'd', 'l', 'e', 'y'};
        myname[1] = new char[] { 'L', '.' };
        myname[2] = new char[] { 'J', 'o', 'n', 'e', 's' };
```

The `myname` array is an array of arrays. It contains three character arrays that are each a different length. Because they are different lengths, you work with their elements differently from the rectangular arrays that you saw before. Figure 7.5 illustrates the `myname` array.

Instead of addressing each element by using index values separated by commas, you instead separate the elements into their own square brackets. For example, the following line of code uses the `WriteLine` method to print the array elements that would be my initials:

```
System.Console.WriteLine("{0}{1}{2}", myname[0][0], myname[1][0], myname[2][0]);
```

It would be wrong to address these as `myname[0,0]`, `myname[1,0]`, and `myname[2,0]`. In fact, you'll get an error if you try to access the elements this way.

7

FIGURE 7.5

An array of different-size arrays.

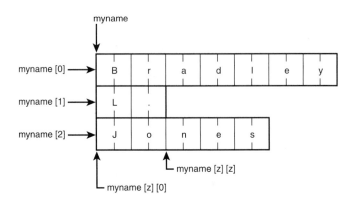

> **Note**
>
> A multidimensional array that contains subarrays of the same size is referred to as *rectangular*. A multidimensional array that has variable-size subarrays stored is referred to as "jagged." In Figure 7.5, you can see where this term comes from.

What happens if you want to declare the `myname` array without initializing it, as was done previously? You know there are three parts to the name, so the first dimension is 3; however, what should the second dimension be? Because of the variable sizes, you must make multiple instantiations to set up the full array. First, you declare the outside array that will hold the arrays:

```
char[][] myname = new char[3][];
```

This declares the `myname` variable as an array with three elements, each holding a character array. After you've done this declaration, you must initialize each of the individual arrays that will be stored in `myname[]`. Figure 7.5 illustrates the `myname` array with the following declarations:

```
myname[0] = new char[7];  // first array of seven elements
myname[1] = new char[2];  // second array of two elements
myname[2] = new char[5];  // third array of five elements
```

Checking Array Lengths and Bounds

Before presenting Listing 7.10 to illustrate the `myname` jagged, multidimensional array, one other item is worth covering: Every array knows its length. The length of an array is stored in a member called `Length`. Like all types in C#, arrays are objects. To get the length of an array, use the `Length` data member. Remember that `Length` is available on any object. The length of a one-dimensional array called `balance` can be obtained from `balance.Length`.

In a multidimensional array, you still use `Length`, or you can use a method of the array called `GetLength()` to get the length of a subarray. You pass the index number of the subarray to identify which length to return. Listing 7.10 illustrates the use of the `Length` member along with a jagged array.

LISTING 7.10   Names.cs—Using a Jagged Two-Dimensional Array

```
 1:  //  Names.cs - Using a two-dimensional array
 2:  //-----------------------------------------------------------
 3:
 4:  using System;
 5:
 6:  public class Names
 7:  {
 8:      public static void Main()
 9:      {
10:          char[][] name = new char[3][];
11:
12:          name[0] = new char[7] {'B', 'r', 'a', 'd', 'l', 'e', 'y'};
13:          name[1] = new char[2] {'L', '.'};
14:          name[2] = new char[5] {'J', 'o', 'n', 'e', 's'};
15:
16:          Console.WriteLine("Display the sizes of the arrays...\n");
17:
18:          Console.WriteLine("Length of name array {0}", name.Length);
19:
20:          for( int ctr = 0; ctr < name.Length; ctr++)
21:              Console.WriteLine("Length of name[{0}] is {1}",
22:                                ctr, name[ctr].Length);
23:  //-----------------------------------------------------------
24:
25:          Console.WriteLine("\nDisplaying the content of the name array...");
26:
27:          for( int ctr = 0; ctr < name.Length; ctr++)
28:          {
29:              Console.Write("\n");  // new line
30:              for( int ctr2 = 0; ctr2 < name[ctr].Length; ctr2++ )
31:              {
32:                  Console.Write("{0}", name[ctr][ctr2]);
33:              }
34:          }
35:          Console.WriteLine("\n...Done displaying");
36:      }
37:  }
```

7

```
Display the sizes of the arrays...

Length of name array 3
Length of name[0] is 7
Length of name[1] is 2
Length of name[2] is 5

Displaying the content of the name array...

Bradley
L.
Jones
...Done displaying
```

ANALYSIS Let's look at this listing in parts. The first part comprises Lines 10–14. In Line 10, a two-dimensional array called name is declared that contains three arrays of characters of possibly different lengths. In Lines 12–14, each of these arrays is instantiated. Although the size of the arrays is included in the square brackets, because the arrays are being initialized, you do not have to include the numbers. It is good practice to include the numbers, however, to be explicit in what you want.

The second part of this listing illustrates the Length member of the arrays. In Line 18, the length of the name array is printed. You might have expected this to print 14; however, it prints 3. The Length member actually prints the number of elements. Three elements are in the name array, and these three elements are each arrays.

In Line 20, the Length member of the name array—which you now know is 3 in this example—is used as the upper limit for looping through each of the arrays. Using an index counter, the length method of each of the subarrays is printed. You can see that these values match what was declared.

The third part of this listing comprises Lines 27–34. This portion of the listing displays the values stored in the individual names. This code has been set up to be dynamic by checking the Length member for each of the subarrays rather than hard-coding any values. If you change the code in Lines 12–14, the rest of this listing still works.

Using Arrays in Classes and Structures

An array is just another type that can be used to create variables. Arrays can be placed and created anywhere other data types can be used. This means that arrays can be used in structures, classes, and other data types.

> **Note**   Although basic data types are used in today's lesson, you can actually create arrays of any of the data elements. You can create arrays using classes, structures, or any other data type.

Using the `foreach` Statement

It's time to address the keyword `foreach`, as promised on Day 4, "Controlling Your Program's Flow." The `foreach` keyword can be used to simplify working with arrays, especially when you want to loop through an entire array. Additionally, instead of using the array name with a subscript, you can use a simple variable to work with the array. The downside of the `foreach` statement is that the simple variable that you get to use is read-only—you can't do assignments to it. The format of the `foreach` command is shown here:

```
foreach( datatype varname in arrayName )
{
    statements;
}
```

`datatype` is the data type for your array. `varname` is a variable name that can be used to identify the individual element of the array. `arrayName` is the name of the array that `foreach` is looping through. Listing 7.11 illustrates using `foreach` to loop through a name array.

LISTING 7.11   ForEach1.cs—Using `foreach` with an Array

```
 1:  // ForEach1.cs - Initializing an array
 2:  //----------------------------------------------------------------
 3:
 4:  using System;
 5:
 6:  public class ForEach1
 7:  {
 8:     public static void Main()
 9:     {
10:         char[] name = new char[] {'B','r','a','d','l','e','y'};
11:
12:         Console.WriteLine("Display content of name array...");
13:
14:         foreach( char x in name )
15:         {
16:             Console.Write("{0}", x);
17:         }
18:
```

7

LISTING 7.11   continued

```
19:        Console.WriteLine("\n...Done.");
20:    }
21: }
```

OUTPUT
Display content of name array...
Bradley
...Done.

ANALYSIS This listing is shorter than the earlier listing. The big focus is in Line 14, which uses the `foreach` keyword to loop through the name array. It loops through each element of the name array and then ends. As it loops, it refers to the individual elements as `x`. In the code in the statements of the `foreach`, you don't have to use `array[index_ctr]`; instead, you use `x`.

Tip

As a reminder, your variable names should be descriptive. The name `x` was used here to keep things simple. A better variable name would have been something like `Letter`.

Summary

Today's lesson covered three key advanced data types: the structure, the enumeration, and the array. You learned that structures operate similarly to classes, with the big difference being that structures are a value type and classes are a reference type. You learned that enumerations—declared with the `enum` keyword—are useful for making your code more readable. Enumerations enable you to create data types that take a range of values that you can control. Additionally, you can give these values more usable names.

In the final lesson today, you learned how to create arrays. You also learned that arrays can have multiple dimensions. On arrays with more than one dimension, you can set the subarrays to have the same size of array (a rectangular array), or you can assign arrays of different sizes (a jagged array).

Today's lesson concluded by covering the `foreach` keyword. You learned how this keyword makes working with arrays much easier.

Q&A

Q Are there other differences between structures and classes that were not mentioned in today's lesson?

A Yes, there are a few other differences that were not mentioned in today's lesson. You now know that structures are stored by value and that classes are stored by references. You also learned that a structure can't have a parameterless constructor. A structure is also not allowed to have a destructor. In addition to these differences, a structure is also different in that it is implicitly sealed. This concept will be explained when you learn about inheritance.

Q I've heard that enumerators can be used with bit fields. How is this done?

A This is a more advanced topic that isn't covered in this book. You can use an enumerator to store the values of a bit. This can be done by using byte members and setting each of the members of the enumerator to one of the positions of the bits in the byte. The enumerator could be this:

```
enum Bits : byte
{
    first = 1,
    second = 2,
    third = 4,
    fourth = 8,
    fifth = 16,
    sixth = 32,
    seventh = 64,
    eighth = 128
}
```

You could then use bitwise operators to do bitwise math using these predefined values.

Q Is an enumerator a value type or a reference type?

A When a variable is declared as an enumerator, it is a value type. The value is actually stored in the enumerator variable.

Q How many dimensions can you store in an array?

A You can store more dimensions than you should. If you declare an array that is more than three dimensions, one of two things happens: Either you waste a lot of memory because you are using rectangular arrays, or your code gets much more complicated. In almost all cases, you can find simpler ways to work with your information that don't require arrays of more than three dimensions.

7

Workshop

The Workshop provides quiz questions to help you solidify your understanding of the material covered and exercises to provide you with experience in using what you've learned. Try to understand the quiz and exercise answers before continuing to the next day's lesson. Answers are provided on the CD.

Quiz

1. What is the difference between a value data type and a reference data type? Which is a structure?

2. What are the differences between a structure and a class?

3. How are structure constructors different from class constructors? (Or are they?)

4. What keyword is used to define an enumeration?

5. What data types can be stored in an enumerator?

6. What is the index value of the first element in an array?

7. What happens if you access an element of an array with an index larger than the number of elements in the array?

8. How many elements are in the array declared as `myArray[4,3,2]`? If this is a character array, how much memory will be used?

9. How can you tell the size of an array?

10. True or false (if false, tell what is wrong): The format of the `foreach` contains the same structure as the `for` statement.

Exercises

1. Modify the `point` and `line` structures used in Listing 7.3 to include properties for the data members.

2. **On Your Own:** Modify the line structure to include a static data value that contains the longest line ever stored. This value should be checked and updated whenever the length method is called.

3. **Bug Buster:** The following code snippet has a problem. Can you fix it? (Assume that `myArray` is an array of decimal values.)

```
foreach( decimal Element in myArray )
{
    System.Console.WriteLine("Element value is: {0}", Element);
    Element *= Element;
    System.Console.WriteLine("Element squared is: {0}", Element);
}
```

4. Write a program for a teacher. The program should have an array that can hold the test scores for 30 students. The program can randomly assign grades from 1 to 100. Determine the average score for the class.

5. Modify the listing that you create in Exercise 4 to keep track of scores for 15 tests used throughout a semester. It should keep track of these tests for the 30 students. Print the average score for each of the 15 tests, and print each student's average score.

6. Modify the listing in Exercise 5 to keep track of the same scores for five years. Do this with a three-dimensional array.

7

WEEK 1

Week in Review

Congratulations! You have finished your first week of learning C#. During this week, you built the foundation for all of the C# applications you will build. You learned how to store basic data, control the flow of the program, repeat pieces of code, and create classes that can store both data and methods—and you've learned a lot more.

Most of the listings and programs you have seen focus on only a single concept. The following code pulls together into a single listing the things you learned this past week. As you can see, when you pull it all together, the listing gets a bit longer.

When you execute this listing, you are presented with a menu on the console from which you can make a selection. This selection is then used to create a class and execute some code.

Note

This listing doesn't use anything that you haven't learned already. Over the next two weeks, you will learn ways to improve this listing. Such improvements will include better ways of performing some of the functionality, other ways to retrieve and convert data from the users, and much more. During Week 3, you'll even learn how to do menuing and such using windows forms.

1

2

3

4

5

6

7

The WR01.cs Program

Enter, compile, and execute the WR01.cs listing. XML comments have been added to the listing. This means that you can produce XML documentation by including the /doc compiler switch that you learned about on Day 2, "Understanding C# Programs."

Note Although I believe the best way to learn is by typing a listing and making mistakes, the source code for the listings in this book are available on the CD as well as at www.TeachYourselfCSharp.com.

LISTING WR1.1 WR01App.cs—Week 1 in Review

```
CH 2     1: //  File:  WR01App.cs
         2: //  Desc:  Week One In Review
         3: //         This program presents a menu and lets the user select a
         4: //         choice from a menu. Based on this choice, the program then
         5: //         executes a set of code that either manipulates a shape or
         6: //         exits the program.
         7: //----------------------------------------------------------------
         8:
CH 6     9: using System;
        10:
        11: //--------------------------------------------------------------
CH 2    12: /// <summary>
CH 2    13: /// This is a point structure. It is for storing and
        14: /// working with an (x,y) value.
        15: /// </summary>
CH 7    16: struct point
        17: {
CH 3    18:    public int x;
        19:    public int y;
        20:
        21:    // A constructor that sets the x and y values
CH 7    22:    public point( int x, int y )
        23:    {
CH 7    24:       this.x = x;
        25:       this.y = y;
        26:    }
        27: }
        28:
        29: //--------------------------------------------------------------
CH 2    30: /// <summary>
        31: /// This class encapsulates line functionality
CH 2    32: /// <see>point</see>
        33: /// </summary>
CH 5    34: class line
```

LISTING WR1.1   continued

```
        35: {
CH 5    36:     private point lineStart;
        37:     private point lineEnd;
        38:
CH 5    39:     public point start
        40:     {
CH 5    41:         get { return lineStart; }
CH 5    42:         set
        43:         {
CH 5    44:             if ( value.x < 0 )
        45:                 lineStart.x = 0;
CH 4    46:             else
CH 5    47:                 lineStart.x = value.x;
        48:             if ( value.y < 0 )
        49:                 lineStart.y = 0;
        50:             else
        51:                 lineStart.y = value.y;
        52:         }
        53:     }
CH 5    54:     public point end
        55:     {
CH 5    56:         get { return lineEnd; }
CH 5    57:         set
        58:         {
        59:             if ( value.x < 0 )
        60:                 lineEnd.x = 0;
        61:             else
        62:                 lineEnd.x = value.x;
        63:             if ( value.y < 0 )
        64:                 lineEnd.y = 0;
        65:             else
        66:                 lineEnd.y = value.y;
        67:         }
        68:     }
        69:
CH 6    70:     public double length()
        71:     {
CH 2    72:         int x_diff;
CH 2    73:         int y_diff;
CH 2    74:         double length;
        75:
CH 3    76:         x_diff = end.x - start.x;
CH 3    77:         y_diff = end.y - start.y;
        78:
CH 3    79:         length = (double) Math.Sqrt((x_diff * x_diff) + (y_diff * y_diff));
CH 6    80:         return (length);
        81:     }
        82:
```

LISTING WR1.1 continued

```
CH 6    83:    public void DisplayInfo()
        84:    {
        85:        Console.WriteLine("\n\n------------------------");
        86:        Console.WriteLine("      Line stats:");
        87:        Console.WriteLine("------------------------");
        88:        Console.WriteLine(" Length:      {0:f3}", length());
        89:        Console.WriteLine(" Start Point: ({0},{1})", start.x, start.y);
        90:        Console.WriteLine(" End Point:   ({0},{1})", end.x, end.y);
        91:        Console.WriteLine("------------------------\n");
        92:    }
        93:
CH 6    94:    public line()
        95:    {
CH 7    96:        lineStart = new point();
CH 5    97:        lineEnd = new point();
        98:    }
        99: }
        100:
        101: //----------------------------------------------------------
CH 2    102: /// <summary>
        103: /// This class encapsulates square functionality
CH 2    104: /// <see>line</see>
        105: /// </summary>
CH 5    106: class square
        107: {
CH 5    108:    private line squareHeight;
CH 5    109:    private line squareWidth;
        110:
CH 5    111:    public line height
        112:    {
CH 5    113:        get { return squareHeight; }
CH 5    114:        set
        115:        {
CH 5    116:            squareHeight.start = value.start;
CH 5    117:            squareHeight.end = value.end;
        118:        }
        119:    }
CH 5    120:    public line width
        121:    {
CH 5    122:        get { return squareWidth; }
CH 5    123:        set
        124:        {
CH 5    125:            squareWidth.start = value.start;
        126:            squareWidth.end = value.end;
        127:        }
        128:    }
        129:
CH 6    130:    public double area()
        131:    {
```

LISTING **WR1.1**   continued

```
CH 2    132:        double total;
        133:
CH 3    134:        total = (width.length() * height.length());
CH 6    135:        return (total);
        136:    }
        137:
CH 6    138:    public double border()
        139:    {
CH 2    140:        double total;
        141:
CH 6    142:        total = ((2 * width.length()) + (2 * (height.length())));
CH 6    143:        return (total);
        144:    }
        145:
CH 6    146:    public void DisplayInfo()
        147:    {
        148:        Console.WriteLine("\n\n--------------------------");
        149:        Console.WriteLine("     Square stats:");
        150:        Console.WriteLine("--------------------------");
        151:        Console.WriteLine(" Area:        {0:f3}", area());
        152:        Console.WriteLine(" Border:      {0:f3}", border());
        153:        Console.WriteLine(" WIDTH Points: ({0},{1}) to ({2},{3})",
        154:            width.start.x, width.start.y, width.end.x, width.end.y);
        155:        Console.WriteLine("        Length: {0:f3}", width.length());
        156:        Console.WriteLine(" HEIGHT Points: ({0},{1}) to ({2},{3})",
        157:            height.start.x, height.start.y, height.end.x, height.end.y);
        158:        Console.WriteLine("        Length: {0:f3}", height.length());
        159:
        160:        Console.WriteLine("--------------------------\n");
        161:    }
        162:
CH 6    163:    public square()
        164:    {
CH 5    165:        squareHeight = new line();
CH 5    166:        squareWidth =  new line();
        167:
CH 7    168:        point tmpPoint = new point(0,0);
        169:
        170:        width.start  = tmpPoint;
        171:        width.end    = tmpPoint;
        172:        height.start = tmpPoint;
        173:        height.end   = tmpPoint;
        174:    }
        175: }
        176:
CH 2    177: //--------------------------------------------------------------
CH 2    178: /// <summary>
        179: /// This class encapsulates circle functionality
CH 2    180: /// <see>line</see>
```

LISTING WR1.1 continued

```
181:  /// </summary>
182:  class circle
183:  {
184:     private point circleCenter;
185:     private long circleRadius;
186:
187:     public point center
188:     {
189:        get { return circleCenter; }
190:        set
191:        {
192:           circleCenter.x = value.x;
193:           circleCenter.y = value.y;
194:        }
195:     }
196:     public long radius
197:     {
198:        get { return circleRadius; }
199:        set {  circleRadius = value; }
200:     }
201:
202:     public double area()
203:     {
204:        double total;
205:
206:        total = 3.14159 * radius * radius;
207:        return (total);
208:     }
209:
210:     public double circumference()
211:     {
212:        double total;
213:
214:        total = 2 * 3.14159 * radius;
215:        return (total);
216:     }
217:
218:     public void DisplayInfo()
219:     {
220:        Console.WriteLine("\n\n-------------------------");
221:        Console.WriteLine("      Circle stats:");
222:        Console.WriteLine("-------------------------");
223:        Console.WriteLine(" Area:         {0:f3}", area());
224:        Console.WriteLine(" Circumference: {0:f3}", circumference());
225:        Console.WriteLine(" Center Points: ({0},{1})", center.x, center.y);
226:        Console.WriteLine(" Radius:       {0:f3}", radius);
227:        Console.WriteLine("-------------------------\n");
228:     }
229:
```

The following chapter markers appear in the left margin:

- CH 5 — line 182
- CH 5 — line 184
- CH 5 — line 185
- CH 5 — line 187
- CH 5 — line 189
- CH 5 — line 190
- CH 5 — line 196
- CH 5 — line 198
- CH 5 — line 199
- CH 6 — line 202
- CH 2 — line 204
- CH 3 — line 206
- CH 6 — line 207
- CH 6 — line 210
- CH 2 — line 212
- CH 3 — line 214
- CH 6 — line 215
- CH 6 — line 218

LISTING **WR1.1** continued

```
Ch 6   230:    public circle()
       231:    {
Ch 6   232:        circleCenter = new point();
       233:
Ch 7   234:        center = new point(0,0);
       235:        radius = 0;
       236:    }
       237: }
       238:
Ch 5   239: class WR01App
       240: {
Ch 2   241:    /// <summary>
Ch 2   242:    /// Main() routine that starts the application
Ch 2   243:    /// </summary>
Ch 2   244:    public static void Main()
       245:    {
Ch 2   246:        int menuChoice = 99;
       247:
Ch 4   248:        do
       249:        {
Ch 6   250:            menuChoice = GetMenuChoice();
       251:
Ch 4   252:            switch( menuChoice )
       253:            {
Ch 4   254:                case 0:  break;
Ch 4   255:                case 1:  WorkWithLine();
Ch 4   256:                    break;
Ch 4   257:                case 2:  WorkWithCircle();
Ch 4   258:                    break;
Ch 4   259:                case 3:  WorkWithSquare();
Ch 4   260:                    break;
Ch 4   261:                case 4:  WorkWithTriangle();
Ch 4   262:                    break;
Ch 4   263:                default: Console.WriteLine("\n\nError... Invalid menu
                     ➡option.");
Ch 4   264:                    break;
       265:            }
       266:
Ch 4   267:            if ( menuChoice !=0 )
       268:            {
       269:                Console.Write("\nPress <ENTER> to continue...");
Ch 6   270:                Console.ReadLine();
       271:            }
       272:
Ch 4   273:        } while ( menuChoice != 0 );
       274:    }
       275:
Ch 2   276:    /// <summary>
Ch 2   277:    /// Displays a menu of choices.
```

LISTING **WR1.1**   continued

```
CH 2      278:    /// </summary>
CH 6      279:    static void DisplayMenu()
          280:    {
          281:        Console.WriteLine("\n            Menu");
          282:        Console.WriteLine("===========================\n");
          283:        Console.WriteLine(" A - Working with Lines");
          284:        Console.WriteLine(" B - Working with Circles");
          285:        Console.WriteLine(" C - Working with Squares");
          286:        Console.WriteLine(" D - Working with Triangles");
          287:        Console.WriteLine(" Q - Quit\n");
          288:        Console.WriteLine("===========================\n");
          289:    }
          290:
CH 2      291:    /// <summary>
CH 2      292:    /// Gets a choice from the user and verifies that it is valid.
CH 2      293:    /// Returns a numeric value to indicate which selection was made.
CH 2      294:    /// </summary>
CH 6      295:    static int GetMenuChoice()
          296:    {
CH 2      297:        int  option = 0;
CH 2      298:        bool cont = true;
CH 2      299:        string buf;
          300:
CH 4      301:        while( cont == true )
          302:        {
CH 6      303:            DisplayMenu();
          304:            Console.Write(" Enter Choice: ");
CH 6      305:            buf = Console.ReadLine();
          306:
CH 4      307:            switch( buf )
          308:            {
CH 4      309:                case "a":
CH 4      310:                case "A":  option = 1;
CH 2      311:                    cont = false;
CH 4      312:                    break;
CH 4      313:                case "b":
CH 4      314:                case "B":  option = 2;
CH 2      315:                    cont = false;
CH 4      316:                    break;
CH 4      317:                case "c":
CH 4      318:                case "C":  option = 3;
          319:                    cont = false;
CH 4      320:                    break;
          321:                case "d":
          322:                case "D":  option = 4;
          323:                    cont = false;
CH 4      324:                    break;
          325:                case "q":
          326:                case "Q":  option = 0;
```

LISTING WR1.1   continued

```
           327:                         cont = false;
           328:                         break;
CH 4       329:                     default:
           330:                         Console.WriteLine("\n\n--> {0} is not valid <--\n\n", buf);
CH 4       331:                         break;
           332:                 }
           333:             }
CH 6       334:         return option;
           335:     }
           336:
CH 2       337:     /// <summary>
CH 2       338:     /// Method to perform code for Working with Line.
CH 2       339:     /// </summary>
CH 6       340:     static void WorkWithLine()
           341:     {
CH 5       342:         line myLine = new line();
           343:
CH 7       344:         point tmpPoint = new point(0,0);
CH 5       345:         myLine.start = tmpPoint;
           346:
CH 5       347:         tmpPoint.x = 3;
CH 5       348:         tmpPoint.y = 3;
CH 5       349:         myLine.end = tmpPoint;
           350:
CH 6       351:         myLine.DisplayInfo();
           352:     }
           353:
           354:     /// <summary>
           355:     /// Method to perform code for Working with Circles.
           356:     /// </summary>
CH 6       357:     static void WorkWithCircle()
           358:     {
CH 5       359:         circle myCircle = new circle();
CH 2       360:
CH 7       361:         myCircle.center = new point(1,1);
CH 5       362:         myCircle.radius = 10;
           363:
CH 6       364:         myCircle.DisplayInfo();
           365:     }
           366:
           367:     /// <summary>
           368:     /// Method to perform code for Working with Squares.
           369:     /// </summary>
CH 6       370:     static void WorkWithSquare()
           371:     {
CH 6       372:         square mySquare = new square();
           373:
CH 7       374:         mySquare.width.start  = new point(1,0);
           375:         mySquare.width.end    = new point(10,0);
```

```
CH 6    376:        mySquare.height.start = new point(0,2);
        377:        mySquare.height.end   = new point(0,8);
        378:
CH 6    379:        mySquare.DisplayInfo();
        380:    }
        381:
        382:    /// <summary>
        383:    /// Method to perform code for Working with Triangles.
        384:    /// </summary>
CH 6    385:    static void WorkWithTriangle()
        386:    {
        387:        Console.WriteLine("\n\nDo Triangle Stuff...\n\n");
        388:        // This section left for you to do
        389:    }
        390: }
CH 2    391:  //-------------------- End of Listing ----------------------
```

When you execute this program, you are presented with the following:

OUTPUT

```
                 Menu
===========================

A - Working with Lines
B - Working with Circles
C - Working with Squares
D - Working with Triangles
Q - Quit


===========================

Enter Choice:
```

If you enter something other than the letters in the menu, you get the following message:

OUTPUT

```
                 Menu
===========================

A - Working with Lines
B - Working with Circles
C - Working with Squares
D - Working with Triangles
Q - Quit


===========================

Enter Choice: g


--> g is not valid <--
```

The menu is then represented. Selecting one of the valid choices produces output like the following (this is the output for entering a choice of `c`):

```
Enter Choice: c



- - - - - - - - - - - - - - - - - - - - - - - -
      Square stats:
- - - - - - - - - - - - - - - - - - - - - - - -
  Area:        54.000
  Border:      30.000
  WIDTH Points: (1,0) to (10,0)
       Length: 9.000
  HEIGHT Points: (0,2) to (0,8)
       Length: 6.000
- - - - - - - - - - - - - - - - - - - - - - - -



  Press <ENTER> to continue...
```

The XML Documentation

As stated earlier, you can produce XML documentation from this listing. The following is the content of the XML file that can be created by using the `/doc` compiler option. Remember to include the filename for the documentation. Using the Microsoft command-line compiler, you would enter the following to place the XML documentation in a file named myfile.xml:

```
csc /doc:myfile.xml WR01.cs
```

> **Note**
> The /doc flag works with the Microsoft compiler. If you are using an IDE or a different compiler, you will need to check the documentation or Help for the specific command for the compiler option.

```
<?xml version="1.0"?>
<doc>
    <assembly>
        <name>WR01</name>
    </assembly>
    <members>
        <member name="T:point">
            <summary>
            This is a point structure. It is for storing and
            working with an (x,y) value.
            </summary>
        </member>
```

```
<member name="T:line">
    <summary>
    This class encapsulates line functionality
    <see>point</see>
    </summary>
</member>
<member name="T:square">
    <summary>
    This class encapsulates square functionality
    <see>line</see>
    </summary>
</member>
<member name="T:circle">
    <summary>
    This class encapsulates circle functionality
    <see>line</see>
    </summary>
</member>
<member name="M:WR01App.Main">
    <summary>
    Main() routine that starts the application
    </summary>
</member>
<member name="M:WR01App.DisplayMenu">
    <summary>
    Displays a menu of choices.
    </summary>
</member>
<member name="M:WR01App.GetMenuChoice">
    <summary>
    Gets a choice from the user and verifies that it is valid.
    Returns a numeric value to indicate which selection was made.
    </summary>
</member>
<member name="M:WR01App.WorkWithLine">
    <summary>
    Method to perform code for Working with Line.
    </summary>
</member>
<member name="M:WR01App.WorkWithCircle">
    <summary>
    Method to perform code for Working with Circles.
    </summary>
</member>
<member name="M:WR01App.WorkWithSquare">
    <summary>
    Method to perform code for Working with Squares.
    </summary>
</member>
<member name="M:WR01App.WorkWithTriangle">
```

```
            <summary>
            Method to perform code for Working with Triangles.
            </summary>
         </member>
      </members>
</doc>
```

The Code at 50,000 Feet

 Now that you've seen some of the output and the XML documentation that can be created, it's time to look at some of the code.

At a 50,000-foot view, there are a few things to notice about this listing. First, Line 9 includes the one namespace in this listing, System. As you learned on Day 5, "The Core of C# Programming: Classes," this means that you don't have to type System when using items from the System namespace. This includes items such as the Console methods. You should also notice that one structure and four classes are declared:

- point structure in Lines 16–27
- line class in Lines 34–99
- square class in Lines 106–174
- circle class in Lines 182–237
- WR01App class in Lines 239–390

The line, square, and circle classes are all similar. The point structure is used to help organize the other classes.

Dissecting the Main Method

Looking closer at the listing, you see that the program flow actually starts in Line 244, where the Main method is declared within the WR01 class. This method uses a do...while statement to continue processing a menu until the appropriate selection is made. The menu is displayed by calling another method, GetMenuChoice. Depending on the value returned from this function, one of a number of different routines is executed. A switch statement in Lines 252–265 is used to direct program flow to the correct statements.

In Lines 267–271, an if statement is used to check the value of the menu choice. If menuChoice is 0, the user chose to exit the program. If it is any other value, information is displayed on the screen. To pause the program before redisplaying the menu, Lines 269–270 were added. Line 269 provides a message to the user saying to press the Enter key to continue. Line 270 uses the Console.ReadLine method to wait for the Enter key to be pressed. If the user entered any text before pressing the key, this listing ignores it. When the user continues, the while statement's condition is checked. If menuChoice is 0, the `while` ends, as does the method and, thus the program. If `menuChoice` is not 0, the `do` statement loops, causing the menu to be redisplayed and the process to continue.

Looking in the `switch` statement, you see that each of the first four cases executes a method that is presented later in the `WR01` class. If the `menuChoice` is not a value from 1 to 4, the `default` statement in the `switch` (Line 263) is executed, thus printing an error.

The `GetMenuChoice` Method

Stepping back, Line 250 calls `GetMenuChoice`. This method is in Lines 295 to 335; it displays the menu and gets the choice from the user. In Line 303, another method is called to do the actual display of the menu. After displaying the menu, Line 305 uses the `Console.ReadLine` method to get the choice from the user and place it in the string variable, `buf`.

A `switch` statement then converts this choice to a numeric value that is passed back to the calling method. This conversion is not absolutely necessary. This method has the purpose of getting the menu choice. You'll notice that there are two correct selections for each menu option. This `switch` statement converts each of these to a single correct option. You could have done this in a number of different ways. Additionally, you could have chosen to return the character value rather than a numeric value. The lesson to learn here is that the functionality for obtaining a menu choice can be placed in its own method. By doing so, you can get the selection any way you want, as long as you return a consistent set of final selection values. You could swap this method with another that returns a value from 0 to 4, and the rest of your code would work exactly the same.

The Main Menu Options

Each of the four main menu options calls a method. Lines 340–352 contain the `WorkWithLine` method. This method declares an object, sets the initial values, and finally calls a method in the declared object that displays the information about the object. The `WorkWithSquare` and `WorkWithCircle` methods work the same way. The `WorkWithTriangle` was not filled coded. Instead, it was left for you to fill.

The `point` Structure

The `point` structure is defined in Lines 16–27. The `point` structure contains two data members, `x` and `y`.

In Line 22, a constructor for the `point` structure is defined. This constructor accepts two values as parameters. In Lines 24–25, these values are set to the `x` and `y` data members. You might notice that the parameters in Line 22 are also named `x` and `y`. To differentiate these from the structure's x and y data members, the `this` keyword is used. The `this` keyword refers to the current structure's x and y values instead of the parameters.

With a structure, you cannot create a default constructor that has no parameters. Because a structure is a value type, it is initially constructed when you declare it.

The `line` Class

The `line` class is declared in Lines 34–99. In Lines 36–37, the data members are declared. In this case, the data members are `point` structures that have been declared as private. To access these data members, you must use the properties declared in Lines 39–68. By using properties as accessors in this class, you hide the internal structure of how you are storing the line information. This provides you with flexibility in case you later decide to change the internal storage structure.

The constructor for the `line` class is in Lines 94–98, which instantiate the two `point` structures for this class. The default values are set to new points.

The `line` class also contains other methods that can be called. The coding in these methods is straightforward.

The Other Classes

The rest of the classes in this program are similar to the `line` class. You can review their code on your own.

Note

> You should understand the code in this listing. If you don't understand a certain area, you should go back and review the appropriate day's lesson. On future days, you will learn how to improve upon this listing.

WEEK 2

At a Glance

You have completed your first week and have only two to go. In this second week, you learn most of the remaining core topics to the C# programming language—not all of them, but most of them. By the end of this week, you will have the tools to build basic C# applications from scratch.

On Day 8, "Advanced Method Access," you will expand on what you learned on Days 6 and 7. You will learn how to overload methods and how to use a variable number of parameters on a method. You will also learn about scope, which will enable you to limit access to your data and other type members. You'll discover the `static` keyword, and you will learn how to create a class that cannot be used to create an object.

Creating programs that don't blow up on the user is important. On Day 9,"Handling Problems in Your Programs: Exceptions and Errors," you will learn how to deal with problems when your programs are running. First, you will learn how about exception handling. Exception handling is a structured approach to catching and stopping problems before they cause your programs to go boom. You follow this by learning ways to find unexpected problems.

One of the key object-oriented features is inheritance. On Day 10, "Reusing Existing Code with Inheritance," you will discover how to use inheritance with the classes you've created (or with someone else's classes). On this day, you will learn several new keywords, including `sealed`, `is`, and `as`.

Day 11, "Formatting and Retrieving Information," steps back from the super- techie stuff and gives you a reprieve. On this day, you will focus on presenting information and retrieving information to and from the console. You will learn how to format the data so that it is much more usable. This chapter contains a number of tables that you will want to refer to.

Day 12, "Tapping into OOP: Interfaces," deals with another core topic for understanding the power of C#. This chapter expands on what you know about classes and structures as well as inheritance. On this day, you will learn how to combine multiple features into a single new class using interfaces.

Day 13, "Making Your Programs React with Delegates, Events, and Indexers," focuses on exactly what its title states—indexers, delegates, and events. You will learn how to use index notation with a class's data. You also will learn about delegates and events, which enable you to dynamically execute methods as well as do event programming. Events are key to your programming Windows-type applications.

The week ends with a day focusing on an interesting topic: Day 14, "Making Operators Do Your Bidding: Overloading." On this day, you are presented with a topic that many people believe to be complex but that is relatively easy to implement in C#. You've already learned how to overload methods. On Day 14, you'll learn how to overload operators.

By the end of this second week, you will have learned most of the core concepts for C# programming. You'll find that by the time you have completed this second week, you will understand most of the core concepts of most C# programs.

DAY **8**

Advanced Method Access

You have learned quite a bit in the past seven days. Today you continue building on this foundation of knowledge by working further with class methods. In Days 5, "The Core of C# Programming: Classes," and 6, "Packaging Functionality: Class Methods and Member Functions," you learned to encapsulate functionality and data into a class. In today's lesson, one of the key things you will learn is how to make your class more flexible. Today you...

- Discover how to overload methods.
- Determine a method's signatures.
- Learn how to pass a variable number of parameters to a method.
- Revisit scope.
- Learn to create your own namespaces.

Overloading Methods

One of the key features of an object-oriented programming language is polymorphism. As you have previously learned, polymorphism is the capability of reaching a result even if different options are provided. One form of polymorphism is overloading. Previously, an example of a circle was provided.

In C#, the easiest place to see overloading in action is with methods. It is possible to create a class that can react to a number of different values and still reach the same conclusion. Consider Figure 8.1. In this figure, the black box illustrates your method for calculating the area of a circle.

FIGURE 8.1

A black box that calculates the area of a circle.

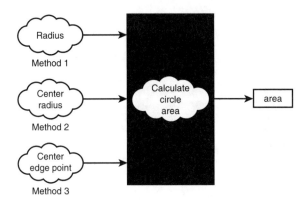

Note that one of three possible solutions can be sent to this circle, and it still provides the appropriate answer. The first option sends just the radius of a circle. The second option sends the center point of the circle and the length of the radius. The third option sends the center point and a point on the circle. All three requests to the circle's area method return the area.

If you wrote a program to have the same functionality as this black box, you might be tempted to create three separate methods. You could call these `CalcArea`, `CalcAreaWithPoints`, and `CalcAreaWithRadius`, or any of a thousand other unique names. If you were programming in a non–object-oriented language such as C, you would have to create multiple functions. In an object-oriented language, there is an easier answer: method overloading.

Overloading Functions

NEW TERM   *Method overloading* is the process of creating multiple methods with the same name. Each of these methods is unique in some way so that the compiler can tell the difference. Listing 8.1 presents a `Circle` class that has its `Area` method overloaded so that each of the calls illustrated in Figure 8.1 will work.

LISTING 8.1   Circle.cs— Method Overloading

```
 1:  // Circle.cs - Overloading the area method
 2:  //-----------------------------------------------------------------
 3:
 4:  using System;
 5:
 6:  public class Circle
 7:  {
 8:      public int x;
 9:      public int y;
10:      public double radius;
11:      private const float PI = 3.14159F;
12:
13:      public double Area()  // Uses values from data members
14:      {
15:          return Area(radius);
16:      }
17:
18:      public double Area( double rad )
19:      {
20:          double theArea;
21:          theArea = PI * rad * rad;
22:          Console.WriteLine("  The area for radius ({0}) is {1}", rad,
            ➥theArea);
23:          return theArea;
24:      }
25:
26:      public double Area(int x1, int y1, double rad)
27:      {
28:           return Area(rad);
29:      }
30:
31:      public double Area( int x1, int y1, int x2, int y2 )
32:      {
33:          int x_diff;
34:          int y_diff;
35:          double rad;
36:
37:          x_diff = x2 - x1;
38:          y_diff = y2 - y1;
39:
40:          rad = (double) Math.Sqrt((x_diff * x_diff) + (y_diff * y_diff));
41:
42:          return Area(rad);
43:      }
44:
45:      public Circle()
46:      {
47:          x = 0;
```

8

LISTING 8.1   continued

```
48:          y = 0;
49:          radius = 0.0;
50:       }
51:  }
52:
53:  class CircleApp
54:  {
55:     public static void Main()
56:     {
57:        Circle myCircle = new Circle();
58:
59:        Console.WriteLine("Passing nothing...") ;
60:        myCircle.Area();
61:
62:        Console.WriteLine("\nPassing a radius of 3...");
63:        myCircle.Area( 3 );
64:
65:        Console.WriteLine("\nPassing a center of (2, 4) and a radius of
            ➥3...");
66:        myCircle.Area( 2, 4, 3 );
67:
68:        Console.WriteLine("\nPassing center of (2, 3) and a point of (4,
            ➥5)...");
69:        myCircle.Area( 2, 3, , 5 );
70:     }
71:  }
```

OUTPUT

```
Passing nothing...
   The area for radius (0) is 0

Passing a radius of 3...
   The area for radius (3) is 28.2743110656738

Passing a center of (2, 4) and a radius of 3...
   The area for radius (3) is 28.2743110656738

Passing center of (2, 3) and a point of (4, 5)...
   The area for radius (2.82842712474619) is 25.1327209472656
```

ANALYSIS   The first things you should look at in this listing are Lines 60, 63, 66, and 69. These lines all call the Area method of the myCircle object. Each of these calls, however, uses a different number of arguments. The program still compiles and works.

This is done using method overloading. If you look at the Circle class, you can see that four Area methods are defined. They differ based on the number of parameters being passed. In Lines 13–16, an Area method is defined that doesn't receive any arguments but that still returns a double. This method's body calls the Area method that contains one parameter. It passes the radius stored in the class radius data member.

In Lines 18–24, the second `Area` method is defined. In this definition, a `double` value is passed into the method. This value is assumed to be the radius. In Line 21, the area is calculated using the passed-in radius value. Line 22 prints the radius and the calculated area to the screen. The method ends by passing the area back to the calling routine.

> **Tip**
>
> Instead of using a literal value for PI throughout this listing, a constant variable was declared in Line 11. This enables you to change the value of PI in one location instead of potentially hard-coding it throughout your application. Maintenance will be much easier in the future.

In Lines 26–29, you see the third defined `Area` method. This definition of the `Area` method is a little silly because only the radius is needed to calculate the area. Instead of repeating functionality in multiple places, this method passes its radius value, `rad`, to the `Area` method that requires only the radius. The area value is then passed back from each of the methods to the previous caller.

Lines 31–43 present the most complicated `Area` method. This method receives the center point of a circle and a point on the circle itself. The radius is the line that goes between these two points (Figure 8.2 illustrates this). Line 40 calculates the length of this line based on the two point values. After the length is obtained, it is passed to the `Area` method that requires only the radius where the rest of the work is done.

FIGURE 8.2

The center point and a point on the circle.

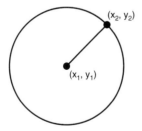

Although each of these methods calls another of the `Area` methods, this does not have to be the case. Each of these might do its coding completely independently of the others. Their individual code is up to you. It is important to know that you can create multiple methods with the same name that can perform operations based on different sets of values.

Caution | Just because you can code completely different functionality in methods with the same name, it doesn't mean that you should. Because the methods are named the same, the end results of each should be similar.

Overloading Constructors

In addition to overloading regular methods, you can overload constructors. An overloaded constructor enables you to pass values to an object at the same time it is created. Listing 8.2 illustrates a `Circle` class that has had the constructor overloaded. This `Circle` class is different from the one in Listing 8.1.

LISTING 8.2   Circle1.cs—Overloading the Constructor

```
 1: // Circle1.cs - A simple circle class with overloaded constructors
 2: //----------------------------------------------------------------
 3:
 4: using System;
 5:
 6: public class Circle
 7: {
 8:     public int x;
 9:     public int y;
10:     public int radius;
11:     private const float PI = 3.14159F;
12:
13:     public double area()
14:     {
15:        double theArea;
16:        theArea = PI * radius * radius;
17:        return theArea;
18:     }
19:
20:     public double circumference()
21:     {
22:        double Circ;
23:        Circ = 2 * PI * radius;
24:        return Circ;
25:     }
26:
27:     public Circle()
28:     {
29:        x = 0;
30:        y = 0;
31:        radius = 0;
32:     }
33:
```

LISTING 8.2   continued

```
34:     public Circle( int r )
35:     {
36:         x = 0;
37:         y = 0;
38:         radius = r;
39:     }
40:
41:     public Circle ( int new_x, int new_y )
42:     {
43:         x = new_x;
44:         y = new_y;
45:         radius = 0;
46:     }
47:
48:     public Circle ( int new_x, int new_y, int r )
49:     {
50:         x = new_x;
51:         y = new_y;
52:         radius = r;
53:     }
54:
55:     public void print_circle_info()
56:     {
57:       Console.WriteLine("Circle: Center = ({0},{1})", x, y);
58:       Console.WriteLine("        Radius = {0}", radius);
59:       Console.WriteLine("        Area   = {0}", area());
60:       Console.WriteLine("        Circum = {0}", circumference());
61:     }
62: }
63:
64: class CircleApp
65: {
66:    public static void Main()
67:    {
68:       Circle first  = new Circle();
69:       Circle second = new Circle(4);
70:       Circle third  = new Circle(3,4);
71:       Circle fourth  = new Circle(1, 2, 5);
72:
73:       Console.WriteLine("\nFirst Circle:");
74:       first.print_circle_info();
75:
76:       Console.WriteLine("\nSecond Circle:");
77:       second.print_circle_info();
78:
79:       Console.WriteLine("\nThird Circle:");
80:       third.print_circle_info();
81:
```

LISTING 8.2 continued

```
82:         Console.WriteLine("\nFourth Circle:");
83:         fourth.print_circle_info();
84:     }
85: }
```

OUTPUT

```
First Circle:
Circle: Center = (0,0)
        Radius = 0
        Area   = 0
        Circum = 0

Second Circle:
Circle: Center = (0,0)
        Radius = 4
        Area   = 50.26544
        Circum = 25.13272

Third Circle:
Circle: Center = (3,4)
        Radius = 0
        Area   = 0
        Circum = 0

Fourth Circle:
Circle: Center = (1,2)
        Radius = 5
        Area   = 78.53975
        Circum = 31.41590001106262
```

ANALYSIS The constructors in the Circle class are the focus of this listing. There are a number of constructors, and each takes a different number of arguments. The first constructor is defined in Lines 27–32. You have seen this constructor before—it takes no parameters. Declared as public and using the class name, this constructor follows the same format that you learned about on Day 6.

In Lines 34–39, you see the first of three additional Circle constructors. This constructor receives an integer that contains the radius. This value is applied to the class's radius field.

The code for the third Circle constructor is presented in Lines 41–46. This constructor differs from the others because it takes two integer values. These are the new values for the x and y coordinates of the center point. In Lines 43–44, these values are set to the object's values.

8

The fourth and final constructor for the `Circle` class in this listing is in Lines 48–53. This constructor takes three values. This includes the radius and the x and y coordinates for the center point.

All of these methods are declared with the same name and in the same manner. The only difference is that each takes different parameters.

In Lines 68–71 of the `CircleApp` class, you see these constructors in action. Line 68 creates a new `Circle` object called `first`. This is declared and created in the same way you've seen objects created before.

In Line 69, the second object is created differently. When this object is created, instead of entering this

```
new Circle()
```

an argument has been added—a `4`. To create the second object, a constructor is required that can accept a single numeric value of `4`. This matches the constructor that starts in Line 34, which has the same format as the call in Line 69.

Based on the description of the creation of the second object, it should be easy to see that the third and fourth objects call the constructors that are appropriate for them. The appropriate constructor is the one with parameters that match the call's arguments.

Consider what happens if you created a `Circle` object as follows:

```
Circle myCircle = new Circle(1, 2, 3, 4);
```

This results in an error because it would pass four values. None of the constructors in the `Circle` class accepts four values, so this declaration will not work.

Understanding Method Signatures

Methods can be overloaded because of the uniqueness of each method's signature. As you learned in the previous section, the number of parameters in the method can determine which method should be called. There are actually other ways in which overloaded methods can differ from each other. Ultimately, these differences comprise a method's signature.

A method's signature is composed of the number of parameters and their types. You saw with the `Circle` constructor that there were four signatures:

```
Circle()
Circle( int )
Circle( int, int )
Circle( int, int, int)
```

The Area method in Listing 8.1 has four signatures:

```
double Area()
```

```
double Area( double )
```

```
double Area(int, int, double )
```

```
double Area( int, int, int, int )
```

The following are other methods that would be valid to overload:

```
MyFunc( int )
```

```
MyFunc( float )
```

```
MyFunc( ref int )
```

```
MyFunc( val int )
```

A number of items cannot be used as part of the signature. The return type cannot be used because it does not have to be used when calling a method.

Additionally, you cannot have a signature that differs because one method has a data type and another has an array of the same data type. For example, if you overload with the following two signatures, you might get an error:

```
int myMethod( int )
```

```
int myMethod( int[] )
```

You also cannot use the params keyword to make signatures different. Using params is covered later today. The following two methods together cause an error:

```
void myMethod( string, float )
```

```
void myMethod( string, params float[] )
```

You can overload a method as many times as you like, as long as each overloaded method has a unique signature.

Using a Variable Number of Parameters

You've now learned how to create and use methods. You've learned how to pass information to methods. You've learned that information can be passed in a number of ways. This includes passing information by value or by reference, and passing variables that can be used to return output. You've even learned to use the return keyword to pass a value back from a method. All these require a structured use of the methods.

What happens when you want to pass an unknown variable number of items to a method? For example, suppose that you want to add a set of numbers, but you don't know how many numbers there will be. You could call a routine multiple times, or you could set up a routine to take a variable number of parameters. Consider the `Console.WriteLine` and `Console.Write` methods. These methods both take a string and then a variable number of different values and data types.

To accept an unknown number of parameters, you can use the `params` keyword. This keyword can be used as the last value in a method's parameters list. The `params` keyword is used with an array data type.

Listing 8.3 presents the `params` keyword used with a method that takes a variable number of integers. The method adds the integers and then returns a `long` value with the total.

LISTING 8.3   Addem.cs—Using the `params` Keyword

```
 1:  //  Addem.cs - Using a variable number of arguments
 2:  //------------------------------------------------------------
 3:
 4:  using System;
 5:
 6:  public class AddEm
 7:  {
 8:      public static long Add( params int[] args )
 9:      {
10:         int ctr = 0;
11:         long Total = 0;
12:
13:         for( ctr = 0; ctr < args.Length; ctr++)
14:         {
15:            Total += args[ctr];
16:         }
17:         return Total;
18:      }
19:  }
20:
21:  class MyApp
22:  {
23:     public static void Main()
24:     {
25:        long Total = 0;   ·
26:
27:        Total = AddEm.Add( 1 );
28:        Console.WriteLine("Total of (1) = {0}", Total);
29:
30:        Total = AddEm.Add( 1, 2 );
31:        Console.WriteLine("Total of (1, 2) = {0}", Total);
```

LISTING 8.3   continued

```
32:
33:          Total = AddEm.Add( 1, 2, 3 );
34:          Console.WriteLine("Total of (1, 2, 3) = {0}", Total);
35:
36:          Total = AddEm.Add( 1, 2, 3, 4 );
37:          Console.WriteLine("Total of (1, 2, 3, 4) = {0}", Total);
38:       }
39:  }
```

OUTPUT
```
Total of (1) = 1
Total of (1, 2) = 3
Total of (1, 2, 3) = 6
Total of (1, 2, 3, 4) = 10
```

ANALYSIS   Your first reaction when looking at this listing should be to say, "Wait a minute—this could be done with a simple array of integers." If you caught this, you are absolutely right. This simple example could have been done without the params keyword and you could have made it work. But... .

If you had declared this without the params keyword, you would not have gotten away with what is in Lines 30, 33, and 36. Instead of being able to pass values to the method, you would have needed to place each of these values into a single int array and then pass that array. The params keyword enabled the compiler to take care of this for you.

If you take a closer look at this listing, you will see that it is not doing anything complex. In Lines 6–19, the class AddEm is created. This class has a single static function named Add that receives a variable number of integers stored in an array named args. Because the params keyword is used, you know that the integers can be passed individually rather than as a single, filled array.

The AddEm method is pretty straightforward. A for loop in Lines 12–16 loops through the args array. Remember, this array was created from the integer values being passed into the AddEm method. Just as with other arrays, you can check standard properties and methods. This includes using args.Length to get the length of the array. The for loop loops from 0 to the end of the args array and adds each of the numbers to a total called Total. This total is then returned in Line 17 to the calling method.

The MyApp class in Lines 21–39 uses the AddEm method to add numbers. You can see that the same method is called with various numbers of integers. You can continue to add integers to the method call, and the method will still work.

> **Note**
>
> No AddEm objects were created. Because the Add method is static, it is called using the class name AddEm. This means that the method can be used even though no objects were created.

Using params with Multiple Data Types

The previous example used all integers within the variable parameter. Because all data types are based on the same class type, an object, you can actually use the object data type to get a variable number of different data types. Listing 8.4 presents a listing that is impractical for everyday use, but it does a great job of illustrating that you can pass a variable number of values that are of any data type. In essence, you can pass anything.

LISTING 8.4 Garbage.cs—Passing Different Data Types

```
 1:  //  Garbage.cs - Using a variable number of arguments
 2:  //              of different types
 3:  //----------------------------------------------------------------
 4:
 5:  using System;
 6:
 7:  public class Garbage
 8:  {
 9:      public static void Print( params object[] args )
10:      {
11:          int ctr - 0;
12:
13:          for( ctr = 0; ctr < args.Length; ctr++)
14:          {
15:              Console.WriteLine("Argument {0} is:  {1}", ctr, args[ctr]);
16:          }
17:      }
18:  }
19:
20:  class MyApp
21:  {
22:      public static void Main()
23:      {
24:          long ALong = 1234567890987654321L;
25:          decimal ADec = 1234.56M;
26:          byte Abyte = 42;
27:          string AString = "Cole McCrary";
28:
29:          Console.WriteLine("First call...");
30:          Garbage.Print( 1 );   // pass a simple integer
31:
```

LISTING 8.4   continued

```
32:          Console.WriteLine("\nSecond call...");
33:          Garbage.Print( );      // pass nothing
34:
35:          Console.WriteLine("\nThird call...");
36:          Garbage.Print( ALong, ADec, Abyte, AString );   // Pass lots
37:
38:          Console.WriteLine("\nFourth call...");
39:          Garbage.Print( AString, "is cool", '!' );      // more stuff
40:      }
41:  }
```

OUTPUT

```
First call...
Argument 0 is:  1

Second call...

Third call...
Argument 0 is:  1234567890987654321
Argument 1 is:  1234.56
Argument 2 is:  42
Argument 3 is:  Cole McCrary

Fourth call...
Argument 0 is:  Cole McCrary
Argument 1 is:  is cool
Argument 2 is:  !
```

ANALYSIS This listing contains a method named Print of the class Garbage in Lines 9–17. The Print method is declared to take a variable number of objects. Any data type can be fitted into an object, so this enables the method to take any data type. The code within the method should be easy to follow. If you look at the output, you will see that in Line 30, the first call to the Garbage.Print method prints a single value, 1.

The second call in Line 32 did not pass any arguments. The Garbage.Print method is still called; however, the logic in the method doesn't print anything. The for statement ends when it checks the args.Length value the first time.

The third and fourth calls to Garbage print various other values. By using a type of object, any data types can be passed in either as variables or as literals.

Note

Recall from the first week that a literal number that ends in an L is considered a long value. A literal number that ends in an M is considered a decimal. (See Lines 24–25 of the listing.)

Taking a More Detailed Look at `params`

It is worth reviewing what the `params` keyword causes to happen in a little more detailed explanation. When values are passed to the method, first the compiler looks to see whether there is a matching method. If a match is found, that method is called. If a match is not found, the compiler checks to see whether there was a method with a `params` argument. If so, that method is used. The compiler then places the values into an array that is passed to the method. For example, using the last call to the `Add` method of `AddEm` in Listing 8.3,

```
AddEm.Add( 1, 2, 3, 4);
```

the compiler does the following behind the scenes:

```
int[] x = new int[4];
int[0] = 1;
int[1] = 2;
int[2] = 3;
int[3] = 4;
AddEm.Add(x);
```

In Listing 8.4, instead of declaring an array of type `int`, an array of type `object` is created and used.

 Caution | Don't forget that array members start at offset 0, not 1.

Working with the `Main` Method and Command-Line Arguments

You have already learned that the `Main` method is a special method because it is always called first. The `Main` method can also receive a variable number of parameters. However, you don't need to use the `params` keyword with `Main`.

You don't need the `params` keyword because the command-line parameters are automatically packed into a string array. As you learned earlier, that is basically the same thing the `params` keyword would do for you. Because the values are already packed into an array, the `params` keyword becomes worthless.

When calling the `Main` method, it is standard practice to use the following format if parameters are expected:

```
public static [int | void] Main( string[] args )
```

Including either `void` or `int` is optional. Generally, your `Main` method either is void or returns an integer. The focus here is in the parameter list: a string array named `args`. The name `args` can be changed to any other name; however, you will find that almost all C# programmers use the variable `args`. Listing 8.5 illustrates the use of command-line parameters.

LISTING 8.5 CommandLine.cs—Using Command-Line Arguments

```
 1:  // CommandLine.cs - Checking for command-line arguments
 2:  //----------------------------------------------------------
 3:
 4:  using System;
 5:
 6:  class CommandLine
 7:  {
 8:      public static void Main(string[] args)
 9:      {
10:          int ctr=0;
11:          if (args.Length <= 0 )
12:          {
13:              Console.WriteLine("No Command Line arguments were provided.");
14:              return;
15:          }
16:          else
17:          {
18:              for( ctr = 0; ctr < args.Length; ctr++)
19:              {
20:                  Console.WriteLine("Argument {0} is {1}", ctr+1, args[ctr]);
21:              }
22:          }
23:      }
24:  }
```

The first output illustrates executing this listing with no arguments.

OUTPUT
```
C:\code\Day08>CommandLine
No Command Line arguments were provided.
```

The second output illustrates calling the program with command-line arguments.

OUTPUT
```
C:\code\Day08>CommandLine xxx 123 456 789.012
Argument 1 is xxx
Argument 2 is 123
Argument 3 is 456
Argument 4 is 789.012
```

ANALYSIS This listing is extremely short and to the point. The Main function, which starts in Line 8, receives command-line arguments. It has been declared with the string[] args parameter, so it is set to capture any command-line arguments sent. In Line 11, the Length data member of the args array is checked. If it is 0, a message is printed saying that no command-line arguments were provided. If the value is something other than 0, Lines 18–21 use a for loop to print each value. In Line 20, instead of printing arguments starting with 0, 1 is added to the counter. This is done so that the end user of the program doesn't have to wonder why the first argument is named 0. After all, the end user might not be a C# programmer.

Do	Don't
Do understand method overloading. **Do** overload methods with the most common ways you believe a method could be used.	**Don't** make things public if you don't need to. Use properties to give public access to private data members. **Don't** ignore command-line parameters in your programs. You can code your programs to accept command-line parameters and to return a value to the operating system.

Understanding Scope

NEW TERM Variables don't last forever. It is important to understand how long a variable exists before the runtime environment throws it out. This lifetime of a variable and its accessibility are referred to as *scope*. Several levels of scope exist; the two most common are *local* and *global*.

A variable with global scope is visible, and thus available, to an entire listing. A variable that is available to a small area only is considered local to that area and, thus, has local scope.

Working with Local Scope

The smallest level of scope is local to a block. A block can include a simple iterative statement, or it can be much longer. Consider the value of x in Listing 8.6. What is the value of x in Line 15? In Line 11?

LISTING 8.6 Scope.cs—Local Variable out of Scope

```
 1:  //  Scope.cs - Local scope with an error
 2:  //  *** You will get a compile error ***
 3:  //-------------------------------------------------------------
 4:
 5:  using System;
 6:
 7:  class Scope
 8:  {
 9:      public static void Main()
10:      {
11:          for( int x; x < 10; x++ )
12:          {
13:              Console.WriteLine("x is {0}", x);
14:          }
15:          Console.WriteLine("Out of For Loop. x is {0}", x);
16:      }
17:  }
```

OUTPUT

```
Scope.cs(15,55): error CS0103: The name 'x' does not exist in the class
               or namespace 'Scope'
```

ANALYSIS Although you might think that x in Line 15 should have a value of 10, x actually
doesn't have a value at that point. It doesn't exist; therefore, using x is actually
an error. The variable is declared as part of the for statement in Line 11. As soon as the
for statement is complete, x goes out of scope. By being out of scope, it can no longer be
used. This generates an error.

Now consider Listing 8.7. This listing contains a declaration in a for statement such as
the one in Listing 8.6; however, it declares x a second time in a second for statement.
Will using x like this lead to an error?

LISTING 8.7 Scope2.cs—Declaring More Than One Local x

```
 1:  //  Scope2.cs - Local scope.
 2:  //-------------------------------------------------------------
 3:
 4:  using System;
 5:
 6:  class Scope2
 7:  {
 8:      public static void Main()
 9:      {
10:          for( int x = 1; x < 5; x++ )
11:          {
```

LISTING 8.7   continued

```
12:                 Console.WriteLine("x is {0}", x);
13:             }
14:
15:         // Second for statement trying to redeclare x...
16:         for( int x = 1; x < 5; x++ )
17:             {
18:                 Console.WriteLine("x is {0}", x);
19:             }
20:     }
21: }
```

OUTPUT

```
x is 1
x is 2
x is 3
x is 4
x is 1
x is 2
x is 3
x is 4
```

ANALYSIS This listing works! Each of the x variables is local to its own block (the for loops). Because of this, each x variable is totally independent of the other.

Now consider Listing 8.8 and its multiple use of x variables.

LISTING 8.8   Scope3.cs—Lots of x Variables

```
 1: //  Scope3.cs - Local scope.
 2: //  *** Error if lines are uncommented ***
 3: //-----------------------------------------------------------------
 4:
 5: using System;
 6:
 7: class Scope3
 8: {
 9:     static int x = 987;
10:
11:     public static void Main()
12:     {
13:         Console.WriteLine("x is {0}", x);
14:
15: //      for( int x = 1; x < 5; x++ )
16: //          {
17: //              Console.WriteLine("x is {0}", x);
18: //          }
19:         Console.WriteLine("x is {0}", x);
20:     }
21: }
```

OUTPUT
```
x is 987
x is 987
```

ANALYSIS
Notice that Lines 15–18 are commented out in this listing. You should enter, compile, and run this listing with the commented lines intact, as presented in the listing. When you do, you get the output shown. The x variable in Lines 13 and 19 print the static x variable contained in the class, as you would expect.

Lines 15–18 contain a local variable x that is declared and used only within the for loop. Based on what you learned in the previous section, you might be tempted to believe that if you uncomment this code and compile, everything will work. The for loop uses its local x variable, and the rest of the method uses the class x variable. Wrong! In Line 17, how would the compiler know that you did not mean to use the class's x variable? It wouldn't. Uncomment Lines 15–18 and recompile the listing. You get the following result:

OUTPUT
```
Scope3.cs(15,17): error CS0136: A local variable named 'x' cannot be
declared in this scope because it would give a different meaning to
'x', which is already used in a 'parent or current' scope to denote
something else
```

The compiler can't tell which x variable to use. The local variable conflicts with the class variable. There is a way around this problem.

Differentiating Class Variables from Local Variables

One way to differentiate class variables from a local variable is to always refer to the class. You learned how to do this in an earlier lesson; however, it is worth reviewing. The error provided in Listing 8.8 can be resolved in two ways: rename the local variable with a different name, or refer to the class variable in Lines 14 and 19 more explicitly.

Depending on how you declared the variable, there are two ways to be more explicit on a class variable's name. If the class variable is a standard, non-static variable, you can use the this keyword. For accessing a class data member, x, you use this.x.

If the data member is static, such as the one in Listing 8.8, you use the class name to reference the variable instead of using the this keyword. For a review on the this keyword and accessing static data variables, go back to Day 6.

Modifying Class Scope with Modifiers

Recall the two modifiers that can be used on methods and data members: private and public. You learned about these during the last three days, and you will learn about others later in this book.

When the `public` modifier is used, a data member or member function can be accessed by methods that are outside a class. You've seen a number of examples of this. When the `private` modifier is used, the data member or method can be accessed only from within the defining class. Data members and methods are private by default.

> **Note**
>
> If you don't declare `private` or `public` on a variable within a class, it is created as `private`.
>
> Also, some languages have the capability to declare variables outside any method or class. Such variables have a different scope then those declared within a function or class. C# cannot declare a variable outside a class.

Creating Classes with No Objects

It is possible to create a class and prevent it from creating an object. You might wonder why you would ever want to do this and how a class can be used if you can't create an object to access it. In reality, you've used a number of classes already that you haven't created objects for. Consider the `Console` class. You have used its `WriteLine` and other methods without declaring a `Console` object. Additionally, classes such as the `Math` class enable you to use them without declaring objects.

How can you use a class without an object? You've learned that `static` methods and data members are assigned to the class, not to the individual objects. If you declare a class with all `static` data and methods, declaring an object is of no value. Listing 8.9 presents the `MyMath` class, which contains a number of methods for doing math operations.

LISTING 8.9   MyMathApp.cs—Math Methods

```
 1:  //  MyMathApp.cs - Static members.
 2:  //----------------------------------------------------------------
 3:
 4:  using System;
 5:
 6:  public class MyMath
 7:  {
 8:      public static long Add( params int[] args )
 9:      {
10:          int ctr = 0;
11:          long Answer = 0;
12:
13:          for( ctr = 0; ctr < args.Length; ctr++)
14:          {
15:              Answer += args[ctr];
```

LISTING 8.9   continued

```
16:            }
17:            return Answer;
18:        }
19:
20:        public static long Subtract( int arg1, int arg2 )
21:        {
22:            long Answer = 0;
23:            Answer = arg1 - arg2;
24:            return Answer;
25:        }
26:    }
27:
28:    class MyMathApp
29:    {
30:        public static void Main()
31:        {
32:            long Result = 0;
33:
34:            Result = MyMath.Add( 1, 2, 3 );
35:            Console.WriteLine("Add result is {0}", Result);
36:
37:            Result = MyMath.Subtract( 5, 2 );
38:            Console.WriteLine("Subtract result is {0}", Result);
39:        }
40:    }
```

OUTPUT   Add result is 6
Subtract result is 3

ANALYSIS   The MyMath class in Lines 6–26 has two methods declared: Subtract and Add. Each of these methods subtracts or adds integers and returns the result. The logic could be more complex; however, that will be left for you to add.

There is no reason to create a MyMath object. Nothing prevents you from creating it, but it's possible to prevent an object from being created.

Using Private Constructors

To prevent an object from being created, you create a private constructor by using the private modifier on the constructor. As you learned earlier, a method with the private keyword can be accessed only from within the class. When you add this modifier, you can't call the constructor from outside the class. Because calling the constructor occurs when you create a class, adding the modifier effectively prevents the class from being created. Listing 8.10 is the MyMath class listing presented again with a private constructor.

LISTING 8.10   MyMathApp2.cs—MyMath Class with a Private Constructor

```
 1:  //  MyMathApp2.cs - Private constructor
 2:  //-------------------------------------------------------------
 3:
 4:  using System;
 5:
 6:  public class MyMath
 7:  {
 8:      public static long Add( params int[] args )
 9:      {
10:          int ctr = 0;
11:          long Answer = 0;
12:
13:          for( ctr = 0; ctr < args.Length; ctr++)
14:          {
15:              Answer += args[ctr];
16:          }
17:          return Answer;
18:      }
19:
20:      public static long Subtract( int arg1, int arg2 )
21:      {
22:          long Answer = 0;
23:          Answer = arg1 - arg2;
24:          return Answer;
25:      }
26:
27:      private MyMath()
28:      {
29:          // nothing to do here since this will never get called!
30:      }
31:  }
32:
33:  class MyMathApp
34:  {
35:      public static void Main()
36:      {
37:          long Result = 0;
38:
39:          // MyMath var = new MyMath();
40:
41:          Result = MyMath.Add( 1, 2, 3 );
42:          Console.WriteLine("Add result is {0}", Result);
43:
44:          Result = MyMath.Subtract( 5, 2 );
45:          Console.WriteLine("Subtract result is {0}", Result);
46:      }
47:  }
```

8

OUTPUT

```
Add result is 6
Subtract result is 3
```

ANALYSIS Lines 27–30 contain a constructor for this class. If you remove the comment from Line 39 and recompile this listing, you get the following error:

```
MyMathApp2.cs(39,20): error CS0122: 'MyMath.MyMath()' is inaccessible due
          to its protection level
```

Creating an object is not possible. The `private` modifier stops you from creating an object. This is not an issue, however, because you can access the `public`, `static` class members anyway.

Revisiting Namespaces

Namespaces can be used to help organize your classes and other types. You've used a number of namespaces that are provided by the framework. This includes the `System` namespace that contains a number of system methods and classes, including the `Console` class that contains the reading and writing routines.

A namespace can contain other namespaces, classes, structures, enumerations, interfaces, and delegates. You are familiar with namespaces, classes, structures, and enumerations. You will learn about interfaces and delegates later in this book.

Naming a Namespace

Namespaces can contain any name that is valid for any other type of identifier. This means that the name should be composed of the standard characters plus underscores. Additionally, namespaces can include periods in their names. As with other identifiers, you should use descriptive names for your namespaces.

Declaring a Namespace

To create a namespace, you use the keyword `namespace` followed by the name that identifies it. You can then use braces to enclose the types that are contained within the namespace. Listing 8.11 contains a listing that declares namespaces.

LISTING 8.11   Routine.cs—Declaring a Namespace

```
1:  // Routine.cs - Declaring namespaces
2:  //---------------------------------------------------------------
3:
4:  using System;
5:
6:  namespace Consts
```

8

LISTING 8.11   continued

```
 7:  {
 8:      public class PI
 9:      {
10:          public static double value = 3.14159;
11:          private PI() {}  // private constructor
12:      }
13:      public class three
14:      {
15:          public static int value = 3;
16:          private three() {} // private constructor
17:      }
18:  }
19:
20:  namespace MyMath
21:  {
22:   public class Routine
23:   {
24:      public static long Add( params int[] args )
25:      {
26:          int ctr = 0;
27:          long Answer = 0;
28:
29:          for( ctr = 0; ctr < args.Length; ctr++)
30:          {
31:              Answer += args[ctr];
32:          }
33:          return Answer;
34:      }
35:
36:      public static long Subtract( int arg1, int arg2 )
37:      {
38:          long Answer = 0;
39:          Answer = arg1 - arg2;
40:          return Answer;
41:      }
42:   }
43:  }
44:
45:  class MyMathApp
46:  {
47:      public static void Main()
48:      {
49:          long Result = 0;
50:
51:          Result = MyMath.Routine.Add( 1, 2, 3 );
52:          Console.WriteLine("Add result is {0}", Result);
53:
54:          Result = MyMath.Routine.Subtract( 5, 2 );
55:          Console.WriteLine("Subtract result is {0}", Result);
56:
```

LISTING 8.11   continued

```
57:            Console.WriteLine("\nThe value of PI is {0}", Consts.PI.value );
58:            Console.WriteLine("The value of three is {0}", Consts.three.value );
59:    }
60: }
```

OUTPUT

```
Add result is 6
Subtract result is 3

The value of PI is 3.14159
The value of three is 3
```

ANALYSIS This listing is a modification of the MyMath listing you saw earlier. Additionally, some additional classes are declared, which is not practical. However, these help illustrate the namespace concepts.

In Line 6, you see the first of two namespaces that are declared in this listing. The Consts namespace contains two classes—PI and three—that are used in Lines 57–58. In these lines, the namespace has to be declared, along with the class and data member name. If you leave off Consts when accessing these classes from a different namespace (such as in Lines 57–58), you get an error:

```
Routinebad.cs(20,1): error CS1529: A using clause must precede all other
        namespace elements
```

However, you can get around this error with the using keyword. You learn about this in the next section.

Note   Every file provides a namespace even if you don't explicitly declare one. Each file contains a global namespace. Anything in this global namespace is available in any named namespace within the file.

using and Namespaces

The using keyword makes using namespaces easier. This keyword provides two functions. First, using can be used to alias a namespace to a different name. Second, using can be used to make it easier to access the types that are located in a namespace by shortcutting the need to fully qualify names.

Shortcutting Fully Qualified Namespace Names

You've already seen how the using keyword can be used to shortcut the need to include a fully qualified name. By including the following line, you no longer have to include the System namespace name when using the classes and types within the System namespace:

```
using System;
```

This enabled you to use Console.WriteLine without the System namespace name being included. In Listing 8.11, you can add the following at Line 5:

```
using Consts;
```

This enables you to use PI.value and three.value without fully qualifying the Consts namespace name.

 Caution

You must include using statements before other code elements. This means that they are best included at the top of a listing. If you try to include them later in a listing, you will get an error.

Aliasing with using

You can also alias a namespace with the using keyword. This enables you to give a namespace—or even a class within a namespace—a different name. This alias can be any valid identifier name. The format of an alias is as follows:

```
using aliasname = namespaceOrClassName;
```

Here, aliasname is the name that you want to use with the alias and namespaceOrClassName is the qualified namespace or class name. For example, consider the following line:

```
using doit = System.Console;
```

If you include this line in your listing, you can use doit in all the places that you would have used System.Console. To write a line to the console, you then type this:

```
doit.WriteLine("blah blah blah");
```

Listing 8.12 illustrates a Hello World program using aliasing of the System.Console class.

LISTING 8.12   AliasApp.cs—Aliasing with using

```
1:  //  AliasApp.cs
2:  //------------------------------------------------------------
3:
4:  using doit = System.Console;
```

LISTING 8.12 continued

```
 5:
 6:  class AliasApp
 7:  {
 8:     public static void Main()
 9:     {
10:         doit.WriteLine("Hello World!");
11:     }
12:  }
```

OUTPUT Hello World!

ANALYSIS This is a very straightforward listing. Line 4 creates a `using` alias called `doit` in the `System.Console` class. The `doit` alias is then used in Line 10 to print a message.

Do	**Don't**
Do understand scope.	**Don't** make data members `public` if they can be kept `private`.
Do use the `using` keyword to make it easier to access members of namespaces.	**Don't** forget that data members are private by default.
Do use namespaces to organize your classes.	

Summary

In today's lesson, you expanded on some of what you learned on previous days. You learned how to overload a method so that it can work with different numbers and types of parameters. You learned that this can be done by creating overloaded methods with unique signatures. In addition to overloading normal methods, you learned how to overload a class's constructor.

You also learned more about the scope of class members. You learned that the `private` keyword isolates a member to the class itself. You learned that the `public` modifier enables the member to be accessed outside the class. You also learned that you can create local variables that exist only within the life of a block of code. You learned that the `this` keyword can be used to identify a data member that is part of a specific instance of a class.

In addition, you learned about namespaces. This includes learning how to create your own namespaces. The `using` keyword was also addressed within the namespace discussion. The `using` keyword enables you to avoid the need to include the fully qualified name to a namespace's members, and it also can be used to alias a namespace or class.

Q&A

Q Can you declare the `Main` method as `private`?

A You can declare the `Main` method as `private`; however, you would be unable to access the `Main` method. To run a program, you need a `Main` method that is publicly accessible. If you can't access the `Main` method from outside the class, you can't run the program.

Q What happens if you don't declare the `Main` method as `public`?

A Although it was stated that methods and data types default to private, the `Main` method actually defaults to public. If you don't include the `public` modifier (and tools such as Visual Studio don't include it), it will still be `public`. To be explicit, it is best to always include the modifier.

Q Scope was briefly discussed in today's lesson. What are the default values of variables if they are not explicitly given a value?

A A number of variable types are not initially assigned a value. This includes instance variables of an initially unassigned structure, output parameters, and local variables. A number of variable types are initially assigned. This includes static variables, instance variables of an object, instance variables of a structure variable that is initially assigned, array elements, value variables used as parameters in a method, and reference. Even though these are initially assigned, you should always set a value initially into all the variables you use.

Q Why not keep things simple and declare everything public?

A One of the benefits of an object-oriented language is to have the capability to encapsulate data and functions into a class that can be treated as a black box. By keeping members private, you make it possible to change the internals without impacting any programs that use the class.

Workshop

The Workshop provides quiz questions to help you solidify your understanding of the material covered and exercises to provide you with experience in using what you've learned. Try to understand the quiz and exercise answers before continuing to the next day's lesson. Answers are provided on the CD.

Quiz

1. Is overloading functions an example of encapsulation, inheritance, polymorphism, or reuse?

2. How many times can a member function be overloaded?

3. Which of the following can be overloaded?

   a. Data members

   b. Member methods

   c. Constructors

   d. Destructors

4. What keyword is used to accept a variable number of parameters in a method?

5. What can you do to receive a variable number of parameters of different, and possibly unknown, data types?

6. To accept a variable number of parameters from the command line, what keyword do you include?

7. What is the default scope for a member of a class?

8. What is the difference between the `public` and `private` modifiers?

9. How can you prevent a class from being instantiated into an object?

10. What are two uses of the `using` keyword?

Exercises

1. Write the line of code for a method header for a `public` function called `abc` that takes a variable number of short values. This method returns a byte.

2. Write the line of code needed to accept command-line parameters.

3. If you have a class called `aClass`, what code can you include to prevent the class from being instantiated into an object?

4. **Bug Buster:** Does the following program have a problem? Enter it in your editor and compile it. If there is a problem, what is it?

```
1:  using doit = System.Console.WriteLine;
2:
3:  class MyApp
4:  {
5:     public static void Main()
6:     {
7:        doit("Hello World!");
8:     }
9:  }
```

5. Create a namespace that contains a class and another namespace. This second namespace should also contain a class. Create an application class that uses both of these classes.

6. Create a program that has a number of overloaded methods. The overloaded method should have the following signatures. Are all these signatures legal? (overload.cs)

```
public myFunc()
public myFunc( int )
public myFunc( float )
public myFunc( ref int )
public myFunc ( ref float )
```

DAY 9

Handling Problems in Your Programs: Exceptions and Errors

If everyone wrote perfect code, if all users entered the correct information the first time, and if all computers disallowed errors, a large number of programmers today would be out of job. The reality is that computers, users, and programmers are not infallible. Because of this, you must write your programs to expect the unexpected. You must write your programs to handle the one thing that is different—the exception. When problems do occur in your programs, you need to find the problems and remove them—a concept known as debugging. Today you will cover a lot. More specifically, you will...

- Learn about the concept of exception handling.
- Discover the `try` and `catch` keywords.
- Implement finality with the `finally` keyword.
- Explore some common exceptions and their causes.

- Understand how to pass an exception to a different routine.
- Define your own exceptions.
- Throw and rethrow exceptions.
- Learn what debugging is.
- Review the primary types of errors that your programs can have.
- Discover how to tell the compiler to ignore parts of your listings.
- Generate your own warnings and errors when compiling.
- Understand how to define symbols both in your code and when compiling.

Understanding the Concept of Handling Problems

When you create a program, you need to consider all possible problems that could arise. When creating programs that obtain information from a file, from a user, from a service, or even from another part of your own program, you should always check to make sure that what you received or what you are using is what you expect. Consider a program that requires you to use a disk file. What happens when the file doesn't exist? If you don't prepare your program for unexpected—or even expected—errors, it could crash.

You can choose not to worry about issues such as these; however, you might find that people quit using your programs. Results of these types of errors can vary. When you write a program, you need to decide which issues are severe enough to worry about and which are not. A good programmer plans for the unusual or unwanted things that might happen.

Preventing Errors via Logical Code

You will find that you can handle a lot of issues within your code with simple programming logic. If simple programming logic can prevent an error, you should add it. For example, you can check the length of a value, you can check for the presence of a command-line argument, or you can verify that a number is within a valid range. These types of checks can easily be performed using the programming constructs you learned in the first week.

Consider the following items. How would you handle these in your code?

- The user tries to open a file that doesn't exist.
- Too many items are assigned to an array.

- The code within a program assigns a string to an integer variable.

- A routine tries to use a reference variable that contains a null (empty) value.

You can write code to avoid these problems, but what happens when you miss one?

What Causes Exceptions?

If you don't programmatically catch problems, an exception can occur. An exception is an uncaught programming error. This excludes logic errors, which are errors because of results that occur, not because of a coding issue. When an uncaught error occurs, the runtime can choke and an exception is thrown. Listing 9.1 contains an error that throws an exception. Run this listing and see what happens when you access the nonexistent sixth element of a five-element array.

LISTING 9.1   Error.cs—Causing an Exception

```
1:  // Error.cs
2:  // A program that throws an exception
3:  //==========================================
4:  using System;
5:
6:  class Error
7:  {
8:     public static void Main()
9:     {
10:        int [] myArray = new int[5];
11:
12:        for ( int ctr = 0; ctr < 10; ctr++ )
13:        {
14:            myArray[ctr] = ctr;
15:        }
16:     }
17:  }
```

ANALYSIS This listing compiles with no errors. It is not very practical because it doesn't create any real output or do anything of value. In Line 10, an array of five integers, named myArray, is created. In Lines 12–15, a for loop assigns the value of a counter to each value in the array. The value of 0 is assigned to myArray[0], 1 is assigned to myArray[1], and so on.

What happens when ctr becomes equal to 5? The conditional statement in Line 12 enables ctr to continue to be incremented as long as it is less than 10. When ctr reaches 5, however, there is a different problem. In Line 14, myArray[5] is not valid—the array's highest element is myArray[4]. The runtime knows that the array cannot have an index value of 5, so it throws an error to indicate that something unusual, or *exceptional*, happened. When you run this program, you might receive a window that gives you an exception error such as the one shown in Figure 9.1. Additionally, you will see a message similar to the following displayed by the runtime:

```
Unhandled Exception: System.IndexOutOfRangeException: Index was outside the boun
ds of the array.
   at Error.Main()
```

The text was actually generated from an underlying object that you are using in your program—the array.

FIGURE 9.1

An exception error being displayed by the runtime.

The results of Listing 9.1 are not pretty and are not what you want your users to see. For a program to be user-friendly, you need to be able to handle these exception errors in a much friendlier manner. Additionally, this program abruptly stopped when the exception occurred. You will also want to be able to maintain control of your programs if these exceptions occur.

Tip	Make a modification to Listing 9.1: Print the value of each array element after it is assigned. This can be done by adding the following after Line 14: `Console.WriteLine("myArray[{0}] equals {1}", ctr, myArray[ctr]);` You will see that the listing stops before printing `myArray[5]`.

Exception Handling

 Exception handling refers to handling runtime errors such as the one created in Listing 9.1. You can add code to your programs that catch the problems and provide cleaner results than pop-up boxes, terminated programs, and cryptic messages. To do this, you use the `try` and `catch` keywords.

Using `try` and `catch`

The `try` and `catch` keywords are the key to exception handling. The `try` command enables you to put a wrapper around a block of code that helps you route any problems (exceptions) that might occur.

The `catch` keyword enables you to catch the exceptions that the `try` command routes. By using a `catch`, you get the chance to execute code and control what happens rather than letting the program terminate. Listing 9.2 illustrates a basic use of the `try` and `catch` commands.

9

LISTING 9.2   TryIt.cs—Using `try-catch`

```
 1:  // TryIt.cs
 2:  // A program that throws an exception
 3:  //=============================================
 4:  using System;
 5:
 6:  class TryIt
 7:  {
 8:     public static void Main()
 9:     {
10:        int [] myArray = new int[5];
11:
12:        try
13:        {
14:           for ( int ctr = 0; ctr < 10; ctr++ )  // Array only has 5 ele-
                 ➥ments!
15:           {
16:              myArray[ctr] = ctr;
17:           }
18:        }
19:
20:        catch
21:        {
22:           Console.WriteLine("The exception was caught!");
23:        }
24:
25:     Console.WriteLine("At end of class");
25:     }
27:  }
```

OUTPUT

```
The exception was caught!
At end of class
```

ANALYSIS This listing is similar to Listing 9.1, but it has basic exception handling added using try and catch. In this version of the listing, the main code is wrapped in a try statement, which starts in Line 12. It uses braces (Lines 13 and 18) to enclose a block of code that is to be watched for exceptions. In this listing, the code that manipulates the array is enclosed in the try statement.

Following the try statement is a catch statement that starts in Line 20 and includes the statements between its braces (Lines 21 and 23). If an exception is found while executing the code within the try statement, control immediately goes to the catch statement. Instead of the results you saw in Listing 9.1, in which a cryptic message was displayed and the program ended, in this listing the code within the catch statement's block executes. The program then continues to operate. In Listing 9.2, the catch statement prints a message and the program flow then continues. Line 25, which contains a call to the WriteLine method, is still executed.

Catching Exception Information

In Listing 9.2, the catch statement catches any exception that might occur within the try statement's code. In addition to generically catching thrown exceptions, you can determine which exception was thrown by including a parameter on your catch. The format of the catch is as follows:

```
catch( System.Exception e ) {}
```

The catch statement can receive the exception as a parameter. In this example, the exception is a variable named e. You could call this something more descriptive, but for this example, the name e works.

You can see that e is of type System.Exception, a fully qualified name meaning that the Exception type is defined in the System namespace. If you include the System statement with a using statement, you can shorten the catch call to this:

```
catch(Exception e) {}
```

The Exception type variable e contains descriptive information on the specific exception that was caused. Listing 9.3 is a modified version of Listing 9.2, containing a catch statement that receives any exceptions as a parameter. The changed lines are in boldface.

LISTING 9.3   TryIt2.cs—Catching Exception Information

```
1:  // TryIt2.cs
2:  // A program that throws an exception
3:  //===========================================
4:  using System;
```

LISTING 9.3   continued

```
 5:
 6:  class TryIt2
 7:  {
 8:      public static void Main()
 9:      {
10:          int [] myArray = new int[5];
11:
12:          try
13:          {
14:              for ( int ctr = 0; ctr < 10; ctr++ )  // Array only has 5 ele-
                 ➥ments!
15:              {
16:                  myArray[ctr] = ctr;
17:              }
18:          }
19:
20:          catch( Exception e)
21:          {
22:              Console.WriteLine("The following exception was caught:\n{0}", e);
23:          }
24:
25:          Console.WriteLine("At end of class");
26:      }
27: }
```

OUTPUT

```
The following exception was caught:
System.IndexOutOfRangeException: Index was outside the bounds of the
array.
    at TryIt2.Main()


At end of class
```

ANALYSIS Listing 9.3 doesn't do much with the exception; however, you can gain a lot of information from what it does. In Line 22, e is printed using the WriteLine method. This displays information on the exception. Looking at the output, you see that the value of e indicates that the exception thrown was an IndexOutOfRangeException and occurred in the Main() method of the MyAppClass—which is your program's class.

This listing catches all exceptions that occur within the try statement. The error printed is based on the type of exception executed. You can actually add code to your program to work with specific errors.

9

Note

Once again, the exception was caught and the program continued to execute. Using a `catch` statement, you can prevent weird error messages from
being automatically displayed. Additionally, the program doesn't terminate
at the moment the exception occurs.

Using Multiple catches for a Single try

The `catch` statement in Listing 9.2 is rather general. It can catch any exception that might
have occurred in the code within the `try` statement code. You can include a `catch` statement that is more specific—in fact, you can write a `catch` statement for a specific exception. Listing 9.4 includes a `catch` statement that captures the exception you are already
familiar with—`IndexOutOfRangeException`.

LISTING 9.4   CatchIndex.cs—Catching a Specific Exception

```
 1:  // CatchIndex.cs
 2:  // A program that throws an exception
 3:  //==========================================
 4:  using System;
 5:
 6:  class CatchIndex
 7:  {
 8:     public static void Main()
 9:     {
10:        int [] myArray = new int[5];
11:
12:        try
13:        {
14:           for ( int ctr = 0; ctr < 10; ctr++ )  // Array only has 5 ele-
              ➥ments!
15:           {
16:              myArray[ctr] = ctr;
17:           }
18:        }
19:
20:        catch (IndexOutOfRangeException e)
21:        {
22:           Console.WriteLine(
              ➥"You were very goofy trying to use a bad array index!!", e);
23:        }
24:
25:        catch (Exception e)
26:        {
27:           Console.WriteLine("Exception caught: {0}", e);
28:        }
```

LISTING 9.4 continued

```
29:
30:         Console.WriteLine("\nDone with the catch statements. Done with pro-
       ➥gram.");
31:     }
32: }
```

OUTPUT

```
You were very goofy trying to use a bad array index!!

Done with the catch statements. Done with program.
```

ANALYSIS This listing uses the same array and the same `try` command that you used in the previous listings, but Lines 20–23 feature something new. Instead of having a parameter for a general exception, the `catch` statement in Line 20 has a parameter for an `IndexOutOfRangeException` type. Like the general `Exception` type, this is in the `System` namespace. Just as its name implies, this exception type is specifically for indexes that go out of range. This `catch` statement captures only this type of exception, though.

To be prepared for other exceptions that might occur, a second `catch` statement is included in Lines 25–28. This `catch` includes the general `Exception` type parameter, so it will catch any other exceptions that might occur. Replace Line 16 of Listing 9.4 with the following:

```
16:         myArray[ctr] = 100/ctr;   // division by zero....
```

When you recompile and run the program, you will get the following output:

```
Exception caught: System.DivideByZeroException: Attempted to divide by zero.
   at CatchIndex2.Main()

Done with the catch statements. Done with program.
```

The new Line 16 causes a different error. The first time through the `for` loop in Line 14, `ctr` is equal to 0. Line 16 ends up dividing 100 by 0 (`ctr`). Division by 0 is not legal because it creates an infinite number, and thus an exception is thrown. This is not an index out of range, so the `catch` statement in Line 20 is ignored because it doesn't match the `IndexOutOfRangeException` type. The `catch` in Line 25 can work with any exception and thus is executed. Line 27 prints the statement `"Exception Caught"`, followed by the exception description obtained with the variable `e`. As you can see by the output, the exception thrown is a `DivideByZeroException`.

Understanding the Order of Handling Exceptions

In Listing 9.4, the order of the two `catch` statements is very important. You always include the more specific exceptions first and the most general exception last. Starting with the original Listing 9.4, if you change the order of the two `catch` statements:

```
catch (Exception e)
{
    Console.WriteLine("Exception caught: {0}", e);
}

catch (IndexOutOfRangeException e)
{
    Console.WriteLine(
"You were very goofy trying to use a bad array index!!", e);
}
```

When you recompile, you get an error. Because the general `catch(Exception e)` catches all the exceptions, no other `catch` statements are executed.

Adding Finality with `finally`

Sometimes you will want to execute a block of code regardless of whether the code in a `try` statement succeeds or fails. C# provides the `finally` keyword to take care of this (see Listing 9.5). The code in a `finally` block always executes.

LISTING 9.5   Final.cs—Using the `finally` Keyword

```
 1:  // Final.cs
 2:  // A program that throws an exception
 3:  //=============================================
 4:  using System;
 5:
 6:  class Final
 7:  {
 8:      public static void Main()
 9:      {
10:          int [] myArray = new int[5];
11:
12:          try
13:          {
14:              for ( int ctr = 0; ctr < 10; ctr++ )  // Array only has 5 ele-
                 ments!
15:              {
16:                  myArray[ctr] = ctr;
17:              }
18:          }
19:
20: //      catch
21: //      {
22: //          Console.WriteLine("Exception caught");
23: //      }
24:
25:          finally
```

LISTING 9.5 continued

```
26:        {
27:            Console.WriteLine("Done with exception handling");
28:        }
29:
30:        Console.WriteLine("End of Program");
31:    }
32: }
```

OUTPUT
```
Unhandled Exception: System.IndexOutOfRangeException: Index was outside
➥ the bounds of the array.
.IndexOutOfRangeException was thrown.
   at Final.Main()
Done with exception handling
```

ANALYSIS Listing 9.5 is the same listing you saw before. The key change to this listing is in Lines 25–28: A `finally` clause has been added. In this listing, the `finally` clause prints a message. It is important to note that even though the exception was not caught by a `catch` clause (Lines 20–23 are commented out), the `finally` still executed before the program terminated. The `WriteLine` command in Line 30, however, doesn't execute.

Remove the comments from Lines 20–23 and rerun the program. This time, you receive the following output:

OUTPUT
```
Exception caught.
Done with exception handling
End of Program
```

The use of a `catch` does not preclude the `finally` code from happening. Now change Line 14 to the following:

```
14:            for ( int ctr = 0; ctr < 5; ctr++ )
```

Then recompile and run the program; you will get the following output:

OUTPUT
```
Done with exception handling
End of Program
```

Notice that this change to Line 14 removed the problem that was causing the exception to occur. This means that the listing ran without problems. As you can see from the output, the `finally` block was still executed. The `finally` block will be executed regardless of what else happens.

Now is a good time to show a more robust example that uses exception handling. Listing 9.6 illustrates a more practical program.

LISTING 9.6   ListFile.cs—Using Exception Handling

```
 1:  // ListFile.cs - program to print a listing to the console
 2:  //-----------------------------------------------------------
 3:
 4:  using System;
 5:  using System.IO;
 6:
 7:  class ListFile
 8:  {
 9:    public static void Main(string[] args)
10:    {
11:      try
12:      {
13:
14:          int ctr=0;
15:          if (args.Length <= 0 )
16:          {
17:              Console.WriteLine("Format: ListFile filename");
18:              return;
19:          }
20:          else
21:          {
22:              FileStream fstr = new FileStream(args[0], FileMode.Open);
23:              try
24:              {
25:                  StreamReader sReader = new StreamReader(fstr);
26:                  string line;
27:                  while ((line = sReader.ReadLine()) != null)
28:                  {
29:                      ctr++;
30:                      Console.WriteLine("{0}:  {1}", ctr, line);
31:                  }
32:              }
33:              catch( Exception e )
34:              {
35:                  Console.WriteLine("Exception during read/write: {0}\n", e);
36:              }
37:              finally
38:              {
39:                  fstr.Close();
40:              }
41:          }
42:      }
43:
44:      catch (System.IO.FileNotFoundException)
45:      {
46:          Console.WriteLine ("ListFile could not find the file {0}", args[0]);
47:      }
48:      catch (Exception e)
```

LISTING 9.6   continued

```
49:      {
50:          Console.WriteLine("Exception: {0}\n\n", e);
51:      }
52:    }
53: }
```

OUTPUT

```
Format: ListFile filename
```

ANALYSIS   If you run this program, you get the output displayed. You need to include a filename as a parameter to the program. If you run this program with ListFile.cs as
the parameter, the output will be the listing with line numbers:

OUTPUT

```
 1: // ListFile.cs - program to print a listing to the console
 2: //------------------------------------------------------------
 3:
 4: using System;
 5: using System.IO;
 6:
 7: class ListFile
 8: {
 9:   public static void Main(string[] args)
10:   {
11:     try
12:     {
13:
14:         int ctr-0,
15:         if (args.Length <= 0 )
16:         {
17:             Console.WriteLine("Format: ListFile filename");
18:             return;
19:         }
20:         else
21:         {
22:             FileStream fstr = new FileStream(args[0], FileMode.Open);
23:             try
24:             {
25:                 StreamReader sReader = new StreamReader(fstr);
26:                 string line;
27:                 while ((line = sReader.ReadLine()) != null)
28:                 {
29:                     ctr++;
30:                     Console.WriteLine("{0}:  {1}", ctr, line);
31:                 }
32:             }
33:             catch( Exception e )
34:             {
35:                 Console.WriteLine("Exception during read/write:
                    ➥{0}\n", e);
```

```
36:                    }
37:                    finally
38:                    {
39:                        fstr.Close();
40:                    }
41:                }
42:            }
43:
44:            catch (System.IO.FileNotFoundException)
45:            {
46:                Console.WriteLine ("ListFile could not find the file {0}",
                   ➥args[0]);
47:            }
48:            catch (Exception e)
49:            {
50:                Console.WriteLine("Exception: {0}\n\n", e);
51:            }
52:        }
53:    }
```

You can add different filenames and get the same results if the file exists. If you enter a file that doesn't exist, you get the following message (the filename xxx was used):

```
ListFile could not find the file xxx
```

Notice that the program isn't presenting the user with cryptic exception messages from the runtime. Instead, it is trying to provide useful information back to the user on what happened. This is done with a combination of programming logic and exception handling.

This listing incorporates everything you've been learning. In Lines 4–5, you see that not only is the System namespace being used, but so is the IO namespace within System. The IO namespace contains routines for sending and receiving information (input/output).

In Line 7, you see the start of the main application class, ListFile. This class has a Main routine, where program execution starts. In Line 9, the Main method receives a string array named args as a parameter. The values within args are obtained from the command-line arguments that you include when you run the program.

Line 11 starts the code that is the focus of today's lesson. In this line, a try block is declared. This try block encompasses the code from Line 11 to Line 42. You can see that this try block has lots of code in it, including another try command. If any of the code within this try block causes an exception to occur—and not be handled— the try statement fails and control goes to its catch blocks. It is important to note that only unhandled exceptions within this try block cause flow to go to this try's catch statements.

Two catch blocks are defined for this overriding try statement. The first, in Lines 44–47, catches a specific exception, FileNotFoundException. For clarity's sake, the exception name is fully qualified; however, you could have chosen to shorten this to just the exception type because System.IO was included in Line 5. The FileNotFoundException occurs when you try to use a file that does not exist. In this case, if the file doesn't exist, a simple message is printed in Line 46 that states the file couldn't be found.

Although the FileNotFoundException is expected with this program, Lines 48–51 were added in case an unexpected exception happens. This allows a graceful exit instead of relying on the runtime.

Digging deeper into the code within the try statement, you get a better understanding of what this program is doing. In Line 14, a simple counter variable, ctr, is created, which is used to place line numbers on a listing.

Line 15 contains programming logic that checks to make sure that users include a filename when they run the program. If a filename is not included, you want to exit the program. In Line 15, an if statement checks the value of the Length property of the args string. If the length is less than or equal to 0, no command-line parameters were entered. The user should have entered at least one item as a command-line parameter. If no items were entered, a descriptive message is presented to the reader and the object is ended using the return statement.

If a command-line parameter is entered—args.Length is greater than 0—the else statement in Lines 20–41 is executed. In Line 22, a new object named fstr is created. This object is of type FileStream, which has a constructor that takes two arguments. The first is a filename. The filename that you are passing is the filename entered by the user and, thus, is available in the first element of the args array. This is args[0]. The second parameter is an indicator of what to do. In this case, you are passing a value named FileMode.Open, which indicates to the FileStream object that it should open a file so that you can read its contents. The file that is opened is referenced using the FileStream object that you are creating, fstr.

If Line 22 fails and throws an exception, it goes to the catch in Line 44. Line 44 contains the catch for the closest try statement (without having gone past it).

Line 23 starts a new try block that has its own catch statement in Line 33. Line 25 creates a variable named t of type StreamReader. This variable is associated to the file that you opened in Line 22 with the variable fstr. The file is treated as a stream of characters flowing into your program. The t variable is used to read this stream of characters.

Line 26 contains a string variable named line, which is used to hold a group of characters that are being streamed into your program. In Line 27, you see how line is used.

Line 27 does a lot, so it is worth dissecting. First, a line of characters is streamed into your program using sReader. The StreamReader type has a method named ReadLine that provides a line of characters. A line of characters is all the characters up until a newline character is found. Because t was associated with fstr and fstr is associated with the file the reader entered, the ReadLine method returns the next line of characters from the user's file. This line of characters is then assigned to the line string variable. After reading this line of characters and placing it into the line variable, the value is compared to null. If the string returned was null, it was either the end of the file or a bad read. Either way, there is no reason to continue processing the file after the null value is encountered.

If the characters read and placed into line are not equal to null, the while statement processes its block commands. In this case, the line counter, ctr, is incremented and the line of text is printed. The printing includes the line number, a colon, and the text from the file that is in the line variable. This processing continues until a null is found.

If anything goes wrong in reading a line of the file, an exception most likely is thrown. Lines 33–36 catch any exceptions that might occur and add additional descriptive text to the exception message. This catch prevents the runtime from taking over. Additionally, it helps you and your users by giving additional information on where the error occurred.

Lines 37–40 contain a finally that is also associated with the try in Line 23. This finally does one thing: It closes the file that was opened in Line 22. Because Line 22 was successful—if it had not been successful, it would have tossed an exception and program flow would have gone to Line 44's catch statement—the file needs to be closed before the program ends. Whether an exception occurs in Lines 24–32 or not, the file should still be closed before leaving the program. The finally clause makes sure that the Close method is called.

As you can see from this listing, try-catch-finally statements can be nested. Not only that, but they also can be used to make your programs much more friendly for your users.

 Note   A program very similar to ListFile was used to add the line numbers to the listings in this book.

Common Exceptions

A number of exceptions are defined in the .NET Framework classes. You have seen a couple already. Table 9.1 lists many of the common exception classes within the System namespace.

TABLE 9.1 Common Exceptions in the `System` Namespace

Exception Name	Description
`MemberAccessException`	Access error. A type member, such as a method, cannot be accessed.
`ArgumentException`	Argument error. A method's argument is not valid.
`ArgumentNullException`	Null argument. A method was passed a null argument that cannot be accepted.
`ArithmeticException`	Math error. An exception caused because of a math operation. This is more general than `DivideByZeroException` and `OverflowException`.
`ArrayTypeMismatchException`	Array type mismatch. This is thrown when you try to store an incompatible type into an array.
`DivideByZeroException`	Divide by zero. Caused by an attempt to divide by zero.
`FormatException`	Format is incorrect. An argument has the wrong format.
`IndexOutOfRangeException`	Index is out of range. Caused when an index is used that is less than 0 or higher than the top value of the array's index.
`InvalidCastException`	Invalid cast. This is caused when an explicit conversion fails.
`MulticastNotSupportedException`	Multicast not supported. This is caused when the combination of two non-null delegates fails. (Delegates are covered on Day 13, "Making Your Programs React with Delegates, Events, and Indexers.")
`NotFiniteNumberException`	Not a finite number. The number is not valid.
`NotSupportedException`	Method is not supported. This indicates that a method is being called that is not implemented within the class.
`NullReferenceException`	Reference to null. This is caused when you refer to a reference object that is null.
`OutOfMemoryException`	Out of memory. This is caused when memory is not available for a new statement to allocate.

9

TABLE 9.1   continued

Exception Name	Description
OverflowException	Overflow. This is caused by a math operation that assigns a value that is too large (or too small) when the checked keyword is used.
StackOverflowException	Stack overflow. This is caused when too many commands are on the stack.
TypeInitializationException	Bad type initialization. This is caused when a static constructor has a problem.

> **Note**   Table 9.1 provides the name with the assumption that you've included a
> using statement with the System namespace; otherwise, you need to fully
> qualify these names using System.*ExceptionName,* where *ExceptionName* is
> the name provided in the table.

Defining Your Own Exception Classes

In addition to the exceptions that have been defined in the framework, you can create
your own. In C#, it is preferred that you throw an exception instead of pass back a lot of
different error codes. Because of this, it is also important that your code always include
exception handling in case an exception is thrown. Although this adds more lines of code
to your programs, it can make them much more friendly to your users.

After you create your own exception, you will want to cause it to occur. To cause an
exception to occur, you *throw* the exception. To throw your own exception, you use the
throw keyword.

You can throw a predefined exception or your own exception. Predefined exceptions are
any that have been previously defined in any of the namespaces you are using. For example, you can actually throw any of the exceptions that were listed in Table 9.1. To do this,
you use the throw keyword in the following format:

```
throw( exception );
```

If the exception doesn't already exist, you also will need to include the new keyword to
create the exception. For example, Listing 9.7 throws a new DivideByZeroException
exception. Granted, this listing is pretty pointless; however, it does illustrate the throw
keyword in its most basic form.

> **Note**
>
> The use of parentheses with the throw keyword is optional. The following two lines are the equivalent:
>
> ```
> throw( exception );
> ```
>
> ```
> throw exception;
> ```

9

LISTING 9.7   Zero.cs—Throwing an Exception

```
 1:  // Zero.cs
 2:  // Throwing a predefined exception.
 3:  // This listing gives a runtime exception error!
 4:  //================================================
 5:  using System;
 6:
 7:  class Zero
 8:  {
 9:     public static void Main()
10:     {
11:        Console.WriteLine("Before Exception...");
12:        throw( new DivideByZeroException() );
13:        Console.WriteLine("After Exception...");
14:     }
15:  }
```

OUTPUT

```
Before Exception...

Unhandled Exception: System.DivideByZeroException: Attempted to divide
➡by zero.
   at Zero.Main()
```

ANALYSIS This listing does nothing other than print messages and throw a DivideByZeroException exception in Line 12. When this program executes, you get a runtime error that indicates the exception was thrown. It's simple but impractical.

When you compile this listing, you get a compiler warning:

```
Zero.cs(13,7): warning CS0162: Unreachable code detected
```

This is because Line 13 will never be executed: The throw command terminates the program. Remember, a throw command leaves the current routine immediately. You can remove Line 13 from the listing—because it would never execute anyway—to avoid the compiler warning. It was added to this listing to emphasize what an exception does to program flow.

]You could replace the `DivideByZeroException` with any of the exceptions listed in Table 9.1. The output would display the appropriate information.

Throwing Your Own Exceptions

Also possible—and more valuable—is being able to create and throw your own exceptions. To create your own exception, you must first declare it. Use the following format:

```
class ExceptionName : Exception {}
```

Here, *ExceptionName* is the name your exception will have. You can tell from this line of code that your exception is a class type. The rest of this line tells you that your exception is related to an existing class named `Exception`. You will learn more about this relationship in tomorrow's lessons on inheritance.

End your exception name with the word `Exception`. If you look at Table 9.1, you will see that this tip follows suit with the predefined exceptions.

One line of code is all that it takes to create your own exception that can then be caught. Listing 9.8 illustrates creating and throwing your own exception.

LISTING 9.8   MathApp.cs—Creating and Throwing Your Own Exception

```
 1: // MathApp.cs
 2: // Throwing your own error.
 3: //=============================================
 4: using System;
 5:
 6: class MyThreeException : Exception {}
 7:
 8: class MathApp
 9: {
10:    public static void Main()
11:    {
12:       int result;
13:
14:       try
15:       {
16:          result = MyMath.AddEm( 1, 2 );
17:          Console.WriteLine( "Result of AddEm(1, 2) is {0}", result);
18:
19:          result = MyMath.AddEm( 3, 4 );
```

LISTING 9.8   continued

```
20:                 Console.WriteLine( "Result of AddEm(3, 4) is {0}", result);
21:         }
22:
23:         catch (MyThreeException)
24:         {
25:             Console.WriteLine("Ack!  We don't like adding threes.");
26:         }
27:
28:         catch (Exception e)
29:         {
30:             Console.WriteLine("Exception caught: {0}", e);
31:         }
32:
33:         Console.WriteLine("\nAt end of program");
34:     }
35: }
36:
37: class MyMath
38: {
39:     static public int AddEm(int x, int y)
40:     {
41:         if(x == 3 || y == 3)
42:             throw( new MyThreeException() );
43:
44:         return( x + y );
45:     }
46: }
```

OUTPUT   Result of AddEm(1, 2) is 3
Ack! We don't like adding threes.

At end of program

ANALYSIS   This listing shows you how to create your own exception named
MyThreeException. This exception is defined in Line 6 using the format you
learned earlier. This enables you to throw a basic exception.

Before jumping into MathApp, first look at the second class in Lines 37–46. This class
named MyMath contains only a simple static method named AddEm. The AddEm method adds
two numbers and returns the result. In Line 41, an if condition checks to see whether
either of the values passed to AddEm is equal to 3; if so, an exception is thrown. This is the
MyThreeException that you declared in Line 6.

In Lines 8–34, you have the Main routine for MathApp. This routine calls the AddEm method.
These calls are done within a try statement, so if any exceptions are thrown, it is ready to
react. In Line 16, the first call to AddEm occurs using the values 1 and 2. These values

don't throw an exception, so program flow continues. Line 19 calls the AddEm method again. This time the first argument is a 3, which results in the AddEm method throwing the MyThreeException. Line 23 contains a catch statement that is looking for a MyThreeException and thus catches and takes care of it.

If you don't catch the exception, the runtime throws an exception message for you. If you comment out Lines 23–26 of Listing 9.8, you get output similar to the following when you compile and rerun the program:

```
Result of AddEm(1, 2) is 3
Exception caught: MyThreeException: Exception of type MyThreeException was
➥thrown.
   at MyMath.AddEm(Int32 x, Int32 y)
   at MathApp.Main()
At end of program
```

This is the same type of message that any other exception receives. You can also pass a parameter to the catch class that handles your exception. This parameter contains the information for the general system message. For example, change Lines 23–26 to the following:

```
23:        catch (MyThreeException e )
24:        {
25:            Console.WriteLine("Ack!  We don't like adding threes. \n {0}" ,
           ➥e);
26:        }
```

You will see the following results (this assumes that you uncommented the lines as well):

```
Result of AddEm(1, 2) is 3
Ack!  We don't like adding threes.
MyThreeException: An exception of type MyThreeException was thrown.
   at MathApp.Main()

At end of program
```

Your new exception is as fully functioning as any of the existing exceptions.

 Tip

Listing 9.8 creates a basic exception. To be more complete, you should include three constructors for your new exception. The details of these overloads will become clearer after tomorrow's lesson on inheritance. For now, you should know that you are being more complete by including the following code, which contains three constructors:

```
class MyThreeException : Exception
{
  public MyThreeException()
  {
```

```
   }

   public MyThreeException( string e ) : base (e)
   {
   }

   public MyThreeException( string e, Exception inner ) :
          base ( e, inner )
   {
   }
}
```

You can replace the exception name of `MyThreeException` with your own exception.

Rethrowing an Exception

It should come as no surprise that if you can throw your own exceptions, and if you can throw system expressions, it is also possible to rethrow an existing exception. Why might you want to do this? And *when* would you want to do this?

As you have seen, you can catch an exception and execute your own code in reaction. If you do this in a class that was called by another class, you might want to let the caller know there was a problem. Before letting the caller know, you might want to do some processing of your own.

Consider an example based on an earlier program. You could create a class that opens a file, counts the number of characters in the file, and returns this to a calling program. If you get an error when you open the file to begin your count, an exception will be thrown. You can catch this exception, set the count to 0, and return to the calling program. However, the calling program won't know that there was a problem opening the file. It will see only that the number of bytes returned was 0.

A better action to take is to set the number of characters to 0 and then rethrow the error for the calling program. This way, the calling program knows exactly what happened and can react, if necessary.

To rethrow the error, you need to include a parameter in your `catch` statement. This parameter should be of the error type. The following code illustrates how the generic `catch` statement could rethrow an exception that was caught:

```
catch (Exception e)
{
    // My personal exception logic here
```

```
throw ( e );   // e is the argument received by this catch
}
```

Note

As you begin to build more detailed applications, you might want to look deeper into exception handling. You have learned the most important features of exception handling today, but you can do a lot more with them. Such topics are beyond the scope of this book, however.

Using checked Versus unchecked Statements

Two additional C# keywords can make an impact on exceptions being thrown. These are checked and unchecked. If the code is checked and a value is placed in a variable that is too big or too small, an exception will occur. If the code is unchecked, the value placed will be truncated to fit within the variable. Listing 9.9 illustrates these two keywords in use.

LISTING 9.9   CheckIt.cs—Using the checked Keyword

```
 1:  // CheckIt.cs
 2:  //=============================================
 3:
 4:  using System;
 5:
 6:  class CheckIt
 7:  {
 8:     public static void Main()
 9:     {
10:         int result;
11:         const int topval = 2147483647;
12:
13:         for( long ctr = topval - 5L;  ctr < (topval+10L); ctr++ )
14:         {
15:            checked
16:            {
17:                result = (int) ctr;
18:                Console.WriteLine("{0} assigned from {1}", result, ctr);
19:            }
20:         }
21:     }
22:  }
```

OUTPUT   You get the following error output; you also get an exception:

```
2147483642 assigned from 2147483642
2147483643 assigned from 2147483643
2147483644 assigned from 2147483644
2147483645 assigned from 2147483645
2147483646 assigned from 2147483646
2147483647 assigned from 2147483647

Unhandled Exception: System.OverflowException: Arithmetic operation
    resulted in an overflow.
    at CheckIt.Main()
```

9

ANALYSIS   In Line 11 of this listing, a variable named topval is created as a constant variable that contains the largest value that a regular integer variable can hold, 2147483647. The for loop in Line 13 loops to a value that is 10 higher than this top value. This is being placed in a long variable, which is okay. In Line 17, however, the ctr value is being explicitly placed into result, which is an integer. When you execute this listing, you receive an error because the code in Lines 16–19 is checked. This code tries to assign a value to result that is larger than the largest value it can hold.

Note

> If you remove the +10 from Line 13 of the listing and compile it, you will see that the listing works. This is because there is nothing wrong. It is when you try to go above the topVal that the overflow error occurs.

You should now change this listing to use the unchecked keyword. Change Line 15 in the listing to the following:

```
13:     unchecked
```

Recompile and execute the listing. The listing will compile this time; however, the output might be unexpected results. The output this time is as follows:

OUTPUT
```
2147483642 assigned from 2147483642
2147483643 assigned from 2147483643
2147483644 assigned from 2147483644
2147483645 assigned from 2147483645
2147483646 assigned from 2147483646
2147483647 assigned from 2147483647
-2147483648 assigned from 2147483648
-2147483647 assigned from 2147483649
-2147483646 assigned from 2147483650
-2147483645 assigned from 2147483651
-2147483644 assigned from 2147483652
-2147483643 assigned from 2147483653
```

```
-2147483642 assigned from 2147483654
-2147483641 assigned from 2147483655
-2147483640 assigned from 2147483656
```

You should notice that this time, an exception was not thrown because the code was unchecked. The results, however, are not what you would want.

Formats for checked and unchecked

Within Listing 9.9, checked and unchecked were used as statements. The format of these was as follows:

```
[un]checked { //statements }
```

You can also use these as operators. The format of using these keywords as operators is shown here:

```
[un]checked ( expression )
```

Here, the expression being checked, or unchecked, is between the parentheses.

> **Caution**
>
> You should not assume that checked or unchecked is the default. checked is generally defaulted; however, factors can change this. You can force checking to occur by including /checked in your command-line compiler. If you are using an integrated development tool, you should be able to select a checked item on your compile options. You can force checking to be ignored by using /checked- at the command line.

What Is Debugging?

When something goes unexpectedly wrong with the compilation or execution of a program, it is up to you to determine what the problem is. In small programs such as those used as examples in this book, it is usually relatively easy to look through the listing to figure out what the problem is. In larger programs, finding the error can be much harder.

 The process of looking for and removing an error is called *debugging*. An error is often referred to as a bug in a program. One of the first computer problems was caused by a bug—specifically, a moth. This bug was found in the computer and removed. Although this error was caused by an actual bug, it has become common to refer to all computer errors as bugs.

> **Note** Knowing that this bug was a moth was a million-dollar question on *Who Wants to Be a Millionaire?* It is good to know that such trivial facts can sometimes become very valuable to know.

Understanding the Types of Errors

NEW TERM As you learned on one of the first days of this book, a number of different types of errors exist. Most errors must be caught before you can run your program. The compiler catches these problems and lets you know about them in the form of errors and warnings. Other errors are harder to find. For example, you can write a program that compiles with no errors but that doesn't perform as you expect. These errors are called *logic errors*. You can also cleanly compile a listing but run into errors when the end user enters bad information, when data is received that your program does not expect, when data is missing, or when any of a nearly infinite number of things is not quite right.

Finding Errors

You will find two standard types of errors: syntax errors and runtime errors.

Encountering Syntax Errors

Syntax errors are generally identified when you compile your listing. At compile time, the compiler identifies these problems with errors and warnings. The compiler provides the location of these errors with a description.

Encountering Runtime Errors

Runtime errors are caused by several issues. You've learned to prevent some of these from crashing your programs by adding exception handling to your programs. For example, if a program tries to open a file that doesn't exist, an exception is thrown. By adding exception handling, you can catch and handle runtime exception errors.

Other runtime errors can be caused by a user entering bad information. For example, if you use an integer to capture a person's age, the user could theoretically enter 30,000 or some other invalid number. This won't throw an exception or cause any other type of error. However, it is still a problem for your program because it is bad data. This type of issue is easily resolved with a little extra programming logic to check the value entered by the user of the program.

A number of runtime errors are harder to find. These are logic errors that are syntactically correct and that don't cause the program to crash. Instead, they provide you with erroneous results. These runtime errors, along with some of the more complex exceptions, might require you to employ more effort to find them than simply reading through your listing's code. These errors require serious debugging.

Some of the ways you can find these more complex errors include walking through your code line by line. You can do this by hand or you can use an automated tool such as a *debugger*. You can also use a few of the features provided within C# to find the errors. This includes using directives or using a couple of built-in classes.

Tracing Code with Code Walkthroughs

 A *code walkthrough* involves reading your code one line at a time. You start at the first line of code that would execute and read each line as it would be encountered. You can also read through each class definition to verify that the logic is contained correctly within the class. This is a tedious, long process that, when done by hand, can take a lot of time and is prone to errors. The positive side of doing these manual code walkthroughs is that you should understand fully the code within your program.

> **Note**
>
> Many companies have code walkthroughs as a standard part of the development process. Generally, these involve sitting down with one or more other people on a project and reading through the code together. It is your job in these walkthroughs to explain the code to the other participants. You might think that there is little value to this; however, often you will find better ways to complete the same task.

Working with Preprocessor Directives

C# provides a number of directives that can be used within your code. These directives can determine how the compiler treats your code. If you have programmed in C or C++, you might be familiar with directives such as these. In C#, however, there are fewer directives. Table 9.2 presents the directives available in C#. The following sections cover the more important of these.

Note

In C and C++, these directives are called *preprocessor* directives because, before compiling the code, the compiler preprocesses the listing and evaluates any preprocessor directives. The name preprocessor is still associated with these directives; however, preprocessing isn't necessary for the compiler to evaluate them.

TABLE 9.2   C# Directives

Directive	Description
#define	Defines a symbol.
#else	Starts an else block.
#elif	Combination of an else statement and an if statement.
#endregion	Identifies the end of a region.
#endif	Ends an #if statement.
#if	Tests a value.
#error	Sends a specified error message when compiled.
#line	Specifies a line source code line number. It can also include a filename that will appear in the output.
#region	Identifies the start of a region. A region is a section of code that can be expanded or collapsed in an IDE.
#undef	Undefines a symbol.
#warning	Sends a specified warning message when compiled.

Preprocessing Declarations

Directives are easy to identify: They start with a pound sign and are the first item on a coding line. However, directives don't end with a semicolon.

The first directives to be aware of are #define and #undef. These directives enable you to define or undefine a symbol that can be used to determine what code is included in your listings. By being able to exclude or include code in your listing, you can allow the same code to be used in multiple ways.

One of the most common ways to use these directives is for debugging. When you are creating a program, you often would like to have it generate extra information that you won't want displayed when in production. Instead of adding and removing this code all the time, you can use defining directives and then define or undefine a value.

The basic format of `#define` and `#undef` is

```
#define xxxx
```

and

```
#undef xxxx
```

Here, *xxxx* is the name of the symbol being defined or undefined. Listing 9.10 uses a listing from earlier in the book. This listing displays the contents of a file provided on the command line.

 Caution   This listing does not include exception-handling code, so you can create errors. For example, if you try to open a file that doesn't exist, an exception will be thrown.

LISTING 9.10   Reading.cs—Using the `#define` Directive

```
 1:  //  Reading.cs - Read text from a file.
 2:  //  Exception handling left out to keep listing short.
 3:  //---------------------------------------------------
 4:
 5:  #define DEBUG
 6:
 7:  using System;
 8:  using System.IO;
 9:
10:  public class Reading
11:  {
12:     public static void Main(String[] args)
13:     {
14:        if( args.Length < 1 )
15:        {
16:            Console.WriteLine("Must include file name.");
17:        }
18:        else
19:        {
20:
21:  #if DEBUG
22:
23:        Console.WriteLine("==============DEBUG INFO==============");
24:        for ( int x = 0; x < args.Length ; x++ )
25:        {
26:            Console.WriteLine("Arg[{0}] = {1}", x, args[x]);
27:        }
28:        Console.WriteLine("=====================================");
29:
```

LISTING 9.10   continued

```
30:  #endif
31:
32:          string buffer;
33:
34:          StreamReader myFile = File.OpenText(args[0]);
35:
36:          while ( (buffer = myFile.ReadLine()) != null )
37:          {
38:  #if DEBUG
39:    Console.Write( "{0:D3} - ", buffer.Length);
40:  #endif
41:              Console.WriteLine(buffer);
42:          }
43:
44:          myFile.Close();
45:      }
46:   }
47: }
```

OUTPUT
```
==============DEBUG INFO==============
Arg[0] = Reading.cs
========================================
041 - //  Reading.cs - Read text from a file.
054 - //  Exception handling left out to keep listing short.
054 - //--------------------------------------------------
000 -
013 - #define DEBUG
000 -
013 - using System;
016 - using System.IO;
000 -
023 - public class Reading
001 - {
041 -     public static void Main(String[] args)
004 -     {
027 -        if( args.Length < 1 )
007 -        {
055 -            Console.WriteLine("Must include file name.");
007 -        }
010 -        else
007 -        {
000 -
009 - #if DEBUG
000 -
064 -        Console.WriteLine("==============DEBUG INFO==============");
043 -        for ( int x = 0; x < args.Length ; x++ )
004 -        {
054 -            Console.WriteLine("Arg[{0}] = {1}", x, args[x]);
004 -        }
```

9

```
065 -    Console.WriteLine("========================================");
000 -
006 - #endif
000 -
023 -         string buffer;
000 -
054 -         StreamReader myFile = File.OpenText(args[0]);
000 -
055 -         while ( (buffer = myFile.ReadLine()) != null )
010 -         {
010 - #if DEBUG
046 -    Console.Write( "{0:D3} - ", buffer.Length);
006 - #endif
039 -             Console.WriteLine(buffer);
010 -         }
000 -
024 -         myFile.Close();
007 -     }
004 -   }
001 - }
```

ANALYSIS This listing includes a number of directive commands within it. When DEBUG is defined, this listing provides additional output. DEBUG is defined in Line 5, so every time this is compiled, it produces the extra output. If you comment out Line 5 (or remove it) and recompile, the extra information does not get displayed.

What is the extra information? In Line 21, you see another directive being used: the #if directive. If the value after the #if is defined, this evaluates to true. If it isn't defined, it evaluates to false. Because DEBUG was defined in Line 5, the if code is included. If it had not been, control would have jumped to the #endif statement in Line 30.

Lines 22–29 print the command-line parameters so that you can see what was entered. Again, when released to production, the DEBUG statement will be left out and this information won't be displayed because it will be dropped out of the listing when compiled.

Line 38 contains a second #if check, again for DEBUG. This time, a value is printed at the beginning of each line. This value is the length of the line being printed. This length information can be used for debugging purposes. Again, when the listing is released, by undefining DEBUG, this information won't be included.

As you can see, defining a value is relatively easy. One of the values of using directives was to prevent the need to change code; yet, to change whether DEBUG is defined, you must change Line 5 in Listing 9.10. An alternative to this is to define a value when compiling.

Defining Values on the Command Line

Remove Line 5 from Listing 9.10 and recompile. You will see that the extra debugging information is left out. To define DEBUG without adding Line 5 back into the listing, you can use the /define flag on the compile option. The format of this compile option is as follows:

```
csc /define:DEBUG Reading.cs
```

Here, DEBUG is any value that you want defined in the listing and Reading.cs is your listing name. If you compile Listing 9.10 using the /define switch, DEBUG is again defined without the need to change your code. Leaving the /define off the command line stops the debugging information from being displayed. The end result is that you can turn the debugging information on and off without needing to change your code.

9

Tip

You can use /d as a shortcut for /define.

Note

If you are using an IDE, check its documentation regarding the defining of directives. A dialog box should enable you to enter symbols to define.

Impact of the Position of #define and #undef

Although it has not been shown, you can also undefine values using #undef. From the point where the #undef is encountered to the end of the program, the symbol in the #undef command no longer is defined.

The #undef and the #define directives must occur before any real code in the listing. They can appear after comments and other directives, but not after a declaration or other code occurs.

Caution

Neither #define nor #undef can appear in the middle of a listing.

Conditional Processing (#if, #elif, #else, #endif)

As you have already seen, you can use if logic with defined values. C# provides full if logic by including #if, #elif, #else, and #endif. This gives you if, if...else, and if...else if logic structures. Regardless of which format you use, you always end with an #endif directive. You've seen #if used in Listing 9.10. A common use of the if logic is to determine whether the listing being compiled is a development version or a release version:

```
#if DEBUG
// do some debug stuff
#elif PRODUCTION
// do final release stuff
#else
// display an error regarding the compile
#endif
```

The listing can produce different results based on the defined values.

Preprocessing Expressions (!, ==, !=, &&, ||)

The if logic with directives can include several operators: !, ==, !=, &&, and ||. These operate exactly as they do with a standard if statement. The ! checks for the not value. The == operator checks for equality. The != checks for inequality. Using && checks to see whether multiple conditions are all true. Using || checks to see whether either condition is true.

A common check that can be added to your listings is the following:

```
#if DEBUG && PRODUCTION
//Produce an error and stop compiling
```

If both DEBUG and PRODUCTION are defined, there is most likely a problem. The next section shows you how to indicate that there was a problem in the preprocessing.

Reporting Errors and Warning in Your Code (#error, #warning)

Because the directives are a part of your compiling, it makes sense that you would want them to be capable of indicating warnings and errors. If both DEBUG and PRODUCTION are defined, there is most likely a serious problem and, thus, an error should occur. You can cause such an error using the #error directive. If you want the listing to still compile—if everything else was okay—you can simply produce a warning. You can produce this warning by using the #warning directive. Listing 9.11 is a modified version of the reading listing that uses some of these new directives.

LISTING 9.11   Reading2.cs—Using #warning and #error

```
 1:  //   Reading2.cs · Read text from a file.
 2:  //   Exception handling left out to keep listing short.
 3:  //   Using the #error & #warning directives
 4:  //------------------------------------------------
 5:
 6:  #define DEBUG
 7:  #define BOOKCHECK
 8:
 9:  #if DEBUG
10:     #warning Compiled listing in Debug Mode
11:  #endif
12:  #if BOOKCHECK
13:     #warning Compiled listing with Book Check on
14:  #endif
15:  #if DEBUG && PRODUCTION
16:     #error Compiled with both DEBUG and PRODUCTION!
17:  #endif
18:
19:  using System;
20:  using System.IO;
21:
22:  public class Reading2
23:  {
24:      public static void Main(String[] args)
25:      {
26:          if( args.Length < 1 )
27:          {
28:              Console.WriteLine("Must include file name.");
29:          }
30:          else
31:          {
32:
33: #if DEBUG
34:
35:      Console.WriteLine("==============DEBUG INFO==============");
36:      for ( int x = 0; x < args.Length ; x++ )
37:      {
38:         Console.WriteLine("Arg[{0}] = {1}", x, args[x]);
39:      }
40:      Console.WriteLine("=====================================");
41:
42: #endif
43:
44:              string buffer;
45:
46:              StreamReader myFile = File.OpenText(args[0]);
47:
48:              while ( (buffer = myFile.ReadLine()) != null )
```

LISTING 9.11   continued

```
49:          {
50:
51:  #if BOOKCHECK
52:
53:      if (buffer.Length > 72)
54:      {
55:          Console.WriteLine("*** Following line too wide to present in book
             ➥***");
56:      }
57:      Console.Write( "{0:D3} - ", buffer.Length);
58:
59:  #endif
60:              Console.WriteLine(buffer);
61:          }
62:
63:          myFile.Close();
64:      }
65:   }
66: }
```

OUTPUT   When you compile this listing, you receive two warnings:

```
Reading2.cs(10,12): warning CS1030: #warning: 'Compiled listing in
➥Debug Mode'
Reading2.cs(13,12): warning CS1030: #warning: 'Compiled listing with
➥Book Check
          on'
```

If you define PRODUCTION on the command line or within your IDE, you get the following
warnings plus an error:

```
Reading2.cs(10,12): warning CS1030: #warning: 'Compiled listing in Debug Mode'
Reading2.cs(13,12): warning CS1030: #warning: 'Compiled listing with Book Check
          on'
Reading2.cs(16,10): error CS1029: #error: 'Compiled with both DEBUG and
          PRODUCTION!'
```

> **Note**   PRODUCTION is defined on the command line using /d:PRODUCTION when com-
> piling.

ANALYSIS   This listing uses the #warning and #error directives in the first few lines of the
              listing. Warnings are provided to let the person compiling the listing know what
modes are being used. In this case, there is a DEBUG mode and a BOOKCHECK mode. In
Line 15, a check is done to verify that the listing is not being compiled with both DEBUG
and PRODUCTION defined.

Most of this listing is straightforward. The addition of the BOOKCHECK is for me, as the author of this book. There is a limitation to the width of a line that can be displayed on a page. This directive is used to include code in Lines 52–58 that check to see whether the length of the code lines is okay. If a line is longer than 72 characters, a message is written to the screen, followed by the line of code with its width included. If the line is not too long, the line prints normally. By undefining BOOKCHECK, I can have this logic removed.

9

Changing Line Numbers

Another directive that is provided is the #line directive. This directive enables you to change the number of the lines in your code. The impact of this can be seen when you print error messages. Listing 9.12 presents a listing using the #line directive.

LISTING 9.12   Lines.cs—Using the #line Directive

```
 1:  //  Lines.cs -
 2:  //------------------------------------------------
 3:
 4:  using System;
 5:
 6:  public class Lines
 7:  {
 8:     #line 100
 9:     public static void Main(String[] args)
10:     {
11:        #warning In Main...
12:        Console.WriteLine("In Main....");
13:        myMethod1();
14:        myMethod2();
15:        #warning Done with main
16:        Console.WriteLine("Done with Main");
17:     }
18:
19:     #line 200
20:     static void myMethod1()
21:     {
22:        Console.WriteLine("In Method 1");
23:        #warning In Method 1...
24:        int x;   // not used. Will give warning.
25:     }
26:
27:     #line 300
28:     static void myMethod2()
29:     {
30:        Console.WriteLine("in Method 2");
31:        #warning In Method 2...
```

LISTING 9.12   continued

```
32:        int y;  // not used. Will give warning.
33:     }
34:  }
```

OUTPUT   You will receive the following warnings when you compile this listing:

```
Lines.cs(102,16): warning CS1030: #warning: 'In Main...'
Lines.cs(106,16): warning CS1030: #warning: 'Done with main'
Lines.cs(203,16): warning CS1030: #warning: 'In Method 1...'
Lines.cs(303,16): warning CS1030: #warning: 'In Method 2...'
Lines.cs(204,11): warning CS0168: The variable 'x' is declared but
➥never used
Lines.cs(304,11): warning CS0168: The variable 'y' is declared but
➥never used
```

The following is the output of the listing:

```
In Main....
In Method 1
in Method 2
Done with Main
```

ANALYSIS   This listing has no practical use; however, it illustrates the #line directive. Each method is started with a different line number. The main listing starts at Line 100 and goes from there. myMethod1 starts at Line 200 and is numbered from there. myMethod2 starts with Line 300. This enables you to tell which location in the listing has a problem based on the line number.

You can see in the compiler output that the warnings are numbered based on the #line values, not on the actual line numbers. Obviously, there are not 100 lines in this listing. These directive line numbers are used in the #warning directives, as well as warnings and errors produced by the compiler.

You also can return line numbers within a section of the listing back to their default values:

```
#line default
```

This returns the line numbers to their default values from that point in the listing forward.

Tip

|]If you do ASP.NET development with C#, you will find line numbers useful; otherwise, it is generally better to stick with the actual line numbers.

A Brief Look at Regions

The other directives that you saw in Table 9.2 were `#region` and `#endregion`. These directives are used to block in regions of a code listing. These regions are used by graphical development environments, such as Visual Studio .NET, to open and collapse code. `#region` indicates the beginning of a block. `#endregion` indicates the end of a block.

Using Debuggers

One of the primary purposes of a debugger is to automate the process of walking through a program line by line. A debugger enables you to do exactly this—run a program one line at a time. You can view the value of variables and other data members after each line of a program lists. You can jump to different parts of the listing, and you can even skip lines of code to prevent them from happening.

> **Note**
>
> It is beyond the scope of this book to cover the use of debuggers. IDEs such as Visual Studio have built-in debuggers. Additionally, the Microsoft .NET Framework ships with a command-line debugger called CORDBG.

> **Note**
>
> The base class libraries include some classes that do tracing and debugging. These classes use DEBUG and TRACE symbols to help display information on what is happening in a listing. It is beyond the scope of this book to cover these classes; however, you can check the class library reference for information on the `Systems.Diagnostics` namespace, which includes classes named `Trace` and `Debug`.

Summary

Today you learned about controlling errors and keeping them out of your programs. Specifically, you learned about exception handling and preprocessor directives.

You learned that the `try` command is used to check for exceptions that occur. If an exception is thrown, you can use the `catch` statement to handle the error in a more controlled fashion. You learned that you can have multiple `catch` statements, to customize what you do for different exceptions, and that you can catch the type `Exception`, which will catch any basic exception.

You also learned that you can create a block of code that will be executed after exception-handling code (both `try` and `catch`) statements have executed. This block can be executed regardless of whether an exception was thrown. This block is tagged with the `finally` keyword.

In the later part of today's lessons, you learned about using directives to indicate to the compiler what should and should not happen while your listing is compiled. This included learning how to include or exclude code by defining or undefining symbols. It also included learning about the `#if`, `#ifel`, `#else`, and `#endif` statements, which can be used to make decisions. You learned how to change the line numbers that are used by the compiler to indicate errors. You also learned how to generate your own errors or warnings when compiling, by using the `#error` and `#warning` directives.

Q&A

Q **Using `catch` by itself seems to be the most powerful. Why shouldn't I just use `catch` with no parameters and do all my logic there?**

A Although using `catch` by itself is the most powerful, it loses all the information about the exception that was thrown. Because of this, it is better to use `catch(Exception e)`. This enables you to get to the exception information that was thrown. If you chose not to use this information, you can then pass it on to any other classes that might call yours. This gives those classes the option to do something with the information.

Q **Are all exceptions treated equally?**

A No. Actually two classes of exceptions exist: system exceptions and application exceptions. Application exceptions will not terminate a program; system exceptions will. For the most part, today's lesson covered the more common exceptions, at the system level. For more details on exceptions and the differences between these two classes of exceptions, see the .NET Framework or C# documentation.

Q **You said there was a lot more to learn about exception handling. Do I need to learn it?**

A Today's lesson about exception handling will get you through the coding you will do. By learning more about exception handling, you will be better able to manipulate errors and messages. Additionally, you can learn how to embed an exception within an exception—and more. It is not critical to know these advanced concepts; however, knowing them will make you a better, more expert C# programmer.

Q Which is better, to define values in a listing or to define them on the compile line?

A If you define a value in a listing, you must remove it or undefine it in the listing. By defining on the command line, you don't have to mess with the code when switching between defining and undefining values.

Q What happens if I undefine a symbol that was never defined?

A Nothing. You also can undefine a symbol more than once without an error.

9

Workshop

The Workshop provides quiz questions to help you solidify your understanding of the material covered and exercises to provide you with experience in using what you've learned. Try to understand the quiz and exercise answers before continuing to the next day's lesson. Answers are provided on the CD.

Quiz

1. What keyword(s) are used with exceptions?

2. Which of the following should be handled by exception handling and which should be handled with regular code?

   a. A value entered by a user is not between a given range.

   b. A file cannot be read correctly.

   c. An argument passed to a method contains an invalid value.

   d. An argument passed to a method contains an invalid type.

3. What causes an exception?

4. When do exceptions occur?

   a. During coding

   b. During the compile

   c. During runtime

   d. When requested by the end user

5. When does the `finally` block execute?

6. Does the order of `catch` statements matter? Why or why not?

7. What does the `throw` command do?

8. What is debugging?

9. Do preprocessing directives end with a semicolon?

10. What are the directives for defining and undefining a symbol in your code listing?

11. What flag is used to define a symbol on the command line?

Exercises

1. What code could be used to check the following line to see whether it causes an exception?

```
GradePercentage = MyValue/Total
```

2. **Bug Buster:** The following program has a problem. What is the cause of the error?

```
int zero = 0;
try
{
    int result = 1000 / zero;
}

catch (Exception e)
{
    Console.WriteLine("Exception caught: {0}", e);
}
catch (DivideByZeroException e)
{
    Console.WriteLine("This is my error message. ", e);
}
finally
{
    Console.WriteLine("Can't get here");
}
```

3. Write the code to create an exception class of your own that includes the three overloaded constructors suggested in the tip in today's lesson. Call the exception NegativeValueException.

4. Use the NegativeValueException that you created in Exercise 3 in a complete listing. Base this program on Listing 9.8. Create a class named SubtractEm that throws your NegativeValueException if the result of a subtraction operation is negative.

5. What code would you use to define a symbol to be used for preprocessing? Call the symbol SYMBOL.

6. Write the code that you would need to add to your listing to have the line numbers start with 1,000.

7. Does the following compile? If so, what does this listing do?

```
1:   // Fun.cs - Using Directives in a goofy way
2:   //-------------------------------------------------
3:
4:   #define AAA
```

```
 5:  #define BBB
 6:  #define CCC
 7:  #define DDD
 8:  #undef  CCC
 9:  using System;
10:  #warning This listing is not practical...
11:  #if DDD
12:  public class
13:  #endif
14:  #if CCC
15:  destroy();
16:  #endif
17:  #if BBB || EEE
18:  myApp { public static void
19:  #endif
20:  #region
21:  #if GGG
22:  Main(){Console.WriteLine("Lions");
23:  #elif AAA
24:  Main(){Console.WriteLine(
25:  #elif GGG
26:  Console.ReadLine(
27:  #else
28:  Console.DumpLine(
29:  #endif
30:   "Hello"
31:  #if AAA
32:  + " Goofy "
33:  #else
34:  + " Strange "
35:  #endif
36:  #if CCC && DDD
37:  + "Mom"
38:  #else
39:  + "World"
40:  #endif
41:  );}
42:  #endregion
43:  }
```

8. **Bug Buster:** Does the following program have a problem? If so, which line(s) generate error messages? You should define the symbol MYLINES when you compile this listing.

```
1:  //  bugbust.cs -
2:  //------------------------------------------------
3:
4:  using System;
5:
6:  public class ReadingApp
7:  {
```

```
 8:     #if MYLINES
 9:     #line 100
10:     #endif
11:     public static void Main(String[] args)
12:     {
13:         Console.WriteLine("In Main....");
14:         myMethod1();
15:         myMethod2();
16:         Console.WriteLine("Done with Main");
17:     }
18:
19:     #if MYLINES
20:     #line 200
21:     #endif
22:     static void myMethod1()
23:     {
24:         Console.WriteLine("In Method 1");
25:     }
26:
27:     #if MYLINES
28:     #line 300
29:     #endif
30:     static void myMethod2()
31:     {
32:         Console.WriteLine("in Method 2");
33:     }
34:     #undef MYLINES
35: }
```

TYPE & RUN **3**

Lines and Circles and Squares, "Oh My!"

Okay, it is a goofy title, but it describes this Type & Run. This Type & Run presents yet another listing for you to use and modify. As with previous Type & Runs, this section presents a listing that is longer than the listings within the daily lessons.

As promised, these programs generally do something either fun or practical. The program included here, named GraphicsTest, uses a simple windows form with five buttons. Three of the buttons display graphics in the window, a fourth colors the form by drawing lines (solid), and the fifth exits the program. You'll learn more about buttons and forms on Days 16, "Creating Windows Forms," and 17, "Creating Windows Applications." In the meantime, you can play with the GraphicsTest listing.

Note   Be aware that not all .NET implementations support windows forms. If yours does not, this listing will not work. Microsoft's .NET Framework supports this listing.

LISTING T&R 3.1   GraphicsTest—A Program to Draw Colored Shapes

```
001: // GraphicsTest.cs
002: //

003: using System;
004: using System.Drawing;
005: using System.ComponentModel;
006: using System.Windows.Forms;
007:
008: namespace GraphicsTest
009: {
010:     public class frmGraphics : System.Windows.Forms.Form
011:     {
012:         private Bitmap DrawingArea;   // Area to draw on.
013:
014:         private Button btnCircle;
015:         private Button btnLine;
016:         private Button btnRectangle;
017:         private Button btnOK;
018:         private Button btn_Solid;
019:
020:         private System.ComponentModel.Container components = null;
021:
022:         private System.Random rnd;
023:         private Pen myPen;
024:
025:         public frmGraphics()
026:         {
027:             InitializeComponent();
028:             rnd   = new System.Random();
029:             myPen = new Pen(Color.Blue);
030:         }
031:
032:         protected override void Dispose( bool disposing )
033:         {
034:             if( disposing )
035:             {
036:                 if (components != null)
037:                 {
038:                     components.Dispose();
039:                 }
040:             }
```

```
041:            base.Dispose( disposing );
042:        }
043:
044:        private void InitializeComponent()
045:        {
046:            this.btnCircle = new System.Windows.Forms.Button();
047:            this.btnLine = new System.Windows.Forms.Button();
048:            this.btnRectangle = new System.Windows.Forms.Button();
049:            this.btnOK = new System.Windows.Forms.Button();
050:            this.btn_Solid = new System.Windows.Forms.Button();
051:            this.SuspendLayout();
052:            //
053:            // btnCircle
054:            //
055:            this.btnCircle.Location = new System.Drawing.Point(8, 32);
056:            this.btnCircle.Name = "btnCircle";
057:            this.btnCircle.Size = new System.Drawing.Size(40, 40);
058:            this.btnCircle.TabIndex = 0;
059:            this.btnCircle.Text = "Circ";
060:            this.btnCircle.Click += new System.EventHandler(
061:                                  this.btnCircle_Click);
062:            //
063:            // btnLine
064:            //
065:            this.btnLine.Location = new System.Drawing.Point(8, 88);
066:            this.btnLine.Name = "btnLine";
067:            this.btnLine.Size = new System.Drawing.Size(40, 40);
068:            this.btnLine.TabIndex = 1;
069:            this.btnLine.Text = "Line";
070:            this.btnLine.Click += new System.EventHandler(this.btnLine_Click);
071:            //
072:            // btnRectangle
073:            //
074:            this.btnRectangle.Location = new System.Drawing.Point(8, 144);
075:            this.btnRectangle.Name = "btnRectangle";
076:            this.btnRectangle.Size = new System.Drawing.Size(40, 40);
077:            this.btnRectangle.TabIndex = 2;
078:            this.btnRectangle.Text = "Rect";
079:            this.btnRectangle.Click += new System.EventHandler(
080:                                  this.btnRectangle_Click);
081:            //
082:            // btnOK
083:            //
084:            this.btnOK.Location = new System.Drawing.Point(296, 296);
085:            this.btnOK.Name = "btnOK";
086:            this.btnOK.TabIndex = 0;
087:            this.btnOK.Text = "OK";
088:            this.btnOK.Click += new System.EventHandler(this.btnOK_Click);
089:            //
```

```
090:          // btn_Solid
091:          //
092:          this.btn_Solid.Location = new System.Drawing.Point(8, 200);
093:          this.btn_Solid.Name = "btn_Solid";
094:          this.btn_Solid.Size = new System.Drawing.Size(40, 40);
095:          this.btn_Solid.TabIndex = 3;
096:          this.btn_Solid.Text = "Solid";
097:          this.btn_Solid.Click += new
     ➥              System.EventHandler(this.btn_Solid_Click);
098:          //
099:          // frmGraphics
100:          //
101:          this.AutoScaleBaseSize = new System.Drawing.Size(5, 13);
102:          this.ClientSize = new System.Drawing.Size(376, 334);
103:          this.Controls.Add(this.btn_Solid);
104:          this.Controls.Add(this.btnOK);
105:          this.Controls.Add(this.btnRectangle) ;
106:          this.Controls.Add(this.btnLine);
107:          this.Controls.Add(this.btnCircle);
108:          this.FormBorderStyle = FormBorderStyle.Fixed3D;
109:          this.Name = "frmGraphics";
110:          this.Text = "Drawing";
111:          this.Load += new System.EventHandler(this.frmGraphics_Load);
112:          this.Closed += new System.EventHandler(this.frmGraphics_Closed);
113:          this.Paint += new System.Windows.Forms.PaintEventHandler(
114:                                  this.frmGraphics_Paint);
115:          this.ResumeLayout(false);
116:
117:      }
118:
119:      /// <summary>
120:      /// The main entry point for the application.
121:      /// </summary>
122:      public static void Main()
123:      {
124:          Application.Run(new frmGraphics());
125:      }
126:
127:      private void btnLine_Click(object sender, System.EventArgs e)
128:      {
129:          Graphics oGraphics;
130:          oGraphics = Graphics.FromImage(DrawingArea);
131:
132:          myPen.Color = Color.Blue;
133:
134:          for ( int x = 1; x < 50; x++)
135:          {
136:              oGraphics.DrawLine(
137:                      myPen,
```

LISTING T&R 3.1 continued

```
138:                        (int) rnd.Next(0, this.Width),
139:                        (int) rnd.Next(0, this.Height),
140:                        (int) rnd.Next(0, this.Width),
141:                        (int) rnd.Next(0, this.Height));
142:             }
143:          oGraphics.Dispose();
144:          this.Invalidate();
145:       }
146:
147:
148:       private void btnCircle_Click(object sender, System.EventArgs e)
149:       {
150:          Graphics oGraphics;
151:          oGraphics = Graphics.FromImage(DrawingArea);
152:
153:          // get a radius for circle - up to 1/2 the width of form
154:          int radius = rnd.Next(0, (this.Width / 2));
155:
156:          for ( int x = 1; x < 50; x++)
157:          {
158:             myPen.Color = Color.FromArgb (
159:                (rnd.Next(0,255)),
160:                (rnd.Next(0,255)),
161:                (rnd.Next(0,255)));
162:
163:             oGraphics.DrawEllipse(
164:                myPen,
165:                rnd.Next(0, this.Width),
166:                rnd.Next(0, this.Height),
167:                radius, radius);
168:          }
169:          oGraphics.Dispose();
170:
171:          this.Invalidate();
172:       }
173:
174:       private void btnRectangle_Click(object sender, System.EventArgs e)
175:       {
176:          Graphics oGraphics;
177:          oGraphics = Graphics.FromImage(DrawingArea);
178:
179:          myPen.Color = Color.Red;
180:
181:          for ( int x = 1; x < 50; x++)
182:          {
183:             oGraphics.DrawRectangle(
184:                   myPen,
185:                   (int) rnd.Next(0, this.Width),
186:                   (int) rnd.Next(0, this.Height),
```

LISTING T&R 3.1   continued

```
187:                          (int) rnd.Next(5, this.Width),
188:                          (int) rnd.Next(5, this.Height));
189:            }
190:            oGraphics.Dispose();
191:
192:            this.Invalidate();
193:        }
194:
195:        private void btn_Solid_Click(object sender, System.EventArgs e)
196:        {
197:            Graphics oGraphics;
198:            oGraphics = Graphics.FromImage(DrawingArea);
199:
200:            myPen.Color = Color.Chartreuse;
201:
202:            for ( int x = 0; x < this.Width; x++)
203:            {
204:                oGraphics.DrawLine(myPen, x, 0, x, this.Height);
205:            }
206:            oGraphics.Dispose();
207:
208:            this.Invalidate();
209:        }
210:
211:        private void btnOK_Click(object sender, System.EventArgs e)
212:        {
213:            Application.Exit();
214:        }
215:
216:        private void frmGraphics_Load(object sender, System.EventArgs e)
217:        {
218:            DrawingArea = new Bitmap(
219:                    this.ClientRectangle.Width,
220:                    this.ClientRectangle.Height,
221:                    System.Drawing.Imaging.PixelFormat.Format24bppRgb);
222:            InitializeDrawingArea();
223:        }
224:
225:        private void InitializeDrawingArea()
226:        {
227:            Graphics oGraphics;
228:            oGraphics = Graphics.FromImage(DrawingArea);
229:
230:            myPen.Color = Color.AliceBlue;
231:
232:            for ( int x = 0; x < this.Width; x++)
233:            {
234:                oGraphics.DrawLine(myPen, x, 0, x, this.Height);
235:            }
```

LISTING T&R 3.1   continued

```
236:            oGraphics.Dispose();
237:
238:            this.Invalidate();
239:        }
240:
241:        private void frmGraphics_Closed(object sender, System.EventArgs e)
242:        {
243:            DrawingArea.Dispose();
244:        }
245:
246:        private void frmGraphics_Paint( object sender,
247:                                        System.Windows.Forms.PaintEventArgs
e)
248:        {
249:            Graphics oGraphics;
250:
251:            oGraphics = e.Graphics;
252:
253:            oGraphics.DrawImage( DrawingArea,
254:                                 0, 0,
255:                                 DrawingArea.Width,
256:                                 DrawingArea.Height);
257:            oGraphics.Dispose();
258:        }
259:    }
260: }
```

When you click the different buttons, shapes are drawn on the window's background. Figures T&R3.1–T&R3.3 show some results. Because the location and the size of shapes are random, your output will be different. If you click a button again, more shapes will be drawn.

OUTPUT

FIGURE TR3.1

Circle output from GraphicsTest.

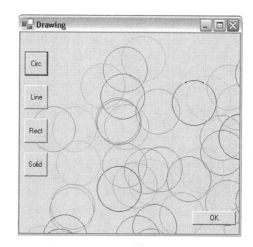

FIGURE TR3.2

Line output from GraphicsTest.

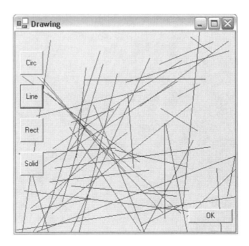

FIGURE TR3.3

Lines, circles, and squares from GraphicsTest.

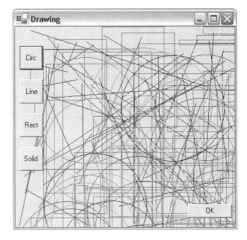

Remember, analysis of listings is not included with Type & Runs. For this listing, however, a couple comments deserve to be made. Again, you will learn about all the code related to buttons and forms on Days 16 and 17. On Day 15, "Using Existing Routines from the .NET Base Classes," you will learn about a number of classes that have been created that you can use. The classes used in this listing are like the classes that will be discussed on that day; they are a part of the .NET Framework.

This program also uses a set of classes used to create and draw graphics. The graphics are drawn onto a basic graphics object named DrawingArea. This is a simple bitmap image that was declared in Line 14. All the graphics are drawn onto this bitmap, which then is copied to the form.

Stepping back, you'll see that in Line 4, the System.Drawing namespace is included. This namespace contains many of the graphic routines. Also included are a number of other namespaces, including Windows.Forms, which contains information for doing the windows form logic.

In Lines 12–23, a number of variables are declared that will be used in drawing the graphics and creating controls on the form. Line 22 contains a variable for getting random numbers. In Line 23, myPen is declared as a Pen object. This object will be assigned colors and used to draw shapes later in the listing. In Line 29, you see a new Pen object actually created and the color blue is assigned to it. You can assign any color to the pen.

Note   Lots of colors are listed in the Color enumeration. You can assign them in the same way that the color blue was assigned. You can see a list of many of the colors in Table 16.2 (on Day 16).

In Lines 127–145, you can see the method btnLine_Click defined. This is actually an event that is executed when the line button is clicked. Because the color of the pen could have been changed, in Line 132, the pen defined earlier is set to the color blue. Before that, in Line 129, a graphics object was created and assigned the DrawingArea graphic created earlier. This new graphic, oGraphics, will be used to draw upon.

In Lines 134–142, there is a loop that executes 50 times. This loop draws a single line each time through the loop by calling the DrawLine method in the graphics object that was created. The parameters being passed are not as complicated as they look in Lines 137–141. The first parameter is the pen, myPen. The next four parameters are random numbers. The first and third are numbers between 0 and the width of the form. The second and fourth are between 0 and the height of the form. The first two numbers are the starting point of the line. The last two are the ending point.

After the lines have been drawn, calling the Dispose method cleans up the oGraphics object. This is done in Line 143. Because the graphics object uses a lot of system resources, it is good to force this cleanup.

The disposal of the graphics object is followed by a call to this.Invalidate in Line 144. Invalidate makes the current form redraw itself. This causes a paint event to occur. An event handler is created in Lines 246–259. In this method, the DrawingArea image is copied to the form's background image.

The other method events in this listing operate in much the same as in the earlier line listing: Random numbers are used to draw shapes. One other difference is in

Lines 158–161. In these lines, instead of setting the pen to a specific color, it is set to a random color. The FromArgb method sets red, green, and blue values for a single color. Because random numbers are used, the result is a random color.

This is a fun listing to play with. You should be able to change the colors, modify the shape sizes and locations, and work with these basic graphics. As with all Type & Runs, make changes, experiment, and have some fun with this listing.

Note
The areas of this listing associated with windows forms will make sense after you cover Days 16 and 17. For now, however, you can still play around with this listing and have some fun.

Note
The source code for this listing is available on the included CD. Any updates to the code will be available at www.TeachYourselfCSharp.com.

DAY 10

Reusing Existing Code with Inheritance

One of the key constructs of an object-oriented language is the capability to extend pre-existing classes. This extending can be done through the concept of inheritance. Today you will...

- Discover base classes.

- Expand base classes with inheritance.

- Learn to expand the functionality of a class using inheritance.

- Protect, yet share, your data members with derived classes.

- Discover how to be virtual and abstract with your class members.

- Learn to seal a class.

- Manipulate objects as different types using keywords `is` and `as`.

Understanding the Basics of Inheritance

Each of us inherits characteristics from our parents—for example, eye color, hair color and texture, and so forth. In addition to these characteristics, we have our own characteristics that extend beyond our parents. Just as we derive and extend characteristics from our parents, classes can derive from other classes. Some of those characteristics are overridden with our own characteristics, and some are not.

The concept of inheritance gives us the ability to create a new class based on an existing class. The new class can use all the features of the original class, it can override existing features, it can extend existing features, or it can add its own features.

A number of new classes can inherit from an original class; however, only one class can be inherited from. For example, you can have a base class named control that can be inherited by a number of different control types. Figure 10.1 helps illustrate this one-to-many relationship. Note from the figure that, reading from left to right, there can be a one-to-many relationship; however, reading from right to left, there is only one original class.

FIGURE 10.1

Inheriting relation-
ships.

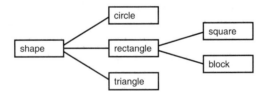

Several basic terms are commonly used when discussing inheritance:

Base class	The original class.
Parent class	Another name for a base class.
Derived class	A new class, created by inheriting from a base class.
Child class	Another name for a derived class.
Single inheritance	A derived class created from only one base class. C# supports only single inheritance. The illustration in Figure 10.1 is for single inheritance.
Multiple inheritance	A derived class created from two or more base classes. C# does not support multiple inheritance.

These are not the only important terms related to inheritance. Throughout today's lesson, you will learn a number of additional terms.

Single Versus Multiple Inheritance

Unlike C++, C# does not support multiple inheritance. Multiple inheritance occurs when a new, derived class is created by more than one base class. For example, you could use a name class and an address class, and derive a business contact class from those two classes. The business class would include characteristics of both base classes. A number of issues, as well as additional complexities, accrue from multiple inheritance. Using interfaces, which are covered on Day 12, "Tapping into OOP: Interfaces," you can obtain many of the same results without some of the downfalls.

Delving into Simple Inheritance

The best way to understand inheritance is to see it in action. With inheritance, you need to start with a base class. Listing 10.1 illustrates a class that will be used to illustrate inheritance in today's lessons. A subset of this listing will also be used.

LISTING 10.1   inherit01.cs—A Base Class and a Class to Illustrate Its Use

```
 1:  // inherit01.cs
 2:  // A relatively simple class to use as a starting point
 3:  //=======================================================
 4:  using System;
 5:  using System.Text;
 6:
 7:  class Person
 8:  {
 9:      private string firstName;
10:      private string middleName;
11:      private string lastName ;
12:      private int    age;
13:
14:      // ToDo: Add properties to access the data members
15:
16:      public Person()
17:      {
18:      }
19:
20:      public Person(string fn, string ln)
21:      {
22:         firstName = fn;
23:         lastName = ln;
24:      }
```

LISTING **10.1**   continued

```
25:
26:    public Person(string fn, string mn, string ln)
27:    {
28:       firstName = fn;
29:       middleName = mn;
30:       lastName = ln;
31:    }
32:
33:    public Person(string fn, string mn, string ln, int a)
34:    {
35:       firstName = fn;
36:       middleName = mn;
37:       lastName = ln;
38:       age = a;
39:    }
40:
41:    public void displayAge()
42:    {
43:       Console.WriteLine("Age {0}", age);
44:    }
45:
46:    public void displayFullName()
47:    {
48:       StringBuilder FullName = new StringBuilder();
49:
50:       FullName.Append(firstName);
51:       FullName.Append(" ");
52:       if( middleName != "" )
53:       {
54:           FullName.Append(middleName[0]);
55:           FullName.Append(". ");
56:       }
57:       FullName.Append(lastName);
58:
59:       Console.WriteLine(FullName);
60:    }
61: }
62:
63: // NameApp class. Illustrates the use of the Person class
64: class NameApp
65: {
66:    public static void Main()
67:    {
68:        Person me = new Person("Bradley", "Lee", "Jones");
69:        Person myWife = new Person("Melissa", "Anne", "Jones", 21);
70:
71:        me.displayFullName();
72:        me.displayAge();
```

LISTING 10.1 continued

```
73:
74:          myWife.displayFullName();
75:          myWife.displayAge();
76:     }
77: }
```

OUTPUT
```
Bradley L. Jones
Age 0
Melissa A. Jones
Age 21
```

ANALYSIS The class that will be used for inheritance is the Person class defined in Lines
7–61. Although this class is more complex than what is needed to illustrate
inheritance, it is practical. In Lines 9–12, you see four data members within the class.
These store information about the person. The access modifier for each of these data
members is private. Remember that private restricts access to the data members to
within the class. To change these values outside the class, you should add properties to
this listing.

Note
> To cut down on the listing size, properties were left out of this listing. You
> should include properties in your own listings. You could change the access
> modifiers to public to give access to the data members; however, it is rec-
> ommended that you don't. It is best to encapsulate your data members and
> use properties. Properties were covered on Day 5, "The Core of C#
> Programming: Classes."

In Lines 16–39, four constructors are created for this listing. This enables the user to
create a Person object in a number of ways. Two member methods are also included in
the class. In Lines 41–44, a simple method, displayAge, displays the age of the person.
Lines 46–60 present a more complex method, displayFullName.

The displayFullName method uses a new class type that you have not seen. The
StringBuilder class is available within the System.Text namespace. In Line 5, you see that
the System.Text namespace is being used in the listing. This namespace in Line 5 was
added for the StringBuilder class. The StringBuilder class creates a stringlike object that
can be manipulated in ways that a normal string cannot. For example, the length of the
string can be increased or decreased. You should know that it is easier to append to or
change a StringBuilder object than a normal string.

10

In Line 48, an object named `FullName` is being created that will be of type `StringBuilder`. This object will be used to hold the formatted full name of the person. In Line 50, you append the first name, `firstName`, to the newly created `FullName` string. Because `FullName` will be blank, Line 50 basically copies the first name into the `FullName`. Line 51 appends a space to the end of the first name. Lines 52–56 add the middle initial instead of the full middle name to `FullName`. In Line 52, an `if` statement is used to make sure that the middle name is not equal to `""` (which is a blank string). If there is a middle name, Line 54 appends the first character of the middle name (the initial). Line 55 then appends a period and a space. Finally, Line 57 appends the last name.

The last line of the method displays the full name to the console. In your own listing, you might want to change the name of this method to `getFullName` and have it return the formatted name instead. This would enable calling programs to use the full name in other ways.

The rest of the listing contains the `NameApp` class. This class is provided so that you can see the `Person` class being used. In Lines 68–69, two objects of type `Person` are declared: `me` and `myWife`. In Lines 71–75, the methods of the objects are called.

Inheritance in Action

Although there is a lot of code in Listing 10.1, you should be able to understand all of it. Nothing new is being presented here other than the `StringBuilder` class. Listing 10.2, however, presents several new features. For example, to inherit from a class, you use this format:

```
class derived_class : base_class
```

The colon (:) is used to indicate inheritance by separating the new, *derived_class,* from the original, *base_class.*

LISTING 10.2   inherit02.cs—Basic Inheritance

```
 1:  // inherit02.cs
 2:  // Basic inheritance.
 3:  //================================================
 4:  using System;
 5:  using System.Text;
 6:
 7:  class Person
 8:  {
 9:      protected string firstName;
10:      protected string middleName;
11:      protected string lastName;
12:      private int    age;
```

LISTING 10.2   continued

```
13:
14:        //ToDo: Add properties to access data members
15:
16:        public Person()
17:        {
18:        }
19:
20:        public Person(string fn, string ln)
21:        {
22:            firstName = fn;
23:            lastName = ln;
24:        }
25:
26:        public Person(string fn, string mn, string ln)
27:        {
28:            firstName = fn;
29:            middleName = mn;
30:            lastName = ln;
31:        }
32:
33:        public Person(string fn, string mn, string ln, int a)
34:        {
35:            firstName = fn;
36:            middleName = mn;
37:            lastName = ln;
38:            age = a;
39:        }
40:
41:        public void displayAge()
42:        {
43:            Console.WriteLine("Age {0}", age);
44:        }
45:
46:        public void displayFullName()
47:        {
48:            StringBuilder FullName = new StringBuilder();
49:
50:            FullName.Append(firstName);
51:            FullName.Append(" ");
52:            if( middleName != "" )
53:            {
54:                FullName.Append(middleName[0]);
55:                FullName.Append(". ");
56:            }
57:            FullName.Append(lastName);
58:
59:            Console.WriteLine(FullName);
60:        }
61: }
```

10

LISTING 10.2 continued

```
62:
63:    class Employee : Person
64:    {
65:       private ushort hYear;
66:
67:       public ushort hireYear
68:       {
69:         get { return(hYear); }
70:         set { hYear = value; }
71:       }
72:
73:       public Employee() : base()
74:       {
75:       }
76:
77:       public Employee( string fn, string ln ) : base( fn, ln)
78:       {
79:       }
80:
81:       public Employee(string fn, string mn, string ln, int a) :
82:                   base(fn, mn, ln, a)
83:       {
84:       }
85:
86:       public Employee(string fn, string ln, ushort hy) : base(fn, ln)
87:       {
88:          hireYear = hy;
89:       }
90:
91:       public new void displayFullName()
92:       {
93:          Console.WriteLine("Employee: {0} {1} {2}",
94:                               firstName, middleName, lastName);
95:       }
96:    }
97:
98:    class NameApp
99:    {
100:      public static void Main()
101:      {
102:          Person myWife = new Person("Melissa", "Anne", "Jones", 21);
103:          Employee me = new Employee("Bradley", "L.", "Jones", 23);
104:          Employee you = new Employee("Kyle", "Rinni", 2000);
105:
106:          myWife.displayFullName();
107:          myWife.displayAge();
108:
109:          me.displayFullName();
```

LISTING **10.2** continued

```
110:            Console.WriteLine("Year hired: {0}", me.hireYear);
111:            me.displayAge();
112:
113:            you.displayFullName();
114:            Console.WriteLine("Year hired of him: {0}", you.hireYear);
115:            you.displayAge();
116:       }
117:  }
```

Tip

> Okay, the listings are getting long. If you don't want to enter all this code, feel free to download the latest source code from the publisher's Web site at www.samspublishing.com or from my own Web site at www.teachyourselfcsharp.com. You can also find the listing on the included CD in the Day10 directory.

10

OUTPUT

```
Melissa A. Jones
Age 21
Employee: Bradley L. Jones
Year hired: 0
Age 23
Employee: Kyle  Rinni
Year hired of him: 2000
Age 0
```

ANALYSIS This listing illustrates inheritance in its simplest form. As you will learn later in today's lessons, some issues can arise as you begin to write more complex programs. For now, you should focus on understanding what is being done in this listing.

Lines 4–61 contain nearly the same Person class as in Listing 10.1. A change was made to this class—did you notice it? In Lines 9–11, the accessor type of the name variables was changed. Instead of private, these are now protected. Because a derived class is a new class outside the base class, it does not have access to the base class's private variables. private variables in the base class are accessible only within the base class. The protected modifier is still restrictive; however, it enables derived classes to also access the data members. This was the only change in the Person class. Later in today's lesson, you learn of a few changes that should be made to a class if you know that it will be used as a base class.

In Lines 63–96, you see the new, derived class, Employee. Line 63 uses the colon notation mentioned earlier. A new class, named Employee, is derived from a base class named Person. The Employee class contains all the functionality of the Person class.

In Line 65, the Employee class adds a data member named hYear that will contain the year in which the employee was hired. This is a private variable that is accessed through the use of the properties declared in Lines 67–71.

Lines 73–89 contain constructors for the Employee class. These also contain a colon notation in what appears to be a different manner. In Line 77, a constructor for Employee is being declared that takes two string parameters: fn and ln. Following the colon, you see the use of the keyword base. The base keyword can be used in this manner to call the base class's constructor. In Line 77, the base class constructor, Person, is called using the two variables passed to the Employee constructor, fn and ln. When the base class constructor is finished executing, any code within the Employee constructor Lines 78–79 will execute. In this case, there is no additional code. In the constructor in Lines 86–89, the hireYear property is used to set the hYear value.

In Lines 91–95, the Employee class has a method named displayFullName. The word new has been included in its declaration. Because this class has the same name as a base member and because the new keyword was used, this class overrides the base class's method. Any calls by an Employee object to the displayFullName method will execute the code in Lines 91–95, instead of the code in Lines 46–60.

In the last part of the listing, a NameApp class declares to illustrate the use of the derived class. In Lines 102–104, three objects are declared. In the rest of the listing, calls to the objects are made. Line 106 calls to the displayFullName method for the myWife object. Because myWife was declared as a person, you receive the Person class's method output, which abbreviates the middle name. In Line 107, a call to the myWife object's displayAge method is made.

In Line 109, the displayFullName method is called for the me object. This time, the Employee class's method is called because me was declared as an Employee in Line 103. In Line 111, a call to the displayAge method is made for the me object. Because the Employee class doesn't have a displayAge method, the program automatically checked to see whether the method was available in the base class. The base class's displayAge was then used.

Line 110 displayed hireYear, using the property created in the Employee class. What happens if you try to call the hireYear property using myWife? If you add the following line after Line 107, what would you expect to happen:

```
110:        Console.WriteLine("Year hired: {0}", myWife.hireYear);
```

This generates an error. A base class does not have any access to the routines in a derived class. Because Person does not have a hireYear, this line of code is not valid.

Using Base Methods in Inherited Methods

The base keyword can also be used to directly call a base class's methods. For example, change Lines 91–95 to the following:

```
public new void displayFullName()
{
    Console.Write("Employee: ");
    base.displayFullName();
}
```

This changes the new displayFullName method in the derived class. Now instead of doing all the work itself, it adds a little text and then calls the base class's version of displayFullName. This enables you to expand on the functionality of the base class without having to rewrite everything.

Exploring Polymorphism and Inherited Classes

To this point, you've learned a very simple use of inheritance. You have seen that you can extend a base class by adding additional data members and methods. You have also seen that you can call routines in the base class by using the base keyword. Finally, you have learned that you override a previous version of a method by declaring a new method of the same name with the new keyword added.

All of this works, but there are reasons to do things differently. One of the key concepts of an object-oriented language is polymorphism. If inheritance is done correctly, it can help you to gain polymorphic benefits within your classes. More specifically, you will be able to create a hierarchy of classes that can be treated in much the same way.

Consider the Employee and Person classes. An Employee is a Person. Granted, an employee is more than a Person, but an Employee is everything that a Person is and more. Listing 10.3 scales back the Person and Employee example to the bare minimum. Notice the declarations in the NameApp of this listing (Lines 53 and 55).

LISTING 10.3   inherit03.cs—Assigning a Person and Employee

```
1:  // inherit03.cs
2:  //==============================================
3:  using System;
4:
5:  class Person
6:  {
7:      protected string firstName;
```

LISTING 10.3 continued

```
 8:     protected string lastName;
 9:
10:     public Person()
11:     {
12:     }
13:
14:     public Person(string fn, string ln)
15:     {
16:         firstName = fn;
17:         lastName = ln;
18:     }
19:
20:     public void displayFullName()
21:     {
22:         Console.WriteLine("{0} {1}", firstName, lastName);
23:     }
24: }
25:
26: class Employee : Person
27: {
28:     public ushort hireYear;
29:
30:     public Employee() : base()
31:     {
32:     }
33:
34:     public Employee( string fn, string ln ) : base( fn, ln)
35:     {                          .
36:     }
37:
38:     public Employee(string fn, string ln, ushort hy) : base(fn, ln)
39:     {
40:         hireYear = hy;
41:     }
42:
43:     public new void displayFullName()
44:     {
45:         Console.WriteLine("Employee: {0} {1}", firstName, lastName);
46:     }
47: }
48:
49: class NameApp
50: {
51:     public static void Main()
52:     {
53:         Employee me = new Employee("Bradley", "Jones", 1983);
54:
55:         Person Brad = me;
56:
```

LISTING 10.3 continued

```
57:            me.displayFullName();
58:            Console.WriteLine("Year hired: {0}", me.hireYear);
59:
60:            Brad.displayFullName();
61:    }
62: }
```

OUTPUT

```
Employee: Bradley Jones
Year hired: 1983
Bradley Jones
```

ANALYSIS
The key point of this listing is in Lines 53 and 55. In Line 53, an Employee object named me was created and assigned values.

In Line 55, a Person object named Brad was created and was set equal to the Employee object, me. An Employee object was assigned to a Person object. How can this be done? Remember the statement earlier—an Employee *is* a Person. An Employee is a Person and more. All the functionality of a Person is contained within an Employee. Stated more generically, all aspects of a base class are a part of a derived class.

The Brad object can be used just as any other Person object can be used. In Line 60, you see that the displayFullName method is called. Sure enough, the full name is displayed using the Person class's displayFullName method.

Because the Person object, Brad, had an Employee object assigned to it, can you call methods or use data members in the Employee class? For example, can you use Brad.hireYear? This is easily tested by adding the following after Line 60:

```
Console.WriteLine("Year hired: ", Brad.hireYear);
```

You might think that 1983 will be displayed, but Brad is a Person object. The Person class does not have a hireYear member, so this results in an error:

```
inherit03b.cs(61,45): error CS0117:  'Person' does not contain a definition
for 'hireYear'
```

Although an Employee is everything that a Person is, a Person—even if assigned an Employee—is not everything that an Employee is. Said more generically, a derived class is everything that a base class is, but a base class is *not* everything that a derived class is.

How is this polymorphic? Simply put, you can make the same method call to multiple object types, and the method call works. In this example, you called the displayFullName method on both a Person and an Employee object. Even though both were assigned the same values, the displayFullName method associated with the appropriate class type was called. You didn't have to worry about specifying which class's method to call.

Working with Virtual Methods

The use of the base class references to derived objects is common in object-oriented programming. Consider this question. In the previous example, Brad was declared as a Person, but was assigned an Employee. In the case of the call to the displayFullName method, which class's method was used to display the name? The base class method was used, even though the value assigned to method was of an Employee.

 In most cases, you will want the assigned class type's methods to be used. This is done using virtual methods in C#. A *virtual method* enables you to call the method associated with the actual assigned type rather than the base class type.

A method is declared as virtual within the base class. Using the virtual keyword in the method's definition does this. If such a method is overloaded, the actual class type of the data will be used at runtime instead of the data type of the declared variable. This means that a base class can be used to point at multiple derived classes, and the appropriate method will be used. In the case of the displayFullName methods, the appropriate data is displayed.

A deriving class must indicate when a virtual method is overridden. This is done using the override keyword when declaring the new method. Listing 10.4 is a modification of Listing 10.3. Notice the difference in the output.

> **Note** A few of the constructors were removed from this listing to shorten the code. This has no impact on the example.

LISTING 10.4   inherit04.cs—Using Virtual Methods

```
 1:  // inherit04.cs - Virtual Methods
 2:  //=============================================
 3:  using System;
 4:
 5:  class Person
 6:  {
 7:      protected string firstName;
 8:      protected string lastName;
 9:
10:      public Person()
11:      {
12:      }
13:
14:      public Person(string fn, string ln)
15:      {
```

LISTING 10.4   continued

```
16:          firstName = fn;
17:          lastName = ln;
18:      }
19:
20:      public virtual void displayFullName()
21:      {
22:          Console.WriteLine("{0} {1}", firstName, lastName);
23:      }
24:  }
25:
26:  class Employee : Person
27:  {
28:      public ushort hireYear;
29:
30:      public Employee() : base()
31:      {
32:      }
33:
34:      public Employee(string fn, string ln, ushort hy) : base(fn, ln)
35:      {
36:          hireYear = hy;
37:      }
38:
39:      public override void displayFullName()
40:      {
41:          Console.WriteLine("Employee: {0} {1}", firstName, lastName);
42:      }
43:  }
44:
45:  // A new class derived from Person...
46:  class Contractor : Person
47:  {
48:      public string company;
49:
50:      public Contractor() : base()
51:      {
52:      }
53:
54:      public Contractor(string fn, string ln, string c) : base(fn, ln)
55:      {
56:          company = c;
57:      }
58:
59:      public override void displayFullName()
60:      {
61:          Console.WriteLine("Contractor: {0} {1}", firstName, lastName);
62:      }
63:  }
64:
```

10

LISTING **10.4**   continued

```
65:  class NameApp
66:  {
67:     public static void Main()
68:     {
69:
70:         Person Brad = new Person("Bradley", "Jones");
71:         Person me   = new Employee("Bradley", "Jones", 1983);
72:         Person worker = new Contractor("Carolyn", "Curry", "UStorIT");
73:
74:         Brad.displayFullName();
75:         me.displayFullName();
76:         worker.displayFullName();
77:     }
78:  }
```

OUTPUT
Bradley Jones
Employee: Bradley Jones
Contractor: Carolyn Curry

ANALYSIS First, take a look at the changes that were made to this listing. A few constructors were removed to shorten the amount of code. More important, in Line 20, you see the first key change. The displayFullName method of the Person class has been declared as virtual. This is an indicator that if the data assigned to a Person object is from a derived class, the derived class's method should be used instead.

In Line 39, of the Employee class—which is derived from Person—you see the second key change. Here, the keyword override has been included instead of the keyword new. This indicates that for any data of the Employee type, this specific version of the displayFullName method should be used.

To make this listing a little more interesting and to help illustrate this example, a second class is derived from Person in Lines 46–63. This class is for Contractors, and it has a data member of its own used to store the company from which the consultant has been hired. This class also contains an overridden version of the displayFullName method. When called, it indicates that the person is a contractor.

The Main method within NameApp has been changed to be straightforward. In Lines 70–72, three objects of type Person are declared. However, each of these is assigned a different data object. In Line 70, a Person object is assigned; in Line 71, an Employee object is assigned; and in Line 72, a Contractor object is assigned.

> **Caution**
>
> Although each of the variables in Lines 70–72 (Brad, me, and worker) is assigned an object of a different types, only the data members and methods within its declared type, Person, are available.

In Lines 74–76, you see the results of using virtual and overridden methods. Although all three of the variables calling `displayFullName` are `Person` types, each is calling the overridden method associated with the actual data that was assigned. They don't all call the `displayFullName` method of the `Person` class. This is almost always the result that you will want.

Working with Abstract Classes

In Listing 10.4, nothing required you to declare the `displayFullName` methods in the `Employee` and `Contractor` classes with `override`. Change Lines 39 and 59 to use `new` instead of `override`:

```
public new void displayFullName()
```

You will find that the results are different:

```
Bradley Jones
Bradley Jones
Carolyn Curry
```

What happened? Although the base class was declared as virtual, for it to be polymorphic—and thus use the method based on the data type assigned to the variable—you must use the `override` keyword in derived methods.

You can force a class to override a method by declaring the base class's method as abstract. An abstract method in the base class is declared with the keyword `abstract`. An abstract method is not given a body; derived classes are expected to supply the body.

Whenever a method is declared as `abstract`, the class must also be declared as `abstract`. Listing 10.5 presents the use of the `abstract` class, again using the `Person`, `Employee`, and `Contract` classes.

> **Note**
>
> Line 20 ends with a semicolon.

LISTING 10.5   inherit05.cs—Using Abstract Classes

```
 1:  // inherit05.cs - Abstract Methods
 2:  //===============================================
 3:  using System;
 4:
 5:  abstract class Person
 6:  {
 7:     protected string firstName;
 8:     protected string lastName;
 9:
10:     public Person()
11:     {
12:     }
13:
14:     public Person(string fn, string ln)
15:     {
16:        firstName = fn;
17:        lastName = ln;
18:     }
19:
20:     public abstract void displayFullName();
21:  }
22:
23:  class Employee : Person
24:  {
25:     public ushort hireYear;
26:
27:     public Employee() : base()
28:     {
29:     }
30:
31:     public Employee(string fn, string ln, ushort hy) : base(fn, ln)
32:     {
33:        hireYear = hy;
34:     }
35:
36:     public override void displayFullName()
37:     {
38:        Console.WriteLine("Employee: {0} {1}", firstName, lastName);
39:     }
40:  }
41:
42:  // A new class derived from Person...
43:  class Contractor : Person
44:  {
45:     public string company;
46:
47:     public Contractor() : base()
48:     {
```

LISTING 10.5 continued

```
49:    }
50:
51:    public Contractor(string fn, string ln, string c) : base(fn, ln)
52:    {
53:       company = c;
54:    }
55:
56:    public override void displayFullName()
57:    {
58:       Console.WriteLine("Contractor: {0} {1}", firstName, lastName);
59:    }
60: }
61:
62: class NameApp
63: {
64:    public static void Main()
65:    {
66:
67: //      Person Brad = new Person("Bradley", "Jones");
68:         Person me   = new Employee("Bradley", "Jones", 1983);
69:         Person worker = new Contractor("Bryce", "Hatfield", "EdgeQuest");
70:
71: //      Brad.displayFullName();
72:         me.displayFullName();
73:         worker.displayFullName();
74:    }
75: }
```

OUTPUT
Employee: Bradley Jones
Contractor: Bryce Hatfield

ANALYSIS
Line 20 is the critical point to notice in this listing. The `displayFullName` method is declared as `abstract`. This indicates that the method will be implemented in a derived class. Therefore, there is no body for the method.

Because the `Person` class now has an abstract method, the class itself must be declared as `abstract`. In Line 5, you can see that the `abstract` keyword has been added.

In Lines 36 and 56, you see overriding `displayFullName` methods for both the `Employee` and `Contractor` classes. Finally, in the main application, you see in Lines 68 and 69 that, again, two variables of type `Person` are being explicitly assigned data of type `Employee` and `Contractor`. When Lines 72–73 call the `displayFullName` method, the method of the data type is again displayed instead of the variable type.

Lines 67 and 71 were commented to prevent them from executing. If you uncomment Line 67 and try to create data with the `Person` class, you get an error:

```
Inherit05b.cs(67, 22): error CS0144: Cannot create an instance of the abstract
➥class or interface 'Person'
```

An abstract class cannot be used to create an object.

You should also try to change the override keywords in Lines 36 and 56 to new, as you could do with Listing 10.4. Using abstract in your base class causes an error:

```
inherit05c.cs(23,7): error CS0534: 'Employee' does not implement inherited
➥ abstract member 'Person.displayFullName()'
inherit05c.cs(20,25): (Location of symbol related to previous error)
inherit05c.cs(43,7): error CS0534: 'Contractor' does not implement inherited
➥ abstract member 'Person.displayFullName()'
inherit05c.cs(20,25): (Location of symbol related to previous error)
```

The complier ensures that your base class abstract methods are overridden correctly.

Sealing Classes

Abstract classes are created with the expectation that other classes will be derived from them. What if you want to prevent inheritance from a class? What if you want to seal off a class so that other classes cannot extend it?

C# provides the sealed keyword to prevent derivation from a class. By including the sealed modifier when defining a class, you effectively prevent it from being inherited from. Listing 10.6 presents a very simple illustration of using a sealed class.

LISTING 10.6   inherit06.cs—Creating Keyword to a Sealed Class

```
 1:  // inherit06.cs - Sealed Classes
 2:  //==============================================
 3:  using System;
 4:
 5:  sealed public class number
 6:  {
 7:      private float pi;
 8:
 9:      public number()
10:      {
11:        pi = 3.14159F;
12:      }
13:
14:      public float PI
15:      {
16:        get {
17:          return pi;
18:        }
19:      }
```

LISTING 10.6 continued

```
20:  }
21:
22:  //public class numbers : number
23:  //{
24:  //    public float myVal = 123.456F;
25:  //}
26:
27:  class myApp
28:  {
29:     public static void Main()
30:     {
31:         number myNumbers = new number();
32:         Console.WriteLine("PI = {0}", myNumbers.PI);
33:
34:  //       numbers moreNumbers = new numbers();
35:  //       Console.WriteLine("PI = {0}", moreNumbers.PI);
36:  //       Console.WriteLine("myVal = {0}", moreNumbers.myVal);
37:     }
38:  }
```

OUTPUT

```
PI = 3.14159
```

ANALYSIS
Most of this listing is straightforward. In Line 5, the number class is declared with the sealed modifier. When a number object is created, the constructor in Lines 9–12 set the data member, pi, to the value of 3.14159. The user can access this value by using the PI accessor defined in Lines 14–19. You see an object created called myNumbers in Line 31. The value of PI is accessed in Line 32.

If you remove the comments from Lines 22–25 and recompile, you get the following error:

```
inherit06b.cs(22,14): error CS0509: 'numbers' : cannot inherit from sealed class
       'number'
inherit06b.cs(5,21): (Location of symbol related to previous error)
```

This happens because you cannot inherit from a sealed class. Line 22 tries to inherit from number but can't.

Note

If you try to declare a data type as protected within a sealed class, you will get a compiler warning. You should declare your data as private because the class won't (can't) be inherited.

10

The Ultimate Base Class: Object

Everything within C# is a class. The ultimate base class in C# is Object. The Object class is the root class in the .NET Framework class hierarchy. This means that it is the first base class.

Based on what you've learned today so far, everything is an Object in C#. This means that all data types and other classes are derived from the Object class. It also means that any methods available in the Object class are available in all .NET classes.

A Look at the Object Class Methods

An Object—and, therefore, all classes—can have two methods of interest: GetType and ToString. The GetType method returns the data type of an object. The ToString method returns a string that represents the current object. Listing 10.7 illustrates using these properties with one of the classes created earlier.

LISTING 10.7   obj.cs—Everything Is an Object

```
 1:  // obj.cs - Object Properties
 2:  //================================================
 3:  using System;
 4:
 5:  sealed class PI
 6:  {
 7:     public static float nbr;
 8:
 9:     static PI()
10:     {
11:         nbr = 3.14159F;
12:     }
13:
14:     static public float val()
15:     {
16:         return(nbr);
17:     }
18:  }
19:
20:  class myApp
21:  {
22:     public static void Main()
23:     {
24:         Console.WriteLine("PI = {0}", PI.val());
25:
26:         Object x = new PI();
27:         Console.WriteLine("ToString: {0}", x.ToString());
28:         Console.WriteLine("Type: {0}", x.GetType());
```

LISTING 10.7 continued

```
29:
30:         Console.WriteLine("ToString: {0}", 123.ToString());
31:         Console.WriteLine("Type: {0}", 123.GetType());
32:     }
33: }
```

OUTPUT

```
PI = 3.14159
ToString: PI
Type: PI
ToString: 123
Type: System. Int32
```

ANALYSIS In Line 26, a new variable named x is declared. This variable is an Object data type; however, it points to a PI object. Because Object is a base class for all classes, including the PI class created in this listing, it is okay to use it to point to a new PI object. In Lines 27–28, two of the Object class's methods are called, GetType and ToString. These methods tell you that x is of type PI and that x is holding a PI class.

In Lines 30–and 31, you see something that might look strange. Remember, everything—including literals—is based on classes in C#, and all classes derive from Object. This means that a literal value such as the number 123 is, in reality, an object—an object that is ultimately derived from the Object class. Using the methods available from the Object class, you can convert the number 123 to a string by using the ToString method. Not surprisingly, this yields the value 123 (as a string). You also see that the data type for the number 123 is a System.Int32 (which is the .NET Framework equivalent of a standard int in C#).

Boxing and Unboxing

Now that you have a better understanding of the relationship between derived classes, there is another topic to explore: boxing and unboxing.

Earlier, it was stated that everything in C# is an object. That is not exactly true; however, everything can be *treated* as an object. On previous days, you learned that value data types are stored differently than reference data types and that objects are reference types. In Listing 10.7, however, you treated a literal value as if it were an object. How was this possible?

In C#, you have the capability to convert a value type to an object, and thus a reference type. This can happen automatically. In Listing 10.7, the value 123 was explicitly converted to an object.

NEW TERM *Boxing* is the conversion of a value type to a reference type (object). *Unboxing* is the explicit conversion of a reference type to a value type. A value that is unboxed must be put into a data type equivalent to the data stored.

Unboxing requires that that you explicitly convert an object to a value type. This can be done using a cast. Listing 10.8 illustrates the simple boxing and unboxing of a value. Figures 10.2 and 10.3 help to illustrate what is happening in the listing.

LISTING 10.8   boxIt.cs—Boxing and Unboxing

```
 1:  // boxIt.cs - boxing and unboxing
 2:  //=================================================
 3:  using System;
 4:
 5:  class myApp
 6:  {
 7:     public static void Main()
 8:     {
 9:
10:        float val = 3.14F;       // Assign a value type a value
11:        object boxed = val;      // boxing val into boxed
12:
13:        float unboxed = (float) boxed;   // unboxing boxed into unboxed
14:
15:        Console.WriteLine("val: {0}", val);
16:        Console.WriteLine("boxed: {0}", boxed);
17:        Console.WriteLine("unboxed: {0}", unboxed);
18:
19:        Console.WriteLine("\nTypes...");
20:        Console.WriteLine("val: {0}", val.GetType());
21:        Console.WriteLine("boxed: {0}", boxed.GetType());
22:        Console.WriteLine("unboxed: {0}", unboxed.GetType());
23:     }
24:  }
```

OUTPUT
```
val: 3.14
boxed: 3.14
unboxed: 3.14

Types...
val: System.Single
boxed: System.Single
unboxed: System. Single
```

ANALYSIS This listing focuses on boxing and unboxing. In Line 10, a value data type is declared and assigned the value of 3.14. In Line 11, boxing occurs. The value type, val, is boxed into the variable, boxed. The boxed variable is an object. Figure 10.2 illustrates how these are different by showing how val and boxed are stored.

FIGURE **10.2**

Boxing a value.

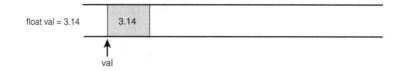
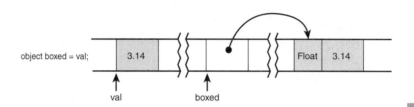

In Line 13, the value in `boxed` is unboxed into a variable named `unboxed`. The `unboxed` variable is a value type that is given a copy of the value stored in `boxed`. In this listing, that value is `3.14`. Figure 10.3 helps illustrate how these are stored in memory.

FIGURE **10.3**

Unboxing a value.

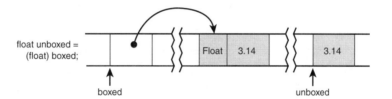

Line 19 uses a method of the object type on each of the three variables. As you should know, `val` and `unboxed` are both value types. As such, you might wonder how the `GetType` method can work because the value types don't really store their type—they store only their value. In Lines 20 and 22, the value types are automatically boxed, thus changing them to objects. This then enables methods such as `GetType` to be called.

Using the `is` and `as` Keywords with Classes—Class Conversions

Two keywords can be used with classes: `is` and `as`. The following sections teach you how you can use these keywords.

Using the `is` Keyword

Sometimes you will want to do a comparison to see whether an object is of a certain type. To help in this comparison, C# has the `is` keyword. You use the `is` keyword to determine whether a variable is of a specified type. The format for using this keyword is as follows:

(*expression* is *type*)

Here, *expression* evaluates to a reference type and *type* is a valid *type*. Generally, *type* will be a class type.

If *expression* is compatible with *type*, this returns true. If *expression* is not compatible with *type*, false is returned. Listing 10.9 is not a practical listing; however, it illustrates the value of is.

LISTING 10.9   islist.cs—Using the is Keyword

```
 1:  // islist.cs - Using the is keyword
 2:  //=================================================
 3:  using System;
 4:
 5:  class Person
 6:  {
 7:      protected string Name;
 8:
 9:      public Person()  { }
10:
11:      public Person(string n)  { Name = n; }
12:
13:      public virtual void displayFullName()
14:      {
15:          Console.WriteLine("Name: {0}", Name);
16:      }
17:  }
18:
19:  class Employee : Person
20:  {
21:      public Employee() : base()   { }
22:
23:      public Employee(string n) : base(n)  { }
24:
25:      public override void displayFullName()
26:      {
27:          Console.WriteLine("Employee: {0}", Name);
28:      }
29:  }
30:
31:  class IsApp
32:  {
33:      public static void Main()
34:      {
35:          Person pers = new Person();
```

LISTING 10.9   continued

```
36:        Object emp = new Employee();
37:        string str = "String";
38:
39:        if( pers is Person )
40:            Console.WriteLine("pers is a Person");
41:        else
42:            Console.WriteLine("pers is NOT a Person");
43:
44:        if( pers is Object )
45:            Console.WriteLine("pers is an Object");
46:        else
47:            Console.WriteLine("pers is NOT an Object");
48:
49:        if( pers is Employee )
50:            Console.WriteLine("pers is an Employee");
51:        else
52:            Console.WriteLine("pers is NOT an Employee");
53:
54:        if( emp is Person )
55:            Console.WriteLine("emp is a Person");
56:        else
57:            Console.WriteLine("emp is NOT a Person");
58:
59:        if( str is Person )
60:            Console.WriteLine("str is a Person");
61:        else
62:            Console.WriteLine("str is NOT a Person");
63:    }
64: }
```

OUTPUT

```
pers is a Person
pers is an Object
pers is NOT an Employee
emp is a Person
str is NOT a Person
```

ANALYSIS   This listing might give you warnings when you compile it. Some of the `is` comparisons are obvious to the compiler; thus, it tells you that they always will be valid. The `is` keyword is a great tool for testing the type of a reference variable when a program is running.

This listing declares a couple of classes before getting to the `Main` method. These classes do very little. The first class is `Person`. The second class, `Employee`, is derived from `Person`. These classes are then used in the `Main` method.

In Lines 35–37, three variables are declared. The first, `pers`, is a `Person` that is assigned a `Person`. The second, `emp`, is of type `Object` and is assigned an `Employee` type. As you learned earlier, you can assign a type to any of its base types. This means that an Employee can be assigned to an Object type, a Person type, or an Employee type. In Line 37, a string is declared.

The rest of this listing does comparisons of the three variables against different types. You can review the output to see which passed the comparisons and which did not.

Note

> The pers variable is an Object and a Person. The emp variable is an Employee, a Person, and an Object. If this doesn't make sense, you should reread today's lesson.

Using the as Keyword

The as operator works similarly to a cast. The as keyword cast an object to a different type. The type being cast to must be compatible with the original type. Remember, a cast is simply a way to force a value to a different type. The format of as is as follows:

expression as *DataType*

Here, *expression* results in a reference type and *DataType* is a reference type. A similar cast would take this form:

(*DataType*) *expression*

Although using the as keyword is similar to a cast, it is not the same. If you use a cast and there is a problem—such as trying to cast a string as a number—an exception is thrown.

With as, if there is an error in changing the expression to the *DataType*, the expression is set to the value of null and converted to the *DataType* anyway. However, no exception is thrown. This makes using the as keyword safer than doing a cast.

Working with Arrays of Different Object Types

Before ending today's lesson, one additional topic deserves discussion. Using the keywords as and is, you can actually gain a lot of power. You can create an array of objects that are of different types. You do this by using a base type to define the variables. Listing 10.10 illustrates the use of the as keyword and also illustrates the storage of different object types in a single array. Be aware, however, that the different data types all must be within the same inheritance hierarchy.

LISTING 10.10   objs.cs—An Array of Objects

```
 1: // objs.cs - Using an array containing different types
 2: //=======================================================
 3: using System;
 4:
 5: public class Person
 6: {
 7:    public string Name;
 8:
 9:    public Person()
10:    {
11:    }
12:
13:    public Person(string nm)
14:    {
15:       Name = nm;
16:    }
17:
18:    public virtual void displayFullName()
19:    {
20:        Console.WriteLine("Person: {0}", Name);
21:    }
22: }
23:
24: class Employee : Person
25: {
26: //   public ushort hireYear;
27:
28:    public Employee() : base()
29:    {
30:    }
31:
32:    public Employee(string nm) : base(nm)
33:    {
34:    }
35:
36:    public override void displayFullName()
37:    {
38:        Console.WriteLine("Employee: {0}", Name);
39:    }
40: }
41:
42: // A new class derived from Person...
43: class Contractor : Person
44: {
45: //   public string company;
46:
47:    public Contractor() : base()
48:    {
```

LISTING 10.10   continued

```
49:      }
50:
51:      public Contractor(string nm) : base(nm)
52:      {
53:      }
54:
55:      public override void displayFullName()
56:      {
57:          Console.WriteLine("Contractor: {0}", Name);
58:      }
59:  }
60:
61:  class NameApp
62:  {
63:      public static void Main()
64:      {
65:          Person [] myCompany = new Person[5];
66:          int ctr = 0;
67:          string buffer;
68:
69:          do
70:          {
71:              do
72:              {
73:                  Console.Write(
➥"\nEnter \'c\' for Contractor, \'e\' for Employee then press ENTER: ");
74:                  buffer = Console.ReadLine();
75:              } while (buffer == "");
76:
77:              if ( buffer[0] == 'c' || buffer[0] == 'C' )
78:              {
79:                  Console.Write("\nEnter the contractor\'s name: ");
80:                  buffer = Console.ReadLine();
81:                  // do other Contractor stuff...
82:                  Contractor contr = new Contractor(buffer);
83:                  myCompany[ctr] = contr as Person;
84:              }
85:              else
86:              if ( buffer[0] == 'e' || buffer[0] == 'E' )
87:              {
88:                  Console.Write("\nEnter the employee\'s name: ");
89:                  buffer = Console.ReadLine();
90:                  // Do other employee stuff...
91:                  Employee emp = new Employee(buffer);
92:                  myCompany[ctr] = emp as Person;
93:              }
94:              else
95:              {
```

LISTING 10.10 continued

```
 96:                    Person pers = new Person("Not an Employee or Contractor");
 97:                    myCompany[ctr] = pers;
 98:                }
 99:
100:                ctr++;
101:
102:          } while ( ctr < 5 );
103:
104:          // Display the results of what was entered....
105:
106:          Console.WriteLine( "\n\n\n===========================");
107:
108:          for( ctr = 0; ctr < 5; ctr++ )
109:          {
110:              if( myCompany[ctr] is Employee )
111:              {
112:                  Console.WriteLine("Employee: {0}", myCompany[ctr].Name);
113:              }
114:              else
115:              if( myCompany[ctr] is Contractor )
116:              {
117:                  Console.WriteLine("Contractor: {0}", myCompany[ctr].Name);
118:              }
119:              else
120:              {
121:                  Console.WriteLine("Person: {0}", myCompany[ctr].Name);
122:              }
123:          }
124:          Console.WriteLine( "===========================");
125:      }
126:  }
```

OUTPUT

```
Enter 'c' for Contractor, 'e' for Employee then press ENTER: C

Enter the contractor's name: Amber Jones

Enter 'c' for Contractor, 'e' for Employee then press ENTER: E

Enter the employee's name: Benjamin Andrews

Enter 'c' for Contractor, 'e' for Employee then press ENTER: e

Enter the employee's name: Jacob Sams

Enter 'c' for Contractor, 'e' for Employee then press ENTER: c
```

```
Enter the contractor's name: Matt Hebron

Enter 'c' for Contractor, 'e' for Employee then press ENTER: Z



============================
Contractor: Amber Jones
Employee: Bejamin Andrews
Employee: Jacob Sams
Contractor: Matt Hebron
Person: Not an Employee or Contractor
============================
```

ANALYSIS This is a long listing compared to what you have been seeing. This listing only partially implements everything it could do. One of today's exercises will have you expand on this listing.

The purpose of the listing is to enable you to enter people into the program. This is set up to take five people; however, you could have the user enter people until a set value is entered. The program prompts you to enter either an 'e' or a 'c' to indicate whether the person is an employee or a contractor. Based on what you enter, it gives you a custom prompt to enter the person's name. You could also ask for additional information; however, this hasn't been done here.

If the user enters a value other than an 'e' or 'c', the program fills the person's name with an error message. You most likely would want different logic than this. You should also notice that although the program prompts for lowercase 'e' or 'c', uppercase letters also work.

Most of the code should be familiar to you. The classes defined in this listing have been scaled back to a minimum amount of code. Lines 26 and 45 were left in the listing as comments. You will be asked to use these data members in one of today's exercises.

In Line 63, you see the beginning of the Main method for this application. Lines 69–102 contain a do...while that loops for each person being entered. Lines 71–75 contain a nested do...while, which prompts the user to enter either an 'e' or a 'c' to indicate the type of person being entered. Using a ReadLine in Line 74, the user's answer is obtained. Users who press Enter are prompted again.

When a value is entered, if...else statements are used to determine what processing should occur. In Line 77, only the first character of the text entered by the user is reviewed. The first character is stored in the 0 position of the string—buffer[0].

If the value entered starts with a c, Lines 79–84 are executed. In Line 79, the user is asked to enter a contractor's name. The Write method is used instead of WriteLine so that the reader can enter the name on the same line as the prompt. If you use WriteLine, a carriage return, line feed occurs and the user must enter the name on the next line.

In Line 80, the name is retrieved using the ReadLine method. In Line 82, a contractor object is created named contr. This object is initialized with the name obtained from the ReadLine method. In Line 83, this new object is then assigned to the myCompany array. Because myCompany is an array of Person, the contr variable is assigned to the array as a Person type. Because Person is a base type for Contractor, you can do this, as you learned earlier today.

In Lines 106–123, the program again loops through the myCompany array. This time, each element in the array is printed to the screen. In Line 110, the element in the array is checked to see whether it is an Employee. If it is, a custom output for employees is displayed. If not, the if statement in Line 115 is checked to see whether it is a Contractor. If so, a message is printed. If not, a message is printed indicating that it is just a Person.

Line 124 prints a dashed line to help format the output. The program then ends.

Using is and as enables you to store different data types in a single array, provided that they work with the same base class. Because all objects inherit from Object, you will always have a base class that works in this manner. This listing illustrates key features of object-oriented programming.

Summary

Today's lesson was long; however, it is also one of the most important. In today's lesson, you learned about inheritance. You learned how to create base classes and how to derive from them. Additionally, you learned different keywords—such as abstract, virtual, and protected—that can impact what you can do with a base class and a derived class. You also learned how to seal a class to prevent inheritance.

Later in the day, you learned how to work with objects using types other than their own. You learned that an object can be assigned or accessed using a type in any of its base classes. Additionally, you learned that you can cast an object to a different type using the as keyword. The as keyword operates similarly to a cast operation, except that, with an error, a null is set instead of an exception being thrown. You also learned that you can use the is keyword to evaluate what type an object is.

Q&A

Q Can you inherit from a base class written in a language other than C#?

A Yes. One of the features of .NET is that classes can inherit from classes written in other languages. This means that your C# classes can be derived from classes of other languages. Additionally, programmers of other languages can use your C# classes as base classes.

Q Today's lesson presented an example of assigning a derived class to a base class in Listing 10.3. Can you assign a base class to a derived class?

A Yes, if you are careful. In Listing 10.3, a base class was assigned an object from a derived class. Although only the items available via the base class constructs can be used, the other portions of the derived class are not lost. It is possible to assign a derived class the value of a base class if you know that the base class was assigned an object of the derived class's type. This assignment is done with a cast. In Listing 10.3, it would not be an error to do the following after Line 55:

```
Employee you = (Employee) Brad;
```

This is valid because Brad was assigned with an Employee object. If Brad was not an Employee object, this line of code would throw an invalid cast exception, (System.InvalidCastException).

Q What is data or method hiding?

A Data or method hiding occurs when you create a method or data element in a derived class that replaces a base method or data element. This occurs when the new keyword is used to create the new class.

Q What are upcasting and downcasting?

A Downcasting is forcing an object to a type of a class derived from it. Upcasting is casting an object to a data type of a base class. Upcasting is considered safe to do and is an implicit operation in C#. Downcasting is considered unsafe. To downcast, you must explicitly force the conversion.

Q What is composition? Is it an object-oriented term?

A Many people confuse inheritance with composition, but they are different. With composition, one object is used within another object. Figure 10.4 is a composition of many circles. This is different from the sphere in the previous example. The sphere is not composed of a circle; it is an extension of the circle. To summarize the difference between composition and inheritance, composition occurs when one class (object) has another within it. Inheritance occurs when one class (object) is an expansion of another.

FIGURE 10.4

A snowman made of circles.

10

Workshop

The Workshop provides quiz questions to help you solidify your understanding of the material covered and exercises to provide you with experience in using what you've learned. Try to understand the quiz and exercise answers before continuing to tomorrow's lesson. Answers are provided on the CD.

Quiz

1. In C#, how many classes can be used to inherit from to create a single new class?

2. Which of the following is the same as a base class?

    a. Parent class

    b. Derived class

    c. Child class

3. What access modifier is used to protect data from being used outside a single class? What access modifier will enable data to be used by only a base class and classes derived from the base class?

4. How is a base class's method hidden?

5. What keyword can be used in a base class to ensure that a derived class creates its own version of a method?

6. What keyword is used to prevent a class from being inherited?

7. Name two methods that all classes have.

8. What class is the ultimate base class from which all other classes are derived?

9. What does boxing do?

10. What is the as keyword used for?

Exercises

1. Write a method header for declaring a constructor for the ABC class that receives two arguments, ARG1 and ARG2, that are both integers. This constructor should call a base constructor and pass it to the ARG2 integer. This should be done in the method header:

```
public ABC( int ARG1, int ARG2) : base( ARG2 )
{
}
```

2. Modify the following class to prevent it from being used as a base class:

```
 1:  class aLetter
 2:  {
 3:      private static char A_ch;
 4:
 5:      public char ch
 6:      {
 7:        get { return A_ch; }
 8:        set { A_ch = value; }
 9:      }
10:
11:      static aLetter()
12:      {
13:         A_ch = 'X';
14:      }
15:  }
```

3. **Bug Buster:** There is a problem with the following code. Which lines are in error?

```
// Bug Buster

//  Class definition for Person would need to be included here...

class NameApp
{
   public static void Main()
   {
```

```
            Person me = new Person();
            Object you = new Object();

            me = you;

            System.Console.WriteLine("Type: {0}", me.GetType());
        }
    }
```

4. **On Your Own**: Modify Listing 10.9 to set the value of `hireyear` or `company`. Print these values, when appropriate, with the output that is displayed.

10

DAY 11

Formatting and
Retrieving Information

The last few days, you covered a lot of hard-core C# development topics that
will be critical to your development of professional-level applications. Before
trudging into additional hard-core topics, today's lesson offers some diversion.
Today you...

- Review the difference between input and output.
- Discover more of the formatting options available when displaying information in the console.
- Get a detailed explanation of reading information from the console.
- Learn how to parse information read from the console.
- Format and work with strings.
- Examine the concept of streams.
- Manipulate basic file information.

> **Note**   Today's lesson contains much more reference information than most of the
> other days in this book. You should find this reference material valuable.

Understanding Console Input and Output

You've seen the terms *input* and *output*. In today's lesson, you step back and focus on providing output in a much better presentation format. Additionally, you learn a little more about getting information from your users via input from the console.

You also learn a lot more about strings in today's lessons. The Write and WriteLine methods actually do string formatting behind the scenes. In today's lesson, you learn how to format these strings using other methods.

Formatting Information

When displaying information, it is often easiest to convert the information to a string first. As you have already seen, the Write and WriteLine methods for the Console class use strings for displaying output. Additionally, the .NET Framework provides a number of methods and specifiers that can be used with strings. A *specifier* indicates that information is to be formatted.

Format specifiers can be used with any string. The following sections cover a number of format specifiers. This includes specifiers for working with each of the following:

- Standard numeric formats
- Currency
- Exponential numbers
- Exponentials
- Custom numeric formats
- Dates and times
- Enumerators

You can use these format specifiers in several ways. The most obvious way is to use the specifiers with the Write and WriteLine methods to provide additional formatting.

You also can use the format specifiers when calling the ToString method. As you learned in yesterday's lesson, the Object class contains a ToString method. As you know, because all classes are derived from Object, all objects have access to a ToString method. In classes such as the Int32 class, this method can be passed a formatting specifier to format the data. For example, if var is an integer variable containing the value 123, by using the currency formatter ("c"), the following line

```
var.ToString("C");
```

returns this value:

```
$123.00
```

A third time to use a specifier is with the string data type. string has a static method named Format. Because Format is a static method, it can be used directly with the class as string.Format. The format for using this method follows the same format as the parameters of the Console display methods:

```
string newString = string.Format("format_string", value(s) );
```

Here, newString is the new string that will be formatted. format_string is a string that contains formatting specifiers. These specifiers are the same as those that can be used in Write and WriteLine. value(s) contains the values that will be formatted into the string.

> **Note**   You will learn more about formatting values as you learn about some of the specifiers.

11

The character c is the format specifier for currency. As stated previously, you can indicate this format to the ToString method by passing it between quotes as an argument. When formatting information within a string, such as with WriteLine, you include this format specifier with the variable placeholder. The following is the basic format:

```
{hldr:X#}
```

Here, hldr is the placeholder number for the variable. x is the specifier used to format the number. To format the number as currency, this would be c. The # is an optional value, which is the number of digits you want. This number can do different types of padding, depending on the specifier. With the currency specifier, this number indicates the number of decimal places. Listing 11.1 presents the three ways of using specifiers that were mentioned earlier. It presents a small example of using the currency and other specifiers. More details are provided later today on these and other specifiers.

LISTING 11.1   FormatIt.cs—Basic Formatting Methods

```
 1:  // FormatIt.cs - Different places for specifiers
 2:  //              to be used.
 3:  //-----------------------------------------------
 4:
 5:  using System;
 6:
 7:  class FormatIt
 8:  {
 9:    public static void Main()
10:    {
11:        int var = 12345;
12:
13:        // Format using WriteLine
14:
15:        Console.Write("You can format text using Write");
16:        Console.WriteLine(" and WriteLine. You can insert");
17:        Console.Write("variables (such as {0}) into a string", var );
18:        Console.WriteLine(" as well as do other formatting!");
19:        Console.WriteLine("\n{0:C}\n{0:C4}", var);
20:        Console.WriteLine("\n{0:f}\n{0:f3}", var);
21:
22:
23:        // Format using ToString
24:
25:        string str1 = var.ToString("C");
26:        string str2 = var.ToString("C3");
27:        string str3 = var.ToString("E8");
28:
29:        Console.WriteLine("\nYou can also format using ToString");
30:        Console.WriteLine(str1);
31:        Console.WriteLine(str2);
32:        Console.WriteLine(str3);
33:
34:        // Formatting with string.Format
35:
36:        string str4 = string.Format("\nOr, you can use string.Format: ");
37:        string str5 = string.Format("Nbr {0:F3} \n{0:C} \n{0:C0}", var);
38:
39:        Console.WriteLine(str4);
40:        Console.WriteLine(str5);
41:    }
42:  }
```

OUTPUT   You can format text using Write and WriteLine. You can insert
variables (such as 12345) into a string as well as do other formatting!

```
$12,345.00
$12,345.0000
```

```
12345.00
12345.000

You can also format using ToString
$12,345.00
$12,345.000
1.23450000E+004

Or, you can use string.Format:
Nbr 12345.000
$12,345.00
$12,345
```

ANALYSIS A full analysis of this listing isn't provided here. Instead, this listing is presented to touch on some of the formatting you can do. You can see that formatting is done in this listing: The var number is formatted as currency, a decimal number, and an exponential. More important to notice here is that the numbers included after the specifier helped determine the number of decimals or zero positions included.

Formatting Numbers

You can use a number of format specifiers to format numeric values. Table 11.1 lists these specifiers.

11

TABLE 11.1 Characters Used for Numeric Formatting

Specifier	Description	Default Format	Example Output
C or c	Currency	$xx,xxx.xx	$12,345.67
		($xx,xxx.xx)	($12,345.67)
D or d	Decimal	xxxxxxx	1234567
		-xxxxxxx	-1234567
E or e	Exponential	x.xxxxxxE+xxx	1.234567E+123
		x.xxxxxxe+xxx	1.234567e+123
		-x.xxxxxxxE+xxx	-1.234567E+123
		-x.xxxxxxxe+xxx	-1.234567e+123
		x.xxxxxxE-xxx	1.234567E-123
		x.xxxxxxe-xxx	1.234567e-123
		-x.xxxxxxxE-xxx	-1.234567E-123
		-x.xxxxxxxe-xxx	-1.234567e-123
F or f	Fixed point	xxxxxx.xx	1234567.89
		-xxxxx.xx	-1234567.89

TABLE 11.1   continued

Specifier	Description	Default Format	Example Output
N or n	Numeric	xx,xxx.xx	12,345.67
		-xx,xxx.xx	-12,345.67
X or x	Hexadecimal	12d687	12D687
G or g	General	Varies (uses the most compact format)	
R or r	Round-trip	Maintains precession when numbers are converted to and then back from a string	

You can use these and the other format specifiers in today's lesson in the ways described earlier. When using the specifiers with the ToString method, you enclose the appropriate character in quotation marks and pass it as a parameter. You saw the earlier example of 123 being formatted as currency:

```
string newString = var.ToString("C");
```

This line of code results in newString containing the value $123.00. The following sections discuss each of these formats briefly.

 Caution

> The formatting specifiers might differ depending on your system's locale settings.

Standard Formats (Fixed, Decimal, Numeric)

The standard format specifiers work with their related number types. F works for floating-point numbers. D works with standard whole numbers, such as integers and longs. If you try to use D with a floating-point number, you will get an exception.

The number specifier (N) adds two decimal places and commas to the number's format. This can be used to obtain a much nicer format than the default format for numbers.

Formatting Currency

By now, you should know that the currency specifier is C. You can use C by itself to have currency displayed with two decimal positions. If you want to avoid decimals, use C0. The 0 indicates that no decimal positions should be included. If you want to get a different number of decimal places in your currency display, simply change the 0 to the number of decimal places you would like.

Formatting Exponential Numbers

Exponential numbers are often presented in scientific notation because of their overly large, or overly small, size. The E and e specifiers can be used to format these numbers. You should note that the case of the E in the format specifier is the same case that will be used in the output.

General Formatting of Numbers

The general formatting specifier (G or g) is used to format a number into the smallest string representation possible. Based on the number, this formatter determines whether an exponential representation or a standard format results in the smallest string. Whichever is smaller is returned. Listing 11.2 illustrates the different formats that this specifier can return.

LISTING 11.2   General.cs—Using the General Specifier

```
 1:  // General.cs - Using the General format specifier
 2:  //----------------------------------------------
 3:  using System;
 4:
 5:  class General
 6:  {
 7:    public static void Main()
 8:    {
 9:       float fVal1 = .000000789F;
10:       float fVal2 = 1.2F;
11:
12:       Console.WriteLine("f1   ({0:f}). Format (G): {0:G}", fVal1);
13:       Console.WriteLine("f2   ({0:f}). Format (G): {0:G}", fVal2);
14:    }
15:  }
```

OUTPUT
```
f1   (0.00). Format (G): 7.89E-07
f2   (1.20). Format (G): 1.2
```

ANALYSIS This listing initializes and prints two variables. In Lines 9–10, two float variables are created. One is a very small decimal value, and the other is a simple number.

In Lines 12–13, these values are written to the console. The first placeholder in each of these lines displays the floating-point value as a fixed-point number using the F specifier. The second placeholder prints the same variable in the general format using the G format. In the output, fVal1 is much more concise as an exponential number, and fVal2 is more concise as a regular number.

Formatting Hexadecimal Numbers

Hexadecimal numbers are numbers based on the base 16 number system. This number system is often used with computers. Appendix C, "Understanding Number Systems" covers using hexadecimal. The letter x—either uppercase or lowercase—is used to specify a hexadecimal number. The hexadecimal specifier automatically converts and prints a value as a hexadecimal value.

Maintaining Precession (Round-Tripping)

When you convert a number from one format to another, you run the risk of losing precision. A specifier has been provided to help maintain precision in case you want to convert a string back to a number: the R (or r) specifier. By using this specifier, the runtime tries to maintain the precision of the original number.

Creating Custom Formats Using Picture Definitions

Sometimes you will want to have more control over a number's format. For example, you might want to format a driver's license number or Social Security number with dashes. You might want to add parentheses and dashes to a phone number. Table 11.2 presents some of the formatting characters that can be used with the specifiers to create custom formats for output. Listing 11.3 provides examples of these specifiers.

TABLE 11.2   Formatting Characters for Picture Definitions

Specifier	Description
0	Zero placeholder. Filled with digit, if available.
#	Blank placeholder. Filled with digit, if available.
.	Displays a period. Used for decimal points.
,	Uses a comma for separating groups of numbers. It can also be used as a multiplier (see Listing 11.3).
%	Displays the number as a percentage value (for example, 1.00 is 100%).
\	Used to indicate that a special character should be printed. This can be one of the escape characters, such as the newline character (\n).
'xyz'	Displays text within the apostrophes.
"xyz"	Displays text within the quotes.

LISTING 11.3   Picts.cs—Using the Picture Specifiers

```
 1: // Picts.cs - Using picture specifiers
 2: //----------------------------------------------
 3:
 4: using System;
 5:
 6: class Picts
 7: {
 8:   public static void Main()
 9:   {
10:     int var1 = 1234;
11:     float var2 = 12.34F;
12:
13:     // Zero formatter
14:     Console.WriteLine("\nZero...");
15:     Console.WriteLine("{0} -->{0:0000000}", var1);
16:     Console.WriteLine("{0} -->{0:0000000}", var2);
17:
18:     // Space formatter
19:     Console.WriteLine("\nSpace...");
20:     Console.WriteLine("{0} -->{0:0#####}<--", var1);
21:     Console.WriteLine("{0} -->{0:0#####}<--", var2);
22:
23:     // Group separator and multiplier (,)
24:     Console.WriteLine("\nGroup Multiplier...");
25:     Console.WriteLine("{0} -->{0:0,,}<--", 1000000);
26:     Console.WriteLine("Group Separator...");
27:     Console.WriteLine("{0} -->{0:##,###,##0}<--", 2000000);
28:     Console.WriteLine("{0} -->{0:##,###,##0]< ", 3);
29:
30:     // Percentage formatter
31:     Console.WriteLine("\nPercentage...");
32:     Console.WriteLine("{0} -->{0:0%}<--", var1);
33:     Console.WriteLine("{0} -->{0:0%}<--", var2);
34:
35:     // Literal formatting
36:     Console.WriteLine("\nLiteral Formatting...");
37:     Console.WriteLine("{0} -->{0:'My Number: '0}<--", var1);
38:     Console.WriteLine("{0} -->{0:'My Number: '0}<--", var2);
39:     Console.WriteLine("\n{0} -->{0:Mine: 0}<--", var1);
40:     Console.WriteLine("{0} -->{0:Mine: 0}<--", var2);
41:   }
42: }
```

11

OUTPUT

```
Zero...
1234 -->0001234
12.34 -->0000012

Space...
1234 -->01234<--
12.34 -->00012<--

Group Multiplier...
1000000 -->1<--
Group Separator...
2000000 -->2,000,000<--
3 -->3<--

Percentage...
1234 -->123400%<--
12.34 -->1234%<--

Literal Formatting...
1234 -->My Number: 1234<--
12.34 -->My Number: 12<--

1234 -->Mine: 1234<--
12.34 -->Mine: 12<--
```

ANALYSIS This listing uses the format specifiers in Table 11.2 and applies them to two variables. Looking at the comments and the output, you can see how a number of the specifiers work.

Formatting Negative Numbers

Sometimes you also when you want a negative number treated differently than a positive number. The specifiers that you have learned about will work with both positive and negative numbers.

The placeholder for specifying the format can actually be separated into either two or three sections. If the placeholder is separated into two sections, the first is for positive numbers and 0, and the second is for negative numbers. If it is broken into three sections, the first is for positive values, the middle is for negative values, and the third is for 0.

The placeholder is broken into these sections using a semicolon. The placeholder number is then included in each. For example, to format a number to print with three levels of precision when positive, five levels when negative, and no levels when 0, you do the following:

```
{0:D3;D5;'0'}
```

Listing 11.4 presents this example in action, along with a couple of additional examples.

LISTING 11.4   ThreeWay.cs.

```
1:  // ThreeWay.cs - Controlling the formatting of numbers
2:  //-------------------------------------------------
3:
4:  using System;
5:
6:  class ThreeWay
7:  {
8:    public static void Main()
9:    {
10:       Console.WriteLine("\nExample 1...");
11:       for ( int x = -100; x <= 100; x += 100 )
12:       {
13:          Console.WriteLine("{0:000;-00000;'0'}", x);
14:       }
15:
16:       Console.WriteLine("\nExample 2...");
17:       for ( int x = -100; x <= 100; x += 100 )
18:       {
19:          Console.WriteLine("{0:Pos: 0;Neg: -0;Zero}", x);
20:       }
21:
22:       Console.WriteLine("\nExample 3...");
23:       for ( int x = -100; x <= 100; x += 100 )
24:       {
25:          Console.WriteLine("{0:You Win!;You Lose!;You Broke Even!}", x);
26:       }
27:    }
28:  }
```

11

OUTPUT

```
Example 1...
-00100
0
100

Example 2...
Neg: -100
Zero
Pos: 100

Example 3...
You Lose!
You Broke Even!
You Win!
```

ANALYSIS This listing helps illustrate how to break the custom formatting into three pieces. A for loop is used to create a negative number, increment the number to 0, and finally increment it to a positive number. The result is that the same WriteLine can be used to display all three values. This is done three separate times for three different examples.

In Line 13, you see that the positive value will be printed to at least three digits because there are three zeros in the first formatting position. The negative number will include a negative sign followed by at least five numbers. You know this because the dash is included in the format for the negative sign, and there are five zeros. If the value is equal to 0, a 0 will be printed.

In the second example, text is included with the formatting of the numbers. This is also done in the third example. The difference is that, in the second example, zero placeholders are also included so that the actual numbers will print. This is not the case with the third example, in which only text is displayed.

As you can see by all three of these examples, it is easy to cause different formats to be used based on the sign (positive or negative) of a variable.

Formatting Date and Time Values

Date and time values can also be formatted. A number of specifiers can help you format everything from the day of the week to the full data and time string. Before learning about these format characters, you should understand how to obtain the date and time.

Getting the Date and Time

C# and the .NET Framework provide a class for storing dates and times—the `DateTime` class located in the `System` namespace. The `DateTime` class stores both the full date and the full time.

The `DateTime` class has a number of properties and methods that you will find useful. Additionally, there are a couple of static members. The two static properties that you will likely use are `Now` and `Today`. `Now` contains the date and time for the moment the call is made. `Today` returns just the current date. Because these are static properties, their values can be obtained using the class name rather than an instant name:

```
DateTime.Now
```

```
DateTime.Today
```

You can review the online documents for information on all the methods and properties of the `DateTime` class. A few of the ones that you might find useful are shown here:

`Date`	Returns the date portion of a `DateTime` object
`Month`	Returns the month portion of a `DateTime` object
`Day`	Returns the day of the month of a `DateTime` object

Year	Returns the year portion of the DateTime object
DayOfWeek	Returns the day of the week of a DateTime object
DayOfYear	Returns the day of the year of a DateTime object
TimeOfDay	Returns the time portion of a DateTime object
Hour	Returns the hour portion of a DateTime object
Minute	Returns the minutes portion of a DateTime object
Second	Returns the seconds portion of a DateTime object
Millisecond	Returns the milliseconds component of a DateTime object
Ticks	Returns a value equal to the number of 100-nanosecond ticks for the given DateTime object

Note Although the DateTime.Today property includes a time value, it is not the current time. The DateTime.Today property gives you only a valid date—it does not give you the current time.

Formatting the Date and Time

A number of specifiers can be used with dates, times, or both. These include the capability to display information in short and long format. Table 11.3 contains the date and time specifiers.

TABLE 11.3 Date and Time Formatting Characters

Specifier	Description	Default Format	Example Output
d	Short date	mm/dd/yyyy	5/6/2001
D	Long date	day, month dd, yyyy	Sunday, May 06, 2001
f	Full date/ short time	day, month dd, yyyy hh:mm AM/PM	Sunday, May 06, 2001 12:30 PM
F	Full date/ full time	day, month dd, yyyy HH:mm:ss AM/PM	Sunday, May 06, 2001 12:30:54 PM
g	Short date/ short time	mm/dd/yyyy HH:mm	6/5/2001 12:30 PM
G	Short date/ long time	mm/dd/yyyy hh:mm:ss	6/5/2001 12:30:54 PM
M or m	Month day	month dd	May 06

TABLE 11.3 continued

Specifier	Description	Default Format	Example Output
R or r	RFC1123	ddd, dd Month yyyy hh:mm:ss GMT	Sun, 06 May 2001 12:30:54 GMT
s	Sortable	yyyy-mm-dd hh:mm:ss	2001-05-06T12:30:54
t	Short time	hh:mm AM/PM	12:30 PM
T	Long time	hh:mm:ss AM/PM	12:30:54 PM
u	Sortable (universal)	yyyy-mm-dd hh:mm:ss	2001-05-06 12:30:54Z
U	Sortable (universal)	day, month dd, yyyy hh:mm:ss AM/PM	Sunday, May 06, 2001 12:30:54 PM
Y or y	Year/month	month, yyyy	May, 2001

 Caution s is used as a specifier for printing a sortable date. Note that this is a lower-case *s*. An uppercase *S* is not a valid format specifier and generates an exception if used.

The date and time specifiers are easy to use. Listing 11.5 defines a simple date variable and then prints it in all the formats presented in Table 11.3.

LISTING 11.5 DtFormat.cs—The Date Formats

```
 1: // DtFormat.cs - date/time formats
 2: //----------------------------------------------
 3:
 4: using System;
 5:
 6: class DtFormat
 7: {
 8:   public static void Main()
 9:   {
10:     DateTime CurrTime = DateTime.Now;
11:
12:     Console.WriteLine("d: {0:d}", CurrTime );
13:     Console.WriteLine("D: {0:D}", CurrTime );
14:     Console.WriteLine("f: {0:f}", CurrTime );
15:     Console.WriteLine("F: {0:F}", CurrTime );
16:     Console.WriteLine("g: {0:g}", CurrTime );
17:     Console.WriteLine("G: {0:G}", CurrTime );
18:     Console.WriteLine("m: {0:m}", CurrTime );
19:     Console.WriteLine("M: {0:M}", CurrTime );
```

LISTING 11.5 continued

```
20:         Console.WriteLine("r: {0:r}", CurrTime );
21:         Console.WriteLine("R: {0:R}", CurrTime );
22:         Console.WriteLine("s: {0:s}", CurrTime );
23:  //     Console.WriteLine("S: {0:S}", CurrTime );   // error!!!
24:         Console.WriteLine("t: {0:t}", CurrTime );
25:         Console.WriteLine("T: {0:T}", CurrTime );
26:         Console.WriteLine("u: {0:u}", CurrTime );
27:         Console.WriteLine("U: {0:U}", CurrTime );
28:         Console.WriteLine("y: {0:y}", CurrTime );
29:         Console.WriteLine("Y: {0:Y}", CurrTime );
30:     }
31: }
```

OUTPUT

```
d: 1/24/2003
D: Friday, January 24, 2003
f: Friday, January 24, 2003 8:43 PM
F: Friday, January 24, 2003 8:43:04 PM
g: 1/24/2003 8:43 PM
G: 1/24/2003 8:43:04 PM
m: January 24
M: January 24
r: Fri, 24 Jan 2003 20:43:04 GMT
R: Fri, 24 Jan 2003 20:43:04 GMT
s: 2003-01-24T20:43:04
t: 8:43 PM
T: 8:43:04 PM
u: 2003-01-24 20:43:04Z
U: Saturday, January 25, 2003 1:43:04 AM
y: January, 2003
Y: January, 2003
```

11

Note

Note that, on some systems, the date formatting might include zero padding. For example, using the mono compiler, dates appear as 01/24/2003 instead of 1/24/2003.

ANALYSIS In Line 10, this listing declares an object to hold the date and time. This is done using the DateTime class. This object is named CurrTime, and it is assigned the static value from the DateTime class, Now, which provides the current date and time. Looking at the output, you can see that I ran this listing midday in May. Lines 12–29 present this same date and time in all the date/time formats.

Line 23 is commented. This line uses the s specifier, which is not legal. If you uncomment this line, you will see that the listing throws an exception.

Displaying Values from Enumerations

When you worked with enumerators on Day 7, "Storing More Complex Stuff: Structures, Enumerators, and Arrays," you saw that the output when using Write and WriteLine displayed the descriptive value of the enumerator rather than the numeric value. With string formatting, you can control the numeric value or the text value. You can also force a hexadecimal representation to be displayed. Table 11.4 presents the formatting characters for enumerators. Listing 11.6 presents a listing using these key values in this table.

TABLE 11.4 Formatting Characters for Enumerators

Specifier	Description
D or d	Displays the numeric value from the enumerator element
G or g	Displays the string value from the enumerator element
X or x	Displays the hexadecimal equivalent of the numeric value from the enumerator element

LISTING 11.6 Enums.cs—Formatting Enumeration Values

```
 1:  // Enums.cs - enumerator formats
 2:  //-----------------------------------------------
 3:
 4:  using System;
 5:
 6:  class Enums
 7:  {
 8:     enum Pet
 9:     {
10:        Cat,
11:        Dog,
12:        Fish,
13:        Snake,
14:        Rat,
15:        Hamster,
16:        Bird
17:     }
18:
19:     public static void Main()
20:     {
21:        Pet myPet = Pet.Fish;
22:        Pet yourPet = Pet.Hamster;
23:
24:        Console.WriteLine("Using myPet: ");
25:        Console.WriteLine("d: {0:d}", myPet );
26:        Console.WriteLine("D: {0:D}", myPet );
```

LISTING 11.6 continued

```
27:        Console.WriteLine("g: {0:g}", myPet );
28:        Console.WriteLine("G: {0:G}", myPet );
29:        Console.WriteLine("x: {0:x}", myPet );
30:        Console.WriteLine("X: {0:X}", myPet );
31:
32:        Console.WriteLine("\nUsing yourPet: ");
33:        Console.WriteLine("d: {0:d}", yourPet );
34:        Console.WriteLine("D: {0:D}", yourPet );
35:        Console.WriteLine("g: {0:g}", yourPet );
36:        Console.WriteLine("G: {0:G}", yourPet );
37:        Console.WriteLine("x: {0:x}", yourPet );
38:        Console.WriteLine("X: {0:X}", yourPet );
39:    }
40: }
```

OUTPUT

```
Using myPet:
d: 2
D: 2
g: Fish
G: Fish
x: 00000002
X: 00000002

Using yourPet:
d: 5
D: 5
g: Hamster
G: Hamster
x: 00000005
X: 00000005
```

11

ANALYSIS This listing creates an enum that holds pets. In Lines 21–22, two objects are created, myPet and yourPet, that are used to illustrate the format specifiers. Lines 24–30 use the specifiers with the myPet object. Lines 32–38 use yourPet. As you can see by the output, the case of the specifiers doesn't matter.

Working More Closely with Strings

Now that you know all about formatting strings, it is worth stepping back and learning a few more details about string specifics. Recall that strings are a special data type that can hold textual information.

As you should know, string is a C# keyword; it is simply a different name for the String class in the System namespace. As such, string has all the methods and properties of the String class.

A value stored in a string cannot be modified. When string methods are called or when you make changes to a string, a new string is actually created. If you try to change a character in a string, you get an error. Listing 11.7 is a simple listing that you can enter to prove this point.

LISTING 11.7   Str_Err.cs—Strings Cannot Be Changed

```
 1:  // Str_Err.cs - Bad listing. Generates error
 2:  //----------------------------------------------
 3:  using System;
 4:
 5:  class Str_Err
 6:  {
 7:    public static void Main()
 8:    {
 9:        string str1 = "abcdefghijklmnop";
10:
11:        str1[5] = 'X';        //  ERROR!!!
12:
13:        Console.WriteLine( str1 );
14:    }
15:  }
```

OUTPUT   This listing generates the following error:

```
Str_Err.cs(11,6): error CS0200: Property or indexer 'string.this[int]'
➥cannot be assigned to -- it is read only
```

ANALYSIS   This listing helps illustrate that you can't change a string. Remember, a string is a specialized array of characters. Line 11 attempts to change the sixth character to a capital x. This generates an error because you can't modify a string's value.

If strings can't be modified, you might believe that their usefulness is greatly limited. You might wonder how methods and properties can work with strings if a string can't be changed. You will find that methods that make modifications to a string actually create a new string. If you really need to modify a string, C# provides another class that can be used—the StringBuilder class, which is covered later today.

Note   Strings are said to be immutable, which means that they can't be changed.

String Methods

A number of extremely useful methods can be used with string comparisons. Table 11.5 presents some of the key string methods, along with descriptions of their use.

TABLE 11.5   Common String Methods

Method	Description
Static Methods of `String/string`	
Compare	Compares the values of two strings.
CompareOrdinal	Compares the values of two strings without compensating for language or other internationalization issues.
Concat	Concatenates (joins) two or more strings into one string.
Copy	Creates a new string from an existing string.
Equals	Compares two strings to determine whether they contain the same value. Returns `true` if the two values are equal; otherwise, returns `false`.
Format	Replaces format specifiers with their corresponding string values. Specifiers were covered earlier today.
Join	Concatenates two or more strings. A specified "separator string" is placed between each of the original strings.
Methods and Properties of Each Instance	
Char	Returns the character at a given location.
Clone	Returns a copy of the stored string.
CompareTo	Compares the value of this string with the value of another string. Returns a negative number if this string is less than the compared string, `0` if equal, and a positive number if the value of this string is greater.
CopyTo	Copies a portion of or all of a string to a new string or character array.
EndsWith	Determines whether the end of the value stored in the string is equal to a string value. If they are equal, `true` is returned; otherwise, `false` is returned.
Equals	Compares two strings to determine whether they contain the same value. Returns `true` if the two values are equal; otherwise, returns `false`.
IndexOf	Returns the index (location) of the first match for a character or string. Returns `-1` if the value is not found.
Insert	Inserts a value into a string. This is done by returning a new string.
LastIndexOf	Returns the index (location) of the last match for a character or a string. Returns `-1` if the value is not found.
Length	Returns the length of the value stored in the string. The length is equal to the number of characters contained.

11

TABLE 11.5   continued

Method	Description
Methods and Properties of Each Instance	
PadLeft	Right-justifies the value of a string and then pads any remaining spaces with a specified character (or space).
PadRight	Left-justifies the value of a string and then pads any remaining spaces with a specified character (or space).
Remove	Deletes a specified number of characters from a specified location within a string.
Split	The opposite of Join. Breaks a string into substrings based on a specified value. The specified value is used as a breaking point.
StartsWith	Determines whether the value stored in a string starts with a specified character or set of characters. Returns true if there is a match and false if not. If specified character is null, true is also returned.
Substring	Returns a substring from the original string starting at a specified location. The number of characters for the substring might also be specified but is not required.
ToCharArray	Copies the characters in the current string value to a char array.
ToLower	Returns a copy of the current value in all lowercase letters.
ToUpper	Returns a copy of the current value in all uppercase characters.
Trim	Removes copies of a specified string from the beginning and end of the current string.
TrimEnd	Removes copies of a specified string from the end of the current string.
TrimStart	Removes copies of a specified string from the beginning of the current string.

Many of these methods and properties are used throughout the rest of this book.

The Special String Formatter—@

You have seen a number of special characters used in many of the listings. For example, to use a quote in a string, you use an escape character. The following prints "Hello World", including quotes:

```
System.Console.WriteLine("\"Hello World\"");
```

To use a backslash, you also must use an escape character:

```
System.Console.WriteLine("My Code: C:\\Books\\TYCSharp\\Originals\\");
```

C# provides a special formatting character that you can use to shortcut using the escape characters: @. When this precedes a string, the string's value is taken literally. In fact, this string is referred to as a *verbatim string literal*. The following is equivalent to the previous directory strings:

```
System.Console.WriteLine(@"My Code: C:\Books\TYCSharp\Originals\");
```

When using the @ string formatter, you will find that the only tricky issue is using a double quote. If you want to use a double quote in a string formatted with @, you must use two double quotes. The following is the equivalent code for the "Hello World" example:

```
System.Console.WriteLine(@"""Hello World!""");
```

> **Note**
>
> You might be thinking, "Wait a minute—he said use two double quotes, but he used three!" One of the quotes is for enclosing the string. In this example, the first quote starts the string. The second quote would normally end the string; however, because it is followed by another quote, the system knows to display a quote. The fourth quote would then normally end the string, but because it also is followed by a quote, it is converted to display a quote. The sixth quote checks to see whether it can end the string. Because it is not followed by another quote, the string value is ended.

11

Building Strings

The StringBuilder class is provided in the System.Text namespace to create an object that can hold a string value that can be changed. An object created with the StringBuilder class operates similarly to a string. The difference is that methods of a StringBuilder can directly manipulate the value stored. The methods and properties for a StringBuilder object are listed in Table 11.6.

TABLE 11.6 The StringBuilder Methods and Properties

Method	Method or Property
Append	Appends an object to the end of the current StringBuilder.
AppendFormat	Inserts objects into a string base on formatting specifiers.
Capacity	Sets or gets the number of characters that can be held. Capacity can be increased up to the value of MaxCapacity.
Chars	Sets or gets the character at a given index position using indexer notation.
EnsureCapacity	Ensures that the capacity of StringBuilder is at least as big as a provided value. If the value is passed to EnsureCapacity, the value of the Capacity property is set to this new value. If MaxCapacity is less than the value passed, an exception is thrown.

TABLE 11.6   continued

Method	Method or Property
Equals	Determines whether the current StringBuilder is equal to the value passed.
Insert	Places an object into StringBuilder at a given location.
Length	Sets or gets the length of the current value stored in StringBuilder. Length cannot be larger than the Capacity of StringBuilder. If the current value is shorter than Length, the value is truncated.
MaxCapacity	Gets the maximum capacity for StringBuilder.
Remove	Removes a specified number of characters, starting at a specified location within the current StringBuilder object.
Replace	Changes all copies of a given character with a new character.
ToString	Converts StringBuilder to String.

The StringBuilder class can be used like other classes. Listing 11.8 uses the StringBuilder object and several of the methods and properties presented in Table 11.6. This listing has a user enter first, last, and middle names. The values are combined into a StringBuilder object.

LISTING 11.8   BuildName.cs—Using the StringBuilder Class

```
 1:  // BuildName.cs - String Builder
 2:  //------------------------------------------
 3:  using System;
 4:  using System.Text;      //For StringBuilder
 5:
 6:  class BuildName
 7:  {
 8:    public static void Main()
 9:    {
10:        StringBuilder name = new StringBuilder();
11:        string buffer;
12:        int marker = 0;
13:
14:        Console.Write("\nEnter your first name: ");
15:        buffer = Console.ReadLine();
16:
17:        if ( buffer != null )
18:        {
19:          name.Append(buffer);
20:          marker = name.Length;
21:        }
22:
23:        Console.Write("\nEnter your last name: ");
```

LISTING 11.8 continued

```
24:      buffer = Console.ReadLine();
25:
26:      if ( buffer != null )
27:      {
28:        name.Append(" ");
29:        name.Append(buffer);
30:      }
31:
32:      Console.Write("\nEnter your middle name: ");
33:      buffer = Console.ReadLine();
34:
35:      if ( buffer != null )
36:      {
37:        name.Insert(marker+1, buffer);
38:        name.Insert(marker+buffer.Length+1, " ");
39:      }
40:
41:      Console.WriteLine("\n\nFull name: {0}", name);
42:
43:      // Some stats....
44:      Console.WriteLine("\n\nInfo about StringBuilder string:");
45:      Console.WriteLine("value: {0}", name);
46:      Console.WriteLine("Capacity: {0}", name.Capacity);
47:      Console.WriteLine("Maximum Capacity: {0}", name.MaxCapacity);
48:      Console.WriteLine("Length: {0}", name.Length);
49:    }
50:  }
```

11

OUTPUT

```
Enter your first name: Bradley

Enter your last name: Jones

Enter your middle name: Lee


Full name: Bradley Lee Jones


Info about StringBuilder string:
value: Bradley Lee Jones
Capacity: 32
Maximum Capacity: 2147483647
Length: 17
```

ANALYSIS The first thing to note about this listing is that Line 4 includes a `using` statement for the `System.Text` namespace. Without this, you would need to fully qualify the `StringBuilder` class as `System.Text.StringBuilder`.

In Line 10, a new `StringBuilder` object named `name` is created. This is used to hold the string that the listing will be building. In Line 11, a string is created named `buffer` that will be used to get information from the user. This information is obtained in Lines 15, 24, and 33 using the `ReadLine` method in `Console`. The first value obtained is the first name. This is appended into the name `StringBuilder` object. Because `name` was empty, this is placed at the beginning. The length of the first name is placed in a variable named `marker` that will be used to determine where to place the middle name.

The last name is obtained second. This is appended to the `name` object (Line 29) right after a space is appended (Line 28). Finally, the middle name is obtained and inserted into the middle of `name` using the `Insert` method. The marker saved earlier is used to determine where to insert the middle name.

The resulting full name is displayed in Line 41. Lines 44–48 display some general information. In Line 45, the value of the `StringBuilder` `name` object is printed. In Line 46, you see the current capacity that the `name` object can hold. In Line 47, you see the maximum value that this can be extended to. In Line 48, the current length of the value is stored in `name`.

Getting Information from the Console

So far, today's lesson has focused on formatting and displaying information. In addition to producing output, you need to have more flexibility in obtaining input—information entered into your program.

You have seen the `Read` and `ReadLine` methods of the `Console` class used in this book. The following sections provide more information on obtaining input from `Console` and converting it to a more usable format.

 Note   Starting on Day 16, "Creating Windows Forms," you learn about getting information from a Windows application.

Using the `Read` Method

Two methods in the `Console` class in the `System` namespace can be used to get information from your users: `ReadLine` and `Read`.

The `Read` method reads a single character at a time from the input stream. The method returns the character as an integer (`int`). If the end of the stream is read, `-1` is returned. Listing 11.9 reads characters from the console using `Read`.

Tip | To end the stream of characters coming from the console, you can press Ctrl+Z. You might need to press the Enter key after pressing Ctrl+Z.

LISTING 11.9   ReadIt.cs—The Read Method

```
 1:  // ReadIt.cs - Read information from Console
 2:  //---------------------------------------------
 3:  using System;
 4:  using System.Text;
 5:
 6:  class ReadIt
 7:  {
 8:    public static void Main()
 9:    {
10:        StringBuilder Input = new StringBuilder();
11:
12:        int ival;
13:        char ch = ' ';
14:
15:        Console.WriteLine("Enter text. When done, press CTRL+Z:");
16:
17:        while ( true )
18:        {
19:          ival = Console.Read();
20:          if ( ival == - 1 )
21:            break;
22:          ch = ( char ) ival;
23:
24:          Input.Append(ch);
25:        }
26:        Console.WriteLine("\n\n=========>\n");
27:        Console.Write( Input );
28:        Console.Write("\n\n");
29:    }
30:  }
```

OUTPUT
```
Enter text. When done, press CTRL+Z:
Mary Had a little lamb,
Its fleece was white as snow.
Everywhere that Mary went,
that lamb was sure to go!
=========>

Mary Had a little lamb,
Its fleece was white as snow.
Everywhere that Mary went,
that lamb was sure to go!
```

The output shows that four lines of text were entered. Afterward, Ctrl+Z was pressed to end the input.

In Lines 17–25, a `while` loop is used to read characters. Line 19 does the actual read. The value read is placed in the `ival` variable. If `ival` is equal to `-1`, the end of the input has been reached and a `break` command is used to get out of the `while` loop. If the `ival` character is valid, this numeric value is cast to a character value in Line 22. The character value is then appended to the string `Input`.

After the entry of characters is completed, Line 27 prints the full value of the `Input` string. All the characters were stored, in addition to the carriage returns and line feeds.

> **Note**
>
> For Windows and Web applications, you obtain information differently. On Days 16–20, you learn more about obtaining data on these platforms.

Using the `ReadLine` Method

The `ReadLine` method has been used a number of times in this book. You should already be aware of what it does; however, in review, the `ReadLine` method reads a line of text up to a carriage return, a line feed, or both. The `ReadLine` method then returns all characters read except the carriage return and line feed. If the end of the stream is reached, the value `null` is returned.

The following is similar to Listing 11.9. To end this listing, you can use Ctrl+Z. You might need to follow Ctrl+Z by pressing the Enter key.

LISTING **11.10**   ReadLine.cs—Using `ReadLine` to Read Characters

```
 1:  // ReadLine.cs - Read information from Console
 2:  //----------------------------------------------
 3:  using System;
 4:  using System.Text;
 5:
 6:  class ReadLine
 7:  {
 8:    public static void Main()
 9:    {
10:       StringBuilder Input = new StringBuilder();
11:       string buff;
12:
13:       Console.WriteLine("Enter text. When done, press Ctrl+Z:");
14:
15:       while ( (buff = Console.ReadLine()) != null )
```

LISTING **11.10**   continued

```
16:        {
17:            Input.Append(buff);
18:            Input.Append("\n");
19:        }
20:        Console.WriteLine("\n\n=========>\n");
21:        Console.Write( Input );
22:        Console.Write("\n\n");
23:    }
24: }
```

OUTPUT

```
Enter text. When done, press Ctrl+Z:
Twinkle, twinkle little star
How I wonder where you are
up above the sky so high
like a diamond in the sky

=========>

Twinkle, twinkle little star
How I wonder where you are
up above the sky so high
like a diamond in the sky
```

11

ANALYSIS   This listing provides the same functionality as in the previous listing. Instead of reading a character at a time, a line is read (Line 15). If the line read is equal to null, the input is ended. If information is read, it is appended to the Input string (Line 17). Because line-feed information is removed from the string, Line 18 adds a line feed back to the string being created so that the final output displayed in Line 21 matches what the user entered.

How could you prevent Ctrl+Z from being used? Suppose that you wanted to end this listing by entering a blank line. Exercise 3 at the end of today's lessons asks you how to change this listing so that a blank line ends the input. The answer is provided on the CD-ROM, "Answers."

Using the Convert Class

The key to using information read in by the Read and ReadLine methods is not in just getting the data, but in converting it to the format that you want to use. This can be meshing the text in a string to a different string value or converting it to a different data type.

The System namespace contains a class that can be used to convert data to a different data type: the Convert class.

The Convert class is a sealed class that contains a large number of static methods. These convert information to different data types. Because they are static, the format for using these methods is as shown:

```
Convert.method( orig_val );
```

This assumes that you have included a using statement with the System namespace. method is the name of the conversion method that you want to use. orig_val is the original value that you are converting to the new type. It is very important to know that this is a class in the base class library. This means that the class also can be used with other programming languages. Instead of converting to C# data types, the Convert class converts to a .NET base data type. Not to fret—as you learned in the section on storing information in Day 2, "Understanding C# Programs," there are equivalent base types for each of the C# data types.

Table 11.7 contains several of the methods in the Convert class. You should consult the .NET Framework documentation for a complete list of methods. Listing 11.11 presents a brief example of using a Convert method. This listing converts a string value entered by ReadLine into an integer.

 Note   The Convert class is being used to convert from strings to numbers in this lesson; however, it can be used to convert from other data types as well.

TABLE 11.7   The Conversion Methods

Method	Converts To
ToBoolean	Boolean
ToByte	8-bit unsigned integer
ToChar	Unicode character
ToDateTime	DateTime
ToDecimal	Decimal number
ToDouble	Double number
ToInt16	16-bit signed integer
ToInt32	32-bit signed integer
ToInt64	64-bit signed integer
ToSByte	8-bit signed integer
ToSingle	Single-precision floating-point number
ToString	String

TABLE 11.7   continued

Method	Converts To
ToUInt16	16-bit unsigned integer
ToUInt32	32-bit unsigned integer
ToUInt64	64-bit unsigned integer

LISTING 11.11   Converts.cs—Using a Convert Method

```
 1:  // Converts.cs - Converting to a data type
 2:  //-----------------------------------------------
 3:  using System;
 4:  using System.Text;
 5:
 6:  class Converts
 7:  {
 8:    public static void Main()
 9:    {
10:       string buff;
11:       int age;
12:
13:       Console.Write("Enter your age: ");
14:
15:       buff = Console.ReadLine();
16:
17:       try
18:       {
19:          age = Convert.ToInt32(buff);
20:
21:          if( age < 21 )
22:             Console.WriteLine("You are under 21.");
23:          else
24:             Console.Write("You are 21 or older.");
25:       }
26:       catch( ArgumentException )
27:       {
28:          Console.WriteLine("No value was entered... (equal to null)");
29:       }
30:       catch( OverflowException )
31:       {
32:          Console.WriteLine(
➥"You entered a number that is too big or too small.");
33:       }
34:       catch( FormatException )
35:       {
36:          Console.WriteLine("You didn't enter a valid number.");
37:       }
```

11

LISTING 11.11   continued

```
38:        catch( Exception e )
39:        {
40:          Console.WriteLine("Something went wrong with the conversion.");
41:          throw(e);
42:        }
43:    }
44: }
```

OUTPUT   The following is output from running the listing several times from the command line:

```
C:\Day11>Converts
Enter your age: 12
You are under 21.

C:\Day11>Converts
Enter your age: 21
You are 21 or older.

C: \Day11>Converts
Enter your age: 65
You are 21 or older.

C:\Day11>Converts
Enter your age: 9999999999999999
You entered a number that is too big or too small.

C:\\Day11>Converts
Enter your age: abc
You didn't enter a valid number.

C:\Day11>Converts
Enter your age: abc123
You didn't enter a valid number.

C:\Day11>Converts
Enter your age: 123abc
You didn't enter a valid number.

C:\Day11>Converts
Enter your age: 123 123
You didn't enter a valid number.
```

ANALYSIS   The first thing you will notice about this listing is that exception handling was used. You should use exception handling whenever there is a possibility of an exception being thrown. The conversion method being used in Line 19, ToInt32, has the possibility of throwing three exceptions if bad information is entered. Lines 26, 30, and 34 catch these three different types of exceptions. Line 38 catches any other unexpected exceptions. If an exception is not thrown, a message is displayed based on whether the age is less than 21.

This sets up the foundation for you to be able to get information from the end user, convert it to a more usable format, and verify the information to make sure it is valid.

Summary

You explored a lot today. Mark the pages that contain the tables of methods; having them handy will help as you continue your programming.

In today's lesson, you learned how to format information to make it more presentable. In addition to learning how to format regular data types, you learned how to get and format dates and times.

The second half of today's lesson focused more on working with strings and the methods available to use with them. Because strings are immutable—they can't be changed—you also learned about the StringBuilder class. Using this class, you learned how to manipulate string information.

Today ended by focusing on obtaining information from the console. You revisited the Read and ReadLine methods. To these you combined what you learned with formatting strings and with a new conversion class. You now know how to retrieve information from the console and format it into a usable format, which can include different data types.

Q&A

Q I'm confused. You said strings can't be changed, yet there are a number of string methods that seem to change strings. What gives?

A The methods that work directly with a string type do not change the original string. Instead, they create a new string with the changes and then replace the original. With the StringBuilder class, the original string information can be manipulated.

Q You said that the Convert class works with the base data types. I didn't follow what you meant. Please explain.

A You should review Day 2. When you compile your programs, the C# data types are all converted to data types in the runtime. For instance, a C# type int is converted to a System.Int32. You can actually use int or System.Int32 interchangeably in your programs.

Workshop

The Workshop provides quiz questions to help you solidify your understanding of the material covered and exercises to provide you with experience in using what you've learned. Try to understand the quiz and exercise answers before continuing to the next day's lesson. Answers are provided on the CD.

Quiz

1. What method can be used to convert and format an integer data type to a string?

2. What method within the `string` class can be used to format information into a new string?

3. What specifier can be used to indicate that a number should be formatted as currency?

4. What specifier can be used to indicate that a number should be formatted as a decimal number with commas and should contain one decimal place (for example, `123,890.5`)?

5. What will the following display be if x is equal to `123456789.876`?

```
Console.WriteLine("X is {0:'a value of '#,.#'.'}", x);
```

6. What would be the specifier used to format a number as a decimal with a minimum of five characters displayed if positive, a decimal with a minimum of eight characters displayed if negative, and the text `<empty>` if the value is `0`?

7. How would you get today's date?

8. What is the key difference between a string and a `StringBuilder` object?

9. What special character is used for the string formatter, and what does this do to the string?

10. How can you get a numeric value out of a string?

Exercises

1. Write the line of code to format a number so that it has at least three digits and two decimal places.

2. Write the code to display a date value written as day of week, month, day, full year (for example, `Monday, January 1, 2002`).

3. Modify Listing 11.10 so that the input ends when a blank line is entered.

4. Modify Listing 11.11. If the user enters information with a space, crop the information and use the first part of the string. For example, if the user enters 123 456, crop to 123 and then convert.

5. **On Your Own:** Write a program that has a person enter a full name, age, and phone number. Display this information with formatting. Also display the person's initials.

11

WEEK 2

DAY 12

Tapping into OOP:
Interfaces

Today you expand your understanding of the object-oriented programming.
This includes expanding your use of inheritance and polymorphism with the
use of interfaces. Today you learn how to inherit traits from multiple sources
and how to perform methods on a number of different data types. More specifically, today you...

- Learn about interfaces.
- Discover what the basic structure of an interface is.
- Define and use interfaces.
- Understand how to implement multiple interfaces.
- Derive new interfaces from existing ones.
- See how to hide interface members from a class.

On Day 5, "The Core of C# Programming: Classes," you began learning about
classes. On Day 10, "Reusing Existing Code with Inheritance," you learned
how to inherit from one class to another. Today you learn how to inherit characteristics from multiple sources into a single new class.

Interfaces: A First Look

Consider the following code. What do you notice about this class?

```
public abstract class cShape
{
    public abstract long Area();
    public abstract long Circumference();
    public abstract int sides();
}
```

You should notice that this is an abstract class and that all its methods are abstract. You learned about abstract classes on Day 10.

To review, abstract classes are classes that generally contain at least one abstract method. Abstract methods are methods that must be overridden when inherited.

Interfaces are another reference type similar to classes and are very similar to the cShape class shown previously. An interface defines what will be contained within a class that will be declared; however, an interface does not define the actual functionality. An interface is like an abstract method and is very similar to the class shown.

In fact, the cShape class can be changed to an interface by dropping the abstract modifiers on the methods and class and by changing the word class to interface:

```
public interface IShape
{
    long Area();
    long Circumference();
    int sides();
}
```

Classes Versus Interfaces

An interface is like a pure abstract class, but its interface differs from a class in a number of ways.

First and foremost, an interface does not provide any implementation code. A class that implements an interface *is* required to include the implementation code. An interface is said to provide a specification or guideline for what will be happening, but not the details.

An interface also differs from a class in that all of an interface's members are assumed to be public. If you try to declare a different scope modifier for a member of an interface, you will get an error.

Interfaces contain only methods, properties, events, and indexers; they do not contain data members, constructors, or destructors. They also cannot contain any static members.

An abstract class has similar traits to those described for interfaces. However, an abstract class differs in what you can do with it versus an interface. By the end of today's lesson, you'll understand these differences.

Using Interfaces

An interface might not seem as all-powerful as a class, but interfaces can be used where a class can't. A class can inherit from only one other class and can implement multiple interfaces. Additionally, structures cannot inherit from other structures or classes. They can, however, implement interfaces. You'll learn more about implementing multiple interfaces later today.

 Note

C# does not support multiple inheritance of classes as C++ and other object-oriented languages do. The capability of multiple inheritance was intentionally left out because of the trouble caused by its complex implementation. C# provides the functionality and benefit of multiple inheritance by enabling multiple interfaces to be implemented.

Why Use Interfaces?

Some benefits can be gained by using interfaces. You probably figured out a couple from the previous sections.

First, you can use interfaces as a means of providing inheritance features with structures. Additionally, you can implement multiple interfaces with a class, thus gaining functionality that you can't obtain with an abstract class.

One of the biggest benefits of using an interface is that you can add characteristics to a class—or set of classes—that a class—or set of classes—would not otherwise have. By adding the same characteristics to other classes, you can begin to make assumptions about your class's functionality. Actually, by using interfaces, you can *avoid* making assumptions.

Another benefit is that by using an interface, you force the new class to implement all the defined characteristics of the interface. If you inherit from a base class with virtual members, you can get away with not implementing code for them. This opens your new class, and the programs that use it, to errors.

12

Defining Interfaces

As you saw earlier, an interface is declared as a guide to what will need to be implemented by classes. The basic structure is shown here:

```
interface IName
{
    members;
}
```

Here, *IName* is the name of the interface. This can be any name that you want to give it. *members* designates the members of the interface. These are any of the types mentioned before: properties, events, methods (virtual methods that is), and indexers. You'll learn about events and indexers tomorrow.

 Tip

> I recommend that you use an I at the beginning of the name to indicate that this is an interface. This is in line with what most programmers generally do.

Methods are specified without the need for a scope modifier. As stated earlier, the methods are assumed public. Additionally, you don't implement the bodies for the methods. In most cases, you state the return type and the method name, followed by a parenthesis and a semicolon:

```
interface IFormatForPrint
{
    void FormatForPrint(PrintClass PrinterType);
    int  NotifyPrintComplete();
}
```

This interface, called `IFormatForPrint`, defines two methods that need to be defined by any classes implementing it: `FormatForPrint`, which takes a `PrintClass` object and returns nothing, and `NotifyPrintComplete`, which returns an integer.

Defining an Interface with Method Members

Enough theory—it's time to take a look at code. Listing 12.1 contains code to define an interface named `IShape`. The `IShape` interface is then implemented by two classes, `Circle` and `Square`.

The definition for the `IShape` interface is as follows:

```
public interface IShape
{
    double Area();
```

```
    double Circumference();
    int   Sides();
}
```

By using this interface, you agree to a couple of things. First, you guarantee that Circle and Square will both fully implement the methods in the interface. In this case, you guarantee that both classes will contain implementations for Area, Sides, and Circumference. Just as important, you guarantee that both contain the characteristic of IShape. You'll see the impact of this in Listing 12.1.

LISTING 12.1   Shape.cs—Using the IShape Interface

```
 1:  //  Shape.cs -
 2:  //------------*------------------------------------------------
 3:
 4:  using System;
 5:
 6:  public interface IShape
 7:  {
 8:      double Area();
 9:      double Circumference();
10:      int    Sides();
11:  }
12:
13:  public class Circle : IShape
14:  {
15:      public int x;
16:      public int y;
17:      public double radius;
18:      private const float PI = 3.14159F;
19:
20:      public double Area()
21:      {
22:          double theArea;
23:          theArea = PI * radius * radius;
24:          return theArea;
25:      }
26:
27:      public double Circumference()
28:      {
29:          return ((double) (2 * PI * radius));
30:      }
31:
32:      public int Sides()
33:      {
34:          return 1;
35:      }
36:
37:      public Circle()
```

12

LISTING 12.1   continued

```
38:       {
39:          x = 0;
40:          y = 0;
41:          radius = 0.0;
42:       }
43:    }
44:
45:    public class Square : IShape
46:    {
47:       public int side;
48:
49:       public double Area()
50:       {
51:          return ((double) (side * side));
52:       }
53:
54:       public double Circumference()
55:       {
56:          return ((double) (4 * side));
57:       }
58:
59:       public int Sides()
60:       {
61:          return 4;
62:       }
63:
64:       public Square()
65:       {
66:          side = 0;
67:       }
68:    }
69:
70:    public class Shape
71:    {
72:       public static void Main()
73:       {
74:          Circle myCircle = new Circle();
75:          myCircle.radius = 5;
76:
77:          Square mySquare = new Square();
78:          mySquare.side = 4;
79:
80:          Console.WriteLine("Displaying Circle information:");
81:          displayInfo(myCircle);
82:
83:          Console.WriteLine("\nDisplaying Square information:");
84:          displayInfo(mySquare);
85:       }
86:
```

LISTING 12.1   continued

```
87:     static void displayInfo( IShape myShape )
88:     {
89:         Console.WriteLine("Area: {0}", myShape.Area());
90:         Console.WriteLine("Sides: {0}", myShape.Sides());
91:         Console.WriteLine("Circumference: {0}", myShape.Circumference());
92:     }
93: }
```

OUTPUT   Displaying Circle information:
Area: 78.5397529602051
Sides: 1
Circumference: 31.415901184082

Displaying Square information:
Area: 16
Sides: 4
Circumference: 16

ANALYSIS   This listing defines the IShape interface in Lines 6–11. As you can see, this is the same interface as presented earlier. In Line 13, you see how an interface is implemented:

```
public class Circle : IShape;
```

An interface is implemented in the same manner that a class is inherited—you include it after your new class's name, using a colon as a separator.

Within the Circle class (Lines 13–43), you can see that there are a number of data members. Additionally, you can see that the methods from the IShape interface have been defined and provided code in the Circle class. Each of these methods includes the same parameter types and return types as the method names in the interface.

In Line 45, you see that the same is true of the Square class. It also implements the IShape interface. Therefore, it also includes definitions for the three IShape methods.

In Line 70, the application class starts. The Main method for this class creates a Circle object in Line 74 and a Square object in Line 77. Each of these is assigned a value. In Line 81, the displayInfo method is called. This method is passed the myCircle Circle object. In Line 84, the displayInfo method of the application class is called again, this time with the mySquare Square object.

Is this method overloaded to take both Circle and Square objects? No. The displayInfo method takes an IShape value. Technically, there is no such thing as an IShape object. *However, some objects have IShape characteristics.* This method is polymorphic; it can work with any object that has implemented the IShape interface. It can then use the methods that were defined within the IShape interface.

Note

You can also use the is and as keywords within the `displayInfo` method to determine whether different class methods can be used. See Day 10 for information on how to use these keywords.

Specifying Properties in Interfaces

A specification for a property can also be included in an interface. As with other members of an interface, no specific implementation code is included. The format for declaring a property within an interface is as follows:

```
modifier(s) datatype name
{
   get;
   set;
}
```

Listing 12.2 is a scaled-down listing that shows how to define a property within an interface and then how to use that property from a class. This listing is of no real value other than to illustrate this concept.

LISTING 12.2   Props.cs—Defining Properties in an Interface

```
 1:  //  Props.cs - Using properties in an interface
 2:  //------------------------------------------------------------------
 3:
 4:  using System;
 5:
 6:  public interface IShape
 7:  {
 8:     int Sides
 9:     {
10:        get;
11:        set;
12:     }
13:
14:     double Area();
15:  }
16:
17:  public class Square : IShape
18:  {
19:     private int InSides;
20:     public  int SideLength;
21:
22:     public double Area()
23:     {
24:        return ((double) (SideLength * SideLength));
```

LISTING 12.2   continued

```
25:      }
26:
27:      public int Sides
28:      {
29:         get { return InSides; }
30:         set { InSides = value; }
31:      }
32:
33:      public Square()
34:      {
35:         Sides = 4;
36:      }
37:   }
38:
39:   public class Props
40:   {
41:      public static void Main()
42:      {
43:         Square mySquare = new Square();
44:         mySquare.SideLength = 5;
45:
46:         Console.WriteLine("\nDisplaying Square information:");
47:         Console.WriteLine("Area: {0}", mySquare.Area());
48:         Console.WriteLine("Sides: {0}", mySquare.Sides);
49:      }
50:   }
```

OUTPUT
```
Displaying Square information:
Area: 25
Sides: 4
```

12

ANALYSIS   This listing focuses on the use of a property rather than all the other code in the previous listing. You can see that the number of sides for the shape is now accessed via a property instead of a method. In Lines 8–12, the IShape interface has a declaration for a property named Sides that will be used with an integer. This will have both the get and set methods. You should note that you are not required to specify both here; it would be perfectly acceptable to specify just a get or just a set. If both are specified in the interface, all classes that implement the interface must implement both.

Note

In the IShape interface used here, it would make sense to specify only the get property for Sides. Many shapes have a specific number of sides that could be set in the constructor and then never changed. The get method could still be used. If set were not included in the interface, a class could still implement set.

The IShape interface is implemented in a Square class starting in Line 17. In Lines 27–31, the actual definitions for the get and set properties are defined. The code for the Square class's implementation is straightforward. The Sides property sets the InSides data member.

Using a property that has been implemented via an interface is no different than using any other property. You can see the use of the Sides property in the previous listing in a number of lines. This includes getting the value in Line 48. The value is set in line 35 of the constructor.

Note

Many people will say that a class inherits from an interface. In a way, this is true; however, it is more correct to say that a class *implements* an interface.

Using Multiple Interfaces

One of the benefits of implementing interfaces instead of inheriting from a class is that you can implement more than one interface at a time. This gives you the power to do multiple inheritance without some of the downside.

To implement multiple interfaces, you separate each interface with a comma. To include both an IShape and an IShapeDisplay interface in a Square class, you use the following:

```
class Square : IShape, IShapeDisplay
{
    ...
}
```

You then need to implement all the constructs within both interfaces. Listing 12.3 illustrates the use of multiple interfaces.

LISTING 12.3   Multi.cs—Implementing Multiple Interfaces in a Single Class

```
 1:  // Multi.cs -
 2:  //-----------------------------------------------------------
 3:
 4:  using System;
 5:
 6:  public interface IShape
 7:  {
 8:      // Cut out other methods to simplify example.
 9:      double Area();
10:      int Sides { get; }
11:  }
```

LISTING 12.3   continued

```
12:
13:    public interface IShapeDisplay
14:    {
15:        void Display();
16:    }
17:
18:    public class Square : IShape, IShapeDisplay
19:    {
20:        private int InSides;
21:        public  int SideLength;
22:
23:        public int Sides
24:        {
25:            get { return InSides; }
26:        }
27:
28:        public double Area()
29:        {
30:            return ((double) (SideLength * SideLength));
31:        }
32:
33:        public double Circumference()
34:        {
35:            return ((double) (Sides * SideLength));
36:        }
37:
38:        public Square()
39:        {
40:            InSides = 4;
41:        }
42:
43:        public void Display()
44:        {
45:            Console.WriteLine("\nDisplaying Square information:");
46:            Console.WriteLine("Side length: {0}", this.SideLength);
47:            Console.WriteLine("Sides: {0}", this.Sides);
48:            Console.WriteLine("Area: {0}", this.Area());
49:        }
50:    }
51:
52:    public class Multi
53:    {
54:        public static void Main()
55:        {
56:            Square mySquare = new Square();
57:            mySquare.SideLength = 7;
58:
59:            mySquare.Display();
60:        }
61:    }
```

12

OUTPUT
```
Displaying Square information:
Side length: 7
Sides: 4
Area: 49
```

ANALYSIS   You can see that two interfaces are declared and used in this listing. In Line 18, you can see that the square class will implement the two interfaces. Because both are included, all members of both interfaces must be implemented by the square class. In looking at the code in Lines 23–49, you see that all the members are implemented.

Using Explicit Interface Members

So far, everything has gone smoothly with implementing interfaces. What happens, however, when you implement an interface that has a member name that clashes with another name already in use? For example, what would happen if the two interfaces in Listing 12.3 both had a Display method?

If a class includes two or more interfaces with the same member name, that member needs to be implemented only once. This single implementation of the method satisfies both interfaces.

Sometimes you want to implement the method independently for both interfaces. In this case, you need to use explicit interface implementations. An explicit implementation is done by including the interface name with the member name when you define the member. You must also use casting to call the method, as shown in Listing 12.4.

LISTING 12.4   Explicit.cs

```
 1:  // Explicit.cs -
 2:  //-------------------------------------------------------------
 3:
 4:  using System;
 5:
 6:  public interface IShape
 7:  {
 8:     double Area();
 9:     int Sides { get; }
10:     void Display();
11:  }
12:
13:  public interface IShapeDisplay
14:  {
15:     void Display();
16:  }
17:
```

LISTING 12.4   continued

```
18:   public class Square : IShape, IShapeDisplay
19:   {
20:      private int InSides;
21:      public  int SideLength;
22:
23:      public int Sides
24:      {
25:         get { return InSides; }
26:      }
27:
28:      public double Area()
29:      {
30:         return ((double) (SideLength * SideLength));
31:      }
32:
33:      public double Circumference()
34:      {
35:         return ((double) (Sides * SideLength));
36:      }
37:
38:      public Square()
39:      {
40:         InSides = 4;
41:      }
42:
43:      void IShape.Display()
44:      {
45:         Console.WriteLine("\nDisplaying Square Shape\'s information:");
46:         Console.WriteLine("Side length: {0}", this.SideLength);
47:         Console.WriteLine("Sides: {0}", this.Sides);
48:         Console.WriteLine("Area: {0}", this.Area());
49:      }
50:      void IShapeDisplay.Display()
51:      {
52:         Console.WriteLine("\nThis method could draw the shape...");
53:      }
54:
55:   }
56:
57:   public class Explicit
58:   {
59:      public static void Main()
60:      {
61:         Square mySquare = new Square();
62:         mySquare.SideLength = 7;
63:
64:         IShape ish = (IShape) mySquare;
65:         IShapeDisplay ishd = (IShapeDisplay) mySquare;
66:
```

12

LISTING 12.4   continued

```
67:        ish.Display();
68:        ishd.Display();
69:    }
70: }
```

OUTPUT

```
Displaying Square Shape's information:
Side length: 7
Sides: 4
Area: 49

This method could draw the shape...
```

ANALYSIS This listing is a bit more complicated, but the result is that you can explicitly declare and then use methods from different interfaces with the same name within a single class.

This listing has two methods named Display. Each of these is explicitly defined within the Square class. You can see in Lines 43 and 50 that the explicit definitions use the explicit name of the method. The explicit name is the interface name and the member name separated by a period.

Using these explicit interfaces requires more work than calling the method. After all, if you call the method using the standard class name, which Display method would be used? To use one of the methods, you must cast the class to the interface type. In this case, it is a matter of casting the class to either IShape or IShapeDisplay. In Line 64, a variable, ish, is declared that is of type IShape. This is assigned to the mySquare class. A cast makes sure that the mySquare class is treated as an IShape type.

In Line 65, the myShape class is cast to a variable, ishd, that is of type IShapeDisplay. You can see in Lines 67–68 that these variables of interface types can then be used to call the appropriate Display method.

The end result of this listing is that you can have multiple interfaces with similarly named methods. Using explicit definitions and a little casting, you can make sure that the correct method is called. Why might you do this? For the previous listing, the IShapeDisplay interface might be used with shapes to ensure that all the classes have the capability of doing a graphical display method. The Display method in the IShape might have the purpose of providing detailed textual information. By implementing both, you have the capability to get both types of display.

Deriving New Interfaces from Existing Ones

As with classes, an interface can be derived from another interface. This inheritance of interfaces is done in a similar manner to inheriting classes. The following snippet shows how the IShape interface created earlier could be extended:

```
public interface IShape
{
    long Area();
    long Circumference();
    int Sides{ get; set; };
}
interface I3DShape : IShape

{
   int Depth { get; set; }
}
```

The I3DShape contains all the members of the IShape class and any new members that it adds. In this case, a Depth property member is added. You can then use the I3DShape interface as you would any other interface. Its members would be Area, Circumference, Sides, and Depth.

Hiding Interface Members

It is possible to implement an interface member and yet hide its access from the base class. This can be done to meet the requirement of implementing the interface and to avoid cluttering up your class with additional members.

To hide an interface, you explicitly define it in the class. Listing 12.5 provides an example of hiding an interface member.

LISTING 12.5   Hide.cs—Hiding an Interface Member from a Class

```
 1:  // Hide.cs -
 2:  //-------------------------------------------------------------
 3:
 4:  using System;
 5:
 6:  public interface IShape
 7:  {
 8:     // members left out to simplify example...
 9:     int ShapeShifter( int val );
10:     int Sides { get; set; }
11:  }
12:
```

12

LISTING 12.5   continued

```
13:   public class Shape : IShape
14:   {
15:      private int InSides;
16:
17:      public int Sides
18:      {
19:        get { return InSides; }
20:        set { InSides = value; }
21:      }
22:
23:      int IShape.ShapeShifter( int val )
24:      {
25:        Console.WriteLine("Shifting Shape....");
26:        val += 1;
27:        return val;
28:      }
29:
30:      public Shape()
31:      {
32:        Sides = 5;
33:      }
34:   }
35:
36:   public class Hide
37:   {
38:      public static void Main()
39:      {
40:        Shape myShape = new Shape();
41:
42:        Console.WriteLine("My shape has been created.");
43:        Console.WriteLine("Using get accessor. Sides = {0}", myShape.Sides);
44:
45: //     myShape.Sides = myShape.ShapeShifter(myShape.Sides);   // error
46:
47:        IShape tmp = (IShape) myShape;
48:        myShape.Sides = tmp.ShapeShifter( myShape.Sides);
49:
50:        Console.WriteLine("ShapeShifter called. Sides = {0}", myShape.Sides);
51:      }
52:   }
```

OUTPUT

```
My shape has been created.
Using get accessor. Sides = 5
Shifting Shape....
ShapeShifter called. Sides = 6
```

ANALYSIS This listing uses a scaled-down version of the Ishape interface that you've seen used throughout today's lessons. The focus of this listing is to illustrate the point of hiding an interface's member from a class. In this case, the ShapeShifter method is hidden from the Shape class. Line 45, which is commented out, is an attempt to use the ShapeShifter method as a member of the Shape class. If you remove the comments from the beginning of this line and try to compile and run this program, you get the following error:

```
Hide2.cs(45,23): error CS0117: 'Shape' does not contain a definition for
        'ShapeShifter'
```

As you can see, Shape objects can't directly access the ShapeShifter method—it is hidden from them.

How is this done? When defining the interface member, you need to do it explicitly. In Line 23, you see that the definition of the ShapeShifter method includes such an explicit definition. The name of the interface is explicitly included in this line.

When calling the explicitly defined member, you need to do what was done in Lines 47–48: You need to declare a variable of the interface type and then use a cast of the interface type using the object that you want to access. In Line 47, you see that a variable named tmp is created that is of the interface type Ishape. The myShape object is then cast to this variable using the same interface type. In Line 48, you see that this variable of the interface type (Ishape) can be used to get to the ShapeShifter method. The output from Line 50 proves that the method was appropriately called.

The tmp variable can access the method because it is of the same type as the explicit declaration in Line 23.

Summary

In today's lesson you learned about interfaces, a construct that enables you to define what must be implemented. Interfaces can be used to ensure that different classes have similar implementations within them. You learned a number of things about interfaces, including how to use them, how to extend them, and how to implement—yet hide—some of their members from the base classes.

Q&A

Q Is it important to understand interfaces?

A Yes. You will find interfaces used through C# programming. Many of the preconstructed methods provided within the class libraries include the use of interfaces.

12

Q You said that the `as` and `is` keywords can be used with interfaces, yet you did not show an example. How does the use of these keywords differ from what was shown with classes?

A The use of `as` and `is` with interfaces is nearly identical to their use with classes. Because the use is so similar, the coding examples with interfaces would be virtually the same as what was shown on Day 11.

Workshop

The Workshop provides quiz questions to help you solidify your understanding of the material covered and exercises to provide you with experience in using what you've learned. Try to understand the quiz and exercise answers before continuing to tomorrow's lesson. Answers are provided on the CD.

Quiz

1. Are interfaces a reference type or a value type?
2. What is the purpose of an interface?
3. Are members of an interface declared as public, private, or protected?
4. What is the primary difference between an interface and a class?
5. What inheritance is available with structures?
6. What types can be included in an interface?
7. How would you declare a public class named `AClass` that inherits from a class named `baseClass` and implements an interface named `IMyInterface`?
8. How many classes can be inherited at one time?
9. How many interfaces can be inherited (implemented) at one time?
10. How is an explicit interface implementation done?

Exercises

1. Write the code for an interface named `Iid` that has a property named `ID` as its only member.
2. Write the code that would declare an interface named `IPosition`. This interface should contain a method that takes a `Point` value and returns a Boolean.
3. **Bug Buster:** The following code snippet might have a problem. If so, what is it?
```
public interface IDimensions
{
    long   Width;
```

```
    long   Height;
    double Area();
    double Circumference();
    int    Sides();
}
```

4. Implement the `IShape` interface declared in Listing 12.1 into a class named
   `Rectangle`.

DAY **13**

Making Your Programs React with Delegates, Events, and Indexers

You've learned many of the foundational topics related to C# programming. In today's lesson, you learn about several additional topics that are foundational for your full understanding of C#. Today you...

- Learn about indexers.
- Build your own indexers.
- Explore delegates.
- Discover event programming.
- Create your own events and event handlers.
- Learn to multicast.

Using an Indexer

NEW TERM On Day 7, "Storing Complex Stuff: Structures, Enumerators, and Arrays," you learned about arrays. Today you learn about indexers. An *indexer* enables you to use an index on an object to obtain values stored within the object. In essence, this enables you to treat an object like an array.

An indexer is also similar to a property. As with properties, you use `get` and `set` when defining an indexer. Unlike properties, you are not obtaining a specific data member; instead, you are obtaining a value from the object itself. When you define a property, you define a property name. With indexers, instead of creating a name as you do with properties, you use the `this` keyword, which refers to the object instance and, thus, the object name is used. The format for defining an indexer is shown here:

```
public dataType this[int index]
{
    get
    {
        // Do whatever you want...
        return aValue;
    }
    set
    {
        // Do whatever you want
        // Generally you should set a value within the class
        // based on the index and the value they assign.
    }
}
```

Creating an indexer enables you to use bracket notation (`[]`) with an object to set and get a value from an object. As you can see in the format shown earlier, you state the *dataType* that will be set and returned by the indexer. In the `get` section, you return a value that is of *dataType*. In the `set` block, you can do something with a value of *dataType*.

As with properties and member functions, you can use the `value` keyword. This is the value passed as the argument to the `set` routine. The best way to understand all of this is to take a look at a simple example of using an indexer, as shown in Listing 13.1.

LISTING 13.1 Indexer.cs—Using an Indexer

```
1:  // Indexer.cs - Using an indexer
2:  //-------------------------------------------------------------------
3:
4:  using System;
5:
6:  public class SpellingList
```

LISTING **13.1**   continued

```
 7:  {
 8:      protected string[] words = new string[size];
 9:      static public int size = 10;
10:
11:      public SpellingList()
12:      {
13:          for (int x = 0; x < size; x++ )
14:              words[x] = String.Format("Word{0}", x);
15:      }
16:
17:      public string this[int index]
18:      {
19:          get
20:          {
21:              string tmp;
22:
23:              if( index >= 0 && index <= size-1 )
24:                  tmp = words[index];
25:              else
26:                  tmp = "";
27:
28:              return ( tmp );
29:          }
30:          set
31:          {
32:              if( index >= 0 && index <= size-1 )
33:                  words[index] = value;
34:          }
35:      }
36:  }
37:
38: public class Indexer
39: {
40:     public static void Main()
41:     {
42:         SpellingList myList = new SpellingList();
43:
44:         myList[3] = "=====";
45:         myList[4] = "Brad";
46:         myList[5] = "was";
47:         myList[6] = "Here!";
48:         myList[7] = "=====";
49:
50:         for ( int x = 0; x < SpellingList.size; x++ )
51:             Console.WriteLine(myList[x]);
52:     }
53: }
```

13

```
Word0
Word1
Word2
=====
Brad
was
Here!
=====
Word8
Word9
```

ANALYSIS This listing creates an indexer to be used with the SpellingList class. This class contains an array of strings named words that can be used to store a list of words. This list is set to the size of the variable declared in Line 9.

Lines 11–15 contain a constructor for SpellingList that sets initial values into each element of the array. You could just as easily have requested the words from the reader or read them from a file. This constructor assigns the string value Word## to each of the elements in the array, where ## is the element number of the array.

Jumping down to the Indexer class in Lines 38–53, you see how the SpellingList class will be used. In Line 42, the SpellingList class is used to instantiate the myList object that will hold the words. Line 42 also causes the constructor to be executed. This initializes the Word## values. Lines 44–48 then change some of these values.

If you think back to how you worked with arrays, you should be saying, "wait a minute" as you look at Lines 44–48. To access the value of one of the words, you would normally have to access the data member within the object. When using arrays as a data member, you learned that you would assign a value to the fourth element as follows:

```
MyList.words[3] = "=====";
```

Line 44, however, is accessing the fourth element within the object, which has been set to be the fourth element in the words array.

An indexer has been created for the SpellingList class in Lines 17–35. This indexer enables you to access the elements within the words array using just the object name.

Line 17 is the defining line for the indexer. You know that this is an indexer rather than a property because the this keyword is used instead of a name. Additionally, this is given an index (named index). The indexer will return a string value.

Lines 19–29 contain the get portion of the indexer. The get block returns a value based on the index. In this class, this value is an element from the words array. You can return any value that you want, but the value should make sense. In Line 23, a check is done to make sure that the index value is valid. If you don't check the value of the index, you risk having an exception thrown. In this listing, if the `index` is out of the range, a null value is returned (in Line 26). If the `index` is valid, the value stored in the `words` array at the `index` location will be returned.

The `set` portion of the indexer is in Lines 30–34. This block can be used to set information within the object. As with properties, the `value` keyword contains the value being assigned. In this code, the `index` value is again checked to make sure it is valid. If it is, a word in the `words` array is updated at the `index` location with the value assigned.

Looking again at the test class, you see that the `set` indexer block is used to assign values in Lines 44–48. For Line 44, the `set` indexer block will be called with `value` equal to ===== and will be passed with an `index` value of 3. In Line 45, `value` is `Brad` and the `index` is 4. In Line 51, the `get` indexer block is called with an `index` value of x. The value returned will be the string value returned by the `get` indexer block.

Tip

> You should use indexers when it makes your code more readable and easier to understand. For example, you can create a stack that can have items placed on it and taken off of it. Using an indexer, you could access items within the stack.

Exploring Delegates

NEW TERM   You now will learn about a more advanced topic: delegates. A *delegate* is a reference type that defines the signature for a method call. The delegate can then accept and execute methods that are of the same format as this signature.

You learned in yesterday's lesson that an interface is a reference type that defines the layout for a class, but it does not itself define any of the functionality. Delegates are often compared to interfaces. A delegate defines the layout for a method but does not actually define a method. Instead, a delegate can accept and work with methods that match its layout (signature).

An example will help make delegates clearer. In this example, a program will be created that sorts two numbers, either ascending or descending. The sorting direction is determined in the code presented; however, you could ask the reader to enter the direction of the sort. Based on the direction—ascending or descending—a different method will be used. Despite this, only one call, to a delegate, will be made. The delegate will be given the appropriate method to execute.

The format for declaring a delegate is shown here:

```
public delegate returnType DelegateName(parameters);
```

13

Here, public can be replaced with appropriate access modifiers, and delegate is the keyword used to indicate that this is a delegate. The rest of the definition is for the signature of the method that the delegate will work with. As you should know from previous lessons, the signature includes the data type to be returned by the method (returnType), as well as the name of the parameters that will be received by the method (parameters). The name of the delegate goes where the method name would normally go. Because the delegate will be used to execute multiple methods that fit the return type and parameters, you don't know the specific method names.

The example used here creates a delegate named Sort that can take multiple sorting methods. These methods will not return a value, so their return type will be void. The methods that will be used for sorting will pass in two integer variables that will be reference types. This enables the sorting functions to switch the values, if necessary. The delegate definition for the example is as follows:

```
public delegate void Sort(ref int a, ref int b);
```

Notice the semicolon at the end. Although this looks similar to a method definition, it is *not* a method definition. There is no body—a delegate is just a template for methods that can be executed. Methods are actually applied, or delegated, to this delegate to be executed.

A delegate is a template for multiple methods. For example, the Sort delegate in the example can be used with methods that don't return a value and that take two reference integers as parameters. The following is an example of a method that can be used with the Sort delegate:

```
public static void Ascending( ref int first, ref int second )
{
    if (first > second )
    {
        int tmp = first;
        first = second;
        second = tmp;
    }
}
```

This method, Ascending, is of type void. Additionally, it receives two values that are both ref int. This matches the signature of the Sort delegate so that it can be used. This method takes the two values and checks to see whether the first is greater than the second. If it is, the two values are swapped using a simple sort routine. Because these values are ref types, the calling routine will have the values swapped as well.

A second method named Descending can also be created:

```
public static void Descending( ref int first, ref int second )
{
   if (first < second )
   {
      int tmp = first;
      first = second;
      second = tmp;
   }
}
```

This method is similar to Ascending, except that the larger value is kept in the first position. You could declare additional sort routines to use with this delegate, as long as the signature of your methods matches. Additionally, different programs could use the Sort delegate and have their own logic within their methods.

Now that a delegate has been declared and multiple functions can be used with it, what is next?

You need to associate your methods with the delegate. Instantiating delegate objects can do this. A delegate object is declared like other objects, with the parameter for the initializer being the method name that you are assigning (delegating) to the delegate. For example, to declare a delegate that can be used with the Ascending method, you code the following:

```
Sort up = new Sort(Ascending);
```

This creates a delegate object named up that can then be used. up is associated with the Ascending method that was declared. The following creates a Sort delegate associated with the Descending method. This delegate is called down.

```
Sort down = new Sort(Descending);
```

Now you've declared your delegate, created methods that can be used with it, and associated these methods to delegate objects. How do you get the delegated methods to execute? You create a method that receives a delegate object as a parameter. This generic method can then execute the method from the delegate:

```
public void DoSort(Sort ar)
{
    ar(ref val1, ref val2);
}
```

As you can see, the DoSort method receives a delegate named ar as its parameter. This method then executes ar. You should notice that ar has the same signature as your

13

delegate. If your delegate has a return type, ar will have a return type. The method of the ar call also matches your delegate. In essence, the DoSort method executes whichever method is passed as a Sort delegate object. For our example, if up is passed, ar(...) is equivalent to calling the Ascending method. If down is passed, ar(...) is equivalent to calling the Descending method.

You've now seen all the key pieces to working with a delegate. Listing 13.2 pulls the entire sample together into a workable solution.

LISTING 13.2   SortClass.cs—Using a Simple Delegate

```
 1:  //  SortClass.cs - Using a delegates
 2:  //-------------------------------------------------------------------
 3:
 4:  using System;
 5:
 6:  public class SortClass
 7:  {
 8:      static public int val1;
 9:      static public int val2;
10:
11:      public delegate void Sort(ref int a, ref int b);
12:
13:      public void DoSort(Sort ar)
14:      {
15:          ar(ref val1, ref val2);
16:      }
17:  }
18:
19:  public class SortProgram
20:  {
21:      public static void Ascending( ref int first, ref int second )
22:      {
23:          if (first > second )
24:          {
25:              int tmp = first;
26:              first = second;
27:              second = tmp;
28:          }
29:      }
30:
31:      public static void Descending( ref int first, ref int second )32:      {
33:          if (first < second )
34:          {
35:              int tmp = first;
36:              first = second;
37:              second = tmp;
38:          }
```

LISTING 13.2   continued

```
39:     }
40:
41:     public static void Main()
42:     {
43:         SortClass.Sort up = new SortClass.Sort(Ascending);
44:         SortClass.Sort down = new SortClass.Sort(Descending);
45:
46:         SortClass doIT = new SortClass();
47:
48:         SortClass.val1 = 310;
49:         SortClass.val2 = 220;
50:
51:         Console.WriteLine("Before Sort: val1 = {0}, val2 = {1}",
52:                           SortClass.val1, SortClass.val2);
53:         doIT.DoSort(up);
54:         Console.WriteLine("After Sort: val1 = {0}, val2 = {1}",
55:                           SortClass.val1, SortClass.val2);
56:
57:         Console.WriteLine("Before Sort: val1 = {0}, val2 = {1}",
58:                           SortClass.val1, SortClass.val2);
59:         doIT.DoSort(down);
60:         Console.WriteLine("After Sort: val1 = {0}, val2 = {1}",
61:                           SortClass.val1, SortClass.val2);
62:     }
63: }
```

OUTPUT
```
Before Sort: val1 = 310, val2 = 220
After Sort: val1 = 220, val2 = 310
Before Sort: val1 = 220, val2 = 310
After Sort: val1 = 310, val2 = 220
```

ANALYSIS This listing starts by declaring a sorting class that will contain the Sort delegate. This class holds two static public variables in Lines 8–9 that will be used to hold the two values to be sorted. These were declared as static to make the coding easier in the rest of the listing. Line 11 contains the delegate definition, followed by the method that will execute the delegated methods, DoSort, in Lines 13–16. As you can see, the DoSort method receives a delegate object as its parameter. The delegate object is used in Line 15 as a method call using the same signature that was used with the delegate definition in Line 11.

The SortProgram class uses the Sort delegate. This class defines the methods that will be delegated—Ascending and Descending. The class also contains a Main method that will perform the key logic. In Lines 43–44, two delegate objects are created; these are the up and down objects that you saw earlier.

13

In Line 46, an object is created of type `SortClass`. This is necessary to use the `DoSort` method. In Lines 48 and 49, two values are set into the sorting variables. Line 51 prints these values to the console. Line 53 then calls the `DoSort` method, passing a delegate object. In this case, the `up` object is passed. This causes the `Ascending` method to be used. As the output from Line 57 shows, the sort was accomplished. Line 59 then calls the `DoSort` method again, this time with the `down` object. This causes the `Descending` method to be used, as can be seen by the final output.

You could actually get around declaring a `doIT` object in Line 46 by declaring the `DoSort` method as static. The `DoSort` method could then be accessed using the class name instead of an object:

```
SortClass.DoSort(...);
```

This example uses delegates with hard-coded values and with specific calls. The value of delegates becomes more apparent when you begin to create more dynamic programs. For example, Listing 13.2 could be modified to use data from a file or information entered by the user. This would give the sorting more value. Additionally, you could have your user enter a preference for sorting ascending, descending, or some other way. Based on what is entered, you could then make a single call to `DoSort` with the appropriate delegate object being passed.

 Note

In today's exercises, you are asked to create a delegate that can accept a method for sorting an array of integers. An answer for this will be provided. You could actually take the answer one step further by making the array work with objects. You could then create a delegate for sorting data of any type.

Working with Events

You will find that you will use delegates primarily when you are working with events. An event is a notification from a class that something has occurred. You—or, more appropriately, your other classes—can then do something based on this notification.

The most common example of event processing is within a Windows-based operating system. Within a system such as Microsoft Windows, a dialog box or window is displayed in which a users can do a number of different things: click a button, select a menu, enter text, and so forth. Whenever the user does one of these actions, an event occurs. Event handlers within Windows then react based on the event that occurred. For example, if a user selects a button, a `ButtonClick` event notification might occur. A `ButtonClick` event handler could then handle any actions that need to occur.

Creating Events

Several steps are involved in creating and using an event. This includes setting up the delegate for the event, creating a class to pass arguments for the event handlers, declaring the code for the event, creating code that should occur when the event happens (the handler), and finally causing the event to occur.

Understanding an Event's Delegate

The first step to working with events is to create a delegate for the event. The delegates that you create for an event follow a specific format:

```
delegate void EventHandlerName(object source, xxxEventArgs e);
```

EventHandlerName is the name of the delegate for the event handler. A delegate for an event always takes two parameters. The first parameter, `object source`, contains the source that raised the event. The second parameter, *xxxEventArgs e*, is a class containing data that can be used by a handler for the event. This class is derived from the `EventArgs` class, which is part of the `System` namespace.

The following line of code creates a delegate for an event. This event checks assigned characters. If a certain character is assigned, an event is executed. The delegate could be defined as follows:

```
delegate void CharEventHandler(object source, CharEventArgs e);
```

This declares the delegate named `CharEventHandler`. From this declaration, you can see that a class named `CharEventArgs` needs to be created by deriving it from `EventArgs`.

Deriving from the `EventArgs` Class

The `EventArgs` class is used to pass data to an event handler. This class can be inherited into a new class that contains data members for any values that your new event may need. The format of a derived class should be as follows:

```
public class xxxEventArgs : EventArgs
{
    // Data members

    public xxxEventArgs( type name )
    {
        //Set up values
    }
}
```

As you can see, *xxxEventArgs* inherits from `EventsArgs`. You can rename *xxxEventArgs* to any name you want; using a name that ends with `EventArgs` makes it obvious as to what this class is used for.

Tip Although you can name the *xxxEventArgs* class anything you want, you should end your class name with EventsArgs. This indicates the purpose of the classand is the more commonly accepted naming convention.

You can add data members to this derived class and add logic to initialize these values within the class's constructor. This class is passed to the event handler. Any data that your event handler will need should be included in this class.

In the example from the previous section, you saw that a delegate was created named CharEventHandler. This delegate passed an object of class CharEventArgs. Code for CharEventArgs follows:

```
public class CharEventArgs : EventArgs
{
    public char CurrChar;
    public CharEventArgs(char CurrChar)
    {
        this.CurrChar = CurrChar;
    }
}
```

As you can see, CharEventArgs is a new class derived from EventArgs. Regardless of the event you are doing, you must create a class that is derived in the same fashion from EventArgs. This class contains a single char value, CurrChar, which is usable by the code that will be written to handle this event. This class also contains a constructor that receives a character when the class is created. The character passed to the constructor is assigned the data member within the class.

Working with the Event Class Code

A class can be created to kick off the event. This class contains a declaration for the event, which takes the following format:

```
public event xxxEventHandler EventName;
```

Here, *xxxEventHandler* is the delegate definition that was created for this event. *EventName* is the name of the event being declared. In summary, this line of code uses the event keyword to create an event instance named *EventName* that is a delegate of type *xxxEventHandler*. *EventName* will be used to assign methods to the delegate, as well as to do the execution of the methods.

Here is an example of creating an event class:

```
 1:  class CharChecker
 2:  {
 3:      char curr_char;
 4:      public event CharEventHandler TestChar;
 5:      public char Curr_Char
 6:      {
 7:          get { return curr_char; }
 8:          set
 9:          {
10:              if (TestChar != null )
11:              {
12:                  CharEventArgs args = new CharEventArgs(value);
13:                  TestChar(this, args);
14:                  curr_char = args.CurrChar;
15:              }
16:          }
17:      }
18:  }
```

This class contains the code that will kick off the event if the appropriate condition is met. Your code can vary from this example; however, a couple of things are similar. In Line 4, an event object is created using the delegate CharEventHandler, which was created earlier. This event object will be used to execute any assigned event handlers. The next section of this class is a properties definition for Curr_Char (Lines 5–17). As you can see, a get property returns the value of the curr_char data member from this class (Line 7).

The set property in Lines 8–16 is unique. The first thing done is to verify that the TestChar object is not equal to null (Line 10). Remember, the TestChar object was just declared as an event. This event object will be null only if there are no event handlers created. You'll learn more about event handlers in the next section. If there is an event handler, Line 12 creates a CharEventArgs object. As you learned in the previous section, this object will hold any values needed for the event-handling routines. The value entered into the set routine is passed to the CharEventArgs constructor. As you saw in the previous section, for this example, this value is a character that will be available to the event handlers.

Line 13 is the call to the event delegate. Using the event object created in Line 4, a call to the delegate is being made. Because this is an event, it checks for all the methods that have been associated with this event object. As you can see, two values are passed to this event object. The first is this, which is the object that is making the call to the event. The second value is args, which is the CharEventArgs object that you declared in the previous line.

13

Line 14 is specific to this particular event. This line assigns the character that is in the
CharEventArgs object back to the curr_char data member. If any event handlers called in
Line 13 change the data, this makes sure that the event class has an updated value and is
thus set—which is the purpose of the set property.

Creating Event Handlers

You have now created a delegate, created a structure to pass information to your event
handlers, and created code to execute the event. Now you code what will get executed if
an event happens. You need event handlers. Specifically, an event handler is a piece of
code that gets notified when an event occurs. An event handler is a method created using
the same format as your delegate. The format of the method is the following:

```
void handlername(object source, xxxEventArgs argName)
{
    // Event Handler code
}
```

handlername is the name of the method that will be called when an event occurs. The two
parameters being passed should look very familiar by this time. The first is the object
that executed the event. The second is the class derived from EventArgs that contains the
values for the event handler to use. The Event Handler code can be any code you want. If
the event was a button click, this would be the code executed when the button is clicked.
If it was a Cancel button, this code would do the logic for canceling. If it were an OK
button, this code would do the logic for things being okay.

Going back to our Character event example, an event can be declared to replace the letter
A whenever it is entered with an x. This is a goofy example, but it is easy to follow:

```
static void Drop_A(object source, CharEventArgs e)
{
    if(e.CurrChar == 'a' || e.CurrChar == 'A' )
    {
        Console.WriteLine("Don't like 'a'!");
        e.CurrChar = 'X';
    }
}
```

As you can see, this event handler receives the CharEventArgs parameter. The CurrChar
value is retrieved from this object and checked for its value. If the user enters an A or an
a, the event handler displays a message and changes the current character to an x instead.
If it is any other character, nothing happens.

Associating Events and Event Handlers

Now you have almost all the pieces. It's time to associate your event handler with the event—in case it happens. This occurs in your primary program.

To associate a handler with an event, you must first declare an object containing an event. For the `Character` example, this is done by declaring a `CharChecker` object:

```
CharChecker tester = new CharChecker();
```

As you can see, this object is instantiated like any other object. When this object is created, your event is available. Whenever the `set` logic of a `CharChecker` object is called, the logic within it is followed, including the creation of the event and the execution of the event object in its `set` statements.

Right now, however, you still have not associated your event handler with this object. To associate an event handler with the object, you need to use the `+=` operator. This is used in the following format:

```
ObjectWithEventName.EventObj += new EventDelegateName(EventName);
```

Here, `ObjectWithEventName` is the object that you just declared using the event class. For the example, this is `tester`. `EventObj` is the event object that you declared in the event class. For the example, this is `TestChar`. The `+=` operator follows as an indicator that the following is an event to be added to the event handler. The `new` keyword indicates that the following handler should be created. Finally, the name of the event handler, `EventName`, is passed to the delegate, `EventDelegateName`. The final statement for the example is as follows:

```
tester.TestChar += new CharEventHandler(Drop_A);
```

Pulling It All Together

Whew! That is a lot to do. however, when this is completed, a line as simple as the following can be used to execute the event:

```
tester.Curr_Char = 'B';
```

Listing 13.3 pulls it all together.

13

LISTING 13.3   Events.cs—Using an Event and Event Handlers

```
1:  // Events.cs - Using events
2:  //-------------------------------------------------------------
3:
4:  using System;
5:
```

LISTING 13.3   continued

```
 6:  delegate void CharEventHandler(object source, CharEventArgs e);
 7:
 8:  public class CharEventArgs : EventArgs
 9:  {
10:      public char CurrChar;
11:      public CharEventArgs(char CurrChar)
12:      {
13:         this.CurrChar = CurrChar;
14:      }
15:  }
16:
17:  class CharChecker
18:  {
19:     char curr_char;
20:     public event CharEventHandler TestChar;
21:     public char Curr_Char
22:     {
23:        get { return curr_char; }
24:        set
25:        {
26:           if (TestChar != null )
27:           {
28:               CharEventArgs args = new CharEventArgs(value);
29:               TestChar(this, args);
30:               curr_char = args.CurrChar;
31:           }
32:        }
33:     }
34:  }
35:
36:  class Events
37:  {
38:     public static void Main()
39:     {
40:        CharChecker tester = new CharChecker();
41:
42:        tester.TestChar += new CharEventHandler(Drop_A);
43:
44:        tester.Curr_Char = 'B';
45:        Console.WriteLine("{0}", tester.Curr_Char);
46:
47:        tester.Curr_Char = 'r';
48:        Console.WriteLine("{0}", tester.Curr_Char);
49:
50:        tester.Curr_Char = 'a';
51:        Console.WriteLine("{0}", tester.Curr_Char);
52:
53:        tester.Curr_Char = 'd';
```

LISTING 13.3   continued

```
54:         Console.WriteLine("{0}", tester.Curr_Char);
55:
56:     }
57:
58:     static void Drop_A(object source, CharEventArgs e)
59:     {
60:         if(e.CurrChar == 'a' || e.CurrChar == 'A' )
61:         {
62:             Console.WriteLine("Don't like 'a'!");
63:             e.CurrChar = 'X';
64:         }
65:     }
66: }
```

OUTPUT

```
B
r
Don't like 'a'!
X
d
```

ANALYSIS If you look at this listing, it contains all the sections of code discussed in the previous sections. The only real new code is in the Main routine in Lines 44–54. This code assigns characters to the Curr_Char value in the tester class. If an a or an A is found, a message is printed and the character is changed to an x. The change is shown by displaying the Curr_Char value using a Console.WriteLine call.

The event class can be any class that you want to create. For example, I could have changed the CharChecker class in this example to a class that stores a full name or other textual information. In other words, this example doesn't do much: Your code can.

Multiple Event Handlers (Multicasting)

You can declare multiple event handlers for a single event with multicasting. Additional event handlers should follow the same format of receiving an object and a derived object of type EventArgs, as well as returning void. To add the additional events, you use the += operator in the same way you saw earlier. Listing 13.4 is a new version of Listing 13.3, with a second event handler added.

13

LISTING 13.4   Events2.cs—Multiple Event Handlers

```
1:  // Events2.cs - Using multiple event handlers
2:  //-------------------------------------------------------------
3:
4:  using System;
5:
```

LISTING **13.4**   continued

```
 6:  delegate void CharEventHandler(object source, CharEventArgs e);
 7:
 8:  public class CharEventArgs : EventArgs
 9:  {
10:      public char CurrChar;
11:      public CharEventArgs(char CurrChar)
12:      {
13:          this.CurrChar = CurrChar;
14:      }
15:  }
16:
17:  class CharChecker
18:  {
19:      char curr_char;
20:      public event CharEventHandler TestChar;
21:      public char Curr_Char
22:      {
23:          get { return curr_char; }
24:          set
25:          {
26:              if (TestChar != null )
27:              {
28:                  CharEventArgs args = new CharEventArgs(value);
29:                  TestChar(this, args);
30:                  curr_char = args.CurrChar;
31:              }
32:          }
33:      }
34:  }
35:
36:  class Events2
37:  {
38:      public static void Main()
39:      {
40:          CharChecker tester = new CharChecker();
41:
42:          tester.TestChar += new CharEventHandler(Drop_A);
43:          tester.TestChar += new CharEventHandler(Change_D);
44:
45:          tester.Curr_Char = 'B';
46:          Console.WriteLine("{0}", tester.Curr_Char);
47:
48:          tester.Curr_Char = 'r';
49:          Console.WriteLine("{0}", tester.Curr_Char);
50:
51:          tester.Curr_Char = 'a';
52:          Console.WriteLine("{0}", tester.Curr_Char);
53:
54:          tester.Curr_Char = 'd';
```

LISTING **13.4**   continued

```
55:            Console.WriteLine("{0}", tester.Curr_Char);
56:        }
57:
58:        static void Drop_A(object source, CharEventArgs e)
59:        {
60:            if(e.CurrChar == 'a' || e.CurrChar == 'A' )
61:            {
62:                Console.WriteLine("Don't like 'a'!");
63:                e.CurrChar = 'X';
64:            }
65:        }
66:
67:    // new event handler....
68:        static void Change_D(object source, CharEventArgs e)
69:        {
70:            if(e.CurrChar == 'd' || e.CurrChar == 'D' )
71:            {
72:                Console.WriteLine("D's are good!");
73:                e.CurrChar = 'Z';
74:            }
75:        }
76:    }
```

OUTPUT

```
B
r
Don't like 'a'!
X
D's are good!
Z
```

ANALYSIS   Lines 68–75 add a new event handler named Change_D. As you can see, it follows the format required—it returns void and receives the appropriate two parameters. This event checks for the letters D or d. If any is found, it converts each character to a z after displaying a message. It's not exciting, but it's effective.

This event handler is added to the event object in Line 43. As you can see, it is added in the same manner as the original event, Drop_A. Now when a letter is assigned, both events are executed.

Removing an Event Handler

Event handlers can be added, and they can also be removed. To remove an event, use the -= operator instead of the += operator. Listing 13.5 contains a new Main routine for the CharChecker program.

13

Caution   Listing 13.5 is not a complete listing; it is only the `Main` routine. You can sub-
stitute this code for the main routine in Listing 13.4 (Lines 38–56).
Alternatively, you can obtain the listing, Events3.cs, from the source code
available on the CD or online at www.TeachYourselfCSharp.com.

LISTING 13.5   Events3.cs—Removing an Event

```
 1:    public static void Main()
 2:    {
 3:        CharChecker tester = new CharChecker();
 4:
 5:        tester.TestChar += new CharEventHandler(Drop_A);
 6:        tester.TestChar += new CharEventHandler(Change_D);
 7:
 8:        tester.Curr_Char = 'B';
 9:        Console.WriteLine("{0}", tester.Curr_Char);
10:
11:        tester.Curr_Char = 'r';
12:        Console.WriteLine("{0}", tester.Curr_Char);
13:
14:        tester.Curr_Char = 'a';
15:        Console.WriteLine("{0}", tester.Curr_Char);
16:
17:        tester.Curr_Char = 'd';
18:        Console.WriteLine("{0}", tester.Curr_Char);
19:
20:        // Remove event handler...
21:        Console.WriteLine("\nRemoving event handler....");
22:        tester.TestChar -= new CharEventHandler(Change_D);
23:
24:        // Try D-a-d...
25:
26:        tester.Curr_Char = 'D';
27:        Console.WriteLine("{0}", tester.Curr_Char);
28:
29:        tester.Curr_Char = 'a';
30:        Console.WriteLine("{0}", tester.Curr_Char);
31:
32:        tester.Curr_Char = 'd';
33:        Console.WriteLine("{0}", tester.Curr_Char);
34:    }
```

OUTPUT

```
B
r
Don't like 'a'!
X
```

```
D's are good!
Z

Removing event handler....
D
Don't like 'a'!
X
d
```

 As you can see by the output, when Line 22 is executed, the Change_D event is no longer active. However, the Change_A event handler continues to work.

> **Caution**
>
> If multiple event handlers are assigned to an event, there is no guarantee for which will be executed first. In Listing 13.5, there is no guarantee that Change_A will execute before Change_D.
>
> Additionally, event handlers and events can throw exceptions and do all the things other code can do. If an exception is thrown, there is no guarantee that other event handlers will be executed.

Summary

In today's lesson, you learned about some of the more complicated topics within C#. You first learned about indexers. Indexers can be used with a class so that you can access the class using index notation. This makes your classes "arraylike."

You then learned about delegates. You learned that delegates are like interfaces: They state a definition for accessing but don't actually provide the implementation. Delegates set up a format for using methods. You learned that a delegate can be used to dynamically call different methods with a single method call.

The last part of today's lesson focused on events. You learned that code can be created to cause an event to happen. More important, you learned that code—event handlers—can be created to react when an event happens.

Q&A

Q Today's concepts were hard. How important is it to understand them?

A You can do a lot with C# without understanding the concepts presented today; however, there is a lot more that you won't be able to do. If you plan to program applications for Windows or other graphical environments, you will find that events are critical. And as you learned today, delegates are critical for working with events.

13

Many of the C# editors, such as Visual Studio .NET, will help by automatically creating a lot of the code for you. For example, Visual Studio .NET adds code for many of the standard events.

Q In today's lesson, events were declared in properties. Do they have to be declared in a property?

A No. You can declare an event call within a property or a method.

Q Multiple event handlers were assigned to an event. Can multiple methods be assigned to a single delegate?

A Yes. It is possible to assign more than one method to a single delegate so that multiple methods execute with a single call. This is also called multicasting.

Q What is a function pointer?

A In languages such as C and C++, there is a construct called a function pointer. A function pointer is used to accomplish the same task as a delegate. A delegate, however, is type-safe and secure. In addition to being used to reference methods, delegates are used by events.

Workshop

The Workshop provides quiz questions to help you solidify your understanding of the material covered and exercises to provide you with experience in using what you've learned. Try to understand the quiz and exercise answers before continuing to tomorrow's lesson. Answers are provided on the CD.

Quiz

1. You are in your living room and the phone rings. You get up and answer the phone. The ringing of the phone is best associated with which of the following concepts?

    a. Indexer

    b. Delegate

    c. Event

    d. Event handler

    e. Exception handler

2. Your answering the phone is best associated with which of the following concepts:

   a. Indexer

   b. Delegate

   c. Event

   d. Event handler

   e. Exception handler

3. What is the point of an indexer?

4. When declaring an indexer, what keyword is used?

5. An indexer definition is similar to which of the following:

   a. A class definition

   b. An object definition

   c. A property definition

   d. A delegate definition

   e. An event definition

6. What are the different steps to creating and using an event?

7. What operator is used to add an event handler?

8. What is it called when multiple event handlers are added to an event?

9. Which is true (note—None and Both are possible answers):

   An event is an instantiation based on a delegate.

   A delegate is an instantiation based on an event.

10. Where within a class can an event be instantiated?

Exercises

1. Add an indexer to the following class. Use the class in a simple program.

```
public class SimpleClass
{
    int[] numbers;

    public SimpleClass(int size)
    {
        numbers = new int[size];        // declare size elements
        for ( int x = 0; x < size; x++ )  // initialize values to 0.
            numbers[x] = 0;
    }
}
```

13

2. Rewrite Listing 13.1 without using indexers.

3. Modify Listing 13.2 so that you don't have to declare a `doIT` object.

4. Write a program using a delegate that sorts an array of integers. You can use Listing 13.2 as a starting point.

5. Add an event handler to the code in Listing 13.5. This event handler should change any lowercase vowels to uppercase.

DAY 14

Making Operators Do Your Bidding: Overloading

In today's lesson, you delve deeper into some of the functionality available when working with classes. This includes exploring overloading in much greater detail. You've seen method overloading earlier. Today you...

- Revisit method and constructor overloading.
- Learn about overloading operators.
- Discover how to overload unary, binary, relational, and logical operators.
- Understand the difference in overloading the logical operators.
- Review the individual operators that can and can't be overloaded.

Overloading Functions Revisited

On Day 8, "Advanced Method Access," you learned that you can overload a method multiple times. The key issue with overloading a method is that you must ensure that each time you overload the method, it has a different signature. A signature is determined by the return type and parameters of a method. For example, all of the following are different signatures:

```
int mymethod( int x, int y )

int mymethod( int x )

int mymethod( long x )

int mymethod( char x, long y, long z )

int mymethod( char x, long y, int z )
```

On Day 8, you learned that you could overload constructors as well as regular methods. Today you go beyond overloading methods: You learn how to overload a class's operators.

Overloading Operators

In addition to overloading constructors and accessors, many object-oriented languages give you the capability to overload operators. C# is no exception: It enables you to overload many of the mathematical operators—such as addition (+) and subtraction (-)—as well as many of the relational and logical operators.

Why would you want to overload these operators? You do not ever *have* to overload them. Sometimes, however, it can make your program's code easier to follow and your classes easier to use.

The string class is a great example of a class that has an operator that is overloaded. Normally, the addition operator would not work on a class type, but in C#, you can actually add two strings with the addition operator. This addition does what you would expect: It concatenates two strings. For example:

```
"animal" + " " + "crackers"
```

results in this string:

```
"animal crackers"
```

To accomplish this, the string class and the string data type overload the addition operator.

You will find that overloading operators can make some of your programs work better as well. Take a look at Listing 14.1. This listing gives you an error when you compile. The error is shown in the listing's output.

Note This listing is not a great example of using operator overloading; however, it is simple so that you can focus on the concepts instead of trying to understand the code in a complex listing. A few of the later listings in today's lesson are much more practical.

LISTING 14.1 over1a.cs—A Program with a Problem

```
 1: // over1a.cs - A listing with a problem
 2: //----------------------------------------------------
 3:
 4: using System;
 5:
 6: public class AChar
 7: {
 8:     private char private_ch;
 9:
10:     public AChar() { this.ch = ' '; }
11:     public AChar(char val) { this.ch = val; }
12:
13:     public char ch
14:     {
15:         get{ return this.private_ch, }
16:         set{ this.private_ch = value; }
17:     }
18: }
19:
20: public class myAppClass
21: {
22:
23:     public static void Main(String[] args)
24:     {
25:         AChar aaa = new AChar('a');
26:         AChar bbb = new AChar('b');
27:
28:         Console.WriteLine("Original value: {0}, {1}", aaa.ch, bbb.ch);
29:
30:         aaa = aaa + 3;
31:         bbb = bbb - 1;
32:
33:         Console.WriteLine("Final values: {0}, {1}", aaa.ch, bbb.ch);
34:     }
35: }
```

14

OUTPUT   The following errors are generated when you try to compile this listing:

```
over1a.cs(30,13): error CS0019: Operator '+' cannot be applied to
    ➥operands of type 'AChar' and 'int'
over1a.cs(31,13): error CS0019: Operator '-' cannot be applied to
    ➥operands of type 'AChar' and 'int'
```

ANALYSIS   This listing is easy to follow. A class is created named AChar. This class is not practical, but its simplicity makes it easy to use as an illustration for overloading.

The AChar class stores a single character. The class has two constructors in Lines 10–11. The first is called when no arguments are provided; it sets the character value stored in a newly instantiated object to a space. The second constructor takes a single character that is placed in a new object's private character variable. The class uses an accessor in Lines 13–17 to do the actual setting of the character value.

The AChar class is used in the myAppClass class. In Lines 25–26, two AChar objects are created. aaa will contain a, and bbb will contain b. In Line 33, these values are printed. In Line 30, the value of 3 is added to aaa. What would you expect would happen when you add 3 to an AChar object? Note that this is not a type char object or even a numeric object. It is an AChar object.

This listing is trying to add 3 to the actual object, not to a member of the object. The result, as you can see by the compiler output, is an error.

In Line 31, the value of 1 is subtracted from an AChar object. An error is produced because you can't add or subtract from an object like this. If Lines 30–31 had worked, Line 33 would have printed their values.

You can make the addition work by manipulating an object's members instead of the class itself. Changing Lines 30–31 to the following allows the listing to compile:

```
aaa.ch = (char) (aaa.ch + 3);
bbb.ch = (char) (bbb.ch - 1);
```

Although this works, it is not the ultimate solution. There is too much casting, and the code is not as simple as it could be. Another solution to make this clear is to add methods to the class that allow addition and subtraction—or other types of operations—to be done with the class's objects. Listing 14.2 presents this approach.

LISTING **14.2**   over1b.cs—Operators for Mathematical Functions

```
 1: // over1b.cs - Using methods for mathematic operations
 2: //-------------------------------------------------------
 3:
 4: using System;
 5:
 6: public class AChar
 7: {
 8:    private char private_ch;
 9:
10:    public AChar() { this.ch = ' '; }
11:    public AChar(char val) { this.ch = val; }
12:
13:    public char ch
14:    {
15:       get{ return this.private_ch; }
16:       set{ this.private_ch = value; }
17:    }
18:
19:    static public AChar Add ( AChar orig, int val )
20:    {
21:       AChar result = new AChar();
22:       result.ch = (char)(orig.ch + val);
23:       return result;
24:    }
25:    static public AChar Subtract ( AChar orig, int val )
26:    {
27:       AChar result = new AChar();
28:       result.ch = (char)(orig.ch - val);
29:       return result;
30:    }
31: }
32:
33: public class myAppClass
34: {
35:    public static void Main(String[] args)
36:    {
37:       AChar aaa = new AChar('a');
38:       AChar bbb = new AChar('b');
39:
40:       Console.WriteLine("Original value: {0}, {1}", aaa.ch, bbb.ch);
41:
42:       aaa = AChar.Add( aaa, 3 );
43:       bbb = AChar.Subtract( bbb, 1 );
44:
45:       Console.WriteLine("Final values: {0}, {1}", aaa.ch, bbb.ch);
46:    }
47: }
```

14

OUTPUT
```
Original value: a, b
Final values: d, a
```

ANALYSIS   This listing is better than the last listing—this one compiles! It also provides routines for doing mathematical operations on the class. This is accomplished with the static methods Add and Subtract declared in Lines 19–24 and 25–30, respectively.

The Add method increments the original AChar character value (ch) by the number specified. In the myAppClass class, the AChar.Add method is called to increment aaa by 3, which results in an a becoming a d. The Add method returns a new AChar class that can overwrite the original. In this way, a number can be added to the class and returned to overwrite the original value. The Subtract method works in the same manner, except that the ch value is decremented by the given number.

This listing is relatively simple. If there were other data members as a part of the class, the Add and Subtract operations would become more complex; however, they would also become more valuable. Consider a few examples:

- A deposit class that contains members for the person making the deposit, an account number, and the value being deposited. In this case, the Add method could manipulate the value being deposited.

- A currency class that contains an enumeration value that indicates the type of currency and multiple numeric values to store different money types, such as dollars and cents.

- A salary class that contains an employee name, the employee ID number, the date of the last salary increase, and the actual salary for the employee.

Creating Overloaded Operators

Using methods such as those presented in Listing 14.2 is a perfectly acceptable way to increment and decrement values of a class. Sometimes, however, overloading an operator makes the class easier to use. The three examples given are such cases, as is the String concatenation example from earlier.

The AChar class is probably not a good class to overload the operators with. Simply put, if you overload an operator, it should be obvious to everyone using the class what the overloaded operator is doing. Consider the following lines of code. What would you expect the results to be? What would everyone else expect the results to be?

```
Salary = Salary + 1000;

MyChar = MyChar + 3;

MyChar = MyChar + 'a';

Deposit = Deposit - 300;
```

The `Salary` and the `Deposit` lines should be obvious. The `MyChar + 3` line might seem obvious, but is it? `MyChar + 'a'` is even more cryptic. The + operator could be overloaded for all of these cases, thus making these examples work. The `MyChar` example would be better using a descriptive named method instead of overloading an operator.

A number of operators can be overloaded. This includes the basic binary mathematics operators, most of the unary operators, the relational operators, and the logical operators.

Overloading the Basic Binary Mathematical Operators

The binary operators are operators that use two values. These operators include addition (+), subtraction (-), multiplication (*), division (/), and modulus (%). All of these can be overloaded within your classes. The total list of binary operators that can be overloaded is as follows:

+	Addition
-	Subtraction
*	Multiplication
/	Division
%	Modulus
&	AND
|	OR
^	Not
<<	Shift left
>>	Shift right

The format for overloading a binary operator is similar to the format for creating methods. The general format for overloading an operator is shown here:

```
public static return_type operator op ( type x, type y )
{
    ...
    return return_type;
}
```

Here, `return_type` is the data type that is being returned by the overloaded operator. For the `AChar` class in the earlier example, `return_type` was the class type—`AChar`. The return type is preceded by the `public` and `static` modifiers. An overloaded operator must always be public so that it can be accessed. It also must always be static so that it can be accessed at the class level rather than at an individual object level.

The term `operator` is then used to indicate that this is an operator-overloading method. The operator being overloaded (`op`) then is presented. If you were overloading the

14

addition operator, for example, this would be a plus sign. Finally, the parameters for the operation are presented.

In this example, a binary operator is being overloaded, so there are two parameters. One of the parameters must be of the type of the class whose operator is being overloaded. The other parameter's type can be of any type. When setting up operator overloading, you will often set these two types as the same. It is perfectly acceptable to make the second type a different type as well. In fact, if you are overloading an operator, you should be sure to set up overloaded methods for any possible data types that might be added to the original class.

Looking back at the AChar class, the following is the method header for overloading the addition operator so that you can add an integer value to an AChar value:

```
public static AChar operator+ (AChar x, int y)
```

Although x and y are used as the parameter names, you can use any variable names that you want. An integer value is the second parameter because that is what was added to the AChar objects in the earlier listings. Listing 14.3 presents the AChar class one more time. This time, however, the addition and subtraction operators are overloaded to allow an integer to be added to an AChar.

 Note

You may have noticed that the format description earlier had a space between the word operator and the *op* sign. In the example just presented for the AChar class, there is no space; the operator is connected to the word operator. Either format works.

LISTING 14.3 over1c—Overloading the Binary Operators

```
1:  // over1c.cs - Overloading an operator
2:  //----------------------------------------------------
3:
4:  using System;
5:
6:  public class AChar
7:  {
8:      private char private_ch;
9:
10:     public AChar() { this.ch = ' '; }
11:     public AChar(char val) { this.ch = val; }
12:
13:     public char ch
14:     {
15:         get{ return this.private_ch; }
```

LISTING 14.3   continued

```
16:          set{ this.private_ch = value; }
17:      }
18:
19:      static public AChar operator+ ( AChar orig, int val )
20:      {
21:          AChar result = new AChar();
22:          result.ch = (char)(orig.ch + val);
23:          return result;
24:      }
25:      static public AChar operator- ( AChar orig, int val )
26:      {
27:          AChar result = new AChar();
28:          result.ch = (char)(orig.ch - val);
29:          return result;
30:      }
31:  }
32:
33:  public class myAppClass
34:  {
35:      public static void Main(String[] args)
36:      {
37:          AChar aaa = new AChar('a');
38:          AChar bbb = new AChar('b');
39:
40:          Console.WriteLine("Original value: {0}, {1}", aaa.ch, bbb.ch);
41:
42:          aaa = aaa + 25;
43:          bbb = bbb - 1;
44:
45:          Console.WriteLine("Final values: {0}, {1}", aaa.ch, bbb.ch);
46:      }
47:  }
```

OUTPUT

```
Original value: a, b
Final values: z, a
```

ANALYSIS Lines 19–30 contain the overloading of the addition and subtraction operators of the AChar class. In Line 19, the overloading follows the format presented earlier and an AChar type is returned. The first type being added is also an AChar.

In this example, an integer value is being added to an AChar type. You could have used another AChar object or any other type that would make sense instead of the integer. You can overload the addition operator multiple times, each time adding a different data type to the AChar type, as long as the resulting overloads have unique signatures. In fact, you will need to overload any types that might be used.

14

The overloaded addition operator's functionality is presented in Lines 21–23. A new AChar object is instantiated in Line 21. The ch value within this new AChar object is assigned a value based upon the values received with the addition operator. When this value is updated, the new AChar object, result, is returned. The code in this method could be changed to anything you want; however, it should be related to the values received by the addition operator.

The subtraction operator is set up in the same manner as the addition operator. In an exercise at the end of today's lesson, you create a second overloaded method for the subtraction operator. The second method takes two AChar values and returns the number of positions between them.

This listing overloaded only the addition and subtraction operators. Overloading the multiplication, division, modulus, and other binary operators is done in the same way.

Overloading the Basic Unary Mathematical Operators

The unary operators work with only one element. The unary operators that can be overloaded are listed here:

```
+

-

++

--

!

~

true

false
```

The unary operators are overloaded similarly to the binary operators. The difference is that only one value is declared as a parameter. This single value is of the same data type as the class containing the overload. A single parameter is all that is passed because a unary operator operates on a single value. Two examples are presented in Listings 14.4 and 14.5. Listing 14.4 presents the positive (+) and negative (-) unary operators. These are used with the AChar class that you've already seen. A positive AChar capitalizes the character. A negative AChar converts the character to lowercase.

Caution Again, the + and – operators to change the case of a character are not obvious functions. Although these operations make good examples, they aren't good in practical usage because they are not obvious. Again, you would be better served using methods with descriptive names.

Listing 14.5 uses the increment and decrement (- -) operators. This listing increments the character to the next character value or decrements the character to the preceding value. Note that this is moving through the character values, so incrementing z or decrementing A will take you to a nonletter character. You could add logic, however, to prevent the incrementing or decrementing past the end or beginning of the alphabet.

LISTING 14.4   over2.cs—Overloading the + and - Unary Operators

```
 1:  // over2.cs - Overloading
 2:  //-------------------------------------------------
 3:
 4:  using System;
 5:  using System.Text;
 6:
 7:  public class AChar
 8:  {
 9:      private char private_ch;
10:
11:      public AChar() { this.ch = ' '; }
12:      public AChar(char val) { this.ch = val; }
13:
14:      public char ch
15:      {
16:         get{ return this.private_ch; }
17:         set{ this.private_ch = value; }
18:      }
19:
20:      static public AChar operator+ ( AChar orig )
21:      {
22:         AChar result = new AChar();
23:         if( orig.ch >= 'a' && orig.ch <='z' )
24:            result.ch = (char) (orig.ch - 32 );
25:         else
26:            result.ch = orig.ch;
27:
28:         return result;
29:      }
30:      static public AChar operator- ( AChar orig )
31:      {
32:         AChar result = new AChar();
```

14

LISTING **14.4**   continued

```
33:           if( orig.ch >= 'A' && orig.ch <='Z' )
34:               result.ch = (char) (orig.ch + 32 );
35:           else
36:               result.ch = orig.ch;
37:
38:           return result;
39:       }
40:
41:   }
42:
43:   public class myAppClass
44:   {
45:       public static void Main(String[] args)
46:       {
47:           AChar aaa = new AChar('g');
48:           AChar bbb = new AChar('g');
49:           AChar ccc = new AChar('G');
50:           AChar ddd = new AChar('G');
51:
52:           Console.WriteLine("ORIGINAL:");
53:           Console.WriteLine("aaa value: {0}", aaa.ch);
54:           Console.WriteLine("bbb value: {0}", bbb.ch);
55:           Console.WriteLine("ccc value: {0}", ccc.ch);
56:           Console.WriteLine("ddd value: {0}", ddd.ch);
57:
58:           aaa = +aaa;
59:           bbb = -bbb;
60:           ccc = +ccc;
61:           ddd = -ddd;
62:
63:           Console.WriteLine("\n\nFINAL:");
64:           Console.WriteLine("aaa value: {0}", aaa.ch);
65:           Console.WriteLine("bbb value: {0}", bbb.ch);
66:           Console.WriteLine("ccc value: {0}", ccc.ch);
67:           Console.WriteLine("ddd value: {0}", ddd.ch);
68:       }
69:   }
```

OUTPUT

```
ORIGINAL:
aaa value: g
bbb value: g
ccc value: G
ddd value: G


FINAL:
aaa value: G
bbb value: g
```

```
ccc value: G
ddd value: g
```

ANALYSIS As you can see by the output of Listing 14.4, using the + operator changes a low-ercase letter to uppercase. It has no effect on a letter that is already uppercase. Using the - operator does the opposite: It changes an uppercase letter to lowercase. It has no effect on a character that is lowercase.

Lines 20–39 contain the overloaded operator methods. You know that these are unary overloaded operator methods because they each have only one parameter (see Lines 20 and 30). The code within these overloaded operators is relatively straightforward. The code checks to see whether the original character is an alphabetic character that is either uppercase (Line 33) or lowercase (Line 24). If the character is one of these, it is changed to the other case by either adding 32 or subtracting 32.

Note
> Remember that characters are stored as numeric values. The letter A is stored as 65. The letter a is stored as 97. Each letter of the same case is stored sequentially afterward.

Listing 14.4 overloaded the unary positive and negative operators; Listing 14.5 overloads the increment and decrement operators.

LISTING 14.5   over2b.cs—Overloading the Increment and Decrement Operators

```
 1:  //  over2b.cs - Overloading
 2:  //---------------------------------------------------
 3:
 4:  using System;
 5:
 6:  public class AChar
 7:  {
 8:     private char private_ch;
 9:
10:     public AChar() { this.ch = ' '; }
11:     public AChar(char val) { this.ch = val; }
12:
13:     public char ch
14:     {
15:        get{ return this.private_ch; }
16:        set{ this.private_ch = value; }
17:     }
18:
19:     static public AChar operator++ ( AChar orig )
20:     {
```

14

LISTING 14.5   continued

```
21:            AChar result = new AChar();
22:            result.ch = (char)(orig.ch + 1);
23:            return result;
24:        }
25:        static public AChar operator-- ( AChar orig )
26:        {
27:            AChar result = new AChar();
28:            result.ch = (char)(orig.ch - 1);
29:            return result;
30:        }
31:
32:    }
33:
34:    public class myAppClass
35:    {
36:        public static void Main(String[] args)
37:        {
38:            AChar aaa = new AChar('g');
39:            AChar bbb = new AChar('g');
40:
41:            Console.WriteLine("Original value: {0}, {1}", aaa.ch, bbb.ch);
42:
43:            aaa = ++aaa;
44:            bbb = --bbb;
45:
46:            Console.WriteLine("Current values: {0}, {1}", aaa.ch, bbb.ch);
47:
48:            aaa = ++aaa;
49:            bbb = --bbb;
50:
51:            Console.WriteLine("Final values: {0}, {1}", aaa.ch, bbb.ch);
52:
53:        }
54:    }
```

OUTPUT
```
Original value: g, g
Current values: h, f
Final values: i, e
```

ANALYSIS This listing is similar to the previous listing. Instead of overloading the - and + operators, this listing overloads the -- and ++ operators. When overloaded, these operators can be used with objects of the given class. You see this in Lines 43, 44, 48, and 49. The other unary operators can be overloaded in the same way.

Overloading the Relational and Logical Operators

The relational operators can also be overloaded. This includes the following operators:

```
<

<=

>

>=
```

This also includes the logical operators:

```
==

!=
```

These differ from the previous operators in how they are declared. Instead of returning a value of the class type, these operators return a Boolean value. This should make sense: The idea of these operators is to compare two values and determine a truth about them.

Listing 14.6 uses a more realistic class to illustrate a couple of the relational operators being overloaded. This class defines a `Salary` value. You will notice that the `==` and the `!=` are not illustrated in this listing; they require a slightly different approach, which is covered in the next section.

LISTING 14.6   over3.cs—Overloading the Relational Operators

```
 1:  // over3.cs - Overloading Relational Operators
 2:  //-----------------------------------------------------
 3:
 4:  using System;
 5:  using System.Text;
 6:
 7:  public class Salary
 8:  {
 9:     private int AMT;
10:
11:     public Salary() { this.amount = 0; }
12:     public Salary(int val) { this.amount = val; }
13:
14:     public int amount
15:     {
16:        get{ return this.AMT; }
17:        set{ this.AMT = value; }
18:     }
19:
20:     static public bool operator < ( Salary first, Salary second )
21:     {
```

14

LISTING 14.6   continued

```
22:        bool retval;
23:
24:        if ( first.amount < second.amount )
25:            retval = true;
26:        else
27:            retval = false;
28:
29:        return retval;
30:    }
31:
32:    static public bool operator <= ( Salary first, Salary second )
33:    {
34:        bool retval;
35:
36:        if ( first.amount <= second.amount )
37:            retval = true;
38:        else
39:            retval = false;
40:
41:        return retval;
42:    }
43:
44:    static public bool operator > ( Salary first, Salary second )
45:    {
46:        bool retval;
47:
48:        if ( first.amount > second.amount )
49:            retval = true;
50:        else
51:            retval = false;
52:
53:        return retval;
54:    }
55:
56:    static public bool operator >= ( Salary first, Salary second )
57:    {
58:        bool retval;
59:
60:        if ( first.amount >= second.amount )
61:            retval = true;
62:        else
63:            retval = false;
64:
65:        return retval;
66:    }
67:
68:    public override string ToString()
69:    {
```

LISTING 14.6   continued

```
70:            return( this.amount.ToString() );
71:        }
72:    }
73:
74: public class myAppClass
75: {
76:     public static void Main(String[] args)
77:     {
78:         Salary mySalary   = new Salary(24000);
79:         Salary yourSalary = new Salary(24000);
80:         Salary PresSalary = new Salary(200000);
81:
82:         Console.WriteLine("Original values: ");
83:         Console.WriteLine("     my salary: {0}", mySalary);
84:         Console.WriteLine("   your salary: {0}", yourSalary);
85:         Console.WriteLine(" a Pres' salary: {0}", PresSalary);
86:         Console.WriteLine("\n-------------------------\n");
87:
88:         if ( mySalary < yourSalary )
89:             Console.WriteLine("My salary less than your salary");
90:         else if ( mySalary > yourSalary )
91:             Console.WriteLine("My salary is greater than your salary");
92:         else
93:             Console.WriteLine("Our Salaries are the same");
94:
95:         if ( mySalary >= PresSalary )
96:             Console.WriteLine("\nI make as much or more than a president.");
97:         else
98:             Console.WriteLine("\nI don't make as much as a president.");
99:     }
100: }
```

OUTPUT

```
Original values:
        my salary: 24000
      your salary: 24000
    a Pres' salary: 200000


-------------------------

Our Salaries are the same

I don't make as much as a president.
```

ANALYSIS   This listing creates a `Salary` class that contains a person's salary. Although this
example doesn't include it, you could also include information such as the last
time the person received a raise, the amount of the raise, and more. Regardless of what
you include, the basic information that you would expect from this class is a person's
salary.

14

For this example, several of the relational operators are overloaded. Each is overloaded in the same manner, so only one needs to be reviewed here. Line 20 overloads the less-than operator (<).

The return type is a Boolean (type `bool`). The result of the method is to return `true` or `false`. The method also receives two `Salary` objects as parameters: the value before and the value after the less-than sign when it is used in code:

```
first < second
```

Using these two values, you can make the determinations that fit for the class. In this case, a check is done in Line 24 to see whether the first `Salary` object's `amount` is less than the second `Salary` object's `amount`. If so, `true` is set for a return value. If not, `false` is set for the return value. Line 29 then returns the value.

In the `myAppClass` class, using the overloaded relational operators is no different than using relational operators with the basic data types. You can easily compare one salary to another, as done in Lines 88, 90, and 95.

Another part of this listing that needs to be covered is not related to operator overloading. In Lines 68–71, the `ToString()` method is overridden by using the `override` keyword. The `ToString` method was inherited automatically from the base class, `Object`. Remember from the days on inheritance that all classes derive from `Object` automatically. As such, all classes contain the functionality of methods that were contained in `Object`. This includes the `ToString` method.

The `ToString` method can be overridden in any class. It should always return a string representation of a class. In the case of a `Salary` class that could contain lots of members, you could return a number of possible items. Returning a string representation of the actual value makes the most sense, however. This is exactly what Line 70 does.

More important, by overloading the `ToString` method (Lines 83–85), you gain the capability to "print" the class. When you display the class as shown in these lines, the `ToString` method is automatically called.

Overloading the Logical Operators

Overloading the equality and inequality logical operators takes more effort than overloading the other relational operators. First, you can't overload just one of these; if you want to overload one, you must overload both. Additionally, if you want to overload these operators, you must also overload two methods, `Equals()` and `GetHashCode()`. Like the `ToString` method, these methods are a part of the base object (`Object`) and are automatically inherited when you create a class. These methods must be overloaded because the logical operators use them behind the scenes.

When comparing two objects of the same class, you should define an Equals method that overrides the base class's Equals method. This method takes the following format:

```
public override bool Equals(object val)
{
   // determine if classes are equal or not
   // return (either true or false)
}
```

This method can be used to see whether one object is equal to another. You can do whatever logic that you want within this method. This might include checking a single value or checking multiple values. For example, are two salaries equal if the amount is equal? If the salary class includes hire dates, would two salaries that are of the same annual amount be equal if the hire dates were different? These are the type of decisions that you must make to code the logic within the Equals method.

The GetHashCode must also be overridden if you want to override the == and != operators. The GetHashCode method returns an integer value used to identify a specific instance of a class. In general, you will not want to make any changes to this method. You can override this method and return the hash code of the current instance by including the following override method:

```
public override int GetHashCode()
{
   return this.ToString().GetHashCode();
}
```

After you have overridden the Equals and GetHashCode methods, you must define the overload methods for == and !=. This is done with the same initial method structure as used with the relational operators. One difference is that you should use the Equals method instead of repeating any comparison code. In Listing 14.7, the != operator basically calls the Equals method and returns the not (!) value of it.

Note

The Equals method actually uses the return values from the GetHashCode method to determine whether two objects are equal.

LISTING 14.7 over4.cs—Overloading Equals and Not Equals

```
1:  // over4.cs - Overloading
2:  //---------------------------------------------------
3:
4:  using System;
5:  using System.Text;
6:
```

14

LISTING 14.7   continued

```
 7:  public class Salary
 8:  {
 9:     private int AMT;
10:
11:     public Salary() { this.amount = 0; }
12:     public Salary(int val) { this.amount = val; }
13:
14:     public int amount
15:     {
16:        get{ return this.AMT; }
17:        set{ this.AMT = value; }
18:     }
19:
20:     public override bool Equals(object val)
21:     {
22:        bool retval;
23:
24:        if( ((Salary)val).amount == this.amount )
25:           retval = true;
26:        else
27:           retval = false;
28:
29:        return retval;
30:     }
31:
32:     public override int GetHashCode()
33:     {
34:        return this.ToString().GetHashCode();
35:     }
36:
37:     static public bool operator == ( Salary first, Salary second )
38:     {
39:        bool retval;
40:
41:        retval = first.Equals(second);
42:
43:        return retval;
44:     }
45:     static public bool operator != ( Salary first, Salary second )
46:     {
47:        bool retval;
48:
49:        retval = !(first.Equals(second));
50:
51:        return retval;
52:     }
53:
54:     public override string ToString()
55:     {
```

LISTING **14.7** continued

```
56:            return( this.amount.ToString() );
57:        }
58:
59:  }
60:
61:  public class myAppClass
62:  {
63:      public static void Main(String[] args)
64:      {
65:          string tmpstring;
66:
67:          Salary mySalary   = new Salary(24000);
68:          Salary yourSalary = new Salary(24000);
69:          Salary PresSalary = new Salary(200000);
70:
71:          Console.WriteLine("Original values: {0}, {1}, {2}",
72:              mySalary, yourSalary, PresSalary);
73:
74:          if (mySalary == yourSalary)
75:              tmpstring = "equals";
76:          else
77:              tmpstring = "does not equal";
78:
79:          Console.WriteLine("\nMy salary {0} your salary", tmpstring);
80:
81:          if (mySalary == PresSalary)
82:              tmpstring = "equals";
83:          else
84:              tmpstring = "does not equal";
85:
86:          Console.WriteLine("\nMy salary {0} a president\'s salary",
87:                                                  tmpstring);
88:      }
89:  }
```

OUTPUT

```
Original values: 24000, 24000, 200000

My salary equals your salary

My salary does not equal a president's salary
```

ANALYSIS Most of the code in this listing was analyzed before the listing. You'll find the overloaded Equals method in Lines 20–30. The overloaded GetHashCode method is in Lines 32–35. For fun, you can remove one of these two methods and try to compile the listing; you will see that your listing will generate errors without them.

14

Line 27 starts the method for overloading the == operator. Earlier, I stated that you should use the Equals method for comparing classes. This is exactly what the overloaded == method is doing: It calls the Equals method and returns the value from it. The != method does the same thing in Lines 45–52, except that the value is changed by using the ! operator.

In the Main method of the myAppClass class, using the == and != operators is as easy as using the other overloaded operators. If you compare two classes, you'll receive a response of true or false.

 Caution

When overloading the logical operators, == and !=, you must always overload both. You can't overload just one.

Summarizing the Operators to Overload

A number of operators can be overloaded. To repeat an earlier point, you should overload operators only when the resulting functionality will be clear to a person using the class. If in doubt, you should use regular methods instead. The operators that are available to overload are presented in Table 14.1. The operators that cannot be overloaded are presented in Table 14.2.

TABLE 14.1   Operators That Can Be Overloaded

```
+   -   ++   --   !   ~   true   false

+   -   *   /   %   &   |   ^   <<   >>

<   <=   >   >=   ==   !=
```

TABLE 14.2   Operators That Cannot Be Overloaded

```
=   .   ?:   &&   ||   new   is

sizeof   typeof   checked   unchecked
```

You also cannot overload parentheses or any of the compound operators (+=, -=, and so forth). The compound operators use the binary overloaded operators.

The only operators that are left are the brackets, []. As you learned earlier in the book, these are overloaded by using indexers.

Summary

Today's lessons covered another OOP topic: overloading operators. Although many people believe that operator overloading is complex, as you saw today, it can be quite simple. You learned to overload the unary, binary, relational, and logical operators. The final section of today's lessons presented two tables containing the operators that can and can't be overloaded.

With today's lessons, you have learned nearly all the basics of C#. This includes having learned nearly all the basic constructs of the language, as well as their use. Over the next several days, you will learn about classes that have been created as part of the .NET Framework. These are classes that you can use in your C# applications. You'll come back to a number of additional advanced C# language topics. Although you have all the building blocks needed to create complex C# applications, there are a few additional advanced topics worth being exposed to. These are covered on Day 21, "A Day for Reflection and Attributes."

Q&A

Q Which is better, using methods such as Add() or overloading operators?

A Either works. Many people expect operators to be overloaded when working with advanced languages such as C++ and C#. As long as it is clear what should be expected when two classes are added or manipulated with an operator, you should consider overloading the operator. In the end, it can actually make your code easier to follow and understand.

Q Why can't compound operators such as += be overloaded?

A This was actually answered in today's lesson. The compound operators are always broken out into:

xxx = xxx *op* yyy

So,

x += 3

is broken out to

x = x + 3

This means the overloaded binary operator can be used. If you overload the addition operator (+), you essentially also overload the compound addition operator (+=).

14

Q I want a different method for postfix and prefix versions of the decrement and increment operators. What do I do?

A Sorry—C# doesn't support this. You get to define only a single overloaded method for the increment and decrement operators.

Workshop

The Workshop provides quiz questions to help you solidify your understanding of the material covered and exercises to provide you with experience in using what you've learned. Try to understand the quiz and exercise answers before continuing to tomorrow's lesson. Answers are provided on the CD.

Quiz

1. How many times can a single operator be overloaded in a single class?

2. What determines how many times an operator can be overloaded?

3. What method or methods must be overloaded to overload the equality operator (==)?

4. Which of the following are good examples of using overloaded operators?

   a. Overloading the plus operator (+) to concatenate two string objects.

   b. Overloading the minus operator (-) to determine the distance between two MapLocation objects.

   c. Overloading the plus operator (+) to increment an amount once, and incrementing the ++ operator to increment the amount twice.

5. How do you overload the /= operator?

6. How do you overload the [] operator?

7. What relational operators can be overloaded?

8. What unary operators can be overloaded?

9. What binary operators can be overloaded?

10. What operators cannot be overloaded?

11. What modifiers are always used with overloaded operators?

Exercises

1. What would the method header be for the overloaded addition operator used to add two type XYZ objects?

2. Modify Listing 14.3. Add an additional subtraction overloaded method that takes two AChar values. The result should be the numerical difference between the character values stored in the two AChar objects.

3. **Bug Buster:** Does the following code snippet have a problem? If so, what is the problem? If not, what does this snippet do?

```
static public int operator >= ( Salary first, Salary second )
{
    int retval;

    if ( first.amount <= second.amount )
        retval = 1;
    else
        retval = 0;

    return retval;
}
```

4. Modify Listing 14.7 to include a method that will compare a salary to an integer value. Also add a method to compare a salary to a long value.

14

WEEK 2

Week in Review

You've succeeded in making it through the second week of learning C#! At this point, you have learned most of the key foundational topics in C#.

The following listing pulls together many of these concepts into a program that is a little more functional than the examples in the lessons. This program is longer, but as you will see, it is a little more fun.

This listing presents a limited blackjack, or "21," card game. This program displays the cards in your hand and the first card in the computer dealer's hand. The idea of blackjack is to accumulate cards totaling as close to 21 as you can without going over. Face cards (jacks, queens, and kings) are worth 10 points, and the other cards are worth their basic value. An ace can be worth 1 point or 11 points—you decide.

The computer dealer must have a total of at least 17. If the computer's hand is less than 17, the dealer must draw another card. If the dealer goes over 21, it busts. If you go over 21, you bust and the computer automatically wins.

LISTING WR2.1   CardGame.cs—The Game of Blackjack

```
 1:  //  CardGame.cs -
 2:  //      Blackjack
 3:  //------------------------------------------------
     --------------------
 4:
 5:  using System;
 6:
 7:  public enum CardSuit
 8:  {
 9:      Zero_Error,
```

CH 7

CH 7

LISTING WR2.1   continued

```
CH 7   10:        clubs,
CH 7   11:        diamonds,
CH 7   12:        hearts,
CH 7   13:        spades
       14:    }
       15:
CH 7   16:    public enum CardValue
       17:    {
       18:        Zero_Error,
       19:        Ace,
       20:        two,
       21:        three,
       22:        four,
       23:        five,
       24:        six,
       25:        seven,
       26:        eight,
       27:        nine,
       28:        ten,
       29:        Jack,
       30:        Queen,
       31:        King
       32:    }
       33:
       34:    // Structure: Card
       35:    //===============================================
CH 7   36:    struct Card
       37:    {
CH 7   38:        public CardSuit suit;  // 1 - 4
CH 7   39:        public CardValue val;  // 1 - 13
       40:
       41:        public int CardValue
       42:        {
       43:          get
       44:          {
       45:            int retval;
       46:
       47:            if( (int) this.val >= 10)
       48:                retval = 10;
       49:            else
       50:            if( (int) this.val == 1 )
       51:                retval = 11;
       52:            else
       53:                retval = (int) this.val;
       54:
       55:            return retval;
       56:          }
       57:        }
       58:
```

```
Сн 10     59:     public override string ToString()
          60:     {
Сн 11     61:         return (string.Format("{0} of {1}", this.val.ToString("G"),
Сн 11     62:                                          this.suit.ToString("G")));
          63:     }
          64: }
          65:
          66: // Class: Deck
          67: //==============================================
          68: class Deck
          69: {
Сн 7      70:     public Card [] Cards = new Card[53] ;
          71:     int next;
          72:
          73:     // Deck()
          74:     //   Constructor for setting up a regular deck
          75:     //==============================================
          76:     public Deck()
          77:     {
          78:         next = 1;   // initialize pointer to point to first card.
          79:
          80:         // Initialize the cards in the deck
Сн 7      81:         Cards[0].val = 0;   // card 0 is set to 0.
Сн 7      82:         Cards[0].suit = 0;
          83:
Сн 8      84:         int currcard = 0;
Сн 8      85:         for( int suitctr = 1; suitctr < 5; suitctr++ )
          86:         {
Сн 8      87:             for( int valctr = 1; valctr < 14; valctr++ )
          88:             {
          89:                 currcard = (valctr) + ((suitctr - 1) * 13);
          90:                 cards[currcard].val = (CardValue) valctr;
          91:                 cards[currcard].suit  = (CardSuit) suitctr;
          92:             }
          93:         }
          94:     }
          95:
          96:     // shuffle()
          97:     //   Randomizes a deck's cards
          98:     //===============================================
          99:     public void shuffle()
         100:     {
         101:         Random rnd = new Random();
         102:         int sort1;
         103:         int sort2;
         104:         Card tmpcard = new Card();
         105:
Сн 8     106:         for( int ctr = 0; ctr < 100; ctr++)
         107:         {
```

```
108:              sort1 = (int) ((rnd.NextDouble() * 52) + 1);
109:              sort2 = (int) ((rnd.NextDouble() * 52) + 1);
110:
111:              tmpcard = this.Cards[sort1];
112:              this.Cards[sort1] = this.Cards[sort2];
113:              this.Cards[sort2] = tmpcard;
114:           }
115:
116:        this.next = 1;  // reset pointer to first card
117:      }
118:
119:      // dealCard()
120:      //    Returns next card in deck
121:      //=============================================
122:      public card dealCard()
123:      {
124:         if( next > 52 )
125:         {
126:            // At end of deck
127:            return (this.Cards[0]);
128:         }
129:         else
130:         {
131:            // Returns current card and increments next
132:            return this.Cards[next++];
133:         }
134:      }
135: }
136:
137: // Class: CardGame
138: //=============================================
139:
140: class CardGame
141: {
142:    static Deck mydeck = new Deck();
143:    static Card [] pHand = new Card[10];
144:    static Card [] cHand = new Card[10];
145:
146:    public static void Main()
147:    {
148:       int pCardCtr = 0;
149:       int pTotal = 0;
150:       int cTotal = 0;
151:
152:       bool playing = true;
153:
154:       while ( playing == true )
155:       {
```

Cн 7 (line 111)
Cн 7 (line 112)
Cн 7 (line 113)

Cн 7 (line 132)

Cн 7 (line 143)
Cн 7 (line 144)

LISTING WR2.1   continued

```
156:            //CLEAR HANDS
157:            pTotal = 0;
158:            cTotal = 0;
159:            pCardCtr = 0;
160:
161:            for ( int ctr = 0; ctr < 10; ctr++)
162:            {
163:                pHand[ctr].val = 0;
164:                pHand[ctr].suit = 0;
165:            }
166:
167:            Console.WriteLine("\nShuffling cards...");
168:            mydeck.shuffle();
169:
170:            Console.WriteLine("Dealing cards...");
171:
172:            pHand[0] = mydeck.dealCard();
173:            cHand[0] = mydeck.dealCard();
174:            pHand[1] = mydeck.dealCard();
175:            cHand[1] = mydeck.dealCard();
176:
177:            // Set computer total equal to its first card...
178:            cTotal = cHand[0].CardValue;
179:
180:            bool playersTurn = true;
181:
182:            do
183:            {
184:                Console.WriteLine("\nPlayer\'s Hand:");
185:                pCardCtr = 0;
186:                pTotal = 0;
187:
188:                do
189:                {
190:                    Console.WriteLine("  Card {0}:  {1}",
191:                            pCardCtr + 1,
192:                            pHand[pCardCtr].ToString());
193:
194:                    // Add card value to player total
195:                    pTotal += pHand[pCardCtr].CardValue;
196:
197:                    pCardCtr++;
198:
199:                } while ((int) pHand[pCardCtr].val != 0);
200:
201:                Console.WriteLine("Dealer\'s Hand:");
202:
203:                Console.WriteLine("  Card 1:  {0}",
```

CH 8 (line 161)
CH 7 (line 163)
CH 7 (line 164)
CH 7 (line 172)
CH 7 (line 178)
CH 8 (line 180)
CH 11 (line 190)
CH 11 (line 203)

LISTING WR2.1   continued

```
204:                                    cHand[0].ToString());
205:
206:
207:             Console.WriteLine("----------------------------");
208:             Console.WriteLine("Player Total = {0} \nDealer Total = {1}",
209:                                 pTotal, cTotal);
210:
211:
212:             if( pTotal <= 21 )
213:             {
214:                 playersTurn = GetPlayerOption(pCardCtr);
215:             }
216:             else
217:             {
218:                 playersTurn = false;
219:             }
220:
221:         } while(playersTurn == true);
222:
223:         // Player's turn is done
224:
225:         if ( pTotal > 21 )
226:         {
227:             Console.WriteLine("\n\n**** BUSTED ****\n");
228:         }
229:         else // Determine computer's score
230:         {
231:             // Tally Computer's current total...
232:             cTotal += cHand[1].CardValue;
233:
234:             int cCardCtr = 2;
235:
236:             Console.WriteLine("\n\nPlayer\'s Total:  {0}", pTotal);
237:             Console.WriteLine("\nComputer: ");
238:             Console.WriteLine("  {0}", cHand[0].ToString());
239:             Console.WriteLine("  {0} TOTAL: {1}",
240:                                 cHand[1].ToString(),
241:                                 cTotal);
242:
243:             while ( cTotal < 17 )   // Less than 17, must draw
244:             {
245:                 cHand[cCardCtr] = mydeck.dealCard();
246:                 cTotal += cHand[cCardCtr].CardValue;
247:                 Console.WriteLine("  {0} TOTAL: {1}",
248:                                     cHand[cCardCtr].ToString(),
249:                                     cTotal);
250:                 cCardCtr++;
251:             }
252:
```

Margin labels:
- CH 11 (line 208)
- CH 7 (line 232)
- CH 8 (line 234)
- CH 11 (line 238)
- CH 11 (line 239)
- CH 7 (line 240)
- CH 7 (line 246)
- CH 11 (line 247)

LISTING **WR2.1** continued

```
253:                    if (cTotal > 21 )
254:                    {
255:                        Console.WriteLine("\n\nComputer Busted!");
256:                        Console.WriteLine("YOU WON!!!");
257:                    }
258:                    else
259:                    {
260:                        if( pTotal > cTotal)
261:                        {
262:                            Console.WriteLine("\n\nYOU WON!!!");
263:                        }
264:                        else
265:                        if( pTotal == cTotal )
266:                        {
267:                            Console.WriteLine("\n\nIt\'s a push");
268:                        }
269:                        else
270:                        {
271:                            Console.WriteLine("\n\nSorry, The Computer won");
272:                        }
273:                    }
274:                }
275:
276:                Console.Write("\n\nDo you want to play again?  ");
277:                string answer = Console.ReadLine();
278:
279:                try
280:                {
281:                    if( answer[0] != 'y' && answer[0] != 'Y' )
282:                    {
283:                        //Quitting
284:                        playing = false;
285:                    }
286:                }
287:                catch( System.IndexOutOfRangeException )
288:                {
289:                    // Didn't enter a value so quit
290:                    playing = false;
291:                }
292:            }
293:        }
294:
295:        // GetPlayerOption()
296:        //    Returns true to hit, false to stay
297:        //==============================================
298:
299:        static bool GetPlayerOption( int cardctr )
300:        {
301:            string buffer;
```

Ch 8 (line 277)
Ch 9 (line 279)
Ch 7 (line 281)
Ch 9 (line 287)

```
302:        bool cont = true;
303:        bool retval = true;
304:
305:        while(cont == true)
306:        {
307:           Console.Write("\n\nH = Hit, S = Stay ");
308:           buffer = Console.ReadLine();
309:
310:           try
311:           {
312:              if ( buffer[0] == 'h' || buffer[0] == 'H')
313:              {
314:                 pHand[cardctr] = mydeck.dealCard();
315:                 cont = false;
316:              }
317:              else if( buffer[0] == 's' || buffer[0] == 'S' )
318:              {
319:                 // Turn is over, return false...
320:                 retval = false;
321:                 cont = false;
322:              }
323:              else
324:              {
325:                 Console.WriteLine("\n*** Please enter an H or S and press
                     ⇒ENTER...");
326:              }
327:           }
328:           catch( System.IndexOutOfRangeException )
329:           {
330:              // Didn't enter a value, so ask again
331:              cont = true;
332:           }
333:        }
334:        return retval;
335:     }
336: }
337: //------------- END OF LISTING -------------//
```

CH 9 (line 310)
CH 7 (line 312)
CH 7 (line 317)
CH 9 (line 328)

OUTPUT

```
Shuffling cards...
Dealing cards...

Player's Hand:
  Card 1:  four of clubs
  Card 2:  six of hearts
Dealer's Hand:
  Card 1:  Jack of hearts
---------------------------
Player Total = 10
Dealer Total = 10
```

```
H = Hit, S = Stay h

Player's Hand:
  Card 1:  four of clubs
  Card 2:  six of hearts
  Card 3:  King of diamonds
Dealer's Hand:
  Card 1:  Jack of hearts
---------------------------
Player Total = 20
Dealer Total = 10


H = Hit, S = Stay s


Player's Total:  20

Computer:
  Jack of hearts
  seven of diamonds TOTAL: 17


YOU WON!!!


Do you want to play again?


Shuffling cards...
Dealing cards...

Player's Hand:
  Card 1:  three of clubs
  Card 2:  Jack of spades
Dealer's Hand:
  Card 1:  seven of clubs
---------------------------
Player Total = 13
Dealer Total = 7


H = Hit, S = Stay h

Player's Hand:
  Card 1:  three of clubs
  Card 2:  Jack of spades
  Card 3:  five of hearts
Dealer's Hand:
```

```
        Card 1:  seven of clubs
        · · · · · · · · · · · · · · · · · · · · · · · · · ·
        Player Total = 18
        Dealer Total = 7


        H = Hit, S = Stay s


        Player's Total:  18

        Computer:
           seven of clubs
           two of diamonds TOTAL: 9
           three of diamonds TOTAL: 12
           five of clubs TOTAL: 17


        YOU WON!!!


        Do you want to play again?
```

ANALYSIS   This output chooses cards from a standard 52-card deck that has been randomly
shuffled, so your output will be different. This program is not a perfect blackjack
game. For example, this game does not indicate whether you actually get a blackjack (21
with two cards). This game also does not keep track of history—how many wins you
have had versus the computer. These are enhancements that you can feel free to add.

This listing uses a number of the concepts you have learned throughout the previous 14
days. The following sections analyze some of the parts of this listing.

Enumerations for the Cards

This review makes use of a lot of information from Day 7, "Storing More Complex
Stuff: Structures, Enumerators, and Arrays." As such, these references were left on the
listing as well. From that day, this program uses enumerations to make it easier to work
with individual cards. Two enumerations are used. First, an enumeration is used in
Lines 7–14 to hold the different values for suits. To make it easier numerically to work
with the cards, the first position is set as an error. Each of the suits, starting with clubs, is
assigned a value from 1 to 4. You could have left out Line 9 and made these same numerical assignments by changing Line 10 to the following:

```
clubs = 1,
```

I chose to include the 0 position to use as an error value, if needed, in card games that I can create with this structure.

The second enumeration is for card values. The CardValue enumeration is defined in Lines 16–32. This enables each card to be represented. Notice that again I skipped 0 and provided a placeholder. This was so that an ace would be equal to 1, a 2 would be equal to 2, and so on. Again, I could have obtained this numbering by assigning 1 to the ace, as the following shows, and by removing Line 18:

```
Ace = 1,
```

A Card Type

The Card type is defined in Lines 36–64, as a structure instead of a class. You could just as easily declare a card as a class; however, because of its small size, it is more efficient to use a structure.

The Card structure has just a few members. In Lines 38–39, a member variable is created to store a CardSuit and a CardValue. These are variables based on the enumerators you just created. Additionally, the Card type contains a property that enables you to get the value of a card. This is based on each face card being valued at 10 (Lines 47–48), an ace at 11 (Lines 50–51), and any other card at its standard value (Lines 52–53).

The final member of the Card structure is the ToString method. As you learned in the previous week, all classes derive from the base class Object. The Object class includes a number of existing methods that your classes can use. One of those methods is ToString. You also learned on Day 10, "Reusing Existing Code with Inheritance," that you can override an existing method with your own functionality by using the override keyword. Lines 59–63 override the ToString method.

The overriding prints the value of an individual card in a more readable manner, using a formatting string of "G". This string prints the textual value of an enumeration. You learned about using formatting strings with enumerations and other data types on Day 11, "Formatting and Retrieving Information."

A Deck Class

Having a card is great, but to play a game, you need a deck of cards. A class is used to define a deck of cards. If you were asked what type should be used to hold a deck of cards, you might be tempted to answer an array. Although you could create an array of cards—and the Deck class actually does—a deck needs to do more than just hold card information.

A class is more appropriate for a deck of cards because, in addition to holding the cards, you will also want to create a couple of methods to work with the cards in the deck. The Deck class in this listing includes methods to shuffle the deck as well as to deal a card. The class also keeps track of the current card position and more.

The Deck class includes an array of cards in Line 70. The individual card structures in this array are initialized in the constructor of the deck (Lines 76–94). This initialization is done by looping through the suits and through the card values. In Lines 90–91, the actual assignments take place. The numeric values are cast to the CardValue or CardSuit types and are placed into the card structure within the deck's card array.

The location in the array where CardValue and CardSuit are being placed is tracked using currcard. The calculation in Line 89 might seem strange; however, this is used to create a number from 1 to 52. If you follow this line's logic, you will see that with each increment of the loops, the value calculated into currcard increments one higher.

The Deck class also contains a method for shuffling the cards in Lines 99–118. This method determines two random numbers from 1 to 52 in Lines 108–109. These cards in the card array, in these two locations, are then switched in Lines 111–113. The number of times that this is done is determined by the for loop started in Line 106. In this case, there will be 100 switches, which is more than enough to randomize the deck.

The Card Game

The main application portion of this program is called CardGame. As stated earlier, this is a simplified version of 21. You could create a number of other card games that use the Deck class and its methods. You could even create a program that uses multiple decks.

This listing has a number of comments and display commands to help you understand the code. I'll highlight only a few points within the game itself. In Lines 143–144, a player and a computer hand are both created. The hands are declared to hold as many as 10 cards; it is rare to have a hand with 5 cards. The chance of needing 10 cards is so low that this should be sufficient.

Most of the code in the card game is straightforward. In Lines 279–291, exception handling has been added. In Line 279, a try statement encloses a check to see whether an answer array's first character is a y or a Y. If it is one of these values, the player wants to play again. If it isn't, it is assumed that the player doesn't want to continue. What happens, however, if the user presses Enter without entering any value? If this happens, the answers array will not have a value in the first position, and an exception will be thrown when you try to access the first character. This exception is an `IndexOutOfRangeException`, which is caught with the `catch` in Line 287. Similar logic is used to determine whether the player wants to hit or stay in Lines 310–332.

Looking at the Entire Deck

You can take a quick look at all the cards in the deck by cycling through it. The listing currently does not do this; however, you can with just a few lines of code:

```
Deck aDeck = new Deck();
Card aHand;

for( int ctr = 1; ctr < 53; ctr++)
{
   aHand = aDeck.dealCard();
   Console.WriteLine(aHand.ToString());
}
```

This declares a new deck named `aDeck`. A temporary card named `aCard` is also declared. This holds a card that is dealt from the deck, `aDeck`. A `for` loop then loops through the deck, dealing a card to the temporary card, and the card is displayed on the screen. This code prints the cards in the deck whether they have been shuffled or not.

Summary

This listing uses only some of the complex topics learned in the last few days. You can do a lot with the basic constructs of the C# language. You'll also find that parts of this code can be reused. This includes the `Card` and `Deck` classes, which you can use to create other card games. Additionally, when you combine this listing with what you'll learn next week, you'll be able to create a graphical interface that makes playing the card game much more fun and easier to follow.

Although this listing is not perfect, it does accomplish quite a bit in a few lines of code. You'll find that in your coding, you will want to include lots of comments, including XML documentation comments. You will also want to include more exception handling than this listing has.

WEEK 3

15

16

17

18

19

20

21

At a Glance

You have now completed two weeks and have only one remaining. You learned a lot of details about C# in Week 2. Week 3 moves away from the basics of the C# language and focuses on some of the pre-existing code that is available for you to use. This is followed by quickly hitting on a number of advanced topics.

More specifically, on the first day of your third week, you will jump into the Base Class Libraries (BCL). These are a set of pre-existing classes and types that you can use within your program. On Day 15, "Using Existing Routines from the .NET Base Classes," you will work with your computer's directories, work with math routines, and do basic file manipulation. You will do all of this with the help of the BCL.

On Days 16, "Creating Windows Forms," and 17, "Creating Windows Applications," you will have fun learning about forms-based programming. You will learn how to create and customize a basic form and how to add some of the basic controls and functionality to your form. This includes adding menus and dialog boxes. These two days are not intended to be all-inclusive; covering just Windows-based form programming could take a book larger than this one. These two days will give you the foundation to apply your C# knowledge to Windows-based form programming.

Day 18, "Working with Databases: ADO.NET," gives you the insights into one of the most important development topics: databases. You will learn to retrieve and store information in a database, as well as how to access that data from a database.

On Days 19 and 20, you learn about Web-based programming. On Day 19, "Creating Remote Procedures (Web Services)," you create and use a Web Service. On Day 20, "Creating Web Applications," you follow up the discussion of Windows-based form programming with an overview of what you can do with C# regarding Web-based forms and applications. These two days assume that you have some Web experience. If you don't, you might find this day's lesson tough to digest. Don't fret, though. Entire books have been written on the topics presented on this day.

The book ends with Day 21, "A Day for Reflection and Attributes." By the time you reach this day, you will have a basic understanding of most of the key topics within C#, as well as an overview of many of the key topics related to C# development. This final day's lesson presents a few advanced-level C# topics for your basic understanding, including attributes and versioning. By the time you finish reviewing Day 21, you will find that you are well equipped to build C# applications.

A Caution on Week 3

Everything in Week 3 is supported by the Microsoft Visual C# .NET compiler and by Microsoft Visual Studio .NET. At the time this book was written, there were plans to support all of the features in Week 3 on other platforms as well; however, the base class libraries and other parts of the .NET Framework had yet to be implemented. As such, if you are not using Microsoft's .NET Framework and runtime, you will need to verify that you have support for these libraries of classes.

DAY 15

Using Existing Routines from the .NET Base Classes

On the previous 14 days, you learned how to create your own types, including classes, interfaces, enumerators, and more. During this time, you used a number of classes and types that were a part of the C# class libraries. This week starts by focusing on these existing base classes. Today you…

- Learn about the Base Class Library.
- Review namespaces and their organization.
- Discover many of the standardized types by working with the following:
  - Timers
  - Directory information
  - The system environment
  - Math routines
  - Files and data
  - Much more

Today and over the several days, you will dig into a number of classes and other types that have already been written by Microsoft and provided within a set of libraries. Today's lesson presents a variety of pre-existing classes and other types that you will find interesting. During the next several days, the focus tightens to cover specific topics such as Windows programming, Web development (including coverage of creating Web forms and Web services), and database development.

Classes in the .NET Framework

The .NET Framework contains a number of classes, enumerators, structures, interfaces, and other data types. In fact, there are thousands of them. These classes are available for you to use in your C# programs.

You'll learn about several of these types today. Today you will see several small example listings that show how to use a number of different classes. You'll be able to easily expand on these examples within your own programs.

The Common Language Specification

The classes within the framework have been written with the Common Language Specification (CLS) in mind. The CLS was mentioned at the beginning of this book when discussing the C# runtime.

The CLS is a set of rules that all languages that run on the .NET platform must follow. This set of rules also includes the Common Type System (CTS) that you learned about when you were working with the basic data types on Day 2, "Understanding C# Programs." By adhering to this set of rules, the common runtime can execute a program regardless of the language syntax used.

The advantage of following the CLS is that code written in one language can be called using another language. Because the routines within the framework follow the CLS, they can be used not only by C#, but also by any other CLS-compliant language, such as Visual Basic .NET and JScript .NET.

Note

> More than 20 languages can use the code within the .NET Framework. The way each language calls a piece of code in the framework may be slightly different; however, the code performs the same functionality.

Namespace Organization of Types

The code within the framework is organized within namespaces. Hundreds of namespaces within the framework are used to organize the thousands of classes and other types.

Some of the namespaces are stored within other namespaces. For example, you have used the DateTime type, which is located in the System namespace. You have also used the Random type, also located in the System namespace. Many of the input and output types are stored in a namespace called IO that is within the System namespace. Many of the routines for working with XML data are within the System.XML namespace. You can check the online documents for a complete list of all the namespaces within the framework.

Using the ECMA Standards

Not all of the types within namespaces are necessarily compatible with all other languages. Additionally, development tools created by other companies for doing C# might not include equivalent code routines.

When C# was developed, Microsoft submitted a large number of classes to the same standards board that was given C# to standardize. This opened the door for other developers to create tools and compilers for C# that use the same namespaces and types. This makes the code created within Microsoft's tools compatible with any other company's tools.

 Note

Submitting the C# language and the Base Class Library to the standards boards means that other people and companies have the ability to create tools for C#—including compilers and runtimes. When this book was written, there were C# compilers that worked on a number of platforms. This includes the Mac OS, FreeBSD, Linux, and more. Additionally, projects are in place to convert the complete System namespace and even a few others to platforms such as Linux. Most of these ports use the ECMA standard and the classes that Microsoft created as the guideline for the new classes. This means that C# programs written for Microsoft Windows should be compatible with other operating systems.

The classes that were standardized are located within the System namespace. Other namespaces include classes that have not been standardized. If a class is not part of the standard, it might not be supported on all operating systems and runtimes that are written to support C#. For example, Microsoft includes several namespaces with its SDK, including

`Microsoft.VisualBasic`, `Microsoft.CSharp`, `Microsoft.JScript`, and `Microsoft.Win32`. These namespaces were not a part of the ECMA standard submission, so they might not be available in all development environments.

> **Note**
>
> Information on ECMA and the C# standard can be found at `Msdn.Microsoft.com/net/ecma`.

> **Note**
>
> In addition to being standardized by ECMA, much of the .NET functionality is being standardized by the ISO.

Checking Out the Framework Classes

Thousands of classes and other types exist within the Base Class Libraries. It would fill several books this size to effectively cover all of them. Before you start writing your own programs, take the time to review the online documentation to check whether similar functionality already exists. All the classes and other types covered in today's lessons are a part of the standards that were submitted to ECMA.

> **Note**
>
> Not only can you directly use the types within the class libraries, but you also can extend many of them.

> **Note**
>
> A set of books has been created by Microsoft press documenting most of the .NET Framework's `System` class. This is approximately seven books that average roughly 2,000 pages each. That is a lot of pages!

Working with a Timer

Listing 15.1 presents a neat little program that is not well designed. It is simple, and nothing new is presented in it.

LISTING 15.1   Timer.cs—Displaying the Time

```
 1:  //  Timer.cs - Displaying Date and Time
 2:  //      Not a great way to do the time.
 3:  //      Press Ctrl+C to end program.
 4:  //-----------------------------------------
 5:  using System;
 6:
 7:  class Timer
 8:  {
 9:     public static void Main()
10:     {
11:        while (true)
12:        {
13:           Console.Write("\r{0}", DateTime.Now);
14:        }
15:     }
16:  }
```

15

OUTPUT   2/22/2003 9:34:19 PM

ANALYSIS   As you can see, this listing was executed at 9:34 on February 22. This listing presents a clock on the command line, which seems to update the time every second. Actually, it updates much more often than that; however, you notice the changes every second only when the value being displayed actually changes. This program runs until you break out of it by using Ctrl+C.

The focus of today's lesson is on using classes and types from the Base Class Libraries. In Line 13, a call to DateTime is made. DateTime is a structure available from the System namespace within the base class libraries. This structure has a static property named Now that returns the current time. Many additional data members and methods exist within the DateTime structure. You can check out the .NET Framework class library documentation for information on these.

NEW TERM   A better way to present a date on the screen is to use a timer. A *timer* enables a process—in the form of a delegate—to be called at a specific time or after a specific period of time has passed. The framework includes a class for timers within the System.Timers namespace. This class is appropriately called Timer. Listing 15.2 is a rewrite of Listing 15.1 using a timer.

LISTING 15.2 NetTimer.cs—Using a Timer with the `DateTime`

```
 1:  // NetTimer.cs - Displaying Date and Time
 2:  //       Using the Timer class.
 3:  //       Press Ctrl+C  or 'q' followed by Enter to end program.
 4:  //------------------------------------------------------------
 5:  using System;
 6:  using System.Timers;
 7:
 8:  class NetTimer
 9:  {
10:     public static void Main()
11:     {
12:        Timer myTimer = new Timer();
13:        myTimer.Elapsed += new ElapsedEventHandler( DisplayTimeEvent );
14:        myTimer.Interval = 1000;
15:        myTimer.Start();
16:
17:        while ( Console.Read() != 'q' )
18:        {
19:           ;    // do nothing...
20:        }
21:     }
22:
23:     public static void DisplayTimeEvent( object source, ElapsedEventArgs e )
24:     {
25:        Console.Write("\r{0}", DateTime.Now);
26:     }
27:  }
```

OUTPUT 2/22/2003 10:04:13 PM

ANALYSIS As you can see, this listing's output is like that of the previous listing. However, this listing operates much better. Instead of constantly updating the date and time being displayed, this listing updates it only every 1,000 ticks, which is equal to 1 second.

Looking closer at this listing, you can see how a timer works. In Line 12, a new `Timer` object is created. In Line 14, the interval to be used is set. In Line 13, the method to be executed after the interval is associated to the timer. In this case, `DisplayTimeEvent` will be executed. This method is defined in Lines 23–26.

In Line 15, the `start` method is called, which starts the interval. Another member for the `Timer` class is the `AutoReset` member. If you change the default value from `true` to `false`, the `Timer` event happens only once. If the `AutoReset` is left at its default value of `true` or is set to `true`, the timer fires an event and thus executes the method every time the given interval passes.

Lines 17–20 contain a loop that continues to operate until the reader enters the letter q and presses Enter. Then the end of the routine is reached and the program ends; otherwise, the program continues to spin in this loop. Nothing is done in this loop in this program. You can do other processing in this loop if you want. There is no need to call the DisplayTimeEvent in this loop because it automatically is called at the appropriate interval.

This timer is used to display the time on the screen. Timers and timer events also can be used for numerous other programs. You could create a timer that fires off a program at a given time. You could create a backup routine that copies important data at a given interval. You could also create a routine to automatically log off a user or end a program after a given time period with no activity. Timers can be used in numerous ways.

 Note   Listing 15.2 uses events with slightly different names than what you saw on Day 13, "Making Your Programs React with Delegates, Events, and Indexers." These slightly different names are customized versions of the routines you learned about on Day 13.

Getting Directory and System Environment Information

A plethora of information is available to your programs about the computer running a program. How you choose to use this information is up to you. Listing 15.3 shows information about a computer and its environment. This is done using the Environment class, which has a number of static data members that you will find interesting.

LISTING 15.3   EnvApp.cs—Using the Environment Class

```
 1:  //  EnvApp.cs - Displaying information with the
 2:  //             Environment class
 3:  //-----------------------------------------------
 4:  using System;
 5:
 6:  class EnvApp
 7:  {
 8:     public static void Main()
 9:     {
10:        // Some Properties...
11:        Console.WriteLine("=================================");
12:        Console.WriteLine(" Command: {0}", Environment.CommandLine);
13:        Console.WriteLine("Curr Dir: {0}", Environment.CurrentDirectory);
14:        Console.WriteLine(" Sys Dir: {0}", Environment.SystemDirectory);
```

LISTING 15.3   continued

```
15:        Console.WriteLine(" Version: {0}", Environment.Version);
16:        Console.WriteLine(" OS Vers: {0}", Environment.OSVersion);
17:        Console.WriteLine(" Machine: {0}", Environment.MachineName);
18:        Console.WriteLine("  Memory: {0}", Environment.WorkingSet);
19:
20:    // Some methods...
21:        Console.WriteLine("=================================");
22:        string [] args = Environment.GetCommandLineArgs();
23:        for ( int x = 0; x < args.Length; x++ )
24:        {
25:            Console.WriteLine("Arg {0}: {1}", x, args[x]);
26:        }
27:
28:        Console.WriteLine("=================================");
29:        string [] drives = Environment.GetLogicalDrives();
30:        for ( int x = 0; x < drives.Length; x++ )
31:        {
32:            Console.WriteLine("Drive {0}: {1}", x, drives[x]);
33:        }
34:
35:        Console.WriteLine("=================================");
36:        Console.WriteLine("Path: {0}",
37:                        Environment.GetEnvironmentVariable("Path"));
38:        Console.WriteLine("=================================");
39:
40:    }
41: }
```

OUTPUT   This is the output from my notebook computer:

```
=================================
 Command: EnvApp
Curr Dir: C:\DOCUME~1\Brad\MYDOCU~1\Books\TYCS2E\99-code\Day15
 Sys Dir: C:\WINDOWS\System32
 Version: 1.0.3705.288
 OS Vers: Microsoft Windows NT 5.1.2600.0
 Machine: NOTE-750III
  Memory: 3911680
=================================
Arg 0: EnvApp
=================================
Drive 0: A:\
Drive 1: C:\
Drive 2: D:\
=================================
Path:
C:\WINDOWS\system32;C:\WINDOWS;C:\WINDOWS\System32\Wbem;C:\Windows\
➥Microsoft.NET\Framework\v1.0.3705\;C:\Program Files\
```

```
➥Microsoft SQL Server\80\Tools\Binn\;C:\Program Files\
➥Microsoft Visual Studio\Common\Tools\WinNT;C:\Program Files\
➥Microsoft Visual Studio\Common\MSDev98\Bin;C:\Program Files\
➥Microsoft Visual Studio\Common\Tools;C:\Program Files\
➥Microsoft Visual Studio\VC98\bin;C:\Program Files\SharpDevelop\bin
==================================
```

This is the output from my desktop computer:

```
==================================
 Command: EnvApp aaa bbbbb ccccc
Curr Dir: C:\DOCUME~1\Brad\WorkArea
 Sys Dir: C:\WINDOWS\System32
 Version: 1.1.4322.510
 OS Vers: Microsoft Windows NT 5.1.2600.0
 Machine: HP400
  Memory: 4136960
==================================
Arg 0: EnvApp
Arg 1: aaa
Arg 2: bbbbb
Arg 3: ccccc
==================================
Drive 0: A:\
Drive 1: C:\
Drive 2: D:\
Drive 3: E:\
Drive 4: F:\
==================================
Path: C:\WINDOWS\system32;C:\WINDOWS;C:\WINDOWS\System32\Wbem;
➥C:\PROGRA~1\MICROS~2\00\Tools\BINN
==================================
```

ANALYSIS The operation of the `Environment` class is pretty straightforward. Lots of static members provide information about the user's system. This application was run on two different machines. The first output was done on my notebook computer, which is running Windows XP (although the output said Windows NT 5.1). I have three drives in this machine: A, C, and D. You can also see the current directory and the system directory. The drives on my machine and additional directory information also are presented in the output.

I ran the second set of output also on Windows XP. You can see lots of other information about this desktop machine. One thing you can tell that is different about this output is that three command-line parameters were used: `aaa`, `bbbbb`, and `ccccc`.

Most of the information can be obtained by calling a static member from the `Environment` class. A number of static members are called in Lines 12–18. A couple of the methods within this class return string arrays. This includes the command-line arguments method GetCommandLineArgs and the GetLogicalDrives method. Simple loops are used in Listing 15.3 to print the values from these string arrays. Lines 22–26 print the command-line arguments, and Lines 29–33 display the valid drives.

The Environment class includes a couple of other methods that you might be interested in. GetEnvironmentVariable gets the environment variables and their values from the current system. GetEnvironmentVariable can be used to get the value stored in one of the current system's environment variables.

Working with Math Routines

Basic math operators—such as plus, minus, and modulus—can get you only so far. It is only a matter of time before you find that you need more robust math routines. C# has access to a set of math routines within the base classes. These are available from within the System.Math namespace. Table 15.1 presents a number of the math methods available.

The Math class is sealed. Recall that a sealed class cannot be used for inheritance. Additionally, all the classes and data members are static, so you can't create an object of type Math. Instead, you use the members and methods with the class name.

TABLE 15.1 Math Routines in the Math Class

Method	Returns
Abs	The absolute value of a number.
Ceiling	A value that is the smallest whole number greater than or equal to a given number.
Exp	E raised to a given power. This is the inverse of Log.
Floor	A value that is the largest whole number that is less than or equal to the given number.
IEEERemainder	The result of a division of two specified numbers. (This division operation conforms to the remainder operation stated within Section 5.1 of ANSI/IEEE Std. 754-1985; IEEE Standard for Binary Floating-Point Arithmetic; Institute of Electrical and Electronics Engineers, Inc; 1985.)
Log	A value that is the logarithmic value of the given number.
Log10	A value that is the base 10 logarithm of a given value.
Max	The larger of two values.
Min	The smaller of two values.
Pow	The value of a given value raised to a given power.

TABLE 15.1   continued

Method	Returns
Round	A rounded value for a number. You can specify the precision of the rounded number. The number .5 would be rounded down.
Sign	A value indicating the sign of a value. -1 is returned for a negative number, 0 is returned for zero, and 1 is returned for a positive number.
Sqrt	The square root for a given value.
Acos	The value of an angle whose cosine is equal to a given number.
Asin	The value of an angle whose sine is equal to a given number.
Atan	The value of an angle whose tangent is equal to a given number.
Atan2	The value of an angle whose tangent is equal to the quotient of two given numbers.
Cos	A value that is the cosine of a given angle.
Cosh	A value that is the hyperbolic cosine for a given angle.
Sin	The sine for a given angle.
Sinh	The hyperbolic sine for a given angle.
Tan	The tangent of a specified angle.
Tanh	The hyperbolic tangent of a given angle.

The Math class also includes two constants: PI and E. PI returns the value of π as 3.14159265358979323846. The E data member returns the value of the logarithmic base, 2.7182818284590452354.

Most of the math methods in Table 15.1 are easy to understand. Listing 15.4 presents a couple of the routines in use.

LISTING 15.4   MathApp.cs—Using Some of the Math Routines

```
 1:  //  MathApp.cs - Using a Math routine
 2:  //----------------------------------------------
 3:  using System;
 4:
 5:  class MathApp
 6:  {
 7:     public static void Main()
 8:     {
 9:        int val2;
10:        char disp;
11:
```

LISTING 15.4   continued

```
12:         for (double ctr = 0.0; ctr <= 10; ctr += .2)
13:         {
14:            val2 = (int) Math.Round( ( 10 * Math.Sin(ctr))) ;
15:            for( int ctr2 = -10; ctr2 <= 10; ctr2++ )
16:            {
17:               if (ctr2 == val2)
18:                  disp = 'X';
19:               else
20:                  disp = ' ';
21:
22:               Console.Write("{0}", disp);
23:            }
24:            Console.WriteLine(" ");
25:         }
26:      }
27:  }
```

OUTPUT

ANALYSIS This listing maps out the `Sin` method. A `for` statement in Lines 12–25 loops through double values, incrementing them by `.2` each iteration. The sine of this value is obtained using the `Math.Sin` method in Line 14. The sine is a value from `-1.0` to `1.0`. To make the display easier, this value is converted to a value from `-10` to `10`. This conversion is done by multiplying the returned sine value by 10 and then rounding the value with the `Math.Round` method.

The result of doing the multiplication and rounding is that `val2` is a value from `-10` to `10`. A `for` loop in Line 15 displays a single line of characters. This line of characters is spaces, with the exception of the character in the position equal to `val2`. Line 24 prints another space to start a new line. The result of this work is a rough display of a sine curve.

Working with Files

The ability to write information to a file or to read information from a file can make your programs much more usable. Additionally, many times you will want to be able to work with existing files. The following sections touch on a few basic features of working with files. This is followed by an explanation of a key file concept called streams.

Note

Day 18, "Working with Databases: ADO.NET," goes into more detail on working with database files. The following sections focus more on standard text and system files.

Copying a File

A file class exists within the base class named `File`, located within the `System.IO` namespace. The `File` class contains a number of static methods that can be used to work with files. In fact, all the methods within the `File` class are static. Table 15.2 lists many of the key methods.

TABLE 15.2 File Methods

Method	Description
AppendText	Appends text to a file.
Copy	Creates a new file from an existing file.
Create	Creates a new file at a specified location.
CreateText	Creates a new file that can hold text.
Delete	Deletes a file at a specified location. The file must exist or an exception is thrown.
Exists	Determines whether a file actually exists at a specified location.
GetAttributes	Returns information on the given file's attributes. This includes information on whether the file is compressed, whether it is a directory name, whether it is hidden or read-only, whether it is a system file, whether it is temporary, and much more.
GetCreationTime	Returns the date and time the file was created.
GetLastAccessTime	Returns the date and time the file was last accessed.
GetLastWriteTime	Returns the date and time of the last write to the file.
Move	Enables a file to be moved to a new location and enables the file to be renamed.
Open	Opens a file at a given location. By opening a file, you then can write information to it or read information from it.
OpenRead	Creates a file that can only be read.
OpenText	Opens a file that can be read as text.
OpenWrite	Opens a specified file for writing to.
SetAttributes	Sets file attributes for a specified file.

TABLE 15.2   continued

Method	Description
SetCreationTime	Sets the date and time of a file's creation.
SetLastAccessTime	Sets the date and time the file was last accessed.
SetLastWriteTime	Sets the date and time that the file was last updated.

Listing 15.5 presents a small listing that uses the File class to create a copy of a file.

LISTING 15.5   FileCopy.cs—Copying a File

```
 1:  //  FileCopy.cs - Copies a file
 2:  //--------------------------------------------
 3:  using System;
 4:  using System.IO;
 5:
 6:  class FileCopy
 7:  {
 8:     public static void Main()
 9:     {
10:         string[] CLA = Environment.GetCommandLineArgs();
11:
12:         if ( CLA.Length < 3 )
13:         {
14:             Console.WriteLine("Format: {0} orig-file new-file", CLA[0]);
15:         }
16:         else
17:         {
18:           string origfile = CLA[1];
19:           string newfile  = CLA[2];
20:
21:           Console.Write("Copy....");
22:
23:           try
24:           {
25:               File.Copy(origfile, newfile);
26:           }
27:
28:           catch (System.IO.FileNotFoundException)
29:           {
30:             Console.WriteLine("\n{0} does not exist!", origfile);
31:             return;
32:           }
33:
34:           catch (System.IO.IOException)
35:           {
36:             Console.WriteLine("\n{0} already exists!", newfile);
```

LISTING 15.5   continued

```
37:            return;
38:        }
39:
40:        catch (Exception e)
41:        {
42:            Console.WriteLine("\nAn exception was thrown trying to copy
                 ➥file.");
43:            Console.WriteLine(e);
44:            return;
45:        }
46:
47:        Console.WriteLine("...Done");
48:        }
49:    }
50: }
```

OUTPUT

```
Copy....... Done
```

ANALYSIS   This output is a result of running this program with the following command line:

```
FileCopy FileCopy.cs FileCopy.bak
```

FileCopy.cs existed and FileCopy.bak did not exist before this command was executed. After the program executes, FileCopy.bak is created and, therefore, exists. If you execute this same command a second time—with FileCopy.bak already existing—you get the following output:

```
Copy....
FileCopy.bak already exists!
```

If you execute this program without any parameters or with only one parameter, you get the following output:

```
Format: FileCopy orig-file new-file
```

Finally, it is worth looking at the output you get if the file you are trying to copy does not exist:

```
Copy....
BadFileName does not exist!
```

As you can see by all this output, Listing 15.5 does a great job of trying to react to all the possible situations that could be thrown at it. You'll see that this is done with both programming logic and exception handling.

Looking at the listing, you see that Line 4 includes the `System.IO` namespace. This enables the program to use the `File` class without fully qualifying it. In Line 10, you see the first key line of the `Main` method. In this line, the command-line arguments are obtained using the `Environment` class method that you saw earlier today.

Line 12 checks to verify that there are at least three values in the command-line arguments variable, `CLA`. If there are less than three, the user didn't provide enough information. Remember, using the `GetCommandLineArgs` method, you are given the name of the program as the first value. The rest of the values on the command line follow. This means that you need three values to have the program name, original file, and new file. If there are not three values, a "usage" method is presented to the user (see Line 14). This usage method includes passing the actual name of the program read in by `GetCommandLineArgs`.

Tip

> The value of using `GetCommandLineArgs` is that it gives you the actual program name that the user executed. You can then use this actual name to present your "usage" message rather than a hard-coded value. The benefit of this is that the FileCopy program can be renamed, and yet the usage information will still be correct—it presents the actual name of the executed program.

If the necessary number of parameters is there, the processing of the files occurs. Lines 18–19 assign the information from the command line to file variables with easier-to-follow names. Technically, you do not need to do this; however, it makes the rest of the program easier to read.

In Line 21, a simple message is presented to the reader stating that the copy has started. Line 25 does the actual copy with the `Copy` method of the `File` class. As you can see, this copy is very straightforward.

Although the use of `Copy` is straightforward, it is important to notice what this listing has done. It has wrapped the copy in exception handling logic. This includes the `try` in Line 23 and the three instances of `catch` that follow. Because so many things can go wrong with a file operation, it is critical that you prepare your programs to react appropriately. The best way to do so is with exception handling.

Most of the `File` methods have exceptions already defined for a number of key errors that can occur. When you look at the online documentation for a class, you will find that any exceptions that are defined for a given method call are also included. It is a good programming practice to include exception handling whenever an exception is possible.

In Line 28, you see the first exception handler for the call to the Copy method. This exception is thrown when the file you are trying to copy is not found. It is named, appropriately, FileNotFoundException.

Note

In this listing, the exception name is fully qualified. Because the System.IO namespace was included, you could have left off System.IO.

Line 34 catches an IOException. This exception is thrown as a result of a number of other exceptions. This includes a directory not being found (DirectoryNotFoundException), an end of a file being found (EndOfStreamException), a problem loading a file (FileLoadException), or a file-not-found exception, which would have been caught by the earlier exception. This exception was thrown when the new filename already existed.

Finally, Line 40 catches the unexpected error by using the standard, generic exception. Because it is unknown what would cause this exception, it presents a general message followed by a display of the exception itself.

If an exception was not thrown, the file was successfully copied. Line 47 displays a messaging stating this success.

Do	**Don't**
Do use exception handling when using file routines.	**Don't** assume that the user provided you with everything you need when using command-line arguments.

Getting File Information

In addition to the File class, the FileInfo class is available for working with files. Listing 15.6 presents the FileInfo class in use. This program takes a single filename and displays the size and key dates regarding it. For the output, the FileSize.cs file was used.

LISTING 15.6 FileSize.cs—Using the FileInfo Class

```
1:  // FileSize.cs -
2:  //----------------------------------------------
3:  using System;
4:  using System.IO;
5:
6:  class FileSize
```

LISTING 15.6   continued

```
 7: {
 8:     public static void Main()
 9:     {
10:         string[] CLA = Environment.GetCommandLineArgs();
11:
12:         FileInfo fiExe = new FileInfo(CLA[0]);
13:
14:         if ( CLA.Length < 2 )
15:         {
16:             Console.WriteLine("Format: {0} filename", fiExe.Name);
17:         }
18:         else
19:         {
20:           try
21:           {
22:             FileInfo fiFile = new FileInfo(CLA[1]);
23:
24:             if(fiFile.Exists)
25:             {
26:               Console.WriteLine("===================================");
27:               Console.WriteLine("{0} - {1}", fiFile.Name, fiFile.Length );
28:               Console.WriteLine("===================================");
29:               Console.WriteLine("Last Access: {0}", fiFile.LastAccessTime);
30:               Console.WriteLine("Last Write:  {0}", fiFile.LastWriteTime);
31:               Console.WriteLine("Creation:    {0}", fiFile.CreationTime);
32:               Console.WriteLine("===================================");
33:             }
34:             else
35:             {
36:               Console.WriteLine("{0} doesn't exist!", fiFile.Name);
37:             }
38:           }
39:
40:           catch (System.IO.FileNotFoundException)
41:           {
42:             Console.WriteLine("\n{0} does not exist!", CLA[1]);
43:             return;
44:           }
45:           catch (Exception e)
46:           {
47:             Console.WriteLine("\nAn exception was thrown trying to copy
                 ➥file.");
48:             Console.WriteLine(e);
49:             return;
50:           }
51:         }
52:     }
53: }
```

OUTPUT

```
=====================================
FileSize.cs - 1551
=====================================
Last Access: 2/22/2003 11:40:30 PM
Last Write:  2/22/2003 11:40:19 PM
Creation:    2/22/2003 11:39:45 PM
```

ANALYSIS This listing is similar to the `FileCopy` listing presented earlier. The `FileInfo` class creates an object that is associated to a specific file. In Line 12, a `FileInfo` object named `fiExe` was created that is associated with the program being executed (fileinfo.exe). If the user doesn't enter an argument on the command line, the value of `fiExe` is printed with program usage information (see Line 14).

In Line 22, a second `FileInfo` object is created using the argument passed to the program. In Lines 26–32, information is displayed about this file.

Working with Simple Data Files

Getting information about files and copying files is great, but it's more valuable to read and write information to and from files. In C#, working with files usually involves working with streams.

Understanding Streams

The term *file* is generally associated with information stored on a disk drive or in memory. When working with files, you generally employ the use of a stream. Many people are confused about the difference between files and streams. A stream is a flow of information. It does not have to be associated with a file, nor does it have to be text.

A stream can be used to send or receive information from memory, the network, the Web, a string, and more. A stream is also used to go to and from a data file.

Understanding the Order for Reading Files

When reading or writing to a file, you need to follow a process. You must first open the file. If you are creating a new file, you generally open the file at the same time you create it. When it's open, you need to use a stream to place information into the file or to pull information out of the file. When you create the stream, you need to indicate the direction that information will be flowing. After you have the stream associated to the file, you can begin the actual reading or writing of data. If you are reading information from a file, you might need to check for the end of the file. When you are done reading or writing, you need to close the file.

Basic Steps to Working with a File

Step 1: Open or create the file.

Step 2: Set up a stream to or from the file.

Step 3: Place information into or read information from the file.

Step 4: Close the stream or file.

Creating and Opening Files

Different types of streams exist. You will use different streams and different methods depending on the type of data within your file. In this section, you focus on reading and writing text information. In the next section, you learn how to read and write binary information. Binary information includes the capability to store numeric values and any of the other data types.

To open a disk file for reading or writing text, you can use either the `File` or the `FileInfo` classes. Several methods can be used from either of these classes, including the ones listed in Table 15.3.

TABLE 15.3   File Methods for Reading and Writing Text

Method	Description
AppendText	Opens a file that can be used to have text appended to it (creates a StreamWriter to be used to append the text)
Create	Creates a new file
CreateText	Creates and opens a file to use with text (actually creates a StreamWriter Stream)
Open	Opens a file for reading or writing (actually opens a FileStream)
OpenRead	Opens a file for reading
OpenText	Opens an existing file to be used to read from (creates a StreamReader to be used)
OpenWrite	Opens a file for reading and writing

How do you know when to use the `File` class instead of the `FileInfo` class if they both contain similar methods? These two classes are different. The `File` class contains all static methods. Additionally, the `File` class automatically checks permissions on a file. The `FileInfo` class is used to create instances of `FileInfo`. If you are opening a file once, using the `File` class is okay. If you plan to use a file multiple times within a program, you are better off using the `FileInfo` class. If in doubt, you can use the `FileInfo` class.

Writing to a Text File

The best way to understand working with files is to jump right into the code. Listing 15.7 creates a text file and then writes information to it.

LISTING 15.7 Writing.cs—Writing to a Text File

```
 1:  //  Writing.cs - Writing to a text file.
 2:  //  Exception handling left out to keep listing short.
 3:  //-----------------------------------------------------
 4:  using System;
 5:  using System.IO;
 6:
 7:  public class Writing
 8:  {
 9:     public static void Main(String[] args)
10:     {
11:        if( args.Length < 1 )
12:        {
13:           Console.WriteLine("Must include file name.");
14:        }
15:        else
16:        {
17:           StreamWriter myFile = File.CreateText(args[0]);
18:
19:           myFile.WriteLine("Mary Had a Little Lamb,");
20:           myFile.WriteLine("Whose Fleece Was White as Snow.");
21:
22:           for ( int ctr = 0; ctr < 10; ctr++ )
23:              myFile.WriteLine ("{0}", ctr);
24:
25:           myFile.WriteLine("Everywhere that Mary Went,");
26:           myFile.WriteLine("That Lamb was sure to go.");
27:
28:           myFile.Close();
29:        }
30:     }
31:  }
```

OUTPUT Running this listing does not produce any viewable output unless you don't include a filename. You need to include a filename as a parameter. This file then is created and contains the following:

```
Mary Had a Little Lamb,
Whose Fleece Was White as Snow.
0
1
2
```

```
3
4
5
6
7
8
9
Everywhere that Mary Went,
That Lamb was sure to go.
```

This listing does not contain exception handling. This means that it is possible for this listing to throw unhandled exceptions. The exception handling was left out to enable you to focus on the file methods. This also cuts down the size of the listing for the example.

Looking at the listing, you can see that Lines 11–14 check whether a filename was included as a command-line parameter. If not, an error message is displayed. If a filename was included, processing continues in Line 17.

In Line 17, you see that the CreateText method of the File class is called to create a new StreamWriter object named myFile. The argument passed is the name of the file being created. The end result of this line is that a file is created that can hold text. This text is sent to the file through the StreamWriter named myFile. Figure 15.1 illustrates the result of this statement.

> **Caution**
>
> If a file already exists with the same name as the filename that you pass into this listing, that original file is overwritten.

FIGURE 15.1

Using a stream to write a file.

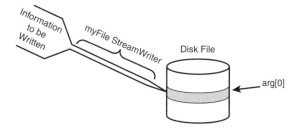

When the stream is set up and points to the file, you can write to the stream and thus write to the file. Line 19 indicates that you can write to the stream in the same way that you write to the Console. Instead of using Console, though, you use the stream name—in this case, myFile. Lines 19–20 call the WriteLine method to write sentences to the stream. Lines 22–23 write numbers to the stream; these numbers are written as text. Finally, Lines 25–26 write two more lines to the file.

When you are done writing to the file, you need to close the stream. Line 28 closes the stream by calling the Close method.

The steps to working with a file are all followed in this example.

Reading Text from a File

Reading information from a text file is very similar to writing information. Listing 15.8 can be used to read the file you created with Listing 15.7. This program reads text data.

LISTING 15.8   Reading.cs—Reading a Text File

```
 1:  //  Reading.cs - Read text from a file.
 2:  //  Exception handling left out to keep listing short.
 3:  //----------------------------------------------------
 4:  using System;
 5:  using System.IO;
 6:
 7:  public class Reading
 8:  {
 9:     public static void Main(String[] args)
10:     {
11:        if( args.Length < 1 )
12:        {
13:            Console.WriteLine("Must include file name.");
14:        }
15:        else
16:        {
17:           string buffer;
18:
19:           StreamReader myFile = File.OpenText(args[0]);
20:
21:           while ( (buffer = myFile.ReadLine()) != null )
22:           {
23:               Console.WriteLine(buffer);
24:           }
25:
26:           myFile.Close();
27:        }
28:     }
29:  }
```

OUTPUT

```
Mary Had a Little Lamb,
Whose Fleece Was White as Snow.
0
1
2
3
4
```

```
5
6
7
8
9
Everywhere that Mary Went,
That Lamb was sure to go.
```

Jumping right into this listing, you can see that a string is declared in Line 17. This string, buffer, will be used to hold the information being read from the file. Line 19 presents a line similar to the one in the Writing.cs listing. Instead of using the CreateText method, you use the OpenText method of the File class. This opens the file passed into the program (arg[0]). Again, a stream is associated to this file. In Line 21, a while loop is used to loop through the file. The ReadLine method is used to read lines of text from the myFile stream until a line is read that is equal to null. The null indicates that the end of the file has been reached.

As each line is read, it is printed to the Console (in Line 23). After all the lines have been read, the file is closed in Line 26.

Writing Binary Information to a File

If you use a text file, you must convert all your numbers to and from text. Many times you would be better off if you could write values directly to a file and read them back in. For example, if you write a bunch of integer numbers to a file as integers, you can pull them out of the file as integers. If you write them as text, you have to read the text from the file and then convert each value from a string to an integer. Instead of going through the extra steps of converting text, you can associate a binary stream type (BinaryStream) to a file and then read and write binary information through this stream.

Listing 15.9 writes binary data to a file. Although this file writes 100 simple integers to a file, it could just as easily write any other data type.

Note

Binary information is information that retains its data type's storage format rather than being converted to text.

LISTING 15.9   MyStream.cs—Writing to a Binary File

```
1:  //  MyStream.cs -
2:  //  Exception handling left out to keep listing short.
3:  //-------------------------------------------------
4:  using System;
5:  using System.IO;
6:
```

LISTING 15.9   continued

```
 7:  class MyStream
 8:  {
 9:    public static void Main(String[] args)
10:    {
11:      if( args.Length < 1 )
12:      {
13:        Console.WriteLine("Must include file name.");
14:      }
15:      else
16:      {
17:        FileStream myFile = new FileStream(args[0], FileMode.CreateNew);
18:        BinaryWriter bwFile = new BinaryWriter(myFile);
19:
20:        // Write data to Test.data.
21:        for (int i = 0; i < 100 ; i++)
22:        {
23:          bwFile.Write(i );
24:        }
25:
26:        bwFile.Close();
27:        myFile.Close();
28:      }
29:    }
30:  }
```

Caution

Like previous listings in today's lesson, this listing does not include exception handling. If you try to write to an existing file, the program will throw an exception. There are other ways to get exceptions as well. You should include exception handling in your applications.

ANALYSIS   A filename should be included as a command-line parameter. If it is included, no output is written to the console. Instead, information is written to a file. If you look at the file, you will see extended characters displayed; you won't see readable numbers.

This listing also lacks exception handling. If you try to write this information to an existing file, an exception will be thrown because of Line 17. In this listing, you open a file differently than the way you opened it for text. In Line 17, you create a FileStream object named myFile. This file stream is associated with a file using the constructor for FileStream. The first argument of the constructor is the name of the file you are creating (arg[0]). The second parameter is the mode you are opening the file in. This second parameter is a value from the `FileMode` enumerator. In this listing, the value being used is `CreateNew`. This means that a new file will be created. Table 15.4 lists other mode values that can be used from the `FileMode` enumeration.

TABLE 15.4 `FileMode` Enumeration Values

Value	Definition
Append	Opens an existing file or creates a new file.
Create	Creates a new file. If the filename already exists, it is deleted and a new file is created with the same name.
CreateNew	Creates a new file. If the filename already exists, an exception is thrown.
Open	Opens an existing file.
OpenOrCreate	Opens a file or creates a new file if the file doesn't already exist.
Truncate	Opens an existing file and deletes its contents.

After you create the `FileStream`, you need to set it up to work with binary data. Line 18 accomplishes this by connecting a type that can be used to write binary data to a stream: the `BinaryWriter` type. In Line 18, a `BinaryWriter` named `bwFile` is created. `myFile` is passed to the `BinaryWriter` constructor, thus associating `bwFile` with `myFile`.

Line 23 indicates that information can be written directly to the `BinaryWriter`, `bwFile`, using a `Write` method. The data being written can be of a specific data type. In this listing, an integer is being written. When you are done writing to the file, you need to close the streams that you have opened.

Reading Binary Information from a File

Now that you have written binary data to a file, you will most likely want to read it. Listing 15.10 presents a program that reads binary information from a file.

LISTING 15.10 BinReader.cs—Reading Binary Information

```
 1: // BinReader.cs -
 2: // Exception handling left out to keep listing short.
 3: //-------------------------------------------------
 4: using System;
 5: using System.IO;
 6:
 7: class BinReader
 8: {
 9:    public static void Main(String[] args)
10:    {
11:       if( args.Length < 1 )
```

LISTING **15.10**   continued

```
12:        {
13:            Console.WriteLine("Must include file name.");
14:        }
15:        else
16:        {
17:            FileStream myFile = new FileStream(args[0], FileMode.Open);
18:            BinaryReader brFile = new BinaryReader(myFile);
19:
20:            // Read data
21:            Console.WriteLine("Reading file....");
22:            while( brFile.PeekChar() != -1 )
23:            {
24:                Console.Write("<{0}> ", brFile.ReadInt32());
25:            }
26:
27:            Console.WriteLine("....Done Reading.");
28:
29:            brFile.Close();
30:            myFile.Close();
31:        }
32:    }
33: }
```

OUTPUT

```
Reading file....
<0> <1> <2> <3> <4> <5> <6> <7> <8> <9> <10> <11> <12> <13> <14> <15>
<16> <17><18> <19> <20> <21> <22> <23> <24> <25> <26> <27> <28> <29>
<30> <31> <32> <33><34> <35> <36> <37> <38> <39> <40> <41> <42> <43>
<44> <45> <46> <47> <48> <49><50> <51> <52> <53> <54> <55> <56> <57>
<58> <59> <60> <61> <62> <63> <64> <65><66> <67> <68> <69> <70> <71>
<72> <73> <74> <75> <76> <77> <78> <79> <80> <81><82> <83> <84> <85>
<86> <87> <88> <89> <90> <91> <92> <93> <94> <95> <96> <97><98> <99>
....Done Reading.
```

ANALYSIS   With this application, you can read the data you wrote with the previous listing. In Line 17, you create your FileStream. This time, the file mode being used is Open. You then associate this to a BinaryReader stream in Line 18, which helps you read binary information.

In Line 22, you see something a little different. The PeekChar method of the BinaryReader class is used. This method takes a look at the next character in the stream. If the next character is the end of the file, -1 is returned; otherwise, the next character is returned. It does this without changing the location within the stream. It lets you peek at the next character.

As long as the next character is not the end of the file, Line 24 is used to read an integer from the `BinaryStream` object, `brFile`. The method being used to read the integer, `ReadInt32`, uses a type name from the framework rather than the C# name. Remember, these are all classes from the framework being called by C#—they are not a part of the C# languages. These classes are usable by languages other than C# as well.

The `BinaryReader` class has methods similar to the `ReadInt32` for each of the other base data types. Each of these read methods is used in the same manner that `ReadInt32` is being used in this listing.

Working with Other File Types

The previous sections showed you how to read and write basic text and binary data. There are also classes for reading other types of data, including XML. A few more of these classes for reading other types of data are covered on Day 18.

A number of other namespaces contain classes, and other types support more advanced file access. Although these classes offer greater functionality with less coding, you need to know the trade-off for using them. Such classes might not follow the .NET standards and thus might not be portable.

Summary

Today you took a look at some of the base classes available through the .NET Framework. At the time this book was written, all of the classes presented in today's lesson had been submitted as a part of the standardization for portions of the .NET Framework. This means that they should eventually be as portable as your C# programs.

You started the day by looking at timers, which can be used to kick off an event after a given amount of time. You then learned how to obtain information about the current directories and files, as well as about the system itself. Math routines are often needed, and today you learned about a bunch of methods available through the `Math` class.

Finally, you focused on accessing files. You learned how to read and write to both text and binary files.

Q&A

Q I tried to use one of the classes in the help documents; however, when I compiled, I was told that I was missing an assembly. What do I need to do?

A If you find that you have done all the appropriate coding but you are still getting an error saying that you are missing a file or assembly, you might need to include a reference to an assembly from the framework in the compile command. This is done by using the `/r:` switch along with the name of the disk file containing the namespace you want included. The help documents will tell you what file is needed for each class. For example, the `System.TextReader` type is stored in the Mscorlib.dll assembly. To compile the xxx.cs program with this assembly, use this command line:

```
csc /r:Mscorlib.dll xxx.cs
```

Q Today I learned that I could get the command-line arguments using the `GetCommandLineArgs` method of the `Environment` class. I learned earlier in the book that I could get the command-line values by using a string parameter within the `Main` method. Which is better?

A Either method works. The difference is that using the `GetCommandLineArgs`, you can also get the name of the program that was executed. The `Main` argument's first value is the first parameter—not the name of the program being executed.

Q Are XML and ADO both a part of the standard classes?

A No. A number of classes are being standardized for XML; however, ADO is a Microsoft technology that is not part of the standards. Day 18 talks about ADO (and ADO.NET) in a little more detail.

Workshop

The Workshop provides quiz questions to help you solidify your understanding of the material covered and exercises to provide you with experience in using what you've learned. Try to understand the quiz and exercise answers before continuing to the next day's lesson. Answers are provided on the CD.

Quiz

1. How many ticks are needed to make a second?
2. Which of the following does a timer use?

    a. A delegate

    b. An event

    c. An orphomite

    d. An exception

3. Which standards organization is standardizing C# and the Base Class Libraries?
4. What is the difference between using `Environment.GetCommandLineArgs` and using `Main( String args[] )`?
5. When would you create an instance of the `Math` class (when would you create a `Math` object)?
6. What class or method can be used to determine whether a file actually exists?
7. What is the difference between a file and a stream?
8. Which `FileMode` value can be used to create a new file?
9. What are some of the classes for working with XML?

Exercises

1. Create a program that uses the binary file methods to write to a file. Create a structure to hold a person's name, age, and membership status. Write this information to the file. (*Note:* Age can be an integer. Membership can be a Boolean).
2. Rewrite Listing 15.4 to use the `Cosine` method of the `Math` class.
3. Create a program that reads text from the console and writes it to the file. The user should enter a blank line to end input.
4. **Bug Buster:** Does the following program have a problem?

```
1:  using System;
2:  using System.IO;
3:
4:  class MyStream
5:  {
6:     public static void Main(String[] args)
7:     {
8:          FileStream myFile = new FileStream(args[0], FileMode.Open);
9:          BinaryReader brFile = new BinaryReader(myFile);
```

```
10:          while( brFile.PeekChar() != -1 )
11:          {
12:              Console.Write("<{0}> ", brFile.ReadInt32());
13:          }
14:      }
15:  }
```

DAY **16**

Creating Windows Forms

The Base Class Libraries in the .NET Framework provide a number of classes for creating and working with forms-based windows applications, including the creation of windows forms and controls. Today you...

- Learn how to create a windows form.
- Customize the appearance of a form.
- Add controls to a windows form.
- Work with text boxes, labels, and more.
- Customize the look of a control by setting its properties.
- Associate events with a control.

 Caution

At the time this book was written, Microsoft's .NET Framework and runtime was the only framework that supported windows forms. If you are using a different runtime and framework, you will need to check whether support has been built. Most of the .NET implementations, including the mono project, are adding support for these classes.

Working with Windows and Forms

Most operating systems today use event-driven programming and forms to interact with users. If you have done development for Microsoft Windows, you most likely used a set of routines within the Win32 libraries that helped you to create windows and forms. Yesterday you learned about the Base Class Libraries (BCL). Within the BCL is a set of classes for doing similar windows forms development. The benefit of the base classes is that they can be used by any of the programming languages within the framework. Additionally, they have been created to make developing forms-based applications simple. Additionally, as the .NET Framework and runtime are ported to other platforms, your forms based applications will also port.

Creating Windows Forms

To create a windows form application, you create a class that inherits from the Form class. The Form class is located within the System.Windows.Forms namespace. Listing 16.1 presents FirstFrm.cs, which is the code required to create a minimal windows form application.

LISTING 16.1   FirstFrm.cs—A Simple Windows Form Application

```
 1:  // FirstFrm.cs - A super simplistic windows form application
 2:  //-----------------------------------------------------------
 3:
 4:  using System.Windows.Forms;
 5:
 6:  public class FirstFrm : Form
 7:  {
 8:      public static void Main( string[] args )
 9:      {
10:         FirstFrm frmHello = new FirstFrm();
11:         Application.Run(frmHello);
12:      }
13:  }
```

As you can see, this listing is extremely short when you consider what it can do. To see what it can do, though, you need to compile it. In the next section, you learn what you need to do to compile this listing.

Compiling Options

Compiling Listing 16.1 must be done differently than you have done before. You might need to include a reference in the compile command to the base classes you are using. Adding this reference was briefly covered yesterday.

The Form classes are contained within an assembly named System.Windows.Forms.dll. You might need to include a reference to this assembly when you compile the program. Including the using statement at the top of a listing does not actually include any files in your program; it only provides a reference to a point within the namespace stored in the file. As you have learned and seen, this enables you to use a shortened version of the name rather than a fully qualified name.

Most of the common windows forms controls and forms functionality is within this assembly. To ensure that this assembly is used when you compile your program, you use a reference when you compile. If you are using an Integrated Development Environment, this reference automatically is added when you choose to create a windows forms application. If you are using the Microsoft command-line compiler, you add /reference: filename to the command line, where filename is the name of the assembly. Using the forms assembly to compile the FirstFrm.cs program in Listing 16.1, you type the following command line:

16

```
csc /reference:System.Windows.Forms.dll FirstFrm.cs
```

Alternatively, you can shorten /reference: to just /r:. When you execute the compile command, your program will be compiled.

> **Note**
>
> The C# compiler included with the Microsoft .NET Framework 1.1 and later may automatically include some references, including the System.Windows.Forms.dll.

If you execute the FirstFrm application from the command prompt, you will see the window in Figure 16.1 displayed.

FIGURE 16.1

The FirstFrm application's form.

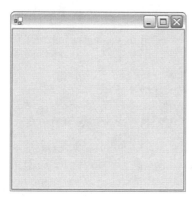

This is exactly what you want. But wait: If you run this program from directly within an operating system such as Microsoft Windows, you will notice a slightly different result. The result will be a command-line box as well as the windows form (See Figure 16.2). The command-line dialog box is not something you want created.

FIGURE 16.2

The actual display from the FirstFrm application.

To stop this from displaying, you need to tell the compiler that you want the program created to be targeted to a Windows system. This is done using the /target: flag with the winexe option. You can use /t: as an abbreviation. Recompiling the FirstFrm.cs program in Listing 16.1 with the following command results in the desired solution:

```
csc /r:System.Windows.Forms.dll /t:winexe FirstFrm.cs
```

When you execute the program, it does not first create a command window.

Note

> You should be aware that some of the assemblies might be automatically included when you compile. For example, development tools such as Microsoft Visual C# .NET include a few assemblies by default. If an assembly is not included, you get an error when you compile, stating that an assembly might be missing.

Analyzing Your First Windows Form Application

Now that you can compile and execute a windows form application, you should begin understanding the code. Look back at the code in Listing 16.1.

In Line 4, the listing uses the `System.Windows.Forms` namespace, which enables the `Form` and `Application` class names to be shortened. In Line 6, this application is in a class named `FirstFrm`. The new class you are creating inherits from the `Form` class, which provides all the basic functionality of a windows form.

> **Note**
>
> As you will learn in today's lesson, the `System.Windows.Forms` namespace also includes controls, events, properties, and other code that will make your windows forms more usable.

With the single line of code (Line 6), you have actually created the form's application class. In Line 10, you instantiate an object from this class. In Line 11, you call the `Run` method of the `Application` class. This is covered in more detail in a moment. For now, know that it causes the application to display the form and keep running until you close the form. You could call the `Show` method of the `Form` class instead by replacing Line 11 with the following:

```
frmHello.Show();
```

Although this seems more straightforward, you will find that the application ends with a flaw. When using the `Show` method, the program shows the form and then moves on to the next line, which is the end of the program. Because the end of the program is reached, the processing ends and the form closes. This is not the result you want. The `Application` class gets around this problem.

> **Note**
>
> Later today, you will learn about a form method that displays a form and waits.

Understanding the `Application.Run` Method

A Windows application is an event-driven program that generally displays a form containing controls. The program then spins in a loop until the user does something on the form or within the windowed environment. Messages are created whenever something occurs. These messages cause an event to occur. If there is an event handler for a given message, it is executed. If there is not, the loop continues. Figure 16.3 illustrates this looping.

FIGURE 16.3

*Flow of a standard
Windows program.*

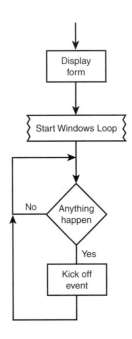

As you can see, the loop never seems to end. Actually, an event can end the program. The basic form that you inherit from (Form) includes the close control as well as a Close item in the Command menu. These controls can kick off an event that closes the form and ends the loop.

By now you should be guessing what the Application class does for you—or, more specifically, what the Application class's Run method does for you. The Run method takes care of creating the loop and keeping the program running until an event that ends the program loop is executed. In the case of Listing 16.1, selecting the Close button on the form or selecting the Close option on the command menu causes an event to be fired that ends the loop and thus closes the form.

The Application.Run method also displays a form for you. Line 11 of Listing 16.1 receives a form object—frmHello. This is an object derived from the Form class (see Line 6 of Listing 16.1). The Application.Run method displays this form and then loops.

Note

The loop created by the Application class's Run method actually processes messages that are created. These messages can be created by the operating system, your application, or other applications that are running. The loop processes these methods. For example, when you click a button, a number of messages are created. This includes messages for a mouse down, a mouse up, a button click, and more. If a message matches with an event handler, the event handler is executed. If no event handler is defined, the message is ignored.

Customizing a Form

In the previous listing, you saw a basic form presented. A number of properties, methods, and events are associated with the Form class—too many to cover in this book. However, it is worth touching on a few of them. You can check the online documentation for a complete accounting of all the functionality available with this class.

Customizing the Caption Bar on a Form

Listing 16.1 presented a basic, blank form. The next few listings continue to work with this blank form; however, with each listing in today's lesson, you learn to take a little more control of the form.

The form from Listing 16.1 comes with a number of items already available, including the control menu and the Minimize, Maximize, and Close buttons on the title bar. You can control whether these features are on or off with your forms by setting properties:

ControlBox	Determines whether the control box is displayed.
HelpButton	Indicates whether a help button is displayed on the caption of the form. This is displayed only if both the MaximizeBox and MinimizeBox values are false.
MaximizeBox	Indicates whether the Maximum button is included.
MinimizeBox	Indicates whether the Minimize button is included.
Text	Includes the caption for the form.

Some of these values impact others. For example, the HelpButton displays only if both the MaximizeBox and MinimizeBox properties are false (turned off). Listing 16.2 gives you a short listing that enables you to play with these values; Figure 16.4 shows the output. Enter this listing, compile it, and run it. Remember to include the /t:winexe flag when compiling.

LISTING 16.2   FormApp.cs—Sizing a Form

```
1:  // FormApp.cs - Caption Bar properties
2:  //-------------------------------------------------------------------
3:
```

LISTING 16.2 continued

```
 4:   using System.Windows.Forms;
 5:
 6:   public class FormApp : Form
 7:   {
 8:       public static void Main( string[] args )
 9:       {
10:           FormApp frmHello = new FormApp();
11:
12:           // Caption bar properties
13:           frmHello.MinimizeBox = true;
14:           frmHello.MaximizeBox = false;
15:           frmHello.HelpButton = true;
16:           frmHello.ControlBox = true;
17:           frmHello.Text = @"My Form's Caption";
18:
19:           Application.Run(frmHello);
20:       }
21:   }
```

OUTPUT

FIGURE 16.4

*Output for Listing
16.2.*

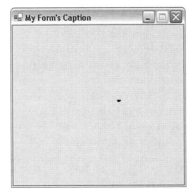

ANALYSIS This listing is easy to follow. In Line 6, a new class is created named FormApp that inherits from the Form class. In Line 10, a new form object is instantiated from the Application class. This form has a number of values set in Lines 13–17 that change items on the caption bar. In Line 19, the Run method of the Application class is called to display the form. You should look at the output in Figure 16.4. Both the Maximize and Minimize buttons are displayed; however, the Maximize button is inactive. This is because you set it to false in Line 14. If you set both values to false, neither button shows.

You should also notice that the Help button is turned to `true` in Line 15. The Help button displays only if both the Minimize and Maximize buttons are turned off (`false`). This means that Line 15 is ignored. Change the property in Line 13 so that the resulting properties in Lines 14–16 are as follows:

```
13:         frmHello.MinimizeBox = false;
14:         frmHello.MaximizeBox = false;
15:         frmHello.HelpButton = true;
16:         frmHello.ControlBox = true;
```

Recompile and run this program. The new output is shown in Figure 16.5.

FIGURE 16.5

Output with a Help button.

As you can see, the output reflects the values that have been set.

One additional combination is worth noting. When you set `ControlBox` to `false`, the Close button and the control box are both hidden. Additionally, if `ControlBox`, `MinimizeBox`, and `MaximizeBox` are all set to `false` and if there is no text for the caption, the caption bar disappears. Remove Line 17 from Listing 16.2 and set the values for the properties in Lines 13–16 to `false`. Recompile and run the program. The output you receive is displayed in Figure 16.6.

You might wonder why you would want to remove the caption bar. One possible reason is to display a splash screen. You'll learn more about creating a splash screen later.

Note

In Microsoft Windows, Alt+F4 closes the current window. If you disable the control box, you end up removing the Close button as well. You'll need Alt+F4 to close the window.

FIGURE 16.6

Output without the caption bar.

Sizing a Form

The next thing to take control of is the form's size. You can use a number of methods and properties to manipulate a form's shape and size. Table 16.1 presents the ones used here.

TABLE 16.1 Sizing Functionality in the Form Class

AutoScale	The form automatically adjusts itself, based on the font or controls used on it.
AutoScaleBaseSize	The base size used for autoscaling the form.
AutoScroll	The form has the automatic capability of scrolling.
AutoScrollMargin	The size of the margin for the autoscroll.
AutoScrollMinSize	The minimum size of the autoscroll.
AutoScrollPosition	The location of the autoscroll position.
ClientSize	The size of the client area of the form.
DefaultSize	The protected property that sets the default size of the form.
DesktopBounds	The size and location of the form.
DesktopLocation	The location of the form.
Height	The height of the form
MaximizeSize	The maximum size for the form.
MinimizeSize	The minimum size for the form.
Size	The size of the form. set or get a Size object that contains an x, y value.
SizeGripStyle	The style of the size grip used on the form. A value from the SizeGripStyle enumerator. Values are Auto (automatically displayed when needed), Hide (hidden), or Show (always shown).

TABLE 16.1   continued

StartPosition	The starting position of the form. This is a value from the FormStartPosition enumerator. Possible FormStartPosition enumeration values are CenterParent (centered within the parent form), CenterScreen (centered in the current display screen), Manual (location and size determined by starting position), WindowsDefaultBounds (positioned at the default location), and WindowsDefaultLocation (positioned at the default location, with dimensions based on specified values for the size).
Width	The width of the form.

The items listed in Table 16.1 are only a few of the available methods and properties that work with a form's size. Listing 16.3 presents some of these in another simple application; Figure 16.7 shows the output.

LISTING 16.3   FormSize.cs—Sizing a Form

```
 1:  // FormSize.cs - Form Size
 2:  //-----------------------------------------------------------
 3:
 4:  using System.Windows.Forms;
 5:  using System.Drawing;
 6:
 7:  public class FormSize : Form
 8:  {
 9:      public static void Main( string[] args )
10:      {
11:          FormSize myForm = new FormSize();
12:          myForm.Text = "Form Sizing";
13:
14:          myForm.Width = 400;
15:          myForm.Height = 100;
16:
17:          Point FormLoc = new Point(200,350);
18:          myForm.StartPosition = FormStartPosition.Manual;
19:          myForm.DesktopLocation = FormLoc;
20:
21:          Application.Run(myForm);
22:      }
23:  }
```

FIGURE 16.7

Positioning and sizing the form.

ANALYSIS Setting the size of a form is simple. Lines 14–15 set the size of the form in Listing 16.3. As you can see, the Width and Height properties can be set. You can also set both of these at the same time by using a Size object.

Positioning the form takes a little more effort. In Line 17, a Point object is created that contains the location on the screen where you want the form positioned. This is then used in Line 19 by applying it to the DesktopLocation property. To use the Point object without fully qualifying its name, you need to include the System.Drawing namespace, as in Line 5.

In Line 18, you see that an additional property has been set. If you leave out Line 18, you will not get the results you want. You must set the starting position for the form by setting the StartPosition property to a value in the FormStartPosition enumerator. Table 16.1 contained the possible values for this enumerator. You should note the other values for FormStartPosition. If you want to center a form on the screen, you can replace Lines 17–19 with one line:

```
myForm.StartPosition = FormStartPosition.CenterScreen;
```

This single line of code takes care of centering the form on the screen, regardless of the screen's resolution.

Changing the Colors and Background of a Form

Working with the background color of a form requires setting the BackColor property to a color value. The color values can be taken from the Color structure located in the System.Drawing namespace. Table 16.2 lists some of the common colors.

TABLE 16.2 Colors

AliceBlue	AntiqueWhite	Acua	Aquamarine	Azure	Beige
Bisque	Black	BlanchedAlmond	Blue	BlueViolet	Brown
BurlyWood	CadetBlue	Chartreuse	Chocolate	Coral	CornflowerBlue
Cornsilk	Crimson	Cyan	DarkBlue	DarkCyan	DarkGoldenrod
DarkGray	DarkGreen	DarkKhaki	DarkMagenta	DarkOliveGreen	DarkOrange
DarkOrchid	DarkRed	DarkSalmon	DarkSeaGreen	DarkSlateBlue	DarkSlateGray
DarkTurquoise	DarkViolet	DeepPink	DeepSkyBlue	DimGray	DodgerBlue
Firebrick	FloralWhite	ForestGreen	Fuchsia	Gainsboro	GhostWhite
Gold	Goldenrod	Gray	Green	GreenYellow	Honeydew
HotPink	IndianRed	Indigo	Ivory	Khaki	Lavender
LavenderBlush	LawnGreen	LemonChiffon	LightBlue	LightCoral	LightCyan
LightGoldenrodYellow	LightGray	LightGreen	LightPink	LightSalmon	LightSeaGreen
LightSkyBlue	LightSlateGray	LightSteelBlue	LightYellow	Lime	LimeGreen
Linen	Magenta	Maroon	MediumAquamarine	MediumBlue	MediumOrchid
MediumPurple	MediumSeaGreen	MediumSlateBlue	MediumSpringGreen	MediumTurquoise	MediumVioletRed
MidnightBlue	MintCream	MistyRose	Moccasin	NavajoWhite	Navy
OldLace	Olive	OliveDrab	Orange	OrangeRed	Orchid
PaleGoldenrod	PaleGreen	PaleTurquoise	PaleVioletRed	PapayaWhip	PeachPuff
Peru	Pink	Plum	PowderBlue	Purple	Red
RosyBrown	RoyalBlue	SaddleBrown	Salmon	SandyBrown	SeaGreen
SeaShell	Sienna	Silver	SkyBlue	SlateBlue	SlateGray
Snow	SpringGreen	SteelBlue	Tan	Teal	Thistle
Tomato	Transparent	Turquoise	Violet	Wheat	White
WhiteSmokeYellow	YellowGreen				

16

Setting a color is as simple as assigning a value from Table 16.2:

```
myForm.BackColor = Color.HotPink;
```

Of equal value to setting the form's color is placing a background image on the form. An image can be set into the form's BackgroundImage property. Listing 16.4 sets an image onto the background; Figure 16.8 shows the output. The image placed is passed as a parameter to the program.

 Caution | Be careful with this listing. For brevity, it does not contain exception handling. If you pass a filename that doesn't exist, the program will throw an exception.

LISTING 16.4   PicForm.cs—Using Background Images

```
 1:  // PicForm.cs - Form Backgrounds
 2:  //-------------------------------------------------
 3:
 4:  using System.Windows.Forms;
 5:  using System.Drawing;
 6:
 7:  public class PicForm : Form
 8:  {
 9:      public static void Main( string[] args )
10:      {
11:          PicForm myForm = new PicForm();
12:          myForm.BackColor = Color.HotPink;
13:          myForm.Text = "PicForm - Backgrounds";
14:
15:          if (args.Length >= 1)
16:          {
17:              myForm.BackgroundImage = Image.FromFile(args[0]);
18:
19:              Size tmpSize = new Size();
20:              tmpSize.Width = myForm.BackgroundImage.Width;
21:              tmpSize.Height = myForm.BackgroundImage.Height;
22:              myForm.ClientSize = tmpSize;
23:
24:              myForm.Text = "PicForm - " + args[0];
25:          }
26:
27:          Application.Run(myForm);
28:      }
29:  }
```

OUTPUT

FIGURE 16.8

Using a background image.

ANALYSIS This program presents an image on the form background. This image is provided on the command line. If no image is entered on the command line, the background color is set to Hot Pink. I ran the listing using a picture of my nephews. I entered this command line:

```
PicForm pict1.jpg
```

pict1.jpg was in the same directory as the PicForm executable. If it were in a different directory, I would have needed to enter the full path. You can pass a different image, as long as the path is valid. If you enter an invalid filename, you get an exception.

Looking at the listing, you can see that creating an application to display images is extremely easy. The framework classes take care of all the difficult work for you. In Line 12, the background color was set to be Hot Pink. This is done by setting the form's BackColor property with a color value from the Color structure.

In Line 15, a check is done to see whether a value was included on the command line. If a value was not included, Lines 17–24 are skipped and the form is displayed with a hot pink background. If a value was entered, this program makes the assumption (which your programs should not do) that the parameter passed was a valid graphics file. This file is then set into the BackgroundImage property of the form. The filename needs to be converted to an actual image for the background by using the Image class. More specifically, the Image class includes a static method, FromFile, that takes a filename as an argument and returns an Image. This is exactly what is needed for this listing.

16

Note　If you want a specific image for your background, you could get rid of the if statement and replace Line 17's arg[0] value with the hard-coded name of the file you want as the background.

The BackgroundImage property holds an Image value. Because of this, properties and methods from the Image class can be used on this property. The Image class includes Width and Height properties that are equal to the width and height of the image contained. Lines 20–21 use these values to a temporary Size variable that, in turn, is assigned to the form's client size in Line 22. The size of the form's client area is set to the same size as the image. The end result is that the form displayed always displays the full image. If you don't do this, you will see either only part of the image or tiled copies of the image.

Changing the Form's Borders

Controlling the border of a form not only impacts the look, but it also determines whether the form can be resized. To modify the border, you set the Form class's BorderStyle property with a value from the FormBorderStyle enumeration. Possible values for the BorderStyle property are listed in Table 16.3. Listing 16.5 presents a form with the border modified; Figure 16.9 shows the output.

TABLE 16.3　FormBorderStyle Enumerator Values

Value	Description
Fixed3D	The form is fixed (not resizable) and has a 3D border.
FixedDialog	The form is fixed (not resizable) and has a thick border.
FixedSingle	The form is fixed (not resizable) and has a single-line border.
FixedToolWindow	The form is fixed (not resizable) and has a tool window border.
None	The form has no border.
Sizeable	The form is resizable.
SizeableToolWindow	The form has a resizable tool window border.

LISTING 16.5　BorderForm.cs—Modifying a Form's Border

```
1:  // BorderForm.cs - Form Borders
2:  //------------------------------------------------------------
3:
4:  using System.Windows.Forms;
5:  using System.Drawing;
```

LISTING 16.5 continued

```
 6:
 7:   public class BorderForm : Form
 8:   {
 9:       public static void Main( string[] args )
10:       {
11:           BorderForm myForm = new BorderForm();
12:           myForm.BackColor = Color.SteelBlue;
13:           myForm.Text = "Borders";
14:
15:           myForm.FormBorderStyle = FormBorderStyle.Fixed3D;
16:
17:           Application.Run(myForm);
18:       }
19:   }
```

OUTPUT

FIGURE 16.9

Modifying a form's border.

ANALYSIS As you can see in the output from Listing 16.5, the border is fixed in size. If you try to resize the form at runtime, you cannot do so.

If you do make the form resizable, you have another option that you can set: SizeGripStyle. SizeGripStyle determines whether the form is marked with a resize indicator. Figure 16.10 has the resize indicator circled. You can set your form to automatically show this indicator or to always hide or always show it. This is done using one of three values in the SizeGripStyle enumerator: Auto, Hide, or Show. The indicator in Figure 16.10 was shown by including this line:

```
myForm.SizeGripStyle = SizeGripStyle.Show;
```

FIGURE 16.10

The size grip.

> Don't get confused by using conflicting properties. For example, if you use a fixed-size border and you set the size grip to display, your results will not match these settings. The fixed border means that the form cannot be resized; therefore, the size grip will not display, regardless of how you set it.

Adding Controls to a Form

Up to this point, you have been working with the look and feel of a form. However, without controls, a form is virtually worthless. Controls are what make a windows application usable.

A control can be a button, a list box, a text box, an image, or even simple plain text. The easiest way to add such controls is to use a graphical development tool such as Microsoft's Visual C# .NET or SharpDevelop. A graphical tool enables you to drag and drop controls onto a form. It also adds all the basic code needed to display the control.

A graphical development tool, however, is not needed. Even if you use a graphical tool, it is still valuable to understand what the tool is doing for you. Some of the standard controls provided in the framework are listed in Table 16.4. Additional controls can be created and used as well.

TABLE 16.4   *Some Standard Controls in the Base Class Libraries*

Button	CheckBox	CheckedListBox	ComboBox
ContainerControl	DataGrid	DateTimePicker	DomainUpDown
Form	GroupBox	HScrollBar	ImageList
Label	LinkLabel	ListBox	ListView
MonthCalendar	NumericUpDown	Panel	PictureBox
PrintReviewControl	ProgressBar	PropertyGrid	RadioButton
RichTextBox	ScrollableControl	Splitter	StatusBar
StatusBarPanel	TabControl	TabPage	TabStrip
TextBox	Timer	ToolBar	ToolBarButton
ToolTip	TrackBar	TreeView	VScrollBar
UserControl			

16

The controls in Table 16.4 are defined in the `System.Windows.Forms` namespace. The following sections cover some of these controls. Be aware, however, that the coverage here is very minimal. Hundreds of properties, methods, and events are associated with the controls listed in Table 16.4. It would take a book bigger than this one to cover all the details of each control. Here, you will learn how to use some of the key controls. The process of using the other controls is very similar to those presented here. Additionally, you will see only a few of the properties. All the properties can be found in the help documentation available with the C# compiler or with your development tool.

Working with Labels and Text Display

You use the `Label` control to display simple text on the screen. The `Label` control is in the `System.Windows.Forms` namespace with the other built-in controls.

To add a control to a form, you first create the control. Then you can customize the control via its properties and methods. When you have made the changes you want, you can then add it to your form.

NEW TERM   A *label* is a control that displays information to the user but does not allow the user to directly change its values (although you can programmatically change its value). You create a label as you do any other object:

```
Label myLabel = new Label();
```

After it's created, you have an empty label that can be added to your form. Listing 16.6 illustrates a few of the label's properties, including setting the textual value with the Text property; Figure 16.11 shows the output. Creating a label does not actually put it on a form; you have to add the label to a form. To add the control to your form, you use the Add method with the form's Controls property. To add the myLabel control to the myForm you've used before, you use this line:

```
myForm.Controls.Add(myLabel);
```

To add other controls, you replace myLabel with the name of the control object that you want to add.

LISTING 16.6   ControlApp.cs—Using a Label Control

```
 1:  // ControlApp.cs - Working with controls
 2:  //----------------------------------------------------------
 3:
 4:  using System;
 5:  using System.Windows.Forms;
 6:  using System.Drawing;
 7:
 8:  public class ControlApp : Form
 9:  {
10:      public static void Main( string[] args )
11:      {
12:          ControlApp myForm = new ControlApp();
13:
14:          myForm.Text = Environment.CommandLine;
15:          myForm.StartPosition = FormStartPosition.CenterScreen;
16:
17:          // Create the controls...
18:          Label myDateLabel = new Label();
19:          Label myLabel = new Label();
20:
21:          myLabel.Text = "This program was executed at:";
22:          myLabel.AutoSize = true;
23:          myLabel.Left = 50;
24:          myLabel.Top = 20;
25:
26:          DateTime currDate = DateTime.Now;;
27:          myDateLabel.Text = currDate.ToString();
28:
29:          myDateLabel.AutoSize = true;
30:          myDateLabel.Left = 50 + myLabel.PreferredWidth + 10;
31:          myDateLabel.Top = 20;
32:
33:          myForm.Width = myLabel.PreferredWidth +
             ➥myDateLabel.PreferredWidth + 110;
```

LISTING 16.6   continued

```
34:            myForm.Height = myLabel.PreferredHeight+ 100;
35:
36:            // Add the control to the form...
37:            myForm.Controls.Add(myDateLabel);
38:            myForm.Controls.Add(myLabel);
39:
40:            Application.Run(myForm);
41:        }
42:    }
```

16

OUTPUT

FIGURE 16.11

Using a Label
control.

ANALYSIS This program creates two label controls and displays them in a form. Instead of just plopping the labels anywhere, this listing positions them somewhat centered in the form.

Stepping back and looking at the code, you can see that the program starts by creating a new form in Line 12. The title on the control bar is set equal to the command-line value from the Environment class. You used the Environment class in yesterday's lesson. In Line 15, the StartPosition property for the form is set to center the form on the screen. At this point, no size for the form has been indicated. That will be done in a minute.

In Lines 18–19, two label controls are created. The first label, myDateLabel, will be used to hold the current date and time. The second label control will be used to hold descriptive text. Recall that a label is a control that displays information to the user but does not allow the user to directly change its values—so these two uses of a label are appropriate.

In Lines 21–24, properties for the myLabel label are set. In Line 21, the text to be displayed is assigned to the Text property of the label. In Line 22, the AutoSize property is set to true. You can control the size of the label or let it determine the best size for itself. Setting the AutoSize property to true gives the label the capability to resize itself. In Lines 23–24, the Left and Top properties are set to values for the location on the form where the control should be placed. In this case, the myLabel control is placed 50 pixels from the left side of the form and 20 pixels down into the client area of the form.

The next two lines of the listing (Lines 26–27) are a roundabout way to assign the current date and time to the Text property of your other label control, myDateLabel. As you can see, a `DateTime` object is created and assigned the value of `Now`. This value is then converted to a string and assigned to the `myDateLabel`.

In Line 29, the `AutoSize` property for the `myDateLabel` is also set to `true` so that the label will be sized appropriately. In Lines 30–31, the position of the `myDateLabel` is set. The `Top` position is easy to understand—it will be at the same vertical location as the other label—but the `Left` position is a little more complex. The `myDateLabel` label is to be placed to the right of the other label. To place it to the right of the other label, you need to move it over a distance equal to the size of the other label, plus any offset from the edge of the window to the other label. This is 50 pixels plus the width of the `myLabel` label. Because you have enabled autosizing your labels, the width is equal to the preferred width. A label's preferred width can be obtained from the `PreferredWidth` property of the control. The end result is that, to place the `myDateLabel` to the right of `myLabel`, you add the preferred width of `myLabel` plus the offset added to `myLabel`. To add a little buffer between the two labels, an additional 10 pixels are added. Figure 16.12 helps illustrate what is happening in Line 30.

FIGURE 16.12

Positioning the label.

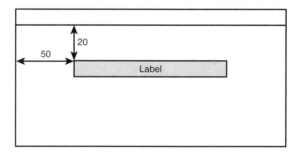

Lines 33–34 set the width and height of the form. As you can see, the width is set to center the labels on the form. This is done by balancing the offsets and using the widths of the two labels. The height is set to make sure there is a lot of space around the text.

In Lines 37–38, you see that adding these controls to the form is simple. The `Add` method of the `Controls` property is called for each of the controls. The `Run` method of the application is then executed in Line 40 so that the form is displayed. The end result is that you now have text displayed on your form.

For the most part, this same process is used for all other types of controls. This involves creating the control, setting its properties, and then adding it to the form.

A Suggested Approach for Using Controls

The process presented in the previous section is appropriate for using controls. One of the most common development tools for creating windowed applications is Microsoft Visual Studio .NET, and thus, for C# applications, Microsoft Visual C# .NET. This development tool provides a unique structure for programming controls. Although it is not necessary, this structure does organize the code so that the graphical design tools can better follow the code. Because the amount of effort needed to follow this approach is minimal, it is worth considering. Listing 16.7 represents Listing 16.6 in this slightly altered structure. This structure is similar to what is generated by Microsoft Visual C# .NET.

16

LISTING 16.7   ControlAppB.cs—Structuring Your Code for Integrated Development Environments

```
 1:  // ControlAppB.cs - Working with controls
 2:  //------------------------------------------------------------
 3:
 4:  using System;
 5:  using System.Windows.Forms;
 6:  using System.Drawing;
 7:
 8:  public class ControlAppB : Form
 9:  {
10:     public ControlAppB()
11:     {
12:        InitializeComponent();
13:     }
14:
15:     private void InitializeComponent()
16:     {
17:        this.Text = Environment.CommandLine;
18:        this.StartPosition = FormStartPosition.CenterScreen;
19:
20:        // Create the controls...
21:        Label myDateLabel = new Label();
22:        Label myLabel = new Label();
23:
24:        myLabel.Text = "This program was executed at:";
25:        myLabel.AutoSize = true;
26:        myLabel.Left = 50;
27:        myLabel.Top = 20;
28:
29:        DateTime currDate = new DateTime();
30:        currDate = DateTime.Now;
31:        myDateLabel.Text = currDate.ToString();
32:
33:        myDateLabel.AutoSize = true;
```

LISTING 16.7   continued

```
34:            myDateLabel.Left = 50 + myLabel.PreferredWidth + 10;
35:            myDateLabel.Top = 20;
36:
37:            this.Width = myLabel.PreferredWidth +
               ➥myDateLabel.PreferredWidth + 110;
38:            this.Height = myLabel.PreferredHeight+ 100;
39:
40:            // Add the control to the form...
41:            this.Controls.Add(myDateLabel);
42:            this.Controls.Add(myLabel);
43:        }
44:
45:        public static void Main( string[] args )
46:        {
47:            Application.Run( new ControlAppB() );
48:        }
49:    }
```

ANALYSIS The output for this listing is identical to that shown in Figure 16.12 for the previous listing. This listing illustrates a different structure for coding. Again, this listing is included and analyzed so that you won't be surprised if you use a tool such as Microsoft Visual C# .NET and see that it follows a different structure than what has been previously presented here.

Looking at this listing, you can see that the code is broken into a couple of methods instead of being placed in the Main method. Additionally, you can see that rather than declaring a specific instance of a form, an instance is created at the same time the Application.Run method is called.

When this application is executed, the Main method in Lines 45–48 is executed first. This method has one line of code that creates a new ControlAppB instance and passes it to the Application.Run method. This one line of code kicks off a series of other activities. The first thing to happen is that the ControlAppB constructor is called to create the new ControlAppB. A constructor has been included in Lines 10–13 of the listing. The constructor again has one simple call, InitializeComponent. This call causes the code in Lines 17–43 to execute. This is the same code that you saw earlier, with one minor exception: Instead of using the name of the form, you use the this keyword. Because you are working within an instance of a form, this refers to the current form. Everywhere you referred to the myForm instance in the previous listing, you now refer to this. When the initialization of the form items is completed, control goes back to the constructor, which is also complete. Control is therefore passed back to Main, which then passes the newly initialized ControlAppB object to the Application.Run method. This displays the form and takes care of the windows looping until the program ends.

The nice thing about this structure is that it moves all your component and form initialization into one method that is separate from a lot of your other programming logic. In larger programs, you will find this beneficial.

Working with Buttons

One of the most common controls used in Windows applications are buttons. Buttons can be created using the—you guessed it—Button class. Buttons differ from labels, in that you will most likely want an action to occur when the user clicks on a button.

Before jumping into creating button actions, it is worth taking a minute to cover creating and drawing buttons. As with labels, the first step to using a button is to instantiate a button object using the Button class:

```
Button myButton = new Button();
```

After you've created the button object, you can set properties to customize its look and feel. As with the Label control, there are too many properties, data members, and methods to list here. You can get the complete list from the help documents. Table 16.5 lists a few of the properties.

TABLE 16.5   A Few Button Properties

Property	Description
BackColor	Returns or sets the background color of the button.
BackgroundImage	Returns or sets an image that will display on the button's background.
Bottom	Returns the distance between the bottom of the button and the top of the container where the button resides.
Enabled	Returns or sets a value indicating whether the control is enabled.
Height	Returns or sets a value indicating the height of the button.
Image	Returns or sets an image on the button.
Left	Returns or sets the position of the left side of the button.
Right	Returns or sets the position of the right side of the button.
Text	Returns or sets the text on the button.
TextAlign	Returns or sets the button's text alignment.
Top	Returns or sets a value indicating the location of the top of the button.
Visible	Returns or sets a value indicating whether the button is visible.
Width	Returns or sets the width of the button.

16

Note Take a close look at the properties in Table 16.5. These should look like some of the same properties you used with Label. There is a good reason for this similarity. All the controls inherit from a more general Control class. This class enables all the controls to use the same methods or the same names to do similar tasks. For example, Top is the property for the top of a control, regardless of whether it is a button, text, or something else.

Adding Button Events

Recall that buttons differ from labels; you generally use a button to cause an action to occur. When the user clicks on a button, you want something to happen. To cause the action to occur, you use events.

After you create a button, you can associate one or more events with it. This is done in the same manner that you learned on Day 13, "Making Your Programs React with Delegates, Events, and Indexers." First, you create a method to handle the event, which will be called when the event occurs. As you learned on Day 13, this method take two parameters, the object that caused the event and a System.EventArgs variable. This method must also be protected and of type void. The format is as follows:

```
protected void methodName( object sender, System.EventArgs args )
```

Note When working with windows, you generally name the method based on what control caused the event, followed by what event occurred. For example, if button ABC was clicked, the method name for the handler could be ABC_Click.

To activate the event, you need to associate it with the appropriate delegate. A delegate object named System.EventHandler takes care of all the windows events. By associating your event handlers to this delegate object, they will be called when appropriate. The format is as follows:

```
ControlName.Event += new System.EventHandler(this.methodName);
```

Here, ControlName.Event is the name of the control and the name of the event for the control. this is the current form, and methodName is the method that will handle the event (as mentioned previously).

Listing 16.8 presents a modified version of Listing 16.7; Figure 16.13 shows the output. You can see that the date and time are still displayed in the form. You can also see, however, that a button has been added. When the button is clicked, an event fires that updates the date and time. Additionally, four other event handlers have been added to this listing for fun. These events are kicked off whenever the mouse moves over or leaves either of the two controls.

LISTING **16.8** ButtonApp.cs—Using Buttons and Events

```
 1:  // ButtonApp.cs - Working with buttons and events
 2:  //------------------------------------------------------------
 3:
 4:  using System;
 5:  using System.Windows.Forms;
 6:  using System.Drawing;
 7:
 8:  public class ButtonApp : Form
 9:  {
10:     private Label  myDateLabel;
11:     private Button btnUpdate;
12:
13:     public ButtonApp()
14:     {
15:        InitializeComponent();
16:     }
17:
18:     private void InitializeComponent()
19:     {
20:         this.Text = Environment.CommandLine;
21:         this.StartPosition = FormStartPosition.CenterScreen;
22:         this.FormBorderStyle = FormBorderStyle.Fixed3D;
23:
24:         myDateLabel = new Label();     // Create label
25:
26:         DateTime currDate = new DateTime();
27:         currDate = DateTime.Now;
28:         myDateLabel.Text = currDate.ToString();
29:
30:         myDateLabel.AutoSize = true;
31:         myDateLabel.Location = new Point( 50, 20);
32:         myDateLabel.BackColor = this.BackColor;
33:
34:         this.Controls.Add(myDateLabel);  // Add label to form
35:
36:         // Set width of form based on Label's width
37:         this.Width = (myDateLabel.PreferredWidth + 100);
38:
39:         btnUpdate = new Button();     // Create a button
40:
41:         btnUpdate.Text = "Update";
42:         btnUpdate.BackColor = Color.LightGray;
43:         btnUpdate.Location = new Point(((this.Width/2) -
```

16

LISTING 16.8   continued

```
44:                          (btnUpdate.Width / 2)),  (this.Height - 75));
45:
46:          this.Controls.Add(btnUpdate);  // Add button to form
47:
48:          // Add a click event handler using the default event handler
49:          btnUpdate.Click += new System.EventHandler(this.btnUpdate_Click);
50:          btnUpdate.MouseEnter +=
    ➥           new System.EventHandler(this.btnUpdate_MouseEnter);
51:          btnUpdate.MouseLeave +=
    ➥           new System.EventHandler(this.btnUpdate_MouseLeave);
52:
53:          myDateLabel.MouseEnter +=
    ➥           new System.EventHandler(this.myDataLabel_MouseEnter);
54:          myDateLabel.MouseLeave +=
    ➥           new System.EventHandler(this.myDataLabel_MouseLeave);
55:      }
56:
57:      protected void btnUpdate_Click( object sender, System.EventArgs e)
58:      {
59:          DateTime currDate =DateTime.Now ;
60:          this.myDateLabel.Text = currDate.ToString();
61:      }
62:
63:
64:      protected void btnUpdate_MouseEnter(object sender, System.EventArgs e)
65:      {
66:          this.BackColor = Color.HotPink;
67:      }
68:
69:      protected void btnUpdate_MouseLeave(object sender, System.EventArgs e)
70:      {
71:          this.BackColor = Color.Blue;
72:      }
73:
74:      protected void myDataLabel_MouseEnter(object sender, System.EventArgs e)
75:      {
76:          this.BackColor = Color.Yellow;
77:      }
78:
79:      protected void myDataLabel_MouseLeave(object sender, System.EventArgs e)
80:      {
81:          this.BackColor = Color.Green;
82:      }
83:
84:
85:      public static void Main( string[] args )
86:      {
87:         Application.Run( new ButtonApp() );
88:      }
89:  }
```

OUTPUT

FIGURE 16.13

Using a button and events.

16

ANALYSIS This listing uses the Windows designer format even though a designer was not used. This is a good way to format your code, so I follow the format here.

You will notice that I made a change to the previous listing. In Lines 10–11, the label and button are declared as members of the form rather than members of a method. This enables all the methods within the form's class to use these two variables. They are private, so only this class can use them.

The Main method and the constructor are no different from those in the previous listing. The InitializeComponent method has changed substantially; however, most of the changes are easy to understand. Line 31 offers the first new item. Instead of using the Top and Left properties to set the location of the myDateLabel control, a Point object was used. This Point object was created with the value (50, 20) and immediately was assigned to the Location property of the label.

> **Tip**
>
> You might find that creating an object and immediately assigning it can be easier to follow than doing multiple assignments. Either method works. Use whichever you are most comfortable with or whichever is easiest to understand.

In Line 39, a button named btnUpdate is created. It is then customized by assigning values to several properties. Don't be confused by the calculations in Lines 43–44; this is just like line 31, except that instead of using literals, calculations are used. Also keep in mind that this is the form, so this.Width is the width of the form.

Line 46 adds the button to the form. As you can see, this is done exactly the same way that any other control would be added to the form.

In Lines 49–54, you see the fun part of this listing. These lines are assigning handlers to various events. On the left side of these assignments, you see the controls and one of their events. This event is assigned to the method name that is being passed to System.EventHandler. For example, in Line 49, the btnUpdate_Click method is being assigned to the Click event of the btnUpdate button. In Lines 50–51, events are being assigned to the MouseEnter and MouseLeave events of btnUpdate. Lines 53–54 assign events to the MouseEnter and MouseLeave events of myDataLabel. Yes, a label control can have events, too. Virtually all controls have events.

> **Note** Too many events are associated with each control type to list in this book. To know which events are available, check the help documentation.

For the event to work, you must actually create the methods you associated with them. In Lines 57–82, you see a number of very simple methods. These are the same methods that were associated in Lines 49–54.

Creating an OK Button

A common button found on many forms is an OK button. This button is clicked when users complete what they are doing. The result of this button is that the form is usually closed.

If you created the form and are using the Application class's Run method, you can create an event handler for a button click that ends the Run method. This method can be as simple as this one:

```
protected void btnOK_Click( object sender, System.EventArgs e)
{
    // Final code logic before closing form
    Application.Exit();   // Ends the Application.Run message loop.
}
```

If you don't want to exit the entire application or application loop, you can use the Close method on the form instead. As its name indicates, the Close method closes the form.

An alternative method exists for implementing the logic of OK. This involves taking a slightly different approach. First, instead of using the Application class's Run method, you can use a Form object's ShowDialog method. The ShowDialog method displays a dialog box and waits for the dialog box to complete. A dialog box is simply a form. All other logic for creating the form is the same.

In general, if a user presses the Enter key on a form, the form activates the OK button. You can associate the Enter key with a button using the AcceptButton property of the form. You set this property equal to the button that will be activated when the Enter key is pressed.

Working with Text Boxes

Another popular control is the text box. The text box control is used to obtain text input from the users. Using a text box control and events, you can obtain information from your users that you can then use. Listing 16.9 illustrates the use of text box controls; Figure 16.14 shows the output.

LISTING 16.9   GetName.cs—Using Text Box Controls

```
 1:  // GetName.cs - Working with text controls
 2:  //-------------------------------------------------------------
 3:
 4:  using System;
 5:  using System.Windows.Forms;
 6:  using System.Drawing;
 7:
 8:  public class GetName : Form
 9:  {
10:      private Button btnOK;
11:
12:      private Label  lblFirst;
13:      private Label  lblMiddle;
14:      private Label  lblLast;
15:      private Label  lblFullName;
16:      private Label  lblInstructions;
17:
18:      private TextBox txtFirst;
19:      private TextBox txtMiddle;
20:      private TextBox txtLast;
21:
22:      public GetName()
23:      {
24:          InitializeComponent();
25:      }
26:
27:      private void InitializeComponent()
28:      {
29:          this.FormBorderStyle = FormBorderStyle.Fixed3D;
30:          this.Text = "Get User Name";
31:          this.StartPosition = FormStartPosition.CenterScreen;
32:
```

LISTING **16.9**   continued

```
33:          // Instantiate the controls...
34:          lblInstructions = new Label();
35:          lblFirst    = new Label();
36:          lblMiddle   = new Label();
37:          lblLast     = new Label();
38:          lblFullName = new Label();
39:
40:          txtFirst    = new TextBox();
41:          txtMiddle   = new TextBox();
42:          txtLast     = new TextBox();
43:
44:          btnOK = new Button();
45:
46:          // Set properties
47:
48:          lblFirst.AutoSize = true;
49:          lblFirst.Text     = "First Name:";
50:          lblFirst.Location = new Point( 20, 20);
51:
52:          lblMiddle.AutoSize = true;
53:          lblMiddle.Text     = "Middle Name:";
54:          lblMiddle.Location = new Point( 20, 50);
55:
56:          lblLast.AutoSize = true;
57:          lblLast.Text     = "Last Name:";
58:          lblLast.Location = new Point( 20, 80);
59:
60:          lblFullName.AutoSize = true;
61:          lblFullName.Location = new Point( 20, 110 );
62:
63:          txtFirst.Width = 100;
64:          txtFirst.Location = new Point(140, 20);
65:
66:          txtMiddle.Width = 100;
67:          txtMiddle.Location = new Point(140, 50);
68:
69:          txtLast.Width = 100;
70:          txtLast.Location = new Point(140, 80);
71:
72:          lblInstructions.Width = 250;
73:          lblInstructions.Height = 60;
74:          lblInstructions.Text = "Enter your first, middle, and last name." +
75:                        "\nYou will see your name appear as you type." +
76:                        "\nFor fun, edit your name after entering it.";
77:          lblInstructions.TextAlign = ContentAlignment.MiddleCenter;
78:          lblInstructions.Location =
79:            new Point(((this.Width/2) - (lblInstructions.Width / 2 )), 140);
80:
```

LISTING **16.9**   continued

```
81:            this.Controls.Add(lblFirst);    // Add label to form
82:            this.Controls.Add(lblMiddle);
83:            this.Controls.Add(lblLast);
84:            this.Controls.Add(lblFullName);
85:            this.Controls.Add(txtFirst);
86:            this.Controls.Add(txtMiddle);
87:            this.Controls.Add(txtLast);
88:            this.Controls.Add(lblInstructions);
89:
90:            btnOK.Text = "Done";
91:            btnOK.BackColor = Color.LightGray;
92:            btnOK.Location = new Point(((this.Width/2) - (btnOK.Width / 2)),
93:                                        (this.Height - 75));
94:
95:            this.Controls.Add(btnOK);  // Add button to form
96:
97:            // Event handlers
98:            btnOK.Click += new System.EventHandler(this.btnOK_Click);
99:            txtFirst.TextChanged +=
        ➥        new System.EventHandler(this.txtChanged_Event);
100:            txtMiddle.TextChanged +=
        ➥        new System.EventHandler(this.txtChanged_Event);
101:            txtLast.TextChanged +=
        ➥        new System.EventHandler(this.txtChanged_Event);
102:    }
103:
104:    protected void btnOK_Click( object sender, System.EventArgs e)
105:    {
106:        Application.Exit();
107:    }
108:
109:    protected void txtChanged_Event( object sender, System.EventArgs e)
110:    {
111:        lblFullName.Text = txtFirst.Text + " " + txtMiddle.Text +
        ➥            " " + txtLast.Text;
112:    }
113:
114:    public static void Main( string[] args )
115:    {
116:        Application.Run( new GetName() );
117:    }
118: }
```

OUTPUT

FIGURE 16.14

Using the text box control.

ANALYSIS As you can see by looking at the output of this listing, the applications that you are creating are starting to look useful. The text box controls in this listing enable your users to enter their name. This name is concatenated and displayed to the screen.

Although Listing 16.9 is long, much of the code is repetitive because of the three similar controls for first, middle, and last names. In Lines 10–20, a number of controls are declared within the frmGetName class. These controls are instantiated (see Lines 34–44) and assigned values within the InitializeComponent method. In Lines 48–58, the three labels for first, middle, and last names are assigned values. They first have their AutoSize property set to true, so the control will be large enough to hold the information. The text value is then assigned. Finally, each is positioned on the form. As you can see, they are each placed 20 pixels from the edge. They also are spaced vertically at different positions.

In Lines 60–61, the full name label is declared. Its Text property is not assigned a value at this point; it obtains its Text assignment when an event is called.

Lines 63–70 assign locations and widths to the text box controls that are being used in this program. As you can see, these assignments are done in the same manner as for the controls you've already learned about.

In Lines 72–79, instructions are added via another label control. Don't be confused by all the code being used here. In Line 74, three lines of text are being added to the control; however, this is really just one very long string of text that has been broken to make it easier to read. The plus sign concatenates the three pieces and assigns them all as a single string to the lblInstructions.Text property. Line 77 uses another property that you have not seen before. This is the TextAlign property that aligns the text within the label control; it is assigned a value from the ContentAlignment enumeration. In this listing,

MiddleCenter was used. Other valid values from the ContentAlignment enumerator include BottomCenter, BottomLeft, BottomRight, MiddleLeft, MiddleRight, TopCenter, TopLeft, and TopRight.

> **Caution**
>
> Although different controls have properties with the same name, such properties might not accept the same values. For example, the label control's TextAlign property is assigned a value from the ContentAlignment enumeration. The text box control's TextAlign is assigned a HorizontalAlignment enumeration value.

16

Lines 98–101 add exception handlers. As you can see, Line 98 adds a handler for the Click event of the btnOK button. The method called is in Lines 104–107. This method exits the application loop, thus helping end the program.

Lines 99–101 add event handlers for the TextChanged event of the text box buttons. Whenever the text within one of the three text boxes is changed, the txtChanged_Event is called. As you can see, the same method can be used with multiple handlers. This method concatenates the three name fields and assigns the result to the lblFullNameText control.

Working with Other Controls

Listing 16.9 provides the basis of what you need to build basic applications. You can use a number of other controls as well. For the most part, basic use of the controls is similar to the use you've seen in the listings in today's lessons. You create the control, modify the properties to be what you need, create event handlers to handle any actions you want to react to, and finally place the control on the form. Some controls, such as list boxes, are a little more complex for assigning initial data, but overall the process of using such controls is the same.

As mentioned earlier, covering all the controls and their functionality would make for a very, very thick book on its own. The online documentation is a great starting point for working the details of these. Although it is beyond the scope of this book to go into too much depth, the popularity of Windows-based programming warrants covering a few additional Windows topics in tomorrow's lesson before moving on to Web forms and services.

Summary

Today's lesson was a lot of fun. As you have learned, using the classes, methods, properties, and events defined in the `System.Windows.Forms` namespace can help you create Windows-based applications with very little code. Today you learned how to create and customize a form. You also learned how to add basic controls to the form and how to work with events to give your forms functionality. Although only a few of the controls were introduced, you will find that using the other controls is similar in a lot of ways to working with the ones presented today.

Tomorrow you continue to expand on what you learned today. On Day 20, "Creating Web Applications," you'll learn how windows forms differ from Web forms.

Q&A

Q Where can I learn more about windows forms?

A You can learn more about windows forms from the documentation that comes with the .NET SDK. Microsoft's .NET SDK includes a Windows Forms Quick Start.

Q Do all .NET Frameworks and runtimes on all platforms support windows, forms, and controls?

A No—at least, not yet. Microsoft's framework fully supports forms. At the time this book was written, frameworks such as the mono project were working to support forms. Although different .NET Frameworks can support windows, forms, and controls in different manners, it is expected that most will try to mimic the classes and controls that Microsoft used.

Q I noticed that `Form` is listed in the table of controls. Why?

A A form is a control. Most of the functionality of a control is also available to a form.

Q Why didn't you cover all the properties, events, and methods for the controls presented today?

A More than 40 controls exist within the framework classes. Additionally, many of these controls have many more than a hundred methods, events, and properties. Covering more than 4,000 items with just a line each would take roughly 80 pages.

Workshop

The Workshop provides quiz questions to help you solidify your understanding of the material covered and exercises to provide you with experience in using what you've learned. Try to understand the quiz and exercise answers before continuing to the next day's lesson. Answers are provided on the CD.

Quiz

1. What is the name of the namespace where most of the windows controls are located?

2. What method can be used to display a form?

3. What three steps are involved in getting a control on a form?

4. What do you enter on the command line to compile the program xyz.cs as a windows program?

5. If you want to include the assembly myAssmb.dll when you compile the program xyz.cs on the command line, what do you include on the command line with your compile command?

6. What does the Show() method of the Form class do? What is the problem with using this method?

7. Which of the following causes the Application.Run method to end?
   a. A method.
   b. An event.
   c. The last line of code in the program is reached.
   d. It never ends.
   e. None of the above.

8. What possible colors can you use for a form? What namespace needs to be included to use such colors?

9. What property can be used to assign a text value to a label?

10. What is the difference between a text box and a label?

Exercises

1. Write the shortest Windows application you can.

2. Create a program that centers a 200 × 200–pixel form on the screen.

3. Create a form that contains a text field that can be used to enter a number. When the user presses a button, display a message in a label that states whether the number is from 0 to 1000.

4. **Bug Buster**: The following program has a problem. Enter it in your editor and compile it. Which lines generate error messages?

```
 1:  using System.Windows.Forms;
 2:
 3:  public class frmHello : Form
 4:  {
 6:      public static void Main( string[] args )
 7:      {
 8:          frmHello frmHelloApp = new frmHello();
 9:          frmHelloApp.Show();
10:      }
11:  }
```

DAY **17**

Creating Windows Applications

Yesterday you learned how to create a windows form and to add controls to it.
Today you will see a couple of additional controls and also learn to enhance
your forms in several ways. Today you...

- Use radio buttons within groups.
- Take a look at containers.
- Add items to a list box control.
- Enhance your applications by adding menus.
- Discover the MessageBox class.
- See how to use a few existing dialog boxes.

Note

> Today's lesson continues yesterday's introduction to windows forms func-
> tionality; however, this is merely a foundation that you can expand upon.
> Effectively covering the controls and the functionality of windows forms
> would take another 1,000-page book. You will find, however, that these two
> days give you a solid foundation for building windows forms–based applica-
> tions.

Working with Radio Buttons

In yesterday's lesson, you learned how to create a couple of basic controls. You were told
that most controls are created and implemented in the same manner:

1. Instantiate a control object.

2. Set property values.

3. Add it to the form.

Radio buttons can be created the same way. Radio buttons are controls that are generally
used in groups. Just like an automobile radio, when one button is selected, any others
grouped with it are generally unselected. As such, they are helpful when the user has a
limited number of choices to make. They are also handy when you want all the choices
to be displayed—for example, when selecting gender (male or female) or selecting mari-
tal status (single or married). To create a radio button, you use the `RadioButton` class.

Grouping Radio Buttons

Radio buttons differ from other controls in that they are generally grouped as a set. If one
button in the group is selected, you want the others to be unselected. Listing 17.1 presents a form that includes two groups of radio buttons. The main form for this listing is
presented in Figure 17.1.

LISTING 17.1   BadRadio.cs—Using and Grouping Radio Buttons

```
1:  // BadRadio.cs - Using Radio Buttons
2:  //             - Not quite right...
3:  //-------------------------------------------------------------
4:
5:  using System.Drawing;
6:  using System.Windows.Forms;
7:
8:  public class BadRadio : Form
9:  {
```

LISTING **17.1** continued

```
10:    private RadioButton rdMale;
11:    private RadioButton rdFemale;
12:    private RadioButton rdYouth;
13:    private RadioButton rdAdult;
14:    private Button btnOK;
15:    private Label lblText1;
16:    private Label lblText2;
17:
18:    public BadRadio()
19:    {
20:        InitializeComponent();
21:    }
22:
23:    private void InitializeComponent()
24:    {
25:        this.rdMale   = new System.Windows.Forms.RadioButton();
26:        this.rdFemale = new System.Windows.Forms.RadioButton();
27:        this.lblText1 = new System.Windows.Forms.Label();
28:        this.rdYouth  = new System.Windows.Forms.RadioButton();
29:        this.rdAdult  = new System.Windows.Forms.RadioButton();
30:        this.lblText2 = new System.Windows.Forms.Label();
31:        this.btnOK    = new System.Windows.Forms.Button();
32:
33:        // Form1
34:        this.ClientSize = new System.Drawing.Size(350, 225);
35:        this.Text       = "Radio Buttons 1";
36:
37:        // rdMale
38:        this.rdMale.Location = new System.Drawing.Point(50, 65);
39:        this.rdMale.Size     = new Size(90, 15);
40:        this.rdMale.TabIndex = 0;
41:        this.rdMale.Text     = "Male";
42:
43:        // rdFemale
44:        this.rdFemale.Location = new System.Drawing.Point(50, 90);
45:        this.rdFemale.Size     = new System.Drawing.Size(90, 15);
46:        this.rdFemale.TabIndex = 1;
47:        this.rdFemale.Text     = "Female";
48:
49:        // lblText1
50:        this.lblText1.Location = new System.Drawing.Point(50, 40);
51:        this.lblText1.Size     = new System.Drawing.Size(90, 15);
52:        this.lblText1.TabIndex = 2;
53:        this.lblText1.Text     = "Sex";
54:
55:        // rdYouth
56:        this.rdYouth.Location = new System.Drawing.Point(220, 65);
```

17

LISTING **17.1**   continued

```
57:          this.rdYouth.Size    = new System.Drawing.Size(90, 15);
58:          this.rdYouth.TabIndex = 3;
59:          this.rdYouth.Text     = "Over 21";
60:
61:
62:          // rdAdult
63:          this.rdAdult.Location = new System.Drawing.Point(220, 90);
64:          this.rdAdult.Size     = new System.Drawing.Size(90, 15);
65:          this.rdAdult.TabIndex = 4;
66:          this.rdAdult.Text     = "Under 21";
67:
68:          // lblText2
69:          this.lblText2.Location = new System.Drawing.Point(220, 40);
70:          this.lblText2.Size     = new System.Drawing.Size(90, 15);
71:          this.lblText2.TabIndex = 5;
72:          this.lblText2.Text     = "Age Group";
73:
74:          // btnOK
75:          this.btnOK.Location = new System.Drawing.Point(130, 160);
76:          this.btnOK.Size     = new System.Drawing.Size(70, 30);
77:          this.btnOK.TabIndex = 6;
78:          this.btnOK.Text     = "OK";
79:          this.btnOK.Click    += new System.EventHandler(this.btnOK_Click);
80:
81:          this.Controls.Add(rdMale);
82:          this.Controls.Add(rdFemale);
83:          this.Controls.Add(lblText1);
84:          this.Controls.Add(rdYouth);
85:          this.Controls.Add(rdAdult);
86:          this.Controls.Add(lblText2);
87:          this.Controls.Add(btnOK);
88:       }
89:
90:    private void btnOK_Click(object sender, System.EventArgs e)
91:    {
92:       Application.Exit();
93:    }
94:
95:    static void Main()
96:    {
97:       Application.Run(new BadRadio());
98:    }
99: }
```

OUTPUT

FIGURE 17.1

Radio buttons in use.

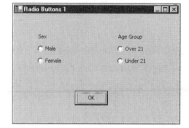

ANALYSIS This listing creates a form with four radio buttons and a command button. There are also two label controls used to provide descriptive information back to the person using the program. When you run this program, you will see that the radio buttons operate as you would expect them to—almost. When you select one radio button, all the others are unselected—that is the standard way radio buttons operate. The problem is that when you select one of the two buttons in the sex category, the choice in the age group category is unselected. It would be better if these two categories were separated. Before showing you how to resolve this issue, it is worth taking a few minutes to review this listing.

In Lines 5–6, the `using` statements include the `Drawing` and `Windows.Forms` namespaces within the `System` namespace. The `Drawing` namespace is used to shorten the names of the `Point` class. The `Windows.Forms` namespace is included to shorten the names of the classes used for forms and controls.

Line 8 presents the beginning statement for the class. In this line, the new form, `BadRadio`, is defined. It inherits from the `Form` class.

In Lines 10–16, a number of private members are declared for the `BadRadio` class. This includes the four radio buttons that will be used (Lines 10–14), the OK button (Line 14), and the two text labels (Lines 15–16). These are instantiated and defined values later in the listing.

Lines 18–21 contain the standard constructor for the form. This should look familiar because it is the same format used in yesterday's later listings. The method `InitializeComponent` is called, which does all the work of setting up the base form for the application.

The `InitializeComponent` method starts by instantiating each of the controls (Lines 25–31). Notice that I included the explicit names for the constructors. Because of the earlier `using` statement, these could have been condensed to just the name of the constructor. For example, Line 25 could have been this:

```
this.rdMail = new RadioButton();
```

I included the full names throughout this listing so you could see which namespaces were being used.

Starting with Line 34, the first values are set for the form. In Line 34, the size of the application's form is set. The ClientSize property of the current form (this) is set by assigning a Size value. In Line 35, the Text for the form is set. Remember, the Text property sets the title that will be used on the form.

In Line 25, the first of the radio buttons is instantiated. It is then set up starting in Line 38. First, the location is set by assigning a Point value to the radio button's Location property. The point will be an (x,y) location on the form. In this case, the button will be positioned 50 pixels over and 65 pixels down. The size of the control is set in Line 39. This is the amount of space given to the little button as well as the text. In Line 40, the TabIndex property is set. Finally, in Line 41, the text included on the radio button is set. In this case, the button is set to equal Male. In the following lines of the listing, the rdFemale, rdYouth, and rdAdult radio buttons are set up in the same manner.

Note

> The TabIndex property is on most controls. This is the order in which the controls will be selected when the Tab button is pressed. The first control is index 0, the second is index 1, the third is index 2, and so on. Setting the tab index enables you to control the order in which the user can navigate through a form's controls.

The two labels on the form are set up in Lines 49–53 and Lines 69–72. In Lines 75–79, the OK button is set up with an event handler that will exit the program when the button is selected.

The final step of initializing the form involves adding all the controls to the actual form. This is done using Controls.Add in Lines 81–87. When this is completed, the form is initialized and ready to display with all the controls.

No logic was needed to actually manipulate the radio buttons. They already contain the code necessary to select and unselect. As mentioned earlier, though, this listing is not operating exactly as you would want. A change needs to be made to enable the two sets of radio buttons to operate independently.

Working with Containers

The answer to the issue in Listing 17.1 is obtained by using containers. A container enables you to group a set of controls. You have already been using a container—your main form. You can also create your own containers, which you can place in the form's container or any other container. By placing your two sets of radio buttons in Listing 17.1 into their own containers, you separate them.

You also can separate the controls by using another control, a group box. The group box operates in the same fashion as a container, and it gives you added functionality, including the capability to display a text label as part of the group box.

Listing 17.2 drops the label controls from Listing 17.2 and replaces them with group boxes. This listing also drops the use of explicit names. The explicit names were included in Listing 17.1 to help you know where different classes and types were stored. Figure 17.2 shows the radio buttons positioned within the group boxes.

LISTING 17.2   GoodRadio.cs—Grouping Radio Buttons

```
 1:  // GoodRadio.cs - Using Radio Buttons
 2:  //               - Using Groups
 3:  //-----------------------------------------------------------
 4:
 5:  using System.Drawing;
 6:  using System.Windows.Forms;
 7:
 8:  public class GoodRadio : Form
 9:  {
10:      private GroupBox gboxAge;
11:      private GroupBox gboxSex;
12:
13:      private RadioButton rdMale;
14:      private RadioButton rdFemale;
15:      private RadioButton rdYouth;
16:      private RadioButton rdAdult;
17:      private Button btnOK;
18:
19:      public GoodRadio()
20:      {
21:          InitializeComponent();
22:      }
23:
24:      private void InitializeComponent()
25:      {
26:          this.gboxAge  = new GroupBox();
27:          this.gboxSex  = new GroupBox();
28:          this.rdMale   = new RadioButton();
29:          this.rdFemale = new RadioButton();
30:          this.rdYouth  = new RadioButton();
31:          this.rdAdult  = new RadioButton();
32:          this.btnOK    = new Button();
33:
```

17

LISTING 17.2   continued

```
34:        // Form1
35:        this.ClientSize = new Size(350, 200);
36:        this.Text       = "Grouping Radio Buttons";
37:
38:        // gboxSex
39:        this.gboxSex.Location = new Point(15, 30);
40:        this.gboxSex.Size     = new Size(125, 100);
41:        this.gboxSex.TabStop  = false;
42:        this.gboxSex.Text     = "Sex";
43:
44:        // rdMale
45:        this.rdMale.Location = new Point(35, 35);
46:        this.rdMale.Size     = new Size(70, 15);
47:        this.rdMale.TabIndex = 0;
48:        this.rdMale.Text     = "Male";
49:
50:        // rdFemale
51:        this.rdFemale.Location = new Point(35, 60);
52:        this.rdFemale.Size     = new Size(70, 15);
53:        this.rdFemale.TabIndex = 1;
54:        this.rdFemale.Text     = "Female";
55:
56:        // gboxAge
57:        this.gboxAge.Location = new Point(200, 30);
58:        this.gboxAge.Size     = new Size(125, 100);
59:        this.gboxAge.TabStop  = false;
60:        this.gboxAge.Text     = "Age Group";
61:
62:        // rdYouth
63:        this.rdYouth.Location = new Point(35, 35);
64:        this.rdYouth.Size     = new Size(70, 15);
65:        this.rdYouth.TabIndex = 3;
66:        this.rdYouth.Text     = "Over 21";
67:
68:        // rdAdult
69:        this.rdAdult.Location = new Point(35, 60);
70:        this.rdAdult.Size     = new Size(70, 15);
71:        this.rdAdult.TabIndex = 4;
72:        this.rdAdult.Text     = "Under 21";
73:
74:        // btnOK
75:        this.btnOK.Location = new Point(130, 160);
76:        this.btnOK.Size     = new Size(70, 30);
77:        this.btnOK.TabIndex = 6;
78:        this.btnOK.Text     = "OK";
79:        this.btnOK.Click    += new System.EventHandler(this.btnOK_Click);
80:
```

LISTING 17.2   continued

```
81:            this.Controls.Add(gboxSex);
82:            this.Controls.Add(gboxAge);
83:
84:            this.gboxSex.Controls.Add(rdMale);
85:            this.gboxSex.Controls.Add(rdFemale);
86:            this.gboxAge.Controls.Add(rdYouth);
87:            this.gboxAge.Controls.Add(rdAdult);
88:
89:            this.Controls.Add(btnOK);
90:        }
91:
92:        private void btnOK_Click(object sender, System.EventArgs e)
93:        {
94:            Application.Exit();
95:        }
96:
97:        static void Main()
98:        {
99:            Application.Run(new GoodRadio());
100:        }
101:    }
```

OUTPUT

FIGURE 17.2

Grouped radio buttons.

ANALYSIS   This listing focuses on the use of the group boxes. If you used containers instead of group boxes, the coding would be similar to this listing, except that you would not set Text and other properties on the container. Instead, you would need to use other controls (such as labels) to create custom look-and-feel attributes on the container.

Lines 10–11 declare the two group box members that will be used in the form. The label controls were removed because a text description can be included on a group box. In Lines 26–27, the two group boxes are instantiated by calling the GroupBox constructor.

Lines 39–42 set the characteristics of the first group box control, gboxSex. Like other controls, the Location, Size, TabStop, and Text properties can be set. You can set other properties as well. Lines 57–60 set the properties for the gboxAge group box.

Tip

> Consult the online documentation for a complete list of all the properties
> and members of the group box. Like all the controls, there are lots—too
> many to cover here.

The big difference to notice in this listing is in Lines 81–87. In Lines 81–82, the two
groups, gboxSex and gboxAge, are added to the form. The radio buttons are not added to
the form. In Lines 84–87, the radio buttons are added to the group boxes instead. The
group box is a part of the form (this), so the radio buttons will appear on the form
within the group box.

By adding the radio buttons within the group buttons, you put them within separate containers. When you run this listing, you will see that selecting a Sex option has no impact
on the Age category.

Note

> You could have a selection of one of the Sex options impact an Age selec-
> tion. To do this, you would include an event that includes code to manipu-
> late the properties of the other control.

Working with List Boxes

Another common control that you want to use on your forms is a list box. A list box is a
control that enables you to list a number of items in a small box. The list box can be set
to scroll through the items. It can also be set to allow the user to select one or more
items. Because a list box requires a little more effort to set the properties with values, it
is worth taking a brief look at its base functionality.

A list box is set up like all the other controls you've seen so far. First, you define the list
box control as part of your form:

```
private ListBox myListBox;
```

You then need to instantiate it:

```
myListBox = new ListBox();
```

Of course, you can do both of these statements on a single line:

```
private ListBox myListBox = new ListBox();
```

After it's created, you can add it to your form—again, the same way you added the other controls:

```
this.Controls.Add(myListBox);
```

A list box is different because you want it to contain a list of items. Of course, you'll need to add these items.

Adding Items to the List

Adding items to a list box is done in a couple of steps. The first step is to let the list box know you are going to update it. This is done by calling the BeginUpdate method on the list box. For a list box named myListBox, this is done as follows:

```
myListBox.BeginUpdate();
```

After you've called this method, you can begin adding items to the list box by calling the Add method of the Items member of the list box. This is easier than it sounds. To add "My First Item" as an item to myListBox, you enter the following:

```
myListBox.Items.Add("My First Item");
```

Other items can be added in the same manner:

```
myListBox.Items.Add("My Second Item");
myListBox.Items.Add("My Third Item");
```

When you are finished adding your items, you need to indicate to the list box that you are done. This is accomplished by calling the EndUpdate method:

```
myListbox.EndUpdate();
```

That is all it takes to add items to the list box. Listing 17.3 uses two list boxes. You can see in the output in Figure 17.3 that they are presented differently.

LISTING 17.3   GetName.cs—Using List Boxes

```
 1:  // GetName.cs - Working with list box controls
 2:  //----------------------------------------------------------
 3:
 4:  using System.Windows.Forms;
 5:  using System.Drawing;
 6:
 7:  public class GetName : Form
 8:  {
 9:      private Button  btnOK;
10:      private Label   lblFullName;
11:      private TextBox txtFullName;
```

17

LISTING 17.3   continued

```
12:        private ListBox lboxSex;
13:        private Label   lblSex;
14:        private ListBox lboxAge;
15:
16:        public GetName()
17:        {
18:            InitializeComponent();
19:        }
20:
21:        private void InitializeComponent()
22:        {
23:            this.FormBorderStyle = FormBorderStyle.Fixed3D;
24:            this.Text = "Get User Info";
25:            this.StartPosition = FormStartPosition.CenterScreen;
26:
27:            // Instantiate the controls...
28:            lblFullName = new Label();
29:            txtFullName = new TextBox();
30:            btnOK       = new Button();
31:            lblSex      = new Label();
32:            lboxSex     = new ListBox();
33:            lboxAge     = new ListBox();
34:
35:            // Set properties
36:            lblFullName.Location = new Point(20, 40);
37:            lblFullName.AutoSize = true;
38:            lblFullName.Text = "Name:";
39:
40:            txtFullName.Width = 170;
41:            txtFullName.Location = new Point(80, 40);
42:
43:
44:            btnOK.Text = "Done";
45:            btnOK.Location = new Point(((this.Width/2) - (btnOK.Width / 2)),
46:                                        (this.Height - 75));
47:
48:            lblSex.Location = new Point(20, 70);
49:            lblSex.AutoSize = true;
50:            lblSex.Text = "Sex:";
51:
52:            // Set up ListBox
53:            lboxSex.Location = new Point(80, 70);
54:            lboxSex.Size = new Size(100, 20);
55:            lboxSex.SelectionMode = SelectionMode.One;
56:
```

LISTING 17.3 continued

```
57:          lboxSex.BeginUpdate();
58:            lboxSex.Items.Add("         ");
59:            lboxSex.Items.Add(" Boy     ");
60:            lboxSex.Items.Add(" Girl    ");
61:            lboxSex.Items.Add(" Man     ");
62:            lboxSex.Items.Add(" Lady    ");
63:          lboxSex.EndUpdate();
64:
65:          // Set up ListBox
66:          lboxAge.Location = new Point(80, 100);
67:          lboxAge.Size     = new Size(100, 60);
68:          lboxAge.SelectionMode = SelectionMode.One;
69:          lboxAge.BeginUpdate();
70:            lboxAge.Items.Add("          ");
71:            lboxAge.Items.Add(" Under 21 ");
72:            lboxAge.Items.Add("    21    ");
73:            lboxAge.Items.Add(" Over 21  ");
74:          lboxAge.EndUpdate();
75:          lboxAge.SelectedIndex = 0;
76:
77:          this.Controls.Add(btnOK);           // Add button to form
78:          this.Controls.Add(lblFullName);
79:          this.Controls.Add(txtFullName);
80:          this.Controls.Add(lboxSex);
81:          this.Controls.Add(lblSex);
82:          this.Controls.Add(lboxAge);
83:
84:          // Event handlers
85:          btnOK.Click += new System.EventHandler(this.btnOK_Click);
86:       }
87:
88:       protected void btnOK_Click( object sender, System.EventArgs e)
89:       {
90:          Application.Exit();
91:       }
92:
93:       public static void Main( string[] args )
94:       {
95:          Application.Run( new GetName() );
96:       }
97:    }
```

17

FIGURE **17.3**

Using list boxes.

ANALYSIS Listing 17.3 uses list boxes to display the selections for the Age and Sex categories. Additionally, the listing contains a text box for users to enter their name. In Figure 17.3, the default selections for the two list boxes are blanks. A blank value was entered as the first item for each list box.

In Lines 9–14, the controls for the form in this application are defined. In Lines 12 and 14, the list boxes are declared. In Lines 28–33, all the controls are instantiated. The two list box controls are instantiated in Lines 32 and 33.

The details of the list boxes are set later in the listing. The first list box, lboxSex, is defined in Lines 53–63. First, the location and size are set up in Lines 53–54. In Line 55, the selection mode is set. The possible selection modes for a list box are listed in Table 17.1. In Line 55, the mode for the lboxSex is SelectionMode.One. Only one item can be selected at a time.

TABLE 17.1   ListBox Selection Modes

Mode	Description
SelectionMode.One	Only one item can be selected at a time.
SelectionMode.MultiExtended	Multiple items can be selected. Shift, Ctrl, and the arrow keys can be used to make multiple selections.
SelectionMode.MultiSimple	Multiple items can be selected.
SelectionMode.None	No items can be selected.

In Lines 57–63, the different selection items are added to the lboxSex list box. This is done as shown earlier. First, the BeginUpdate method is called. Each item is then added by using the Items.Add method. Finally, the additions are ended by calling the EndUpdate method.

In Lines 66–75, the lboxAge is set up in a similar manner. You should notice two distinct differences. The first is that the SelectedIndex is set in Line 75 for the lboxAge control.

This determines which item is to be initially selected in the list box. The second difference is in the size of the control. For the lboxSex control, the size was set to 100×20 (in Line 54). For the lboxAge, the size was set to 100×60 (in Line 67). You can see the results of this on the displayed form (refer to Figure 17.3). The lboxSex control can display only one option at a time because of its smaller vertical size. Because the items don't fit in the size of the control, vertical scroll arrows are automatically added to the control. For the lboxAge box, the control is big enough, so no vertical scrollbar is needed.

Everything else about a list box is similar to the other controls. You can create events to determine when a selection has changed or when the user has left the control. You can add logic to your form to make sure that a selection was made. Or, you can do a lot more.

Adding Menus to Your Forms

Controls are one way to make your forms functional. Another way is to add menus. Most windowed applications include a menu of some sort. At a minimum, there is generally a File or a Help menu item. When selected, these usually list a set of submenu items for selection. You also can add menus to your forms.

Creating a Basic Menu

Listing 17.4 is the form you saw yesterday that displays the current date and time (see Figure 17.4). Instead of using a button to update the current date and time, this form uses a menu item. Although this is not a great use of a menu item, it illustrates a number of key points. First, you add a menu to your form. Second, you explore how the menu items are associated to an event item. Finally, you see how to code a menu item's event.

LISTING 17.4   Menu.cs—Basic Menu

```
 1:  // Menu.cs -
 2:  //------------------------------------------------------------
 3:
 4:  using System;
 5:  using System.Windows.Forms;
 6:  using System.Drawing;
 7:
 8:  public class Menu : Form
 9:  {
10:      private Label myDateLabel;
11:      private MainMenu myMainMenu;
12:
13:      public Menu()
14:      {
```

LISTING **17.4** continued

```
15:          InitializeComponent();
16:      }
17:
18:      private void InitializeComponent()
19:      {
20:         this.Text = "STY Menus";
21:         this.StartPosition = FormStartPosition.CenterScreen;
22:         this.FormBorderStyle = FormBorderStyle.Fixed3D;
23:
24:         myDateLabel = new Label();       // Create label
25:
26:         DateTime currDate = new DateTime();
27:         currDate = DateTime.Now;
28:         myDateLabel.Text = currDate.ToString();
29:
30:         myDateLabel.AutoSize = true;
31:         myDateLabel.Location = new Point( 50, 70);
32:         myDateLabel.BackColor = this.BackColor;
33:
34:         this.Controls.Add(myDateLabel);  // Add label to form
35:
36:         // Set width of form based on Label's width
37:         this.Width = (myDateLabel.PreferredWidth + 100);
38:
39:         myMainMenu = new MainMenu();
40:
41:         MenuItem menuitemFile = myMainMenu.MenuItems.Add("File");
42:         menuitemFile.MenuItems.Add(new MenuItem("Update Date",
43:                         new EventHandler(this.MenuUpdate_Selection)));
44:         menuitemFile.MenuItems.Add(new MenuItem("Exit",
45:                         new EventHandler(this.FileExit_Selection)));
46:         this.Menu = myMainMenu;
47:      }
48:
49:      protected void MenuUpdate_Selection(object sender, System.EventArgs e)
50:      {
51:          DateTime currDate = new DateTime();
52:          currDate = DateTime.Now;
53:          this.myDateLabel.Text = currDate.ToString();
54:      }
55:      protected void FileExit_Selection( object sender, System.EventArgs e )
56:      {
57:          this.Close();
58:      }
59:
60:      public static void Main( string[] args )
61:      {
62:          Application.Run( new Menu() );
63:      }
64: }
```

OUTPUT

FIGURE 17.4

The basic menu selected on the form.

ANALYSIS In Figure 17.4, the listing creates a simple File menu that contains two items, Update Date and Exit. Selecting Update Date updates the date and time on the screen. Selecting Exit ends the program by calling closing the current form using `this.Close()`.

The primary menu on a form is called the main menu, which contains File as well as any other options that appear across the top of the application. In Line 11 of Listing 17.4, a `MainMenu` type named `myMainMenu` is declared for the `Menu` form.

In Line 39, the `myMainMenu` data member is instantiated. In Lines 41–44, it is set up; in Line 46, it is added to the form.

Looking closer, you can see that a lot of work is done in Lines 41–46. In fact, a lot of work is done in Line 41 alone. In Line 41, a new data member is declared named `menuitemFile`. Additionally, the following statement adds a new item—the first item—to the `myMainMenu` menu:

```
MyMainMenu.MenuItems.Add("File");
```

This item is called File, and it is then assigned to the `menuitemFile` data member.

In general terms, to add a menu item, you can call the `MenuItems.Add` method on either a menu data member or another menu item data member. If you call this on the main menu, you get the primary items in the main menu. If you call `MenuItems.Add` on a menu item, you get a submenu menu item.

In Line 42, the menu item containing File, `menuitemFile`, has its `MenuItems.Add` method called. This means that a submenu item is being added to File. In the case of Line 42, this is the item Update Date. In Line 44, the submenu item Exit is added.

Wait a minute: If you look closely, you will see that the call in Line 41 to the `MenuItems.Add` method is different from the ones in Lines 42 and 44. It should be obvious to you that this method has been overloaded. If only one parameter string is passed, it is assumed to be the text item that will be displayed. In the calls in Lines 42 and 44, two parameters are passed. The first is a new MenuItem that is assigned directly to the menu rather than an intermediary variable.

The second is a new event handler. This is the event handler that will be called if and when the menu item is selected. Event-handler methods have been created (starting in Lines 49 and 54) for the two event handlers passed in Lines 43 and 45.

Line 49 contains the event handler for the Update Date menu option. This method call has the same name passed to the MenuItems.Add method in Line 42. Don't forget that when you set up the actual event-handler methods, you will have two parameters, the sender and EventArgs. When the Update Date menu option is selected, the event handler in Lines 49–54 is called. This method updates the date and time on the form. This could just as easily have done something else.

The event handler in Lines 55–58 is called when Exit is selected. This handler exits the application by closing the form.

Creating Multiple Menus

In this section, you add a second menu item to the main menu and control key access to your menu items. Listing 17.5 presents a program that contains both a File and a Help menu option on the main menu (see Figure 17.5). Each of these options contains its own submenu selections.

LISTING 17.5   Menus.cs—Multiple Items on the Main Menu

```
 1:  // Menus.cs -
 2:  //-----------------------------------------------------------
 3:
 4:  using System;
 5:  using System.Windows.Forms;
 6:  using System.Drawing;
 7:
 8:  public class Menus : Form
 9:  {
10:      private Label myDateLabel;
11:      private MainMenu myMainMenu;
12:
13:      public Menus()
14:      {
15:          InitializeComponent();
16:      }
17:
18:      private void InitializeComponent()
19:      {
```

LISTING **17.5**   continued

```
20:          this.Text = "STY Menus";
21:          this.StartPosition = FormStartPosition.CenterScreen;
22:          this.FormBorderStyle = FormBorderStyle.Fixed3D;
23:
24:          myDateLabel = new Label();      // Create label
25:
26:          DateTime currDate = new DateTime();
27:          currDate = DateTime.Now;
28:          myDateLabel.Text = currDate.ToString();
29:
30:          myDateLabel.AutoSize = true;
31:          myDateLabel.Location = new Point( 50, 70);
32:          myDateLabel.BackColor = this.BackColor;
33:
34:          this.Controls.Add(myDateLabel);  // Add label to form
35:
36:          // Set width of form based on Label's width
37:          this.Width = (myDateLabel.PreferredWidth + 100);
38:
39:          CreateMyMenu();
40:       }
41:
42:       protected void MenuUpdate_Selection( object sender, System.EventArgs e)
43:       {
44:          DateTime currDate = new DateTime();
45:          currDate = DateTime.Now;
46:          this.myDateLabel.Text = currDate.ToString();
47:       }
48:
49:       protected void FileExit_Selection( object sender, System.EventArgs e)
50:       {
51:          this.Close();
52:       }
53:
54:       protected void FileAbout_Selection( object sender, System.EventArgs e)
55:       {
56:          // display an about form
57:       }
58:
59:       public void CreateMyMenu()
60:       {
61:          myMainMenu = new MainMenu();
62:
63:          MenuItem menuitemFile = myMainMenu.MenuItems.Add("&File");
64:          menuitemFile.MenuItems.Add(new MenuItem("Update &Date",
65:                              new EventHandler(this.MenuUpdate_Selection),
66:                              Shortcut.CtrlD));
```

17

LISTING 17.5   continued

```
67:           menuitemFile.MenuItems.Add(new MenuItem("E&xit",
68:                               new EventHandler(this.FileExit_Selection),
69:                               Shortcut.CtrlX));
70:
71:           MenuItem menuitemHelp = myMainMenu.MenuItems.Add("&Help");
72:           menuitemHelp.MenuItems.Add(new MenuItem("&About",
73:                               new EventHandler(this.FileAbout_Selection)));
74:
75:           this.Menu = myMainMenu;
76:       }
77:
78:       public static void Main( string[] args )
79:       {
80:           Application.Run( new Menus() );
81:       }
82:   }
```

OUTPUT

FIGURE 17.5

Multiple items on the main menu.

ANALYSIS This listing is similar to Listing 17.4. One major difference is that the menu creation has been pulled into its own method to help organize the code better. This method, CreateMyMenu, is in Lines 59–76. The InitializeComponent method calls CreateMyMenu in Line 39 as a part of its initial form setup.

Lines 42–57 contain the events that might be activated by different menu selections. The first two, MenuUpdate_Selection and FileExit_Selection, are like the ones in Listing 17.4. The third, FileAbout_Selection, is associated with the About menu item on the Help menu. Line 56 does not contain any code; however, any code could be placed here. In the case of an About menu selection, that would most likely be the display of an informative dialog box. Later today, you'll see an example of such a dialog box.

The focus of this listing related to menus is in Lines 59–76, and it takes the same approach as in the previous listing. In Line 61, the main menu is instantiated. In Line 63, the File item is added to myMainMenu. There is one difference in this call: An ampersand

(&) has been added to File. This indicates that a letter—the letter following the ampersand—should be underlined on the display. For a `MainMenu` item, it also indicates that the given item should be selectable by using the Alt key with the letter following the ampersand. In this case, pressing Alt+F automatically selects the File menu option.

In Lines 64 and 67, you see the addition of menu items to the File menu similar to the ones in the previous listing; however, yet another version of the `MenuItems.Add` method is called. This time a third parameter is included, which specifies that the menu item should indicate that a keyboard shortcut can be used to select the given menu item. If you look at the two submenu items on the File menu, you will see that they have additional text indicating that a shortcut key is available (see Figure 17.6).

FIGURE 17.6

Shortcut key indicators on a menu item.

17

> **Note**
>
> Fortunately, there are shortcut keys already defined in the `Shortcut` data type. In general, you can use `Shortcut.Ctrl*`, where * is any letter.

Adding the second menu item to the main menu is done the same way the first item was added. The About menu item was added in Line 71. Because this menu item will have submenu items, you need to assign it to a `MenuItem` variable. In this case, it is `menuitemHelp`. `menuitemHelp` then has its items added using its `MenuItems.Add` method.

Using Checked Menus

One other common feature of using menus is the capability to check or uncheck a menu item. When checked, it is active; when unchecked, it is not active. Listing 17.6 illustrates how to add checking to a menu item and also provides an alternate way of declaring and defining menus (see Figure 17.7). This method requires more code; however, some people consider it easier to read and follow.

LISTING **17.6**   CheckedMenu.cs—Checking Menus

```
 1:  // CheckedMenu.cs - menus
 2:  //----------------------------------------------------------
 3:
 4:  using System;
 5:  using System.Windows.Forms;
 6:  using System.Drawing;
 7:
 8:  public class CheckedMenu : Form
 9:  {
10:      private Label myDateLabel;
11:      private MainMenu myMainMenu;
12:
13:      private MenuItem menuitemFile;
14:      private MenuItem menuitemUD;
15:      private MenuItem menuitemActive;
16:      private MenuItem menuitemExit;
17:      private MenuItem menuitemHelp;
18:      private MenuItem menuitemAbout;
19:
20:      public CheckedMenu()
21:      {
22:          InitializeComponent();
23:      }
24:
25:      private void InitializeComponent()
26:      {
27:          this.Text = "STY Menus";
28:          this.StartPosition = FormStartPosition.CenterScreen;
29:          this.FormBorderStyle = FormBorderStyle.Sizable;
30:
31:          myDateLabel = new Label();        // Create label
32:
33:          DateTime currDate = new DateTime();
34:          currDate = DateTime.Now;
35:          myDateLabel.Text = currDate.ToString();
36:
37:          myDateLabel.AutoSize = true;
38:          myDateLabel.Location = new Point( 50, 70);
39:          myDateLabel.BackColor = this.BackColor;
40:
41:          this.Controls.Add(myDateLabel);  // Add label to form
42:
43:          // Set width of form based on Label's width
44:          this.Width = (myDateLabel.PreferredWidth + 100);
45:
46:          CreateMyMenu();
47:      }
48:
```

LISTING 17.6 continued

```
49:   protected void MenuUpdate_Selection( object sender, System.EventArgs e)
50:   {
51:      if( menuitemActive.Checked == true)
52:      {
53:         DateTime currDate = new DateTime();
54:         currDate = DateTime.Now;
55:         this.myDateLabel.Text = currDate.ToString();
56:      }
57:      else
58:      {
59:         this.myDateLabel.Text = "** " + this.myDateLabel.Text + " **";
60:      }
61:   }
62:
63:   protected void FileExit_Selection( object sender, System.EventArgs e)
64:   {
65:      Application.Exit();
66:   }
67:
68:   protected void FileAbout_Selection( object sender, System.EventArgs e)
69:   {
70:      // display an about form
71:   }
72:
73:   protected void ActiveMenu_Selection( object sender, System.EventArgs e)
74:   {
75:      MenuItem tmp;
76:      tmp = (MenuItem) sender;
77:
78:      if ( tmp.Checked == true )
79:         tmp.Checked = false;
80:      else
81:         tmp.Checked = true;
82:   }
83:
84:   public void CreateMyMenu()
85:   {
86:      myMainMenu = new MainMenu();
87:
88:      // FILE MENU
89:      menuitemFile = myMainMenu.MenuItems.Add("&File");
90:
91:      menuitemUD = new MenuItem();
92:      menuitemUD.Text = "Update &Date";
93:      menuitemUD.Shortcut = Shortcut.CtrlD;
94:      menuitemUD.Click += new EventHandler(this.MenuUpdate_Selection);
95:      menuitemFile.MenuItems.Add( menuitemUD );
96:
```

17

LISTING 17.6   continued

```
97:            menuitemExit = new MenuItem();
98:            menuitemExit.Text = "E&xit";
99:            menuitemExit.Shortcut = Shortcut.CtrlX;
100:           menuitemExit.ShowShortcut = false;
101:           menuitemExit.Click += new EventHandler(this.FileExit_Selection);
102:           menuitemFile.MenuItems.Add( menuitemExit );
103:
104:           // HELP MENU
105:           menuitemHelp = myMainMenu.MenuItems.Add("&Help");
106:
107:           menuitemActive = new MenuItem();
108:           menuitemActive.Text = "Active";
109:           menuitemActive.Click += new EventHandler(this.ActiveMenu_Selection);
110:           menuitemActive.Checked = true;
111:           menuitemHelp.MenuItems.Add( menuitemActive );
112:
113:           menuitemAbout = new MenuItem();
114:           menuitemAbout.Text = "&About";
115:           menuitemAbout.Shortcut = Shortcut.CtrlA;
116:           menuitemAbout.ShowShortcut = false;
117:           menuitemAbout.Click += new EventHandler(this.FileAbout_Selection);
118:           menuitemHelp.MenuItems.Add( menuitemAbout );
119:
120:           this.Menu = myMainMenu;
121:       }
122:
123:       public static void Main( string[] args )
124:       {
125:           Application.Run( new CheckedMenu() );
126:       }
127:   }
```

OUTPUT

FIGURE 17.7

Checked menus.

ANALYSIS   This listing is a little longer than the previous two, partly because of the alternate way of creating the menu.

Instead of declaring a `MainMenu` data item and only the top-level menu items, this listing declares a `MainMenu` item in Line 11 and then `MenuItem` variables for each menu item that will exist. Lines 13–18 declare a `MenuItem` variable to hold each of the individual menu items.

As in the previous listing, the functionality to create the menu is placed in its own method, starting in Line 84. In Line 86, the `MainMenu` item, `myMainMenu`, is declared.

In Line 89, the first menu item, File, is declared in the same way as you've seen. The declaration of the submenu items is different this time. The Update Date menu item is created in Lines 91–95. First, a menu item variable, `menuitemUD`, is instantiated as a menu item. This is followed by setting individual property values on this menu item (Lines 92–93). In Line 94, an event handler is associated with the `Click` event of this menu item. This event handler will be called whenever the menu item is selected. Finally, in Line 95, the menu item is attached to its parent menu item. In this case, the `menuitemUD` is added to the File menu, `menuitemFile`.

All the other menu items are added in the same manner. In some cases, different properties are set.

This listing also incorporates a new feature that you've not used. The Active menu item on the Help menu can be checked on and off. If checked on, the date and time are updated when the Date Update menu item is selected. If checked off, the date and time are enclosed in asterisks when displayed. This is done by setting the Checked property on the menu item, as in Line 110, and by adding a little code to the menu item's event handler, `ActiveMenu_Selection`.

The `ActiveMenu_Selection` event handler is in Lines 73–83. There is nothing new in this routine, but a few lines are worth reviewing. As with other event handlers, this method receives an object as its first argument. Because this event was caused by a menu selection, you know that this object actually contains a `MenuItem`. In Lines 75–76, a temporary `MenuItem` variable is created and the argument is cast to this temporary variable. This temporary variable, `tmp`, can then be used to access all `MenuItem` properties and methods.

You also know that this event was activated by the Active menu selection. In Line 78, you check to see whether the Checked property of the Active menu item is `true` and thus checked. If it is, you uncheck it in Line 79 by setting the Checked property to `false`. If it wasn't checked, you set the Checked property to `true`. The result of this method is that it toggles the Active menu's check on and off.

The `MenuUpdate` event handler has also been modified in this listing. This event handler displays the current date if the active menu item is checked. If it isn't checked, the current date and time value is enclosed in asterisks and is redisplayed. The main point of this event handler is not what is being displayed. Rather, it is that the checked menu item can be used to determine what should occur.

Creating a Pop-Up Menu

In addition to the standard menus you have seen up to this point, you can create pop-up menus. A pop-up menu is a menu that can appear at any location on the screen. Listing 17.7 presents a pop-up menu that is displayed by pressing the right mouse button (see Figure 17.8).

LISTING 17.7   PopUp.cs—Using a Pop-Up Menu

```
 1:  // PopUp.cs - popup menus
 2:  //-------------------------------------------------------------
 3:
 4:  using System;
 5:  using System.Windows.Forms;
 6:  using System.Drawing;
 7:
 8:  public class PopUp : Form
 9:  {
10:     private ContextMenu myPopUp;
11:
12:     public PopUp()
13:     {
14:        InitializeComponent();
15:     }
16:
17:     private void InitializeComponent()
18:     {
19:        this.Text = "STY Pop-up Menu";
20:        this.StartPosition = FormStartPosition.CenterScreen;
21:
22:        CreatePopUp();
23:     }
24:
25:     protected void Popup_Selection( object sender, System.EventArgs e)
26:     {
27:        // Determine menu item and do logic...
28:        this.Text = ((MenuItem) sender).Text;
29:     }
30:
31:     private void CreatePopUp()
32:     {
33:        myPopUp = new ContextMenu();
34:
35:        myPopUp.MenuItems.Add("First Item",
36:                           new EventHandler(this.PopUp_Selection));
```

LISTING 17.7   continued

```
37:
38:            myPopUp.MenuItems.Add("Second Item",
39:                               new EventHandler(this.PopUp_Selection));
40:
41:            myPopUp.MenuItems.Add("-");
42:
43:            myPopUp.MenuItems.Add("Third Item",
44:                               new EventHandler(this.PopUp_Selection));
45:
46:            this.ContextMenu = myPopUp;
47:
48:        }
49:
50:        public static void Main( string[] args )
51:        {
52:            Application.Run( new PopUp() );
53:        }
54:    }
```

17

OUTPUT

FIGURE 17.8

A custom pop-up menu.

ANALYSIS Instead of creating a `MainMenu` object, to create a pop-up menu, you create a `ContextMenu` item. This is done in Listing 17.7 in Line 33, where `myPopUp` is instantiated as a `ContextMenu`. `myPopUp` was declared as a variable in Line 10.

You can add items to a `ContextMenu` the same way that you add them to a `MainMenu`—by using the `MenuItems.Add` method. In this listing, four items are added to this menu. The first, second, and fourth items are added the way you've seen before. The third item in Line 41 is the unique one. In Line 41, it appears that a single dash is being added to the menu. However, adding a single dash actually creates a line across the menu. You can see this in the output in Figure 17.8. When the items are all added to the `ContextMenu` item `myPopUp`, the menu is added as a `ContextMenu` to the current form.

You should also notice that all three of the actual menu items use the same event handler, PopUp_Selection. This event handler is defined in Lines 25–29, with the actual functionality contained on Line 28. Line 28 assigns a new value to the Text property of the current form. Remember, the Text property is the title on the form. The value assigned is the text of the object that called the event handler. This is the text of the menu item that was selected. The code in Line 28 casts the sender object to a MenuItem and then uses the text value of this MenuItem. This is a shortcut way of doing the same thing that was done in Lines 75–76 of the previous listing.

Displaying Pop-Up Dialog Boxes and Forms

You now know how to display controls and menus on your forms. You have also learned to create event handlers to react to events that occur on your forms. The one procedure that has been missing from the examples shown so far is how to display another dialog box or form.

The following sections cover three topics related to displaying a new form or dialog box. First, you use the basic functionality of the MessageBox class. Then you explore a few dialog boxes that exist in Microsoft Windows. Finally, you learn about creating your own dialog box form, which is not nearly the same as using the custom dialog boxes.

Working with the MessageBox Class

A class that is often used when doing Windows programming is a message box class. A message box class is defined in the Base Class Libraries (BCL) as well. This class enables you to display a message in a pop-up box. Listing 17.8 uses the MessageBox class to pop up messages. You can see this by the output in Figures 17.9–17.12.

LISTING 17.8   MsgBox.cs—Using the MessageBox Class

```
 1:  // MsgBox.cs - Using the MessageBox class
 2:  //-------------------------------------------------------------
 3:
 4:  using System;
 5:  using System.Windows.Forms;
 6:  using System.Drawing;
 7:
 8:  public class MsgBox : Form
 9:  {
10:      private ContextMenu myPopUp;
```

LISTING 17.8   continued

```
11:
12:     public MsgBox()
13:     {
14:         MessageBox.Show( "You have started the application.", "Status");
15:         InitializeComponent();
16:         CreatePopUp();
17:         MessageBox.Show( "Form has been initialized.", "Status");
18:     }
19:
20:     private void InitializeComponent()
21:     {
22:          this.Text = "STY C# Pop-up Menu";
23:          this.StartPosition = FormStartPosition.CenterScreen;
24:     }
25:
26:     protected void PopUp_Selection( object sender, System.EventArgs e)
27:     {
28:         // Determine menu item and do logic...
29:         MessageBox.Show( ((MenuItem) sender).Text, this.Text + " Msg Box");
30:     }
31:
32:     private void CreatePopUp()
33:     {
34:         myPopUp = new ContextMenu();
35:
36:         myPopUp.MenuItems.Add("First Item",
37:                             new EventHandler(this.PopUp_Selection));
38:         myPopUp.MenuItems.Add("Second Item",
39:                             new EventHandler(this.PopUp_Selection));
40:         myPopUp.MenuItems.Add("-");
41:         myPopUp.MenuItems.Add("Third Item",
42:                             new EventHandler(this.PopUp_Selection));
43:
44:         this.ContextMenu = myPopUp;
45:     }
46:
47:     public static void Main( string[] args )
48:     {
49:         Application.Run( new MsgBox() );
50:         MessageBox.Show( "You are done with the application", "Status");
51:
52:     }
53: }
```

17

Figure 17.9

A message box displayed at the start of this program.

Figure 17.10

A message box displayed when the form has completed its initialization.

Figure 17.11

A message box displayed by selecting an item from the context menu.

Figure 17.12

A message box displayed at the end of the program.

ANALYSIS This listing uses a MessageBox object to display a message at a number of different times throughout the program's execution.

The basic usage of the MessageBox class enables you to display a text string within a dialog box containing an OK button. You can also specify the title that will appear in the dialog box. Listing 17.8 uses a number of message boxes. The first is called in the constructor at Line 14. Two parameters are used with this basic call to the Show method of MessageBox. The first is the message that will be displayed in the dialog box. The second argument is the title of the dialog box. You can see that this is true by comparing the code in Line 14 to the dialog box presented in Figure 17.9. The dialog box in Line 14 is displayed immediately.

Lines 15–16 initialize the application's main form and set up a pop-up menu. This is followed by another message box, which indicates that the initialization has been completed. This message box is the second that displayed.

When the OK button is clicked in the second message box, the constructor code, MsgBox(), concludes and the application's main form is displayed. This form is an empty form that contains a menu that pops up with a right click of the mouse. When you select an item from this menu, the PopUp_Selection event handler in Lines 26–30 is called. This event handler calls the message box class regardless of which item was selected.

Figure 17.12 shows the final message box that is displayed when you exit this program. This dialog box results from the MessageBox.Show call in Line 50, and it doesn't display until after the main form has exited.

Using Pre-existing Microsoft Windows Dialog Boxes

In addition to the MessageBox class, a number of more complex dialog boxes have been defined. The following are useful dialog boxes:

- Color Selection dialog box (ColorDialog)
- Print Preview dialog box (PrintPreviewDialog)
- Fonts dialog box (FontDialog)
- File Open dialog box (OpenFileDialog)
- File Save dialog box (SaveFileDialog)

 Note When this book was written, only Microsoft Windows supported these dialog boxes. Other platforms such as Linux may support these in the future.

These dialog boxes are within the BCL. Listing 17.9 shows how easy it is to incorporate the basic features of these dialog boxes into your list, as shown in Figures 17.13–17.15.

LISTING 17.9   Canned.cs—Using Some of the Canned Dialog Boxes

```
 1:  // Canned.cs - using existing dialogs
 2:  //------------------------------------------------------------
 3:
 4:  using System;
 5:  using System.Windows.Forms;
 6:  using System.Drawing;
```

LISTING 17.9 continued

```
 7:
 8:  public class Canned : Form
 9:  {
10:      private MainMenu myMainMenu;
11:
12:      public Canned()
13:      {
14:          InitializeComponent();
15:      }
16:
17:      private void InitializeComponent()
18:      {
19:          this.Text = "Canned Dialogs";
20:          this.StartPosition = FormStartPosition.CenterScreen;
21:          this.FormBorderStyle = FormBorderStyle.Sizable;
22:          this.Width = 400;
23:
24:          myMainMenu = new MainMenu();
25:
26:          MenuItem menuitemFile = myMainMenu.MenuItems.Add("&File");
27:          menuitemFile.MenuItems.Add(new MenuItem("Colors Dialog",
28:                                    new EventHandler(this.Menu_Selection)));
29:          menuitemFile.MenuItems.Add(new MenuItem("Fonts Dialog",
30:                                    new EventHandler(this.Menu_Selection)));
31:          menuitemFile.MenuItems.Add(new MenuItem("Print Preview Dialog",
32:                                    new EventHandler(this.Menu_Selection)));
33:          menuitemFile.MenuItems.Add("-");
34:          menuitemFile.MenuItems.Add(new MenuItem("Exit",
35:                                    new EventHandler(this.Menu_Selection)));
36:          this.Menu = myMainMenu;
37:      }
38:
39:      protected void Menu_Selection( object sender, System.EventArgs e )
40:      {
41:          switch (((MenuItem) sender).Text )
42:          {
43:            case "Exit":
44:                  Application.Exit();
45:                  break;
46:
47:            case "Colors Dialog":
48:                  ColorDialog myColorDialog = new ColorDialog();
49:                  myColorDialog.ShowDialog();
50:                  break;
51:
52:            case "Fonts Dialog":
53:                  FontDialog myFontDialog = new FontDialog();
54:                  myFontDialog.ShowDialog();
```

LISTING **17.9**   continued

```
55:                 break;
56:
57:         case "Print Preview Dialog":
58:             PrintPreviewDialog myPrintDialog =
59:                                 new PrintPreviewDialog();
60:             myPrintDialog.ShowDialog();
61:                 break;
62:
63:         default:
64:             MessageBox.Show("DEFAULT", "PopUp");
65:                 break;
66:         }
67:     }
68:
69:     public static void Main( string[] args )
70:     {
71:         Application.Run( new Canned() );
72:     }
73: }
```

17

OUTPUT

FIGURE **17.13**

*Displaying the basic
Color dialog box.*

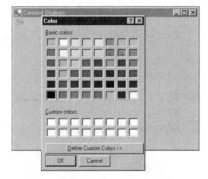

FIGURE **17.14**

*Displaying the basic
Font dialog box.*

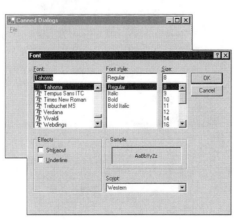

FIGURE 17.15

Displaying the Print Preview dialog box.

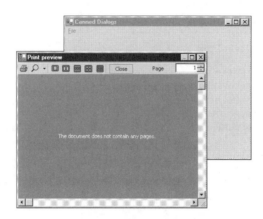

 This listing uses functionality that has been presented in earlier listings to display the dialog boxes. A File menu has been added to the form. This menu contains items for displaying three dialog boxes, each displayed in the same manner. A new object of the dialog box's type is instantiated. The object is then displayed by calling the ShowDialog method, which presents the dialog box. Selecting each of the menu options provides you with the associated precreated dialog box.

> **Note**
>
> To learn more about customizing and using the features of these dialog boxes, check the online help documents.

Popping Up Your Own Dialog Box

You also can create your own dialog boxes. You do this in the same way you create your base form: define a form object, add controls, and then display it.

You can display a form two ways. You can display a form so that it must be responded to before the application will continue. This is done using the ShowDialog method. Alternatively, you can display a form and let the application continue or let other forms continue to be displayed. This is done with the Show method. Listing 17.10 illustrates the difference between using Show and using ShowDialog (see Figure 17.16).

LISTING 17.10   MyForm.cs—Using Show Versus Using ShowDialog

```
1:  // MyForm.cs - displaying subforms
2:  //------------------------------------------------------------
3:
4:  using System;
```

LISTING **17.10** continued

```
 5: using System.Windows.Forms;
 6: using System.Drawing;
 7:
 8: public class MyForm : Form
 9: {
10:     private MainMenu myMainMenu;
11:
12:     public MyForm()
13:     {
14:         InitializeComponent();
15:     }
16:
17:     private void InitializeComponent()
18:     {
19:         this.Text = "Canned Dialogs";
20:         this.StartPosition = FormStartPosition.CenterScreen;
21:         this.FormBorderStyle = FormBorderStyle.Sizable;
22:         this.Width = 400;
23:
24:         myMainMenu = new MainMenu();
25:
26:         MenuItem menuitemFile = myMainMenu.MenuItems.Add("&File");
27:         menuitemFile.MenuItems.Add(new MenuItem("My Form",
28:                             new EventHandler(this.Menu_Selection)));
29:         menuitemFile.MenuItems.Add(new MenuItem("My Other Form",
30:                             new EventHandler(this.Menu_Selection)));
31:         menuitemFile.MenuItems.Add("-");
32:         menuitemFile.MenuItems.Add(new MenuItem("Exit",
33:                             new EventHandler(this.Menu_Selection)));
34:         this.Menu = myMainMenu;
35:     }
36:
37:     protected void Menu_Selection( object sender, System.EventArgs e )
38:     {
39:         switch (((MenuItem) sender).Text )
40:         {
41:           case "Exit":
42:                 Application.Exit();
43:                 break;
44:
45:           case "My Form":
46:                 subForm aForm = new subForm();
47:                 aForm.Text = "A Show form";
48:                 aForm.Show();
49:                 break;
50:
51:           case "My Other Form":
52:                 subForm bForm = new subForm();
```

17

LISTING **17.10**   continued

```
53:                    bForm.Text = "A ShowDialog form";
54:                    bForm.ShowDialog();
55:                    break;
56:
57:            default:
58:                    MessageBox.Show("DEFAULT", "PopUp");
59:                    break;
60:          }
61:      }
62:
63:      public static void Main( string[] args )
64:      {
65:          Application.Run( new MyForm() );
66:      }
67:  }
68:
69:
70:  public class subForm : Form
71:  {
72:      private MainMenu mySubMainMenu;
73:
74:      public subForm()
75:      {
76:          InitializeComponent();
77:      }
78:
79:      private void InitializeComponent()
80:      {
81:          this.Text = "My sub-form";
82:          this.StartPosition = FormStartPosition.CenterScreen;
83:          this.FormBorderStyle = FormBorderStyle.FixedDialog;
84:          this.Width = 300;
85:          this.Height = 250;
86:
87:          mySubMainMenu = new MainMenu();
88:
89:          MenuItem menuitemFile = mySubMainMenu.MenuItems.Add("&File");
90:          menuitemFile.MenuItems.Add(new MenuItem("Close",
91:                             new EventHandler(this.CloseMenu_Selection)));
92:          this.Menu = mySubMainMenu;
93:      }
94:
95:      protected void CloseMenu_Selection( object sender, System.EventArgs e )
96:      {
97:          this.Close();
98:      }
99:  }
```

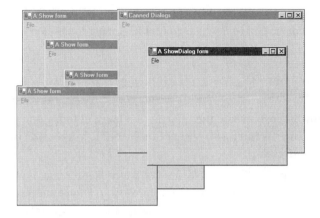

OUTPUT

FIGURE 17.16

Only one ShowDialog *form can be displayed at a time, but multiple* Show *forms can be displayed.*

ANALYSIS When you run this program, you will find that you can create multiple ShowDialog forms. You can even change focus between them and the main application form. When you create a ShowDialog form, you cannot do anything else in this program until you close it.

Note A form that must be responded to before giving up focus is *modal*.

Summary

Today's lesson ended up being among the longest in the book; however, you saw a lot of code. Today you expanded on what you learned yesterday regarding the creation of windows-based development. Although the information covered today is not a part of the ECMA standard C# language, it is applicable to programming on Microsoft Windows. Other platforms supporting .NET will most likely have similar—if not the same—functionality. For example, the mono C# and .NET project is planning to support the windows forms classes.

Today's lesson started with coverage of two more controls, radio buttons and list boxes. You learned how to group controls with the group box. Additionally, you learned how to add both main menus and context (pop-up) menus to your applications. Creating an application with multiple forms and dialog boxes was also demonstrated. Not only did you learn to use the message box dialog box, but you also learned how to create your own dialog boxes and how to use pre-existing dialog boxes.

The two days of windows coverage were not intended to be complete coverage. However, you now have a foundation for beginning to develop windows-based applications.

Q&A

Q How important was the information learned today and yesterday if I use a tool such as Microsoft Visual Studio .NET, Microsoft Visual C# .NET, or SharpDevelop?

A The graphical IDEs will do a lot of the coding for you. For example, using Visual Studio, you can drag and drop controls onto a form and set properties by using a dialog box within the tool. This makes it very easy to create dialog boxes. Yesterday's lesson and today's lesson help you understand the code that these tools are creating for you. By understanding generated code, you can better understand your programs and how they operate.

Q Isn't there a lot more to learn about windows programming?

A Yesterday and today barely scratched the surface of windows-based programming, but they do give you a solid foundation from which to start such programming.

Q Is what I learned yesterday and today portable to other platforms?

A Because all of the routines presented are a part of the Base Class Libraries, it is hoped that they will be ported to new platforms. In reality, these classes were not all part of the ECMA standard created for C#, so there is no guarantee that these window classes or control classes will be converted to other platforms. I believe there is a good chance that they will be ported.

Workshop

The Workshop provides quiz questions to help you solidify your understanding of the material covered and exercises to provide you with experience in using what you've learned. Try to understand the quiz and exercise answers before continuing to the next day's lesson. Answers are provided on the CD.

Quiz

1. What class can be used to create a radio button control?
2. What namespace contains controls such as radio buttons and list boxes?
3. How do you set the tab order for a form's controls?

4. What steps are involved in adding items to a list box?

5. What is the difference between a `MainMenu` and a `ContextMenu` item?

6. What is an easy way to display a dialog box with a simple message in a simple dialog box?

7. What are some of the pre-existing dialog boxes that you can use from the Base Class Library?

8. If you want to display a form and not allow any other forms to be displayed or activated in the same application, what method should you use?

9. How many forms can be displayed with the `Show` method at the same time?

Exercises

1. Write the code to add two radio buttons named `butn1` and `butn2` to a group box named `grpbox`.

2. What code would you use to add a line to the `MYMENU` menu?

3. Create an application that uses the `ColorDialog` form. Set the background of your main form to the color returned from the `ColorDialog` form that you display. The color returned is stored in the `Color` property. *Hint:* Create a variable of type `ColorDialog`. When you return from calling the dialog box, the selected color should be in the `Color` property.

4. **Bug Buster:** Does the following code have a problem? If so, what is it?

```
1:  using System;
2:  using System.Windows.Forms;
3:  using System.Drawing;
4:
5:  public class frmApp : Form
6:  {
7:      private Label myDateLabel;
8:      private MainMenu myMainMenu;
9:
10:     public frmApp()
11:     {
12:         this.Text = "STY Menus";
13:         this.FormBorderStyle = FormBorderStyle.Fixed3D;
14:
15:         myDateLabel = new Label();      // Create label
16:
17:         DateTime currDate = new DateTime();
18:         currDate = DateTime.Now;
19:         myDateLabel.Text = currDate.ToString();
20:         myDateLabel.AutoSize = true;
21:         myDateLabel.Location = new Point( 50, 70);
22:         myDateLabel.BackColor = this.BackColor;
```

```
23:          this.Controls.Add(myDateLabel);   // Add label to form
24:          this.Width = (myDateLabel.PreferredWidth + 100);
25:
26:          CreateMyMenu();
27:      }
28:
29:      protected void MenuUpdate_Selection( object sender,
     ➥System.EventArgs e)
30:      {
31:          DateTime currDate;
32:          currDate = DateTime.Now;
33:          this.myDateLabel.Text = currDate.ToString();
34:      }
35:
36:      protected void FileExit_Selection( object sender, System.
     ➥EventArgs e)
37:      {
38:          this.Close();
39:      }
40:
41:      public void CreateMyMenu()
42:      {
43:          myMainMenu = new MainMenu();
44:
45:          MenuItem menuitemFile = myMainMenu.MenuItems.Add("&File");
46:          menuitemFile.MenuItems.Add(new MenuItem("Update &Date",
47:                                      new
     ➥EventHandler(this.MenuUpdate_Selection),
48:                                         Shortcut.CtrlH));
49:          menuitemFile.MenuItems.Add(new MenuItem("E&xit",
50:                                      new
     ➥EventHandler(this.FileExit_Selection),
51:                                         Shortcut.CtrlX));
52:          this.Menu = myMainMenu;
53:      }
54:
55:      public static void Main( string[] args )
56:      {
57:          Application.Run( new frmApp() );
58:      }
59:  }
```

5. **On Your Own:** Create an application that contains a menu. The menu should display a dialog box that contains a number of controls, including an OK button.

6. Modify Listing 17.6 to include an About dialog box.

TYPE & RUN 4

Tic Tac Toe

This Type & Run is a simple game of Tic Tac Toe. This is done as a windows forms application using standard controls. For the most part, buttons are used. Although this code is very long, you will find that most of it sets up the controls on the form. Because this listing is so long, I suggest that you copy it from the CD.

If you are using an Integrated Development Environment that has a windows forms designer, I suggest that you try to re-create this application from scratch.

Unlike most of the Type & Runs, you have actually covered nearly everything that is in this listing. You should be able to work through this listing and follow what is happening. A few .NET Framework classes are being used that you have not seen before; however, you should find their functionality obvious.

Remember, the purpose of Type & Runs is to provide you with a longer, more complete listing than what is in the individual lessons. More important, they are to provide you with code to modify and play with.

The listing provides the code for a simple Tic Tac Toe game; however, a lot of functionality can be added. You could keep a tally for scoring. You could add menus that have options for starting a game, switching who goes first (X or O), exiting the program, and using Help. The listing is functional; however, there are lots of ways you can enhance it.

The Tic Tac Toe Code

Enter and compile the following program. If you get any errors, make sure you entered the program correctly. You can also copy the code from the CD or pull it from www.TeachYourselfCSharp.com.

LISTING T&R 4.1   TicTac.cs—A Tic Tac Toe Game

```
 1: // TicTac.cs - Simple Windows Tic Tac Toe program
 2: //
 3: //-----------------------------------------------------------
 4:
 5: using System;
 6: using System.Drawing;
 7: using System.Collections;
 8: using System.ComponentModel;
 9: using System.Windows.Forms;
10: using System.Data;
11:
12: namespace TicTac
13: {
14:     /// <summary>
15:     /// Summary description for TicTac.
16:     /// </summary>
17:     public class TicTac : System.Windows.Forms.Form
18:     {
19:         // Buttons for the nine game positions:
20:         private System.Windows.Forms.Button btnTopLeft;
21:         private System.Windows.Forms.Button btnTopMiddle;
22:         private System.Windows.Forms.Button btnTopRight;
23:         private System.Windows.Forms.Button btnMiddleRight;
24:         private System.Windows.Forms.Button btnMiddleMiddle;
25:         private System.Windows.Forms.Button btnMiddleLeft;
26:         private System.Windows.Forms.Button btnBottomRight;
27:         private System.Windows.Forms.Button btnBottomMiddle;
28:         private System.Windows.Forms.Button btnBottomLeft;
29:         // Other controls for the games:
30:         private System.Windows.Forms.Button btnNewGame;
31:         private System.Windows.Forms.Button btnExit;
32:         private System.Windows.Forms.Button btnTurn;
33:         private System.Windows.Forms.Panel panel1;
34:         // variable to keep track of turn
35:         private int turn = 0;
36:
```

LISTING T&R 4.1   continued

```
37:        /// <summary>
38:        /// Required designer variable.
39:        /// </summary>
40:        private System.ComponentModel.Container components = null;
41:
42:        public TicTac()
43:        {
44:            InitializeComponent();
45:        }
46:
47:        /// <summary>
48:        /// Clean up any resources being used.
49:        /// </summary>
50:        protected override void Dispose( bool disposing )
51:        {
52:            if( disposing )
53:            {
54:                if (components != null)
55:                {
56:                    components.Dispose();
57:                }
58:            }
59:            base.Dispose( disposing );
60:        }
61:
62:        private void InitializeComponent()
63:        {
64:            this.btnTopLeft      = new Button();
65:            this.btnTopMiddle    = new Button();
66:            this.btnTopRight     = new Button();
67:            this.btnMiddleRight  = new Button();
68:            this.btnMiddleMiddle = new Button();
69:            this.btnMiddleLeft   = new Button();
70:            this.btnBottomRight  = new Button();
71:            this.btnBottomMiddle = new Button();
72:            this.btnBottomLeft   = new Button();
73:            this.btnNewGame      = new Button();
74:            this.btnExit         = new Button();
75:            this.btnTurn         = new Button();
76:            this.panel1          = new Panel();
77:            this.SuspendLayout();
78:            //
79:            // btnTopLeft
80:            //
81:            this.btnTopLeft.Font =
82:                new System.Drawing.Font("Microsoft Sans Serif",
83:                                        20.25F,
84:                                        System.Drawing.FontStyle.Regular,
85:                                        System.Drawing.GraphicsUnit.Point,
```

```
86:                              ((System.Byte)(0)));
87:        this.btnTopLeft.Location = new System.Drawing.Point(16, 16);
88:        this.btnTopLeft.Name = "btnTopLeft";
89:        this.btnTopLeft.Size = new System.Drawing.Size(64, 56);
90:        this.btnTopLeft.TabIndex = 0;
91:        this.btnTopLeft.Click +=
92:            new System.EventHandler(this.btnTicTac_Click);
93:        //
94:        // btnTopMiddle
95:        //
96:        this.btnTopMiddle.Font =
97:            new System.Drawing.Font("Microsoft Sans Serif",
98:                                    20.25F,
99:                                    System.Drawing.FontStyle.Regular,
100:                                   System.Drawing.GraphicsUnit.Point,
101:                                   ((System.Byte)(0)));
102:       this.btnTopMiddle.Location = new System.Drawing.Point(96, 16);
103:       this.btnTopMiddle.Name = "btnTopMiddle";
104:       this.btnTopMiddle.Size = new System.Drawing.Size(64, 56);
105:       this.btnTopMiddle.TabIndex = 1;
106:       this.btnTopMiddle.Click +=
107:           new System.EventHandler(this.btnTicTac_Click);
108:       //
109:       // btnTopRight
110:       //
111:       this.btnTopRight.Font =
112:           new System.Drawing.Font("Microsoft Sans Serif",
113:                           20.25F, System.Drawing.FontStyle.Regular,
114:                                   System.Drawing.GraphicsUnit.Point,
115:                                   ((System.Byte)(0)));
116:       this.btnTopRight.Location = new System.Drawing.Point(176, 16);
117:       this.btnTopRight.Name = "btnTopRight";
118:       this.btnTopRight.Size = new System.Drawing.Size(64, 56);
119:       this.btnTopRight.TabIndex = 2;
120:       this.btnTopRight.Click +=
121:           new System.EventHandler(this.btnTicTac_Click);
122:       //
123:       // btnMiddleRight
124:       //
125:       this.btnMiddleRight.Font =
126:           new System.Drawing.Font("Microsoft Sans Serif",
127:                           20.25F, System.Drawing.FontStyle.Regular,
128:                                   System.Drawing.GraphicsUnit.Point,
129:                                   ((System.Byte)(0)));
130:       this.btnMiddleRight.Location = new System.Drawing.Point(176, 88);
131:       this.btnMiddleRight.Name = "btnMiddleRight";
132:       this.btnMiddleRight.Size = new System.Drawing.Size(64, 56);
133:       this.btnMiddleRight.TabIndex = 5;
134:       this.btnMiddleRight.Click +=
```

LISTING T&R 4.1   continued

```
135:                    new System.EventHandler(this.btnTicTac_Click) ;
136:            //
137:            // btnMiddleMiddle
138:            //
139:            this.btnMiddleMiddle.Font =
140:                new System.Drawing.Font("Microsoft Sans Serif",
141:                                        20.25F,
142:                                        System.Drawing.FontStyle.Regular,
143:                                        System.Drawing.GraphicsUnit.Point,
144:                                        ((System.Byte)(0)));
145:            this.btnMiddleMiddle.Location = new System.Drawing.Point(96, 88);
146:            this.btnMiddleMiddle.Name = "btnMiddleMiddle";
147:            this.btnMiddleMiddle.Size = new System.Drawing.Size(64, 56);
148:            this.btnMiddleMiddle.TabIndex = 4;
149:            this.btnMiddleMiddle.Click +=
150:                    new System.EventHandler(this.btnTicTac_Click);
151:            //
152:            // btnMiddleLeft
153:            //
154:            this.btnMiddleLeft.Font =
155:                new System.Drawing.Font("Microsoft Sans Serif",
156:                                        20.25F,
157:                                        System.Drawing.FontStyle.Regular,
158:                                        System.Drawing.GraphicsUnit.Point,
159:                                        ((System.Byte)(0)));
160:            this.btnMiddleLeft.Location = new System.Drawing.Point(16, 88);
161:            this.btnMiddleLeft.Name = "btnMiddleLeft";
162:            this.btnMiddleLeft.Size = new System.Drawing.Size(64, 56);
163:            this.btnMiddleLeft.TabIndex = 3;
164:            this.btnMiddleLeft.Click +=
165:                    new System.EventHandler(this.btnTicTac_Click);
166:            //
167:            // btnBottomRight
168:            //
169:            this.btnBottomRight.Font =
170:                new System.Drawing.Font("Microsoft Sans Serif",
171:                                20.25F, System.Drawing.FontStyle.Regular,
172:                                System.Drawing.GraphicsUnit.Point,
173:                                ((System.Byte)(0)));
174:            this.btnBottomRight.Location = new System.Drawing.Point(176, 160);
175:            this.btnBottomRight.Name = "btnBottomRight";
176:            this.btnBottomRight.Size = new System.Drawing.Size(64, 56);
177:            this.btnBottomRight.TabIndex = 8;
178:            this.btnBottomRight.Click +=
179:                    new System.EventHandler(this.btnTicTac_Click);
180:            //
181:            // btnBottomMiddle
182:            //
183:            this.btnBottomMiddle.Font =
```

```
184:                    new System.Drawing.Font("Microsoft Sans Serif",
185:                                      20.25F,
186:                                      System.Drawing.FontStyle.Regular,
187:                                      System.Drawing.GraphicsUnit.Point,
188:                                      ((System.Byte)(0)));
189:         this.btnBottomMiddle.Location = new System.Drawing.Point(96, 160);
190:         this.btnBottomMiddle.Name = "btnBottomMiddle";
191:         this.btnBottomMiddle.Size = new System.Drawing.Size(64, 56);
192:         this.btnBottomMiddle.TabIndex = 7;
193:         this.btnBottomMiddle.Click +=
194:                 new System.EventHandler(this.btnTicTac_Click);
195:         //
196:         // btnBottomLeft
197:         //
198:         this.btnBottomLeft.Font =
199:                 new System.Drawing.Font("Microsoft Sans Serif",
200:                                      20.25F,
201:                                      System.Drawing.FontStyle.Regular,
202:                                      System.Drawing.GraphicsUnit.Point,
203:                                      ((System.Byte)(0)));
204:         this.btnBottomLeft.Location = new System.Drawing.Point(16, 160);
205:         this.btnBottomLeft.Name = "btnBottomLeft";
206:         this.btnBottomLeft.Size = new System.Drawing.Size(64, 56);
207:         this.btnBottomLeft.TabIndex = 6;
208:         this.btnBottomLeft.Click +=
209:                 new System.EventHandler(this.btnTicTac_Click) ;
210:         //
211:         // btnNewGame
212:         //
213:         this.btnNewGame.Location = new System.Drawing.Point(16, 248);
214:         this.btnNewGame.Name = "btnNewGame";
215:         this.btnNewGame.Size = new System.Drawing.Size(80, 24);
216:         this.btnNewGame.TabIndex = 9;
217:         this.btnNewGame.Text = "New Game";
218:         this.btnNewGame.Click +=
219:                 new System.EventHandler(this.btnNewGame_Click);
220:         //
221:         // btnExit
222:         //
223:         this.btnExit.Location = new System.Drawing.Point(160, 248);
224:         this.btnExit.Name = "btnExit";
225:         this.btnExit.Size = new System.Drawing.Size(80, 24);
226:         this.btnExit.TabIndex = 10;
227:         this.btnExit.Text = "Exit";
228:         this.btnExit.Click += new System.EventHandler(this.btnExit_Click);
229:         //
230:         // btnTurn
231:         //
232:         this.btnTurn.FlatStyle = System.Windows.Forms.FlatStyle.Flat;
```

```
233:            this.btnTurn.Font =
234:                new System.Drawing.Font("Microsoft Sans Serif",
235:                                        20.25F,
236:                                        System.Drawing.FontStyle.Regular,
237:                                        System.Drawing.GraphicsUnit.Point,
238:                                        ((System.Byte)(0)));
239:            this.btnTurn.Location = new System.Drawing.Point(112, 232);
240:            this.btnTurn.Name = "btnTurn";
241:            this.btnTurn.Size = new System.Drawing.Size(32, 40);
242:            this.btnTurn.TabIndex = 0;
243:            this.btnTurn.TabStop = false;
244:            this.btnTurn.Text = "X";
245:            //
246:            // panel1
247:            //
248:            this.panel1.BackColor = System.Drawing.Color.Black;
249:            this.panel1.Location = new System.Drawing.Point(16, 16);
250:            this.panel1.Name = "panel1";
251:            this.panel1.Size = new System.Drawing.Size(224, 200);
252:            //
253:            // TicTac
254:            //
255:            this.AutoScaleBaseSize = new System.Drawing.Size(5, 13);
256:            this.ClientSize = new System.Drawing.Size(256, 286);
257:            this.Controls.Add(this.btnTurn);
258:            this.Controls.Add(this.btnExit);
259:            this.Controls.Add(this.btnNewGame);
260:            this.Controls.Add(this.btnBottomRight);
261:            this.Controls.Add(this.btnBottomMiddle);
262:            this.Controls.Add(this.btnBottomLeft);
263:            this.Controls.Add(this.btnMiddleRight);
264:            this.Controls.Add(this.btnMiddleMiddle);
265:            this.Controls.Add(this.btnMiddleLeft);
266:            this.Controls.Add(this.btnTopRight);
267:            this.Controls.Add(this.btnTopMiddle);
268:            this.Controls.Add(this.btnTopLeft);
269:            this.Controls.Add(this.panel1);
270:            this.FormBorderStyle = FormBorderStyle.Fixed3D;
271:            this.MaximizeBox = false;
272:            this.Name = "TicTac";
273:            this.Text = "Tic Tac Toe";
274:            this.ResumeLayout(false);
275:
276:        }
277:
278:        /// <summary>
279:        /// The main entry point for the application.
280:        /// </summary>
281:        public static void Main()
```

```
282:        {
283:           Application.Run(new TicTac());
284:        }
285:
286:        private string setText(string origText)
287:        {
288:           string tmpText = origText;
289:           if (origText == "X" || origText == "O" )
290:           {
291:              // Already a character in section
292:
293:           }
294:           else
295:           {
296:              tmpText = btnTurn.Text;
297:              if ( btnTurn.Text == "X")
298:              {
299:                 btnTurn.Text = "O";
300:              }
301:              else
302:              {
303:                 btnTurn.Text = "X";
304:              }
305:              turn++;  // turn successful, so count.
306:           }
307:           return tmpText;
308:        }
309:
310:        // Check to see if game is over
311:        // val == character for turn.
312:        private void checkEndGame(string val)
313:        {
314:           bool gameover = false;
315:
316:           // First check for a winner....
317:           if( btnTopLeft.Text == val )
318:           {
319:              if( btnTopMiddle.Text == val &&
320:                 btnTopRight.Text == val )
321:              {
322:                 gameover = true;
323:              }
324:              if( btnMiddleLeft.Text == val &&
325:                 btnBottomLeft.Text == val )
326:              {
327:                 gameover = true;
328:              }
329:              if( btnMiddleMiddle.Text == val &&
330:                 btnBottomRight.Text == val)
```

LISTING T&R 4.1 continued

```
331:                {
332:                    gameover = true;
333:                }
334:            }
335:
336:            if(btnTopMiddle.Text == val)
337:            {
338:                if(btnMiddleMiddle.Text == val &&
339:                    btnBottomMiddle.Text == val)
340:                {
341:                    gameover = true;
342:                }
343:            }
344:
345:            if(btnMiddleLeft.Text == val)
346:            {
347:                if(btnMiddleMiddle.Text == val &&
348:                    btnMiddleRight.Text == val)
349:                {
350:                    gameover = true;
351:                }
352:            }
353:
354:            if( btnBottomLeft.Text == val )
355:            {
356:                if( btnBottomMiddle.Text == val &&
357:                    btnBottomRight.Text == val)
358:                {
359:                    gameover = true;
360:                }
361:                if( btnMiddleMiddle.Text == val &&
362:                    btnTopRight.Text == val )
363:                {
364:                    gameover = true;
365:                }
366:            }
367:
368:            if( btnTopRight.Text == val)
369:            {
370:                if( btnMiddleRight.Text == val &&
371:                     btnBottomRight.Text == val)
372:                {
373:                    gameover = true;
374:                }
375:            }
376:
377:            // Check to see if game over because of win...
378:            if( gameover == true)
379:            {
```

```
380:                if ( val == "X" )
381:                    MessageBox.Show( "Game Over - X wins!",
382:                       "Game Over!" );
383:                else
384:                    MessageBox.Show( "Game Over - O wins!",
385:                       "Game Over!");
386:            }
387:        else
388:        {
389:            // no winner, are all nine spaces filled?
390:            if( turn >= 9 )
391:            {
392:                // game over do end game stuff
393:                MessageBox.Show("Game Over - No winner!");
394:                gameover = true;
395:            }
396:        }
397:
398:        // See if board needs reset.
399:        if (gameover == true)
400:        {
401:            resetGame();
402:        }
403:    }
404:
405:    private void btnExit_Click(object sender, System.EventArgs e)
406:    {
407:        Application.Exit();
408:    }
409:
410:    private void btnNewGame_Click(object sender, System.EventArgs e)
411:    {
412:        resetGame();
413:    }
414:
415:    private void resetGame()
416:    {
417:        turn = 0;
418:        btnTopLeft.Text       = " ";
419:        btnTopMiddle.Text     = " ";
420:        btnTopRight.Text      = " ";
421:        btnMiddleLeft.Text    = " ";
422:        btnMiddleMiddle.Text  = " ";
423:        btnMiddleRight.Text   = " ";
424:        btnBottomLeft.Text    = " ";
425:        btnBottomMiddle.Text  = " ";
426:        btnBottomRight.Text   = " ";
427:        btnTurn.Text = "X";
428:    }
```

LISTING T&R 4.1 continued

```
429:
430:        // Set X or O text on grid button
431:        private void btnTicTac_Click(object sender, System.EventArgs e)
432:        {
433:            // convert the sender object to a button:
434:            Button tmpButton = (Button) sender;
435:            // Set the text of this button:
436:            tmpButton.Text = setText(tmpButton.Text);
437:
438:            checkEndGame(tmpButton.Text);
439:        }
440:    }
441: }
442: // End of Listing
```

This is a Windows application, so you will want to target the compiling as a winexe. With the Microsoft C# command-line compiler, this is done by using the /target: or /t: flags. Additionally, you may need to reference the windows forms classes in the command line:

```
csc /r:System.Windows.Forms.dll /t:winexe TicTac.cs
```

Note Depending on your compiler, you may not need to include the reference to System.Windows.Forms.dll in the command line.

After it is compiled, running the program presents the form presented in Figure TR4.1.

FIGURE TR4.1

The Tic Tac Toe application.

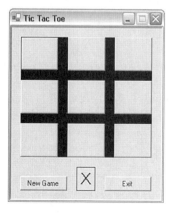

Note   The source code for this listing is available on the included CD. Any updates to the code will be available at www.TeachYourselfCSharp.com.

DAY **18**

Working with Databases: ADO.NET

You've learned about working with classes within the .NET Framework. You've even learned about working with the windows forms classes. Today you continue your learning with a different set of classes within the .NET Framework. These classes are focused on accessing and manipulating data. Today you...

- Review key database terminology.
- Learn about ADO.NET.
- Use ADO.NET to retrieve data from a database.
- Discover how to use a `DataReader`.
- Add data to a database.

> **Note**
>
> Be aware that entire books have been written on the topic of data pro-
> gramming with C# and .NET. In today's lesson, you will learn quite a bit;
> however, this just scratches the surface of everything there is to learn about
> database programming with C#.

Understanding Key Database Concepts

On Day 15, "Using Existing Routines from the .NET Base Classes," you learned how to read and write simple text files using streams. Using classes such as StreamWriter, StreamReader, BinaryWriter, and FileStream, you were able to both read information from different files and write information.

In real-world applications, you will often need a more robust set of classes and routines to work with data and information. Instead of storing everything as pure text or pure binary information, you will want to store items as different data types with different characteristics. You won't want to store integers and strings; instead, you will want to store information such as prices and titles. Information such as this is best stored in a database.

Data becomes more useful when it is stored in a grouping. For example, if you create an application to track videos that are available for a rental, you might have a group of information that describes the videos and a group of information that describes the cus-tomers. For customers, this information may include their name, address, phone number, and membership number, along with the date they obtained rental privileges. You may also keep information on the media in the store. For example, you may keep track of title, rating, length, format, release date, and price to buy. A third set of information that you might want to track is the videos that a customer rented and when he or she rented them. Obviously, a lot more information can be tracked; however, most of this informa-tion can be grouped.

If you started to write programs using the file classes you learned on Day 15, you would find that it would take a lot of work to simply read in a date or a dollar number. Additionally, storing the information in a straight text or binary file would not be very efficient. Instead, information can be stored in databases such as Oracle, Microsoft SQL Server, mySQL, and Microsoft Access. A database system such as these helps organize, store, and access the information.

Understanding the Terminology

NEW TERM   A single piece of information, such as a name or an address, is called a *field*. Another name for a field is a column; you'll understand why in a second. A group of related fields is called a record. Another name for a record is a *column*. An example of a record or column is the information traced on a video—this may be the title, media, price, and other information. A set of records, or information on a number of titles, is kept as a *fil*. A file is also known as a *table*. A group of one or more related files is considered a *database*.

You've just learned a lot of terms. In general, the terms *row*, *column*, and *table* are used within the context of .NET. These terms come from the fact that you can present data in a table format, as shown in Figure 18.1.

> **Note**
>
> One other term worth mentioning here is *dataset*. A dataset is one or more tables that have been copied from a database into memory.

FIGURE 18.1

Tables, rows, and columns.

Table: Videos   Columns/Fields

#	Title	Rating	Price	Sale		Min	Genre	Owner	Media
1	AI - Artificial Intelligence	PG-13	$22.99	$19.99	☐	145	SciFi	Brad Jones	DVD
2	Cider House Rules, The	PG-13	$9.99	$4.99	☑	125	Drama	Brad Jones	DVD
3	Halo Combat Evolved	Mature	$49.99	$39.99	☐	0	Shooter	Brad Jones	XBx
4	Project Gotham Racing	Everyone	$49.99	$39.99	☐	0	Racing	Brad Jones	XBx
5	RalliSport Challenge	Everyone	$49.99	$10.00	☐	0	Racing	Brad Jones	XBx
6	NFL Fever 2002	Everyone	$49.99	$10.00	☐	0	Sports	Brad Jones	XBx
7	OddWorld Munch's Oddysee	Teen	$49.99	$10.00	☐	0	Adventure	Brad Jones	XBx
8	Xbox Game Disk - 07 - June 2002	RP-M	$5.95	$5.95	☐	0	Various	Brad Jones	XBx
9	Xbox Game Disk - 05 - April 2002	RP-M	$5.95	$5.95	☐	0	Various	Brad Jones	XBx
10	Xbox Game Disk - 06 - May 2002	RP-M	$5.95	$5.95	☐	0	Various	Brad Jones	XBx
11	Blood Wake	Teen	$49.99	$39.99	☐	0	Adventure	Brad Jones	XBx
12	amped	Everyone	$49.99	$10.00	☐	0	Sports	Brad Jones	XBx
13	Fuzion Frenzy	Everyone	$49.99	$10.00	☐	0	Game	Brad Jones	XBx
14	NightCaster Defeat the Darkness	Teen	$49.99	$10.00	☐	0	Adventure	Brad Jones	XBx
15	NBA 2002 Inside Drive	Everyone	$49.99	$10.00	☐	0	Sports	Brad Jones	XBx
16	Azurk Rise of Perathia	Teen	$49.99	$10.00	☐	0	Adventure	Brad Jones	XBx
17	Traffic	R	$12.99	$0.00	☑	147	Drama	Brad Jones	DVD
18	Cast Away	PG-13	$19.99	$9.99	☑	107	Drama	Brad Jones	DVD
19	Family Man, The	PG-13	$12.99	$9.99	☑	126	Comedy	Brad Jones	DVD
20	What Women Want	PG-13	$9.99	$7.99	☑	126	Comedy	Brad Jones	DVD
21	Erin Brockovich	R	$9.99	$6.99	☑	132	Drama	Brad Jones	DVD
22	Planet of the Apes	PG-13	$18.99	$14.99	☐	124	SciFi	Brad Jones	DVD
23	StarGate SG1 - Vol 1	NR	$8.99	$8.99	☐	185	SciFi	Brad Jones	DVD
24	Unbreakable	PG-13	$9.99	$7.99	☑	107	SciFi	Brad Jones	DVD

Rows/Records

Introducing ADO.NET

Because most real-world applications use data stored in a database, it shouldn't be a surprise that strong database support is a part of the .NET Framework. Regardless of whether your data is stored on your local machine, on a network, or somewhere across the Internet, routines exist to help you access that information.

The primary data access technology for tapping into a database from .NET is ADO.NET. ADO.NET provides a way to connect to a database and to manipulate the data within it.

Accessing databases is a slow process in terms of how fast your application will execute. Keeping a database open and working with specific data while the database is being accessed is a resource-intensive process. In general, you will want to access and connect to a database for the shortest periods of time possible.

In the past, people opened a database at the beginning of their application. They viewed, added, updated, and deleted information in the application. Finally, when the application was ready to end, they closed the database. This mode of operation is fine if you are the only one using the database and if the database is on your local machine; however, if you are working with a database across the Internet, or if you are sharing the database with others, this method of operation is very inefficient.

One of the key features of ADO.NET is that it provides classes and methods for accessing a database in a disconnected sort of way. Instead of accessing the database the entire time your application is running, you access it only when you really need to. The way this works is that, using ADO.NET classes, information is copied from the database into the memory of your own computer. You can then disconnect from the database. After manipulating the data in memory, you can again connect to the database and have the changes made.

Connecting to and Working with a Database

NEW TERM   Connecting to the database, retrieving data from the database, updating or deleting the data in the database, and performing other functions directly related to the database are all done with a data provider. The *data provider* is used to interact between the database and your program.

A data provider is a set of classes that you use. More specifically, four key classes are used as a part of the data provider:

*xxx*Connection	Used to connect to the database.
*xxx*Command	Used to execute a command against the database.
*xxx*DataReader	A special class used to get a set of data from the database that you can view. This can be viewed only sequentially, and the data can't be changed.
*xxx*DataAdapter	Used to get a set of data from the database that you can then manipulate. You use this to make the changes to the database as well.

The actual names for the key data provider classes are dependent upon the data provider you use. Microsoft's .NET Framework contains two different data providers. The Microsoft SQL Server .NET Data Provider is specifically tailored for Microsoft SQL Server 7.0 or later. The other, OleDb .NET Data Provider, is a more generic provider that connects to a number of different databases, including Microsoft Access and Oracle.

The different data provider classes are accessed from different namespaces. The SQL Server data provider classes can be found in `System.IO.Data.Sql`. The names of the classes within this provider start with the prefix `Sql`. For example, the connection class mentioned previously (*xxx*Connection) would be `SqlConnection` if the SQL Server provider were used.

The OleDb classes can be found in `System.IO.Data.OleDB`. The prefix for these classes is `OleDb`. The connection class for this data provider would be `OleDbConnection`.

Note

In today's lessons, the OleDb data provider is used. If you are using a SQL Server database, you should switch to the SQL Server data provider. It is optimized for Microsoft SQL Server, so it can provide for better performance. If you use the SQL Server provider, you should change the `OleDb` prefix used in the examples to an `Sql` prefix.

18

Making the Connection to the Database

When using a database, the first thing you must do is open it. To open a database, you must first connect to it.

You create a connection by using the *xxx*Connection class mentioned earlier. Using this class, you instantiate a connection object:

```
OleDbConnection myConnection = new OleDbConnection(myConnectionString);
```

As you can see, `myConnection` is created in the same way that other objects are created.

The one unique thing is the `myConnectionString` value that is passed to the constructor. This string contains information about connecting to a database. The exact values placed in this string vary depending on the database, access rights, and other information specific to the database you are opening. For example, if you want to open a Microsoft Access database that does not have any security included, you could set `myConnectionString` as follows:

```
string myConnectionString = @"Provider=Microsoft.Jet.OLEDB.4.0;User Id=;
                             Password=;Data Source=Videos.mdb"
```

You can see that the string is composed of four different areas that are separated by semi-colons:

Provider   This defines the data provider that will be used. In this case, it is
                  Microsoft Jet, which is the provider for Microsoft Access. If you
                  were using a Microsoft Access database, you would most likely use
                  this same provider.

User ID   This is the ID of the account to use to access the database. In the
                  case of the database used here, no ID is needed.

Password   This is the password associated with the User ID. Again, because
                  there is no security being used on the example database, no value is
                  set equal to the Password.

Data Source   This is the database name and location. In the example provided
                  here, the data source is the Videos.mdb database that is in the cur-
                  rent directory.

If you were accessing a different database, your values would be different. You may also
need to include additional values. The values that you will provide are the ones needed
by your database. If you are unsure of what is needed, check with your database admin-
istrator. Examples of other connection strings are shown here:

```
"Provider=MSDAORA; Data Source=ORACLE8i7;Persist Security Info=False;I
➥ntegrated Security=yes"
"Provider=Microsoft.Jet.OLEDB.4.0; Data Source=c:\databases\Contacts.mdb"
"Provider=SQLOLEDB;Data Source=MySQLServer;Integrated Security=SSPI"
```

After you have created your connection object, you can use it to open the database. You
open the database by calling the Open method of the connection object:

```
MyConnection.Open();
```

After Open is called, a connection to the database should be opened and ready to use. Of
course, if the database doesn't exist or if there is something wrong with the database, an
exception will be thrown.

Note   You should always use exception handling when using database routines.
             You want to control your application's reaction to problems such as a miss-
             ing database. In today's examples, exception handling is left out to save
             space. In the exercises, you will see an example of using exception handling
             with database access.

Executing a Command

With a database opened, the next step is to issue one or more commands to the database. Commands are issued to the database by using a command object that is associated to your connection object. You will want to first create the command object. You will then apply a command to the command object. Finally, you will execute the command.

To create the command object, you use the *xxx*Command class. Because you are using the OleDb provider in this chapter, you would use the following statement to create a command object named myCommand:

```
OleDbCommand myCommand = new OleDbCommand();
```

You can then associate the command object with the connection object by setting the command's Connection property:

```
myCommand.Connection = myConnection;
```

You now have a command object that you can use. When the command object is executed, it will use the database associated with myConnection.

Before you can execute the command, you need to associate a SQL query or a stored procedure with the command. To make this association, you assign the SQL query or stored procedure to the CommandText property:

```
myCommand.CommandText = "SELECT * FROM Titles ORDER BY Title";
```

As you can see, this assigns a SQL query to the CommandText of the myCommand object. With this assignment, the command can now be executed.

How you execute a command depends on the result you expect from the command. You will consider executing a command generally in three ways:

- ExecuteReader
- ExecuteNonQuery
- ExecuteScalar

You use ExecuteReader if you plan to retrieve data from the database. If you plan to make changes to the database but don't expect values to be returned, you can use ExecuteNonQuery. Finally, if you want to get just a single value from the database, you can use ExecuteScalar.

Retrieving Data with a DataReader

Most likely, your first foray into a database will be to read information from the database to display. A special class has been created to enable you to easily and efficiently read

18

data from a database. This is the `DataReader`. The downsides to the `DataReader` are that it can only read data (it can't write) and that it does only a forward read. This means you can go through the data only once. With these downsides, it is worth saying again—the benefit of the `DataReader` is that it is easy and efficient.

When you initially create a `DataReader`, you don't need to instantiate it. Instead, when you execute a command against the database, it returns a `DataReader` object to you. The following creates a `DataReader` named `myDataReader` and sets it to `null`:

```
OleDbDataReader myDataReader = null;
```

You can then execute your `Command` object, using the `ExecuteReader` method:

```
myDataReader = myCommand.ExecuteReader();
```

Remember, `myCommand` is associated with your connection, plus it contains the SQL statement or stored procedure that you assigned earlier. After it is executed, `myDataReader` will contain the results of the command that you assigned.

This result will most likely be a set of records from the database. You can now loop through these records by calling the `Read` method of the `DataReader`. Each time you call the `Read` method, the next record is read.

You can access the values in each record by getting their values with a `Getxxx` method. To use most of these methods, you must know the data type of the information you are retrieving. If you don't know the type, you will want to use the `GetValue` method. Table 18.1 presents a list of the `Getxxx` methods that you can use.

TABLE 18.1   The `Getxxx` Methods of the `DataReader`

Method	Returns
GetBoolean	A Boolean value (bool)
GetByte	A byte value
GetBytes	An array of bytes
GetChar	A character value (char)
GetChars	An array of characters
GetDataTypeName	The name of the source's data type
GetDateTime	A `DateTime` object
GetDecimal	A decimal value
GetDouble	A double value
GetFieldType	A `Type` value
GetFloat	A float value

TABLE 18.1   continued

Method	Returns
GetGuid	A Guid object
GetInt16	A short value
GetInt32	An integer value (int)
Get64	A long value
GetName	The column's name
GetOrdinal	The ordinal, when passed the column title
GetSchemaTable	A DataTable object
GetString	A string value
GetTimeSpan	A TimeSpan object
GetValue	The value
GetValues	Gets all the attribute values in the current row

With the DataReader executed, you can easily set up a command to loop through the retrieved information. For example, to print the value of the first item in each row or record retrieved, you could use the following simple loop:

```
while ( myDataReader.Read() )
{
   WriteLine(myDataReader.GetValue(0).ToString());
}
```

When you are done using the DataReader, you should close it using the Close method:

```
myDataReader.Close();
```

Closing the Database

Just as you should close the DataReader when you are finished with it, you should close the database connection. You close the connection by calling its Close method:

```
myConnection.Close();
```

Pulling It All Together

You've covered a lot up to this point. When you pull together all of the snippets, you can create a simple application that can read through a set of records within a database. Listing 18.1 presents an application that uses the code snippets you've seen up to this point. This listing uses a Microsoft Access database named Videos. This database can be found on the CD included with this book.

18

Note

Listing 18.1 does not include exception handling, to keep the listing short. It is highly recommended that you never create a database application without including exception handling because too many things can go wrong. For example, the database could be missing.

Exercise 1 at the end of this chapter instructs you to add exception handling to this listing. The answer to that exercise is provided on the CD-ROM, "Answers."

LISTING 18.1   ReadVids.cs—Using the `DataReader`

```csharp
 1: // ReadVids.cs
 2: // ------
 3: // ------ Note - Exception handling will be added in exercise 1
 4: // ------------------------------------------------------------
 5: using System;
 6: using System.Data;
 7: using System.Data.OleDb;
 8:
 9:
10: public class ReadVids
11: {
12:
13:     public static void Main()
14:     {
15:
16:         string  myConnectionString =
17:                         "Provider=Microsoft.Jet.OLEDB.4.0;" +
18:                         "User Id=;Password=;" +
19:                         @"Data Source=C:\Videos.mdb";
20:         decimal total = 0;
21:         int     count = 0;
22:         string  mySelectQuery = "SELECT * FROM videos Order By Title";
23:
24:         OleDbConnection myConnection =
25:                 new OleDbConnection(myConnectionString);
26:
27:         OleDbCommand myCommand =
28:                 new OleDbCommand(mySelectQuery, myConnection);
29:
30:         myConnection.Open();
31:
32:         OleDbDataReader myDataReader = null;
33:         myDataReader = myCommand.ExecuteReader();
34:
35:         while ( myDataReader.Read() )
36:         {
```

LISTING 18.1   continued

```
37:             Console.WriteLine(
38:                 myDataReader.GetString(9).PadLeft(4,' ') +
39:                 " - " +
40:                 myDataReader.GetString(1) +
41:                 " (" +
42:                 myDataReader.GetString(2) +
43:                 ") - {0:C}", myDataReader.GetDecimal(3) );
44:
45:             total += myDataReader.GetDecimal(3);
46:             count++;
47:         }
48:
49:         // Close when done reading.
50:         myDataReader.Close();
51:
52:         // Close the connection when done with it.
53:         myConnection.Close();
54:
55:         Console.WriteLine("\nTOTAL: {0:C}    AVG PRICE: {1:C}",
56:             total, total/count);
57:     }
58: }
```

OUTPUT

```
VHS - 61* (NR) - $12.99
DVD - A Knight's Tale (PG-13) - $12.99
DVD - AI - Artificial Intelligence (PG-13) - $22.99
XBx - amped (Everyone) - $49.99
VHS - Anywhere But Here (PG-13) - $7.99
DVD - Atlantis (PG) - $20.99
XBx - Azurk Rise of Perathia (Teen) - $49.99
VHS - Billy Elliot (R) - $14.99
XBx - Blood Wake (Teen) - $49.99
DVD - Boys Don't Cry (R) - $9.99
DVD - BraveHeart (R) - $24.99
DVD - Cast Away (PG-13) - $19.99
DVD - Charlie's Angels (PG-13) - $14.99
DVD - Cider House Rules, The (PG-13) - $9. 99
DVD - Contender, The (R) - $9.99
VHS - Contender, The (R) - $9.99
DVD - Crouching Tiger Hidden dragon (PG-13) - $16.99
DVD - Dinotopia (NR) - $14.99
VHS - Double Jeopardy (R) - $12.99
DVD - Enemy of the State (R) - $1.50
DVD - Erin Brockovich (R) - $9.99
DVD - Excallibur (R) - $9.99
DVD - Family Man, The (PG-13) - $12.99
DVD - For Love of the Game (PG-13) - $9.99
XBx - Fuzion Frenzy (Everyone) - $49.99
```

18

```
DVD - GalaxyQuest (PG) - $16.99
DVD - Gladiator (R) - $19.99
XBx - Halo Combat Evolved (Mature) - $49.99
DVD - Harry Potter and the Sorcerer's Stone (PG) - $12.99
VHS - Hollow Man (R) - $9.99
DVD - Independence Day Collector's Edition (PG-13) - $19.99

...

DVD - X-Men (PG-13) - $14.99
VHS - You Can Count On Me (R) - $9.99
DVD - You've Got Mail (PG) - $14.99

TOTAL: $1,727.36   AVG PRICE: $16.77
```

 ANALYSIS Before running this listing, you need to make sure that the Videos.mdb file is located at C:\. If you want this file to be somewhere else, change the path used in the data source shown in Line 19.

This listing uses everything you've read about in today's lesson up to this point. In Line 16, a connection string named myConnectionString is created. This includes information to use Microsoft Access database (see Line 17) as well as the previously mentioned link to the data source.

> **Note** Notice the use of @ in Line 19. This allows the string following to be taken literally. If you leave off the @, you will need to use double forward slashes in the path. You should also note that although this is a single string variable, it looks like three strings are assigned. This is not the case. The plus sign adds the three strings (concatenates them) into a single string.

In Lines 20–21, two variables are set up to track totals. These totals will be filled in as the records are read. In Line 22 a SQL query is created and also assigned to a string variable, mySelectQuery. This query selects all the information from each row in the videos table. It then orders (sorts) them by their titles.

In Line 24, the connection object, myConnection, is created using the connection string that was created in Line 16. In Line 27, an OleDbCommand object is created. This is done slightly differently than what you saw earlier. As you can see, the query (mySelectQuery) is passed as the first item along with the connection object.

Line 30 uses the connection object that you created for the video database to actually open the database using the Open method. After this line is executed, you will have an opened, usable connection to the data.

Line 32 creates the `DataReader` that will be used to read the data. Line 33 calls the `ExecuteReader` method using your command object. This returns the data to your reader object, `myDataReader`. With the reader full of data, you are ready to loop through it. This is accomplished with the `while` loop in Lines 35–47. Each time through, you call the `Read` method to get the next record.

With each loop, Lines 37–43 contain a call to `WriteLine`. Although this looks complicated, it isn't. `Getxxx` methods are used to get data from the records. In this case, the `10` element is the medium type. Because the medium type is a string, `myDataReader` uses the `GetString` method and passes the value `9`, which gives the tenth element because of the zero offset. The `PadLeft` is a standard string function that enables you to pad a value with a character—in this case, a string. Line 40 works in the same way, getting the second element, which is the title. Line 43 uses the `GetDecimal` method to get the fourth value, which is a currency value. This is retrieved as a decimal value and then is displayed using the currency formatter (`{0:C}`).

In Line 45, the fourth value is used a second time. In this line, the value is added to a total accumulator. In Line 46, a counter is being used to count the number of records that are being counted.

After the loop completes, Line 50 closes the `DataReader` that you were using. You should always close your `DataReader`s. Line 53 closes the connection to the database. Again, this is something you should always do.

This listing ends with the values of the counter variables being printed in Line 55. This prints the total value of the videos along with the average value.

I may sound like a broken record (or a CD with a skip), but this listing is missing exception handling. In an exercise at the end of today, exception handling will be added. You should always include exception handling in your applications.

Adding, Updating, and Deleting Data

Earlier, the `Command` class was mentioned. In Listing 18.1, you used the `ExecuteReader` method to read data from a database. You can also use the command object to execute other commands against the database. This includes using it to do inserts, updates, and deletes.

Instead of using `ExecuteReader`, you use the `ExecuteNonQuery` method. This method enables you to execute a SQL query or a stored procedure against the database. This method returns the number of records impacted by the query. Because it doesn't return data, you can't use it for retrieving information. However, this is perfect for inserts, updates, and deletes.

The ExecuteNonQuery command is used similarly to the ExecuteReader command. You connect to and open the database, create a command object, and associate both the connection and the query you want to execute with the Command object. You then call ExecuteNonQuery. You should close the connection before exiting.

The queries that you can assign are any valid SQL query or stored procedure. This query needs to be valid for the specific database that you are using. SQL is not exactly the same across databases.

In Listing 18.2, a simple insert query is created for Microsoft Access. To make this listing simpler, a different table from within the Videos database is used. When this listing is executed, two additional rows are added to the Names table.

LISTING 18.2   Customers.cs—Updating with a SQL query

```
 1:  // Customers.cs
 2:  // --------------------------------------------------------------
 3:  using System;
 4:  using System.Data;
 5:  using System.Data.OleDb;
 6:
 7:  public class Customers
 8:  {
 9:    public static void Main()
10:    {
11:       Customers myCustomer = new Customers();
12:       myCustomer.Add("Kyle", "Rinni", DateTime.Now.Date);
13:       myCustomer.Add("Kaylee", "Rinni", DateTime.Now.Date);
14:     }
15:
16:    public void Add( string FirstName,
17:                     string LastName,
18:                     DateTime Joined)
19:    {
20:       int rv = 0;
21:       OleDbConnection myConnection = null;
22:
23:       string  myConnectionString =
24:          "Provider=Microsoft.Jet.OLEDB.4.0;" +
25:          "User Id=;Password=;" +
26:          @"Data Source=C:\Videos.mdb";
27:
28:       string  myAddQuery = @"INSERT INTO [Names] " +
29:                            @"(FirstName, LastName, JoinDate ) " +
30:                             "VALUES ( \"" + FirstName + "\",\"" +
31:                                LastName + "\",\"" + Joined + "\")";
32:
33:       try
```

LISTING 18.2 continued

```
34:          {
35:              myConnection = new OleDbConnection(myConnectionString);
36:
37:              OleDbCommand myCommand =
38:                  new OleDbCommand(myAddQuery, myConnection);
39:
40:              myConnection.Open();
41:
42:              rv = myCommand.ExecuteNonQuery();
43:          }
44:          catch (OleDbException e )
45:          {
46:              Console.WriteLine("OleDb Error: {0}", e.Message );
47:          }
48:          finally
49:          {
50:              if ( myConnection != null )
51:                  myConnection.Close();
52:          }
53:
54:          Console.WriteLine("Record added ({0})", rv );
55:      }
56:  }
```

18

OUTPUT
Record added (1)
Record added (1)

Note that this listing also writes two additional rows into the Names table in the Videos.mdb Microsoft Access Database located at C:\.

ANALYSIS The first thing you should notice is that a little bit of exception handling was added to this listing. The code for connecting and accessing the database is contained within a try statement starting in Line 33. If an error occurs with the database, instead of having the application crash with an error, the exception is caught. In Line 44, a check is done to catch an OleDbException. This is a general exception class for database errors that may have occurred. You can actually catch more specific errors if you want. If a database error is caught, it is simply printed to the console.

Stepping back, you can see that much of the logic for connecting and opening the database is the same as in the previous listing. Where things start to truly differ is in Line 42. Instead of calling the ExecuteReader method, this line calls the ExecuteNonQuery method. This executes the myAddQuery that was associated to myCommand in Lines 37–38. The call to ExecuteNonQuery results in the query being executed and a number being returned that is equal to the number of rows affected. In this case, a single line was added, so the value 1 should be returned.

After Line 42 completes, the exception-handling logic directs the program's flow to the `finally` clause in Line 48. In Line 50, a check is made to see whether the connection to the database was actually made. If it was, it is closed in Line 51. If an exception had been thrown before the connection had been made or opened, you wouldn't have wanted to close it because it wouldn't have been opened.

With the record updated and everything closed, the listing ends with Line 54. This simply prints the return value from having called `ExecuteNonQuery`. This was done to show you that the returned value did equal the number of records impacted: one.

This same logic can be used to do updates and deletes. All you need to do is prepare the information that you want to update or delete and then associate it with the command object that you create.

 Caution　　The SQL commands that you use must be appropriate for your database. Although SQL for different databases looks similar, it often is not.

Other Database Concepts

As mentioned at the beginning of today's lesson, covering database topics and ADO could fill several books. I've provided you with a means of accessing and manipulating data in a database. However, this is not the only means. There are other ways, including a more robust way to work with data from databases. This includes the use of `DataSets` and `DataAdapters`. There is also the capability to do data binding to controls. Finally, you can work with data in other formats, including XML. This can be done in the same manner as working with databases.

 A `DataSet` is a copy of data from a database that is stored in the memory of your computer. Data is often manipulated by retrieving data and placing it into a `DataSet`. This set may include multiple data tables as well as relationships between them. Unlike the `DataReader`, you are not locked into just reading data, nor are you forced to read the data only from beginning to end.

Although `DataSets` are on your local machine, they are not directly connected to a database. Again, they are a copy of the data. To pull this data from the database (and to put changes back into the database), you use a `DataAdapter`.

When working with `DataSets`, you often use a `DataAdapter`. A `DataAdapter` is an object that contains a set of commands and a database connection. You use a `DataAdapter` as an intermediary for working with the data and a database.

Data binding is the process of associating a data to a control. This is usually a control on a form such as a `DataGrid`. The binding of data makes it easy to present the data on the control. However, it doesn't remove the need to do the adding, updating, and deleting logic.

Summary

In today's lesson, you learned a little about working with ADO.NET and databases. You learned to use a number of key classes for manipulating data. You learned an efficient way to retrieve data using the `DataReader`. You also learned a method for adding, updating, and deleting information from a database. The lesson ended by exposing you to a few of the terms that were not covered in regard to database programming.

Q&A

Q What does ADO stand for?

A ADO stands for Active Data Objects.

Q Isn't ADO.NET a Microsoft standard? If so, will it be portable?

A ADO is a Microsoft standard; however, it is still being ported to other platforms. For example, the mono project (www.go-mono.com) is including a port of ADO.NET within its scope. This should result in ADO.NET being supported on platforms such as Red Hat Linux, FreeBSD, and the Mac.

Q Is ADO.NET just a newer version of ADO?

A Yes and no. ADO.NET continued what ADO started. ADO.NET, however, is based on the premise that the database may be disconnected from the application. To accomplish this, ADO.NET was written from the ground up.

Q How comprehensive was today's lessons in regard to databases and ADO.NET?

A Today's lessons barely scratched the surface of ADO.NET and database development with .NET. Entire books focus on just ADO.NET.

Workshop

The Workshop provides quiz questions to help you solidify your understanding of the material covered and exercises to provide you with experience in using what you've learned. Try to understand the quiz and exercise answers before continuing to the next day's lesson. Answers are provided on the CD.

18

Quiz

1. What is the difference between a column and a field?

2. Put the following in order from largest to smallest:

   a. Table

   b. Row/record

   c. Database

   d. Column/field

3. What four key classes are generally used by a data provider?

4. What is the difference between `OleDbConnection` and `SqlConnection`?

5. In the following, what is the name of the database being used?

```
string myConnectionString = @"Provider=Microsoft.Jet.OLEDB.4.0;User Id=;
                               Password=;Data Source=Bobby.mdb"
```

6. What would the connection string be for accessing a Microsoft Access database named Customers using the password secret and the user ID BradJ?

7. What method of `OleDbCommand` would you use with a `DataReader`?

8. What method of `OleDbCommand` would you use to delete a record from a table?

9. What method of the `DataReader` would you use to get an double value from a record?

10. Why is exception handling important when working with databases?

Exercises

1. Add exception handling to Listing 18.1.

2. Modify the listing in Exercise 1 so that the class contains a method that will accept any valid connection string and still work. *Hint:* From the `Main` method, pass a connection string value to a new method.

3. **On Your Own:** Using a database, create the tables for tracking data for a video store. Write the code for reading the information in the different tables.

4. **On Your Own:** Create a windows form application that displays the information from the `DataReader`.

5. **On Your Own:** Create a windows form that allows the user to enter a first name and a last name as well as a date. Add the values to the Names table in the Videos.mdb database when the user clicks a button. Make sure that the three values have been entered before actually adding the information.

DAY 19

Creating Remote Procedures: Web Services

Over the last couple of days, you have learned about creating applications that use windows forms. If you are building applications for the Internet—or, more specifically, the Web—you might not be able to use windows-based forms that use the System.Windows.Forms namespace. Instead, you might want to take advantage of the Web's capability of working with numerous different systems by using general standards, such as HTML and XML. Today you begin the first of two days that dig into developing applications focused at the Web. Today you…

- Learn the basics about Web services.
- Create a simple Web service using C#.
- Understand how to generate a proxy file for using a Web service.
- Use your Web service from a client program.

> The topic of today's lesson and tomorrow's lesson—Web development—could fill entire books on its own. To avoid adding a large number of pages to these lessons, I make some assumptions. If you don't fit all these assumptions, don't fret—you will still find lots of value in the concepts and code presented in today's lessons.
>
> My assumptions are as follows:
>
> - You have access to a Web server or a Web service provider that can host Web services written to the .NET runtime.
> - You are familiar with basic Web development concepts, including the use of HTML and basic client-side scripting.
> - You are using a computer that has a Web server running that supports Active Server Pages and ASP.NET (such as Microsoft Internet Information Server [IIS]).
> - Your Web server is set up with the standard Inetpub/wwwroot directory. Today's lesson references this directory as the base directory or root directory of your Web server. If you know how to set up virtual directories, you can use those as well.

Creating Web Applications

Two types of Web applications are covered: Web services and Web forms. Each of these has its own use and its own applications. Today you start with Web services.

Examining the Concept of a Component

NEW TERM Before tackling the concept of a Web service, it is worth looking at the concept of components. A *component* is a piece of software that has a well-defined interface, hidden internals, and the capability of being discovered. By "discovered," I mean that you can determine what the component does without needing to see the code within it. In a lot of ways, a component is similar to a method. It can be called with arguments that fit a set of parameters, and it has the capability of returning results.

Web Services

NEW TERM The use of methods as components has been moved to the Web. A Web component can be referred to as a Web service. A *Web service* is a component that performs a function or service. A Web service may also return information to the caller. This service resides somewhere on the Web and can be accessed from other locations on the

Web. For this service to be called, a number of elements must be in place. First, the caller must know how to call the service. Second, the call must be made across the Web (otherwise, it is just a service, not a *Web* service). Finally, the Web service must know how to respond. Figure 19.1 illustrates the Web service process.

FIGURE 19.1

Web services.

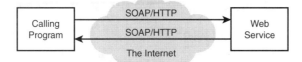

In the figure, the Simple Object Access Protocol (SOAP) has been created to communicate between a program and a Web service. SOAP is a standardized way of formatting information about method calls and data. This formatting is based on the XML standard. Using SOAP, a program can communicate to a Web service, and the Web service can communicate back.

The calling program can be a C# program or a program written in any other programming language. Additionally, the calling program can be a browser or even another Web service, and the Web service can be written in C# or any other language. Because a standardized protocol—SOAP—is being used, the calling program can interact with the Web service and vice versa.

Note
Although understanding SOAP is valuable, it is not critical for creating Web services.

19

Three basic steps are involved in setting up and using a Web service:

1. Create the actual Web service.
2. Create a program to use the service.
3. Create a file that can help your program call the service. This helper program is called a *Web proxy*. **NEW TERM**

You'll learn about creating each of these three parts in the following sections.

Creating a Simple Component

Before creating a Web service, you create a simple class. This class then is used as the basis of your first Web service. This class also is compiled as a routine within a library. Listing 19.1 contains the simple routine that will be used.

LISTING 19.1 Calc.cs—A Basic Component

```
 1:  // Calc.cs
 2:  //-------------------------------
 3:
 4:  using System;
 5:
 6:  public class Calc
 7:  {
 8:     public static int Add( int x, int y )
 9:     {
10:        return x + y;
11:     }
12:     public static int Subtract( int x, int y )
13:     {
14:        return x - y;
15:     }
16:  }
```

To make this an external class that you can call, you need to compile the listing as a library. You create a library by targeting the output as a library. This is done by using library with the command-line target flag:

```
csc /t:library Calc.cs
```

The result is a file named Calc.dll instead of Calc.exe.

 Note

> If you are using Visual Studio .NET 2003, you can set the output type to target a library (Class Library) by selecting the properties of the project. You can see the project properties in several ways. One is to right-click the name of the project in the Solutions Explorer and select Properties from the pop-up menu. Alternatively, you can select the Properties option on the Project menu. When you have the project's Properties page displayed, change the Output Type to Class Library.
>
> If you are using SharpDevelop, to set the project to create a library, select Project Options from the Project menus. Within the Project Options dialog box, select the Configurations folder and then Code Generation. In the Code Generation dialog box, you can change the compile target to Library. Clicking OK applies this change.
>
> If you are using another editor, consult your documentation or the help files. In many Integrated Development Environments, including Visual Studio .NET and SharpDevelop, you can select a library project type when initially creating the project.

ANALYSIS Looking at the listing, you see that the component will contain two methods in a class named `Calc`. `Add` in Lines 8–11 add two numbers. `Subtract` in Lines 12–15 returns the difference of two numbers. Listing 19.2 presents a routine that can use these methods.

LISTING 19.2 myApp.cs—Using `Add` and `Subtract`

```
 1:  // myApp.cs
 2:  // Calling a component
 3:  //--------------------------
 4:
 5:  using System;
 6:
 7:  public class myApp
 8:  {
 9:     public static void Main()
10:     {
11:        Console.WriteLine("Using Calc component");
12:        Console.WriteLine("Calc.Add( 11, 33); = {0}",
13:                          Calc.Add(33, 11));
14:        Console.WriteLine("Calc.Subtract(33, 11); = {0}",
15:                          Calc.Subtract(33,11));
16:     }
17:  }
```

OUTPUT
```
Using Calc component
Calc.Add( 11, 33); = 44
Calc.Subtract(33, 11); - 22
```

If you compile this routine the normal way, you get an error saying that a type or namespace could not be found:

`csc myApp.cs`

As you learned earlier in this book, you need to include a reference to the component that you will be using—in this case, `Calc`. Compile the main listing by including a reference to the file with the component that you created in Listing 19.1. This is done by using the reference compile flag:

`csc /r:Calc.dll myApp.cs`

The `/r:` is the reference flag. It tells the compiler to include the identified file, Calc.dll. The result is that myApp.cs will be capable of using the classes and methods in Calc.dll.

If you are using an Integrated Development Environment, you can add a reference to your library in the same manner as the other libraries you've referenced. If your library is in a different directory, you may need to browse to that directory.

19

Note

In Visual Studio .NET, you can add a reference by first selecting Add Reference from the Project menu. You then can click the Browse button in the displayed Add Reference dialog box. Browse and select the library file that you created earlier. You will see the file added to the Solution Explorer.

In SharpDevelop, you can add a reference as well. In the Project window, right-click References and then select Add Reference. This displays the Add Reference dialog box. Select the .NET Assembly Browser. Use the Browse button to find and select the library file that you created earlier. The library will be added to your project.

ANALYSIS Looking at the code in Listing 19.2, you can see that there is nothing different from what you have done before. The Main routine makes calls to the classes that are available. Because you included the Calc.dll in your compile command, the Calc class and its Add and Subtract methods are available.

Creating a Web Service

The Calc class and its methods are nice, but the example in Listings 19.1 and 19.2 are for a class located on a local machine. A Web service uses a component across the Web. You want to have the Calc methods operate as Web services so that they will be accessible across the Web by any Web-based application. This obviously adds complexity to the use of the class.

To create a Web service based on the Calc class, you need to make some changes. Listing 19.3 presents the Calc routine as a Web service.

LISTING 19.3   WebCalc.asmx—Making Calc a Web Service

```
 1: <%@WebService Language="C#" Class="Calc"%>
 2:
 3: //-----------------------------------
 4: // WebCalc.asmx
 5: //-----------------------------------
 6:
 7: using System;
 8: using System.Web.Services;
 9:
10: public class Calc : WebService
11: {
12:     [WebMethod]
13:     public int Add( int x, int y )
14:     {
15:         return x + y;
```

LISTING 19.3 continued

```
16:     }
17:
18:     [WebMethod]
19:     public int Subtract( int x, int y )
20:     {
21:        return x - y;
22:     }
23: }
```

ANALYSIS Several changes were made to this listing to make it a Web service. As you can see by glancing at the listing, none of the changes was major.

The first change is in the name of the file. Instead of ending with a .cs extension, a Web service always ends with an .asmx extension. This extension is a signal to the runtime and to a browser that this is a Web service.

The first coding change is in Line 1—a line with lots of stuff that may seem weird:

```
%@WebService Language="C#" Class="Calc"%
```

The <%@ and %> are indicators to the Web server. The Web server will see that this is a Web service written in the language C#. It will also know that the primary routine is named Calc. Because the language is specified as C#, the server will know to read the rest of the file as C# and not as some other language.

When this service is first called, it is compiled. You do not need to do the actual compile yourself. The Web server calls the correct compiler based on the language specified in the Language= command.

The next change that you can see is the inclusion of the System.Web.Service namespace in Line 8. This is included so that the use of WebMethod and WebService can be done without explicitly including the namespace name throughout the rest of the listing.

In Line 10, the Calc class is derived from WebService. This gives your class the Web service traits as defined within the .NET Framework.

The only remaining change is to identify each of the methods that you want to have available to anyone accessing your service. These are identified by including [WebMethod] before the method, as has been done in Lines 12 and 18.

That's it: This Web service is ready to go.

19

Note

> If you are using Visual Studio .NET, you have the option to create a Web service project. This project provides you with the basic infrastructure for a Web service. Like many other Visual Studio .NET projects, it includes a lot of additional code.
>
> SharpDevelop also includes a file template for creating Web services. Selecting File, New, File takes you to the New File dialog box. You can then select the category for Web services files. This gives you several options for Web service files.
>
> Other development environments may also include templates for creating Web services.

In the following sections, you learn how to create a proxy and how to call your Web service. You probably can't wait to see your Web service in action—and you don't have to.

If you are running a Web server such as Microsoft's Internet Information Server (IIS), you have a directory on your machine named Inetpub. This directory has a subdirectory named wwwroot. You can copy your Web service (WebCalc.asmx) to this directory.

When your new Web service is in that directory, you can call it by using your browser. You use the following address to call the WebCalc.asmx service:

```
http://localhost/WebCalc.asmx
```

When you use this address, you get a page similar to the page in Figure 19.2. If you have an error in your Web service, you might get a different page, indicating the error.

FIGURE 19.2

The WebCalc.asmx Web service displayed in Internet Explorer.

Looking at this page, you can see that a lot of information is displayed regarding your Web service. Most important is that this page lists the two operations that can be performed, Add and Subtract. These are the two methods from your Web services class.

If you click on either of these methods, you are taken to a second screen (see Figure 19.3), which enables you to enter the parameters that your method expects.

FIGURE 19.3

The Add *method within the Web service.*

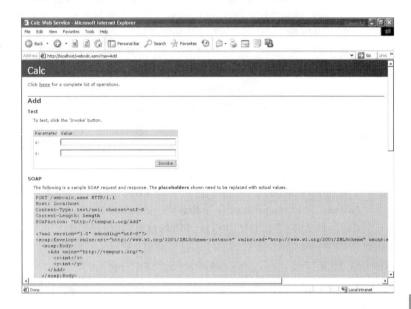

In the case of the Add method, two parameters are expected: x and y. This matches your code in Listing 19.3. If you enter the values of 5 and 10, as you did in Listing 19.2, you will see the result:

```
<?xml version="1.0" encoding="utf-8" ?>
<int xmlns="http://tempuri.org/">15</int>
```

The result of 15 is in there, but so is a bunch of other stuff. The other stuff is the SOAP information needed to send the information back to the calling routine.

Creating a Proxy

The previous section showed you how to see your Web service in action by using your browser on your local machine; however, it is more likely that you will want to use the service from another program. To do this, you need to set up a Web proxy.

As mentioned earlier, this proxy helps your local program know where on the Web to find the Web service. It also contains the details for communicating to the Web service (the SOAP stuff).

19

Writing a proxy can be a lot of work; however, there are utilities to help make this easier. One such utility is wsdl.exe, provided by Microsoft in its framework. This command-line tool can be run using the following parameters:

```
wsdl WebService_file?wsdl /out:proxyfile
```

Here, `wsdl` is the name of the utility that you are executing and `WebService_file` is the name and location of your Web service file. The Web service name is followed by `?wsdl`, which indicates that this is to generate a file using the wsdl standard. For the `Calc` programming example, this is currently on your `localhost` server; this could easily be on a different server, in which case this would be the URL to the service.

The `/out:` flag is optional and is used to give your proxy a name. If you don't use the `/out:` flag, your proxy will be named the same as your service. I suggest adding `proxy` to the name of your proxy. The following line creates the proxy file for the `WebCalc.asmx` service and places it in the `inetpub\wwwroot\` directory with the name of `CalcProxy.cs`:

```
wsdl http://localhost/WebCalc.asmx?wsdl /out:c:\inetpub\wwwroot\CalcProxy.cs
```

The proxy file has a .cs extension, which means that it is C# code that can be compiled. Listing 19.4 contains the code that was generated by wsdl using the WebCalc.asmx file that you created earlier (no line numbers are provided).

LISTING 19.4   CalcProxy.cs—Generated Code from wsdl

```
//-------------------------------------------------------------------------
// <autogenerated>
//     This code was generated by a tool.
//     Runtime Version: 1.1.4322.510
//
//     Changes to this file may cause incorrect behavior and will be lost if
//     the code is regenerated.
// </autogenerated>
//-------------------------------------------------------------------------

//
// This source code was auto-generated by wsdl, Version=1.1.4322.510.
//
using System.Diagnostics;
using System.Xml.Serialization;
using System;
using System.Web.Services.Protocols;
using System.ComponentModel;
using System.Web.Services;
```

LISTING **19.4**   continued

```
/// <remarks/>
[System.Diagnostics.DebuggerStepThroughAttribute()]
[System.ComponentModel.DesignerCategoryAttribute("code")]
[System.Web.Services.WebServiceBindingAttribute(Name="CalcSoap",
➥Namespace="http://tempuri.org/")]
public class Calc : System.Web.Services.Protocols.SoapHttpClientProtocol {

    /// <remarks/>
    public Calc() {
        this.Url = "http://localhost/WebCalc.asmx";
    }

    /// <remarks/>

[System.Web.Services.Protocols.SoapDocumentMethodAttribute("http://tempuri.org/
➥Add", RequestNamespace="http://tempuri.org/", ResponseNamespace="http://
➥tempuri.org/", Use=System.Web.Services.Description.SoapBindingUse.Literal,
ParameterStyle=System.Web.Services.Protocols.SoapParameterStyle.Wrapped)]
    public int Add(int x, int y) {
        object[] results = this.Invoke("Add", new object[] {
                    x,
                    y});
        return ((int)(results[0]));
    }

    /// <remarks/>
    public System.IAsyncResult BeginAdd(int x, int y, System.AsyncCallback
➥callback, object asyncState) {
        return this.BeginInvoke("Add", new object[] {
                    x,
                    y}, callback, asyncState);
    }

    /// <remarks/>
    public int EndAdd(System.IAsyncResult asyncResult) {
        object[] results = this.EndInvoke(asyncResult);
        return ((int)(results[0]));
    }

    /// <remarks/>

[System.Web.Services.Protocols.SoapDocumentMethodAttribute("http://tempuri.org/
➥Subtract", RequestNamespace="http://tempuri.org/", ResponseNamespace="http://
➥tempuri.org/", Use=System.Web.Services.Description.SoapBindingUse.Literal,
ParameterStyle=System.Web.Services.Protocols.SoapParameterStyle.Wrapped)]
    public int Subtract(int x, int y) {
```

19

LISTING **19.4**   continued

```
        object[] results = this.Invoke("Subtract", new object[] {
                    x,
                    y});
        return ((int)(results[0]));
    }

    /// <remarks/>
    public System.IAsyncResult BeginSubtract(int x, int y, System.AsyncCallback
callback, object asyncState) {
        return this.BeginInvoke("Subtract", new object[] {
                    x,
                    y}, callback, asyncState);
    }

    /// <remarks/>
    public int EndSubtract(System.IAsyncResult asyncResult) {
        object[] results = this.EndInvoke(asyncResult);
        return ((int)(results[0]));
    }
}
```

It is beyond the scope of this book to explain the code in this listing. The important thing to note is that it takes care of the SOAP stuff for you. Before you can use it, however, you need to compile it. As you've done before, you need to compile this listing as a library. Remember, this is done using the target flag (/t:library):

```
csc /t:library CalcProxy.cs
```

The result is a file named CalcProxy.dll that you will use with the programs that call your Web service.

Calling a Web Service

The final step in using a Web service is to create the program that will call the service. Listing 19.5 presents a simple program that can use the WebCalc service.

LISTING **19.5**   WebClient.cs—Client to Use WebCalc

```
1:  // WebClient.cs
2:  // Calling a Web service
3:  //---------------------------
4:
5:  using System;
6:
7:  public class WebClient
8:  {
```

LISTING 19.5   continued

```
 9:     public static void Main()
10:     {
11:         Calc cSrv = new Calc();
12:
13:         Console.WriteLine("cSrv.Add( 11, 33); = {0}",
14:                             cSrv.Add(33, 11));
15:         Console.WriteLine("cSrv.Subtract(33, 11); = {0}",
16:                             cSrv.Subtract(33,11));
17:     }
18: }
```

OUTPUT
```
cSrv.Add( 11, 33); = 44
cSrv.Subtract(33, 11); = 22
```

ANALYSIS   When you compile this listing, you need to include a reference to the proxy file that you previously compiled. You do this the same way that you include any library, with the /r: flag:

```
csc /r:CalcProxy.dll WebClient.cs
```

After it's compiled, you have a program that can use the Web proxy (via the CalcProxy program that you generated) to access the Web service that you created (WebCalc.cs). You can see in Listing 19.5 that using the Web service is very easy. In Line 11, you create a Calc object named cSrv. This is then used to call the methods within the service. In reality, this is the same as if you were using a local library. The difference is that you created and used the Web proxy file that took care of connecting to the calc routines on the Web server.

> **Note**
> You can move the WebCalc.asmx file to a different Web server. You would then need to create a new proxy file and recompile your local program.

19

Summary

Today's lesson was broken into two parts. You spent the first part setting up and using a simple Web service. You learned that a Web service is a piece of code residing somewhere on the Web that you can call from your program. Because of communication standards that have been developed, calling and using such Web services has become relatively easy.

In tomorrow's lesson, you will continue working with Web-based applications. Rather than focusing on services, tomorrow you will focus on building Web applications that use forms.

Q&A

Q The code in the Web service and in the client using the Web service is not very different from normal code. Shouldn't this be more complex?

A The code presented in today's Web service and client was very simple. A lot of work has gone into creating standards for communicating across the Web. The complexity of Web services is in the communication. The wsdl tool created the complex code for you. By creating standards for communicating interaction, much of the complexity has been removed from the applications. Your applications can focus on what they need to do rather than on communicating.

Q Do I have to use wsdl.exe to generate the proxy code file?

A No. You can write this code by hand, or you can use a development tool such as Visual Studio .NET that can help generate some of the code needed.

Q Can windows forms, database routines, and other .NET Framework classes be used with Web services?

A Because a Web service is accessed across the Web, and because a Web service could be called from any platform, you should avoid using a graphical user interface (GUI) within a Web service. You can use database routines or .NET Framework classes in your Web services. Any routines can be used that are supported by the server running the Web service.

Workshop

The Workshop provides quiz questions to help you solidify your understanding of the material covered and exercises to provide you with experience in using what you've learned. Try to understand the quiz and exercise answers before continuing to the next day's lesson. Answers are provided on the CD.

Quiz

1. What is a Web service?
2. What is the file called that helps a client application communicate with a Web service?
3. What program can be used to create the code to communicate with a Web server?

4. How can you tell a Web service from an ASP.NET page?

5. How do you execute an ASP.NET page?

6. What is the SOAP returned from the WebCalc Web service if you enter 20 for x and 10 for y?

7. If you have a Web Service in a file named myService.asmx on a server named www.myserver.com, what wsdl command would you use to create a proxy file named myProxy in the wwwroot directory on your C: drive?

8. If you were using Microsoft's command-line compiler, how would you compile the proxy file generated in question 7?

9. How would you compile a program in a file named myClient.cs that uses the proxy from question 8?

Exercises

1. What is the first line of a C# program that will be used as a Web service? Assume that the Web service class name is DBInfo and that the first method is named GetData.

2. What changes need to be made to a method to use it in a Web service?

3. Add a Multiply method and a Subtract method to the WebCalc Web service.

4. Create a new client that uses the Multiply and Divide classes created in Exercise 3.

5. **On Your Own:** Amazon.com is one of many sites that have provided a Web service. At the time this book was written, you could access this Web service on the Amazon.com Web site (www.Amazon.com). Incorporate this Web service into an application. Your application should allow you to see how well your favorite books are doing at Amazon.

19

Type & Run 5

Quote of the Day Web Service

Throughout this book, you will find a number of Type & Run sections. These sections present a listing that is a little longer than the listings within the daily lessons. The purpose of these listings is to give you a program to type in and run.

This Type & Run builds off of Day 19, "Creating Remote Procedures: Web Services." In this Type & Run, you are presented with a Web service that reads quotes from an XML file. A small application is then presented that uses the service.

The Web Service File

The following listing presents the Web Service file.

LISTING T&R 5.1   QuoteService.asmx—The Quotes Web Service

```
 1: <%@ WebService Language="c#" Class="JustCSharp.QuoteService.Quote" %>
 2:
 3: using System;
 4: using System.Data;
 5: using System.Web;
 6: using System.Web.Services;
 7: using System.Text.RegularExpressions;
 8:
 9: namespace JustCSharp.QuoteService
10: {
11:   /// <summary>
12:   /// Summary description for Service1.
13:   /// </summary>
14:   public class Quote : WebService
15:   {
16:     [WebMethod]
17:     public string GetQuote()
18:     {
19:       // Load quotes...
20:       // Create a DataSet
21:       DataSet dsQuotes = new DataSet();
22:
23:       // Read an XML file into the DataSet
24:       dsQuotes.ReadXml( Regex.Replace (
25:             Context.Request.PhysicalPath.ToString(),
26:             "QuoteService.asmx",
27:             "verses.xml",
28:             RegexOptions.IgnoreCase) );
29:
30:        Random rnd = new Random();
31:
32:        string strQuote = null;  // string to hold quote
33:
34:        // Get a random number from 1 to the number of rows in the table
35:        int QuoteRow = rnd.Next(1, dsQuotes.Tables[0].Rows.Count );
36:
37:        // Get a quote by grabbing a row out of the XML table.
38:        strQuote += Server.HtmlEncode (
39:              dsQuotes.Tables[0].Rows[QuoteRow][0].ToString());
40:
41:        return strQuote;
42:     }
43:   }
44: }
```

Remember, Type & Runs don't include full analysis. Like the Web service presented on Day 19, the Quote Web service is entered into a file with an .asmx extension. This listing can be placed in the Inetpub\wwwroot directory. Because this listing reads an XML file, you need to also place the XML file into the Inetpub\wwwroot directory. Listing T&R 2 contains the verses XML file. You can replace the text with any quotes you would like.

LISTING T&R 5.2   verses.xml—XML File of Verses

```xml
<?xml version="1.0" encoding="utf-8" ?>
<quotes>
    <quote>He is good; his love endures forever. 2 Chronicles 5:13
    </quote>
    <quote>But I lead a blameless life; redeem me and be merciful to
    me. Psalm 26:13</quote>
    <quote>Listen carefully to my words; let this be the consolation
    you give me. Job 21:2</quote>
    <quote>Resentment kills a fool, and envy slays the simple.
    Job 5:2</quote>
    <quote>Blessed is the man who does not walk in the counsel of
    the wicked or stand in the way of sinners or sit in the seat
    of mockers. Psalms 1:1</quote>
    <quote>No one remembers you when he is dead. Who praises you from
    the grave? Psalms 6:5</quote>
    <quote>Do not fret because of evil men or be envious of those who

    do wrong; Psalms 37:1</quote>
    <quote>This is a message you heard from the beginning: We should
    love one another. 1 John 3:13</quote>
    <quote>What good is it, my brothers, if a man claims to have faith
    but has no deeds? Can such faith save him? James 2:14</quote>
    <quote>If a man is lazy, the rafters sag; if his hands are idle,
    the house leaks. Ecclesiastes 10:18</quote>
    <quote>No one knows what is coming - who can tell him what will
    happen after him? Ecclesiastes 10:14</quote>
    <quote>Since no man knows the future, who can tell him what is to
    come? Ecclesiastes 8:7</quote>
    <quote>The evil deeds of a wicked man ensnares him; the cords of his
    sin hold him fast. Proverbs 5:22</quote>
</quotes>
```

Note   The quotes come from the Holy Bible, New International Version, ©1978 by New York International Bible Society, 144 Tices Lane, East Brunswick, New Jersey 08816.

With both the XML and Web service files in the wwwroot directory, you can use Internet Explorer to test the service by opening the asmx file in the Internet Explorer address bar:

```
http://localhost/QuoteService.asmx
```

This results in what you see in Figure T&R5.1.

FIGURE TR5.1

QuoteService.asmx running in Internet Explorer.

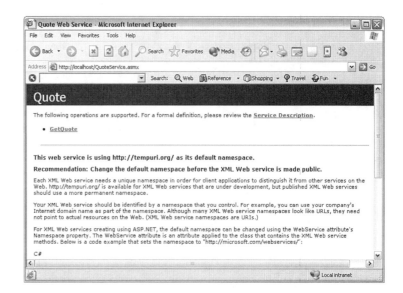

The Proxy File

To use the Web service, you need to create a proxy file. Day 19 walks you through this process. To create the proxy, use wsdl:

```
wsdl http://localhost/QuoteService.asmx?wsdl
➥/out:c:\inetpub\wwwroot\QuoteProxy.cs
```

This generates the QuoteProxy.cs file that is shown in Listing T&R 5.3.

LISTING T&R 5.3   QuoteProxy.cs—The wsdl-Generated Proxy Class

```
//-------------------------------------------------------------------------
// <autogenerated>
//      This code was generated by a tool.
//      Runtime Version: 1.1.4322.510
//
//      Changes to this file may cause incorrect behavior and will be lost if
//      the code is regenerated.
// </autogenerated>
```

```
//---------------------------------------------------------------------------
//
// This source code was auto-generated by wsdl, Version=1.1.4322.510.
//
using System.Diagnostics;
using System.Xml.Serialization;
using System;
using System.Web.Services.Protocols;
using System.ComponentModel;
using System.Web.Services;


/// <remarks/>
[System.Diagnostics.DebuggerStepThroughAttribute()]
[System.ComponentModel.DesignerCategoryAttribute("code")]
[System.Web.Services.WebServiceBindingAttribute(Name="QuoteSoap",
Namespace="http://tempuri.org/")]
public class Quote : System.Web.Services.Protocols.SoapHttpClientProtocol {

    /// <remarks/>
    public Quote() {
        this.Url = "http://localhost/QuoteService.asmx";
    }

    /// <remarks/>
    [System.Web.Services.Protocols.SoapDocumentMethodAttribute
("http://tempuri.org/GetQuote", RequestNamespace="http://tempuri.org/",
ResponseNamespace="http://tempuri.org/", Use=System.Web.Services.Description.
SoapBindingUse.Literal, ParameterStyle=System.Web.Services.Protocols.
SoapParameterStyle.Wrapped)]
    public string GetQuote() {
        object[] results = this.Invoke("GetQuote", new object[0]);
        return ((string)(results[0]));
    }

    /// <remarks/>
    public System.IAsyncResult BeginGetQuote(System.AsyncCallback callback,
        object asyncState) {
        return this.BeginInvoke("GetQuote", new object[0], callback,
asyncState);
    }

    /// <remarks/>
    public string EndGetQuote(System.IAsyncResult asyncResult) {
        object[] results = this.EndInvoke(asyncResult);
        return ((string)(results[0]));
    }
}
```

You will want to compile this proxy file as a library. If you are using the Microsoft Visual C# .NET command-line compiler, enter the following to create the library:

```
csc t:/library QuoteService.cs
```

This results in a DLL file being created.

Using the Service

Now that you have a service and a proxy, you'll want to use it. Listing T&R 5.4 contains a client program that uses the Quote service. Remember from Day 19 that you need to include a reference to the compiled proxy library when you compile this. If you are using the Microsoft command-line compiler, enter this:

```
csc /r:QuoteService.dll frmQuotes.cs
```

LISTING T&R 5.4   frmQuote.cs—An Application to Use the Web Service

```
 1: /// frmQuote.cs
 2:
 3: using System;
 4: using System.Drawing;
 5: using System.Collections;
 6: using System.ComponentModel;
 7: using System.Windows.Forms;
 8: using System.Data;
 9:
10: //using QuoteService
11: namespace UsingQuotes
12: {
13:     /// <summary>
14:     /// Summary description for Form1.
15:     /// </summary>
16:     public class frmQuotes : System.Windows.Forms.Form
17:     {
18:         private Label  lblQuote;
19:         private Button btnGetQuote;
20:         private string CurrentQuote;
21:
22:         private System.ComponentModel.Container components = null;
23:
24:         public frmQuotes()
25:         {
26:             InitializeComponent();
27:         }
28:
29:         /// <summary>
30:         /// Clean up any resources being used.
```

LISTING T&R 5.4   continued

```
31:       /// </summary>
32:       protected override void Dispose( bool disposing )
33:       {
34:          if( disposing )
35:          {
36:             if (components != null)
37:             {
38:                components.Dispose();
39:             }
40:          }
41:          base.Dispose( disposing );
42:       }
43:
44:       private void InitializeComponent()
45:       {
46:          this.lblQuote    = new Label();
47:          this.btnGetQuote = new Button();
48:          this.SuspendLayout();
49:          //
50:          // lblQuote
51:          //
52:          this.lblQuote.Location = new Point(16, 16);
53:          this.lblQuote.Name     = "lblQuote";
54:          this.lblQuote.Size     = new Size(256, 88);
55:          this.lblQuote.TabIndex = 0;
56:          this.lblQuote.Text     = "xxx";
57:          //
58:          // btnGetQuote
9:           //
60:          this.btnGetQuote.Location = new Point(88, 184);
61:          this.btnGetQuote.Name     = "btnGetQuote";
62:          this.btnGetQuote.Size     = new Size(112, 32);
63:          this.btnGetQuote.TabIndex = 1;
64:          this.btnGetQuote.Text     = "Get Quote";
65:          this.btnGetQuote.Click +=
           ➥     new System.EventHandler(this.btnGetQuote_Click);
66:          //
67:          // frmQuotes
68:          //
69:          this.AutoScaleBaseSize = new Size(5, 13) ;
70:          this.ClientSize        = new Size(292, 230);
71:          this.Controls.AddRange(new Control[] { this.btnGetQuote,
72:                                                 this.lblQuote});
73:          this.Name = "frmQuotes";
74:          this.Text = "Quotes";
75:          this.ResumeLayout(false);
76:
77:       }
78:
```

LISTING T&R 5.4   continued

```
 79:        /// <summary>
 80:        /// The main entry point for the application.
 81:        /// </summary>
 82:        static void Main()
 83:        {
 84:            Application.Run(new frmQuotes());
 85:        }
 86:
 87:        private void btnGetQuote_Click(object sender, System.EventArgs e)
 88:        {
 89:            CurrentQuote = "zzz";
 90:
 91:            Quote myQuoteService = new Quote();
 92:
 93:            try
 94:            {
 95:              CurrentQuote = myQuoteService.GetQuote();
 96:            }
 97:            catch ( Exception ex)
 98:            {
 99:              MessageBox.Show("Error getting quote: " + ex.Message,
100:                    "error", MessageBoxButtons.OK,
101:                     MessageBoxIcon.Error);
102:            }
103:            lblQuote.Text = CurrentQuote;
104:        }
105:    }
106: }
```

Figure TR5.2 presents output from compiling and running the frmQuote application. This is the result from clicking the button. Because a random quote is returned, your output may be different.

OUTPUT

FIGURE TR5.2

Output from the Web service.

Note The source code for these listings is available on the included CD. Any updates to the code will be available at `www.TeachYourselfCSharp.com`.

DAY **20**

Creating Web Applications

A couple of days ago, you learned about creating applications that use windows forms. If you are building applications for the Internet—or, more specifically, the Web—you might not be able to use windows-based forms that use the `System.Windows.Forms` namespace. Instead you might want to take advantage of the Web's capability of working with numerous different systems by using general standards, such as HTML and XML. Today you...

- Obtain an overview of what Web forms are.
- Evaluate some of the basic controls used in Web forms.
- Discover the differences between server and client controls.
- Create a basic Web form application.

Caution Like yesterday's topic, the topic of today's lesson—Web application develop-ment—could fill an entire book on its own. To avoid adding a large number of pages to today's lesson, I make some assumptions. If you don't fit all these assumptions, don't fret—you will still find lots of value in the concepts and code presented in today's lessons.

My assumptions are as follows:

- You are familiar with basic Web development concepts, including the use of HTML and basic client-side scripting.

- You are using a computer that has a Web server running that sup-ports Active Server Pages and ASP.NET (such as Microsoft Internet Information Server [IIS]).

- Your Web server is set up with the standard Inetpub/wwwroot direc-tory. Today's lesson references this directory as the base directory or root directory of your Web server. If you know how to set up virtual directories, you can use those as well.

Creating Regular Web Applications

Yesterday Web services were covered. In today's lesson, a second type of Web application is covered—Web forms. As a technology, Web forms are closer to windows forms and the standard applications that you are accustomed to. A Web form is a build-ing block to creating dynamic Web sites.

A Web form application is not created as a file with a .cs extension. Instead, it is created as a part of ASP.NET. ASP.NET stands for Active Server Pages *dot* NET, or Active Server Pages for *dot* NET. As such, Web form applications end with an .aspx extension.

ASP.NET applications, and thus Web forms, are applications that generate what an end user sees from within a browser. These applications can use any general markup lan-guage, such as HTML. Additionally, they can be viewed in any standard browser. Most importantly, they can use programming code that can be executed on a Web server.

You should already be familiar with HTML and how a Web page is displayed. You should also be aware of how a basic browser works. You should know that a browser (the client) sends a request for a Web page. This request is routed and received by the appro-priate Web server (the server). The Web server then processes the request and sends the HTML for the Web page across the Internet back to the browser machine (the client) that made the request. The delivered HTML can then be processed and displayed by the browser (see Figure 20.1).

FIGURE 20.1

Request for a Web page.

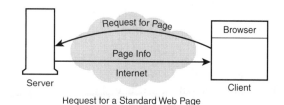

Request for a Standard Web Page

Request for an ASP.NET Page

In a basic Web page, the request received by the server causes the server to send HTML back to the browser. Microsoft provided Active Server Pages to intervene in this process. ASP enables greater control over what is being sent to a browser.

When the request is made for an ASP.NET page, rather than simply returning the page, the server executes the ASP.NET code. This runs on the server, not on the browser. This means that an ASP.NET page does not have to be compatible with a browser. This enables you to include real code, such as C#, in the ASP.NET file. The ASP.NET program generates the Web page that will be returned to the browser. The result of this processing is that you can do lots of cool things before sending the HTML. This includes customizing the HTML before sending it. Such customization might include adding current database information, modeling the Web page with browser-specific features, and creating dynamic pages. There are no limits to what the server-side programming can do.

> **Note**
>
> Although I call it an ASP.NET page, it is really an ASP.NET application. Because they are accessed in the same manner as an HTML or other standard Web page, ASP.NET *applications* are often referred to as ASP.NET *pages*.

20

With ASP.NET, a lot of the features of the .NET platform can be carried into these ASP.NET applications. This is because the ASP.NET file is executed on the server, not on the client's machine or the client's Web browser. I've repeated this several times—it is the key to the power of ASP.NET. As long as the server is running a .NET runtime and Web server, it can generate Web sites that virtually any browser can view.

The results of the ASP.NET application are sent to the client's Web browser, so you will want to make sure that the results are compatible with most browsers. Windows forms are not compatible with a machine that is not running the .NET runtime; therefore, they don't make a very good solution for generating a Web page. Don't fret: You can use the standard HTML controls. Better yet, .NET provides two additional types of controls that you can use on the server. These server-side controls generate appropriate standard HTML controls or, if supported, newer and better ways of displaying information.

Working with Web Forms

Web forms are generally broken into two pieces: a visual piece and a code piece. The visual piece is generally the look of the Web page or form that will be created. This is the layout, including where controls or text may be presented. The code piece is generally the logic (code) that ties all the visual pieces together and provides the actual functionality of the Web page.

Creating a Basic ASP.NET Application

Creating a simple ASP.NET application requires a combination of HTML, ASP scripting, and the possible use of controls. Listing 20.1 presents a simple ASP.NET application.

LISTING 20.1   FirstASP.aspx—Simple ASP.NET Application

```
 1:  <%@ Page Language="C#" %>
 2:
 3:  <HTML>
 4:  <HEAD>
 5:      <SCRIPT runat="server">
 6:      protected void btnMyButton_Click(object Source, EventArgs e)
 7:      {
 8:          lblMyLabel.Text="The button was <b>clicked</b>!";
 9:      }
10:      </SCRIPT>
11:  </HEAD>
12:
13:  <BODY>
14:      <H3>Simple Web Form Example</H3>
15:
16:      <FORM runat=server>
17:          <asp:Button id=btnMyButton
18:                      runat="server"
19:                      Text="My Button"
20:                      onclick="btnMyButton_Click" />
```

LISTING 20.1 continued

```
21:              <br>
22:              <br>
23:              <asp:Label id=lblMyLabel
24:                        runat=server />
25:         </FORM>
26:    </BODY>
27:    </HTML>
```

FIGURE 20.2

The result of the FirstASP.aspx application.

Enter this listing and save it as FirstASP.aspx. You don't need to compile this listing. Instead, as with the Web service program, you copy this program to the Web server. If you place this application in the inetpub\wwwroot\ directory, you can call it using localhost. After you copy the program, use the following URL in the browser to execute the ASP.NET application:

```
http://localhost/FirstASP.aspx
```

The initial result is shown in Figure 20.2. As you can see, the page displays standard HTML. The file extension of .aspx identifies this as an ASP.NET page and, thus, a Web form. The Web server knows that any files with an .aspx extension are to be treated as ASP.NET applications.

20

An ASP.NET application can use a number of different languages. The first line of Listing 20.1 includes a standard ASP directive that indicates that this page will use the language C#. Including this line at the top of your page enables you to use C# with your ASP.NET page. If for some strange reason you wanted to use a different language, you would change c# to the language you are going to use. For example, to use Visual Basic, you would change the c# to vb.

This directive is intercepted by the Web server. The Web server knows to process this as an ASP.NET page because of the `<%`. The Web server treats everything between the `<%` and `%>` tags as ASP.NET directives.

The rest of this listing should look similar to a standard Web page that contains a scripting element. The unique items can be seen in Lines 5, 17, 18, 20, 23, and 24. You should notice two things. First are the `runat=server` statements and the use of `asp:` in front of the control names. These items are addressed in the following sections.

The other unique item that you should notice is the slight change in style of the HTML. Instead of regular HTML, an XHTML or XML format is used. You'll see that all the control tags must include an ending tag. This also is a standard for XML. For example, `<html>` is an opening tag and `</html>` is an ending tag. In general, ending tags use the same tag name preceded by a forward slash. With some tags, you can abbreviate this by including the forward slash at the end of the opening tag commands. The controls in Listing 20.1 do this, ending with `/>`. To clarify this, here is an example of the two ways to open and close a generic tag named xxx (note that spacing doesn't matter):

```
< XXX   attributes > text < /XXX >

< XXX   attributes  />
```

The `attributes` are optional, as is the `text`.

Before continuing, you should click the button on the Web page. Doing so causes the `btnMyButton_Click` event to be executed. In Line 8, this event assigns a value to the `Text` property of the label control, `lblMyLabel`. Figure 20.3 shows the results of clicking the button.

Figure 20.3

The browser code after clicking the button.

You should do one more thing before continuing: Within your browser, open the source file using the View Source option. Do you see the FirstASP.aspx code shown earlier? No! You should see the following (after you've clicked the button):

```
<HTML>
<HEAD>

</HEAD>

<BODY>
    <H3>Simple Web Form Example</H3>

    <form name="ctrl0" method="post" action="FirstASP.aspx" id="ctrl0">
<input type="hidden" name="__VIEWSTATE" value="dDw1ODM3NzA0MzM7dDw7bDxpPDI+O
➥z47bDx0PDtsPGk8Mz47PjtsPHQ8cDxwPGw8VGV4dDs+O2w8VGhlIGJ1dHRvbiB3YXMgX
➥DxiXD5jbGlja2VkXDwvYlw+ITs+Pjs+Ozs+Oz4+Oz4=" />

        <input type="submit" name="btnMyButton" value="My Button"
              id="btnMyButton" />
        <br>
        <br>
        <span id="lblMyLabel">The button was <b>clicked</b>!</span>
    </form>
</BODY>
</HTML>
```

Remember, your browser is not getting the ASP.NET file; it is getting the *results generated* by the file. This includes the HTML code and browser-friendly controls. You might notice that the lblMyLabel control was converted to an HTML span tag rather than a control. This is the result that the Web server determined appropriate and thus generated.

Using ASP.NET Controls

When creating Web pages with ASP.NET and C#, you have the capability to use two different sets of controls: HTML server controls and Web form controls. Like ASP.NET in general, both sets of controls execute on the Web server, not on the client's machine.

Exploring HTML Server Controls

If you are familiar with the HTML forms controls, HTML server controls will look very familiar. In fact, the HTML server controls follow pretty close to the standard HTML controls—but they are not the same. Figure 20.4 illustrates the HTML server controls that are in the .NET Framework.

20

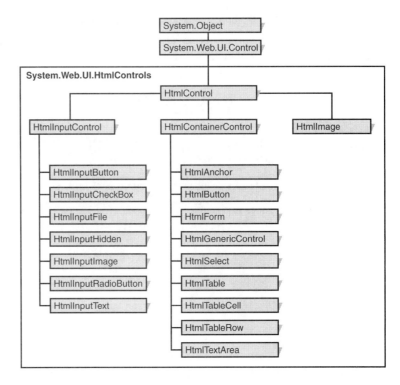

FIGURE 20.4

The HTML server controls.

Even though the primary purpose of these controls is to provide a migration path for previous versions of ASP, you can still use them. Listing 20.1 presented a Web page application that uses HTML server controls.

Table 20.1 shows you which HTML server control maps to which standard HTML control.

TABLE 20.1 HTML Server Controls

Control	Standard HTML Control
HtmlAnchor	`<a>`
HtmlButton	`<button>`
HtmlForm	`<form>`
HtmlGenericControl	`<span>`, `<div>`, `<body>`, `<font>`, or other tags not specified in an existing HTML server control
HtmlImage	`<img>`
HtmlInputButton	`<input type=button>`, `<input type=submit>`, and `<input type=reset>`

TABLE 20.1 continued

Control	Standard HTML Control
HtmlInputCheckBox	`<input type=checkbox>`
HtmlInputFile	`<input type=file>`
HtmlInputHidden	`<input type=hidden>`
HtmlInputImage	`<input type=image>`
HtmlInputRadioButton	`<input type=radio>`
HtmlInputText	`<input type=text>` and `<input type=password>`
HtmlSelect	`<select>`
HtmlTable	`<table>`
HtmlTableCell	`<td>` and `<th>`
HtmlTableRow	`<tr>`
HtmlTextArea	`<textarea>`

Although Figure 20.4 lists a bunch of controls with names that are different from the HTML controls, you will see a pattern. The difference is that each of the standard HTML server controls have been named after the standard HTML control, with Html added to the beginning.

When the ASPX file is originally parsed, all the standard HTML controls in the page are left alone. Yes, left alone. They are assumed to be standard HTML controls that should be passed to the calling Web page. However, if you add runat=server to the control's list of attributes, the parser converts the control to the related HTML server control in Table 20.1. By converting to the HTML server equivalent, you can manipulate the controls on the server. If you don't include runat=server, you can't manipulate the controls on the server; they are sent to the browser instead.

Listing 20.2 is a rather long listing that uses HTML server controls. This listing displays a form that enables you to enter a username and a password. In the code, the username is Brad and the correct password is Swordfish. The form contains two input boxes and two buttons. They all have runat=server included, so all the controls will be executed on the server as HTML server controls.

20

LISTING 20.2 HTMLControls.aspx—Using HTML Server Controls

```
1:  <html>
2:      <script Language="C#"  runat="server">
3:
4:          protected void SubmitBtn_Click(object source, EventArgs e)
```

LISTING 20.2   continued

```
 5:         {
 6:             if ((Name.Value == "Brad") &&
 7:                     (Password.Value == "Swordfish"))
 8:             {
 9:                 Message.InnerHtml = "You Pass!";
10:             }
11:             else
12:             {
13:                 Message.InnerHtml = "Incorrect user name or password.";
14:             }
15:         }
16:
17:         protected void ResetBtn_Click(object source, EventArgs e)
18:         {
19:             Name.Value = "";
20:             Password.Value = "";
21:         }
22:     </script>
23:     <body>
24:         <form method=post runat="server">
25:             Enter Name:         
26:                         <input id="Name"
27:                                 type=text
28:                                 size=50
29:                                 runat="server">
30: <br /><br />
31:             Enter Password: <input id="Password"
32:                                 type=password
33:                                 size=50
34:                                 runat="server">
35: <br /><br />     
36:
37:                 <input type=submit value="Enter"
38:                                 size=30
39:                                 OnServerClick="SubmitBtn_Click"
40:                                 runat="server">
41:      
42:
43:                 <input type=reset OnServerClick="ResetBtn_Click"
44:                                 size=30
45:                                 runat="server">
46:             <h1>
47:             <span id="Message" runat="server"> </span>
48:             </h1>
49:         </form>
50:     </body>
51: </html>
```

FIGURE 20.5

The result of using HTML server controls.

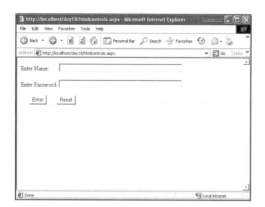

  The structure of this listing is slightly different from the preceding one. Instead of using the ASP.NET `Page` directive at the top of the listing, this one jumps right into HTML. In Line 2, a set of script code is included. This is a standard script tag—or is it? Actually, it includes the `runat=server` directive, so it is actually ASP code that will run on the server. This means that the script functionality will be available when this form executes on the server. If the `runat=server` was not included, this would be a standard script tag that would be sent off to the browser.

The next several lines are C# code used in the script. Because this script is executed on the server, C# is fine to use. The code checks to see whether the password and name are valid. They set a message field based on the results.

The form starts in Line 24. The controls on the form all look standard. The only thing that is unique is that they include `runat="server"` attributes. This changes the controls and the form to HTML server controls. If you know standard HTML, you should be able to follow the rest of this listing.

> **Caution**
>
> If you don't know standard HTML, you should learn it before tackling Web forms and ASP.NET.

20

Run this ASP.NET page. Figure 20.6 shows the output when the correct name and password are entered.

You can use any of the other standard HTML controls in the same manner as the input button. For specific properties that you can manipulate with each control, check the online documentation for each of the controls listed in Table 20.1.

FIGURE 20.6

The HTML server controls program with correct login.

> **Tip**
>
> You should notice that label controls were not used in the form. You are generating HTML. Standard text is treated as part of the HTML file that is sent to the browser. This means that you don't need to use a label control to display information; instead, you can use standard HTML. You should use a label only when you need to change displayed information.

Exploring Web Server Controls

In addition to the HTML server controls, Web server controls can be used with your ASP.NET applications. These controls are very similar to the windows form controls that you learned to use on Days 16, "Creating Windows Forms," and 17, "Creating Windows Applications." The common Web server controls are presented in Figure 20.7.

You generally use the Web server controls to create Web forms. You then can identify the Web server controls in a listing because, in addition to the `runat=server` directive, Web server controls are preceded by `asp:`. You can see this in Listing 20.3, which shows another simple Web form application—this time, using the Web server controls.

> **Caution**
>
> Don't confuse the extensions between Web form applications and Web service applications. Web service programs end in .asmx, whereas Web form applications end in .aspx.

FIGURE 20.7

The Web server controls.

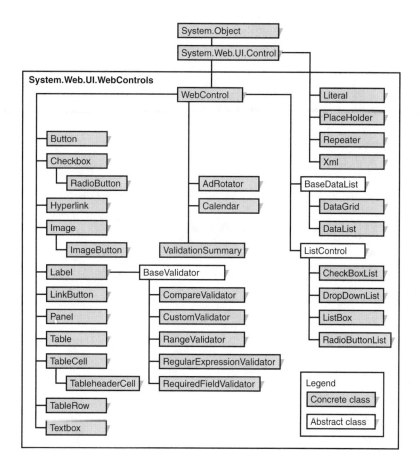

LISTING 20.3 WebForm.aspx—Using Web Server Controls

```
1:  <%@ Page Language="C#" %>
2:
3:  <HTML>
4:  <HEAD>
5:    <SCRIPT RUNAT="SERVER">
6:    protected void Button1_Click(object Source, EventArgs e)
7:    {
8:       DateTime currDate = new DateTime();
9:       currDate = DateTime.Now;
10:      myDateLabel.Text = currDate.ToString();
11:   }
12:   </SCRIPT>
13:  </HEAD>
14:  <BODY>
15:    <H3 align="center">Simple Web Server Controls Example</H3>
```

LISTING 20.3 continued

```
16:
17:        <FORM runat=server>
18:        <center><asp:Label id=myDateLabel runat="server" />
19:        <br><br>
20:            <asp:Button id=Button1 runat="server"
21:                Text="Update"
22:                onclick="Button1_Click" />
23:        </center>
24:        </FORM>
25:   </BODY>
26:   </HTML>
```

OUTPUT

FIGURE 20.8

The results of WebForm.aspx displayed in the browser.

ANALYSIS You'll see that this listing looks very similar to Listing 20.1. The page starts with the Page directive, which indicates the language that will be used. This listing displays the date and time when you click an Update button. This is the same type of application that you created with windows forms, and the code in Lines 8–10 is the same. This code calculates the date value and assigns it to a label control. In Line 18, this label control is a Web server control. You know this because it is preceded by the asp: and ends with a runat=server. Obviously, a timer would make this listing work better; however, that wouldn't allow me to illustrate the use of a Web server button with a label control.

This listing displays the date and time when the Update button is clicked (see Figure 20.9). Is this the time on the server or the time on the browser? The correct answer is that it is the server's time because the code is executed on the server.

FIGURE 20.9

The webform.aspx out-put after the Update button is clicked.

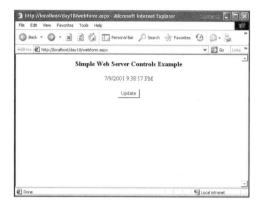

You should again take a look at the HTML sent to the browser. It has been stated a number of times that the Web HTML and server controls execute on the server. Take a look at the source code associated with Listing 20.3's browser output. You can do this by selecting the option to view the source from the browser. You will see something like the following:

```
<HTML>
<HEAD>

</HEAD>
<BODY>
    <H3 align="center">Simple Web Server Controls Example</H3>

    <form name="ctrl0" method="post" action="webform.aspx" id="ctrl0">
<input type="hidden" name="__VIEWSTATE"
value="dDwtMTA2MDQwMDUyMDt0PDtsPGk8Mj47PjtsPHQ8O2w8aTwxPjs+O2w8dDxwPHA8bDxU
➥ZXh00z47bDw3LzkvMjAwMSA5OjQwOjAxIFBNOz4+Oz47Oz47Pj47Pg==" />

    <center><span id="myDateLabel">7/9/2001 9:40:01 PM</span>
    <br><br>
        <input type="submit" name="Button1" value="Update" id="Button1" />
    </center>
    </form>
</BODY>
</HTML>
```

This code is definitely different than the codes included in the original listing.

Summary

Today's lesson continued yesterday's. In today's lesson, you received a very quick overview on Web-based forms applications. You learned that C# can be used with

ASP.NET to create Web-centric dynamic applications. Obviously, this was just enough information to whet your appetite. A number of books are available specifically for programming ASP.NET and Web forms.

Q&A

Q Today's lesson covered a lot of material but barely went into any depth. Why didn't you provide more coverage and more depth?

A As mentioned at the beginning of today's lesson, Web forms could fill a book on their own. Additionally, Web applications are a way of using C# rather than a part of the C# languages. As such, many C# books don't even cover the topic. I believe the Web-based topics are important and of interest to most people, and I think it's worth giving you a taste of the Web technologies associated with Web development.

Q I'm confused. You stated there are server controls and HTML controls, but the HTML controls are not the same as standard HTML controls used in a browser. Which controls are HTML controls?

A Microsoft has created a set of controls called HTML controls that run on the Web server. These controls match up to the original HTML controls that run on a browser. In fact, the HTML server controls generally generate HTML browser controls. The important thing to know is that the HTML controls that run on the server can adapt to what any calling browser can handle.

Workshop

The Workshop provides quiz questions to help you solidify your understanding of the material covered and exercises to provide you with experience in using what you've learned. Try to understand the quiz and exercise answers before continuing to the next day's lesson. Answers are provided on the CD.

Quiz

1. What extension does an ASP.NET application using C# have?
2. What are two ways to close an XHTML tag named SPAN?
3. How can you tell a Web service from an ASP.NET page?
4. How do you execute an ASP.NET page?
5. What two types of controls are used for Web forms?

6. Does Listing 20.1 use HTML controls, HTML server controls, or Web server controls?

7. What is the difference between a standard HTML control and an HTML server control?

8. What is the server equivalent of the standard HTML table tag?

9. How can you tell a server-side HTML control from a standard HTML control?

Exercises

1. Modify Listing 20.1. Add an ASP text box control. When the button is clicked, copy the text that the user entered into the text box to the label.

2. Modify Listing 20.2 to call a method when a successful name and password are entered. This method should display the entered name to the HTML form.

3. **On Your Own:** Create a Web page that uses HTML server controls. Rewrite the application to use ASP server controls.

4. **On Your Own:** Review the online documentation that might have come with your compiler. Look up HTML server controls and Web server controls. Review the different properties, methods, and events that are associated with these controls.

20

DAY 21

A Day for Reflection and Attributes

At this point, you have worked through 14 days of learning fundamentals of the C# programming language and another 6 days of using the C# language with the .NET Framework. You have learned about data types, classes, object-oriented programming, and much more. You have learned all the basics of C# programming. You have the ability to create C# programs, including programs that use the Base Class Library (BCL) classes and more. These can be Windows-based, Web-based, or those within the console. In today's lesson, you touch on a couple of advanced-level topics within C# that you might come across. Today you...

- Discover the concept of reflection.
- Use reflection to determine the contents of a program.
- Learn how to use predefined attributes.
- Explore the creation of custom attributes.
- See how to associate custom attributes with your code.

- Write the code to evaluate attributes at runtime.
- Take a quick look at future enhancements coming to C#.

Reflecting on Reflection

Sometimes it is good to sit back and reflect on life. More specifically, you can sit back and reflect on yourself. Often you will discover information that you didn't realize about yourself.

Just as *you* can reflect, it is possible to have a C# program reflect upon *itself*. You can use such reflection to learn about an application. For example, you can have a class reflect upon itself and tell you the methods or properties it contains. You'll find that being able to reflect on a program, a class, a type, or another item will enable you to take more advantage of it.

The key to getting information on a type (remember, a class is a type) is to use a reflection method. For example, the GetMembers method can be used to get a type's members. You get the list of members by passing GetMembers a Type type. Yes, Type *is a type that holds types*. Read that sentence slowly, and it should make sense.

The first step for reflection is to get the type of a type. You get the type of a class (or other type) using the static method Type.GetType. The return value of this method is a type that can be assigned to a Type object. The GetType method uses virtually any data type as a parameter. For example, to get the type of a class named TestClass and assign it to a Type object named MyTestObject, you do the following:

```
Type MyTypeObject = Type.GetType(TestClass);
```

MyTypeObject then contains the type for TestClass. You can use MyTypeObject to get the members of a TestClass. As stated, this is done using the GetMembers method. The GetMembers method returns an array of MemberItems. To call the GetMember method on the MyTypeObject (which contains the type of a TestClass in this example), you do the following:

```
MemberInfo[] MyMemberArray = MyTypeObject.GetMembers();
```

An array of MemberInfo objects named MyMemberArray is created, which is assigned the return value of the call to GetMembers for the type stored in MyTypeObject.

After you've done this assignment, the MyMemberArray contains the members of your type. You can loop through this array and evaluate each member. If you are completely confused, don't worry. Listing 21.1 pulls all this together into a single listing. For fun, this listing reflects on a reflection-related class—the System.Reflection.PropertyInfo class.

The `MemberInfo` type is a part of the `Reflection` namespace. You need to include `System.Reflection` to use the shortened version of the name.

LISTING 21.1   MyMemberInfo.cs—Using Reflection

```
 1: using System;
 2: using System.Reflection;
 3:
 4: class MyMemberInfo
 5: {
 6:    public static int Main()
 7:    {
 8:        //Get the Type and MemberInfo.
 9:        string testclass = "System.Reflection.PropertyInfo";
10:
11:        Console.WriteLine ("\nFollowing is the member info for class: {0}",
12:                                          testclass);
13:
14:        Type MyType = Type.GetType(testclass);
15:
16:        MemberInfo[] MyMemberInfoArray = MyType.GetMembers();
17:
18:        //Get the MemberType method and display the elements
19:
20:        Console.WriteLine("\nThere are {0} members in {1}",
21:                MyMemberInfoArray.GetLength(0),
22:                MyType.FullName);
23:
24:        for ( int counter = 0;
25:                counter < MyMemberInfoArray.GetLength(0);
26:                counter++ )
27:        {
28:          Console.WriteLine( "{0}. {1} Member type - {2}",
29:                    counter,
30:                    MyMemberInfoArray[counter].Name,
31:                    MyMemberInfoArray[counter].MemberType.ToString());
32:        }
33:        return 0;
34:    }
35: }
```

OUTPUT

```
Following is the member info for class: System.Reflection.PropertyInfo

There are 36 members in System.Reflection.PropertyInfo
0. get_CanWrite Member type - Method
1. get_CanRead Member type - Method
2. get_Attributes Member type - Method
3. GetIndexParameters Member type - Method
4. GetSetMethod Member type - Method
```

21

```
 5. GetGetMethod Member type - Method
 6. GetAccessors Member type - Method
 7. SetValue Member type - Method
 8. SetValue Member type - Method
 9. GetValue Member type - Method
10. GetValue Member type - Method
11. get_PropertyType Member type - Method
12. IsDefined Member type - Method
13. GetCustomAttributes Member type - Method
14. GetCustomAttributes Member type - Method
15. get_ReflectedType Member type - Method
16. get_DeclaringType Member type - Method
17. get_Name Member type - Method
18. get_MemberType Member type - Method
19. GetHashCode Member type - Method
20. Equals Member type - Method
21. ToString Member type - Method
22. GetAccessors Member type - Method
23. GetGetMethod Member type - Method
24. GetSetMethod Member type - Method
25. get_IsSpecialName Member type - Method
26. GetType Member type - Method
27. MemberType Member type - Property
28. PropertyType Member type - Property
29. Attributes Member type - Property
30. IsSpecialName Member type - Property
31. CanRead Member type - Property
32. CanWrite Member type - Property
33. Name Member type - Property
34. DeclaringType Member type - Property
35. ReflectedType Member type - Property
```

Before digging into the code, take a look at the output. You can see that there are 36 members in the System.Reflection.PropertyInfo class. In the line numbered 0 of the output, the first member is the get_CanWrite member, which is a method. Other members are get_CanRead, get_Attributes, GetIndexParameters, and so forth. Look at the lines numbered 13 and 14 of the output. They appear to be the same—both contain GetCustomAttributes. Is this an error? No! Each overloaded method is a separate member, as it should be.

ANALYSIS The first thing to note about the code is that the System.Reflection namespace is included in Line 2. This is necessary for the reflection members that will be used in the listing.

In Line 9, a specific class name is assigned to a variable. This makes it easy for you to reflect on different classes—just change the name stored in this string.

A great enhancement to this listing would be to capture a command-line parameter that indicates which class to reflect upon. I'll leave that to you to add. By using a command-line value, you wouldn't need to recompile each time you wanted to change the class being reflected on. This also illustrates a key point—reflection can happen at runtime.

In Line 14, the name of a class is passed to the `Type.GetType` method. The returned type is assigned to the variable `MyType`. The `MyType` object is then used to get the members of the type it contains. These are assigned to a `MemberInfo` array named `MyMemberInfoArray` in Line 16. Lines 24–32 then loop through this array and print the `Name` and the `MemberType` values for each element. As you can see, the `Name` element contains the name of the member. The `MemberType` when displayed as a string tells you the type of the individual member.

Getting basic information is relatively easy. If you want to get more specific information, a little more work is involved. Before getting to that, look at a second listing illustrating the `MemberInfo` objects. Listing 21.2 presents another look at the process of reflection.

LISTING 21.2   Reflect.cs—A Second Look at Reflection

```
 1: // Reflect.cs
 2: //----------------------------
 3: using System;
 4: using System.Reflection;
 5:
 6: namespace Reflect
 7: {
 8:
 9:   class MyMemberInfo
10:   {
11:      int classMyValue;
12:
13:      public void THIS_IS_A_METHOD()
14:      {
15:         //
16:      }
17:
18:      public int MyValue      // property
19:      {
20:         set { classMyValue = value; }
21:      }
22:
23:      public static int Main()
24:      {
25:         //The following is the class being checked
26:         string testclass = "Reflect.MyMemberInfo";
27:
```

21

LISTING 21.2   continued

```
28:          Console.WriteLine ("\nFollowing is the member info for class: {0}",
29:                                           testclass );
30:
31:          Type MyType = Type.GetType(testclass);
32:
33:          MemberInfo[] MyMemberInfoArray = MyType.GetMembers();
34:
35:          //Get the MemberType method and display the elements
36:
37:          Console.WriteLine("\nThere are {0} members in {1}",
38:                  MyMemberInfoArray.GetLength(0),
39:                  MyType.FullName);
40:
41:          for ( int counter = 0;
42:                  counter < MyMemberInfoArray.GetLength(0);
43:                  counter++ )
44:          {
45:            Console.WriteLine( "{0}. {1} Member type - {2}",
46:                    counter,
47:                    MyMemberInfoArray[counter].Name,
48:                    MyMemberInfoArray[counter].MemberType.ToString());
49:          }
50:        return 0;
51:      }
52:    }
53:  }
```

OUTPUT

```
Following is the member info for class: Reflect.MyMemberInfo

There are 9 members in Reflect.MyMemberInfo
0. GetHashCode Member type - Method
1. Equals Member type - Method
2. ToString Member type - Method
3. THIS_IS_A_METHOD Member type - Method
4. set_myValue Member type - Method
5. Main Member type - Method
6. GetType Member type - Method
7. .ctor Member type - Constructor+
8. myValue Member type - Property
```

ANALYSIS   This listing uses the same reflection that you saw in Listing 21.1. The base of the listing is the same, but in this one, the listing reflects on itself. More important, a few different member types were added to this listing to help illustrate what can be reflected on using the MemberInfo type. This includes a property named myValue.

The MemberInfo type enables you to get general information. You can also use a number of other types to restrict the information you retrieve. For example, you could declare a

`FieldInfo` array and discover information on fields within the type. By using a more focused method—such as `FieldInfo`—you gain the capability to obtain more specific information on each item. For example, the `FieldInfo` type enables you to discover information, such as what the access modifiers are on a field, and provides implementation details. It also enables you to get and set values. Table 21.1 contains some classes that you might find useful for reflection.

TABLE 21.1 Types for Discovering Specific Information

Reflection Types	Description
`Assembly`	Works with assemblies.
`ConstructorInfo`	Works with constructors. Determines information such as name, parameters, access modifiers, and implementation details of constructors.
`EventInfo`	Works with events. Determines information such as name, event-handling information, custom attributes, and more.
`FieldInfo`	Works with fields. Determines information such as name, access modifiers, and implementation of fields.
`MethodInfo`	Works with methods. Determines information such as name, return type, parameters, access modifiers, and the implementation details of methods.
`Module`	Works with modules. Determines information such as classes.
`ParameterInfo`	Works with parameters. Determines information such as a parameter's name, data type, type (for example, input or output), and position of the parameter in a method's signature.
`PropertyInfo`	Works with properties. Determines information such as name, data type, declaring type, and more.

Understanding Attributes

As time passes, things change—just as you are changing topics now. Over the years, programming languages such as BASIC and C have also needed to change. These changes are usually to add new functionality that wasn't initially known or considered. If a language can't easily adapt—without breaking existing programs—the language tends to get left behind. Languages such as C and COBOL were not designed for paradigms such as object-oriented programming.

In addition to things changing, it is not unexpected that you want your programs to interact with other programs. Most programming languages are not set up to be capable of interacting with other systems or languages.

21

What Are Attributes?

The designers of C# have included a way for the language to extend itself. This extensibility is gained through the use of attributes.

One of the key reasons for using attributes is to associate additional information with the code in your C# programs. This information can then be obtained later at runtime.

You've actually already used an attribute in this book without realizing it. On Day 19, "Creating Remote Procedures: Web Services," you included the code [WebMethod] before each method that you wanted exposed in your Web services. You actually associated an attribute to your methods. Later, when the program was executed, these attributes could be queried using reflection to know which methods could be used as WebMethods.

A number of attributes are available throughout the .NET Framework and are defined in the BCL. These include classes for documentation, multithreading, Web services, and much more. In addition to being able to use or extend these, you can create your own custom attributes. Some examples of existing attributes in the framework include these:

- CLSCompliant indicates that the target is compliant with the CLS.
- Conditional indicates whether a method can be called. It is based on a defined value in the calling code.
- Obsolete indicates that a type is no longer current.
- WebMethod indicates that a method should be available within a Web service.

Three steps are usually applied when using attributes. The first step is to define the attribute. You must create an attribute to use it, although there are some pre-existing attributes in the .NET Framework. The second is to associate the attribute with code elements. The third step is to query the attributes at runtime. If you don't use the attributes by querying them, there really is no point in having them.

Using Attributes

As you might have guessed from the usage of the WebMethod attribute, attributes are included in your code listings before the element that you are associating them with. You might have also speculated that attributes are indicated by the use of square brackets to enclose them. On Day 18, "Working with Databases: ADO.NET," you associated the WebMethod attribute to the method within your class as follows:

```
[WebMethod]
public static int Add( int x, int y )
{
    return x + y;
}
```

In general, an attribute is associated with the code element that follows it. Some of the code elements that an attribute can be associated with are listed in Table 21.2.

TABLE 21.2   Elements Associated with Attributes

Element	Explicit Specifier
Assembly	assembly
Event method	event
Field	field
Method	method
Program module	module
Parameter	param
Property	property
Return value	return
Class or structure	type

From Table 21.2, you can see that an attribute can be associated with a number of different elements. Consider the following example:

```
[MyAttribute]
class MyClass {}
```

The MyAttribute attribute appears before a class. The attribute would therefore be associated with the MyClass class.

Now consider a second example:

```
[MyAttribute]
public int MyMethod() {}
```

This looks very similar to the WebMethod attribute. What is this attribute associated with? Table 21.2 lists a number of elements. Is MyAttribute associated to the method? MyAttribute could be associated to either the method or the return type.

C# gives you a way to make explicit where you want the attribute associated. This is done using one of the explicit terms in Table 21.2. The ambiguity can be resolved by including the explicit term at the beginning of the attribute, with a colon for separation. To associate the MyAttribute attribute with the return value, you use the following:

```
[return:MyAttribute]
public int MyMethod() {}
```

21

To associate it with the method, you use the following:

```
[method:MyAttribute]
public int MyMethod() {}
```

Tip	Because there is no harm in using an explicit specifier on an attribute, you should use them liberally.

Using Multiple Attributes

You can associate more than one attribute with a single code element. This can be accomplished by listing each attribute separately:

```
[FirstAttr]
[SecondAttr]
class myClass {}
```

Although this example shows the attributes on separate lines, you could include them on the same line. Additionally, you can combine attributes into a single declaration by separating each with a comma:

```
[FirstAttr, SecondAttr]
class myClass {}
```

Using Attributes That Have Parameters

Attributes can have parameters. The purpose of including parameters with an attribute is to provide additional information.

Two types of parameters are used with attributes: positional parameters and named parameters. Positional parameters are also called *unnamed parameters*.

Positional parameters gain their name from the fact that their position is important. Because they must be placed in a set position, their name becomes less important. The order in which *named parameters* are presented is not important. Named parameters get their name from the fact that their name is included with the specification of the parameter. By including the name, you automatically know what the parameter is.

You can define both positional and named parameters in a single attribute. As you should be able to guess, if you are including positional parameters, they must be declared first because their position is important. Consider the following example:

```
[CodeStatus("Tested", Coder="Brad")]
class MyClass {}
```

The `CodeStatus` attribute has two parameters. These parameters are included in a similar manner to what you use with a method call. All the parameters are enclosed in a single set of parentheses, just as a method's parameters are. Additionally, each parameter is separated by a comma.

In looking at the example, you should be able to tell that the first parameter is a positional parameter. It includes just the data being supplied. In this case, the data is `"Tested"`. The second parameter includes a name that is set equal to a data value. This is a named parameter called `Coder` that is associated with the data `"Brad"`.

> **Note**
> To clarify, positional parameters are just data. Named parameters are the name of the field set equal to the data value.

Defining Your Own Attribute

It is important to understand that although attributes appear somewhat differently from the other C# code in your programs, they are not different. Attributes are simply classes put to a special use. Because they are just classes, you can define your own to use.

Attributes are derived from an existing class in the framework, `System.Attribute`. You derive an attribute just as you would any other class:

```
public myAttribute : System.Attribute
{
   ...
}
```

When you derive a new class, you need to define a public constructor. Any parameters within the constructor are considered positional parameters. You then must define any additional data members to be used with the attribute. Named parameters are associated with public data members within the class. Specifically, the named parameters are public properties or fields. Finally, you must include information to define the usage of the class.

Restricting an Attribute

An attribute can be restricted. You can create an attribute that can be associated with only specific types of code or specific targets. For example, you can create an attribute that can be associated with only constructors. You can also create an attribute that can be associated with only methods or properties. This restriction is done with another attribute, `AttributeUsage`.

21

AttributeUsage is associated with the attribute class that you create. The AttributeUsage class takes a parameter that indicates what your attribute can be associated with—it indicates your attribute's usage. Table 21.3 lists the different targets that an attribute can be restricted to.

> **Caution**
>
> Don't be confused by Tables 21.2 and 21.3. The values in Table 21.2 are used when you place your attributes in your program. The values in Table 21.3 are used when you create the attribute. Obviously, there should be some correlation between the two within your programs. If you create an attribute to work only with properties, you shouldn't place it anywhere other than with properties.

TABLE 21.3   AttributeUsage Targets

Flag	Can Be Used...
All	Anywhere
Assembly	With an assembly
Class	With a class
Constructor	With constructors
Delegate	With delegates
Enum	With enumerators
Event	With events
Field	With fields
Interface	With interfaces
Method	With methods
Module	With modules
Parameter	With a method parameter
Property	With properties
ReturnValue	With a method's return value
Struct	With structures

You can actually associate more than one target with an attribute that you create. The restriction is accomplished by using the attribute with a parameter indicating the specific target. The parameter is composed of values from the AttributeTargets enumeration.

These values in this enumeration are the flags listed in Table 21.3. To include more than one attribute restriction from the table, you use the | operator. The following shows how to use the AttributeUsage attribute to restrict a new attribute to structures and classes:

```
[AttributeUsage(AttributeTargets.Class | AttributeTargets.Struct)]
```

Defining the Attribute Class

You define an attribute similarly to defining a regular class. After all, an attribute is really just another class—an attribute class. You've already seen the class header for declaring an attribute. In addition to the header, you need to set up any parameters and the elements within the body.

There are restrictions on the parameters for an attribute class. You can use only simple types, such as bool, byte, char, short, int, long, float, and double. Additionally, you can use string, System.Type, and enum. A parameter can also be defined as a one-dimensional array, as long as the array type is one of the standard types already mentioned. Finally, a parameter can be of type object. If it is declared of type object, when a value is passed to an instantiated object of the attribute class, it must also be of the types already mentioned.

Listing 21.3 presents a code snippet for a custom attribute that can be used to track the status of a code listing, who the coder is, and who the tester is.

 Caution

Listings 21.3–21.5 are not complete, so you will not be able to successfully compile and execute them. Listing 21.6 pulls together these snippets into a complete solution.

LISTING 21.3   CodeStatus.cs—A Custom Attribute Class

```
 1: using System;
 2:
 3: [AttributeUsage(AttributeTargets.All)]
 4: public class CodeStatusAttribute : System.Attribute
 5: {
 6:    private string pSTATUS;
 7:    private string pTESTER;
 8:    private string pCODER;
 9:
10:    public CodeStatusAttribute( string Status )
11:    {
12:       this.pSTATUS = Status;
13:    }
14:
```

21

LISTING 21.3   continued

```
15:        public string Tester
16:        {
17:          set
18:          {
19:             pTESTER = value;
20:          }
21:          get
22:          {
23:             return pTESTER;
24:          }
25:        }
26:
26:        public string Coder
27:        {
28:          set
29:          {
30:             pCODER = value;
31:          }
32:          get
33:          {
34:             return pCODER;
35:          }
36:        }
37:
38:        public override string ToString()
39:        {
40:          return pSTATUS;
41:        }
42:    }
```

> **Note**
>
> C# enables you to use an attribute named *xxx*Attribute by simply typing
> [*xxx*()].

ANALYSIS   Listing 21.3 creates a custom attribute class named CodeStatusAttribute. You can see in Line 3 that this class is restricted to All, which really means that it isn't restricted—it can be used at all the locations specified in Listing 21.3. You can see that AttributeUsage is an attribute that is passed one positional parameter. You know that it is an attribute because it is enclosed in square brackets.

The attribute class actually starts in Line 4. As you can see, the CodeStatusAttribute class inherits from System.Attribute and thus is an attribute class. The rest of the class contains standard code that you should be able to follow. Three private variables are all accessed using properties.

You should note a few things. Parameters that are defined as part of the constructor are positional. The first parameter used in the CodeStatusAttribute attribute is the Status parameter. Two named parameters are also available: the other two public members, Coder and Tester.

Using a Custom Attribute

Now that you've defined an attribute, you'll want to use it. Using the CodeStatusAttribute attribute in a listing is done just as the attributes used earlier were used. You need to include the positional parameter, and you have the option of including the named parameters. Listing 21.4 presents a code fragment with several classes. These classes use the CodeStatusAttribute attribute to indicate the status of the coding efforts.

 Caution

This is not a complete listing, so it won't compile correctly.

LISTING 21.4 attrUsed.cs—CodeStatusAttribute in Use with a Class

```
 1: // attrUsed.cs - using the CodeStatus attribute
 2: //----------------------------------------------
 3:
 4: [CodeStatus("Beta", Coder="Brad")]
 5: public class Circle
 6: {
 7:     public Circle()
 8:     {
 9:         // Set up and build a circle class
10:     }
11: }
12:
13: [CodeStatus("Final", Coder="Fred", Tester="John")]
14: public class Square
15: {
16:     public Square()
17:     {
18:         // Set up and build a square class
19:     }
20: }
21:
22: [CodeStatus("Alpha")]
23: public class Triangle
24: {
25:     public Triangle()
26:     {
27:         // Set up and build a triangle class
```

21

LISTING 21.4   continued

```
28:      }
29:  }
30:
31:  [CodeStatus("Final", Coder="Bill")]
32:  public class Rectangle
33:  {
34:      public Rectangle()
35:      {
36:          // Set up and build a rectangle class
37:      }
38:  }
```

ANALYSIS   This class uses the `CodeStatusAttribute` attribute. You might wonder whether there is an error in Lines 4, 13, 22, and 31. These lines use `CodeStatus` instead of `CodeStatusAttribute`. This is not an error. You can change all of these to `CodeStatusAttribute` and the program will work; however, you don't have to. The .NET Framework enables you to define attributes with the word `Attribute` at the end of the name. When you do use the attribute, you can drop the word `Attribute`. This helps make your listings a little more readable, and it makes your attribute definitions easy to identify.

In Line 4, the `CodeStatus` attribute is called with the positional attribute parameter filled with `"Beta"`, and one named parameter is used, `Coder`. It is assigned the value `"Brad"`. In Line 13, you can see that a `Tester` named parameter is also included. Line 21 contains the minimum parameters—it contains only a positional value.

Accessing the Associated Attribute Information

If you couldn't access the attribute information at runtime, there would be little point of using attributes. You can access the attribute information via reflection. Listing 21.5 presents the code that can be used to see what attributes are associated with a class.

LISTING 21.5   reflAttr.cs—Reflection on the `CodeStatus` Attributes

```
1:  // reflAttr.cs -
2:  //------------------------------------------------------------
3:  class reflAttr
4:  {
5:      public static void Main()
6:      {
7:          PrintAttributes(typeof(Rectangle));
8:      }
9:
```

LISTING 21.5   continued

```
10:      public static void PrintAttributes(Type psdType )
11:      {
12:         Console.WriteLine("\nAttributes for: {0}", psdType.ToString());
13:
14:         Attribute[] attribs = Attribute.GetCustomAttributes(psdType);
15:         foreach (Attribute attr in attribs)
16:         {
17:            CodeStatus item = (CodeStatus) attr;
18:            Console.WriteLine(
19:               "Status is {0}. Coder is {1}. Tester is {2}.",
20:               item.ToString(), item.Coder, item.Tester);
21:         }
22:      }
23:   }
```

ANALYSIS   This code snippet enables you to evaluate what attributes are associated with a class. The bulk of the listing is in the PrintAttributes method in Lines 10–22. This method takes a type and then prints the types associated with that type. The Main method of this code snippet shows how the PrintAttributes method can be called with the Rectangle class. You should remember from Day 6, "Packaging Functionality: Class Methods and Member Functions," that a class is itself a type. This means that a Rectangle object is a Rectangle type. Because you can't pass the name, a method from the .NET Framework is used to convert the class name to a Type. This is the typeof operator.

First, in the PrintAttributes method, the name of the type passed into the method, psdType, is printed. For the Rectangle class, this is Rectangle.

In Line 14, an array of type Attribute is created. This array is named attribs. It is assigned the value of the attributes from the type that was passed into the method. This is done using a method within the Attribute class named GetCustomAttributes, which returns the individual attributes associated with the argument. In the case of psdType, which contains the Rectangle type, there was one attribute (in Line 31 of Listing 21.4). If there were additional attributes, they would be assigned to this array as well.

In Lines 15–21, a foreach statement is used to loop through the attribs array of Attribute values. A variable named attr is defined as a single Attribute in Line 15 as a part of the foreach statement. This is assigned the current value from the attribs array. For each Attribute in the array (attr), the three possible parameter values are printed. This is done by first changing the current attr value to be a CodeStatus value using casting (in Line 17). If Line 15 is confusing, review the inheritance lessons in Days 10, "Reusing Existing Code with Inheritance," and 12, "Tapping into OOP: Interfaces." When you have cast the attr to a CodeStatus, you can then use the methods, properties, and fields as if it were a normal CodeStatus type (which it is).

21

Pulling It All Together

Up to this point, you have seen all the parts of creating an attribute, associating it with your classes, and getting the information at runtime. Listing 21.6 pulls this all together into a listing that can be compiled and executed. You'll see that this listing is composed of the previous three listings and nothing more.

LISTING 21.6   complete.cs—Using a Custom Attribute

```
 1: // complete.cs -
 2: //------------------------------------------------------------
 3: using System;
 4:
 5: [AttributeUsage(AttributeTargets.All)]
 6: public class CodeStatusAttribute : System.Attribute
 7: {
 8:     private string pSTATUS;
 9:     private string pTESTER;
10:     private string pCODER;
11:
12:     public CodeStatusAttribute( string Status )
13:     {
14:         this.pSTATUS = Status;
15:     }
16:
17:     public string Tester
18:     {
19:        set
20:        {
21:            pTESTER = value;
22:        }
23:        get
24:        {
25:            return pTESTER;
26:        }
27:     }
28:
29:     public string Coder
30:     {
31:        set
32:        {
33:            pCODER = value;
34:        }
35:        get
36:        {
37:            return pCODER;
38:        }
39:     }
40:
```

LISTING 21.6 continued

```
41:    public override string ToString()
42:    {
43:        return pSTATUS;
44:    }
45: }
46:
47: // attrUsed.cs - using the CodeStatus attribute
48: //-----------------------------------------------
49:
50: [CodeStatus("Beta", Coder="Brad")]
51: public class Circle
52: {
53:    public Circle()
54:    {
55:        // Set up and build a circle class
56:    }
57: }
58:
59: [CodeStatus("Final", Coder="Fred", Tester="John")]
60: public class Square
61: {
62:    public Square()
63:    {
64:        // Set up and build a square class
65:    }
66: }
67:
68: [CodeStatus("Alpha")]
69: public class Triangle
70: {
71:    public Triangle()
72:    {
73:        // Set up and build a triangle class
74:    }
75: }
76:
77: [CodeStatus("Final", Coder="Bill")]
78: public class Rectangle
79: {
80:    public Rectangle()
81:    {
82:        // Set up and build a rectangle class
83:    }
84: }
85:
86: class reflAttr
87: {
88:    public static void Main()
89:    {
```

21

LISTING 21.6 continued

```
 90:          PrintAttributes(typeof(Circle));
 91:          PrintAttributes(typeof(Triangle));
 92:          PrintAttributes(typeof(Square));
 93:          PrintAttributes(typeof(Rectangle));
 94:      }
 95:
 96:      public static void PrintAttributes( Type psdType )
 97:      {
 98:          Console.WriteLine("\nAttributes for: {0}", psdType.ToString());
 99:
100:          Attribute[] attribs = Attribute.GetCustomAttributes(psdType);
101:          foreach (Attribute attr in attribs)
102:          {
103:              CodeStatusAttribute item = (CodeStatusAttribute) attr;
104:              Console.WriteLine(
105:                  "Status is {0}. Coder is {1}. Tester is {2}.",
106:                  item.ToString(), item.Coder, item.Tester);
107:          }
108:      }
109:  }
```

OUTPUT

```
Attributes for: Circle
Status is Beta. Coder is Brad. Tester is .

Attributes for: Triangle
Status is Alpha. Coder is . Tester is .

Attributes for: Square
Status is Final. Coder is Fred. Tester is John.

Attributes for: Rectangle
Status is Final. Coder is Bill. Tester is .
```

ANALYSIS The first part of the listing defines the custom attribute CodeStatusAttribute. This attribute is then used with its shortened name, CodeStatus, with the classes throughout the middle part of the listing. Finally, the reflAttr class checks the attributes on each of the classes.

Lines 90–91 are additions. In the previous listing, only the Rectangle class was included. In this listing, each of the different class types is used with the PrintAttributes method. The output shows that the appropriate attributes are printed for each.

Note   Although this is all included in a single listing, you could have included the custom attribute with a `using` statement in a separate file or namespace.

Single-Use Versus Multiuse Attributes

One other point regarding attributes deserves some attention. If you try to associate the `CodeStatus` with the same class more than once, you will get an error. For example, consider the following:

```
[CodeStatus("Beta", Coder="Brad")]
[CodeStatus("Testing", Tester="Bill")]
class Rectangle()
...
```

This generates an error. However, what if you changed the attribute to be information on the coder of the class? The attribute could contain the coder's name as a positional parameter. Additional named parameters could include information such as the last date modified or the status. It would make sense that you could then have multiple coders on a single class.

Using multiple attributes of the same type on an item is simple. All you need to do is specify that multiple associates are allowed when you initially declare the attribute. When you declared an attribute earlier, you included the following information as an attribute on your attribute declaration:

```
[AttributeUsage(AttributeTargets)]
```

Here, `AttributeTargets` is a positional parameter that specifies the valid targets for your attribute. You can also include the `AllowMultiple` named parameter. Setting this parameter to `true` enables you to use the same attribute multiple times on the same target. Although the default is `false`, you can state this value by assigning `false` to `AllowMultiple`.

To allow multiple `CodeStatus` attributes to be used, you change a single line in the complete.cs listing. Changing Line 5 to the following is all that is required:

```
5: [AttributeUsage(AttributeTargets.All, AllowMultiple=true)]
```

When you've done this, you can add multiple `CodeStatus` attributes to your listing.

21

Reflecting on the Future of C#

Although the C# programming language has been standardized by ECMA and ISO, it is not locked in stone. A number of features are being considered as enhancements to the language. These are changes—or enhancements—that will make C# an even more powerful language. Most of these changes are advanced features to the language. Four big changes that may happen are listed here:

- Generics
- Iterators
- Partial types
- Anonymous methods

At the time this book was written, these features were not a part of the current standard for C#, nor had they been incorporated into any public products. However, these are being considered for a future standard.

 Note

> The coverage provided here is not intended to be complete coverage. Rather, it is provided to help make you aware of future changes to C#.

Generics

Generics are used to help make the code in your software components much more reusable. Generics are a type of data structure that contains code that remains the same; however, the data type of the parameters can change with each use. Additionally, the usage within the data structure adapts to the different data type of the passed variables. In summary, a generic is a code template that can be applied to use the same code repeatedly. Each time the generic is used, it can be customized for different data types without needing to rewrite any of the internal code.

The functionality that is provided by generics can be obtained in C# today. This functionality is done by using type casts and polymorphism, similar to what you learned about on Day 12. With generics, however, you can avoid the messy and intensive conversions from reference types to native types. Additionally, you can create routines that are much more type-safe.

A generic is defined using a slightly different notation. The following is the basic code for a generic named Compare that can compare two items of the same type and return the larger or smaller value, depending on which method is called:

```
public class Compare<ItemType, ItemType>
{
    public ItemType Larger(ItemType data, ItemType data2)
    {
            // logic...
    }

    public ItemType Smaller(ItemType data, ItemType data2)
    {
            // logic...
    }
}
```

> **Note**   This is incomplete code; however, the important part is shown.

This generic could be used with any data type, ranging from basic data types such as integers to complex classes and structures. When you use the generic, you identify what data type you are using with it. For example, to use an integer with the previous Compare generic, you would enter code similar to the following:

```
Compare<int, int> compare = new Compare<int, int>;
int MyInt = compare.Larger(3, 5);
```

You could use the type with other types as well. One thing to be aware of is that a declared generic such as the Compare in the previous example is strongly typed. This means if you pass a different data type than an integer to compare.Larger, the compiler will display an error. If you wanted to use a different data type, you would need to declare another instance of the generic:

```
Compare<float, float> f_compare = new Compare<float, float>;
float MyFloat = f_compare.Larger(1.23f, 4.32f);
```

Because you can use this with different types, you don't need to change the original generic code.

The example here is a simplification of what can be done with generics. You will find that to truly create a generic type that can be used with any data type as a parameter, you will need to ensure that a number of requirements are met. One way to do this—the appropriate way—is with a constraint. A constraint is a class or interface that must be included as a part of the type used for the parameter. For example, in the previous Compare class, to make sure that any data type will work as a parameter when declaring the delegate, you can force the data types to have implemented the IComparable interface from the .NET Framework.

21

You can add a constraint by including it after the generic class declaration. You indicate a constraint using the new keyword where:

```
public class Compare<ItemType, ItemType> where ItemType : IComparable
{
   public ItemType Larger(ItemType data, ItemType data2)
   {
      // logic...
   }

   public ItemType Smaller(ItemType data, ItemType data2)
   {
      // logic...
   }
}
```

What Are Iterators?

An iterator is a construct that helps a foreach statement loop through a class. Although this can be done with C# today, it requires a number of complex pieces of code to be included. With the new standard, the inclusion of an additional keyword, yield, is being added to simplify the capability to add iterators to your data types.

What Are Partial Types?

Partial types are being added to allow a single class to be defined in more than one file. Although it is recommended that a class be stored in a single source file, sometimes that is just not practical. You also can rewrite the class to inherit some of the code from a subclass, but this also is not always practical.

Partial types resolve this by allowing multiple files to be used to declare a single class. When compiled, the classes can be combined so that a single class is created.

Note

> If you use a tool to generate some of your code, you can use partial types to combine the generated code with your own additions to the class. You can keep both pieces in separate files. You won't have to worry about inadvertently changing some of the generated code.

Partial types are implemented using yet another new keyword, partial. The partial keyword is added to the class declaration in each file that will be combined. For example, the following declares a class named MyClass within parts in two different source files named FileOne.cs and FileTwo.cs:

LISTING 21.7 FileOne.cs— Not a Complete Listing

```
public class partial MyClass
{
   // Class stuff...
   public void FunctionInMyClass()
   {
      // Logic...
   }
   // more stuff...
}
```

LISTING 21.8 FileTwo.cs—Not a Complete Listing

```
public class partial MyClass
{
   // Class stuff...
   public void AntherFunctionInMyClass()
   {
      // Logic...
   }
   // more stuff...
}
```

When these listings are compiled together, the logic is combined into a single class.

What Are Anonymous Methods?

Anonymous methods allow snippets of code to be created that can be called dynamically at a later time. These methods are similar to delegates that you learned about on Day 13, "Making Your Programs React with Delegates, Events, and Indexers." They differ from delegates in that the code for the method is included as a part of the delegate declaration instead of as a separate method. This provides the benefit of not having to declare a separate method for the delegate.

Anonymous methods can access other variables within the same class they are located, yet outside their own declaration. Additionally, anonymous methods can receive parameters.

Summary

In this last day, you covered two advanced topics within C# programming. Both enable you to get technical programming information at runtime. First you discovered reflection.

21

You learned that through reflection, you can learn what methods, properties, events, and other members are available within a program.

After discovering reflection, you learned about attributes. Attributes enable the C# language to be extended in a structured manner. Additionally, attributes enable you to associate additional information to portions of your programs. You learned how to create custom attributes. You learned how to associate them with your own classes. Finally, you learned how to query the information about attributes on a program at runtime.

The day's lesson ended with just a brief overview of some of the features being considered in the future of C#. This included a brief mention of generics, iterators, partial types, and anonymous methods. This also mentioned the addition of three new keywords: `partial`, `yield`, and `where`.

Congratulations!

Congratulations, you've made it through 21 days of C#. You've learned a lot in just 21 lessons. There is more to learn—like today's topics, most of what you could continue to learn is an extension of what you already know. Attributes are just another application of classes within your listings. Reflection uses classes and information in the Base Class Library. If you understood most of what was in this book, you are ready to tackle almost any basic C# project. The best way to become an expert or guru is to apply what you've learned. Write programs. The more programs you write, the quicker you will most likely go from simply knowing C# to being a full-fledged expert.

Q&A

Q If an attribute is supposed to appear before the element it is associated with, where do you put an attribute associated to an assembly?

A Attributes for assemblies and modules are placed in your code listings after your `using` clauses for namespaces and before your code. This is the only location they can go for an assembly.

Q Can reflection be used with attributes?

A Reflection is used to determine attribute values.

Q Can I use generics, iterators, partial types, and anonymous methods today?

A The versions of C# available at the time this book was written did not support these new features, nor were they a part of the initial C# standards. However, Microsoft has publicly stated that these features will be submitted for standardization. You should check your C# compiler's documentation to see whether these features are supported yet. Microsoft is planning to support the features in the version of Visual Studio .NET after Visual Studio .NET 2003.

Workshop

The Workshop provides quiz questions to help you solidify your understanding of the material covered and exercises to provide you with experience in using what you've learned. Answers are provided on the CD.

Quiz

1. What can be used to get the type of an object, class, or other item?

2. What type can be used to hold a type value? What namespace is this type in?

3. What concept provides information about a class at runtime?

4. What type would you use to get detailed information on a method's parameter(s)?

5. What has been included in C# to help the language be expanded in the future or to help the language handle concepts not currently discovered?

6. Was the `WebMethod` tag that you used in creating Web services on Day 16 an example of reflection or an example of attributes?

7. Name three predefined attributes.

8. What five things within a program can an attribute be associated with?

9. What two types of parameters are used with attributes? What is the difference between the two?

10. How can you limit what items an attribute can be assigned to?

11. **Bonus:** What data types can an attribute parameter be?

Exercises

1. Modify the MyMemberInfo.cs listing (Listing 21.1) to reflect on the `Object` class (`System.Object`).

2. What methods are available in the `Object` class? Which methods in the `Object` type are also in the types you displayed in today's exercises?

3. Modify Listing 22.2 to use the `FieldInfo` type instead of the `MemberInfo` type. Use this type to evaluate a listing for its field values.

4. Modify the complete.cs listing to allow multiple attributes to be assigned to a single target. Assign two `CodeStatus` attributes to a single class.

21

WEEK 3

Week in Review

Congratulations! You have come to the end of this book. In addition to learning the fundamentals of C#, you learned to use some of the classes and other types within the standard class libraries, including the Base Class Libraries (BCL).

You learned that by using pre-existing classes, you have the capability to create applications that are windows-based, Web-based, or services-based. You learned that you can use a number of existing classes to instantly gain large amounts of functionality.

Apply What You Know

The best way to ensure that you have learned C# is to apply what you have learned. You should create as many C# programs as you can. You will find that the more you use C#, the easier it becomes.

Show What You Know

As you continue to use C#, you will most likely create a number of programs or classes that you are proud of or that you believe will be useful to others. If so, I recommend that you share your code with others. You can send a copy of your listing along with a couple of paragraphs of text detailing what your listing does and what is special about it. Send copies to sites such as www.CodeGuru.com, which will post your listing so that thousands of others can also see and use it. At the same time, you will be able to review the listings that have been submitted by others to these sites. For specific submission guidelines, see the Web site.

Appendices

Answers are located on the CD-ROM.

A

B

C

D

APPENDIX **A**

C# Keywords

Keywords have specific meanings and use, and are reserved in the C# language. The following are C# keywords:

abstract

A modifier that can be used to indicate that a class is to be used only as a base class to another class.

as

An operator used to perform conversions between compatible types. The value to the left of the operator is cast as the type on the right.

base

A keyword that enables values and types in a base class to be accessed.

bool

A logical data type that can be either `true` or `false`. `bool` is equivalent to `System.Boolean` in the .NET Framework.

break

A program flow keyword that enables program control to exit a loop or a conditional block (`switch` or `if`).

byte

A data type that stores an unsigned integer in 1 byte—a value from `0` to `255`. `byte` is equivalent to `System.Byte` in the .NET Framework.

case

A program flow keyword that defines a logical condition within a `switch` statement.

catch

Part of the `try-catch` error-handling logic of a program. The `catch` blocks are used to specify exceptions to be handled and the code to be executed when such exceptions occur.

char

A data type that stores a single Unicode character in 2 bytes. `char` is equivalent to `System.Char` in the .NET Framework.

checked

A program flow keyword that indicates that overflow-checking for integral-type arithmetic operations and conversions should occur.

class

A reference data type that can contain both data and method definitions. A class can contain constructors, constants, fields, methods, properties, indexers, operators, and nested types.

A

const

A modifier that is applied to a data member or variable. When used, the value of the data type is constant and, therefore, cannot be changed.

continue

A program flow keyword that enables program control to automatically go to the next iteration of a loop.

decimal

A data type that stores a floating-point number in 16 bytes. The precision of a `decimal` variable is better than that of the other floating-point types. This generally makes it better for storing financial values. The suffixes `m` and `M` designate a decimal literal. `decimal` is equivalent to `System.Decimal` in the .NET Framework.

default

A label within a `switch` statement to which program flow goes when there is no matching `case` statement.

delegate

A reference type that can receive a method based on a specified method signature. This signature of methods is based on the declaration of the delegate (similar to function pointers in languages such as C and C++).

do

A looping program flow construct that causes execution of a statement or block of statements until a condition at the end of the block evaluates to `false`. Often called a `do...while` statement because the condition at the end of the block is contained with the `while` keyword.

double

A data type that stores a floating-point number in 8 bytes. The suffixes `d` and `D` designate a `double` literal. `double` is equivalent to `System.Double` in the .NET Framework.

else

A conditional program flow statement that contains a statement or block of statements that is executed when a preceding `if` statement evaluates to `false`.

enum

A value data type that can store a number of predetermined constant values.

event

A keyword used to specify an event. The `event` keyword enables a delegate to be specified that can be called when an "event" occurs in a program.

explicit

A keyword used to declare an explicit conversion operator for a user-defined type.

extern

A modifier that indicates that a method is external and, thus, outside the current C# code.

false

A Boolean literal value. Can also be used as an operator that can be overloaded.

finally

Part of a `try-catch` statement. The `finally` block executes after the `try` block's scope ends. It is generally used to clean up any resources allocated in the `try` block.

fixed

A keyword used within unmanaged code to lock a reference type in memory so that the garbage collector won't move it.

float

A data type that stores a floating-point number in 4 bytes. The suffixes f and F designate a `float` literal. `float` is equivalent to `System.Single` in the .NET Framework.

for

A program flow statement used for looping. This statement contains an initializer, a conditional, and an iterator. The statements within the `for` construct's block execute until the conditional evaluates to `false`. The initializer is executed at the start of the `for`. The iterator is executed after each execution of the `for` statement's statement block.

foreach

An iterative program flow construct that enables you to loop through a collection or array.

get

A special word used for creating an accessor that gets the value from a property. This is not a reserved word.

goto

A program flow construct that jumps program flow from the current location to a labeled location elsewhere in the program.

if

A program flow construct that executes a block of code when a condition evaluates to `true`.

implicit

A keyword used to declare a user-defined type conversion operator that does not have to be specified (it is called implicitly).

in

A keyword used with the `foreach` keyword. The `in` keyword identifies the collection or array that the `foreach` will loop through.

int

A data type that stores a signed integer in 4 bytes. The range of possible values is from –2,147,483,648 to 2,147,483,647. `int` is equivalent to `System.Int32` in the .NET Framework. Literal numbers with no suffix are of type `int` by default if the value fits within the given range for an `int`.

interface

A keyword used to declare a reference type that defines a set of members but does not declare them.

internal

An access modifier that enables a data type to be accessible only from within files in the same assembly.

is

An operator used to determine at runtime whether an object is a specified type.

lock

A keyword used to make a block of code critical. This section of code does not enable more than one thread to access it at a time.

long

A data type that stores a signed integer in 8 bytes. The range of possible values is from –9,223,372,036,854,775,808 to 9,223,372,036,854,775,807. `long` is equivalent to `System.Int64` in the .NET Framework. The suffixes `l` and `L` designate a `long` literal.

A

namespace

A keyword that enables you to organize a number of types into a group. Used to help prevent name collisions and to make it easier to reference types.

new

An operator used to create an object. Also used as a modifier to hide a member inherited from a base class.

null

A literal used to represent reference value points to nothing.

object

A type based on the `System.Object` class in the .NET Framework. All other types are derived from `object`.

operator

A keyword used to create or overload an operator's functionality in a class or structure.

out

A parameter modifier that enables the parameter reference variable to be used to return a value from a method. The variable must be assigned a value in the method.

override

A keyword used to provide a new implementation of a method or property, which replaces a base class's existing method or property with the same signature.

params

A parameter modifier that indicates that a variable number of values can be contained in the parameter. This modifier can be used only with the final parameter in a method's parameter list.

partial

A potential future keyword used to indicate that the associated class is only partially defined in the current listing. This allows a single class to be broken across multiple source listings.

private

An access modifier that indicates that a method, property, or other member of a structure or class is accessible only within the same class or structure.

protected

An access modifier that indicates that a method, property, or other member of a class is accessible only within the same class or within classes that are derived from this class.

public

An access modifier that indicates that a method, property, or other member of a class or structure is accessible.

readonly

A data member modifier that indicates that after the initial assignment—either at the time of declaration or within the constructor—the value within the data member cannot be changed.

ref

A parameter modifier that indicates that changes to the parameter variable will also be reflected in the variable that was passed as the ref argument.

return

A keyword used to return a value from a method. Process flow is changed back to the calling method upon execution of this keyword.

A

sbyte

A data type that stores a signed integer in 1 byte. This is a value from –128 to 127. `sbyte` is equivalent to `System.SByte` in the .NET Framework.

sealed

A modifier for classes that prevents you from deriving from the class.

set

A special word used for creating an accessor that sets the value in a property. This is not a reserved word.

short

A data type that stores a signed integer in 2 bytes. The range of possible values is from –32,768 to 32,767. `short` is equivalent to `System.Int16` in the .NET Framework.

sizeof

An operator used to determine the size of a value type in bytes.

stackalloc

A keyword used to allocate a block of memory on the stack. This block's size is determined by the data type and expression included with the keyword. This allocated memory is assigned to a pointer and is not subject to garbage collection.

static

A modifier used to indicate that only a single value will be stored for the type. Used with fields, methods, properties, operators, and constructors.

string

A data type that stores Unicode characters. `string` is an alias for `System.String` in the .NET Framework.

struct

A value data type that can contain both data and method definitions. A structure can contain constructors, constants, fields, methods, properties, indexers, operators, and nested types.

switch

A program flow construct that changes program flow based on a value of a variable. Flow can go to either a `case` statement or a `default` statement.

this

A keyword used within a non-`static` method that associates a variable with the current instance of a class or structure.

throw

A program flow statement that is used to throw an exception, which indicates that something abnormal has occurred. Used with `try` and `catch`.

true

A Boolean literal value. Can also be used as an operator, which can be overloaded.

try

The keyword used for exception handling. The `try` block contains the code that could potentially throw an exception. Used with `catch` and `finally`.

typeof

An operator that returns the data type of an object. The type is returned as a .NET data type (a `System.Type` object).

A

uint

A data type that stores an unsigned integer in 4 bytes. The range of possible values is from 0 to 4,294,967,295. uint is equivalent to System.UInt32 in the .NET Framework. A suffix of u or U designates a uint literal.

ulong

A data type that stores an unsigned integer in 8 bytes. The range of possible values is from 0 to 18,446,744,073,709,551,615. ulong is equivalent to System.UInt64 in the .NET Framework. The suffix of ul (regardless of the case of the U and L) designates a ulong literal.

unchecked

An operator or statement that can be used to indicate that overflow checking on integer data types should be ignored.

unsafe

A keyword used to identify code that is considered unsafe to execute in the managed environment. For example, unsafe should be used to wrap any code that uses pointers.

ushort

A data type that stores an unsigned integer in 2 bytes. The range of possible values is from 0 to 65,535. ushort is equivalent to System.UInt16 in the .NET Framework.

using

A keyword for creating an alias for a namespace. It can also be used to shortcut the need to use fully qualified names for types within a namespace.

value

The name of the variable being set by a set property accessor. This is not a reserved word.

virtual

A modifier used on a method or property to indicate that the method or property can be overridden.

void

A keyword used in place of a type to indicate that no data type is used. In method declarations, void can be used to declare that no value is returned from the method.

where

A potential future keyword used to declare constraints on generics.

while

A looping program flow construct that causes execution of a statement or block of statements as long as a condition evaluates to true.

yield

A potential future keyword that is used within iterators to indicate a value that should be returned to a foreach statement. The yield keyword also indicates where the foreach statement should continue on its next iteration.

APPENDIX B

Command-Line Compiler Flags for Microsoft Visual C# .NET

You can set options with the Microsoft Visual C# .NET command-line compiler. You can see the options by running the command-line compiler with the `/help` flag.

Output

`/out:<file>`

This flag indicates the name for the final output file. If this flag is not specified, the `out` name is based on the name of the first source file.

`/target:<type>` or `/t:<type>`

This flag states the type of program that will be created. Possible values for `<type>` are shown here:

Type	Description
exe	For a console executable (default)
winexe	To build a Windows executable
library	To build a library
module	To build a module that can be added to an assembly

/define:<symbol list> or /d: <symbol list>

This flag is used to define symbols that can be used with the preprocessing directives. It is similar to using a #define <symbol> directive at the beginning of a source file.

/doc:<file>

This flag specifies that XML documentation should be created. The XML documentation file will be named <file>.

Input

/recurse:<wildcard>

This flag indicates that all files in the current directory and subdirectories should be included according to the wildcard specifications.

/reference:<file list> or /r:<file list>

This flag indicates that metadata should be referenced from the specified assembly files.

/addmodule:<file list>

This flag links the specified modules into the current assembly.

Resource

/win32res:<file>

This flag specifies a Win32 resource file (.res).

/win32icon:<file>

This flag indicates the icon that should be used for the output.

/resource:*<resinfo>* or /res:*<resinfo>*

This flag embeds the specified resource.

/linkresource:*<resinfo>* or /linkres:*<resinfo>*

This flag links the specified resource to this assembly.

Code Generation

/debug[+|-]

This flag indicates whether debugging information should be included (+) or omitted (-).

/debug:{full|pdbonly}

This flag specifies the type of debugging, where full enables attaching a debugger to a running program. full is the default.

/optimize[+|-] or /o[+|-]

This flag specifies whether optimizations should (+) or should not (-) occur.

/incremental[+|-] or /incr[+|-]

This flag indicates whether incremental compilation is enabled (+) or is not enabled (-).

Errors and Warnings

/warnaserror[+|-]

This flag causes warnings to be treated as errors. This means that a final file won't be created if there are any warnings. + turns on, and - leaves off (default).

/warn:*<n>* or /w*<n>*

This flag sets the warning level from 0 to 4. Warnings each contain a severity level. Only warnings at or above the set level are displayed.

/nowarn:*<warning list>*

This flag disables specified warning messages.

Programming Language

/checked[+|-]

This flag generates overflow checks, if set to +, or ignores them, if set to -.

/unsafe[+|-]

This flag allows "unsafe" code, if turned on (+), and doesn't allow this code, if turned off (-).

Miscellaneous

@<*file*>

This flag reads a response file (<*file*>) for more options.

/help or /?

This flag displays help information similar to what is presented in this appendix.

/nologo

This flag suppresses the compiler's copyright message.

/noconfig

This flag prevents the CSC.RSP file from being automatically included.

Advanced

/baseaddress:<*address*>

This flag indicates the base address (<*address*>) for the library to be built.

/bugreport:<*file*>

This flag creates a Bug Report file called <*file*>.

/codepage:<*n*>

This flag specifies the code page to use when opening source files.

/utf8output

This flag causes compiler messages to be output in UTF-8 encoding.

/main:*<type>* or /m:*<type>*

This flag specifies the type (class) that contains the entry point (generally a Main method). All other possible entry points are ignored.

/fullpaths

This flag indicates that the compiler should generate fully qualified paths.

/filealign:*<n>*

This flag specifies the alignment used for output file sections.

/nostdlib[+|-]

This flag indicates that the standard library (mscorlib.dll) should not be referenced or used.

/lib:*<file list>*

This flag specifies additional directories to search for references.

B

APPENDIX C

Understanding Number Systems

As a computer programmer, you might sometimes be required to work with numbers expressed in binary and hexadecimal notation. This appendix explains what these systems are and how they work. To help you understand, let's first review the common decimal number system.

The Decimal Number System

The decimal system is the base-10 system that you use every day. A number in this system—for example, 342—is expressed as powers of 10. The first digit (counting from the right) gives 10 to the 0 power, the second digit gives 10 to the 1 power, and so on. Any number to the 0 power equals 1, and any number to the 1 power equals itself. Thus, continuing with the example of 342, you have:

3        $3 \times 10^2 = 3 \times 100 = 300$

4        $4 \times 10^1 = 4 \times 10 = 40$

2        $2 \times 10^0 = 2 \times 1 = 2$

         Sum = 342

The base-10 system requires 10 different digits, 0 through 9. The following rules apply to base 10 and to any other base number system:

- A number is represented as powers of the system's base.
- The system of base n requires n different digits.

Now let's look at the other number systems.

The Binary System

The binary number system is base 2 and therefore requires only two digits, 0 and 1. The binary system is useful for computer programmers, because it can be used to represent the digital on/off method in which computer chips and memory work. Here's an example of a binary number and its representation in the decimal notation you're more familiar with, writing 1011 vertically:

1        $1 \times 2^3 = 1 \times 8 = 8$

0        $0 \times 2^2 = 0 \times 4 = 0$

1        $1 \times 2^1 = 1 \times 2 = 2$

1        $1 \times 2^0 = 1 \times 1 = 1$

         Sum = 11 (decimal)

Binary has one shortcoming: It's cumbersome for representing large numbers.

The Hexadecimal System

The hexadecimal system is base 16. Therefore, it requires 16 digits. The digits 0 through 9 are used, along with the letters A through F, which represent the decimal values 10 through 15. Here is an example of a hexadecimal number, 2DA, and its decimal equivalent:

2        $2 \times 16^2 = 2 \times 256 = 512$

D $13 \times 16^1 = 13 \times 16 = 208$

A $10 \times 16^0 = 10 \times 1 = 10$

         Sum = 730 (decimal)

The hexadecimal system (often called the hex system) is useful in computer work because it's based on powers of 2. Each digit in the hex system is equivalent to a four-digit binary number, and each two-digit hex number is equivalent to an eight-digit binary number. Table C.1 shows some hex/decimal/binary equivalents.

TABLE C.1 Hexadecimal numbers and their decimal and binary equivalents.

Hexadecimal Digit	Decimal Equivalent	Binary Equivalent
0	0	0000
1	1	0001
2	2	0010
3	3	0011
4	4	0100
5	5	0101
6	6	0110
7	7	0111
8	8	1000
9	9	1001
A	10	1010
B	11	1011
C	12	1100
D	13	1101
E	14	1110
F	15	1111
10	16	00010000
F0	240	11110000
FF	255	11111111

C

APPENDIX **D**

Using SharpDevelop

If you have Microsoft's .NET Framework installed, you can also install and use SharpDevelop. SharpDevelop is an Integrated Development Environment (IDE) for C#. This IDE can be used along with Microsoft's .NET Framework and Common Language Runtime to create complete C# solutions. Unlike Visual Studio .NET, SharpDevelop has been written entirely using .NET. In fact, you can get the C# source code. Also different from Visual Studio .NET, SharpDevelop is free!

You can find a copy of SharpDevelop on the CD included with this book. Additionally, you can go to www.icsharpcode.net to find the latest version.

> **Note**   It is assumed that you are installing SharpDevelop on a machine running Microsoft Windows. At the time this book was written, SharpDevelop was being ported to use the Mono .NET runtime, to allow SharpDevelop to run on other platforms such as Red Hat Linux.

Installing SharpDevelop

Follow the instructions provided on the CD to install SharpDevelop. Alternatively, you can go to the www.icsharpcode.net site and download the latest version to install.

Running SharpDevelop

After it is installed, SharpDevelop is added to your Windows Start menu. When you start SharpDevelop, you are greeted with a splash screen and then placed in the IDE. Figure D.1 shows the startup screen.

FIGURE D.1

The startup screen of SharpDevelop.

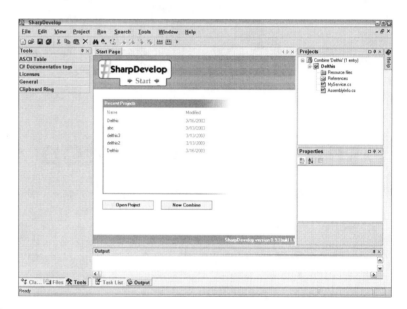

After you've started SharpDevelop, you can begin creating projects. With SharpDevelop, a project is the C# code files and other files that make up a solution. You can also combine multiple projects into what is called a combine.

To create a C# program, you start by selecting File, New, Combine or pressing Ctrl+Shift+N. This opens the dialog box for creating a new project, which will hold your C# program. You must select this to create a project. Figure D.2 presents the New Project dialog box that you are shown.

FIGURE D.2

The New Project dialog box.

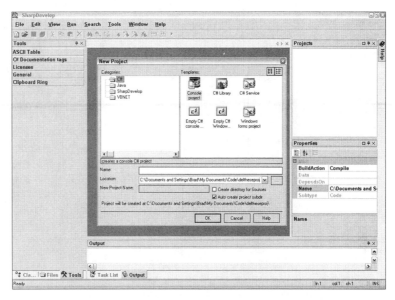

Within this dialog box, you can create the type of project that you want to create. As you can see in the dialog box, you can also do Java and Visual Basic .NET using the SharpDevelop IDE. By clicking one of these categories, you can see the type of projects that you can create.

Within the C# category, you can select from a number of templates. These include a console project, a C# service, a C# library, a C# empty console application, an empty Windows application, and a forms application. Each of these different project types provides default settings.

Creating Applications from This Book

To create the applications within this book, you can shortcut SharpDevelop. Instead of creating a combine or a project, you can simply select File, New, File from the menus. You are presented with the New File dialog box, shown in Figure D.3.

Select the C# category. Then select the Empty C# file template. This adds a C# file to the editor, as shown in Figure D.4.

FIGURE D.3

The New File dialog box.

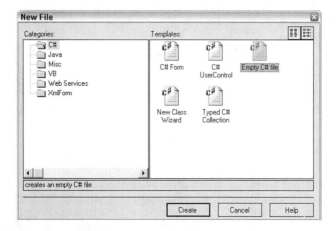

FIGURE D.4

A new C# source file.

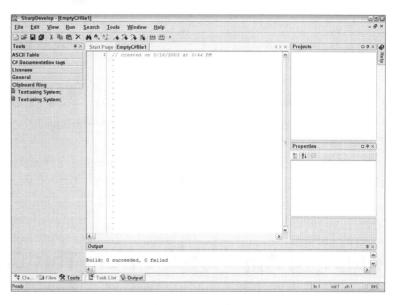

At this point, you can enter the C# code into the form. After doing so, save the form by pressing Ctrl+S or by selecting Save from the File menu. After saving the form, you can compile the project by pressing F8 or by selecting Run, Build Combine. This compiles the listing. If errors exist, they are shown at the bottom of the window in the Output section. If the listing is successful, this also is displayed. Figure E.5 shows the successful entering and compiling of a "Hello World" style of application.

Figure D.5

A Hello application entered, saved, and compiled.

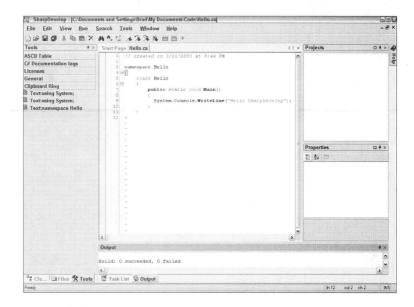

After compiling, you can execute the program by pressing F5 or by selecting Run, Run from the menu. The output is displayed in a console window, as shown in Figure D.6.

Figure D.6

A Hello application's output.

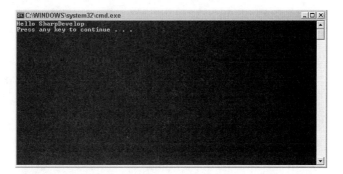

You can see that the window automatically stays open until you press a key. The Press Any Key to Continue text is not a part of your application; it is provided by SharpDevelop.

D

INDEX

Symbols

G

H

I

Your Guide to Computer Technology

informIT

www.informit.com

What's on the CD-ROM

The companion CD-ROM contains all of the source code for the examples developed in the book, SharpDevelop, the Mono compiler and runtime, Microsoft .NET Framework 1.1, and the .NET runtime redistributable.

Windows Installation Instructions

1. Insert the disc into your CD-ROM drive.
2. From the Windows desktop, double-click the My Computer icon.
3. Double-click the icon representing your CD-ROM drive.
4. Double-click on `start.exe`. Follow the on-screen prompts to access the CD-ROM information.

Note
> If you have the AutoPlay feature enabled, `start.exe` will be launched automatically whenever you insert the disc into your CD-ROM drive.

License Agreement

By opening this package, you are also agreeing to be bound by the following agreement:

You may not copy or redistribute the entire CD-ROM as a whole. Copying and redistribution of individual software programs on the CD-ROM is governed by terms set by individual copyright holders.

The installer and code from the author(s) are copyrighted by the publisher and the author(s). Individual programs and other items on the CD-ROM are copyrighted or are under an Open Source license by their various authors or other copyright holders.

This software is sold as-is without warranty of any kind, either expressed or implied, including but not limited to the implied warranties of merchantability and fitness for a particular purpose. Neither the publisher nor its dealers or distributors assumes any liability for any alleged or actual damages arising from the use of this program. (Some states do not allow for the exclusion of implied warranties, so the exclusion may not apply to you.)

Microsoft .NET Framework 1.1 and .NET Framework 1.1 Redistributable

This program was reproduced by Sams Publishing under a special arrangement with Microsoft Corporation. For this reason, Sams Publishing is responsible for the product warranty and support. If your disc is defective, please return it to Sams Publishing, which will arrange for its replacement. PLEASE DO NOT RETURN IT TO MICROSOFT CORPORATION. Any product support will be provided, if at all, by Sams Publishing. PLEASE DO NOT CONTACT MICROSOFT CORPORATION FOR PRODUCT SUP-PORT. End users of this Microsoft program shall not be considered "registered owners" of a Microsoft product and therefore shall not be eligible for upgrades, promotions or other benefits available to "registered owners" of Microsoft products.

NOTE: This CD-ROM uses long and mixed-case filenames requiring the use of a protected-mode CD-ROM Driver.